SELECTED

NEW RIVERSIDE EDITIONS

Series Editor for the American Volumes
Paul Lauter

Charles W. Chesnutt, *Selected Writings*
Edited by SallyAnn H. Ferguson

Stephen Crane, *The Red Badge of Courage, Maggie: A Girl of the Streets,*
and Other Selected Writings
Edited by Phyllis Frus and Stanley Corkin

Ralph Waldo Emerson and Margaret Fuller, *Selected Works*
Edited by John Carlos Rowe

Olaudah Equiano, Mary Rowlandson, and Others,
American Captivity Narratives
Edited by Gordon M. Sayre

Nathaniel Hawthorne, *The Scarlet Letter*
Edited by Rita K. Gollin

Henry James, *The Portrait of a Lady*
Edited by Jan Cohn

Henry David Thoreau, *Walden and Civil Disobedience*
Edited by Paul Lauter

Mark Twain, *Adventures of Huckleberry Finn*
Edited by Susan K. Harris

Edith Wharton, *The Age of Innocence*
Edited by Carol J. Singley

For a complete listing of our American and British New Riverside
Editions, visit our web site at **http://college.hmco.com.**

NEW RIVERSIDE EDITIONS

Series Editor for the American Volumes

Paul Lauter, Trinity College

RALPH WALDO EMERSON
AND MARGARET FULLER

Selected Works

Essays, Poems, and Dispatches with Introduction

Edited by John Carlos Rowe

UNIVERSITY OF CALIFORNIA — IRVINE

Houghton Mifflin Company

BOSTON • NEW YORK

FOR STUDENTS OF EMERSON AND FULLER

Sponsoring Editor: Michael Gillespie
Editorial Associate: Bruce Cantley
Associate Project Editor: Martha Rogers
Editorial Assistant: Reba Frederics
Cover Design Manager: Diana Coe
Manufacturing Manager: Florence Cadran
Marketing Manager: Cindy Graff Cohen

Cover image: © Judith Rosenbaum/Nonstock

Library of Congress Control Number: 99-72002
ISBN: 0-395-98075-5
1   2   3   4   5   6   7   8   9-FFG-06   05   04   03   02

CONTENTS

ABOUT THIS SERIES
Paul Lauter

The Riverside name dates back well over a century. Readers of this book may have seen—indeed, may own—Riverside Editions of works by the best-known nineteenth-century American writers, such as Emerson, Thoreau, Lowell, Longfellow, and Hawthorne. Houghton Mifflin and its predecessor, Ticknor & Fields, were the primary publishers of the New England authors who constituted much of the undisputed canon of American literature until well into the twentieth century. The Riverside Editions of works by these writers, and of some later writers such as Amy Lowell, became benchmarks for distinguished and useful editions of standard American authors for home, library, and classroom.

In the 1950s and 1960s, the Riverside name was used for another series of texts, primarily for the college classroom, of well-known American and British literary works. These paperback volumes, edited by distinguished critics of that generation, were among the most widely used and appreciated of their day. They provided carefully edited texts in a handsome and readable format, with insightful critical introductions. They were books one kept beyond the exam, the class, or even the college experience.

In the last quarter century, however, ideas about the American literary canon have changed. Many scholars want to see a canon that reflects a broader American heritage, including significant literary works by previously marginalized writers, many of them women or men of color. These changes began to be institutionalized in curricula as well as in textbooks such as *The Heath Anthology of American Literature*, which Houghton Mifflin started publishing in 1998. The older Riverside series, excellent in its day, ran the risk of appearing outdated; the editors were long retired or deceased, and the authors were viewed by some as too exclusive.

Yet the name Riverside and the ideas behind it continued to have appeal. The name stood for distinction and worth in the publication of America's literary heritage. Houghton Mifflin's New Riverside Series, initiated in the year 2000, is designed to uphold the Riverside reputation for excellence while offering a more inclusive range of authors. The Series also provides today's reader with books that contain, in addition to notable literary works, introductions by influential critics, as well as a variety of stimulating materials that bring alive the debates, the conversations, the social and cultural movements within which America's literary classics were formed.

Thus emerged the book you have in hand. Each volume of the New Riverside Editions will contain the basic elements that we think today's readers find interesting and useful: important literary works by significant authors, incisive introductions, and a variety of contextual materials to make the literary text fully engaging. These books will be useful in many kinds of classrooms, but they are also designed to offer the casual reader the enjoyment of a good read in a fresh and accessible format. Among the first group of New Riverside Editions are familiar titles, such as Henry David Thoreau's *Walden* and Mark Twain's *Adventures of Huckleberry Finn*. There are also works in fresh new combinations, such as the collection of early captivity narratives. And there are well-known works in distinctively interesting formats, such as the volume containing Edith Wharton's *The Age of Innocence* and the volume of writings by Stephen Crane. Future books will include classics as well as works drawing renewed attention.

The New Riverside Editions will provide discriminating readers with a wide range of important literary works, contextual materials that vividly illuminate those works, and the best of recent critical commentary and analysis. And because we have not confined our editors to a single monotonous format, we think our readers will find that each volume in this new series has a character appropriate to the literary work it presents.

We expect the New Riverside Editions to bring to the twenty-first century the same literary publishing distinction of its nineteenth- and twentieth-century predecessors.

INTRODUCTION
John Carlos Rowe

R alph Waldo Emerson occupies a unique position in U.S. history as a nineteenth-century public intellectual who has exerted a continuous, shaping influence on U.S. culture for more than a century and a half. The extent and persistence of Emerson's legacy have often baffled scholars, because Emerson is a difficult thinker whose writings rely on the highly allusive and rhetorically subtle conventions of nineteenth-century religion and philosophy. In contrast, Margaret Fuller, until recently, remained a figure of primarily scholarly interest, despite her contributions to the nineteenth-century women's movement and to American Transcendentalism. The usual reason given for the neglect of Fuller is the "difficulty" of her prose style, even though it resembles the rhetorically complex, highly allusive style of Emerson. Of course, Fuller was a woman who was a political activist for women's rights, abolition, and republican movements (and thus was opposed to monarchism in general) around the world, and such nineteenth-century radicalism marginalized her in her own era and possibly in subsequent periods. Yet what is often most prized about Emerson is his "radicalism" on such issues as abolition, even though, as Stephen Whicher points out, "whenever confronted with a specific choice between political possibilities he instinctively preferred the conservative opinion" (*Selections* xviii).

Emerson's capacity to be both radical and conservative may account in part for his enduring appeal and for Margaret Fuller's primarily historical interest. Emerson epitomizes the liberalism that many identify with the "American consensus" and others criticize as a middle-class ethos characterized by what Herbert Marcuse termed its "repressive tolerance."[1] I would add to this interpretation of liberalism what I have termed "aesthetic dissent" as the particular quality of entertaining in writing and thought

---

[1] Marcuse actually uses the phrase "repressive desublimation" (76–102).

1

social problems—slavery, women's rights, rights of labor—that demand political, legal, economic, and other material reforms (Rowe, *Emerson's Tomb* 1–3). Although Margaret Fuller shared with Emerson many of the idealist tenets fundamental to American Transcendentalism, she believed that thought and writing succeeded only when complemented by particular social and political actions. In Fuller's view, women's rights would be improved in the United States not merely as a consequence of reading her *Woman in the Nineteenth Century* (1845), but only if such reading prompted the creation of educational curricula more suited to women's interests and needs, including the study of influential women in history and literature such as those Fuller interprets in this work.

Although Emerson staunchly supported abolition as a cause, he refused to join specific political groups organized to abolish slavery, even when he became so infuriated by Daniel Webster's part in the Compromise of 1850 as to assume a radical abolitionist posture in his lectures and writings. In response to William Henry Channing's efforts to involve him more directly in the politics of abolition, Emerson wrote "Ode, Inscribed to W. H. Channing" (reprinted in this volume), in which he defends as necessary the poet's distance from direct political action. Nevertheless, Emerson's reputation as the source of American liberalism cannot be attributed entirely or even primarily to Emerson himself. "Emersonianism" has a complex genealogy that includes the many intellectuals, politicians, and corporate leaders who have relied on their own interpretations, some quite fantastic, of Emerson's philosophy. Divided as Emerson may have been over the politics of abolition, he rose on several dramatic occasions to meet that historical crisis and contributed materially to the defeat of an immoral system. Less compelling is Emerson's record with regard to women's rights, despite his friendship with Margaret Fuller, which dates from 1836 through their work together on the transcendentalist journal *The Dial* (1842–44), to his part in editing her posthumously published *Memoirs of Margaret Fuller Ossoli* (1852).[2] Indeed, he turned down an invitation to address a women's rights convention on the grounds that he was too busy editing Fuller's memoirs, although he later delivered the lecture "Woman" (1855) to the Woman's Rights Convention in Boston on 20 September 1855 (Rowe, *Emerson's Tomb* 37). Emerson's views in that lecture (also reprinted in this volume) are obviously meliorist and contradictory, at first advocating the self-evident worthiness of the rights demanded by women at the Seneca Falls Convention of 1848 and later insisting that women do not really want these rights at that historical moment.

---

[2] See Emerson et al., *Memoirs*.

Fuller herself is by no means free of such contradictions. On the one hand, she called for specific reforms of legal slavery and wage slavery, genocidal policies toward native peoples, wife abuse, child abuse, alcoholism, educational institutions and practices, and religious intolerance. On the other hand, in her writings she offers a wide range of transcendentalist palliatives for such problems, ranging from feminine "sacrifice" and abjection to versions of dubious sexual sublimation, including "spiritual" (read "Platonic") relationships between men and women. Surprisingly modern as Fuller can be—a quality I try to stress in the explanatory notes to her writings—she can also be perversely abstract and anachronistic, even in the relatively old-fashioned United States of the 1840s, as well as predictably conventional with respect to the myth of the "Vanishing American" and Euroamerican cultural superiority. Fuller's writings, especially *Woman in the Nineteenth Century*, deserve the modern reader's attention and not exclusively for their historical value. Her neglect, however, has not been entirely the work of liberal culture intent on suppressing women's history and her political radicalism.

There are numerous editions of Emerson's writings and several recent excellent editions of Fuller's.[3] This New Riverside Edition, however, is the first volume to include Emerson's and Fuller's writings in the same volume. One reason for this pairing is to change the public perception of American Transcendentalism as primarily a male phenomenon. Another is to call attention to the contradictions in the philosophies and social practices of two of the most important transcendentalists. These contradictions are illustrated in the selections from Emerson's writings by my emphasis on his political essays, few of which have been included in modern anthologies. In the original Riverside Edition of Emerson's writings, edited by James Elliot Cabot, and in the Centenary Edition, edited by Edward Waldo Emerson, the majority of Emerson's political writings on slavery, women's rights, and Cherokee rights appeared in the volume *Miscellanies*, in part because Emerson had not collected most of these essays into the several volumes of his work to be published during his lifetime.

To make space for essays on specific political issues, such as abolition and women's rights, I excluded several famous essays in the Emerson canon. In this regard, I have been particularly sensitive to the changes I made to the texts in Whicher's modern Riverside Edition, which appeared in 1957. Subtitled "An Organic Anthology," Whicher's anthology was carefully composed to represent Emerson as an international romantic whose

---

[3] In the case of Fuller, two recent editions—one edited by Donna Dickenson, the other by Larry J. Reynolds—are especially valuable.

poetic identity—the "Orphic poet"—epitomized the ideals of romantic organicism. Whicher's edition is a scholarly and artistic work that deserves study in its own right, and his care in preparing it is justly renowned. Yet the "organic" Emerson belongs to an earlier generation of scholars, critics, and readers, for whom romanticism was the foundation of modern culture and thus of much contemporary thought. Whicher demonstrated the complementarity of Emerson's journals, letters, published essays, and poems, in keeping with the critical tradition that viewed the *oeuvre* of the genius to be coherent and articulable as a grand work.

I do not share Whicher's aesthetic assumptions, even though I am sensitive to what is lost by substituting "my" Emerson, divided between practical politics and philosophical idealism, for Whicher's.[4] Yet there are considerable advantages for the contemporary reader to understand Emerson apart from either the cultural heritage of "Emersonianism" or the romantic tradition of "organicism," in both of which Emerson represents transcendent "genius." By identifying the significant contradictions in Emerson's career and by encouraging the reader to compare and contrast his ideas with those of his more politically radical, albeit often contradictory, contemporary Margaret Fuller, I am rehistoricizing both authors as representatives of the political and social conflicts in the critical first half of the nineteenth century, when the United States was defining itself as a nation while grappling with the major social issues of abolition and women's rights.

Ralph Waldo Emerson (1803–82)

Ralph Waldo Emerson was born on 25 May 1803, the fourth child of William and Ruth Haskins Emerson. His father died of tuberculosis in 1811, just before Ralph's eighth birthday. Ruth had to take in boarders and call periodically on her sister-in-law, Mary Moody Emerson, to help her raise five sons. William Emerson had been the minister at the First Church of Boston, so there was some expectation that one son might follow his profession. In 1812, Ralph entered the Boston Public Latin School, where he received a sound education in Latin and Greek, supplemented by work in writing and mathematics at a Boston grammar school.

---

[4] By the same token, I find Whicher's version of Emerson nearly unteachable in any course except one dedicated to Emerson or to the American transcendentalists. Having embedded the famous essays in sections framed by his introduction and selections from Emerson's journals and letters, Whicher vastly complicated the reader's (especially the beginning reader's) task. By dehistoricizing Emerson's essays and locating them totally within Emerson's "organic" *oeuvre*, Whicher made it very difficult for the reader (or teacher) to take essays out of Whicher's context.

In 1817, at the age of fourteen, Emerson passed the entrance examination for Harvard and was admitted to the class of 1821 as its youngest member. In college, he followed the nineteenth-century curriculum of classical languages and rhetoric, history, English, and philosophy. He studied with such well-known professors as Edward Everett (Greek), George Ticknor (European literature), and Edward Tyrell Channing (rhetoric and composition). In 1820, while still at Harvard, he began to keep a journal, which he entitled "The Wide World." In it he would record quotations (in the manner of a copy-book) followed by his reflections on them. The method would serve him well throughout his life, providing the basic format and context for developing his lectures and eventually his published essays. The journals are remarkably similar to notes taken by modern scholars in the humanities to prepare lectures, papers, essays, and books. Indeed, there is much in Emerson's method and writing that anticipates modern scholarship in the humanities.[5]

After his graduation from Harvard in 1821, Emerson (who now preferred to be called "Waldo") taught at his brother William's school for girls in Boston. In 1824, he resolved to follow his father's vocation and in the spring of 1825 enrolled in Harvard Divinity School, where he suffered problems with his eyes that almost caused him to go blind, respiratory difficulties probably tied to the family's chronic bouts with tuberculosis, and muscle and joint problems. Despite these health problems, all of which recurred throughout his life, Emerson was licensed to preach in October 1826 by the Middlesex Association of Unitarian Ministers. Strongly influenced by Enlightenment reason, the Unitarian Church was the most liberal Protestant sect in New England. Unitarianism in general secularized, if not outright rejected, many of the central doctrines of Calvinism on which New England Puritanism was based, including such notions as human beings' utter sinfulness (our "fallen" condition) and God's absolute authority (especially the doctrine of supralapsarian election) (Whicher, *Selections* xv).

Like other young ministers yet to be ordained, Emerson traveled the countryside giving sermons as a visitor at different churches, until 1828, when he was asked to replace temporarily the ailing minister of the Second Church of Boston. In March 1829, he was ordained minister there. In

---

[5]This impression may also be an indirect consequence of the influence of such romantic idealists as Immanuel Kant, Georg Wilhelm Friedrich Hegel, and others (including Emerson) on the theoretical and practical development of the modern liberal arts university. Kant's *Conflict of the Faculties* (1798) and *Education* (1803), the latter composed of his lectures at the University of Königsberg on pedagogy between 1776 and 1787, and Hegel's contributions to the founding of the University of Berlin in the early nineteenth century are good examples of such work.

September, he married Ellen Louisa Tucker of Concord, New Hampshire, whom he had met in 1827 during his traveling ministry. At the time of their marriage, he was twenty-six and she was seventeen. A year and a half later (1831), Ellen died of tuberculosis, and Emerson haunted her tomb, recording in his journal that during one of his visits he had opened her coffin, an event modern scholars treat variously as metaphorical or literal. Ellen's death was certainly a critical event in Emerson's young adulthood, and he began to question his ministry, especially such residual Calvinist rituals as Communion. In 1832, he asked the elders of his church for permission not to administer Communion. When permission was denied, he delivered a sermon called "The Last Supper," in which he resigned his position in the church.

With the prospect of his share of Ellen's estate, Emerson traveled in 1833 to Europe, moving north from the Mediterranean through Italy and France, where he was impressed with the natural history and botany on display in Paris at the Jardin des Plantes. He would remember this visit in his last project, *The Natural History of the Intellect* (1893). In Great Britain, he met such international figures as William Wordsworth, Samuel Taylor Coleridge, and Thomas Carlyle; with Carlyle, Emerson developed a lifelong friendship and correspondence. In the fall, he sailed home and on shipboard planned his first major work, *Nature*, which was published three years later (and is reprinted in this volume).

Back in Boston, Emerson continued to earn his living as a traveling preacher and met Lidian Jackson. He proposed to her by letter in January 1835, and they were married in September. In that same year, he joined the new American Lyceum lecturing circuit, which spread through the Northeast, Mid-Atlantic, and even into the Midwest as a means of bringing culture and education to small villages and midsize towns. Lyceum lectures were also meant to be entertaining; some listeners at the time judged them be superficial. In his journals Emerson repeatedly reminded himself not to surrender to the organizers' basest wishes for such lectures. In fact, his journals and his years as an itinerant preacher prepared him very well for the format of the Lyceum, and he soon became an established figure who earned a significant percentage of his income from his lectures. The lectures provided him with the germs for his published works, not unlike the ways in which professional conferences enable modern scholars to draft ideas that they later develop into published essays and books.

The lecture format is evident in the style of Emerson's published essays, or perhaps Emerson's modes of thinking and writing were simply well adapted to the lecture. In either case, Emerson's prose style in *Nature* (1836), *Essays* (1841), and *Essays: Second Series* (1844) is typically digressive, resists analytic categories (even when Emerson divided the writing into sections, as he did in *Nature*), and is prone to repetition and occasional contradictions. His style is not architectonic, like Kant's, or rigorously dialectical, like Hegel's. Instead, it proceeds by metaphoric and other figurative changes, in which certain themes are elaborated as you might adopt different perspectives of a single object or scene in order to understand it more fully. The style even of Emerson's most philosophical subjects, such as *Nature*, or religious topics, such as the work known as the "Divinity School Address" (1838) (also reprinted here), is literary, and it is fair to say that Emerson's greatest poetry and most successful uses of figurative language are his essays rather than his poems.

The book Emerson had planned on his return from Europe was *Nature*; it was published in 1836 as a single volume and made him famous. It enunciates the basic ideas of American Transcendentalism, which certainly resemble those of European romanticism but with crucial differences. In *Nature*, Emerson relies on the idealist philosophy of Kant, including Kant's rigorous "transcendental deduction" of the constitutive categories of human consciousness and Kant's method of overcoming apparent oppositions or "antinomies." *Nature* begins with a classic antinomy or opposition between "Me" (mind, philosophical subjectivity) and "Nature," which Emerson terms the "Not-Me." The task of the transcendentalist is to demonstrate the relationship between these two opposites. Kant demonstrated the mind's independence from a determining and scientifically accessible natural world, but he never adequately proved the imbrication of mind and Nature. Emerson does so by claiming, rather than proving, the symbolic matrix that humans share with Nature. In other words, language links humans and Nature, and Emerson draws on and modifies the Puritan conception of the natural world as the expression of a providential will, written obliquely in time and space but readable nonetheless by those with refined interpretive skills. For the Puritans, this ideal reader was the minister or the elder of the church; for Emerson, it is the poet or man of sufficient imagination. Emerson's transcendentalism is progressive, like Hegel's, and rational, like Kant's, but it is also pragmatist in its acknowledgment of the incompletion that any theory of progress or of human consciousness requires. For all his loving references to Plato, Emerson is an idealist who is also a pragmatist and insists on the entanglements of the ideal and the actual, of Plato's noumenal truth with the deceptions of the phenomenal.[6]

---

[6] Emerson's pragmatism has certainly influenced many philosophers, especially Americans, more recognizably identifiable with the pragmatist tradition (often termed America's only "original" philosophy), such as William James, John Dewey, and more recently Richard Rorty.

Emerson's ideas helped organize and focus similar views by many of his contemporaries and younger writers and intellectuals, including his friends Amos Bronson Alcott, William Ellery Channing, Theodore Parker, Henry David Thoreau, Margaret Fuller, William Henry Channing, Orestes Brownson, and Walt Whitman. His growing fame brought invitations to lecture on distinguished occasions, such as the Phi Beta Kappa lecture he gave at Harvard in 1837, "The American Scholar" (reprinted here), and his address to the Divinity School in 1838, whose audience was deeply divided between criticism and praise of Emerson's radical challenge to organized religion. For many scholars, the years from *Nature* (1836) to *Essays* (1841) to *Essays: Second Series* (1844) encompass Emerson at his most powerful and original. Many published works followed, of course, including *Poems* (1846), *Representative Men* (1850), *English Traits* (1856), *The Conduct of Life* (1860), *May-Day and Other Pieces* (1867), *Society and Solitude* (1870), *Social Aims* (1875), and *Selected Poems* (1876). But many scholars judge Emerson's philosophy to grow conventional and more didactic, less vigorous and optimistically "transcendentalist," after 1844.

As Emerson developed his version of transcendentalism, he and Lidian had three children: Waldo, Jr., born in 1836; Ellen Tucker, born in 1839; Edward Waldo, born in 1844. When Waldo, Jr., died in 1842 of scarlet fever at just over five years of age, Emerson went into a deep depression. Some scholars consider this loss the source of the growing skepticism evident in lectures and essays after 1842. But there were additional reasons for Emerson's pessimism in the 1840s and 1850s, many of which had more to do with social and political than with personal issues.

Emerson's friends and colleagues among the transcendentalists and many other northern intellectuals, such as William Lloyd Garrison and Wendell Phillips, were active abolitionists, critics of urban capitalism in Jacksonian America, and women's rights activists. Many of the transcendentalists understood their philosophy to result in social reforms. Thoreau's famous civil disobedience in protest of U.S. efforts to annex Texas from Mexico and his two-year, two-month "experiment" at Walden Pond (on land owned by Emerson) were anticipations of his support of John Brown's effort to initiate violent rebellion against slavery, first in Kansas and finally in his raid on the federal arsenal at Harpers Ferry. Emerson's friend Bronson Alcott started a utopian community called Fruitlands, and George Ripley in 1841 founded the Brook Farm Institute of Agriculture and Education. In 1848, women's rights activists organized the first national convention at Seneca Falls, New York, and drew up a list of civil, economic, and political rights. When the Fugitive Slave Law was made part of the Compromise of 1850, Boston radicals sought opportunities to test the federal law against state laws, especially in Massachusetts, by challenging in court and on the streets the legal return to slavery of such fugitives as Anthony Burns.[7]

With its emphasis on individual self-consciousness and rhetorical performativity, Emerson's transcendentalism was not well suited to address these political urgencies, even if many influenced by Emerson's thought were major antebellum political reformers. While crowds demonstrated in Boston against the federal troops brought in to ensure the return of Anthony Burns to slavery, Emerson remained in Concord, complaining that he was busy with his own writing. Shy and introspective, he was personally averse to confrontational politics; he also believed that education and "moral suasion," especially as they were represented in his public lectures and published essays, offered the best long-term solutions to political and social problems (Gougeon and Myerson xi). Yet as a deeply moral thinker, Emerson was strongly motivated by himself and others to lecture and write about such urgent issues as slavery, women's rights, and industrialization.

Emerson's political writings range from his lecture on the ten-year celebration of the abolition of slavery in the British West Indies, "An Address . . . on . . . the Emancipation of the Negroes in the British West Indies" (1844), to his eulogy in 1862 for his friend Henry David Thoreau, in which he praises Thoreau for his political activism, betraying even a hint of regret that Emerson himself had not been publicly political (Rowe, *Emerson's Tomb* 17–41).[8] These essays cover an impressive range of political issues, including his protest against the forcible expulsion of the Cherokee from Georgia, the imperialism of the United States in the Mexican-American War, the evils of slavery, and the social inequality of women. In all of these essays, however, Emerson struggles to preserve the coherence of his basic transcendentalism, including the radical individualism of the "self-reliant" man — "Man Thinking" in "The American Scholar" — and the active or performative qualities of thought and rhetorical language. The results are uneven, often demonstrably contradictory, and they may well account for scholars' preferences for Emerson's writings before 1844. In "American Civilization" (1862), Emerson criticizes U.S. materialism and commercialism while defending spiritual ideas of progress. In "Woman" (1855), he attacks patriarchy and endorses women's rights but concludes that the ideal woman should "want" no more than the emancipation of her

---

[7] For a comprehensive account of the transcendentalists' political activism, see Packer, "The Transcendentalists." For an account of the transcendentalists' role in the trial of the fugitive slave Anthony Burns, see von Frank, *The Trials of Anthony Burns*.

[8] Both of these works and the other essays mentioned in this and the following paragraph are reprinted in this volume.

"brother," on whose freedom she herself depends. In "Man the Reformer" (1841), he defends the right of every man to his own labor but concludes that material labor is trivial and that only the "work" of the spirit has lasting value. In "Emancipation of the Negroes in the British West Indies" and "The Fugitive Slave Law" (1854), the evils of slavery are palpable in the suffering, exploitation, and murder of millions, but the sins of the slave-owner stubbornly remain consequences of Emerson's transcendentalist theodicy: their "lack" of education or "failure" to see their economic self-interest in abolition.[9]

The enduring value of Emerson, the founder of American Transcendentalism, still rests on such celebrated works as *Nature*, "The American Scholar," "The Divinity School Address," "Self-Reliance" (1841), "Circles" (1841), "The Transcendentalist" (1842), "Experience" (1844), and "The Poet" (1844). But the Emerson who has the most to teach us in our late modernity and postmodernity is the idealist who struggled with political and social urgencies that are still very much with us: racism, sexism, class distinctions, xenophobia, and nationalism without rationalism. His efforts to come to terms with these issues are often less than satisfactory, but his failures may teach us how better to relate philosophy, literature, and the humanities to the social problems of our times.

Margaret Fuller (1810–50)

Margaret Fuller offers an alternative to Emerson's anxious responses to political and social activism, but the contradictions within her own transcendentalism as well as in her social practice suggest she offers less an answer to Emerson's meliorism than another perspective on some of the crucial problems within the social theory of transcendentalism. Emerson and Fuller are rightly termed friends in most of the scholarship, but Emerson often expresses his friendship in patriarchal, patronizing ways. In the *Memoirs of Margaret Fuller Ossoli*, which he coedited with William Henry Channing and with James Freeman Clarke two years after her death, Emmerson suggests that Fuller failed to realize her potential, not simply because she died young but because she was a woman (1: 279–80). Emerson was not alone among the male transcendentalists in his tendency to trivialize Margaret Fuller, but he helped perpetuate the myth of her "tragic" fatality as a woman intellectual who was unable to produce the enduring

---

[9]Whicher tries hard to defend Emerson against the familiar charge that he "was not aware of evil" by claiming that Emerson "felt keenly — *his* evil" (xix). But Emerson's personal sense of evil I would argue was insufficient for him to take into account the sins of the slavocracy and of patriarchy.

work of her male contemporaries. Henry James, Jr., following the example of his father Henry James, Sr. (a minor transcendentalist), compared Fuller with Beatrice Cenci (1577–99)—especially as the Italian painter Guido Reni (1575–1642) portrayed her. Cenci typified the tragic feminine in the Victorian imagination.[10]

When the male transcendentalists praised Fuller, they often followed Emerson, who stressed her special facility as a conversationalist.[11] In "Woman" (247),[12] he generalizes that women's best talent is for conversation: "Wise, cultivated, genial conversation is the last flower of civilization." Emerson, of course, knew that between 1839 and 1844 Fuller had sponsored seminars for women in Boston and that she had called her seminars "Conversations." Modeled on the pedagogy of Emerson's friend Bronson Alcott, for whom Fuller had taught in 1836, her "Conversations" were like university seminars in an alternative curriculum for women without access to Harvard or its equivalent. Yet in referring to women's talent for conversation, Emerson clearly means the "blue-stocking" or salon woman (neither of whom Fuller scorns), whose knowledge may be profound but whose conversation does not endure.

It is little wonder, then, that Fuller's greatest weaknesses as a writer and intellectual are not her superficiality or lack of profundity, but her complexity, scholarly rigor, and pedantry. Fuller worked hard to demonstrate her learning, both to refute popular clichés about women's superficiality and to emphasize the long history of women's achievements ignored by most of her contemporaries. *Woman in the Nineteenth Century* is a difficult book for the modern reader, because it makes so many references to so many unfamiliar figures in such a wide variety of cultures. In her frequent catalogues of examples, often weaving five or six different figures (or books or historical events) into a single sentence, she differs little from other transcendentalists, who were prone to such overburdened periodic sentences. All of them anticipate modern scholarship, whose sentences are often clogged with evidence and whose pages are peppered with footnotes and fractured by block quotations. In short, Fuller was a scholar, and her most enduring work is best read as a major contribution to both the theory and the practice of comparative literature and cultural studies. Read together with Erich Auerbach's *Mimesis* and Ernst Robert Curtius's *European*

---

[10] See Rowe, *The Other Henry James* 38–55.

[11] Emerson writes in *Memoirs of Margaret Fuller Ossoli*: "Her talk was a comedy in which dramatic justice was done to everybody's foibles. I remember that she made me laugh more than I liked. [. . .] She had an incredible variety of anecdotes, and the readiest wit to give an absurd turn to whatever passed" (1: 270).

[12] All parenthetical citations are to this New Riverside Edition.

Literature and the Latin Middle Ages—both foundations of post–World War II comparative literature—Fuller's *Woman in the Nineteenth Century* does not appear as difficult or pedantic as when it is read together with Thoreau's *Walden* and Hawthorne's *The Scarlet Letter*.

Margaret Fuller was educated as a scholar, even though as a woman she could not have the Harvard education of her father, Timothy Fuller, who graduated in 1801. Born on 23 May 1810, Sarah Margaret Fuller was the first of eight children of Timothy and Margarett Crane Fuller (1789–1859). Although five of the Fullers' children (two of whom would die as infants) would be sons, the father was disappointed that their first-born was a daughter and treated Margaret as if she were a son. By age five, she was studying at home with her father—Latin, French, logic, rhetoric, and even some Greek. One year later, she began to memorize all of Virgil in Latin— a typical rhetorical exercise of the times, albeit not for six-year-olds! Her father also sent her to Dr. Park's school in Boston, where her home schooling helped her to distinguish herself.

In 1817, Timothy Fuller was elected to Congress as a Democratic Republican in the James Monroe administration (1817–25). In 1825, he retired from Congress and resumed his law practice in Cambridge, but he still hoped he might return to national politics and strongly supported John Quincy Adams, who was elected sixth president (1825–29) in a narrow victory over Andrew Jackson. Fuller had great hopes that he would be rewarded for his support with an ambassadorship, which would have meant for Margaret an opportunity to continue her studies abroad. The ambassadorship was not offered.

Timothy Fuller feared that he was not responsibly preparing his daughter for a world in which women were expected to be "angels in the house" and graceful fixtures in its parlor. In 1824, Margaret was sent for a year to Miss Prescott's Young Ladies' Seminary (a finishing school) in Groton, Massachusetts, where she obtained a more conventional middle-class education for U.S. women. Yet, as Stern (ix) indicates, Fuller's early education at home and at Dr. Park's school instilled in her a love of reading that led to a lifelong habit of systematic study and reading.

The election of Andrew Jackson in 1828 and his reelection in 1832 destroyed any lingering hopes that Timothy Fuller had for elected or appointed political office. In 1833, he moved his family from Cambridge to a farm in Groton. There, as a young adult, Margaret learned what it really meant to be the "angel in the house." Housework alternated with her efforts to home-school her younger brothers and sister, and she suffered the cultural isolation and daily routines of a small New England farm. Nevertheless, she found the time to translate from German Goethe's play *Torquato Tasso* and plan a European tour. Such plans were dashed, however, when

Timothy Fuller died suddenly of cholera in 1835, leaving the family nearly destitute and forcing Margaret to look for work.

Margaret Fuller met Emerson in 1836, the year he published *Nature*, and she began teaching in Emerson's friend Bronson Alcott's Temple School in Boston. Alcott, who would later publish his "Orphic Sayings" in *The Dial* while Fuller was editor, was a progressive, utopian reformer, and the Temple School emphasized transcendentalist "self-reliance" and spiritual development along with racial integration (Stern x). Unfortunately, Alcott was unable to pay Fuller, so in 1837 she began teaching at the Greene Street School in Providence, Rhode Island, giving about a third of her annual salary to her brother Eugene (born in 1815) to help him begin his career. While in Providence, she heard the radical poet John Neal lecture on women's rights and strongly advocate women's suffrage. After eighteen months in Providence, she returned to Groton to sell the family house and farm and help move the family to Jamaica Plain, Massachusetts (a suburb of Boston).

Later in 1839, Fuller published her translation from German of Johann Eckermann's *Conversations with Goethe* and began in Boston her "Conversations" in what she termed a "Parlatorio" at 13 West Street in Elizabeth Peabody's bookshop. For twenty dollars, women could enroll in seminars organized by Fuller on diverse topics in a curriculum designed by a woman and for women, carrying even further Mary Wollstonecraft's appeal in her *Vindication of the Rights of Woman* (1792) for educational reform as basic to women's liberation.[13] The seminars lasted until 1844, when Fuller became literary editor for the *New York Daily Tribune*. In 1840, she accepted the editorship of *The Dial* and began a period of close intellectual relationships with Emerson, Caroline Sturgis, Anna Barker, Samuel Ward Gray, Thoreau, Theodore Parker, Elizabeth Peabody, and many other leading transcendentalists and New England intellectuals.

In 1842, overworked teaching her seminars while editing *The Dial* and working on still more translations from German, Fuller transferred her editorship to Emerson.[14] Lacking sufficient funds to continue it, Emerson discontinued the journal in 1844, but not before *The Dial* had published some of the most important works of American Transcendentalism, including Fuller's "The Great Lawsuit. Man *versus* Men. Woman *versus* Women" in the July 1843 issue. The core of what became *Woman in the Nineteenth Century* appeared while Fuller was traveling with Sarah Freeman Clarke between May and August to Niagara, Chicago, the Illinois countryside,

---

[13] Wollstonecraft devotes the final two sections of this work to proposals for educational reforms.

[14] In 1842, Fuller and Minna Wesselhoeft published their translation of the *Correspondence of Fräulein Günderrode and Bettina von Arnim*.

Milwaukee (and Wisconsin Territory), and the Great Lakes. That trip became the basis for Fuller's first authored book, *Summer on the Lakes in 1843*, published in 1844. "The Great Lawsuit" constitutes a little more than half of the final text of *Woman in the Nineteenth Century*.[15] Fuller's argument in this first version was sufficiently developed to attract the praise of Emerson, Thoreau, and Sophia Ripley, and favorable reviews in the *New York Daily Tribune*, edited by Horace Greeley (Stern xii–xiii). Privately, Emerson encouraged Fuller to revise the essay, adding an introduction and clarifying and developing her argument ("To Margaret Fuller" 183).

In *Summer on the Lakes*, Fuller criticized U.S. policies toward Native Americans and challenged Manifest Destiny, even as she endorsed her own transcendentalist version of spiritual progress and sadly acknowledged the "inevitablity" of Native Americans' "disappearance." Though a champion of minority and women's rights, Fuller was a product of her times and accepted the myth of the "Vanishing American" and rejected the alternative of "amalgamation" as "the only true and profound means of civilization," on grounds that "those of mixed blood fade early, and are not generally a fine race" (Smith 95–96). Perhaps for some of these contrary reasons, the book attracted the interest of Horace Greeley, editor of the *New York Daily Tribune*, which had favorably reviewed her "Great Lawsuit" in *The Dial*, and Greeley offered Fuller a position as a literary editor, beginning in December 1844.

In October and November 1844, Fuller took seven weeks' respite from her busy life to revise "The Great Lawsuit" for book publication. In the small village of Fishkill Landing on the Hudson River, accompanied by her friend Caroline Sturgis, she stayed at Mr. Van Vliet's boarding house, walked the countryside during the day, and read and wrote in the evenings. She had brought with her "Taylor's translations of the old Greek writers, the Confucious [sic], the Desater, and Alkuna, a Scandinavian mythology," works that Fuller used frequently in her revisions and that were common sources for many transcendentalists.[16] During those seven weeks, she left Fishkill Landing only to visit women convicts, most of them prostitutes, at Sing Sing Prison in upstate New York. In the letter she sent the inmates after her visit, she tells them she has arranged for "the ladies of Boston" to "send you books which may [. . .] encourage the taste for reading which [. . .] so many of you show," underscoring her belief that reading and writ-

---

[15] Dickenson helpfully notes in her modern edition of *Woman in the Nineteenth Century*, p. 245 (n. to p. 85), where *The Dial* publication ends and the later version begins, with the exception of four paragraphs from the former.

[16] Margaret Fuller to Richard F. Fuller, 23 Nov. 1844, Margaret Fuller Papers, Houghton Library (Harvard University), qtd. in Stern xiv.

ing were deeply connected with pedagogy and education as acts of social reform.[17]

Woman in the Nineteenth Century was published in March 1845 by Horace Greeley and his partner, Thomas McElrath, in a volume costing fifty cents and a first edition of probably fifteen hundred copies, which sold out in the first week. There was no subsequent U.S. edition until after Fuller's death in 1850, but the book was promptly pirated in England and "issued as a volume in H. G. Clarke's Library of Choice Reading series" (Stern xxxv). When the book appeared in New York, Fuller was hard at work as literary editor and social critic for Greeley's *New York Daily Tribune*, to which she contributed hundreds of articles and reviews between 1845 and 1846, including her review of Frederick Douglass's *Narrative of the Life of an American Slave, Written by Himself* (1845). In the spring of 1845, she had a close personal relationship with a German businessman, James Nathan, who left Fuller and New York in June.

A little more than a year later, on 1 August 1846, Fuller herself sailed for England with Greeley's commission to write *Tribune* articles about the republican movements in mid-nineteenth-century Europe.[18] Like Emerson in Europe in 1833, and in part thanks to letters of introduction from him, she met in England, Scotland, and France some of the leading intellectuals and artists of the period, including William Wordsworth, Thomas De Quincey, Thomas Carlyle, Giuseppe Mazzini, George Sand, Frédéric Chopin, and the Polish nationalist and poet Adam Mickiewicz. While she was traveling, a collection of her *Papers on Literature and Art*, including her thoughts on "American Literature," was published in the United States in 1846.

Fuller traveled to Italy in February 1847 and met Marchese Giovanni Angelo Ossoli in April in Rome. A staunch republican, a devout Catholic, an Italian aristocrat, and an officer in the Civic Guard, Ossoli could not marry the Protestant American Fuller in Italy. In May, as revolutions broke out all over Europe against the collapsing monarchical orders and Papal control of the Italian peninsula, Fuller left Rome, pregnant by Ossoli, and gave birth to their son, Angelo Eugene Philip Ossoli (Nino), on 5 September 1848 in Rieti. Leaving her newborn with a nurse, Fuller returned to Rome in November to witness the expulsion of Pope Pius IX from the Vatican and Rome as part of the republican attacks on Papal authority and the political legitimacy of the Papal States. In February 1849, the Roman republic was declared and from April through June was besieged by the

---

[17]"Letter to the Women Inmates at Sing Sing," [early Nov.? 1844], included in Reynolds, *Woman* 205; originally published in Hudspeth (3: 238).

[18]Fuller's dispatches from Europe are collected in "*These Sad But Glorious Days*": *Dispatches from Europe, 1846–1850*, ed. Reynolds and Smith.

French. During the siege of Rome, Fuller ran the hospital of Bene Fratelli while Ossoli served as a republican captain in the Civic Guard. When Rome fell to the French on 1 July 1849, the Ossolis fled to Florence, where they were welcomed by Elizabeth Barrett and Robert Browning.

In Florence, Fuller worked on her "History of the Late Revolutionary Movements in Italy" and sent the last of her European dispatches to Greeley. In May 1850, the family embarked for the United States on board the *Elizabeth*. On 19 July 1850, in a hurricane off Fire Island, New York, the ship foundered on a sandbar, and Margaret Fuller, Giovanni Ossoli, and Nino, along with four others, drowned. Her manuscript of the history of the Roman revolution was lost, although Thoreau walked the beach on Fire Island the morning after the shipwreck looking for her last work. Nino's body eventually washed up on shore, but Fuller's and Ossoli's bodies were never found.[19]

Of course, we will never know how Fuller's "History of the Late Revolutionary Movements in Italy" complemented or departed from her thought, method, and style in *Woman in the Nineteenth Century*. Her dispatches from Europe to Horace Greeley's *New York Tribune* undoubtedly provided her with basic materials for her history, especially because she had access in Italy to very few libraries and archives for research. Because these dispatches give the modern reader some sense of how Fuller's lost history might have taken shape, I am including in this edition a selection of her dispatches to Greeley. Larry Reynolds and Susan Belasco Smith have argued that Fuller's dispatches give us a reasonably clear idea that she conceived her "History" in accord with nineteenth-century conventions "about the writing of history—its documentary foundation, its multivolume format, its elevated status." They conclude that Fuller regarded "history as a creative form that combined attention to detail and the use of archival materials with sweeping narrative, heroic figures, and dramatic action."[20]

---

[19] From the nineteenth century to the present, there is a long tradition of identifying in Fuller's published and personal writings "anticipations" of her drowning. It was a tradition that Hawthorne exploited for particularly nasty effects in the drowning of Zenobia in *The Blithedale Romance* (1852) and several references to Fuller in his *Italian Notebooks*. Feminists have followed suit, as if to suggest that she had some preternatural or supernatural anticipation of her own end. Although I note here this tradition, I want to dissociate myself from it and state simply that fear of water and references to death by drowning were quite conventional and entirely understandable in nineteenth-century U.S. and other societies in which few people knew how to swim yet most faced at least occasional encounters with travel over water.

[20] *"These Sad But Glorious Days": Dispatches from Europe, 1846–1850,"* ed. Reynolds and Smith, p. 27.

At the end of her life, Fuller was caught up in the republican revolutions of mid-nineteenth-century Europe, and she had begun her career as a transcendentalist with experiments in feminist pedagogy that she considered cultural aspects of wider political reforms. In these respects, Fuller more resembles Thoreau than Emerson, because she understood reading, writing, and thinking to be parts of social activism that sometimes required more than merely abstract or aesthetic dissent. Yet her greatest published work, *Woman in the Nineteenth Century*, is full of intellectual and political contradictions, and it endorses roles for women that many nineteenth-century women's rights activists did not accept. Although she laid the foundation for modern women's and cultural studies, she celebrates mythic figures like Panthea, whose courage and nobility are finally and fatally sacrificial. While advocating new gender and sexual relations between men and women, she admires the personal freedom Percy Bysshe Shelley exhibited by divorcing his wife to marry Mary Wollstonecraft Godwin, but she condemns the liberated sexuality of Mary Wollstonecraft and George Sand. Although her life exemplifies new, activist roles for nineteenth-century women, her writings often endorse social reforms as "spiritual," as Emerson does and in a style that speaks primarily to an elite, specially educated audience. Thus, reading Fuller together with Ralph Waldo Emerson does not provide a clearly activist alternative to Emersonian abstraction. Both writers complicate and deepen our understanding of American Transcendentalism, which was neither strictly an intellectual movement nor solely a mode of political activism.

A NOTE ON THE TEXTS
John Carlos Rowe

Emerson and Fuller are extremely allusive writers, and their prose styles often rely on figurative, provocative leaps of logic. In addition, each writer was deeply involved in the political currents of the time. In order to make their works accessible to the modern reader, I have provided many footnotes, the majority of which are explanatory. Because of the number of footnotes and because this volume presents two major figures, I do not have the space to include background and secondary materials, such as are included in some New Riverside Editions. A list of further readings is included at the end of this volume to help the reader understand these two complex figures and American Transcendentalism.

Emerson's texts are notoriously difficult to establish as authoritative, because most of his major works went through numerous revisions from delivery as lectures to first publication and collection in nineteenth-century standard editions, such as the Riverside and Centenary Editions. Whenever possible, I have followed the text established by Stephen E. Whicher, editor of the 1957 Riverside Edition, titled *Selections from Ralph Waldo Emerson*. *The Collected Works of Ralph Waldo Emerson*, under the general editorship of Alfred R. Ferguson and published by Harvard University Press, is the authoritative scholarly edition, but it is not yet complete. It also incorporates Emerson's later revisions of many essays and several poems that do not always clarify his argument or improve his poetry. With the help of my research assistant, William Etter, I compared the first book publication and the 1893 Riverside and the 1903–04 Centenary Editions' versions of Emerson's essays and poetry with the texts published so far by Harvard and with Whicher's texts. I then chose the version that seems to me clearest and most accessible for the modern reader, recognizing that this process does not establish an authoritative text.

Emerson's antislavery writings are not yet published in the Harvard scholarly edition, and they pose numerous textual problems because many were not published in book form until collected in the 1893 Riverside

Edition and the Centenary Edition. Fortunately, Len Gougeon and Joel Myerson provide authoritative texts in *Emerson's Anti-Slavery Writings*, and with the permission of Yale University Press I adopted their versions of and notes to "Letter to Martin Van Buren," "An Address . . . on . . . the Emancipation of the Negroes in the British West Indies," and "The Fugitive Slave Law."

The text of Margaret Fuller's *Woman in the Nineteenth Century* is based on the first edition published by Greeley and McElrath in 1845. It incorporates all the corrections suggested by Joel Myerson in his facsimile edition of the work and corrects a few typographical and punctuation errors not identified by him.

Part One

———•——

SELECTED ESSAYS

Selected Essays

Ralph Waldo Emerson

Nature
1836

*"Nature is but an image or imitation of wisdom, the
last thing of the soul; nature being a thing which doth
only do, but not know."*

— Plotinus

A subtle chain of countless rings
The next unto the farthest brings;
The eye reads omens where it goes,
And speaks all languages the rose;
And, striving to be man, the worm
Mounts through all the spires of form.

[*— Emerson, "Nature"*][1]

Introduction

Our age is retrospective. It builds the sepulchres of the fathers.[2] It writes
biographies, histories, and criticism. The foregoing generations beheld God
and nature face to face; we, through their eyes. Why should not we also enjoy an original relation to the universe? Why should not we have a poetry
and philosophy of insight and not of tradition, and a religion by revelation
to us, and not the history of theirs? Embosomed for a season in nature,
whose floods of life stream around and through us, and invite us, by the
powers they supply, to action proportioned to nature, why should we grope
among the dry bones of the past, or put the living generation into masquerade out of its faded wardrobe? The sun shines today also. There is more

---

Selections from Ralph Waldo Emerson: An Organic Anthology. Ed. Stephen E.
Whicher. Riverside Edition. Boston: Houghton, 1957.

[1] The epigraph from Plotinus on the title page of the 1836 edition of *Nature* Emerson
"probably derived from *The True Intellectual System of the Universe* [1678], by Ralph
Cudworth, edited by Thomas Birch, 4 vols. (London, 1820)," which included many quotations from Platonists and Neoplatonists (Ferguson 1:247). For the 1849 edition, Emerson replaced it with his own poem, "Nature," which is also included here. [Ed.]

[2] Emerson is alluding to Daniel Webster's speech at the dedication of the Bunker Hill
Monument on June 17, 1825. [Ed.]

wool and flax in the fields. There are new lands, new men, new thoughts. Let us demand our own works and laws and worship.

Undoubtedly we have no questions to ask which are unanswerable. We must trust the perfection of the creation so far as to believe that whatever curiosity the order of things has awakened in our minds, the order of things can satisfy. Every man's condition is a solution in hieroglyphic to those inquiries he would put.[3] He acts it as life, before he apprehends it as truth. In like manner, nature is already, in its forms and tendencies, describing its own design. Let us interrogate the great apparition that shines so peacefully around us. Let us inquire, to what end is nature?

All science has one aim, namely, to find a theory of nature. We have theories of races and of functions, but scarcely yet a remote approach to an idea of creation. We are now so far from the road to truth, that religious teachers dispute and hate each other, and speculative men are esteemed unsound and frivolous. But to a sound judgment, the most abstract truth is the most practical. Whenever a true theory appears, it will be its own evidence. Its test is, that it will explain all phenomena. Now many are thought not only unexplained but inexplicable; as language, sleep, madness, dreams, beasts, sex.

Philosophically considered, the universe is composed of Nature and the Soul. Strictly speaking, therefore, all that is separate from us, all which Philosophy distinguishes as the NOT ME, that is, both nature and art, all other men and my own body, must be ranked under this name, NATURE.[4] In enumerating the values of nature and casting up their sum, I shall use the word in both senses;—in its common and in its philosophical import. In inquiries so general as our present one, the inaccuracy is not material; no confusion of thought will occur. *Nature,* in the common sense, refers to essences unchanged by man; space, the air, the river, the leaf. *Art* is applied to the mixture of his will with the same things, as in a house, a canal, a statue, a picture. But his operations taken together are so insignificant, a little chipping, baking, patching, and washing, that in an impression so grand as that of the world on the human mind, they do not vary the result.

---

[3] Interest in Egyptian hieroglyphics and ancient Egyptian civilization increased in 1823 with Jean François Champollion's decoding of the Rosetta stone, which provided Greek translations of key hieroglyphs. [Ed.]

[4] Thomas Carlyle uses the terms "me" and "not-me" in *Sartor Resartus,* which was first published in Boston in 1836 "at Emerson's urging and with a preface by him" (Whicher 472). The distinction is typical of German idealist philosophy, which strongly influenced Carlyle's and Emerson's writings. [Ed.]

I. Nature

To go into solitude, a man needs to retire as much from his chamber as from society. I am not solitary whilst I read and write, though nobody is with me. But if a man would be alone, let him look at the stars. The rays that come from those heavenly worlds will separate between him and what he touches. One might think the atmosphere was made transparent with this design, to give man, in the heavenly bodies, the perpetual presence of the sublime. Seen in the streets of cities, how great they are! If the stars should appear one night in a thousand years, how would men believe and adore; and preserve for many generations the remembrance of the city of God which had been shown! But every night come out these envoys of beauty, and light the universe with their admonishing smile.

The stars awaken a certain reverence, because though always present, they are inaccessible; but all natural objects make a kindred impression, when the mind is open to their influence. Nature never wears a mean appearance. Neither does the wisest man extort her secret, and lose his curiosity by finding out all her perfection. Nature never became a toy to a wise spirit. The flowers, the animals, the mountains, reflected the wisdom of his best hour, as much as they had delighted the simplicity of his childhood.

When we speak of nature in this manner, we have a distinct but most poetical sense in the mind. We mean the integrity of impression made by manifold natural objects. It is this which distinguishes the stick of timber of the wood-cutter from the tree of the poet. The charming landscape which I saw this morning is indubitably made up of some twenty or thirty farms. Miller owns this field, Locke that, and Manning the woodland beyond. But none of them owns the landscape. There is a property in the horizon which no man has but he whose eye can integrate all the parts, that is, the poet. This is the best part of these men's farms, yet to this their warranty-deeds give no title.

To speak truly, few adult persons can see nature. Most persons do not see the sun. At least they have a very superficial seeing. The sun illuminates only the eye of the man, but shines into the eye and the heart of the child. The lover of nature is he whose inward and outward senses are still truly adjusted to each other; who has retained the spirit of infancy even into the era of manhood. His intercourse with heaven and earth becomes part of his daily food. In the presence of nature a wild delight runs through the man, in spite of real sorrows. Nature says,—he is my creature, and maugre[5] all

---

[5] "In spite of " ("Maugre," def. 3). [Ed.]

his impertinent griefs, he shall be glad with me. Not the sun or the summer alone, but every hour and season yields its tribute of delight; for every hour and change corresponds to and authorizes a different state of the mind, from breathless noon to grimmest midnight. Nature is a setting that fits equally well a comic or a mourning piece. In good health, the air is a cordial of incredible virtue. Crossing a bare common, in snow puddles, at twilight, under a clouded sky, without having in my thoughts any occurrence of special good fortune, I have enjoyed a perfect exhilaration. I am glad to the brink of fear. In the woods, too, a man casts off his years, as the snake his slough, and at what period soever of life is always a child. In the woods is perpetual youth. Within these plantations[6] of God, a decorum and sanctity reign, a perennial festival is dressed, and the guest sees not how he should tire of them in a thousand years. In the woods, we return to reason and faith. There I feel that nothing can befall me in life,—no disgrace, no calamity (leaving me my eyes), which nature cannot repair. Standing on the bare ground,—my head bathed by the blithe air and uplifted into infinite space,—all mean egotism vanishes. I become a transparent eyeball; I am nothing; I see all; the currents of the Universal Being circulate through me; I am part or parcel of God. The name of the nearest friend sounds then foreign and accidental: to be brothers, to be acquaintances, master or servant, is then a trifle and a disturbance. I am the lover of uncontained and immortal beauty. In the wilderness, I find something more dear and connate[7] than in streets or villages. In the tranquil landscape, and especially in the distant line of the horizon, man beholds somewhat as beautiful as his own nature.[8]

The greatest delight which the fields and woods minister is the suggestion of an occult relation between man and the vegetable. I am not alone and unacknowledged. They nod to me, and I to them. The waving of the boughs in the storm is new to me and old. It takes me by surprise, and yet is not unknown. Its effect is like that of a higher thought or a better emotion coming over me, when I deemed I was thinking justly or doing right.

---

[6] "Assemblage of planted growing plants, especially trees" ("Plantation," def. 2). Emerson was probably contrasting the divinity of nature with the unnaturalness of southern plantations' reliance on slave labor. [Ed.]

[7] Familiar or well known. [Ed.]

[8] Emerson's famous visionary experience of becoming a "transparent eyeball," which was parodied by contemporary critics of American Transcendentalism, draws on a long philosophical and theological tradition that equates the eye with the passage from physical to inner vision, from the material to the spiritual world, and thus from the body to the soul. Emerson also builds on a long tradition from Plato to Kant that links aesthetic beauty with visual perception, as the Greek root *aisthetikon* suggests in its original meaning of "perception." [Ed.]

Yet it is certain that the power to produce this delight does not reside in nature, but in man, or in a harmony of both. It is necessary to use these pleasures with great temperance. For nature is not always tricked in holiday attire, but the same scene which yesterday breathed perfume and glittered as for the frolic of the nymphs is overspread with melancholy today. Nature always wears the colors of the spirit. To a man laboring under calamity, the heat of his own fire hath sadness in it. Then there is a kind of contempt of the landscape felt by him who has just lost by death a dear friend. The sky is less grand as it shuts down over less worth in the population.

II. Commodity

Whoever considers the final cause of the world will discern a multitude of uses that enter as parts into that result. They all admit of being thrown into one of the following classes: Commodity; Beauty; Language; and Discipline.

Under the general name of commodity, I rank all those advantages which our senses owe to nature. This, of course, is a benefit which is temporary and mediate, not ultimate, like its service to the soul. Yet although low, it is perfect in its kind, and is the only use of nature which all men apprehend. The misery of man appears like childish petulance, when we explore the steady and prodigal provision that has been made for his support and delight on this green ball which floats him through the heavens. What angels invented these splendid ornaments, these rich conveniences, this ocean of air above, this ocean of water beneath, this firmament of earth between? this zodiac of lights, this tent of dropping clouds, this striped coat of climates, this four-fold year? Beasts, fire, water, stones, and corn serve him. The field is at once his floor, his work-yard, his play-ground, his garden, and his bed.

"More servants wait on man
Than he'll take notice of." [9]

Nature, in its ministry to man, is not only the material, but is also the process and the result. All the parts incessantly work into each other's hands for the profit of man. The wind sows the seed; the sun evaporates the sea; the wind blows the vapor to the field; the ice, on the other side of the planet, condenses rain on this; the rain feeds the plant; the plant feeds the animal; and thus the endless circulations of the divine charity nourish man.

---

[9] George Herbert, "Man" (1633). Emerson quotes at greater length from this English metaphysical poem in section VIII, "Prospects" (53–54 in this volume). [Ed.]

The useful arts are reproductions or new combinations by the wit of man, of the same natural benefactors. He no longer waits for favoring gales, but by means of steam, he realizes the fable of Aeolus's bag, and carries the two and thirty winds in the boiler of his boat.[10] To diminish friction, he paves the road with iron bars, and, mounting a coach with a ship-load of men, animals, and merchandise behind him, he darts through the country, from town to town, like an eagle or a swallow through the air. By the aggregate of these aids, how is the face of the world changed, from the era of Noah to that of Napoleon! The private poor man hath cities, ships, canals, bridges, built for him. He goes to the post-office, and the human race run on his errands; to the book-shop, and the human race read and write of all that happens, for him; to the court-house, and nations repair his wrongs. He sets his house upon the road, and the human race go forth every morning, and shovel out the snow, and cut a path for him.

But there is no need of specifying particulars in this class of uses. The catalogue is endless, and the examples so obvious, that I shall leave them to the reader's reflection, with the general remark, that this mercenary benefit is one which has respect to a farther good. A man is fed, not that he may be fed, but that he may work.

III. Beauty

A nobler want of man is served by nature, namely, the love of Beauty.

The ancient Greeks called the world Κόσμος,[11] beauty. Such is the constitution of all things, or such the plastic power of the human eye, that the primary forms, as the sky, the mountain, the tree, the animal, give us a delight *in and for themselves;* a pleasure arising from outline, color, motion, and grouping. This seems partly owing to the eye itself. The eye is the best of artists. By the mutual action of its structure and of the laws of light, perspective is produced, which integrates every mass of objects, of what character soever, into a well colored and shaded globe, so that where the particular objects are mean and unaffecting, the landscape which they compose is round and symmetrical. And as the eye is the best composer, so light is the first of painters. There is no object so foul that intense light will not make beautiful. And the stimulus it affords to the sense, and a sort of

---

[10] In Greek mythology, Aeolus, god of the wind, was thought to carry the wind in a bag. Emerson compares the modern industrial harnessing of steam power—Watt patented the first practical steam engine in 1769 and Fulton operated the first steamboat, the *Clermont*, in 1807—with Aeolus' ability to control the wind. [Ed.]

[11] Greek: cosmos. The Greeks used the word to refer to the perfect order of the world or universe. [Ed.]

infinitude which it hath, like space and time, make all matter gay. Even the corpse has its own beauty. But besides this general grace diffused over nature, almost all the individual forms are agreeable to the eye, as is proved by our endless imitations of some of them, as the acorn, the grape, the pine-cone, the wheat-ear, the egg, the wings and forms of most birds, the lion's claw, the serpent, the butterfly, sea-shells, flames, clouds, buds, leaves, and the forms of many trees, as the palm.

For better consideration, we may distribute the aspects of Beauty in a threefold manner.

1. First, the simple perception of natural forms is a delight. The influence of the forms and actions in nature is so needful to man, that, in its lowest functions, it seems to lie on the confines of commodity and beauty. To the body and mind which have been cramped by noxious work or company, nature is medicinal and restores their tone. The tradesman, the attorney comes out of the din and craft of the street and sees the sky and the woods, and is a man again. In their eternal calm, he finds himself. The health of the eye seems to demand a horizon. We are never tired, so long as we can see far enough.

But in other hours, Nature satisfies by its loveliness, and without any mixture of corporeal benefit. I see the spectacle of morning from the hilltop over against my house, from daybreak to sunrise, with emotions which an angel might share. The long slender bars of cloud float like fishes in the sea of crimson light. From the earth, as a shore, I look out into that silent sea. I seem to partake its rapid transformations; the active enchantment reaches my dust, and I dilate and conspire [12] with the morning wind. How does Nature deify us with a few and cheap elements! Give me health and a day, and I will make the pomp of emperors ridiculous. The dawn is my Assyria; the sunset and moon-rise my Paphos, and unimaginable realms of faerie; broad noon shall be my England of the senses and the understanding; the night shall be my Germany of mystic philosophy and dreams. [13]

Not less excellent, except for our less susceptibility in the afternoon, was the charm, last evening, of a January sunset. The western clouds divided and subdivided themselves into pink flakes modulated with tints of unspeakable softness, and the air had so much life and sweetness that it was a pain

---

[12] Breathe. [Ed.]

[13] Emerson compares natural phenomena with historical locations: the dawn with the power of the ancient Assyrian Empire, noted for its military might; sunset and evening with the erotic and romantic powers of Aphrodite, whose primary site of worship in the ancient world was the city of Paphos on the island of Cyprus; noon with the reason and good sense of the modern English nation; night with the mystery of German idealist philosophy (and the spiritualism of his own transcendentalism). [Ed.]

to come within doors. What was it that nature would say? Was there no meaning in the live repose of the valley behind the mill, and which Homer or Shakespeare could not re-form for me in words? The leafless trees become spires of flame in the sunset, with the blue east for their background, and the stars of the dead calices of flowers, and every withered stem and stubble rimed with frost, contribute something to the mute music.

The inhabitants of cities suppose that the country landscape is pleasant only half the year. I please myself with the graces of the winter scenery, and believe that we are as much touched by it as by the genial influences of summer. To the attentive eye, each moment of the year has its own beauty, and in the same field, it beholds, every hour, a picture which was never seen before, and which shall never be seen again. The heavens change every moment, and reflect their glory or gloom on the plains beneath. The state of the crop in the surrounding farms alters the expression of the earth from week to week. The succession of native plants in the pastures and roadsides, which makes the silent clock by which time tells the summer hours, will make even the divisions of the day sensible to a keen observer. The tribes of birds and insects, like the plants punctual to their time, follow each other, and the year has room for all. By watercourses, the variety is greater. In July, the blue pontederia or pickerelweed blooms in large beds in the shallow parts of our pleasant river, and swarms with yellow butterflies in continual motion. Art cannot rival this pomp of purple and gold. Indeed the river is a perpetual gala, and boasts each month a new ornament.

But this beauty of Nature which is seen and felt as beauty, is the least part. The shows of day, the dewy morning, the rainbow, mountains, orchards in blossom, stars, moonlight, shadows in still water, and the like, if too eagerly hunted, become shows merely, and mock us with their unreality. Go out of the house to see the moon, and 'tis mere tinsel; it will not please as when its light shines upon your necessary journey. The beauty that shimmers in the yellow afternoons of October, who ever could clutch it? Go forth to find it, and it is gone; 'tis only a mirage as you look from the windows of diligence.

2. The presence of a higher, namely, of the spiritual element is essential to its perfection. The high and divine beauty which can be loved without effeminacy, is that which is found in combination with the human will. Beauty is the mark God sets upon virtue. Every natural action is graceful. Every heroic act is also decent,[14] and causes the place and the bystanders to shine. We are taught by great actions that the universe is the property of every individual in it. Every rational creature has all nature for his dowry

---

[14] Handsome, morally proper. [Ed.]

and estate. It is his, if he will. He may divest himself of it; he may creep into a corner, and abdicate his kingdom, as most men do, but he is entitled to the world by his constitution. In proportion to the energy of his thought and will, he takes up the world into himself. "All those things for which men plough, build, or sail, obey virtue," said Sallust.[15] "The winds and waves," said Gibbon, "are always on the side of the ablest navigators."[16] So are the sun and moon and all the stars of heaven. When a noble act is done,—perchance in a scene of great natural beauty; when Leonidas and his three hundred martyrs consume one day in dying, and the sun and moon come each and look at them once in the steep defile of Thermopylae,[17] when Arnold Winkelried, in the high Alps, under the shadow of the avalanche, gathers in his side a sheaf of Austrian spears to break the line for his comrades;[18] are not these heroes entitled to add the beauty of the scene to the beauty of the deed? When the bark of Columbus nears the shore of America;—before it the beach lined with savages, fleeing out of all their huts of cane; the sea behind; and the purple mountains of the Indian Archipelago around, can we separate the man from the living picture? Does not the New World clothe his form with her palm-groves and savannahs as fit drapery? Ever does natural beauty steal in like air, and envelope great actions. When Sir Harry Vane[19] was dragged up the Tower-hill, sitting on a sled, to suffer death as the champion of the English laws, one of the multitude cried out to him, "You never sate on so glorious a seat!" Charles II,[20] to intimidate the citizens of London, caused the patriot Lord Russell[21] to be drawn in an open coach through the principal streets of the city on his

---

[15] Sallust (86–35 BCE) is identified as the source for this quote in the 1849 edition, but simply "an ancient historian" in the 1836 edition. The quotation appears exactly in Milton's *Apology for Smectymnuus* (1642), which may be Emerson's source (Ferguson 1:248). [Ed.]

[16] Edward Gibbon, *Decline and Fall of the Roman Empire* (1788). [Ed.]

[17] Leonidas, king of Sparta, together with three hundred soldiers, defended the pass of Thermopylae against the Persians in the Battle of Thermopylae (480 BCE). [Ed.]

[18] In the Battle of Sempach (1386), Arnold von Winkelried was reputed to have brought victory to the Swiss by "gathering all the Austrian pikes he could reach into his own body," enabling the Swiss to break through the Austrian line (Ferguson 1:248). [Ed.]

[19] Vane (1613–1662), a leading English Puritan statesman, who served as the fourth governor of Massachusetts and was executed by Charles II for treason after the Restoration (Whicher 29). [Ed.]

[20] Charles II (r. 1660–85), English monarch who was restored to the throne at the end of the Puritan Commonwealth. [Ed.]

[21] William Russell (1639–83) was accused of high treason for complicity in the Rye House Plot (June 1683) against Charles II and his probable successor, James, Duke of York, and was executed. [Ed.]

way to the scaffold. "But," his biographer says, "the multitude imagined they saw liberty and virtue sitting by his side." In private places, among sordid objects, an act of truth or heroism seems at once to draw to itself the sky as its temple, the sun as its candle. Nature stretches out her arms to embrace man, only let his thoughts be of equal greatness. Willingly does she follow his steps with the rose and the violet, and bend her lines of grandeur and grace to the decoration of her darling child. Only let his thoughts be of equal scope, and the frame will suit the picture. A virtuous man is in unison with her works, and makes the central figure of the visible sphere. Homer, Pindar, Socrates, Phocion, associate themselves fitly in our memory with the geography and climate of Greece. The visible heavens and earth sympathize with Jesus. And in common life whosoever has seen a person of powerful character and happy genius, will have remarked how easily he took all things along with him, — the persons, the opinions, and the day, and nature become ancillary to a man.[22]

3. There is still another aspect under which the beauty of the world may be viewed, namely, as it becomes an object of the intellect. Beside the relation of things to virtue, they have a relation to thought. The intellect searches out the absolute order of things as they stand in the mind of God, and without the colors of affection. The intellectual and the active powers seem to succeed each other, and the exclusive activity of the one generates the exclusive activity of the other. There is something unfriendly in each to the other, but they are like the alternate periods of feeding and working in animals; each prepares and will be followed by the other. Therefore does beauty, which, in relation to actions, as we have seen, comes unsought, and comes because it is unsought, remain for the apprehension and pursuit of the intellect; and then again, in its turn, of the active power. Nothing divine dies. All good is eternally reproductive. The beauty of nature reforms itself in the mind, and not for barren contemplation, but for new creation.

All men are in some degree impressed by the face of the world; some men even to delight. This love of beauty is Taste. Others have the same love in such excess, that, not content with admiring, they seek to embody it in new forms. The creation of beauty is Art.

The production of a work of art throws a light upon the mystery of humanity. A work of art is an abstract or epitome of the world. It is the result or expression of nature, in miniature. For although the works of nature are innumerable and all different, the result or the expression of them all is similar and single. Nature is a sea of forms radically alike and even unique.

---

[22]Emerson uses examples of ancient artists and philosophers, together with Jesus, to suggest how "genius" is a natural phenomenon, in general accord with romantic philosophy's theory of genius. [Ed.]

A leaf, a sunbeam, a landscape, the ocean, make an analogous impression on the mind. What is common to them all,—that perfectness and harmony, is beauty. The standard of beauty is the entire circuit of natural forms,—the totality of nature; which the Italians expressed by defining beauty "il più nell' uno."[23] Nothing is quite beautiful alone; nothing but is beautiful in the whole. A single object is only so far beautiful as it suggests this universal grace. The poet, the painter, the sculptor, the musician, the architect, seek each to concentrate this radiance of the world on one point, and each in his several work to satisfy the love of beauty which stimulates him to produce. Thus is Art a nature passed through the alembic[24] of man. Thus in art does Nature work through the will of a man filled with the beauty of her first works.

The world thus exists to the soul to satisfy the desire of beauty. This element I call an ultimate end. No reason can be asked or given why the soul seeks beauty. Beauty, in its largest and profoundest sense, is one expression for the universe. God is the all-fair. Truth, and goodness, and beauty, are but different faces of the same All. But beauty in nature is not ultimate. It is the herald of inward and eternal beauty, and is not alone a solid and satisfactory good. It must stand as a part, and not as yet the last or highest expression of the final cause of Nature.

IV. Language

Language is a third use which Nature subserves to man. Nature is the vehicle of thought, and in a simple, double, and threefold degree.

1. Words are signs of natural facts.

2. Particular natural facts are symbols of particular spiritual facts.

3. Nature is the symbol of spirit.

1. Words are signs of natural facts. The use of natural history is to give us aid in supernatural history; the use of the outer creation, to give us language for the beings and changes of the inward creation. Every word which is used to express a moral or intellectual fact, if traced to its root, is found to be borrowed from some material appearance. *Right* originally means *straight; wrong* means *twisted. Spirit* primarily means *wind; transgression,* the *crossing of a line; supercilious,* the *raising of the eyebrow.* We say the *heart*

---

[23] Italian: the many in one. Emerson used this expression frequently in Italian and English. [Ed.]

[24] A beaker. [Ed.]

to express emotion, the *head* to denote thought; and *thought* and *emotion* are words borrowed from sensible things, and now appropriated to spiritual nature. Most of the process by which this transformation is made, is hidden from us in the remote time when language was framed; but the same tendency may be daily observed in children. Children and savages use only nouns or names of things, which they convert into verbs, and apply to analogous mental acts.

2. But this origin of all words that convey a spiritual import,—so conspicuous a fact in the history of language,—is our least debt to nature. It is not words only that are emblematic; it is things which are emblematic. Every natural fact is a symbol of some spiritual fact. Every appearance in nature corresponds to some state of the mind, and that state of the mind can only be described by presenting that natural appearance as its picture. An enraged man is a lion, a cunning man is a fox, a firm man is a rock, a learned man is a torch. A lamb is innocence; a snake is subtle spite; flowers express to us the delicate affections. Light and darkness are our familiar expression for knowledge and ignorance; and heat for love. Visible distance behind and before us, is respectively our image of memory and hope.

Who looks upon a river in a meditative hour and is not reminded of the flux of all things? Throw a stone into a stream, and the circles that propagate themselves are the beautiful type of all influence. Man is conscious of a universal soul within or behind his individual life, wherein, as in a firmament, the natures of Justice, Truth, Love, Freedom, arise and shine. This universal soul he calls Reason: it is not mine, or thine, or his, but we are its; we are its property and men. And the blue sky in which the private earth is buried, the sky with its eternal calm, and full of everlasting orbs, is the type of Reason. That which intellectually considered we call Reason, considered in relation to nature, we call Spirit. Spirit is the Creator. Spirit hath life in itself. And man in all ages and countries embodies it in his language as the FATHER.

It is easily seen that there is nothing lucky or capricious in these analogies, but that they are constant, and pervade nature. These are not the dreams of a few poets, here and there, but man is an analogist, and studies relations in all objects. He is placed in the center of beings, and a ray of relation passes from every other being to him. And neither can man be understood without these objects, nor these objects without man. All the facts in natural history taken by themselves, have no value, but are barren, like a single sex. But marry it to human history, and it is full of life. Whole floras, all Linnaeus' and Buffon's volumes, are dry catalogues of facts; but the most trivial of these facts, the habit of a plant, the organs, or work, or noise of an insect, applied to the illustration of a fact in intellectual philosophy, or in any way associated to human nature, affects us in the most lively and agreeable manner. The seed of a plant,—to what affecting analogies in the nature of man is that little fruit made use of, in all discourse, up to the voice of Paul, who calls the human corpse a seed,—"It is sown a natural body; it is raised a spiritual body."[25] The motion of the earth round its axis and round the sun, makes the day and the year. These are certain amounts of brute light and heat. But is there no intent of an analogy between man's life and the seasons? And do the seasons gain no grandeur or pathos from that analogy? The instincts of the ant are very unimportant considered as the ant's; but the moment a ray of relation is seen to extend from it to man, and the little drudge is seen to be a monitor, a little body with a mighty heart, then all its habits, even that said to be recently observed, that it never sleeps, become sublime.

Because of this radical correspondence between visible things and human thoughts, savages, who have only what is necessary, converse in figures. As we go back in history, language becomes more picturesque, until its infancy, when it is all poetry; or all spiritual facts are represented by natural symbols. The same symbols are found to make the original elements of all languages. It has moreover been observed, that the idioms of all languages approach each other in passages of the greatest eloquence and power. And as this is the first language, so is it the last. This immediate dependence of language upon nature, this conversion of an outward phenomenon into a type of somewhat in human life, never loses its power to affect us. It is this which gives that piquancy to the conversation of a strong-natured farmer or back-woodsman, which all men relish.

Thus is nature an interpreter, by whose means man converses with his fellow men. A man's power to connect his thought with its proper symbol, and so to utter it, depends on the simplicity of his character, that is, upon his love of truth and his desire to communicate it without loss. The corruption of man is followed by the corruption of language. When simplicity of character and the sovereignty of ideas is broken up by the prevalence of secondary desires,—the desire of riches, of pleasure, of power, and of praise,—and duplicity and falsehood take place of simplicity and truth, the power over nature as an interpreter of the will is in a degree lost; new imagery ceases to be created, and old words are perverted to stand for things which are not; a paper currency is employed, when there is no bullion in the vaults. In due time the fraud is manifest, and words lose all power to stimulate the understanding or the affections. Hundreds of writers may be found in every long-civilized nation who for a short time believe and make others believe that they see and utter truths, who do not of themselves

---

[25] 1 Cor. 15.44. [Ed.]

clothe one thought in its natural garment, but who feed unconsciously on the language created by the primary writers of the country, those, namely, who hold primarily on nature.

But wise men pierce this rotten diction and fasten words again to visible things; so that picturesque language is at once a commanding certificate that he who employs it is a man in alliance with truth and God. The moment our discourse rises above the ground line of familiar facts and is inflamed with passion or exalted by thought, it clothes itself in images. A man conversing in earnest, if he watch his intellectual processes, will find that a material image more or less luminous arises in his mind, contemporaneous with every thought, which furnishes the vestment of the thought. Hence, good writing and brilliant discourse are perpetual allegories. This imagery is spontaneous. It is the blending of experience with the present action of the mind. It is proper creation. It is the working of the Original Cause through the instruments he has already made.

These facts may suggest the advantage which the country-life possesses, for a powerful mind, over the artificial and curtailed life of cities. We know more from nature than we can at will communicate. Its light flows into the mind evermore, and we forget its presence. The poet, the orator, bred in the woods, whose senses have been nourished by their fair and appeasing changes, year after year, without design and without heed, — shall not lose their lesson altogether, in the roar of cities or the broil of politics. Long hereafter, amidst agitation and terror in national councils, — in the hour of revolution, — these solemn images shall reappear in their morning lustre, as fit symbols and words of the thoughts which the passing events shall awaken. At the call of a noble sentiment, again the woods wave, the pines murmur, the river rolls and shines, and the cattle low upon the mountains, as he saw and heard them in his infancy. And with these forms, the spells of persuasion, the keys of power are put into his hands.

3. We are thus assisted by natural objects in the expression of particular meanings. But how great a language to convey such pepper-corn informations! Did it need such noble races of creatures, this profusion of forms, this host of orbs in heaven, to furnish man with the dictionary and grammar of his municipal speech? Whilst we use this grand cipher to expedite the affairs of our pot and kettle, we feel that we have not yet put it to its use, neither are able. We are like travelers using the cinders of a volcano to roast their eggs. Whilst we see that it always stands ready to clothe what we would say, we cannot avoid the question whether the characters are not significant of themselves. Have mountains, and waves, and skies, no significance but what we consciously give them when we employ them as emblems of our thoughts? The world is emblematic. Parts of speech are metaphors, because the whole of nature is a metaphor of the human mind. The laws of moral

nature answer to those of matter as face to face in a glass. "The visible world and the relation of its parts, is the dial plate of the invisible."[26] The axioms of physics translate the laws of ethics. Thus, "the whole is greater than its part"; "reaction is equal to action"; "the smallest weight may be made to lift the greatest, the difference of weight being compensated by time"; and many the like propositions, which have an ethical as well as physical sense. These propositions have a much more extensive and universal sense when applied to human life, than when confined to technical use.

In like manner, the memorable words of history and the proverbs of nations consist usually of a natural fact, selected as a picture or parable of a moral truth. Thus: A rolling stone gathers no moss; A bird in the hand is worth two in the bush; A cripple in the right way will beat a racer in the wrong; Make hay while the sun shines; 'Tis hard to carry a full cup even; Vinegar is the son of wine; The last ounce broke the camel's back; Long-lived trees make roots first; — and the like. In their primary sense these are trivial facts, but we repeat them for the value of their analogical import. What is true of proverbs, is true of all fables, parables, and allegories.

This relation between the mind and matter is not fancied by some poet, but stands in the will of God, and so is free to be known by all men. It appears to men, or it does not appear. When in fortunate hours we ponder this miracle, the wise man doubts if at all other times he is not blind and deaf;

"Can these things be,
And overcome us like a summer's cloud,
Without our special wonder?"[27]

for the universe becomes transparent, and the light of higher laws than its own shines through it. It is the standing problem which has exercised the wonder and the study of every fine genius since the world began; from the era of the Egyptians and the Brahmins to that of Pythagoras, of Plato, of Bacon, of Leibnitz, of Swedenborg. There sits the Sphinx at the road-side, and from age to age, as each prophet comes by, he tries his fortune at reading her riddle. There seems to be a necessity in spirit to manifest itself in material forms; and day and night, river and storm, beast and bird, acid and alkali, preëxist in necessary Ideas in the mind of God, and are what they are by virtue of preceding affections in the world of spirit. A Fact is the end or last issue of spirit. The visible creation is the terminus or the circumference of the invisible world. "Material objects," said a French philosopher,

---

[26] Emanuel Swedenborg, qtd. by Samuel Sandels in "Emanuel Swedenborg," *New Jerusalem Magazine* 5 (July 1832): 437 (Ferguson 1:249). [Ed.]

[27] *Macbeth* 3.4.110–12. [Ed.]

"are necessarily kinds of *scoriae* of the substantial thoughts of the Creator, which must always preserve an exact relation to their first origin; in other words, visible nature must have a spiritual and moral side."[28]

This doctrine is abstruse, and though the images of "garment," "scoriae," "mirror," etc., may stimulate the fancy, we must summon the aid of subtler and more vital expositors to make it plain. "Every scripture is to be interpreted by the same spirit which gave it forth,"—is the fundamental law of criticism.[29] A life in harmony with Nature, the love of truth and of virtue, will purge the eyes to understand her text. By degrees we may come to know the primitive sense of the permanent objects of nature, so that the world shall be to us an open book, and every form significant of its hidden life and final cause.

A new interest surprises us, whilst, under the view now suggested, we contemplate the fearful extent and multitude of objects; since "every object rightly seen, unlocks a new faculty of the soul."[30] That which was unconscious truth, becomes, when interpreted and defined in an object, a part of the domain of knowledge,—a new weapon in the magazine of power.

V. Discipline

In view of this significance of nature, we arrive at once at a new fact, that nature is a discipline. This use of the world includes the preceding uses, as parts of itself.

Space, time, society, labor, climate, food, locomotion, the animals, the mechanical forces, give us sincerest lessons, day by day, whose meaning is unlimited. They educate both the Understanding and the Reason. Every property of matter is a school for the understanding,—its solidity or resistance, its inertia, its extension, its figure, its divisibility. The understanding adds, divides, combines, measures, and finds nutriment and room for its activity in this worthy scene. Meantime, Reason transfers all these lessons into its own world of thought, by perceiving the analogy that marries Matter and Mind.

1. Nature is a discipline of the understanding in intellectual truths. Our dealing with sensible objects is a constant exercise in the necessary lessons of difference, of likeness, of order, of being and seeming, of progressive arrangement; of ascent from particular to general; of combination to one

---

[28] G. Oegger, *The True Messiah; or The Old and New Testaments, Examined According to The Principles of the Language of Nature,* trans. E. P. Peabody (Boston, 1842) (Ferguson 1:250) *Scoriae:* Latin for dross or waste. [Ed.]

[29] George Fox, founder of the Quakers. [Orig. ed.]

[30] Samuel Taylor Coleridge, *Aids to Reflection* (1825). [Ed.]

end of manifold forces. Proportioned to the importance of the organ to be formed, is the extreme care with which its tuition is provided,—a care pretermitted in no single case. What tedious training, day after day, year after year, never ending, to form the common sense; what continual reproduction of annoyances, inconveniences, dilemmas; what rejoicing over us of little men; what disputing of prices, what reckonings of interest,—and all to form the Hand of the mind;—to instruct us that "good thoughts are no better than good dreams, unless they be executed!"[31]

The same good office is performed by Property and its filial systems of debt and credit. Debt, grinding debt, whose iron face the widow, the orphan, and the sons of genius fear and hate;—debt, which consumes so much time, which so cripples and disheartens a great spirit with cares that seem so base, is a preceptor whose lessons cannot be foregone, and is needed most by those who suffer from it most. Moreover, property, which has been well compared to snow,—"if it fall level today, it will be blown into drifts tomorrow,"—is the surface action of internal machinery, like the index on the face of a clock. Whilst now it is the gymnastics of the understanding, it is hiving, in the foresight of the spirit, experience in profounder laws.

The whole character and fortune of the individual are affected by the least inequalities in the culture of the understanding; for example, in the perception of differences. Therefore is Space, and therefore Time, that man may know that things are not huddled and lumped, but sundered and individual. A bell and a plough have each their use, and neither can do the office of the other. Water is good to drink, coal to burn, wool to wear; but wool cannot be drunk, nor water spun, nor coal eaten. The wise man shows his wisdom in separation, in gradation, and his scale of creatures and of merits is as wide as nature. The foolish have no range in their scale, but suppose every man is as every other man. What is not good they call the worst, and what is not hateful, they call the best.

In like manner, what good heed Nature forms in us! She pardons no mistakes. Her yea is yea, and her nay, nay.

The first steps in Agriculture, Astronomy, Zoölogy (those first steps which the farmer, the hunter, and the sailor take), teach that Nature's dice are always loaded; that in her heaps and rubbish are concealed sure and useful results.

How calmly and genially the mind apprehends one after another the laws of physics! What noble emotions dilate the mortal as he enters into the councils of the creation, and feels by knowledge the privilege to Be! His

---

[31] Francis Bacon, "Of Great Place" (1612). [Ed.]

insight refines him. The beauty of nature shines in his own breast. Man is greater that he can see this, and the universe less, because Time and Space relations vanish as laws are known.

Here again we are impressed and even daunted by the immense Universe to be explored. "What we know is a point to what we do not know."[32] Open any recent journal of science, and weigh the problems suggested concerning Light, Heat, Electricity, Magnetism, Physiology, Geology, and judge whether the interest of natural science is likely to be soon exhausted.

Passing by many particulars of the discipline of nature, we must not omit to specify two.

The exercise of the Will, or the lesson of power, is taught in every event. From the child's successive possession of his several senses up to the hour when he saith, "Thy will be done!" he is learning the secret that he can reduce under his will not only particular events but great classes, nay, the whole series of events, and so conform all facts to his character. Nature is thoroughly mediate. It is made to serve. It receives the dominion of man as meekly as the ass on which the Saviour rode. It offers all its kingdoms to man as the raw material which he may mold into what is useful. Man is never weary of working it up. He forges the subtile and delicate air into wise and melodious words, and gives them wing as angels of persuasion and command. More and more, with every thought, does his kingdom stretch over things until the world becomes at last only a realized will, — the double of the man.

2. Sensible objects conform to the premonitions of Reason and reflect the conscience. All things are moral; and in their boundless changes have an unceasing reference to spiritual nature. Therefore is nature glorious with form, color, and motion; that every globe in the remotest heaven, every chemical change from the rudest crystal up to the laws of life, every change of vegetation from the first principle of growth in the eye of a leaf, to the tropical forest and antediluvian coal-mine, every animal function from the sponge up to Hercules, shall hint or thunder to man the laws of right and wrong, and echo the Ten Commandments. Therefore is Nature ever the ally of Religion: lends all her pomp and riches to the religious sentiment. Prophet and priest, David, Isaiah, Jesus, have drawn deeply from this source.

This ethical character so penetrates the bone and marrow of nature, as to seem the end for which it was made. Whatever private purpose is answered by any member or part, this is its public and universal function, and is never omitted. Nothing in nature is exhausted in its first use. When a

---

[32] Bishop Joseph Butler, qtd. in Robert Plumer Ward's novel *Tremaine* (1825) (Ferguson 1:250). [Ed.]

thing has served an end to the uttermost, it is wholly new for an ulterior service. In God, every end is converted into a new means. Thus the use of commodity, regarded by itself, is mean and squalid. But it is to the mind an education in the doctrine of Use, namely, that a thing is good only so far as it serves; that a conspiring of parts and efforts to the production of an end is essential to any being. The first and gross manifestation of this truth is our inevitable and hated training in values and wants, in corn and meat.

It has already been illustrated, that every natural process is a version of a moral sentence. The moral law lies at the center of nature and radiates to the circumference. It is the pith and marrow of every substance, every relation, and every process. All things with which we deal, preach to us. What is a farm but a mute gospel? The chaff and the wheat, weeds and plants, blight, rain, insects, sun, — it is a sacred emblem from the first furrow of spring to the last stack which the snow of winter overtakes in the fields. But the sailor, the shepherd, the miner, the merchant, in their several resorts, have each an experience precisely parallel and leading to the same conclusion: because all organizations are radically alike. Nor can it be doubted that this moral sentiment which thus scents the air, grows in the grain, and impregnates the waters of the world, is caught by man and sinks into his soul. The moral influence of nature upon every individual is that amount of truth which it illustrates to him. Who can estimate this? Who can guess how much firmness the sea-beaten rock has taught the fisherman? how much tranquillity has been reflected to man from the azure sky, over whose unspotted deeps the winds forevermore drive flocks of stormy clouds, and leave no wrinkle or stain? how much industry and providence and affection we have caught from the pantomime of brutes? What a searching preacher of self-command is the varying phenomenon of Health!

Herein is especially apprehended the unity of Nature, — the unity in variety, — which meets us everywhere. All the endless variety of things make an identical impression. Xenophanes[33] complained in his old age, that, look where he would, all things hastened back to Unity. He was weary of seeing the same entity in the tedious variety of forms. The fable of Proteus[34] has a cordial truth. A leaf, a drop, a crystal, a moment of time, is related to the whole, and partakes of the perfection of the whole. Each particle is a microcosm, and faithfully renders the likeness of the world.

Not only resemblances exist in things whose analogy is obvious, as when we detect the type of the human hand in the flipper of the fossil saurus, but

---

[33] Xenophanes of Elea (570–480 BCE), a Greek philosopher. [Ed.]

[34] Greek mythological prophet known for his ability to change his form to avoid prophesying. When forced to tell the truth, he would assume his original form. "Cordial" means in this context "living," as in "still relevant." [Ed.]

also in objects wherein there is great superficial unlikeness. Thus architecture is called "frozen music," by De Staël and Goethe. Vitruvius[35] thought an architect should be a musician. "A Gothic church," said Coleridge, "is a petrified religion." Michael Angelo maintained, that, to an architect, a knowledge of anatomy is essential. In Haydn's oratorios, the notes present to the imagination not only motions, as of the snake, the stag, and the elephant, but colors also; as the green grass. The law of harmonic sounds reappears in the harmonic colors. The granite is differenced in its laws only by the more or less of heat from the river that wears it away. The river, as it flows, resembles the air that flows over it; the air resembles the light which traverses it with more subtle currents; the light resembles the heat which rides with it through Space. Each creature is only a modification of the other; the likeness in them is more than the difference, and their radical law is one and the same. A rule of one art, or a law of one organization, holds true throughout nature. So intimate is this Unity, that, it is easily seen, it lies under the undermost garment of Nature, and betrays its source in Universal Spirit. For it pervades Thought also. Every universal truth which we express in words, implies or supposes every other truth. *Omne verum vero consonat.*[36] It is like a great circle on a sphere comprising all possible circles; which, however, may be drawn and comprise it in like manner. Every such truth is the absolute Ens[37] seen from one side. But it has innumerable sides.

The central Unity is still more conspicuous in actions. Words are finite organs of the infinite mind. They cannot cover the dimensions of what is in truth. They break, chop, and impoverish it. An action is the perfection and publication of thought. A right action seems to fill the eye, and to be related to all nature. "The wise man, in doing one thing, does all; or, in the one thing he does rightly, he sees the likeness of all which is done rightly."[38]

Words and actions are not the attributes of brute nature. They introduce us to the human form, of which all other organizations appear to be degradations. When this organization appears among so many that surround it, the spirit prefers it to all others. It says, "From such as this have I drawn joy and knowledge; in such as this have I found and beheld myself; I will speak to it; it can speak again; it can yield me thought already formed and alive." In fact, the eye, —the mind, —is always accompanied by

[35]Vitruvius was a "first century BC Roman architect, engineer, and writer on architecture," to whom Emerson attributes the origin of the idea expressed by Madame de Staël and Goethe (Ferguson 1:251). [Ed.]

[36]Latin for "All truth accords with truth". [Orig. ed.]

[37]Latin: being, in the philosophical sense. [Ed.]

[38]Thomas Carlyle's translation of Goethe's *Wilhelm Meister's Travels* (1821–29) (Ferguson 1:251). [Ed.]

these forms, male and female; and these are incomparably the richest informations of the power and order that lie at the heart of things. Unfortunately every one of them bears the marks as of some injury; is marred and superficially defective. Nevertheless, far different from the deaf and dumb nature around them, these all rest like fountain-pipes on the unfathomed sea of thought and virtue whereto they alone, of all organizations, are the entrances.

It were a pleasant inquiry to follow into detail their ministry to our education, but where would it stop? We are associated in adolescent and adult life with some friends, who, like skies and waters, are coextensive with our idea; who, answering each to a certain affection of the soul, satisfy our desire on that side; whom we lack power to put at such focal distance from us, that we can mend or even analyze them. We cannot choose but love them. When much intercourse with a friend has supplied us with a standard of excellence, and has increased our respect for the resources of God who thus sends a real person to outgo our ideal; when he has, moreover, become an object of thought, and, whilst his character retains all its unconscious effect, is converted in the mind into solid and sweet wisdom, — it is a sign to us that his office is closing, and he is commonly withdrawn from our sight in a short time.

VI. Idealism

Thus is the unspeakable but intelligible and practicable meaning of the world conveyed to man, the immortal pupil, in every object of sense. To this one end of Discipline, all parts of nature conspire.

A noble doubt perpetually suggests itself, —whether this end be not the Final Cause of the Universe; and whether nature outwardly exists. It is a sufficient account of that Appearance we call the World, that God will teach a human mind, and so makes it the receiver of a certain number of congruent sensations, which we call sun and moon, man and woman, house and trade. In my utter impotence to test the authenticity of the report of my senses, to know whether the impressions they make on me correspond with outlying objects, what difference does it make, whether Orion is up there in heaven, or some god paints the image in the firmament of the soul? The relations of parts and the end of the whole remaining the same, what is the difference, whether land and sea interact, and worlds revolve and intermingle without number or end, —deep yawning under deep, and galaxy balancing galaxy, throughout absolute space, —or whether, without relations of time and space, the same appearances are inscribed in the constant faith of man? Whether nature enjoy a substantial existence without, or is only in the apocalypse of the mind, it is alike useful and alike venerable to me. Be it what it may, it is ideal to me so long as I cannot try the accuracy of my senses.

The frivolous make themselves merry with the Ideal theory, as if its consequences were burlesque; as if it affected the stability of nature. It surely does not. God never jests with us, and will not compromise the end of nature by permitting any inconsequence in its procession. Any distrust of the permanence of laws would paralyze the faculties of man. Their permanence is sacredly respected, and his faith therein is perfect. The wheels and springs of man are all set to the hypothesis of the permanence of nature. We are not built like a ship to be tossed, but like a house to stand. It is a natural consequence of this structure, that so long as the active powers predominate over the reflective, we resist with indignation any hint that nature is more short-lived or mutable than spirit. The broker, the wheelwright, the carpenter, the tollman, are much displeased at the intimation.

But whilst we acquiesce entirely in the permanence of natural laws, the question of the absolute existence of nature still remains open. It is the uniform effect of culture on the human mind, not to shake our faith in the stability of particular phenomena, as of heat, water, azote,[39] but to lead us to regard nature as a phenomenon, not a substance; to attribute necessary existence to spirit; to esteem nature as an accident and an effect.

To the senses and the unrenewed understanding, belongs a sort of instinctive belief in the absolute existence of nature. In their view man and nature are indissolubly joined. Things are ultimates, and they never look beyond their sphere. The presence of Reason mars this faith. The first effort of thought tends to relax this despotism of the senses which binds us to nature as if we were a part of it, and shows us nature aloof, and, as it were, afloat. Until this higher agency intervened, the animal eye sees, with wonderful accuracy, sharp outlines and colored surfaces. When the eye of Reason opens, to outline and surface are at once added grace and expression. These proceed from imagination and affection, and abate somewhat of the angular distinctness of objects. If the Reason be stimulated to more earnest vision, outlines and surfaces become transparent, and are no longer seen; causes and spirits are seen through them. The best moments of life are these delicious awakenings of the higher powers, and the reverential withdrawing of nature before its God.

Let us proceed to indicate the effects of culture.

1. Our first institution[40] in the Ideal philosophy is a hint from Nature herself.

---

[39] Nitrogen. [Ed.]

[40] Established practice, law, custom. [Ed.]

Nature is made to conspire with spirit to emancipate us. Certain mechanical changes, a small alteration in our local position, apprizes us of a dualism. We are strangely affected by seeing the shore from a moving ship, from a balloon, or through the tints of an unusual sky. The least change in our point of view gives the whole world a pictorial air. A man who seldom rides, needs only to get into a coach and traverse his own town, to turn the street into a puppet-show. The men, the women, — talking, running, bartering, fighting, — the earnest mechanic, the lounger, the beggar, the boys, the dogs are unrealized[41] at once, or, at least, wholly detached from all relation to the observer, and seen as apparent, not substantial beings. What new thoughts are suggested by seeing a face of country quite familiar, in the rapid movement of the railroad car! Nay, the most wonted objects, (make a very slight change in the point of vision), please us most. In a camera obscura,[42] the butcher's cart, and the figure of one of our own family amuse us. So a portrait of a well-known face gratifies us. Turn the eyes upside down, by looking at the landscape through your legs, and how agreeable is the picture, though you have seen it any time these twenty years!

In these cases, by mechanical means, is suggested the difference between the observer and the spectacle — between man and nature. Hence arises a pleasure mixed with awe; I may say, a low degree of the sublime is felt, from the fact, probably, that man is hereby apprized that whilst the world is a spectacle, something in himself is stable.

2. In a higher manner the poet communicates the same pleasure. By a few strokes he delineates, as on air, the sun, the mountain, the camp, the city, the hero, the maiden, not different from what we know them, but only lifted from the ground and afloat before the eye. He unfixes the land and the sea, makes them revolve around the axis of his primary thought, and disposes them anew. Possessed himself by a heroic passion, he uses matter as symbols of it. The sensual man conforms thoughts to things; the poet conforms things to his thoughts. The one esteems nature as rooted and fast; the other, as fluid, and impresses his being thereon. To him, the refractory world is ductile and flexible; he invests dust and stones with humanity, and makes them the words of the Reason. The Imagination may be defined to be the use which the Reason makes of the material world. Shakespeare possesses the power of subordinating nature for the purposes of expression, beyond all poets. His imperial muse tosses the creation like a bauble from hand to hand, and uses it to embody any caprice of thought

---

[41] Made unreal. [Orig. ed.]

[42] A "dark chamber" with an aperture through which light from external objects enters to form an image on the opposite surface; a pre-photographic system for representing objects. The image formed by the light is the inverse of the original. [Ed.]

that is uppermost in his mind. The remotest spaces of nature are visited, and the farthest sundered things are brought together, by a subtile spiritual connection. We are made aware that magnitude of material things is relative, and all objects shrink and expand to serve the passion of the poet. Thus in his sonnets, the lays of birds, the scents and dyes of flowers he finds to be the *shadow* of his beloved; time, which keeps her from him, is his *chest;* the suspicion she has awakened, is her *ornament;*

> "The ornament of beauty is Suspect,
> A crow which flies in heaven's sweetest air." [43]

His passion is not the fruit of chance; it swells, as he speaks, to a city, or a state.

> "No, it was builded far from accident;
> It suffers not in smiling pomp, nor falls
> Under the brow of thralling discontent;
> It fears not policy, that heretic,
> That works on leases of short numbered hours,
> But all alone stands hugely politic." [44]

In the strength of his constancy, the Pyramids seem to him recent and transitory. The freshness of youth and love dazzles him with its resemblance to morning;

> "Take those lips away
> Which so sweetly were forsworn;
> And those eyes,—the break of day,
> Lights that do mislead the morn." [45]

The wild beauty of this hyperbole, I may say in passing, it would not be easy to match in literature.

This transfiguration which all material objects undergo through the passion of the poet,—this power which he exerts to dwarf the great, to magnify the small,—might be illustrated by a thousand examples from his Plays. I have before me the Tempest, and will cite only these few lines.

> "PROSPERO. The strong based promontory
> Have I made shake, and by the spurs plucked up
> The pine and cedar."

---

[43] Shakespeare, Sonnet 70. [Ed.]

[44] Shakespeare, Sonnet 124. [Ed.]

[45] Shakespeare, *Measure for Measure* 4.1. [Ed.]

Prospero calls for music to soothe the frantic Alonzo, and his companions;

> "A solemn air, and the best comforter
> To an unsettled fancy, cure thy brains
> Now useless, boiled within thy skull."

Again;

> "The charm dissolves apace,
> And, as the morning steals upon the night,
> Melting the darkness, so their rising senses
> Begin to chase the ignorant fumes that mantle
> Their clearer reason.
>   Their understanding
> Begins to swell: and the approaching tide
> Will shortly fill the reasonable shores
> That now lie foul and muddy."[46]

The perception of real affinities between events (that is to say, of *ideal* affinities, for those only are real), enables the poet thus to make free with the most imposing forms and phenomena of the world, and to assert the predominance of the soul.

3. Whilst thus the poet animates nature with his own thoughts, he differs from the philosopher only herein, that the one proposes Beauty as his main end; the other Truth. But the philosopher, not less than the poet, postpones the apparent order and relations of things to the empire of thought. "The problem of philosophy," according to Plato, "is, for all that exists conditionally, to find a ground unconditioned and absolute." It proceeds on the faith that a law determines all phenomena, which being known, the phenomena can be predicted. That law, when in the mind, is an idea. Its beauty is infinite. The true philosopher and the true poet are one, and a beauty, which is truth, and a truth, which is beauty, is the aim of both. Is not the charm of one of Plato's or Aristotle's definitions strictly like that of the Antigone of Sophocles? It is, in both cases, that a spiritual life has been imparted to nature; that the solid seeming block of matter has been pervaded and dissolved by a thought; that this feeble human being has penetrated the vast masses of nature with an informing soul, and recognized itself in their harmony, that is, seized their law. In physics, when this is attained, the memory disburthens itself of its cumbrous catalogues of particulars, and carries centuries of observation in a single formula.

Thus even in physics, the material is degraded before the spiritual. The astronomer, the geometer, rely on their irrefragable analysis, and disdain

---

[46]Shakespeare, *The Tempest* 5.1. [Ed.]

the results of observation. The sublime remark of Euler[47] on his law of arches, "This will be found contrary to all experience, yet is true"; had already transferred nature into the mind, and left matter like an outcast corpse.

4. Intellectual science has been observed to beget invariably a doubt of the existence of matter. Turgot[48] said, "He that has never doubted the existence of matter, may be assured he has no aptitude for metaphysical inquiries." It fastens the attention upon immortal necessary uncreated natures, that is, upon Ideas; and in their presence we feel that the outward circumstance is a dream and a shade. Whilst we wait in this Olympus of gods, we think of nature as an appendix to the soul. We ascend into their region, and know that these are the thoughts of the Supreme Being. "These are they who were set up from everlasting, from the beginning, or ever the earth was. When he prepared the heavens, they were there; when he established the clouds above, when he strengthened the fountains of the deep. Then they were by him, as one brought up with him. Of them took he counsel."[49]

Their influence is proportionate. As objects of science they are accessible to few men. Yet all men are capable of being raised by piety or by passion, into their region. And no man touches these divine natures, without becoming, in some degree, himself divine. Like a new soul, they renew the body. We become physically nimble and lightsome; we tread on air; life is no longer irksome, and we think it will never be so. No man fears age or misfortune or death in their serene company, for he is transported out of the district of change. Whilst we behold unveiled the nature of Justice and Truth, we learn the difference between the absolute and the conditional or relative. We apprehend the absolute. As it were, for the first time, *we exist.* We become immortal, for we learn that time and space are relations of matter; that with a perception of truth or a virtuous will they have no affinity.

5. Finally, religion and ethics, which may be fitly called the practice of ideas, or the introduction of ideas into life, have an analogous effect with all lower culture, in degrading nature and suggesting its dependence on spirit. Ethics and religion differ herein; that the one is the system of human duties commencing from man; the other, from God. Religion includes the personality of God; Ethics does not. They are one to our present design. They both put nature under foot. The first and last lesson of religion is,

---

[47] Leonhard Euler (1707–83), Swiss mathematician, physicist, and speculative philosopher (Ferguson 1:252). [Ed.]

[48] Anne Robert Jacques Turgot (1727–81), French statesman and economist (Ferguson 1:252). [Ed.]

[49] Adapted from Prov. 8.23, 27, 28, 30 (Ferguson 1: 252). [Ed.]

"The things that are seen, are temporal; the things that are unseen, are eternal."[50] It puts an affront upon nature. It does that for the unschooled, which philosophy does for Berkeley and Viasa.[51] The uniform language that may be heard in the churches of the most ignorant sects is, — "Contemn the unsubstantial shows of the world; they are vanities, dreams, shadows, unrealities; seek the realities of religion." The devotee flouts nature. Some theosophists have arrived at a certain hostility and indignation towards matter, as the Manichean and Plotinus.[52] They distrusted in themselves any looking back to these flesh-pots of Egypt. Plotinus was ashamed of his body. In short, they might all say of matter, what Michael Angelo said of external beauty, "It is the frail and weary weed, in which God dresses the soul which he has called into time."[53]

It appears that motion, poetry, physical and intellectual science, and religion, all tend to affect our convictions of the reality of the external world. But I own there is something ungrateful in expanding too curiously the particulars of the general proposition, that all culture tends to imbue us with idealism. I have no hostility to nature, but a child's love to it. I expand and live in the warm day like corn and melons. Let us speak her fair. I do not wish to fling stones at my beautiful mother, nor soil my gentle nest. I only wish to indicate the true position of nature in regard to man, wherein to establish man all right education tends; as the ground which to attain is the object of human life, that is, of man's connection with nature. Culture inverts the vulgar views of nature, and brings the mind to call that apparent which it uses to call real, and that real which it uses to call visionary. Children, it is true, believe in the external world. The belief that it appears only, is an afterthought, but with culture this faith will as surely arise on the mind as did the first.

The advantage of the ideal theory over the popular faith is this, that it presents the world in precisely that view which is most desirable to the mind. It is, in fact, the view which Reason, both speculative and practical, that is, philosophy and virtue take. For seen in the light of thought, the world always is phenomenal; and virtue subordinates it to the mind. Idealism sees the world in God. It beholds the whole circle of persons and things, of actions and events, of country and religion, not as painfully accumulated,

---

[50] 2 Cor. 4.18 (Ferguson 1:252). [Ed.]

[51] George Berkeley (1685–1753), Irish idealist philosopher. Viasa, reputed to be the arranger of the Hindu Vedas. [Ed.]

[52] Manichean, a follower of the Babylonian Manes (c. 213–c. 276), a Christian mystic. Plotinus (c. 204–c. 270), a Neoplatonist Greek philosopher. [Ed.]

[53] Michelangelo, Sonnet 51. [Ed.]

atom after atom, act after act, in an aged creeping Past, but as one vast picture which God paints on the instant eternity for the contemplation of the soul. Therefore the soul holds itself off from a too trivial and microscopic study of the universal tablet. It respects the end too much to immerse itself in the means. It sees something more important in Christianity than the scandals of ecclesiastical history or the niceties of criticism; and, very incurious concerning persons or miracles, and not at all disturbed by chasms of historical evidence, it accepts from God the phenomenon, as it finds it, as the pure and awful form of religion in the world. It is not hot and passionate at the appearance of what it calls its own good or bad fortune, at the union or opposition of other persons. No man is its enemy. It accepts whatsoever befalls, as part of its lesson. It is a watcher more than a doer, and it is a doer, only that it may the better watch.

VII. Spirit

It is essential to a true theory of nature and of man, that it should contain somewhat progressive. Uses that are exhausted or that may be, and facts that end in the statement, cannot be all that is true of this brave lodging wherein man is harbored, and wherein all his faculties find appropriate and endless exercise. And all the uses of nature admit of being summed in one, which yields the activity of man an infinite scope. Through all its kingdoms, to the suburbs and outskirts of things, it is faithful to the cause whence it had its origin. It always speaks of Spirit. It suggests the absolute. It is a perpetual effect. It is a great shadow pointing always to the sun behind us.

The aspect of Nature is devout. Like the figure of Jesus, she stands with bended head, and hands folded upon the breast. The happiest man is he who learns from nature the lesson of worship.

Of that ineffable essence which we call Spirit, he that thinks most, will say least. We can foresee God in the coarse, and, as it were, distant phenomena of matter; but when we try to define and describe himself, both language and thought desert us, and we are as helpless as fools and savages. That essence refuses to be recorded in propositions, but when man has worshipped him intellectually, the noblest ministry of nature is to stand as the apparition of God. It is the organ through which the universal spirit speaks to the individual, and strives to lead back the individual to it.

When we consider Spirit, we see that the views already presented do not include the whole circumference of man. We must add some related thoughts.

Three problems are put by nature to the mind: What is matter? Whence is it? and Whereto? The first of these questions only, the ideal theory answers. Idealism saith: matter is a phenomenon, not a substance. Idealism acquaints us with the total disparity between the evidence of our own being and the evidence of the world's being. The one is perfect; the other, incapable of any assurance; the mind is a part of the nature of things; the world is a divine dream, from which we may presently awake to the glories and certainties of day. Idealism is a hypothesis to account for nature by other principles than those of carpentry and chemistry. Yet, if it only deny the existence of matter, it does not satisfy the demands of the spirit. It leaves God out of me. It leaves me in the splendid labyrinth of my perceptions, to wander without end. Then the heart resists it, because it balks the affections in denying substantive being to men and women. Nature is so pervaded with human life that there is something of humanity in all and in every particular. But this theory makes nature foreign to me, and does not account for that consanguinity which we acknowledge to it.

Let it stand then, in the present state of our knowledge, merely as a useful introductory hypothesis, serving to apprize us of the eternal distinction between the soul and the world.

But when, following the invisible steps of thought, we come to inquire, Whence is matter? and Whereto? many truths arise to us out of the recesses of consciousness. We learn that the highest is present to the soul of man; that the dread universal essence, which is not wisdom, or love, or beauty, or power, but all in one, and each entirely, is that for which all things exist, and that by which they are; that spirit creates; that behind nature, throughout nature, spirit is present; one and not compound it does not act upon us from without, that is, in space and time, but spiritually, or through ourselves: therefore, that spirit, that is, the Supreme Being, does not build up nature around us, but puts it forth through us, as the life of the tree puts forth new branches and leaves through the pores of the old. As a plant upon the earth, so a man rests upon the bosom of God; he is nourished by unfailing fountains, and draws at his need inexhaustible power. Who can set bounds to the possibilities of man? Once inhale the upper air, being admitted to behold the absolute natures of justice and truth, and we learn that man has access to the entire mind of the Creator, is himself the creator in the finite. This view, which admonishes me where the sources of wisdom and power lie, and points to virtue as to

> "The golden key
> Which opens the palace of eternity," [54]

carries upon its face the highest certificate of truth, because it animates me to create my own world through the purification of my soul.

---

[54] John Milton, *Comus*, lines 13–14 (1637). [Ed.]

The world proceeds from the same spirit as the body of man. It is a remoter and inferior incarnation of God, a projection of God in the unconscious. But it differs from the body in one important respect. It is not, like that, now subjected to the human will. Its serene order is inviolable by us. It is, therefore, to us, the present expositor of the divine mind. It is a fixed point whereby we may measure our departure. As we degenerate, the contrast between us and our house is more evident. We are as much strangers in nature as we are aliens from God. We do not understand the notes of birds. The fox and the deer run away from us; the bear and tiger rend us. We do not know the uses of more than a few plants, as corn and the apple, the potato and the vine. Is not the landscape, every glimpse of which hath a grandeur, a face of him? Yet this may show us what discord is between man and nature, for you cannot freely admire a noble landscape if laborers are digging in the field hard by. The poet finds something ridiculous in his delight until he is out of the sight of men.

VIII. Prospects

In inquiries respecting the laws of the world and the frame of things, the highest reason is always the truest. That which seems faintly possible, it is so refined, is often faint and dim because it is deepest seated in the mind among the eternal verities. Empirical science is apt to cloud the sight, and by the very knowledge of functions and processes to bereave the student of the manly contemplation of the whole. The savant becomes unpoetic. But the best naturalist who lends an entire and devout attention to truth, will see that there remains much to learn of his relation to the world, and that it is not to be learned by any addition or subtraction or other comparison of known quantities, but is arrived at by untaught sallies of the spirit, by a continual self-recovery, and by entire humility. He will perceive that there are far more excellent qualities in the student than preciseness and infallibility; that a guess is often more fruitful than an indisputable affirmation, and that a dream may let us deeper into the secret of nature than a hundred concerted experiments.

For the problems to be solved are precisely those which the physiologist and the naturalist omit to state. It is not so pertinent to man to know all the individuals of the animal kingdom, as it is to know whence and whereto is this tyrannizing unity in his constitution, which evermore separates and classifies things, endeavoring to reduce the most diverse to one form. When I behold a rich landscape, it is less to my purpose to recite correctly the order and superposition of the strata, than to know why all thought of multitude is lost in a tranquil sense of unity. I cannot greatly honor minuteness in details, so long as there is no hint to explain the relation between things and thoughts; no ray upon the *metaphysics* of conchology, of botany, of the arts, to show the relation of the forms of flowers, shells, animals, architecture, to the mind, and build science upon ideas. In a cabinet of natural history,[55] we become sensible of a certain occult recognition and sympathy in regard to the most unwieldly and eccentric forms of beast, fish, and insect. The American who has been confined, in his own country, to the sight of buildings designed after foreign models, is surprised on entering York Minster or St. Peter's at Rome, by the feeling that these structures are imitations also, —faint copies of an invisible archetype. Nor has science sufficient humanity, so long as the naturalist overlooks that wonderful congruity which subsists between man and the world; of which he is lord, not because he is the most subtle inhabitant, but because he is its head and heart, and finds something of himself in every great and small thing, in every mountain stratum, in every new law of color, fact of astronomy, or atmospheric influence which observation or analysis lays open. A perception of this mystery inspires the muse of George Herbert, the beautiful psalmist of the seventeenth century. The following lines are part of his little poem on Man.

> "Man is all symmetry,
> Full of proportions, one limb to another,
>   And all to all the world besides.
>   Each part may call the farthest, brother;
> For head with foot hath private amity,
>   And both with moons and tides.
>
>   "Nothing hath got so far
> But man hath caught and kept it as his prey;
>   His eyes dismount the highest star:
>   He is in little all the sphere.
> Herbs gladly cure our flesh, because that they
>   Find their acquaintance there.
>
>   "For us, the winds do blow,
> The earth doth rest, heaven move, and fountains flow,
>   Nothing we see, but means our good,
>   As our delight, or as our treasure;
> The whole is either our cupboard of food,
>   Or cabinet of pleasure.
>
>   "The stars have us to bed:
> Night draws the curtain; which the sun withdraws.

---

[55] A natural history exhibition. [Ed.]

Music and light attend our head.
All things unto our flesh are kind,
In their descent and being; to our mind,
In their ascent and cause.

"More servants wait on man
Than he'll take notice of. In every path,
He treads down that which doth befriend him
When sickness makes him pale and wan.
Oh mighty love! Man is one world, and hath
Another to attend him."[56]

The perception of this class of truths makes the attraction which draws men to science, but the end is lost sight of in attention to the means. In view of this half-sight of science, we accept the sentence of Plato, that "poetry comes nearer to vital truth than history."[57] Every surmise and vaticination[58] of the mind is entitled to a certain respect, and we learn to prefer imperfect theories, and sentences which contain glimpses of truth, to digested systems which have no one valuable suggestion. A wise writer will feel that the ends of study and composition are best answered by announcing undiscovered regions of thought, and so communicating, through hope, new activity to the torpid spirit.

I shall therefore conclude this essay with some traditions of man and nature, which a certain poet sang to me; and which, as they have always been in the world, and perhaps reappear to every bard, may be both history and prophecy.[59]

"The foundations of man are not in matter, but in spirit. But the element of spirit is eternity. To it, therefore, the longest series of events, the oldest chronologies are young and recent. In the cycle of the universal man, from whom the known individuals proceed, centuries are points, and all history is but the epoch of one degradation.

"We distrust and deny inwardly our sympathy with nature. We own and disown our relation to it, by turns. We are like Nebuchadnezzar, de-

---

[56] George Herbert (1593–1633), "Man." Emerson edits the poem by deleting several stanzas. [Ed.]

[57] The idea sounds more like Aristotle's veneration of poetry in his *Poetics* than Plato's condemnation of poetry and exile of poets from the ideal republic in his *Republic.* [Ed.]

[58] Prophecy, foretelling. [Ed.]

[59] Some scholars have speculated that Emerson refers in the following quotations to Bronson Alcott (1799–1888), whose "Orphic Sayings" were published in *The Dial* (1840–41). But Emerson more likely adopts here, as he does elsewhere, the persona of an "Orphic poet" to lend authority and drama to his own wisdom. [Ed.]

throned, bereft of reason, and eating grass like an ox.[60] But who can set limits to the remedial force of spirit?

"A man is a god in ruins. When men are innocent, life shall be longer, and shall pass into the immortal as gently as we awake from dreams. Now, the world would be insane and rabid, if these disorganizations should last for hundreds of years. It is kept in check by death and infancy. Infancy is the perpetual Messiah, which comes into the arms of fallen men, and pleads with them to return to paradise.

"Man is the dwarf of himself. Once he was permeated and dissolved by spirit. He filled nature with his overflowing currents. Out from him sprang the sun and moon; from man the sun, from woman the moon. The laws of his mind, the periods of his actions externized themselves into day and night, into the year and the seasons. But, having made for himself this huge shell, his waters retired; he no longer fills the veins and veinlets; he is shrunk to a drop. He sees that the structure still fits him, but fits him colossally. Say, rather, once it fitted him, now it corresponds to him from far and on high. He adores timidly his own work. Now is man the follower of the sun, and woman the follower of the moon. Yet sometimes he starts in his slumber, and wonders at himself and his house, and muses strangely at the resemblance betwixt him and it. He perceives that if his law is still paramount, if still he have elemental power, if his word is sterling yet in nature,[61] it is not conscious power, it is not inferior but superior to his will. It is instinct." Thus my Orphic poet sang.

At present, man applies to nature but half his force. He works on the world with his understanding alone. He lives in it and masters it by a penny-wisdom; and he that works most in it is but a half-man, and whilst his arms are strong and his digestion good, his mind is imbruted, and he is a selfish savage. His relation to nature, his power over it, is through the understanding, as by manure; the economic use of fire, wind, water, and the mariner's needle; steam, coal, chemical agriculture; the repairs of the human body by the dentist and the surgeon. This is such a resumption of power as if a banished king should buy his territories inch by inch, instead

---

[60] As recounted in Dan. 4.29–33, the Assyrian king Nebuchadnezzar (604–561 BCE) suddenly and unexpectedly departed from public affairs at the height of his power. Emerson uses the legend as an analogy with how we "own and disown" our "relation" to Nature. Emerson also anticipates the next line–"A man is a god in ruins"–by suggesting that the pagan Nebuchadnezzar was driven more by his vanity and whim than by his understanding of his descent from the divinity in Nature. [Ed.]

[61] Shakespeare, *Richard II* 4.1.264: "An if my word be sterling yet in England" (Ferguson 1:253). [Ed.]

of vaulting at once into his throne. Meantime, in the thick darkness, there are not wanting gleams of a better light,—occasional examples of the action of man upon nature with his entire force,—with reason as well as understanding. Such examples are, the traditions of miracles in the earliest antiquity of all nations; the history of Jesus Christ; the achievements of a principle, as in religious and political revolutions, and in the abolition of the slave-trade; the miracles of enthusiasm, as those reported of Swedenborg, Hohenlohe, and the Shakers;[62] many obscure and yet contested facts, now arranged under the name of Animal Magnetism;[63] prayer; eloquence; self-healing; and the wisdom of children. These are examples of Reason's momentary grasp of the scepter; the exertions of a power which exists not in time or space, but an instantaneous in-streaming causing power. The difference between the actual and the ideal force of man is happily figured by the schoolmen, in saying, that the knowledge of man is an evening knowledge, *vespertina cognitio,* but that of God is a morning knowledge, *matutina cognitio.*

The problem of restoring to the world original and eternal beauty is solved by the redemption of the soul. The ruin or the blank that we see when we look at nature, is in our own eye. The axis of vision is not coincident with the axis of things, and so they appear not transparent but opaque. The reason why the world lacks unity, and lies broken and in heaps, is because man is disunited with himself. He cannot be a naturalist until he satisfies all the demands of the spirit. Love is as much its demand as perception. Indeed, neither can be perfect without the other. In the uttermost meaning of the words, thought is devout, and devotion is thought. Deep calls unto deep. But in actual life, the marriage is not celebrated. There are innocent men who worship God after the tradition of their fathers, but their sense of duty has not yet extended to the use of all their faculties. And there are patient naturalists, but they freeze their subject under the wintry light of the understanding. Is not prayer also a study of truth,— a sally of the soul into the unfound infinite? No man ever prayed heartily without learning something. But when a faithful thinker, resolute to de-

---

[62] All visionaries of various sorts. Emanuel Swedenborg (1688–1772), Swedish theologian, scientist, and philosopher, experienced a spiritual crisis (1743–45) and spent his final years writing religious philosophy. Prince Leopold of Hohenlohe-Waldenberg-Schillingsfürst (1794–1849) was a German Catholic bishop known for miraculous cures. Members of Shaker religious communes believed in immediate revelation of the Holy Ghost and also believed that angels and other spirits communicate with those granted God's grace. [Ed.]

[63] Hypnotism, based on the theory of the curative power of the magnet (Ferguson 1:253). [Ed.]

tach every object from personal relations and see it in the light of thought, shall, at the same time, kindle science with the fire of the holiest affections, then will God go forth anew into the creation.

It will not need, when the mind is prepared for study, to search for objects. The invariable mark of wisdom is to see the miraculous in the common. What is a day? What is a year? What is summer? What is woman? What is a child? What is sleep? To our blindness, these things seem unaffecting. We make fables to hide the baldness of the fact and conform it, as we say, to the higher law of the mind. But when the fact is seen under the light of an idea, the gaudy fable fades and shrivels. We behold the real higher law. To the wise, therefore, a fact is true poetry, and the most beautiful of fables. These wonders are brought to our own door. You also are a man. Man and woman and their social life, poverty, labor, sleep, fear, fortune, are known to you. Learn that none of these things is superficial, but that each phenomenon has its roots in the faculties and affections of the mind. Whilst the abstract question occupies your intellect, nature brings it in the concrete to be solved by your hands. It were a wise inquiry for the closet, to compare, point by point, especially at remarkable crises in life, our daily history with the rise and progress of ideas in the mind.

So shall we come to look at the world with new eyes. It shall answer the endless inquiry of the intellect,—What is truth? and of the affections,—What is good? by yielding itself passive to the educated Will. Then shall come to pass what my poet said: "Nature is not fixed but fluid. Spirit alters, molds, makes it. The immobility or bruteness of nature is the absence of spirit; to pure spirit it is fluid, it is volatile, it is obedient. Every spirit builds itself a house, and beyond its house a world, and beyond its world a heaven. Know then that the world exists for you. For you is the phenomenon perfect. What we are, that only can we see. All that Adam had, all that Caesar could, you have and can do. Adam called his house, heaven and earth; Caesar called his house, Rome; you perhaps call yours, a cobbler's trade; a hundred acres of ploughed land; or a scholar's garret. Yet line for line and point for point your dominion is as great as theirs, though without fine names. Build therefore your own world. As fast as you conform your life to the pure idea in your mind, that will unfold its great proportions. A correspondent revolution in things will attend the influx of the spirit. So fast will disagreeable appearances, swine, spiders, snakes, pests, mad-houses, prisons, enemies, vanish; they are temporary and shall be no more seen. The sordor and filths of nature, the sun shall dry up and the wind exhale. As when the summer comes from the south the snow-banks melt and the face of the earth becomes green before it, so shall the advancing spirit create its ornaments along its path, and carry with it the beauty it visits and the song which enchants it; it shall draw beautiful faces, warm hearts, wise discourse, and heroic acts, around its way, until evil is no more seen. The kingdom of man over nature, which cometh not with observation,—a dominion such as now is beyond his dream of God,—he shall enter without more wonder than the blind man feels who is gradually restored to perfect sight."

The American Scholar
1837

Mr. President and Gentlemen:

I greet you on the recommencement of our literary year. Our anniversary is one of hope, and, perhaps, not enough of labor. We do not meet for games of strength or skill, for the recitation of histories, tragedies, and odes, like the ancient Greeks; for parliaments of love and poesy, like the Troubadours;[1] nor for the advancement of science, like our contemporaries in the British and European capitals. Thus far, our holiday has been simply a friendly sign of the survival of the love of letters amongst a people too busy to give to letters any more. As such it is precious as the sign of an indestructible instinct. Perhaps the time is already come when it ought to be, and will be, something else; when the sluggard intellect of this continent will look from under its iron lids and fill the postponed expectation of the world with something better than the exertions of mechanical skill. Our day of dependence, our long apprenticeship to the learning of other lands, draws to a close. The millions that around us are rushing into life, cannot always be fed on the sere remains of foreign harvests. Events, actions arise, that must be sung, that will sing themselves. Who can doubt that poetry will revive and lead in a new age, as the star in the constellation Harp, which now flames in our zenith, astronomers announce, shall one day be the polestar for a thousand years?[2]

In this hope I accept the topic which not only usage but the nature of our association seem to prescribe to this day,—the AMERICAN SCHOLAR.

Selections from Ralph Waldo Emerson: An Organic Anthology. Ed. Stephen E. Whicher. Riverside Edition. Boston: Houghton, 1957.

[1] Poets and musicians of Provence between the eleventh and thirteenth centuries, celebrated for their participation in the so-called courts of love of Eleanor of Aquitaine. [Ed.]

[2] Emerson is probably referring to the constellation Lyra ("Harp") and to the astronomical fact that the North Star (or "pole star") changes over time. His analogy is with the rise and fall of different nations as leaders in different ages, in this case anticipating U.S. authority. [Ed.]

Year by year we come up hither to read one more chapter of his biography. Let us inquire what light new days and events have thrown on his character and his hopes.

It is one of those fables which out of an unknown antiquity convey an unlooked-for wisdom, that the gods, in the beginning, divided Man into men, that he might be more helpful to himself; just as the hand was divided into fingers, the better to answer its end.

The old fable covers a doctrine ever new and sublime; that there is One Man, —present to all particular men only partially, or through one faculty; and that you must take the whole society to find the whole man. Man is not a farmer, or a professor, or an engineer, but he is all. Man is priest, and scholar, and statesman, and producer, and soldier. In the *divided* or social state these functions are parcelled out to individuals, each of whom aims to do his stint of the joint work, whilst each other performs his. The fable implies that the individual, to possess himself, must sometimes return from his own labor to embrace all the other laborers. But, unfortunately, this original unit, this fountain of power, has been so distributed to multitudes, has been so minutely subdivided and peddled out, that it is spilled into drops, and cannot be gathered. The state of society is one in which the members have suffered amputation from the trunk, and strut about so many walking monsters, —a good finger, a neck, a stomach, an elbow, but never a man.

Man is thus metamorphosed into a thing, into many things. The planter, who is Man sent out into the field to gather food, is seldom cheered by any idea of the true dignity of his ministry. He sees his bushel and his cart, and nothing beyond, and sinks into the farmer, instead of Man on the farm. The tradesman scarcely ever gives an ideal worth to his work, but is ridden by the routine of his craft, and the soul is subject to dollars. The priest becomes a form; the attorney a statute-book; the mechanic a machine; the sailor a rope of the ship.

In this distribution of functions the scholar is the delegated intellect. In the right state he is *Man Thinking*. In the degenerate state, when the victim of society, he tends to become a mere thinker, or still worse, the parrot of other men's thinking.

In this view of him, as Man Thinking, the whole theory of his office is contained. Him Nature solicits with all her placid, all her monitory pictures; him the past instructs; him the future invites. Is not indeed every man a student, and do not all things exist for the student's behoof? And, finally, is not the true scholar the only true master? But the old oracle said, "All things have two handles: beware of the wrong one."[3] In life, too

---

[3] Epictetus, *Encheiridion* (Ferguson 1:254). [Ed.]

often, the scholar errs with mankind and forfeits his privilege. Let us see him in his school, and consider him in reference to the main influences he receives.

I. The first in time and the first in importance of the influences upon the mind is that of nature. Every day, the sun; and, after sunset, Night and her stars. Ever the winds blow; ever the grass grows. Every day, men and women, conversing—beholding and beholden. The scholar is he of all men whom this spectacle most engages. He must settle its value in his mind. What is nature to him? There is never a beginning, there is never an end, to the inexplicable continuity of this web of God, but always circular power returning into itself. Therein it resembles his own spirit, whose beginning, whose ending, he never can find,—so entire, so boundless. Far too as her splendors shine, system on system shooting like rays, upward, downward, without center, without circumference,—in the mass and in the particle, Nature hastens to render account of herself to the mind. Classification begins. To the young mind every thing is individual, stands by itself. By and by, it finds how to join two things and see in them one nature; then three, then three thousand; and so, tyrannized over by its own unifying instinct, it goes on tying things together, diminishing anomalies, discovering roots running under ground whereby contrary and remote things cohere and flower out from one stem. It presently learns that since the dawn of history there has been a constant accumulation and classifying of facts. But what is classification but the perceiving that these objects are not chaotic, and are not foreign, but have a law which is also a law of the human mind? The astronomer discovers that geometry, a pure abstraction of the human mind, is the measure of planetary motion. The chemist finds proportions and intelligible method throughout matter; and science is nothing but the finding of analogy, identity, in the most remote parts. The ambitious soul sits down before each refractory fact; one after another reduces all strange constitutions, all new powers, to their class and their law, and goes on forever to animate the last fiber of organization, the outskirts of nature, by insight.

Thus to him, to this schoolboy under the bending dome of day, is suggested that he and it proceed from one root; one is leaf and one is flower; relation, sympathy, stirring in every vein. And what is that root? Is not that the soul of his soul? A thought too bold; a dream too wild. Yet when this spiritual light shall have revealed the law of more earthly natures,—when he has learned to worship the soul, and to see that the natural philosophy that now is, is only the first gropings of its gigantic hand, he shall look forward to an ever expanding knowledge as to a becoming creator. He shall see that nature is the opposite of the soul, answering to it part for part. One is seal and one is print. Its beauty is the beauty of his own mind. Its laws are the laws of his own mind. Nature then becomes to him the measure of his attainments. So much of nature as he is ignorant of, so much of his own mind does he not yet possess. And, in fine, the ancient precept, "Know thyself," and the modern precept, "Study nature," become at last one maxim.

II. The next great influence into the spirit of the scholar is the mind of the Past, — in whatever form, whether of literature, of art, of institutions, that mind is inscribed. Books are the best type of the influence of the past, and perhaps we shall get at the truth, — learn the amount of this influence more conveniently, — by considering their value alone.

The theory of books is noble. The scholar of the first age received into him the world around; brooded thereon; gave it the new arrangement of his own mind, and uttered it again. It came into him life; it went out from him truth. It came to him short-lived actions; it went out from him immortal thoughts. It came to him business; it went from him poetry. It was dead fact; now, it is quick thought. It can stand, and it can go. It now endures, it now flies, it now inspires. Precisely in proportion to the depth of mind from which it issued, so high does it soar, so long does it sing.

Or, I might say, it depends on how far the process had gone, of transmuting life into truth. In proportion to the completeness of the distillation, so will the purity and imperishableness of the product be. But none is quite perfect. As no air-pump can by any means make a perfect vacuum, so neither can any artist entirely exclude the conventional, the local, the perishable from his book, or write a book of pure thought, that shall be as efficient, in all respects, to a remote posterity, as to contemporaries, or rather to the second age. Each age, it is found, must write its own books; or rather, each generation for the next succeeding. The books of an older period will not fit this.

Yet hence arises a grave mischief. The sacredness which attaches to the act of creation, the act of thought, is transferred to the record. The poet chanting was felt to be a divine man: henceforth the chant is divine also. The writer was a just and wise spirit: henceforward it is settled the book is perfect; as love of the hero corrupts into worship of his statue. Instantly the book becomes noxious: the guide is a tyrant. The sluggish and perverted mind of the multitude, slow to open to the incursions of Reason, having once so opened, having once received this book, stands upon it, and makes an outcry if it is disparaged. Colleges are built on it. Books are written on it by thinkers, not by Man Thinking; by men of talent, that is, who start wrong, who set out from accepted dogmas, not from their own sight of principles. Meek young men grow up in libraries, believing it their duty to accept the views which Cicero, which Locke, which Bacon, have given; forgetful that Cicero, Locke, and Bacon were only young men in libraries when they wrote these books.

Hence, instead of Man Thinking, we have the bookworm. Hence the book-learned class, who value books, as such; not as related to nature and the human constitution, but as making a sort of Third Estate[4] with the world and the soul. Hence the restorers of readings, the emendators, the bibliomaniacs of all degrees.

Books are the best of things, well used; abused, among the worst. What is the right use? What is the one end which all means go to effect? They are for nothing but to inspire. I had better never see a book than to be warped by its attraction clean out of my own orbit, and made a satellite instead of a system. The one thing in the world, of value, is the active soul. This every man is entitled to; this every man contains within him, although in almost all men obstructed and as yet unborn. The soul active sees absolute truth and utters truth, or creates. In this action it is genius; not the privilege of here and there a favorite, but the sound estate of every man. In its essence it is progressive. The book, the college, the school of art, the institution of any kind, stop with some past utterance of genius. This is good, say they,— let us hold by this. They pin me down. They look backward and not forward. But genius looks forward: the eyes of man are set in his forehead, not in his hindhead: man hopes: genius creates. Whatever talents may be, if the man create not, the pure efflux of the Deity is not his;—cinders and smoke there may be, but not yet flame. There are creative manners, there are creative actions, and creative words; manners, actions, words, that is, indicative of no custom or authority, but springing spontaneous from the mind's own sense of good and fair.

On the other part, instead of being its own seer, let it receive from another mind its truth, though it were in torrents of light, without periods of solitude, inquest, and self-recovery, and a fatal disservice is done. Genius is always sufficiently the enemy of genius by over-influence. The literature of every nation bears me witness. The English dramatic poets have Shakespearized now for two hundred years.

Undoubtedly there is a right way of reading, so it be sternly subordinated. Man Thinking must not be subdued by his instruments. Books are for the scholar's idle times. When he can read God directly, the hour is too precious to be wasted in other men's transcripts of their readings. But when the intervals of darkness come, as come they must,—when the sun is hid and the stars withdraw their shining,—we repair to the lamps which were kindled by their ray, to guide our steps to the East again, where the dawn

---

[4]The medieval parliament was divided into three "estates"—nobility, clergy, and commons. [Orig. ed.]

is. We hear, that we may speak. The Arabian proverb says, "A fig tree, looking on a fig tree, becometh fruitful."

It is remarkable, the character of the pleasure we derive from the best books. They impress us ever with the conviction that one nature wrote and the same reads. We read the verses of one of the great English poets, of Chaucer, of Marvell, of Dryden, with the most modern joy,—with a pleasure, I mean, which is in great part caused by the abstraction of all *time* from their verses. There is some awe mixed with the joy of our surprise, when this poet, who lived in some past world, two or three hundred years ago, says that which lies close to my own soul, that which I also had well-nigh thought and said. But for the evidence thence afforded to the philosophical doctrine of the identity of all minds, we should suppose some pre-established harmony, some foresight of souls that were to be, and some preparation of stores for their future wants, like the fact observed in insects, who lay up food before death for the young grub they shall never see.

I would not be hurried by any love of system, by any exaggeration of instincts, to underrate the Book. We all know, that as the human body can be nourished on any food, though it were boiled grass and the broth of shoes, so the human mind can be fed by any knowledge. And great and heroic men have existed who had almost no other information than by the printed page. I only would say that it needs a strong head to bear that diet. One must be an inventor to read well. As the proverb says, "He that would bring home the wealth of the Indies, must carry out the wealth of the Indies."[5] There is then creative reading as well as creative writing. When the mind is braced by labor and invention, the page of whatever book we read becomes luminous with manifold allusion. Every sentence is doubly significant, and the sense of our author is as broad as the world. We then see, what is always true, that as the seer's hour of vision is short and rare among heavy days and months, so is its record, perchance, the least part of his volume. The discerning will read, in his Plato or Shakespeare, only that least part,—only the authentic utterances of the oracle;—all the rest he rejects, were it never so many times Plato's and Shakespeare's.

Of course there is a portion of reading quite indispensable to a wise man. History and exact science he must learn by laborious reading. Colleges, in like manner, have their indispensable office,—to teach elements. But they can only highly serve us when they aim not to drill, but to create;

---

[5] Qtd. in James Boswell's *Life of Johnson*, conversation 17 April 1778 (Ferguson 1:254). [Ed.]

when they gather from far every ray of various genius to their hospitable halls, and by the concentrated fires, set the hearts of their youth on flame. Thought and knowledge are natures in which apparatus and pretension avail nothing. Gowns and pecuniary foundations, though of towns of gold, can never countervail the least sentence or syllable of wit. Forget this, and our American colleges will recede in their public importance, whilst they grow richer every year.

III. There goes in the world a notion that the scholar should be a recluse, a valetudinarian,—as unfit for any handiwork or public labor as a penknife for an axe. The so-called "practical men" sneer at speculative men, as if, because they speculate or *see*, they could do nothing. I have heard it said that the clergy,—who are always, more universally than any other class, the scholars of their day,—are addressed as women; that the rough, spontaneous conversation of men they do not hear, but only a mincing and diluted speech. They are often virtually disfranchised; and indeed there are advocates for their celibacy. As far as this is true of the studious classes, it is not just and wise. Action is with the scholar subordinate, but it is essential. Without it he is not yet man. Without it thought can never ripen into truth. Whilst the world hangs before the eye as a cloud of beauty, we cannot even see its beauty. Inaction is cowardice, but there can be no scholar without the heroic mind. The preamble of thought, the transition through which it passes from the unconscious to the conscious, is action. Only so much do I know, as I have lived. Instantly we know whose words are loaded with life, and whose not.

The world,—this shadow of the soul, or *other me*,—lies wide around. Its attractions are the keys which unlock my thoughts and make me acquainted with myself. I run eagerly into this resounding tumult. I grasp the hands of those next me, and take my place in the ring to suffer and to work, taught by an instinct that so shall the dumb abyss be vocal with speech. I pierce its order; I dissipate its fear; I dispose of it within the circuit of my expanding life. So much only of life as I know by experience, so much of the wilderness have I vanquished and planted, or so far have I extended my being, my dominion. I do not see how any man can afford, for the sake of his nerves and his nap, to spare any action in which he can partake. It is pearls and rubies to his discourse. Drudgery, calamity, exasperation, want, are instructors in eloquence and wisdom. The true scholar grudges every opportunity of action past by, as a loss of power. It is the raw material out of which the intellect molds her splendid products. A strange process too, this by which experience is converted into thought, as a mulberry leaf is converted into satin. The manufacture goes forward at all hours.

The actions and events of our childhood and youth are now matters of calmest observation. They lie like fair pictures in the air. Not so with our recent actions, —with the business which we now have in hand. On this we are quite unable to speculate. Our affections as yet circulate through it. We no more feel or know it than we feel the feet, or the hand, or the brain of our body. The new deed is yet a part of life, —remains for a time immersed in our unconscious life. In some contemplative hour it detaches itself from the life like a ripe fruit, to become a thought of the mind. Instantly it is raised, transfigured; the corruptible has put on incorruption. Henceforth it is an object of beauty, however base its origin and neighborhood. Observe too the impossibility of antedating this act. In its grub state, it cannot fly, it cannot shine, it is a dull grub. But suddenly, without observation, the selfsame thing unfurls beautiful wings, and is an angel of wisdom. So is there no fact, no event, in our private history, which shall not, sooner or later, lose its adhesive, inert form, and astonish us by soaring from our body into the empyrean. Cradle and infancy, school and playground, the fear of boys, and dogs, and ferules, the love of little maids and berries, and many another fact that once filled the whole sky, are gone already; friend and relative, profession and party, town and country, nation and world, must also soar and sing.

Of course, he who has put forth his total strength in fit actions has the richest return of wisdom. I will not shut myself out of this globe of action, and transplant an oak into a flower-pot, there to hunger and pine; nor trust the revenue of some single faculty, and exhaust one vein of thought, much like those Savoyards,[6] who, getting their livelihood by carving shepherds, shepherdesses, and smoking Dutchmen, for all Europe, went out one day to the mountain to find stock, and discovered that they had whittled up the last of their pine trees. Authors we have, in numbers, who have written out their vein, and who, moved by a commendable prudence, sail for Greece or Palestine, follow the trapper into the prairie, or ramble round Algiers, to replenish their merchantable stock.

If it were only for a vocabulary, the scholar would be covetous of action. Life is our dictionary. Years are well spent in country labors; in town; in the insight into trades and manufactures; in frank intercourse with many men and women; in science; in art; to the one end of mastering in all their facts a language by which to illustrate and embody our perceptions. I learn immediately from any speaker how much he has already lived, through the poverty or the splendor of his speech. Life lies behind us as the quarry from whence we get tiles and copestones for the masonry of today. This is the way to learn grammar. Colleges and books only copy the language which the field and the work-yard made.

---

[6] Residents of Savoy, a rural region of southeastern France. [Ed.]

But the final value of action, like that of books, and better than books, is that it is a resource. That great principle of Undulation in nature, that shows itself in the inspiring and expiring of the breath; in desire and satiety; in the ebb and flow of the sea; in day and night; in heat and cold; and, as yet more deeply ingrained in every atom and every fluid, is known to us under the name of Polarity, — these "fits of easy transmission and reflection," as Newton called them, are the law of nature because they are the law of spirit.[7]

The mind now thinks, now acts, and each fit reproduces the other. When the artist has exhausted his materials, when the fancy no longer paints, when thoughts are no longer apprehended and books are a weariness, — he has always the resource *to live*. Character is higher than intellect. Thinking is the function. Living is the functionary. The stream retreats to its source. A great soul will be strong to live, as well as strong to think. Does he lack organ or medium to impart his truths? He can still fall back on this elemental force of living them. This is a total act. Thinking is a partial act. Let the grandeur of justice shine in his affairs. Let the beauty of affection cheer his lowly roof. Those "far from fame," who dwell and act with him, will feel the force of his constitution in the doings and passages of the day better than it can be measured by any public and designed display. Time shall teach him that the scholar loses no hour which the man lives. Herein he unfolds the sacred germ of his instinct, screened from influence. What is lost in seemliness is gained in strength. Not out of those on whom systems of education have exhausted their culture, comes the helpful giant to destroy the old or to build the new, but out of unhandselled savage nature; out of terrible Druids and Berserkers come at last Alfred and Shakespeare.[8]

I hear therefore with joy whatever is beginning to be said of the dignity and necessity of labor to every citizen. There is virtue yet in the hoe and the spade, for learned as well as for unlearned hands. And labor is everywhere welcome; always we are invited to work; only be this limitation observed,

---

[7] Emerson is referring to the concept of natural polarity, or the alteration of attractive opposites (as in magnetism), in Newton and Enlightenment science and is using it to justify the opposition between thought and action. [Ed.]

[8] "Unhandseled" suggests someone ("savage nature") uninitiated into culture or civilization. The verb *handsel* comes from OE *handseln*, to "give unto a person's hands," as in a promise, meant here as a social contract. In keeping with this Old English term, Emerson sketches a little genealogy of culture out of "terrible Druids" (ancient Celtic priests) and "Berserkers" (those related to Berserker, "bare of mail," grandson of the Scandinavian Starkader, called such because he fought without armor or wildly), who can produce the culture of modern England from King Alfred to William Shakespeare. [Ed.]

that a man shall not for the sake of wider activity sacrifice any opinion to the popular judgments and modes of action.

I have now spoken of the education of the scholar by nature, by books, and by action. It remains to say somewhat of his duties.

They are such as become Man Thinking. They may all be comprised in self-trust. The office of the scholar is to cheer, to raise, and to guide men by showing them facts amidst appearances. He plies the slow, unhonored, and unpaid task of observation. Flamsteed and Herschel, in their glazed observatories, may catalogue the stars with the praise of all men, and the results being splendid and useful, honor is sure.[9] But he, in his private observatory, cataloguing obscure and nebulous stars of the human mind, which as yet no man has thought of as such, —watching days and months sometimes for a few facts; correcting still his old records; —must relinquish display and immediate fame. In the long period of his preparation he must betray often an ignorance and shiftlessness in popular arts, incurring the disdain of the able who shoulder him aside. Long he must stammer in his speech; often forego the living for the dead. Worse yet, he must accept—how often!—poverty and solitude. For the ease and pleasure of treading the old road, accepting the fashions, the education, the religion of society, he takes the cross of making his own, and, of course, the self-accusation, the faint heart, the frequent uncertainty and loss of time, which are the nettles and tangling vines in the way of the self-relying and self-directed; and the state of virtual hostility in which he seems to stand to society, and especially to educated society. For all this loss and scorn, what offset? He is to find consolation in exercising the highest functions of human nature. He is one who raises himself from private considerations and breathes and lives on public and illustrious thoughts. He is the world's eye. He is the world's heart. He is to resist the vulgar prosperity that retrogrades ever to barbarism, by preserving and communicating heroic sentiments, noble biographies, melodious verse, and the conclusions of history. Whatsoever oracles the human heart, in all emergencies, in all solemn hours, has uttered as its commentary on the world of actions, —these he shall receive and impart. And whatsoever new verdict Reason from her inviolable seat pronounces on the passing men and events of today, —this he shall hear and promulgate.

These being his functions, it becomes him to feel all confidence in himself, and to defer never to the popular cry. He and he only knows the world. The world of any moment is the merest appearance. Some great decorum,

---

[9] John Flamsteed (1646–1719) and Sir William Herschel (1738–1822), noted astronomers. [Ed.]

some fetish of a government, some ephemeral trade, or war, or man, is cried up by half mankind and cried down by the other half, as if all depended on this particular up or down. The odds are that the whole question is not worth the poorest thought which the scholar has lost in listening to the controversy. Let him not quit his belief that a popgun is a popgun, though the ancient and honorable of the earth affirm it to be the crack of doom. In silence, in steadiness, in severe abstraction, let him hold by himself; add observation to observation, patient of neglect, patient of reproach, and bide his own time, — happy enough if he can satisfy himself alone that this day he has seen something truly. Success treads on every right step. For the instinct is sure, that prompts him to tell his brother what he thinks. He then learns that in going down into the secrets of his own mind he has descended into the secrets of all minds. He learns that he who has mastered any law in his private thoughts, is master to that extent of all men whose language he speaks, and of all into whose language his own can be translated. The poet, in utter solitude remembering his spontaneous thoughts and recording them, is found to have recorded that which men in crowded cities find true for them also. The orator distrusts at first the fitness of his frank confessions, his want of knowledge of the persons he addresses, until he finds that he is the complement of his hearers; — that they drink his words because he fulfils for them their own nature; the deeper he dives into his privatest, secretest presentiment, to his wonder he finds this is the most acceptable, most public, and universally true. The people delight in it; the better part of every man feels, This is my music; this is myself.

In self-trust all the virtues are comprehended. Free should the scholar be, — free and brave. Free even to the definition of freedom, "without any hindrance that does not arise out of his own constitution."[10] Brave, for fear is a thing which a scholar by his very function puts behind him. Fear always springs from ignorance. It is a shame to him if his tranquillity, amid dangerous times, arise from the presumption that like children and women his is a protected class; or if he seek a temporary peace by the diversion of his thoughts from politics or vexed questions, hiding his head like an ostrich in the flowering bushes, peeping into microscopes, and turning rhymes, as a boy whistles to keep his courage up. So is the danger a danger still; so is the fear worse. Manlike let him turn and face it. Let him look into its eye and search its nature, inspect its origin, — see the whelping of this lion, — which lies no great way back; he will then find in himself a perfect comprehension of its nature and extent; he will have made his hands meet on the other side, and can henceforth defy it and pass on superior. The world is his who can

[10] ("Freedom," def. 1.e). [Ed.]

see through its pretension. What deafness, what stone-blind custom, what overgrown error you behold is there only by sufferance,—by your sufferance. See it to be a lie, and you have already dealt it its mortal blow.

Yes, we are the cowed,—we the trustless. It is a mischievous notion that we are come late into nature; that the world was finished a long time ago. As the world was plastic and fluid in the hands of God, so it is ever to so much of his attributes as we bring to it. To ignorance and sin, it is flint. They adapt themselves to it as they may; but in proportion as a man has any thing in him divine, the firmament flows before him and takes his signet and form. Not he is great who can alter matter, but he who can alter my state of mind. They are the kings of the world who give the color of their present thought to all nature and all art, and persuade men by the cheerful serenity of their carrying the matter, that this thing which they do is the apple which the ages have desired to pluck, now at last ripe, and inviting nations to the harvest. The great man makes the great thing. Wherever Macdonald sits, there is the head of the table. Linnaeus makes botany the most alluring of studies, and wins it from the farmer and the herb-woman; Davy, chemistry; Cuvier, fossils.[11] The day is always his who works in it with serenity and great aims. The unstable estimates of men crowd to him whose mind is filled with a truth, as the heaped waves of the Atlantic follow the moon.

For this self-trust, the reason is deeper than can be fathomed,—darker than can be enlightened. I might not carry with me the feeling of my audience in stating my own belief. But I have already shown the ground of my hope, in adverting to the doctrine that man is one. I believe man has been wronged; he has wronged himself. He has almost lost the light that can lead him back to his prerogatives. Men are become of no account. Men in history, men in the world of today, are bugs, are spawn, and are called "the mass" and "the herd." In a century, in a millennium, one or two men; that is to say, one or two approximations to the right state of every man. All the rest behold in the hero or the poet their own green and crude being,— ripened; yes, and are content to be less, so *that* may attain to its full stature. What a testimony, full of grandeur, full of pity, is borne to the demands of his own nature, by the poor clansman, the poor partisan, who rejoices in the glory of his chief. The poor and the low find some amends to their immense moral capacity, for their acquiescence in a political and social inferiority. They are content to be brushed like flies from the path of a great

---

[11] Emerson extends a popular Scottish saying to the ways geniuses make their discoveries seem self-evident and central to our knowledge, such as Linnaeus (1707–78) in botany, Sir Humphry Davy (1778–1829) in chemistry, and Georges Cuvier (1769–1832) in ethnography. [Ed.]

person, so that justice shall be done by him to that common nature which it is the dearest desire of all to see enlarged and glorified. They sun themselves in the great man's light, and feel it to be their own element. They cast the dignity of man from their downtrod selves upon the shoulders of a hero, and will perish to add one drop of blood to make that great heart beat, those giant sinews combat and conquer. He lives for us, and we live in him.

Men, such as they are, very naturally seek money or power; and power because it is as good as money,—the "spoils," so called, "of office." And why not? for they aspire to the highest, and this, in their sleep-walking, they dream is highest. Wake them and they shall quit the false good and leap to the true, and leave governments to clerks and desks. This revolution is to be wrought by the gradual domestication of the idea of Culture. The main enterprise of the world for splendor, for extent, is the upbuilding of a man. Here are the materials strewn along the ground. The private life of one man shall be a more illustrious monarchy, more formidable to its enemy, more sweet and serene in its influence to its friend, than any kingdom in history. For a man, rightly viewed, comprehendeth the particular natures of all men. Each philosopher, each bard, each actor has only done for me, as by a delegate, what one day I can do for myself. The books which once we valued more than the apple of the eye, we have quite exhausted. What is that but saying that we have come up with the point of view which the universal mind took through the eyes of one scribe; we have been that man, and have passed on. First, one, then another, we drain all cisterns, and waxing greater by all these supplies, we crave a better and more abundant food. The man has never lived that can feed us ever. The human mind cannot be enshrined in a person who shall set a barrier on any one side to this unbounded, unboundable empire. It is one central fire, which, flaming now out of the lips of Etna, lightens the capes of Sicily, and now out of the throat of Vesuvius, illuminates the towers and vineyards of Naples.[12] It is one light which beams out of a thousand stars. It is one soul which animates all men.

But I have dwelt perhaps tediously upon this abstraction of the Scholar. I ought not to delay longer to add what I have to say of nearer reference to the time and to this country.

Historically, there is thought to be a difference in the ideas which predominate over successive epochs, and there are data for marking the genius of the Classic, of the Romantic, and now of the Reflective or Philosophical age. With the views I have intimated of the oneness or the identity of the

---

[12] Continuing his theme of the human being's potential for genius, Emerson compares the great mind to the volcanoes Vesuvius and Etna, whose tremendous upheavals are illuminating as well as destructive. [Ed.]

mind through all individuals, I do not much dwell on these differences. In fact, I believe each individual passes through all three. The boy is a Greek; the youth, romantic; the adult, reflective. I deny not, however, that a revolution in the leading idea may be distinctly enough traced.[13]

Our age is bewailed as the age of Introversion. Must that needs be evil? We, it seems, are critical; we are embarrassed with second thoughts; we cannot enjoy any thing for hankering to know whereof the pleasure consists; we are lined with eyes; we see with our feet; the time is infected with Hamlet's unhappiness, —

"Sicklied o'er with the pale cast of thought."[14]

It is so bad then? Sight is the last thing to be pitied. Would we be blind? Do we fear lest we should outsee nature and God, and drink truth dry? I look upon the discontent of the literary class as a mere announcement of the fact that they find themselves not in the state of mind of their fathers, and regret the coming state as untried; as a boy dreads the water before he has learned that he can swim. If there is any period one would desire to be born in, is it not the age of Revolution; when the old and the new stand side by side and admit of being compared; when the energies of all men are searched by fear and by hope; when the historic glories of the old can be compensated by the rich possibilities of the new era? This time, like all times, is a very good one, if we but know what to do with it.

I read with some joy of the auspicious signs of the coming days, as they glimmer already through poetry and art, through philosophy and science, through church and state.

One of these signs is the fact that the same movement which effected the elevation of what was called the lowest class in the state, assumed in literature a very marked and as benign an aspect. Instead of the sublime and beautiful, the near, the low, the common, was explored and poetized. That which had been negligently trodden under foot by those who were harnessing and provisioning themselves for long journeys into far countries, is suddenly found to be richer than all foreign parts. The literature of the poor, the feelings of the child, the philosophy of the street, the meaning of household life, are the topics of the time. It is a great stride. It is a sign—is it not?—of new vigor when the extremities are made active, when currents

---

[13]G. W. F. Hegel divided history into three stages—"symbolic," "classic," and "romantic"—universalizing thereby the progressive ethos of the romantic idealist philosophers in the first half of the nineteenth century. Emerson's claim that "each individual passes through all three" stages (or that ontogeny recapitulates phylogeny) is also a conventional romantic idea. [Ed.]

[14]Shakespeare, *Hamlet* 3.1.87. [Ed.]

of warm life run into the hands and the feet. I ask not for the great, the remote, the romantic; what is doing in Italy or Arabia; what is Greek art, or
Provençal minstrelsy; I embrace the common, I explore and sit at the feet
of the familiar, the low. Give me insight into today, and you may have the
antique and future worlds. What would we really know the meaning of?
The meal in the firkin,[15] the milk in the pan; the ballad in the street; the
news of the boat; the glance of the eye; the form and the gait of the body;—
show me the ultimate reason of these matters; show me the sublime presence of the highest spiritual cause lurking, as always it does lurk, in these
suburbs and extremities of nature; let me see every trifle bristling with the
polarity that ranges it instantly on an eternal law; and the shop, the plough,
and the ledger referred to the like cause by which light undulates and poets
sing;—and the world lies no longer a dull miscellany and lumber-room,
but has form and order; there is no trifle, there is no puzzle, but one design
unites and animates the farthest pinnacle and the lowest trench.

This idea has inspired the genius of Goldsmith, Burns, Cowper, and, in
a newer time, of Goethe, Wordsworth and Carlyle. This idea they have differently followed and with various success. In contrast with their writing,
the style of Pope, of Johnson, of Gibbon, looks cold and pedantic.[16] This
writing is blood-warm. Man is surprised to find that things near are not
less beautiful and wondrous than things remote. The near explains the far.
The drop is a small ocean. A man is related to all nature. This perception of
the worth of the vulgar is fruitful in discoveries. Goethe, in this very thing
the most modern of the moderns, has shown us, as none ever did, the genius of the ancients.

There is one man of genius who has done much for this philosophy of
life, whose literary value has never yet been rightly estimated;—I mean
Emanuel Swedenborg.[17] The most imaginative of men, yet writing with the
precision of a mathematician, he endeavored to engraft a purely philosophical Ethics on the popular Christianity of his time. Such an attempt of
course must have difficulty which no genius could surmount. But he saw
and showed the connection between nature and the affections of the soul.
He pierced the emblematic or spiritual character of the visible, audible,

---

[15] A small cask. "Meal" probably means "grain." [Ed.]

[16] Emerson ties his argument to the first generation of English romantics—Oliver Goldsmith, Robert Burns, and William Cowper—and their followers—Johann Wolfgang
Goethe, William Wordsworth, and Thomas Carlyle (as well as Emerson himself). He
contrasts these moderns with the "cold and pedantic" neoclassicism of Alexander Pope,
Samuel Johnson, and Edward Gibbon. [Ed.]

[17] Emanuel Swedenborg (1688–1772), Swedish scientist and religious mystic who had a
profound influence on Emerson and many other romantics. [Ed.]

tangible world. Especially did his shade-loving muse hover over and interpret the lower parts of nature; he showed the mysterious bond that allies
moral evil to the foul material forms, and has given in epical parables a theory of insanity, of beasts, of unclean and fearful things.

Another sign of our times, also marked by an analogous political movement, is the new importance given to the single person. Every thing that
tends to insulate the individual, — to surround him with barriers of natural
respect, so that each man shall feel the world is his, and man shall treat with
man as a sovereign state with a sovereign state, — tends to true union as well
as greatness. "I learned," said the melancholy Pestalozzi,[18] "that no man in
God's wide earth is either willing or able to help any other man." Help must
come from the bosom alone. The scholar is that man who must take up
into himself all the ability of the time, all the contributions of the past, all
the hopes of the future. He must be an university of knowledges. If there
be one lesson more than another which should pierce his ear, it is, The
world is nothing, the man is all; in yourself is the law of all nature, and you
know not yet how a globule of sap ascends; in yourself slumbers the whole
of Reason; it is for you to know all; it is for you to dare all. Mr. President
and Gentlemen, this confidence in the unsearched might of man belongs,
by all motives, by all prophecy, by all preparation, to the American Scholar.
We have listened too long to the courtly muses of Europe. The spirit of the
American freeman is already suspected to be timid, imitative, tame. Public
and private avarice make the air we breathe thick and fat. The scholar is decent, indolent, complaisant. See already the tragic consequence. The mind
of this country, taught to aim at low objects, eats upon itself. There is no
work for any but the decorous and the complaisant. Young men of the
fairest promise, who begin life upon our shores, inflated by the mountain
winds, shined upon by all the stars of God, find the earth below not in unison with these, but are hindered from action by the disgust which the principles on which business is managed inspire, and turn drudges, or die of
disgust, some of them suicides. What is the remedy? They did not yet see,
and thousands of young men as hopeful now crowding to the barriers for
the career do not yet see, that if the single man plant himself indomitably
on his instincts, and there abide, the huge world will come round to him.
Patience, — patience; with the shades of all the good and great for company;
and for solace the perspective of your own infinite life; and for work the
study and the communication of principles, the making those instincts
prevalent, the conversion of the world. Is it not the chief disgrace in the

---

[18] Johann Heinrich Pestalozzi (1746–1827), Swiss educator whose "organic principles of
education were followed by Bronson Alcott and Elizabeth Peabody" and whose works
Emerson would frequently cite (Ferguson 1: 256). [Ed.]

world, not to be an unit; — not to be reckoned one character; — not to yield that peculiar fruit which each man was created to bear, but to be reckoned in the gross, in the hundred, or the thousand, of the party, the section, to which we belong; and our opinion predicted geographically, as the north, or the south? Not so, brothers and friends — please God, ours shall not be so. We will walk on our own feet; we will work with our own hands; we will speak our own minds. The study of letters shall be no longer a name for pity, for doubt, and for sensual indulgence. The dread of man and the love of man shall be a wall of defence and a wreath of joy around all. A nation of men will for the first time exist, because each believes himself inspired by the Divine Soul which also inspires all men.

Letter to Martin Van Buren
April 23, 1838

Concord, Massachusetts, April 23, 1838[1]

Sir: The seat you fill places you in a relation of credit and dearness to every citizen. By right and natural position, every citizen is your friend. Before any acts, contrary to his own judgment or interest, have repelled the affections of any man, each may look with trust and loving anticipations to your government. Each has the highest right to call your attention to such subjects as are of a public nature, and properly belong to the Chief Magistrate; and the good Magistrate will feel a joy in meeting such confidence. In this belief, and at the instance of a few of my friends and neighbors, I crave of your patience, through the medium of the press, a short hearing for their sentiments and my own; and the circumstance that my name will be utterly unknown to you will only give the fairer chance to your equitable construction of what I have to say.[2]

Emerson's Anti-Slavery Writings. Ed. Len Gougeon and Joel Myerson. New Haven: Yale UP, 1995.

[1] First published as "Communication," in the *Daily National Intelligencer* (Washington, D.C.), May 14, 1838: p 2. [Orig. ed.]

[2] Emerson's letter to President Van Buren was the result of a public protest in Concord (on 22 April 1838) against the removal of the Cherokee from Georgia to Oklahoma. In addition, "Emerson (along with 490 other male citizens) signed a petition to the U.S. Congress" protesting the New Echota Treaty and its unconstitutional "'violation of all principles of free government, and of the solemn obligation of the U. States to this dependent people'"; "the women of Concord . . . signed six separate versions of the same petition" (Gougeon and Myerson xxvi). [Ed.]

Sir, my communication respects the sinister rumors that fill this part of the country concerning the Cherokee people. The interest always felt in the aboriginal population — an interest naturally growing as that decays — has been heightened in regard to this tribe. Even to our distant State, some good rumor of their worth and civility has arrived. We have learned with joy their improvement in social arts. We have read their newspapers. We have seen some of them in our schools and colleges. In common with the great body of the American People, we have witnessed with sympathy the painful endeavors of these red men to redeem their own race from the doom of eternal inferiority, and to borrow and domesticate in the tribe the inventions and customs of the Caucasian race.[3] And notwithstanding the unaccountable apathy with which, of late years, the Indians have been sometimes abandoned to their enemies, it is not to be doubted that it is the good pleasure and the understanding of all humane persons in the Republic, of the men and the matrons sitting in thriving families all over the land, that they shall be duly cared for, that they shall taste justice and love from all to whom we have delegated the office of dealing with them.

The newspapers now inform us that in December, 1835, a treaty, contracting for the exchange of the entire Cherokee territory, was pretended to be made by an agent on the part of the United States with some persons appearing on the part of the Cherokees; that the fact afterwards[4] transpired that these individual Indians did by no means represent the will of the nation; and that, out of eighteen thousand souls composing the nation, fifteen thousand six hundred and sixty-eight have protested against the so-called treaty. It now appears that the Government of the United States choose to hold the Cherokees to this sham treaty, and the proceeding to execute the same. Almost the entire Cherokee nation stand up and say, "This is not our act. Behold us! Here are we. Do not mistake that handful of deserters for us."[5] And the President and his Cabinet, the Senate and the

---

[3] The Cherokee had successfully adapted to Euroamerican socioeconomic practices and institutions, including African American slavery. Their successful competition with local white farmers was one reason behind their expulsion from Georgia. The second reason was the discovery of gold on their lands. [Ed.]

[4] "*Note by a friend of the writer.*—The fact that few Cherokee who made the treaty were not authorized to make it, was known to the Executive at the time, not afterwards discovered, as supposed by Mr. Emerson' [printed in the *Daily National Intelligencer*]". [Orig. ed.]

[5] The New Echota Treaty was signed by members of the Ridge-Boudinot faction, notably by John Ridge, Elias Boudinot, and others committed to full accommodation to the dominant white society of Georgia. Members of the John Ross faction vigorously opposed the New Echota Treaty and declared its signers "traitors," who were then subject to execution under Cherokee law. [Ed.]

House of Representatives, neither hear these men nor see them, and are contracting to put this nation into carts and boats, and to drag them over mountains and rivers to a wilderness at a vast distance beyond the Mississippi. And a paper, purporting to be an army order, fixes a month from this day as the hour for this doleful removal.[6]

In the name of God, sir, we ask you if this is so? Do the newspapers rightly inform us? Men and women, with pale and perplexed faces, meet one another in streets and churches here, and ask if this be so? We have inquired if this be a gross misrepresentation from the party opposed to the Government and anxious to blacken it with the People. We have looked into newspapers of different parties, and find a horrid confirmation of the tale. We are slow to believe it. We hoped the Indians were misinformed, and their remonstrance was premature, and would turn out to be a needless act of terror. The piety, the principle, that is left in these United States — if only its coarsest form, a regard to the speech of men — forbid us to entertain it as a fact. Such a dereliction of all faith and virtue, such a denial of justice, and such deafness to screams for mercy, were never heard of in times of peace, and in the dealing of a nation with its own allies and wards, since the earth was made. Sir, does the Government think that the People of the United States are become savage and mad? From their minds are the sentiments of love and of a good nature wiped clean out? The soul of man, the justice, the mercy, that is the heart's heart in all men, from Maine to Georgia, does abhor this business.

In speaking thus the sentiments of my neighbors and my own, perhaps I overstep the bounds of decorum. But would it not be a higher indecorum coldly to argue a matter like this? We only state the fact, that a crime is projected that confounds our understandings by its magnitude — a crime that really deprives us as well as the Cherokees of a country; for how could we call the conspiracy that should crush these poor Indians our Government, or the land that was cursed by their parting and dying imprecations our country, any more? You, sir, will bring down that renowned chair in which you sit into infamy if your seal is set to this instrument of perfidy; and the name of this nation, hitherto the sweet omen of religion and liberty, will stink to the world.

---

[6] During the spring of 1838, the U.S. Army (under the command of General Winfield S. Scott) forced Georgia Cherokee people to walk from Georgia to Oklahoma Territory. Many died. General Scott allowed the remainder of the Cherokee to wait until late summer and fall to move to Oklahoma, and John and Lewis Ross organized the logistics of the move, which lasted from 23 August 1838 to 17 January 1839. Accurate accounts of how many Cherokee died on the so-called Trail of Tears are not available, but estimates range from four thousand to eight thousand. [Ed.]

You will not do us the injustice of connecting this remonstrance with any sectional or party feeling. It is in our hearts the simplest commandment of brotherly love. We will not have this great and solemn claim upon national and human justice huddled aside under the flimsy plea of its being a party act. Sir, to us the questions upon which the Government and the People have been agitated during the past year, touching the prostration of the currency and of trade, seem motes in the comparison.[7] The hard times, it is true, have brought this discussion home to every farmhouse and poor man's table in this town, but it is the chirping of grasshoppers, beside the immortal question whether justice shall be done by the race of civilized to the race of savage man; whether all the attributes of reason, of civility, of justice, and even of mercy, shall be put off by the American People, and so vast an outrage upon the Cherokee nation, and upon human nature, shall be consummated.

One circumstance lessens the reluctance with which I intrude on your attention: my conviction that the Government ought to be admonished of a new historical fact, which the discussion of this question has disclosed, namely, that there exists in a great part of the Northern People a gloomy diffidence of the *moral* character of the Government. On the broaching of this question, a general expression of despondency, of disbelief that any good will accrue from a remonstrance on an act of fraud and robbery, appeared in those men to whom we naturally turn for aid and counsel. Will the American Government steal? will it lie? will it kill? We asked triumphantly. Our wise men shake their heads dubiously. Our counselors and old statesmen here say that, ten years ago, they would have staked their life on the affirmation that the proposed Indian measures could not be executed; that the unanimous country would put them down.[8] And now the steps of this crime follow each other so fast, at such fatally quick time, that the millions of virtuous citizens whose agents the Government are, have no space to interpose, and must shut their eyes until the last howl and wailing of these poor tormented villages and tribes shall afflict the ear of the world.

I will not hide from you as an indication of this alarming distrust, that a letter addressed as mine is, and suggesting to the mind of the Executive the plain obligations of man, has a burlesque character in the apprehension of some of my friends. I, sir, will not beforehand treat you with the contumely

---

[7] Emerson is referring here to the Panic of 1837, "hard times" that may have spurred white enmity toward Cherokee competition in Georgia. [Ed.]

[8] Emerson seems to be referring to the time shortly before President Andrew Jackson's eight-year term (1829–37) during which Jackson and Congress developed Indian removal policies that would result in such human disasters as the Trail of Tears. [Ed.]

of this distrust. I will at least state to you this fact, and show you how plain and humane people whose love would be honor regard the policy of the Government and what injurious inferences they draw as to the mind of the governors. A man with your experience in affairs must have seen cause to appreciate the futility of opposition to the moral sentiment. However feeble the sufferer, and however great the oppressor, it is in the nature of things that the blow should recoil on the aggressor. For, God is in the sentiment, and it cannot be withstood. The potentate and the People perish before it; but with it and as its executors, they are omnipotent.

I write thus, sir, to inform you of the state of mind these Indian tidings have awakened here, and to pray with one voice more, that you, whose hands are strong with the delegated power of fifteen millions of men, will avert, with that might, the terrific injury which threatens the Cherokee tribe.

> With great respect, sir, I am, your fellow-citizen,
> Ralph Waldo Emerson.

An Address Delivered before the Senior Class in Divinity College,
Cambridge [Massachusetts], Sunday Evening, July 15, 1838

In this refulgent summer, it has been a luxury to draw the breath of life. The grass grows, the buds burst, the meadow is spotted with fire and gold in the tint of flowers. The air is full of birds, and sweet with the breath of the pine, the balm-of-Gilead, and the new hay. Night brings no gloom to the heart with its welcome shade. Through the transparent darkness the stars pour their almost spiritual rays. Man under them seems a young child, and his huge globe a toy. The cool night bathes the world as with a river, and prepares his eyes again for the crimson dawn. The mystery of nature was never displayed more happily. The corn and the wine have been freely dealt to all creatures, and the never-broken silence with which the old bounty goes forward has not yielded yet one word of explanation. One is constrained to respect the perfection of this world in which our senses converse. How wide; how rich; what invitation from every property it gives to every fac-

Selections from Ralph Waldo Emerson: An Organic Anthology. Ed. Stephen E. Whicher. Riverside Edition. Boston: Houghton, 1957.

ulty of man! In its fruitful soils; in its navigable sea; in its mountains of metal and stone; in its forests of all woods; in its animals; in its chemical ingredients; in the powers and path of light, heat, attraction and life, it is well worth the pith and heart of great men to subdue and enjoy it. The planters, the mechanics, the inventors, the astronomers, the builders of cities, and the captains, history delights to honor.

But when the mind opens and reveals the laws which traverse the universe and make things what they are, then shrinks the great world at once into a mere illustration and fable of this mind. What am I? and What is? asks the human spirit with a curiosity new-kindled, but never to be quenched. Behold these outrunning laws, which our imperfect apprehension can see tend this way and that, but not come full circle. Behold these infinite relations, so like, so unlike; many, yet one. I would study, I would know, I would admire forever. These works of thought have been the entertainments of the human spirit in all ages.

A more secret, sweet, and overpowering beauty appears to man when his heart and mind open to the sentiment of virtue. Then he is instructed in what is above him. He learns that his being is without bound; that to the good, to the perfect, he is born, low as he now lies in evil and weakness. That which he venerates is still his own, though he has not realized it yet. *He ought.* He knows the sense of that grand word, though his analysis fails to render account of it. When in innocency or when by intellectual perception he attains to say, — "I love the Right; Truth is beautiful within and without for evermore. Virtue, I am thine; save me; use me; thee will I serve, day and night, in great, in small, that I may be not virtuous, but virtue"; — then is the end of the creation answered, and God is well pleased.

The sentiment of virtue is a reverence and delight in the presence of certain divine laws. It perceives that this homely game of life we play, covers, under what seem foolish details, principles that astonish. The child amidst his baubles is learning the action of light, motion, gravity, muscular force; and in the game of human life, love, fear, justice, appetite, man, and God, interact. These laws refuse to be adequately stated. They will not be written out on paper, or spoken by the tongue. They elude our persevering thought; yet we read them hourly in each other's faces, in each other's actions, in our own remorse. The moral traits which are all globed into every virtuous act and thought, — in speech we must sever, and describe or suggest by painful enumeration of many particulars. Yet, as this sentiment is the essence of all religion, let me guide your eye to the precise objects of the sentiment, by an enumeration of some of those classes of facts in which this element is conspicuous.

The intuition of the moral sentiment is an insight of the perfection of the laws of the soul. These laws execute themselves. They are out of time, out of space, and not subject to circumstance. Thus in the soul of man there is a justice whose retributions are instant and entire. He who does a good deed is instantly ennobled. He who does a mean deed is by the action itself contracted. He who puts off impurity, thereby puts on purity. If a man is at heart just, then in so far is he God; the safety of God, the immortality of God, the majesty of God do enter into that man with justice. If a man dissemble, deceive, he deceives himself, and goes out of acquaintance with his own being. A man in the view of absolute goodness, adores, with total humility. Every step so downward, is a step upward. The man who renounces himself, comes to himself.

See how this rapid intrinsic energy worketh everywhere, righting wrongs, correcting appearances, and bringing up facts to a harmony with thoughts. Its operation in life, though slow to the senses, is at last as sure as in the soul. By it a man is made the Providence to himself, dispensing good to his goodness, and evil to his sin. Character is always known. Thefts never enrich; alms never impoverish; murder will speak out of stone walls. The least admixture of a lie, —for example, the taint of vanity, any attempt to make a good impression, a favorable appearance, —will instantly vitiate the effect. But speak the truth, and all nature and all spirits help you with unexpected furtherance. Speak the truth, and all things alive or brute are vouchers, and the very roots of the grass underground there do seem to stir and move to bear you witness. See again the perfection of the Law as it applies itself to the affections, and becomes the law of society. As we are, so we associate. The good, by affinity, seek the good; the vile, by affinity, the vile. Thus of their own volition, souls proceed into heaven, into hell.

These facts have always suggested to man the sublime creed that the world is not the product of manifold power, but of one will, of one mind; and that one mind is everywhere active, in each ray of the star, in each wavelet of the pool; and whatever opposes that will is everywhere balked and baffled, because things are made so, and not otherwise. Good is positive. Evil is merely privative, not absolute: it is like cold, which is the privation of heat. All evil is so much death or nonentity.[1] Benevolence is absolute and real. So much benevolence as a man hath, so much life hath he. For all things proceed out of this same spirit, which is differently named love, justice, temperance, in its different applications, just as the ocean receives different names on the several shores which it washes. All things proceed out of the same spirit, and all things conspire with it. Whilst a man seeks good

---

[1] Emerson borrows from his "Ethics" (1837) and develops his version of Saint Augustine's privation theodicy, in which evil is the absence of the good, or a "turning away" from God. [Ed.]

ends, he is strong by the whole strength of nature. In so far as he roves from these ends, he bereaves himself of power, or auxiliaries; his being shrinks out of all remote channels, he becomes less and less, a mote a point, until absolute badness is absolute death.

The perception of this law of laws awakens in the mind a sentiment, which we call the religious sentiment, and which makes our highest happiness. Wonderful is its power to charm and to command. It is a mountain air. It is the embalmer of the world. It is myrrh and storax, and chlorine and rosemary.[2] It makes the sky and the hills sublime, and the silent song of the stars is it. By it is the universe made safe and habitable, not by science or power. Thought may work cold and intransitive in things, and find no end or unity; but the dawn of the sentiment of virtue on the heart, gives and is the assurance that Law is sovereign over all natures; and the worlds, time, space, eternity, do seem to break out into joy.

This sentiment is divine and deifying. It is the beatitude of man. It makes him illimitable. Through it, the soul first knows itself. It corrects the capital mistake of the infant man, who seeks to be great by following the great, and hopes to derive advantages *from another,*—by showing the fountain of all good to be in himself, and that he, equally with every man, is an inlet into the deeps of Reason. When he says, "I ought"; when love warms him; when he chooses, warned from on high, the good and great deed; then, deep melodies wander through his soul from Supreme Wisdom.—Then he can worship, and be enlarged by his worship; for he can never go behind this sentiment. In the sublimest flights of the soul, rectitude is never surmounted, love is never outgrown.

This sentiment lies at the foundation of society, and successively creates all forms of worship. The principle of veneration never dies out. Man fallen into superstition, into sensuality, is never wholly without the visions of the moral sentiment. In like manner, all the expressions of this sentiment are sacred and permanent in proportion to their purity. The expressions of this sentiment affect us more than all other compositions. The sentences of the oldest time, which ejaculate this piety, are still fresh and fragrant. This thought dwelled always deepest in the minds of men in the devout and contemplative East; not alone in Palestine, where it reached its purest expression, but in Egypt, in Persia, in India, in China. Europe has always

---

[2] Myrrh and storax are fragrant tree resins; rosemary is an herb. All were used in perfumery, medicine, and embalming. Chlorine was used as a medicinal disinfectant. By metaphorizing these herbs and chemicals as religious qualities, Emerson subordinates contemporary science to faith. Whereas modern embalming lends the illusion of life to the dead, Christianity promises genuine resurrection. [Ed.]

owed to oriental genius its divine impulses. What these holy bards said, all sane men found agreeable and true. And the unique impression of Jesus upon mankind, whose name is not so much written as ploughed into the history of this world, is proof of the subtle virtue of this infusion.

Meantime, whilst the doors of the temple stand open, night and day, before every man, and the oracles of this truth cease never, it is guarded by one stern condition; this, namely; it is an intuition. It cannot be received at second hand. Truly speaking, it is not instruction, but provocation, that I can receive from another soul. What he announces, I must find true in me, or reject; and on his word, or as his second, be he who he may, I can accept nothing. On the contrary, the absence of this primary faith is the presence of degradation. As is the flood, so is the ebb. Let this faith depart, and the very words it spake and the things it made become false and hurtful . Then falls the church, the state, art, letters, life. The doctrine of the divine nature being forgotten, a sickness infects and dwarfs the constitution. Once man was all; now he is an appendage, a nuisance. And because the indwelling Supreme Spirit cannot wholly be got rid of, the doctrine of it suffers this perversion, that the divine nature is attributed to one or two persons, and denied to all the rest, and denied with fury. The doctrine of inspiration is lost; the base doctrine of the majority of voices usurps the place of the doctrine of the soul. Miracles, prophecy, poetry, the ideal life, the holy life, exist as ancient history merely; they are not in the belief, nor in the aspiration of society; but, when suggested, seem ridiculous. Life is comic or pitiful as soon as the high ends of being fade out of sight, and man becomes nearsighted, and can only attend to what addresses the senses.

These general views, which, whilst they are general, none will contest, find abundant illustration in the history of religion, and especially in the history of the Christian church. In that, all of us have had our birth and nurture. The truth contained in that, you, my young friends, are now setting forth to teach. As the Cultus, or established worship of the civilized world, it has great historical interest for us.[3] Of its blessed words, which have been the consolation of humanity, you need not that I should speak. I shall endeavor to discharge my duty to you on this occasion, by pointing out two errors in its administration, which daily appear more gross from the point of view we have just now taken.

Jesus Christ belonged to the true race of prophets. He saw with open eye the mystery of the soul. Drawn by its severe harmony, ravished with its

---

[3] "Cultus" refers to the system of worship and has cognate meaning with *culture*. Emerson uses it to support his claim that Christianity is the structural foundation for all religions and thus civilizations. [Ed.]

beauty, he lived in it, and had his being there. Alone in all history he estimated the greatness of man. One man was true to what is in you and me.
He saw that God incarnates himself in man, and evermore goes forth anew
to take possession of his World. He said, in this jubilee of sublime emotion,
"I am divine. Through me, God acts; through me, speaks. Would you see
God, see me; or see thee, when thou also thinkest as I now think." But what
a distortion did his doctrine and memory suffer in the same, in the next,
and the following ages! There is no doctrine of the Reason which will bear
to be taught by the Understanding. The understanding caught this high
chant from the poet's lips, and said, in the next age, "This was Jehovah
come down out of heaven. I will kill you, if you say he was a man." The idioms of his language and the figures of his rhetoric have usurped the place
of his truth; and churches are not built on his principles, but on his tropes.
Christianity became a Mythus, as the poetic teaching of Greece and of
Egypt, before.[4] He spoke of miracles; for he felt that man's life was a miracle, and all that man doth, and he knew that this daily miracle shines as the
character ascends. But the very word Miracle, as pronounced by Christian
churches, gives a false impression; it is Monster. It is not one with the
blowing clover and the falling rain.

He felt respect for Moses and the prophets, but no unfit tenderness at
postponing their initial revelations to the hour and the man that now is; to
the eternal revelation in the heart. Thus was he a true man. Having seen
that the law in us is commanding, he would not suffer it to be commanded.
Boldly, with hand, and heart, and life, he declared it was God. Thus was he
a true man. Thus is he, as I think, the only soul in history who has appreciated the worth of man.

1. In thus contemplating Jesus, we become very sensible of the first defect of historical Christianity. Historical Christianity has fallen into the error that corrupts all attempts to communicate religion. As it appears to us,
and as it has appeared for ages, it is not the doctrine of the soul, but an exaggeration of the personal, the positive, the ritual. It has dwelt, it dwells,
with noxious exaggeration about the *person* of Jesus. The soul knows no
persons. It invites every man to expand to the full circle of the universe,
and will have no preferences but those of spontaneous love. But by this
eastern monarchy of a Christianity, which indolence and fear have built,

---

[4]"Mythus" is Latinate *myth* and is opposed to "Cultus." If we understand the miracles
of Christianity, especially those of Jesus as ideal human, as mere rhetoric or metaphor,
then we are no better than Greek or Egyptian pagans, who did not find religion within
their own natures but as the expression of remote gods. Emerson's sentiments are typically romantic. [Ed.]

the friend of man is made the injurer of man. The manner in which his name is surrounded with expressions which were once sallies of admiration and love, but are now petrified into official titles, kills all generous sympathy and liking. All who hear me, feel that the language that describes Christ to Europe and America is not the style of friendship and enthusiasm to a good and noble heart, but is appropriated and formal,—paints a demigod, as the Orientals or the Greeks would describe Osiris or Apollo.[5] Accept the injurious impositions of our early catechetical instruction, and even honesty and self-denial were but splendid sins, if they did not wear the Christian name. One would rather be

"A pagan, suckled in a creed outworn,"[6]

than to be defrauded of his manly right in coming into nature and finding not names and places, not land and professions, but even virtue and truth foreclosed and monopolized. You shall not be a man even. You shall not own the world; you shall not dare and live after the infinite Law that is in you, and in company with the infinite Beauty which heaven and earth reflect to you in all lovely forms; but you must subordinate your nature to Christ's nature; you must accept our interpretations, and take his portrait as the vulgar draw it.

That is always best which gives me to myself. The sublime is excited in me by the great stoical doctrine, Obey thyself. That which shows God in me, fortifies me. That which shows God out of me, makes me a wart and a wen.[7] There is no longer a necessary reason for my being. Already the long shadows of untimely oblivion creep over me, and I shall decease forever.

The divine bards are the friends of my virtue, of my intellect, of my strength. They admonish me that the gleams which flash across my mind are not mine, but God's; that they had the like, and were not disobedient to the heavenly vision. So I love them. Noble provocations go out from them, inviting me also to emancipate myself; to resist evil; to subdue the world; and to Be. And thus, by his holy thoughts, Jesus serves us, and thus only. To aim to convert a man by miracles is a profanation of the soul. A true conversion, a true Christ, is now, as always, to be made by the reception of beautiful sentiments. It is true that a great and rich soul, like his, falling among the simple, does so preponderate, that, as his did, it names the world. The world seems to them to exist for him, and they have not yet

---

[5] Osiris is the Egyptian and Apollo is the Greek sun-god. [Ed.]

[6] William Wordsworth's sonnet "The world is too much with us," line 10 (Ferguson 1:256). [Ed.]

[7] Goiter or benign skin tumor—an imperfection. [Ed.]

drunk so deeply of his sense as to see that only by coming again to themselves, or to God in themselves, can they grow forevermore. It is a low benefit to give me something; it is a high benefit to enable me to do somewhat of myself. The time is coming when all men will see that the gift of God to the soul is not a vaunting, overpowering, excluding sanctity, but a sweet, natural goodness, a goodness like thine and mine, and that so invites thine and mine to be and to grow.

The injustice of the vulgar tone of preaching is not less flagrant to Jesus than to the souls which it profanes. The preachers do not see that they make his gospel not glad, and shear him of the locks of beauty and the attributes of heaven. When I see a majestic Epaminondas,[8] or Washington; when I see among my contemporaries a true orator, an upright judge, a dear friend; when I vibrate to the melody and fancy of a poem; I see beauty that is to be desired. And so lovely, and with yet more entire consent of my human being, sounds in my ear the severe music of the bards that have sung of the true God in all ages. Now do not degrade the life and dialogues of Christ out of the circle of this charm, by insulation and peculiarity. Let them lie as they befell, alive and warm, part of human life and of the landscape and of the cheerful day.

2. The second defect of the traditionary and limited way of using the mind of Christ is a consequence of the first; this, namely; that the Moral Nature, that Law of laws whose revelations introduce greatness—yea, God himself—into the open soul, is not explored as the fountain of the established teaching in society. Men have come to speak of the revelation as somewhat long ago given and done, as if God were dead. The injury to faith throttles the preacher; and the goodliest of institutions becomes an uncertain and inarticulate voice.

It is very certain that it is the effect of conversation with the beauty of the soul, to beget a desire and need to impart to others the same knowledge and love. If utterance is denied, the thought lies like a burden on the man. Always the seer is a sayer. Somehow his dream is told; somehow he publishes it with solemn joy: sometimes with pencil on canvas, sometimes with chisel on stone, sometimes in towers and aisles of granite, his soul's worship is builded; sometimes in anthems of indefinite music; but clearest and most permanent, in words.

The man enamored of this excellency becomes its priest or poet. The office is coeval with the world. But observe the condition, the spiritual limitation of the office. The spirit only can teach. Not any profane man, not any sensual, not any liar, not any slave can teach, but only he can give, who

---

[8] Epaminondas (c. 418–362 BCE), Theban statesman and general (Ferguson 1:256). [Ed.]

has; he only can create, who is. The man on whom the soul descends, through whom the soul speaks, alone can teach. Courage, piety, love, wisdom, can teach; and every man can open his door to these angels, and they shall bring him the gift of tongues. But the man who aims to speak as books enable, as synods use, as the fashion guides, and as interest commands, babbles. Let him hush.

To this holy office you propose to devote yourselves. I wish you may feel your call in throbs of desire and hope. The office is the first in the world. It is of that reality that it cannot suffer the deduction of any falsehood. And it is my duty to say to you that the need was never greater of new revelation than now. From the views I have already expressed, you will infer the sad conviction, which I share, I believe, with numbers, of the universal decay and now almost death of faith in society. The soul is not preached. The Church seems to totter to its fall, almost all life extinct. On this occasion, any complaisance would be criminal which told you, whose hope and commission it is to preach the faith of Christ, that the faith of Christ is preached.

It is time that this ill-suppressed murmur of all thoughtful men against the famine of our churches;—this moaning of the heart because it is bereaved of the consolation, the hope, the grandeur that come alone out of the culture of the moral nature,—should be heard through the sleep of indolence, and over the din of routine. This great and perpetual office of the preacher is not discharged. Preaching is the expression of the moral sentiment in application to the duties of life. In how many churches, by how many prophets, tell me, is man made sensible that he is an infinite Soul; that the earth and heavens are passing into his mind; that he is drinking forever the soul of God? Where now sounds the persuasion, that by its very melody imparadises my heart, and so affirms its own origin in heaven? Where shall I hear words such as in elder ages drew men to leave all and follow,—father and mother, house and land, wife and child? Where shall I hear these august laws of moral being so pronounced as to fill my ear, and I feel ennobled by the offer of my uttermost action and passion? The test of the true faith, certainly, should be its power to charm and command the soul, as the laws of nature control the activity of the hands,—so commanding that we find pleasure and honor in obeying. The faith should blend with the light of rising and of setting suns, with the flying cloud, the singing bird, and the breath of flowers. But now the priest's Sabbath has lost the splendor of nature; it is unlovely; we are glad when it is done; we can make, we do make, even sitting in our pews, a far better, holier, sweeter, for ourselves.

Whenever the pulpit is usurped by a formalist, then is the worshipper defrauded and disconsolate. We shrink as soon as the prayers begin, which do not uplift, but smite and offend us. We are fain to wrap our cloaks about us, and secure, as best we can, a solitude that hears not. I once heard a preacher who sorely tempted me to say I would go to church no more. Men go, thought I, where they are wont to go, else had no soul entered the temple in the afternoon. A snow-storm was falling around us. The snow-storm was real, the preacher merely spectral, and the eye felt the sad contrast in looking at him, and then out of the window behind him into the beautiful meteor of the snow. He had lived in vain. He had no one word intimating that he had laughed or wept, was married or in love, had been commended, or cheated, or chagrined. If he had ever lived and acted, we were none the wiser for it. The capital secret of his profession, namely, to convert life into truth, he had not learned. Not one fact in all his experience had he yet imported into his doctrine. This man had ploughed and planted and talked and bought and sold; he had read books; he had eaten and drunken; his head aches, his heart throbs; he smiles and suffers; yet was there not a surmise, a hint, in all the discourse, that he had ever lived at all. Not a line did he draw out of real history. The true preacher can be known by this, that he deals out to the people his life, —life passed through the fire of thought. But of the bad preacher, it could not be told from his sermon what age of the world he fell in; whether he had a father or a child; whether he was a freeholder or a pauper; whether he was a citizen or a countryman; or any other fact of his biography. It seemed strange that the people should come to church. It seemed as if their houses were very unentertaining, that they should prefer this thoughtless clamor. It shows that there is a commanding attraction in the moral sentiment, that can lend a faint tint of light to dulness and ignorance coming in its name and place. The good hearer is sure he has been touched sometimes; is sure there is somewhat to be reached, and some word that can reach it. When he listens to these vain words, he comforts himself by their relation to his remembrance of better hours, and so they clatter and echo unchallenged.

I am not ignorant that when we preach unworthily, it is not always quite in vain. There is a good ear, in some men, that draws supplies to virtue out of very indifferent nutriment. There is poetic truth concealed in all the commonplaces of prayer and of sermons, and though foolishly spoken, they may be wisely heard; for each is some select expression that broke out in a moment of piety from some stricken or jubilant soul, and its excellency made it remembered. The prayers and even the dogmas of our church are like the zodiac of Denderah [9] and the astronomical monuments

---

[9] Town in the upper Nile Valley of Egypt, where there is a well-preserved ancient temple with "the signs of the Zodiac [...] sculptured on the ceiling" (Ferguson 1:256). [Ed.]

of the Hindus, wholly insulated from anything now extant in the life and business of the people. They mark the height to which the waters once rose. But this docility is a check upon the mischief from the good and devout. In a large portion of the community, the religious service gives rise to quite other thoughts and emotions. We need not chide the negligent servant. We are struck with pity, rather, at the swift retribution of his sloth. Alas for the unhappy man that is called to stand in the pulpit, and *not* give bread of life. Everything that befalls, accuses him. Would he ask contributions for the missions, foreign or domestic? Instantly his face is suffused with shame, to propose to his parish that they should send money a hundred or a thousand miles, to furnish such poor fare as they have at home and would do well to go the hundred or the thousand miles to escape. Would he urge people to a godly way of living;—and can he ask a fellow-creature to come to Sabbath meetings, when he and they all know what is the poor uttermost they can hope for therein? Will he invite them privately to the Lord's Supper? He dares not. If no heart warm this rite, the hollow, dry, creaking formality is too plain, than that he can face a man of wit and energy and put the invitation without terror. In the street, what has he to say to the bold village blasphemer? The village blasphemer sees fear in the face, form, and gait of the minister.

Let me not taint the sincerity of this plea by any oversight of the claims of good men. I know and honor the purity and strict conscience of numbers of the clergy. What life the public worship retains, it owes to the scattered company of pious men, who minister here and there in the churches, and who, sometimes accepting with too great tenderness the tenet of the elders, have not accepted from others, but from their own heart, the genuine impulses of virtue, and so still command our love and awe, to the sanctity of character. Moreover, the exceptions are not so much to be found in a few eminent preachers, as in the better hours, the truer inspirations of all,—nay, in the sincere moments of every man. But, with whatever exception, it is still true that tradition characterizes the preaching of this country; that it comes out of the memory, and not out of the soul; that it aims at what is usual, and not at what is necessary and eternal; that thus historical Christianity destroys the power of preaching, by withdrawing it from the exploration of the moral nature of man; where the sublime is, where are the resources of astonishment and power. What a cruel injustice it is to that Law, the joy of the whole earth, which alone can make thought dear and rich; that Law whose fatal sureness the astronomical orbits poorly emulate;—that it is travestied and depreciated, that it is behooted and behowled, and not a trait, not a word of it articulated. The pulpit in losing sight of this Law, loses its reason, and gropes after it knows not what. And for want of this culture the soul of the community is sick and faithless. It wants nothing so much as a stern, high, stoical, Christian discipline, to make it know itself and the divinity that speaks through it. Now man is ashamed of himself; he skulks and sneaks through the world, to be tolerated, to be pitied, and scarcely in a thousand years does any man dare to be wise and good, and so draw after him the tears and blessings of his kind.

Certainly there have been periods when, from the inactivity of the intellect on certain truths, a greater faith was possible in names and persons. The Puritans in England and America found in the Christ of the Catholic Church and in the dogmas inherited from Rome, scope for their austere piety and their longings for civil freedom. But their creed is passing away, and none arises in its room. I think no man can go with his thoughts about him into one of our churches, without feeling that what hold the public worship had on men is gone, or going. It has lost its grasp on the affection of the good and the fear of the bad. In the country, neighborhoods, half parishes are *signing off*, to use the local term. It is already beginning to indicate character and religion to withdraw from the religious meetings. I have heard a devout person, who prized the Sabbath, say in bitterness of heart, "On Sundays, it seems wicked to go to church."[10] And the motive that holds the best there is now only a hope and a waiting. What was once a mere circumstance, that the best and the worst men in the parish, the poor and the rich, the learned and the ignorant, young and old, should meet one day as fellows in one house, in sign of an equal right in the soul, has come to be a paramount motive for going thither.

My friends, in these two errors, I think, I find the causes of a decaying church and a wasting unbelief. And what greater calamity can fall upon a nation than the loss of worship? Then all things go to decay. Genius leaves the temple to haunt the senate or the market. Literature becomes frivolous. Science is cold. The eye of youth is not lighted by the hope of other worlds, and age is without honor. Society lives to trifles, and when men die we do not mention them.

And now, my brothers, you will ask, What in these desponding days can be done by us? The remedy is already declared in the ground of our complaint of the Church. We have contrasted the Church with the Soul. In the soul then let the redemption be sought. In one soul, in your soul, there are resources for the world. Wherever a man comes, there comes revolution. The old is for slaves. When a man comes, all books are legible, all things

---

[10] Attributed to Emerson's wife, Lidian. [Orig. ed.]

transparent, all religions are forms. He is religious. Man is the wonder-worker. He is seen amid miracles. All men bless and curse. He saith yea and nay, only. The stationariness of religion; the assumption that the age of inspiration is past, that the Bible is closed; the fear of degrading the character of Jesus by representing him as a man;—indicate with sufficient clearness the falsehood of our theology. It is the office of a true teacher to show us that God is, not was; that He speaketh, not spake. The true Christianity,—a faith like Christ's in the infinitude of man,—is lost. None believeth in the soul of man, but only in some man or person old and departed. Ah me! no man goeth alone. All men go in flocks to this saint or that poet, avoiding the God who seeth in secret. They cannot see in secret; they love to be blind in public. They think society wiser than their soul, and know not that one soul, and their soul, is wiser than the whole world. See how nations and races flit by on the sea of time and leave no ripple to tell where they floated or sunk, and one good soul shall make the name of Moses, or of Zeno, or of Zoroaster, reverend forever.[11] None assayeth the stern ambition to be the Self of the nation and of nature, but each would be an easy secondary to some Christian scheme, or sectarian connection, or some eminent man. Once leave your own knowledge of God, your own sentiment, and take secondary knowledge, as St. Paul's, or George Fox's, or Swedenborg's, and you get wide from God with every year this secondary form lasts, and if, as now, for centuries,—the chasm yawns to that breadth, that men can scarcely be convinced there is in them anything divine.[12]

Let me admonish you, first of all, to go alone; to refuse the good models, even those which are sacred in the imagination of men, and dare to love God without mediator or veil. Friends enough you shall find who will hold up to your emulation Wesleys and Oberlins,[13] Saints and Prophets. Thank God for these good men, but say, "I also am a man." Imitation cannot go above its model. The imitator dooms himself to hopeless mediocrity. The

---

[11] Emerson mixes together the Old Testament prophet Moses with Zeno, the Greek philosopher who founded Stoicism, and Zoroaster, the Persian prophet of Zoroastrianism. Apparently contradicting his earlier claims for the "Cultus" of Christianity, he equates all three with human genius as sign of the divine and thus of true religion. [Ed.]

[12] Citing three of his own favorites, Emerson warns of the dangers in confusing the historical personality with the divine inspiration. George Fox (1624–91) founded the Quakers and is the subject of an Emerson lecture in 1835. Emerson admired Emanuel Swedenborg (1688–1772) for his combination of science and mysticism (see n. 62, p. 56). [Ed.]

[13] John Wesley (1703–91), founder of Methodism. Jean Frédéric Oberlin (1740–1826), Protestant clergyman and religious reformer. [Ed.]

inventor did it because it was natural to him, and so in him it has a charm. In the imitator something else is natural, and he bereaves himself of his own beauty, to come short of another man's.

Yourself a newborn bard of the Holy Ghost, cast behind you all conformity, and acquaint men at first hand with Deity. Look to it first and only, that fashion, custom, authority, pleasure, and money, are nothing to you, — are not bandages over your eyes, that you cannot see, — but live with the privilege of the immeasurable mind. Not too anxious to visit periodically all families and each family in your parish connection, — when you meet one of these men or women, be to them a divine man; be to them thought and virtue; let their timid aspirations find in you a friend; let their trampled instincts be genially tempted out in your atmosphere; let their doubts know that you have doubted, and their wonder feel that you have wondered. By trusting your own soul, you shall gain more confidence in other men. For all our penny-wisdom, for all our soul-destroying slavery to habit, it is not to be doubted that all men have sublime thoughts; that all men value the few real hours of life; they love to be heard; they love to be caught up into the vision of principles. We mark with light in the memory the few interviews we have had, in the dreary years of routine and of sin, with souls that made our souls wiser; that spoke what we thought; that told us what we knew; that gave us leave to be what we inly were. Discharge to men the priestly office, and, present or absent, you shall be followed with their love as by an angel.

And, to this end, let us not aim at common degrees of merit. Can we not leave, to such as love it, the virtue that glitters for the commendation of society, and ourselves pierce the deep solitudes of absolute ability and worth? We easily come up to the standard of goodness in society. Society's praise can be cheaply secured, and almost all men are content with those easy merits; but the instant effect of conversing with God will be to put them away. There are persons who are not actors, not speakers, but influences; persons too great for fame, for display; who disdain eloquence; to whom all we call art and artist, seems too nearly allied to show and by-ends, to the exaggeration of the finite and selfish, and loss of the universal. The orators, the poets, the commanders encroach on us only as fair women do, by our allowance and homage. Slight them by preoccupation of mind, slight them, as you can well afford to do, by high and universal aims, and they instantly feel that you have right, and that it is in lower places that they must shine. They also feel your right; for they with you are open to the influx of the all-knowing Spirit, which annihilates before its broad noon the little shades and gradations of intelligence in the compositions we call wiser and wisest.

In such high communion, let us study the grand strokes of rectitude: a bold benevolence, an independence of friends, so that not the unjust wishes of those who love us shall impair our freedom, but we shall resist for truth's sake the freest flow of kindness, and appeal to sympathies far in advance; and, —what is the highest form in which we know this beautiful element, —a certain solidity of merit, that has nothing to do with opinion, and which is so essentially and manifestly virtue, that it is taken for granted that the right, the brave, the generous step will be taken by it, and nobody thinks of commending it. You would compliment a coxcomb doing a good act, but you would not praise an angel. The silence that accepts merit as the most natural thing in the world, is the highest applause. Such souls, when they appear, are the Imperial Guard of Virtue, the perpetual reserve, the dictators of fortune. One needs not praise their courage, —they are the heart and soul of nature. O my friends, there are resources in us on which we have not drawn. There are men who rise refreshed on hearing a threat; men to whom a crisis which intimidates and paralyzes the majority, —demanding not the faculties of prudence and thrift, but comprehension, immovableness, the readiness of sacrifice, —comes graceful and beloved as a bride. Napoleon said of Massena,[14] that he was not himself until the battle began to go against him; then, when the dead began to fall in ranks around him, awoke his powers of combination, and he put on terror and victory as a robe. So it is in rugged crises, in unweariable endurance, and in aims which put sympathy out of question, that the angel is shown. But these are heights that we can scarce remember and look up to without contrition and shame. Let us thank God that such things exist.

And now let us do what we can to rekindle the smouldering, nigh quenched fire on the altar. The evils of the church that now is are manifest. The question returns, What shall we do? I confess, all attempts to project and establish a Cultus with new rites and forms, seem to me vain. Faith makes us, and not we it, and faith makes its own forms. All attempts to contrive a system are as cold as the new worship introduced by the French to the goddess of Reason, —today, pasteboard and filigree, and ending tomorrow in madness and murder. Rather let the breath of new life be breathed by you through the forms already existing. For if once you are alive, you shall find they shall become plastic and new. The remedy to their deformity is first, soul, and second, soul, and evermore, soul. A whole popedom of forms one pulsation of virtue can uplift and vivify. Two ines-

---

[14] André Masséna, Duke de Rivoli (c. 1758–1817), one of Napoleon's field marshals (Ferguson 1:257). [Ed.]

timable advantages Christianity has given us; first the Sabbath, the jubilee of the whole world, whose light dawns welcome alike into the closet of the philosopher, into the garret of toil, and into prison-cells, and everywhere suggests, even to the vile, a thought of the dignity of spiritual being. Let it stand forevermore, a temple, which new love, new faith, new sight shall restore to more than its first splendor to mankind. And secondly, the institution of preaching,—the speech of man to men,—essentially the most flexible of all organs, of all forms. What hinders that now, everywhere, in pulpits, in lecture-rooms, in houses, in fields, wherever the invitation of men or your own occasions lead you, you speak the very truth, as your life and conscience teach it, and cheer the waiting, fainting hearts of men with new hope and new revelation?

I look for the hour when that supreme Beauty which ravished the souls of those Eastern men, and chiefly of those Hebrews, and through their lips spoke oracles to all time, shall speak in the West also. The Hebrew and Greek Scriptures contain immortal sentences, that have been bread of life to millions. But they have no epical integrity; are fragmentary; are not shown in their order to the intellect. I look for the new Teacher that shall follow so far those shining laws that he shall see them come full circle; shall see their rounding complete grace; shall see the world to be the mirror of the soul; shall see the identity of the law of gravitation with purity of heart; and shall show that the Ought, that Duty, is one thing with Science, with Beauty, and with Joy.

Self-Reliance
1841

"Ne te quaesiveris extra." [1]

"Man is his own star; and the soul that can
Render an honest and a perfect man,
Commands all light, all influence, all fate;
Nothing to him falls early or too late.

Selection from Ralph Waldo Emerson: An Organic Anthology. Ed. Stephen E. Whicher. Riverside Edition. Boston: Houghton, 1957. (All notes are by the present editor.)

[1] Persius, *Satires* 1.7: "Look to no one outside yourself" (Ferguson 2:229).

Our acts our angels are, or good or ill,
Our fatal shadows that walk by us still."
—Epilogue to Beaumont and Fletcher's
Honest Man's Fortune

Cast the bantling on the rocks,
Suckle him with the she-wolf's teat,
. *Wintered with the hawk and fox,*
Power and speed be hands and feet.
[—Emerson, "Power"]

I read the other day some verses written by an eminent painter which were original and not conventional.[2] The soul always hears an admonition in such lines, let the subject be what it may. The sentiment they instil is of more value than any thought they may contain. To believe your own thought, to believe that what is true for you in your private heart is true for all men,—that is genius. Speak your latent conviction, and it shall be the universal sense; for the inmost in due time becomes the outmost, and our first thought is rendered back to us by the trumpets of the Last Judgment. Familiar as the voice of the mind is to each, the highest merit we ascribe to Moses, Plato and Milton is that they set at naught books and traditions, and spoke not what men, but what *they* thought. A man should learn to detect and watch that gleam of light which flashes across his mind from within, more than the lustre of the firmament of bards and sages. Yet he dismisses without notice his thought, because it is his. In every work of genius we recognize our own rejected thoughts; they come back to us with a certain alienated majesty. Great works of art have no more affecting lesson for us than this. They teach us to abide by our spontaneous impression with good-humored inflexibility then most when the whole cry of voices is on the other side. Else tomorrow a stranger will say with masterly good sense precisely what we have thought and felt all the time, and we shall be forced to take with shame our own opinion from another.

There is a time in every man's education when he arrives at the conviction that envy is ignorance; that imitation is suicide; that he must take himself for better for worse as his portion; that though the wide universe is full

---

[2] Washington Allston (Emerson's "eminent painter"), "To the Author of 'The Diary of the Ennuyée,'" published in Allston's *Lectures on Art, and Poems* (1850) (Ferguson 2:229).

of good, no kernel of nourishing corn can come to him but through his toil bestowed on that plot of ground which is given to him to till. The power which resides in him is new in nature, and none but he knows what that is which he can do, nor does he know until he has tried. Not for nothing one face, one character, one fact, makes much impression on him, and another none. This sculpture in the memory is not without preestablished harmony. The eye was placed where one ray should fall, that it might testify of that particular ray. We but half express ourselves, and are ashamed of that divine idea which each of us represents. It may be safely trusted as proportionate and of good issues, so it be faithfully imparted, but God will not have his work made manifest by cowards. A man is relieved and gay when he has put his heart into his work and done his best; but what he has said or done otherwise shall give him no peace. It is a deliverance which does not deliver. In the attempt his genius deserts him; no muse befriends; no invention, no hope.

Trust thyself: every heart vibrates to that iron string. Accept the place the divine Providence has found for you, the society of your contemporaries, the connection of events. Great men have always done so, and confided themselves childlike to the genius of their age, betraying their perception that the absolutely trustworthy was seated at their heart, working through their hands, predominating in all their being. And we are now men, and must accept in the highest mind the same transcendent destiny; and not minors and invalids in a protected corner, not cowards fleeing before a revolution, but guides, redeemers and benefactors, obeying the Almighty effort and advancing on Chaos and the Dark.

What pretty oracles nature yields us on this text in the face and behavior of children, babes, and even brutes! That divided and rebel mind, that distrust of a sentiment because our arithmetic has computed the strength and means opposed to our purpose, these have not. Their mind being whole, their eye is as yet unconquered, and when we look in their faces we are disconcerted. Infancy conforms to nobody; all conform to it, so that one babe commonly makes four or five out of the adults who prattle and play to it. So God has armed youth and puberty and manhood no less with its own piquancy and charm, and made it enviable and gracious and its claims not to be put by, if it will stand by itself. Do not think the youth has no force, because he cannot speak to you and me. Hark! in the next room his voice is sufficiently clear and emphatic. It seems he knows how to speak to his contemporaries. Bashful or bold then, he will know how to make us seniors very unnecessary.

The nonchalance of boys who are sure of a dinner, and would disdain as much as a lord to do or say aught to conciliate one, is the healthy attitude of human nature. A boy is in the parlor what the pit is in the playhouse;

independent, irresponsible, looking out from his corner on such people and facts as pass by, he tries and sentences them on their merits, in the swift, summary way of boys, as good, bad, interesting, silly, eloquent, troublesome. He cumbers himself never about consequences, about interests; he gives an independent, genuine verdict. You must court him; he does not court you. But the man is as it were clapped into jail by his consciousness. As soon as he has once acted or spoken with *éclat* he is a committed person, watched by the sympathy or the hatred of hundreds, whose affections must now enter into his account. There is no Lethe for this. Ah, that he could pass again into his neutrality! Who can thus avoid all pledges and, having observed, observe again from the same unaffected, unbiased, unbribable, unaffrighted innocence, — must always be formidable. He would utter opinions on all passing affairs, which being seen to be not private but necessary, would sink like darts into the ear of men and put them in fear.

These are the voices which we hear in solitude, but they grow faint and inaudible as we enter into the world. Society everywhere is in conspiracy against the manhood of every one of its members. Society is a joint-stock company, in which the members agree, for the better securing of his bread to each shareholder, to surrender the liberty and culture of the eater. The virtue in most request is conformity. Self-reliance is its aversion. It loves not realities and creators, but names and customs.

Whoso would be a man, must be a nonconformist. He who would gather immortal palms must not be hindered by the name of goodness, but must explore if it be goodness. Nothing is at last sacred but the integrity of your own mind. Absolve you to yourself, and you shall have the suffrage of the world. I remember an answer which when quite young I was prompted to make to a valued adviser who was wont to importune me with the dear old doctrines of the church. On my saying, "What have I to do with the sacredness of traditions, if I live wholly from within?" my friend suggested, — "But these impulses may be from below, not from above." I replied, "They do not seem to me to be such; but if I am the Devil's child, I will live then from the Devil." No law can be sacred to me but that of my nature. Good and bad are but names very readily transferable to that or this; the only right is what is after my constitution; the only wrong what is against it. A man is to carry himself in the presence of all opposition as if every thing were titular and ephemeral but he. I am ashamed to think how easily we capitulate to badges and names, to large societies and dead institutions. Every decent and well-spoken individual affects and sways me more than is right. I ought to go upright and vital, and speak the rude truth in all ways. If malice and vanity wear the coat of philanthropy, shall that pass? If an angry bigot assumes this bountiful cause of Abolition, and comes to me with his last news from Barbadoes, why should I not say to him, "Go love thy infant; love thy wood-chopper; be good-natured and modest; have that grace; and never varnish your hard, uncharitable ambition with this incredible tenderness for black folk a thousand miles off. Thy love afar is spite at home."[3] Rough and graceless would be such greeting, but truth is handsomer than the affectation of love. Your goodness must have some edge to it, —else it is none. The doctrine of hatred must be preached, as the counteraction of the doctrine of love, when that pules and whines. I shun father and mother and wife and brother when my genius calls me. I would write on the lintels of the door-post,[4] *Whim.* I hope it is somewhat better than whim at last, but we cannot spend the day in explanation. Expect me not to show cause why I seek or why I exclude company. Then again, do not tell me, as a good man did today, of my obligation to put all poor men in good situations. Are they *my* poor? I tell thee, thou foolish philanthropist, that I grudge the dollar, the dime, the cent I give to such men as do not belong to me and to whom I do not belong. There is a class of persons to whom by all spiritual affinity I am bought and sold; for them I will go to prison if need be; but your miscellaneous popular charities; the education at college of fools; the building of meeting-houses to the vain end to which many now stand; alms to sots, and the thousand-fold Relief Societies; — though I confess with shame I sometimes succumb and give the dollar, it is a wicked dollar, which by and by I shall have the manhood to withhold.

Virtues are, in the popular estimate, rather the exception than the rule. There is the man *and* his virtues. Men do what is called a good action, as some piece of courage or charity, much as they would pay a fine in expiation of daily non-appearance on parade. Their works are done as an apology or extenuation of their living in the world, —as invalids and the insane pay a high board. Their virtues are penances. I do not wish to expiate, but to live. My life is for itself and not for a spectacle. I much prefer that it should be of a lower strain, so it be genuine and equal, than that it should be glittering and unsteady. I wish it to be sound and sweet, and not to need diet and bleeding. I ask primary evidence that you are a man, and refuse this appeal from the man to his actions. I know that for myself it makes no difference whether I do or forbear those actions which are reckoned excellent. I cannot consent to pay for a privilege where I have intrinsic right. Few and mean as my gifts may be, I actually am, and do not need for my own assurance or the assurance of my fellows any secondary testimony.

---

[3] Slavery was abolished in the British West Indies in 1834. See Emerson's memorial address, "Address . . . on . . . the Emancipation of the Negroes in the British West Indies" (1844), in this volume.

[4] Cf. Exod. 12.23.

What I must do is all that concerns me, not what the people think. This rule, equally arduous in actual and in intellectual life, may serve for the whole distinction between greatness and meanness. It is the harder because you will always find those who think they know what is your duty better than you know it. It is easy in the world to live after the world's opinion; it is easy in solitude to live after our own; but the great man is he who in the midst of the crowd keeps with perfect sweetness the independence of solitude.

The objection to conforming to usages that have become dead to you is that it scatters your force. It loses your time and blurs the impression of your character. If you maintain a dead church, contribute to a dead Bible-Society, vote with a great party either for the government or against it, spread your table like base housekeepers, — under all these screens I have difficulty to detect the precise man you are: and of course so much force is withdrawn from your proper life. But do your work, and I shall know you. Do your work, and you shall reinforce yourself. A man must consider what a blind-man's-buff is this game of conformity. If I know your sect, I anticipate your argument. I hear a preacher announce for his text and topic the expediency of one of the institutions of his church. Do I not know beforehand that not possibly can he say a new and spontaneous word? Do I not know that with all this ostentation of examining the grounds of the institution he will do no such thing? Do I not know that he is pledged to himself not to look but at one side, the permitted side, not as a man, but as a parish minister? He is a retained attorney, and these airs of the bench are the emptiest affectation. Well, most men have bound their eyes with one or another handkerchief, and attached themselves to some one of these communities of opinion. This conformity makes them not false in a few particulars, authors of a few lies, but false in all particulars. Their every truth is not quite true. Their two is not the real two, their four not the real four; so that every word they say chagrins us and we know not where to begin to set them right. Meantime nature is not slow to equip us in the prison-uniform of the party to which we adhere. We come to wear one cut of face and figure, and acquire by degrees the gentlest asinine expression. There is a mortifying experience in particular, which does not fail to wreak itself also in the general history; I mean "the foolish face of praise," the forced smile which we put on in company where we do not feel at ease, in answer to conversation which does not interest us. The muscles, not spontaneously moved but moved by a low usurping wilfulness, grow tight about the outline of the face, with the most disagreeable sensation.

For nonconformity the world whips you with its displeasure. And therefore a man must know how to estimate a sour face. The by-standers look askance on him in the public street or in the friend's parlor. If this aversion had its origin in contempt and resistance like his own he might well go home with a sad countenance; but the sour faces of the multitude, like their sweet faces, have no deep cause, but are put on and off as the wind blows and a newspaper directs. Yet is the discontent of the multitude more formidable than that of the senate and the college. It is easy enough for a firm man who knows the world to brook the rage of the cultivated classes. Their rage is decorous and prudent, for they are timid, as being very vulnerable themselves. But when to their feminine rage the indignation of the people is added, when the ignorant and the poor are aroused, when the unintelligent brute force that lies at the bottom of society is made to growl and mow, it needs the habit of magnanimity and religion to treat it godlike as a trifle of no concernment.

The other terror that scares us from self-trust is our consistency; a reverence for our past act or word, because the eyes of others have no other data for computing our orbit than our past acts, and we are loth to disappoint them.

But why should you keep your head over your shoulder? Why drag about this corpse of your memory, lest you contradict somewhat you have stated in this or that public place? Suppose you should contradict yourself; what then? It seems to be a rule of wisdom never to rely on your memory alone, scarcely even in acts of pure memory, but to bring the past for judgment into the thousand-eyed present, and live ever in a new day. In your metaphysics you have denied personality to the Deity, yet when the devout motions of the soul come, yield to them heart and life, though they should clothe God with shape and color. Leave your theory, as Joseph his coat in the hand of the harlot, and flee.

A foolish consistency is the hobgoblin of little minds, adored by little statesmen and philosophers and divines. With consistency a great soul has simply nothing to do. He may as well concern himself with his shadow on the wall. Speak what you think now in hard words and tomorrow speak what tomorrow thinks in hard words again, though it contradict every thing you said today. — "Ah, so you shall be sure to be misunderstood." — Is it so bad then to be misunderstood? Pythagoras was misunderstood, and Socrates, and Jesus, and Luther, and Copernicus, and Galileo, and Newton, and every pure and wise spirit that ever took flesh.[5] To be great is to be misunderstood.

---

[5] Emerson typically illustrates how genius is ahead of its time and often misunderstood by citing Greek philosophers (Pythagoras and Socrates), religious prophets (Jesus and Luther), early modern astronomers (Copernicus and Galileo), and a modern scientist (Newton).

I suppose no man can violate his nature. All the sallies of his will are rounded in by the law of his being, as the inequalities of Andes and Himmaleh are insignificant in the curve of the sphere. Nor does it matter how you gauge and try him. A character is like an acrostic or Alexandrian stanza;—read it forward, backward, or across, it still spells the same thing.[6] In this pleasing contrite wood-life which God allows me, let me record day by day my honest thought without prospect or retrospect, and, I cannot doubt, it will be found symmetrical, though I mean it not and see it not. My book should smell of pines and resound with the hum of insects. The swallow over my window should interweave that thread or straw he carries in his bill into my web also. We pass for what we are. Character teaches above our wills. Men imagine that they communicate their virtue or vice only by overt actions, and do not see that virtue or vice emit a breath every moment.

There will be an agreement in whatever variety of actions, so they be each honest and natural in their hour. For of one will, the actions will be harmonious, however unlike they seem. These varieties are lost sight of at a little distance, at a little height of thought. One tendency unites them all. The voyage of the best ship is a zigzag line of a hundred tacks. See the line from a sufficient distance, and it straightens itself to the average tendency. Your genuine action will explain itself and will explain your other genuine actions. Your conformity explains nothing. Act singly, and what you have already done singly will justify you now. Greatness appeals to the future. If I can be firm enough today to do right and scorn eyes, I must have done so much right before as to defend me now. Be it how it will, do right now. Always scorn appearances and you always may. The force of character is cumulative. All the foregone days of virtue work their health into this. What makes the majesty of the heroes of the senate and the field, which so fills the imagination? The consciousness of a train of great days and victories behind. They shed a united light on the advancing actor. He is attended as by a visible escort of angels. That is it which throws thunder into Chatham's voice, and dignity into Washington's port, and American into Adams's eye.[7]

---

[6] An acrostic is a poem or other composition in which the first letter of each line (or the first and middle [double] or the first and middle and final [triple] letters) compose a readable message. The poets of Alexandria, Egypt—the center of Hellenistic literature from 300 to 200 BCE—were fond of including acrostics, palindromes, and other puzzles in their poems. Emerson's point here is that character is readable in all directions, but also that the most recondite mysteries lurk in the human being.

[7] William Pitt (d. 1778), British prime minister and statesman, was the Earl of Chatham. By linking George Washington and (probably) John Adams with Pitt, Emerson adds a venerable air to American politics.

Honor is venerable to us because it is no ephemera. It is always ancient virtue. We worship it today because it is not of today. We love it and pay it homage because it is not a trap for our love and homage, but is self-dependent, self-derived, and therefore of an old immaculate pedigree, even if shown in a young person.

I hope in these days we have heard the last of conformity and consistency. Let the words be gazetted and ridiculous henceforward. Instead of the gong for dinner, let us hear a whistle from the Spartan fife. Let us never bow and apologize more. A great man is coming to eat at my house. I do not wish to please him; I wish that he should wish to please me. I will stand here for humanity, and though I would make it kind, I would make it true. Let us affront and reprimand the smooth mediocrity and squalid contentment of the times, and hurl in the face of custom and trade and office, the fact which is the upshot of all history, that there is a great responsible Thinker and Actor working wherever a man works; that a true man belongs to no other time or place, but is the center of things. Where he is, there is nature. He measures you and all men and all events. Ordinarily, every body in society reminds us of somewhat else, or of some other person. Character, reality, reminds you of nothing else; it takes place of the whole creation. The man must be so much that he must make all circumstances indifferent. Every true man is a cause, a country, and an age; requires infinite spaces and numbers and time fully to accomplish his design; —and posterity seem to follow his steps as a train of clients. A man Caesar is born, and for ages after we have a Roman Empire. Christ is born, and millions of minds so grow and cleave to his genius that he is confounded with virtue and the possible of man. An institution is the lengthened shadow of one man; as, Monachism, of the Hermit Antony; the Reformation, of Luther; Quakerism, of Fox; Methodism, of Wesley; Abolition, of Clarkson.[8] Scipio, Milton called "the height of Rome"; and all history resolves itself very easily into the biography of a few stout and earnest persons.[9]

Let a man then know his worth, and keep things under his feet. Let him not peep or steal, or skulk up and down with the air of a charity-boy, a bastard, or an interloper in the world which exists for him. But the man in the street, finding no worth in himself which corresponds to the force which built a tower or sculptured a marble god, feels poor when he looks on these. To him a palace, a statue, or a costly book have an alien and forbidding air,

---

[8] Emerson provides a long list of founders of religious and political movements — Saint Anthony, Martin Luther, George Fox, John Wesley, and Thomas Clarkson — to illustrate his point that historical change often depends on geniuses and heroes.

[9] John Milton, *Paradise Lost* 9.510 (1667).

much like a gay equipage, and seem to say like that, "Who are you, Sir?" Yet they all are his, suitors for his notice, petitioners to his faculties that they will come out and take possession. The picture waits for my verdict; it is not to command me, but I am to settle its claims to praise. That popular fable of the sot who was picked up dead-drunk in the street, carried to the duke's house, washed and dressed and laid in the duke's bed, and, on his waking, treated with all obsequious ceremony like the duke, and assured that he had been insane, owes its popularity to the fact that it symbolizes so well the state of man, who is in the world a sort of sot, but now and then wakes up, exercises his reason and finds himself a true prince.[10]

Our reading is mendicant and sycophantic. In history our imagination plays us false. Kingdom and lordship, power and estate, are a gaudier vocabulary than private John and Edward in a small house and common day's work; but the things of life are the same to both; the sum total of both is the same. Why all this deference to Alfred and Scanderbeg and Gustavus?[11] Suppose they were virtuous; did they wear out virtue? As great a stake depends on your private act today as followed their public and renowned steps. When private men shall act with original views, the lustre will be transferred from the actions of kings to those of gentlemen.

The world has been instructed by its kings, who have so magnetized the eyes of nations. It has been taught by this colossal symbol the mutual reverence that is due from man to man. The joyful loyalty with which men have everywhere suffered the king, the noble, or the great proprietor to walk among them by a law of his own, make his own scale of men and things and reverse theirs, pay for benefits not with money but with honor, and represent the law in his person, was the hieroglyphic by which they obscurely signified their consciousness of their own right and comeliness, the right of every man.

The magnetism which all original action exerts is explained when we inquire the reason of self-trust. Who is the Trustee? What is the aboriginal Self, on which a universal reliance may be grounded? What is the nature and power of that science-baffling star, without parallax, without calcula-

---

[10] An ancient tale of switched identities, which is traceable to *The Thousand and One Nights* and would have been familiar to Emerson's readers from the "Induction" to Shakespeare's *The Taming of the Shrew*.

[11] King Alfred is the Saxon reputed to have founded England. "Scanderbeg" is Emerson's version of the Turkish title *Iskander Bey*, held by George Castriota (1403–68), who led the Albanian rebellion against the Turks. Gustavus is probably Gustavus Adolphus (1594–1632), the king of Sweden who led the interventionist forces in the Thirty Years War. All three are heroes of European political history.

ble elements, which shoots a ray of beauty even into trivial and impure actions, if the least mark of independence appear? The inquiry leads us to that source, at once the essence of genius, of virtue, and of life, which we call Spontaneity or Instinct. We denote this primary wisdom as Intuition, whilst all later teachings are tuitions. In that deep force, the last fact behind which analysis cannot go, all things find their common origin. For the sense of being which in calm hours rises, we know not how, in the soul, is not diverse from things, from space, from light, from time, from man, but one with them and proceeds obviously from the same source whence their life and being also proceed. We first share the life by which things exist and afterwards see them as appearances in nature and forget that we have shared their cause. Here is the fountain of action and of thought. Here are the lungs of that inspiration which giveth man wisdom and which cannot be denied without impiety and atheism. We lie in the lap of immense intelligence, which makes us receivers of its truth and organs of its activity. When we discern justice, when we discern truth, we do nothing of ourselves, but allow a passage to its beams. If we ask whence this comes, if we seek to pry into the soul that causes, all philosophy is at fault. Its presence or its absence is all we can affirm. Every man discriminates between the voluntary acts of his mind and his involuntary perceptions, and knows that to his involuntary perceptions a perfect faith is due. He may err in the expression of them, but he knows that these things are so, like day and night, not to be disputed. My wilful actions and acquisitions are but roving;—the idlest reverie, the faintest native emotion, command my curiosity and respect. Thoughtless people contradict as readily the statement of perceptions as of opinions, or rather much more readily; for they do not distinguish between perception and notion. They fancy that I choose to see this or that thing. But perception is not whimsical, but fatal. If I see a trait, my children will see it after me, and in course of time all mankind, —although it may chance that no one has seen it before me. For my perception of it is as much a fact as the sun.

The relations of the soul to the divine spirit are so pure that it is profane to seek to interpose helps. It must be that when God speaketh he should communicate, not one thing, but all things, should fill the world with his voice; should scatter forth light, nature, time, souls, from the center of the present thought; and new date and new create the whole. Whenever a mind is simple and receives a divine wisdom, old things pass away, —means, teachers, texts, temples fall; it lives now, and absorbs past and future into the present hour. All things are made sacred by relation to it, —one as much as another. All things are dissolved to their center by their cause, and in the universal miracle petty and particular miracles disappear. If therefore a man claims to know and speak of God and carries you backward to the phraseology of some old mouldered nation in another country, in another world, believe him not. Is the acorn better than the oak which is its fulness and completion? Is the parent better than the child into whom he has cast his ripened being? Whence then this worship of the past? The centuries are conspirators against the sanity and authority of the soul. Time and space are but physiological colors which the eye makes, but the soul is light: where it is, is day; where it was, is night; and history is an impertinence and an injury if it be any thing more than a cheerful apologue or parable of my being and becoming.

Man is timid and apologetic; he is no longer upright; he dares not say "I think," "I am," but quotes some saint or sage. He is ashamed before the blade of grass or the blowing rose. These roses under my window make no reference to former roses or to better ones; they are for what they are; they exist with God today. There is no time to them. There is simply the rose; it is perfect in every moment of its existence. Before a leaf-bud has burst, its whole life acts; in the full-blown flower there is no more; in the leafless root there is no less. Its nature is satisfied and it satisfies nature in all moments alike. But man postpones or remembers; he does not live in the present, but with reverted eye laments the past, or, heedless of the riches that surround him, stands on tiptoe to foresee the future. He cannot be happy and strong until he too lives with nature in the present, above time.

This should be plain enough. Yet see what strong intellects dare not yet hear God himself unless he speak the phraseology of I know not what David, or Jeremiah, or Paul. We shall not always set so great a price on a few texts, on a few lives. We are like children who repeat by rote the sentences of grandames and tutors, and, as they grow older, of the men of talents and character they chance to see, — painfully recollecting the exact words they spoke; afterwards, when they come into the point of view which those had who uttered these sayings, they understand them and are willing to let the words go; for at any time they can use words as good when occasion comes. If we live truly, we shall see truly. It is as easy for the strong man to be strong, as it is for the weak to be weak. When we have new perception, we shall gladly disburden the memory of its hoarded treasures as old rubbish. When a man lives with God, his voice shall be as sweet as the murmur of the brook and the rustle of the corn.

And now at last the highest truth on this subject remains unsaid; probably cannot be said; for all that we say is the far-off remembering of the intuition. That thought by what I can now nearest approach to say it, is this. When good is near you, when you have life in yourself, it is not by any known or accustomed way; you shall not discern the footprints of any other; you shall not see the face of man; you shall not hear any name; — the way, the thought, the good, shall be wholly strange and new. It shall exclude example and experience. You take the way from man, not to man. All persons that ever existed are its forgotten ministers. Fear and hope are alike beneath it. There is somewhat low even in hope. In the hour of vision there is nothing that can be called gratitude, nor properly joy. The soul raised over passion beholds identity and eternal causation, perceives the self-existence of Truth and Right, and calms itself with knowing that all things go well. Vast spaces of nature, the Atlantic Ocean, the South Sea; long intervals of time, years, centuries, are of no account. This which I think and feel underlay every former state of life and circumstances, as it does underlie my present, and what is called life and what is called death.

Life only avails, not the having lived. Power ceases in the instant of repose; it resides in the moment of transition from a past to a new state, in the shooting of the gulf, in the darting to an aim. This one fact the world hates; that the soul *becomes*; for that forever degrades the past, turns all riches to poverty, all reputation to a shame, confounds the saint with the rogue, shoves Jesus and Judas equally aside. Why then do we prate of self-reliance? Inasmuch as the soul is present there will be power not confident but agent. To talk of reliance is a poor external way of speaking. Speaking rather of that which relies because it works and is. Who has more obedience than I masters me, though he should not raise his finger. Round him I must revolve by the gravitation of spirits. We fancy it rhetoric when we speak of eminent virtue. We do not yet see that virtue is Height, and that a man or a company of men, plastic and permeable to principles, by the law of nature must overpower and ride all cities, nations, kings, rich men, poets, who are not.

This is the ultimate fact which we so quickly reach on this, as on every topic, the resolution of all into the ever-blessed ONE. Self-existence is the attribute of the Supreme Cause, and it constitutes the measure of good by the degree in which it enters into all lower forms. All things real are so by so much virtue as they contain. Commerce, husbandry, hunting, whaling, war, eloquence, personal weight, are somewhat, and engage my respect as examples of its presence and impure action. I see the same law working in nature for conservation and growth. Power is, in nature, the essential measure of right. Nature suffers nothing to remain in her kingdoms which cannot help itself. The genesis and maturation of a planet, its poise and orbit, the bended tree recovering itself from the strong wind, the vital resources of every animal and vegetable, are demonstrations of the self-sufficing and therefore self-relying soul.

Thus all concentrates: let us not rove; let us sit at home with the cause. Let us stun and astonish the intruding rabble of men and books and institutions by a simple declaration of the divine fact. Bid the invaders take the shoes from off their feet, for God is here within.[12] Let our simplicity judge them, and our docility to our own law demonstrate the poverty of nature and fortune beside our native riches.

But now we are a mob. Man does not stand in awe of man, nor is his genius admonished to stay at home, to put itself in communication with the internal ocean, but it goes abroad to beg a cup of water of the urns of other men. We must go alone. I like the silent church before the service begins, better than any preaching. How far off, how cool, how chaste the persons look, begirt each one with a precinct or sanctuary! So let us always sit. Why should we assume the faults of our friend, or wife, or father, or child, because they sit around our hearth, or are said to have the same blood? All men have my blood and I all men's. Not for that will I adopt their petulance or folly, even to the extent of being ashamed of it. But your isolation must not be mechanical, but spiritual, that is, must be elevation. At times the whole world seems to be in conspiracy to importune you with emphatic trifles. Friend, client, child, sickness, fear, want, charity, all knock at once at thy closet door and say, — "Come out unto us." But keep thy state; come not into their confusion. The power men possess to annoy me I give them by a weak curiosity. No man can come near me but through my act. "What we love that we have, but by desire we bereave ourselves of the love."[13]

If we cannot at once rise to the sanctities of obedience and faith, let us at least resist our temptations; let us enter into the state of war and wake Thor and Woden, courage and constancy, in our Saxon breasts.[14] This is to be done in our smooth times by speaking the truth. Check this lying hospitality and lying affection. Live no longer to the expectation of these deceived and deceiving people with whom we converse. Say to them, "O father, O mother, O wife, O brother, O friend, I have lived with you after appearances hitherto. Henceforward I am the truth's. Be it known unto you that henceforward I obey no law less than the eternal law. I will have no covenants but proximities. I shall endeavor to nourish my parents, to support my family, to be the chaste husband of one wife, — but these relations I must fill after a new and unprecedented way. I appeal from your customs. I must be myself. I cannot break myself any longer for you, or you. If you

---

[12]Cf. Exod. 3.5.

[13]An approximate translation of lines in the German poet Friedrich Schiller's (1759–1805) "Liebe und Begierde" ("Love and Desire"): "One loves what one has; one desires what one has not." Emerson has clearly changed the sense of Schiller's lines.

[14]Thor and Woden (or Woten) are gods in Norse mythology. Emerson's frequent invocation of Saxon and Norse backgrounds is typical of a prevailing Anglo-Saxonism in nineteenth-century American culture, especially in the Northeast.

can love me for what I am, we shall be the happier. If you cannot, I will still seek to deserve that you should. I will not hide my tastes or aversions. I will so trust that what is deep is holy, that I will do strongly before the sun and moon whatever inly rejoices me and the heart appoints. If you are noble, I will love you; if you are not, I will not hurt you and myself by hypocritical attentions. If you are true, but not in the same truth with me, cleave to your companions; I will seek my own. I do this not selfishly but humbly and truly. It is alike your interest, and mine, and all men's, however long we have dwelt in lies, to live in truth. Does this sound harsh today? You will soon love what is dictated by your nature as well as mine, and if we follow the truth it will bring us out safe at last." — But so may you give these friends pain. Yes, but I cannot sell my liberty and my power, to save their sensibility. Besides, all persons have their moments of reason, when they look out into the region of absolute truth; then will they justify me and do the same thing.

The populace think that your rejection of popular standards is a rejection of all standard, and mere antinomianism;[15] and the bold sensualist will use the name of philosophy to gild his crimes. But the law of consciousness abides. There are two confessionals, in one or the other of which we must be shriven. You may fulfil your round of duties by clearing yourself in the *direct*, or in the *reflex* way. Consider whether you have satisfied your relations to father, mother, cousin, neighbor, town, cat and dog — whether any of these can upbraid you. But I may also neglect this reflex standard and absolve me to myself. I have my own stern claims and perfect circle. It denies the name of duty to many offices that are called duties. But if I can discharge its debts it enables me to dispense with the popular code. If any one imagines that this law is lax, let him keep its commandment one day.

And truly it demands something godlike in him who has cast off the common motives of humanity and has ventured to trust himself for a taskmaster. High be his heart, faithful his will, clear his sight, that he may in good earnest be doctrine, society, law, to himself, that a simple purpose may be to him as strong as iron necessity is to others!

If any man consider the present aspects of what is called by distinction *society*, he will see the need of these ethics. The sinew and heart of man seem to be drawn out, and we are become timorous, desponding whimperers.

---

[15] The antinomian heresy was the belief that God revealed himself directly to individuals without the mediation of the clergy. Anne Hutchinson (1591–1643), who broke with the Puritan Church of the early Bay Colony, is an example of an American antinomian. Emerson may be suggesting that his break with the Unitarian Church and his secular transcendentalism constitute a version of antinomianism.

We are afraid of truth, afraid of fortune, afraid of death, and afraid of each other. Our age yields no great and perfect persons. We want men and women who shall renovate life and our social state, but we see that most natures are insolvent, cannot satisfy their own wants, have an ambition out of all proportion to their practical force and do lean and beg day and night continually. Our housekeeping is mendicant, our arts, our occupations, our marriages, our religion we have not chosen, but society has chosen for us. We are parlor soldiers. We shun the rugged battle of fate, where strength is born.

If our young men miscarry in their first enterprises, they lose all heart. If the young merchant fails, men say he is *ruined*. If the finest genius studies at one of our colleges and is not installed in an office within one year afterwards in the cities or suburbs of Boston of New York, it seems to his friends and to himself that he is right in being disheartened and in complaining the rest of his life. A sturdy lad from New Hampshire or Vermont, who in turn tries all the professions, who *teams it, farms it, peddles,* keeps a school, preaches, edits a newspaper, goes to Congress, buys a township, and so forth, in successive years, and always like a cat falls on his feet, is worth a hundred of these city dolls. He walks abreast with his days and feels no shame in not "studying a profession," for he does not postpone his life, but lives already. He has not one chance, but a hundred chances. Let a Stoic open the resources of man and tell men they are not leaning willows, but can and must detach themselves; that with the exercise of self-trust, new powers shall appear; that a man is the word made flesh, born to shed healing to the nations; that he should be ashamed of our compassion, and that the moment he acts from himself, tossing the laws, the books, idolatries and customs out of the window, we pity him no more but thank and revere him; — and that teacher shall restore the life of man to splendor and make his name dear to all history.

It is easy to see that a greater self-reliance must work a revolution in all the offices and relations of men; in their religion; in their education; in their pursuits; their modes of living; their association; in their property; in their speculative views.

1. In what prayers do men allow themselves! That which they call a holy office is not so much as brave and manly. Prayer looks abroad and asks for some foreign addition to come through some foreign virtue, and loses itself in endless mazes of natural and supernatural, and mediatorial and miraculous. Prayer that craves a particular commodity, anything less than all good, is vicious. Prayer is the contemplation of the facts of life from the highest point of view. It is the soliloquy of a beholding and jubilant soul. It is the spirit of God pronouncing his works good. But prayer as a means to effect a private end is meanness and theft. It supposes dualism and not unity in nature and consciousness. As soon as the man is at one with God,

he will not beg. He will then see prayer in all action. The prayer of the farmer kneeling in his field to weed it, the prayer of the rower kneeling with the stroke of his oar, are true prayers heard throughout nature, though for cheap ends. Caratach, in Fletcher's "Bonduca," when admonished to inquire the mind of the god Audate, replies, —

"His hidden meaning lies in our endeavors;
Our valors are our best gods."[16]

Another sort of false prayers are our regrets. Discontent is the want of self-reliance: it is infirmity of will. Regret calamities if you can thereby help the sufferer; if not, attend your own work and already the evil begins to be repaired. Our sympathy is just as base. We come to them who weep foolishly and sit down and cry for company, instead of imparting to them truth and health in rough electric shocks, putting them once more in communication with their own reason. The secret of fortune is joy in our hands. Welcome evermore to gods and men is the self-helping man. For him all doors are flung wide; him all tongues greet, all honors crown, all eyes follow with desire. Our love goes out to him and embraces him because he did not need it. We solicitously and apologetically caress and celebrate him because he held on his way and scorned our disapprobation. The gods love him because men hated him. "To the persevering mortal," said Zoroaster, "the blessed Immortals are swift."[17]

As men's prayers are a disease of the will, so are their creeds a disease of the intellect. They say with those foolish Israelites, "Let not God speak to us, lest we die. Speak thou, speak any man with us, and we will obey."[18] Everywhere I am hindered of meeting God in my brother, because he has shut his own temple doors and recites fables merely of his brother's, or his brother's brother's God. Every new mind is a new classification. If it prove a mind of uncommon activity and power, a Locke, a Lavoisier, a Hutton, a Bentham, a Fourier, it imposes its classification on other men, and lo! a new system.[19] In proportion to the depth of the thought, and so to the number of the objects its touches and brings within reach of the pupil, is his complacency. But chiefly is this apparent in creeds and churches, which

---

[16] John Fletcher (1579–1625), *Bonduca* 3.1. Audate is an ancient Briton war-god.

[17] A saying attributed to Zoroaster, founder of Persian Zoroastrianism, a religion based on fundamental dualisms, such as light and dark. Interest in Middle Eastern religions was strong in the first half of the nineteenth century, in part because of the decoding of Egyptian hieroglyphs with the Rosetta stone.

[18] Cf. Exod. 20.19.

[19] As examples of genius, Emerson offers well-known philosophers John Locke (1632–1704) and Jeremy Bentham (1748–1832); a social theorist, Charles Fourier (1772–1837); a

are also classifications of some powerful mind acting on the elemental thought of duty and man's relation to the Highest. Such is Calvinism, Quakerism, Swedenborgism. The pupil takes the same delight in subordinating every thing to the new terminology as a girl who has just learned botany in seeing a new earth and new seasons thereby. It will happen for a time that the pupil will find his intellectual power has grown by the study of his master's mind. But in all unbalanced minds the classification is idolized, passes for the end and not for a speedily exhaustible means, so that the walls of the system blend to their eye in the remote horizon with the walls of the universe; the luminaries of heaven seem to them hung on the arch their master built. They cannot imagine how you aliens have any right to see,—how you can see; "It must be somehow that you stole the light from us." They do not yet perceive that light, unsystematic, indomitable, will break into any cabin, even into theirs. Let them chirp awhile and call it their own. If they are honest and do well, presently their neat new pinfold will be too strait and low, will crack, will lean, will rot and vanish, and the immortal light, all young and joyful, million-orbed, million-colored, will beam over the universe as on the first morning.

2. It is for want of self-culture that the superstition of Traveling, whose idols are Italy, England, Egypt, retains its fascination for all educated Americans. They who made England, Italy, or Greece venerable in the imagination, did so by sticking fast where they were, like an axis of the earth. In manly hours we feel that duty is our place. The soul is no traveler; the wise man stays at home, and when his necessities, his duties, on any occasion call him from his house, or into foreign lands, he is at home still and shall make men sensible by the expression of his countenance that he goes, the missionary of wisdom and virtue, and visits cities and men like a sovereign and not like an interloper or a valet.

I have no churlish objection to the circumnavigation of the globe for the purposes of art, of study, and benevolence, so that the man is first domesticated, or does not go abroad with the hope of finding somewhat greater than he knows. He who travels to be amused, or to get somewhat which he does not carry, travels away from himself, and grows old even in youth among old things. In Thebes, in Palmyra, his will and mind have become old and dilapidated as they. He carries ruins to ruins.

Traveling is a fool's paradise. Our first journeys discover to us the indifference of places. At home I dream that at Naples, at Rome, I can be intoxicated with beauty and lose my sadness. I pack my trunk, embrace my friends, embark on the sea and at last wake up in Naples, and there beside

chemist, Antoine Lavoisier (1743–94); and a geologist, James Hutton (1726–97), who was a precursor of such nineteenth-century geologists as Lyell.

me is the stern fact, the sad self, unrelenting, identical, that I fled from. I seek the Vatican and the palaces. I affect to be intoxicated with sights and suggestions, but I am not intoxicated. My giant goes with me wherever I go.

3. But the rage of traveling is a symptom of a deeper unsoundness affecting the whole intellectual action. The intellect is vagabond, and our system of education fosters restlessness. Our minds travel when our bodies are forced to stay at home. We imitate; and what is imitation but the traveling of the mind? Our houses are built with foreign taste; our shelves are garnished with foreign ornaments; our opinions, our tastes, our faculties, lean, and follow the Past and the Distant. The soul created the arts wherever they have flourished. It was in his own mind that the artist sought his model. It was an application of his own thought to the thing to be done and the conditions to be observed. And why need we copy the Doric or the Gothic model?[20] Beauty, convenience, grandeur of thought and quaint expression are as near to us as to any, and if the American artist will study with hope and love the precise thing to be done by him, considering the climate, the soil, the length of the day, the wants of the people, the habit and form of the government, he will create a house in which all these will find themselves fitted, and taste and sentiment will be satisfied also.

Insist on yourself; never imitate. Your own gift you can present every moment with the cumulative force of a whole life's cultivation; but of the adopted talent of another you have only an extemporaneous half possession. That which each can do best, none but his Maker can teach him. No man yet knows what it is, nor can, till that person has exhibited it. Where is the master who could have taught Shakespeare? Where is the master who could have instructed Franklin, or Washington, or Bacon, or Newton? Every great man is a unique. The Scipionism of Scipio is precisely that part he could not borrow. Shakespeare will never be made by the study of Shakespeare. Do that which is assigned you, and you cannot hope too much or dare too much. There is at this moment for you an utterance brave and grand as that of the colossal chisel of Phidias,[21] or trowel of the Egyptians, or the pen of Moses or Dante, but different from all these. Not possibly will the soul, all rich, all eloquent, with thousand-cloven tongue, deign to repeat itself; but if you can hear what these patriarchs say, surely you can reply to them in the same pitch of voice; for the ear and the tongue are two organs of one nature. Abide in the simple and noble regions of thy life, obey thy heart, and thou shalt reproduce the Foreworld again.

---

[20] Styles of classical and medieval architecture, respectively.

[21] Classical Greek sculptor reputed to have carved the hieratic sculpture of Athena in the Parthenon.

4. As our Religion, our Education, our Art look abroad, so does our spirit of society. All men plume themselves on the improvement of society, and no man improves.

Society never advances. It recedes as fast on one side as it gains on the other. It undergoes continual changes; it is barbarous, it is civilized, it is christianized, it is rich, it is scientific; but this change is not amelioration. For every thing that is given, something is taken. Society acquires new arts and loses old instincts. What a contrast between the well-clad, reading, writing, thinking American, with a watch, a pencil and a bill of exchange in his pocket, and the naked New Zealander, whose property is a club, a spear, a mat and an undivided twentieth of a shed to sleep under! But compare the health of the two men and you shall see that the white man has lost his aboriginal strength. If the traveler tell us truly, strike the savage with a broadaxe and in a day or two the flesh shall unite and heal as if you struck the blow into soft pitch, and the same blow shall send the white to his grave.[22]

The civilized man has built a coach, but has lost the use of his feet. He is supported on crutches, but lacks so much support of muscle. He has a fine Geneva watch, but he fails of the skill to tell the hour by the sun. A Greenwich nautical almanac he has, and so being sure of the information when he wants it, the man in the street does not know a star in the sky. The solstice he does not observe; the equinox he knows as little; and the whole bright calendar of the year is without a dial in his mind. His note-books impair his memory; his libraries overload his wit; the insurance-office increases the number of accidents; and it may be a question whether machinery does not encumber; whether we have not lost by refinement some energy, by a Christianity, entrenched in establishments and forms, some vigor of wild virtue. For every Stoic was a Stoic; but in Christendom where is the Christian?

There is no more deviation in the moral standard than in the standard of height or bulk. No greater men are now than ever were. A singular equality may be observed between the great men of the first and of the last ages; nor can all the science, art, religion, and philosophy of the nineteenth century avail to educate greater men than Plutarch's heroes, three or four and twenty centuries ago. Not in time is the race progressive. Phocion, Socrates, Anaxagoras, Diogenes, are great men, but they leave no class.[23] He who is

---

[22] Emerson is borrowing from Captain James Cook's *The Three Voyages of Captain James Cook round the World* (1821), in which such Enlightenment myths of the "noble savage" are given frequent support. Emerson also is hinting in his indictment of physical travel that Cook died during his voyages.

[23] Plutarch's *Lives* was a popular work in the nineteenth century, providing biographies of leaders such as Solon and Alcibiades in Greece's so-called golden age. Emerson's list

really of their class will not be called by their name, but will be his own man, and in his turn the founder of a sect. The arts and inventions of each period are only its costume and do not invigorate men. The harm of the improved machinery may compensate its good. Hudson and Behring accomplished so much in their fishingboats as to astonish Parry and Franklin, whose equipment exhausted the resources of science and art. Galileo, with an opera-glass, discovered a more splendid series of celestial phenomena than any one since. Columbus found the New World in an undecked boat. It is curious to see the periodical disuse and perishing of means and machinery which were introduced with loud laudation a few years or centuries before.[24] The great genius returns to essential man. We reckoned the improvements of the art of war among the triumphs of science, and yet Napoleon conquered Europe by the bivouac, which consisted of falling back on naked valor and disencumbering it of all aids. The Emperor held it impossible to make a perfect army, says Las Cases, "without abolishing our arms, magazines, commissaries and carriages, until, in imitation of the Roman custom, the soldier should receive his supply of corn, grind it in his hand-mill, and bake his bread himself."[25]

Society is a wave. The wave moves onward, but the water of which it is composed does not. The same particle does not rise from the valley to the ridge. Its unity is only phenomenal. The persons who make up a nation today, next year die, and their experience dies with them.

And so the reliance on Property, including the reliance on governments which protect it, is the want of self-reliance. Men have looked away from themselves and at things so long that they have come to esteem the religious, learned and civil institutions as guards of property, and they deprecate assaults on these, because they feel them to be assaults on property. They measure their esteem of each other by what each has, and not by what each is. But a cultivated man becomes ashamed of his property, out of new respect for his nature. Especially he hates what he has if he see that it is accidental, —came to him by inheritance, or gift, or crime; then he feels that

---

of famous Greek philosophers suggests that each was an original, even though it is obvious that each produced an influential philosophical school or movement.

[24] In his sustained criticism of modern technology, Emerson suggests how much early explorers, such as Henry Hudson, William Behring, and Christopher Columbus, accomplished without the navigational and maritime devices employed by Emerson's contemporaries, the explorers Sir William Edmund Parry (1790–1855) and Sir John Franklin (1786–1847).

[25] Cf. Emmanuel de Las Cases, *Mémoirial de Sainte Hélène*, 4.7.97 (Ferguson 2:233). Las Cases (1766–1842) was a French historian to whom Napoleon, while in exile on St. Helena, dictated a portion of his memoirs.

it is not having; it does not belong to him, has no root in him and merely lies there because no revolution or no robber takes it away. But that which a man is, does always by necessity acquire; and what the man acquires, is living property, which does not wait the beck of rulers, or mobs, or revolutions, or fire, or storm, or bankruptcies, but perpetually renews itself wherever the man breathes. "Thy lot or portion of life," said the Caliph Ali, "is seeking after thee; therefore be at rest from seeking after it." [26] Our dependence on these foreign goods leads us to our slavish respect for numbers. The political parties meet in numerous conventions; the greater the concourse and with each new uproar of announcement, The delegation from Essex! The Democrats from New Hampshire! The Whigs of Maine! the young patriot feels himself stronger than before by a new thousand of eyes and arms. In like manner the reformers summon conventions and vote and resolve in multitude. Not so, O friends! will the God deign to enter and inhabit you, but by a method precisely th reverse. It is only as a man puts off all foreign support and stands alone that I see him to be strong and to prevail. He is weaker by every recruit to his banner. Is not a man better than a town? Ask nothing of men, and, in the endless mutation, thou only firm column must presently appear the upholder of all that surrounds thee. He who knows that power is inborn, that he is weak because he has looked for good out of him and elsewhere, and, so perceiving, throws himself unhesitatingly on his thought, instantly rights himself, stands in the erect position, commands his limbs, works miracles; just as a man who stands on his feet is stronger than a man who stands on his head.

So use all that is called Fortune. Most men gamble with her, and gain all, and lose all, as her wheel rolls. But do thou leave as unlawful these winnings, and deal with Cause and Effect, the chancellors of God. In the Will work and acquire, and thou hast chained the wheel of Chance, and shall sit hereafter out of fear from her rotations. A political victory, a rise of rents, the recovery of your sick or the return of your absent friend, or some other favorable event raises your spirits, and you think good days are preparing for you. Do not believe it. Nothing can bring you peace but yourself. Nothing can bring you peace but the triumph of principles.

---

[26] Emerson is quoting from Simon Ockley, *The History of the Saracens,* 2 vols. (London, 1718), vol. 2 (Ferguson 2:233).

Circles
1841

Nature centers into balls,
And her proud ephemerals,[1]
Fast to surface and outside,
Scan the profile of the sphere;
Knew they what that signified,
A new genesis were here.

The eye is the first circle; the horizon which it forms is the second; and throughout nature this primary figure is repeated without end. It is the highest emblem in the cipher of the world. St. Augustine described the nature of God as a circle whose center was everywhere and its circumference nowhere.[2] We are all our lifetime reading the copious sense of this first of forms. One moral we have already deduced in considering the circular or compensatory character of every human action. Another analogy we shall now trace, that every action admits of being outdone. Our life is an apprenticeship to the truth that around every circle another can be drawn; that there is no end in nature, but every end is a beginning; that there is always another dawn risen on mid-noon, and under every deep a lower deep opens.

This fact, as far as it symbolizes the moral fact of the Unattainable, the flying Perfect, around which the hands of man can never meet, at once the inspirer and the condemner of every success, may conveniently serve us to connect many illustrations of human power in every department.

There are no fixtures in nature. The universe is fluid and volatile. Permanence is but a word of degrees. Our globe seen by God is a transparent

---

Selections from Ralph Waldo Emerson: An Organic Anthology. Ed. Stephen E. Whicher. Riverside Edition. Boston: Houghton, 1957.

[1] Emerson wrote poetic epigraphs or "mottoes" for many of his essays. Epigraphs without quotation marks are his own, as is this one. Nature's "proud ephemerals" are human beings. [Ed.]

[2] Emerson misattributes this idea to Saint Augustine, copying it in his journals from John Norris, *An Essay Towards the Theory of the Ideal of Intelligible World* (London, 1701–04), "where it refers not to God but to Truth" in this manner (Ferguson 2:253). Of course, Emerson may simply be interpreting the passage in such a way as to equate "the nature of God" with truth. [Ed.]

law, not a mass of facts. The law dissolves the fact and holds it fluid. Our culture is the predominance of an idea which draws after it this train of cities and institutions. Let us rise into another idea; they will disappear. The Greek sculpture is all melted away; as if it had been statues of ice; here and there a solitary figure or fragment remaining, as we see flecks and scraps of snow left in cold dells and mountain clefts in June and July. For the genius that created it creates now somewhat else. The Greek letters last a little longer, but are already passing under the same sentence and tumbling into the inevitable pit which the creation of new thought opens for all that is old. The new continents are built out of the ruins of an old planet; the new races fed out of the decomposition of the foregoing. New arts destroy the old. See the investment of capital in aqueducts, made useless by hydraulics; fortifications, by gunpowder; roads and canals, by railways; sails, by steam; steam by electricity.

You admire this tower of granite, weathering the hurts of so many ages. Yet a little waving hand built this huge wall, and that which builds is better than that which is built. The hand that built can topple it down much faster. Better than the hand and nimbler was the invisible thought which wrought through it; and thus ever, behind the coarse effect, is a fine cause, which, being narrowly seen, is itself the effect of a finer cause. Everything looks permanent until its secret is known. A rich estate appears to women a firm and lasting fact; to a merchant, one easily created out of any materials, and easily lost. An orchard, good tillage, good grounds, seem a fixture, like a gold mine, or a river, to a citizen; but to a large farmer, not much more fixed than the state of the crop. Nature looks provokingly stable and secular, but it has a cause like all the rest; and when once I comprehend that, will these fields stretch so immovably wide, these leaves hang so individually considerable? Permanence is a word of degrees. Every thing is medial. Moons are no more bounds to spiritual power than batballs.

The key to every man is his thought. Sturdy and defying though he look, he has a helm which he obeys, which is the idea after which all his facts are classified. He can only be reformed by showing him a new idea which commands his own. The life of man is a self-evolving circle, which, from a ring imperceptibly small, rushes on all sides outwards to new and larger circles, and that without end. The extent to which this generation of circles, wheel without wheel, will go, depends on the force or truth of the individual soul. For it is the inert effort of each thought, having formed itself into a circular wave of circumstance,—as for instance an empire, rules of an art, a local usage, a religious rite,—to heap itself on that ridge and to solidify and hem in the life. But if the soul is quick and strong it bursts over that boundary on all sides and expands another orbit on the great deep, which also runs up into a high wave, with attempt again to stop and to bind. But the heart refuses to be imprisoned; in its first and narrowest pulses it already tends outward with a vast force and to immense and innumerable expansions. Every ultimate fact is only the first of a new series. Every general law only a particular fact of some more general law presently to disclose itself. There is no outside, no inclosing wall, no circumference to us. The man finishes his story,—how good! how final! how it puts a new face on all things! He fills the sky. Lo! on the other side rises also a man and draws a circle around the circle we had just pronounced the outline of the sphere. Then already is our first speaker not man, but only a first speaker. His only redress is forthwith to draw a circle outside of his antagonist. And so men do by themselves. The result of today, which haunts the mind and cannot be escaped, will presently be abridged into a word, and the principle that seemed to explain nature will itself be included as one example of a bolder generalization. In the thought of tomorrow there is a power to upheave all thy creed, all the creeds, all the literatures of the nations, and marshal thee to a heaven which no epic dream has yet depicted. Every man is not so much a workman in the world as he is a suggestion of that he should be. Men walk as prophecies of the next age.

Step by step we scale this mysterious ladder; the steps are actions, the new prospect is power. Every several result is threatened and judged by that which follows. Every one seems to be contradicted by the new; it is only limited by the new. The new statement is always hated by the old, and, to those dwelling in the old, comes like an abyss of skepticism. But the eye soon gets wonted to it, for the eye and it are effects of one cause; then its innocency and benefit appear, and presently, all its energy spent, it pales and dwindles before the revelation of the new hour.

Fear not the new generalization. Does the fact look crass and material, threatening to degrade thy theory of spirit? Resist it not; it goes to refine and raise thy theory of matter just as much.

There are no fixtures to men, if we appeal to consciousness. Every man supposes himself not to be fully understood; and if there is any truth in him, if he rests at last on the divine soul, I see not how it can be otherwise. The last chamber, the last closet, he must feel was never opened; there is always a residuum unknown, unanalyzable. That is, every man believes that he has a greater possibility.

Our moods do not believe in each other. Today I am full of thoughts and can write what I please. I see no reason why I should not have the same thought, the same power of expression, tomorrow. What I write, whilst I write it, seems the most natural thing in the world; but yesterday I saw a dreary vacuity in this direction in which now I see so much; and a month hence, I doubt not, I shall wonder who he was that wrote so many continuous pages. Alas for this infirm faith, this will not strenuous, this vast ebb of a vast flow! I am God in nature; I am a weed by the wall.

The continual effort to raise himself above himself, to work a pitch above his last height, betrays itself in a man's relations. We thirst for approbation, yet cannot forgive the approver. The sweet of nature is love; yet if I have a friend I am tormented by my imperfections. The love of me accuses the other party. If he were high enough to slight me, then could I love him, and rise by my affection to new heights. A man's growth is seen in the successive choirs of his friends. For every friend whom he loses for truth, he gains a better. I thought as I walked in the woods and mused on my friends, why should I play with them this game of idolatry? I know and see too well, when not voluntarily blind, the speedy limits of persons called high and worthy. Rich, noble and great they are by the liberality of our speech, but truth is sad. O blessed Spirit, whom I forsake for these, they are not thou! Every personal consideration that we allow costs us heavenly state. We sell the thrones of angels for a short and turbulent pleasure.

How often must we learn this lesson? Men cease to interest us when we find their limitations. The only sin is limitation. As soon as you once come up with a man's limitations, it is all over with him. Has he talents? has he enterprise? has he knowledge? It boots not. Infinitely alluring and attractive was he to you yesterday, a great hope, a sea to swim in; now, you have found his shores, found it a pond, and you care not if you never see it again.

Each new step we take in thought reconciles twenty seemingly discordant facts, as expressions of one law. Aristotle and Plato are reckoned the respective heads of two schools. A wise man will see that Aristotle Platonizes. By going one step farther back in thought, discordant opinions are reconciled by being seen to be two extremes of one principle, and we can never go so far back as to preclude a still higher vision.

Beware when the great God lets loose a thinker on this planet. Then all things are at risk. It is as when a conflagration has broken out in a great city, and no man knows what is safe, or where it will end. There is not a piece of science but its flank may be turned tomorrow; there is not any literary reputation, not the so-called eternal names of fame, that may not be revised and condemned. The very hopes of man, the thoughts of his heart, the religion of nations, the manners and morals of mankind are all at the mercy of a new generalization. Generalization is always a new influx of the divinity into the mind. Hence the thrill that attends it.

Valor consists in the power of self-recovery, so that a man cannot have his flank turned, cannot be out-generaled, but put him where you will, he stands. This can only be by his preferring truth to his past apprehension of truth, and his alert acceptance of it from whatever quarter; the intrepid conviction that his laws, his relations to society, his Christianity, his world, may at any time be superseded and decease.

There are degrees in idealism. We learn first to play with it academically, as the magnet was once a toy. Then we see in the heyday of youth and poetry that it may be true, that it is true in gleams and fragments. Then its countenance waxes stern and grand, and we see that it must be true. It now shows itself ethical and practical. We learn that God is; that he is in me; and that all things are shadows of him. The idealism of Berkeley[3] is only a crude statement of the idealism of Jesus, and that again is a crude statement of the fact that all nature is the rapid efflux of goodness executing and organizing itself. Much more obviously is history and the state of the world at any one time directly dependent on the intellectual classification then existing in the minds of men. The things which are dear to men at this hour are so on account of the ideas which have emerged on their mental horizon, and which cause the present order of things, as a tree bears its apples. A new degree of culture would instantly revolutionize the entire system of human pursuits.

Conversation is a game of circles. In conversation we pluck up the *termini* which bound the common of silence on every side. The parties are not to be judged by the spirit they partake and even express under this Pentecost.[4] Tomorrow they will have receded from this highwater mark. Tomorrow you shall find them stooping under the old pack-saddles. Yet let us enjoy the cloven flame whilst it glows on our walls. When each new speaker strikes a new light, emancipates us from the oppression of the last speaker to oppress us with the greatness and exclusiveness of his own thought, then yields us to another redeemer, we seem to recover our rights, to become men. O, what truths profound and executable only in ages and orbs, are supposed in the announcement of every truth! In common hours, society sits cold and statuesque. We all stand waiting, empty,—knowing, possibly, that we can be full, surrounded by mighty symbols which are not symbols to us, but prose and trivial toys. Then cometh the god and converts the statues into fiery men, and by a flash of his eye burns up the veil which shrouded all things, and the meaning of the very furniture, of cup and saucer, of chair and clock and tester, is manifest. The facts which loomed so large in the fogs of yesterday,—property, climate, breeding, personal beauty and the like, have strangely changed their proportions. All that we

---

[3] George Berkeley (1685–1753), Irish bishop and philosopher famous for formulating the radically idealist position of "solipsism," from the Latin *solus* ("alone") and *ipse* ("by itself"). [Ed.]

[4] Pentecost celebrates the day "when the disciples of Jesus, fifty days after his resurrection, were filled with the Holy Ghost, which appeared as 'cloven tongues like as of fire'". [Orig. ed.]

reckoned settled shakes and rattles; and literatures, cities, climates, religions, leave their foundations and dance before our eyes. And yet here again see the swift circumscription! Good as is discourse, silence is better, and shames it. The length of the discourse indicates the distance of thought betwixt the speaker and the hearer. If they were at a perfect understanding in any part, no words would be necessary thereon. If at one in all parts, no words would be suffered.

Literature is a point outside of our hodiernal[5] circle through which a new one may be described. The use of literature is to afford us a platform whence we may command a view of our present life, a purchase by which we may move it. We fill ourselves with ancient learning, install ourselves the best we can in Greek, in Punic,[6] in Roman houses, only that we may wiselier see French, English, and American houses and modes of living. In like manner we see literature best from the midst of wild nature, or from the din of affairs, or from a high religion. The field cannot be well seen from within the field. The astronomer must have his diameter of the earth's orbit as a base to find the parallax of any star.

Therefore we value the poet. All the argument and all the wisdom is not in the encyclopaedia, or the treatise on metaphysics, or the Body of Divinity, but in the sonnet or the play. In my daily work I incline to repeat my old steps, and do not believe in remedial force, in the power of change and reform. But some Petrarch or Ariosto, filled with the new wine of his imagination, writes me an ode or a brisk romance, full of daring thought and action.[7] He smites and arouses me with his shrill tones, breaks up my whole chain of habits, and I open my eye on my own possibilities. He claps wings to the sides of all the solid old lumber of the world, and I am capable once more of choosing a straight path in theory and practice.

We have the same need to command a view of the religion of the world. We can never see Christianity from the catechism:—from the pastures, from a boat in the pond, from amidst the songs of wood-birds we possibly may. Cleansed by the elemental light and wind, steeped in the sea of beautiful forms which the field offers us, we may chance to cast a right glance back upon biography. Christianity is rightly dear to the best of mankind;

---

[5] Of the present day—from Latin *hodiernus* ("today"). [Ed.]

[6] Phoenician. Emerson is enunciating an early theory of comparative literature, albeit one shared by most of his romantic contemporaries, in which the "Ancients" are studied in order to understand "modern" circumstances by comparison or contrast. [Ed.]

[7] Ariosto (1474–1533) and Petrarch (1304–1374) are used here simply as examples of inspiring poets, although both are identifiable with the beginnings of modern European literature. [Ed.]

yet was there never a young philosopher whose breeding had fallen into the Christian church by whom that brave text of Paul's was not specially prized: "Then shall also the Son be subject unto Him who put all things under him, that God may be all in all." Let the claims and virtues of persons be never so great and welcome, the instinct of man presses eagerly onward to the impersonal and illimitable, and gladly arms itself against the dogmatism of bigots with this generous word out of the book itself.

The natural world may be conceived of as a system of concentric circles, and we now and then detect in nature slight dislocations which apprise us that this surface on which we now stand is not fixed, but sliding. These manifold tenacious qualities, this chemistry and vegetation, these metals and animals, which seem to stand there for their own sake, are means and methods only,—are words of God, and as fugitive as other words. Has the naturalist or chemist learned his craft, who has explored the gravity of atoms and the elective affinities, who has not yet discerned the deeper law whereof this is only a partial or approximate statement, namely that like draws to like, and that the goods which belong to you gravitate to you and need not be pursued with pains and cost? Yet is that statement approximate also, and not final. Omnipresence is a higher fact. Not through subtle, subterranean channels need friend and fact be drawn to their counterpart, but, rightly considered, these things proceed from the eternal generation of the soul. Cause and effect are two sides of one fact.

The same law of eternal procession ranges all that we call the virtues, and extinguishes each in the light of a better. The great man will not be prudent in the popular sense; all his prudence will be so much deduction from his grandeur. But it behooves each to see, when he sacrifices prudence, to what god he devotes it; if to ease and pleasure, he had better be prudent still; if to a great trust, he can well spare his mule and panniers who has a winged chariot instead. Geoffrey draws on his boots to go through the woods, that his feet may be safer from the bite of snakes; Aaron never thinks of such a peril. In many years neither is harmed by such an accident. Yet it seems to me that with every precaution you take against such an evil you put yourself into the power of the evil. I suppose that the highest prudence is the lowest prudence. Is this too sudden a rushing from the center to the verge of our orbit? Think how many times we shall fall back into pitiful calculations before we take up our rest in the great sentiment, or make the verge of today the new center. Besides, your bravest sentiment is familiar to the humblest men. The poor and the low have their way of expressing the last facts of philosophy as well as you. "Blessed be nothing" and "The worse things are, the better they are" are proverbs which express the transcendentalism of common life.

One man's justice is another's injustice; one man's beauty another's ugliness; one man's wisdom another's folly; as one beholds the same objects from a higher point. One man thinks justice consists in paying debts, and has no measure in his abhorrence of another who is very remiss in this duty and makes the creditor wait tediously. But that second man has his own way of looking at things; asks himself, Which debt must I pay first, the debt to the rich, or the debt to the poor? the debt of money, or the debt of thought to mankind, of genius to nature? For you, O broker, there is no other principle but arithmetic. For me, commerce is of trivial import; love, faith, truth of character, the aspiration of man, these are sacred; nor can I detach one duty, like you, from all other duties, and concentrate my forces mechanically on the payment of moneys. Let me live onward; you shall find that, though slower, the progress of my character will liquidate all these debts without injustice to higher claims. If a man should dedicate himself to the payment of notes, would not this be injustice? Does he owe no debt but money? And are all claims on him to be postponed to a landlord's or a banker's?

There is no virtue which is final; all are initial. The virtues of society are vices of the saint. The terror of reform is the discovery that we must cast away our virtues, or what we have always esteemed such, into the same pit that has consumed our grosser vices: —

"Forgive his crimes, forgive his virtues too,
Those smaller faults, half converts to the right."[8]

It is the highest power of divine moments that they abolish our contritions also. I accuse myself of sloth and unprofitableness day by day; but when these waves of God flow into me I no longer reckon lost time. I no longer poorly compute my possible achievement by what remains to me of the month or the year; for these moments confer a sort of omnipresence and omnipotence which asks nothing of duration, but sees that the energy of the mind is commensurate with the work to be done, without time.

And thus, O circular philosopher, I hear some reader exclaim, you have arrived at a fine Pyrrhonism,[9] at an equivalence and indifference of all ac-

---

[8] Edward Young (1683–1765), *The Complaint; or, Night Thoughts* 9.2316–2317 (Ferguson 2:254). [Ed.]

[9] Thoroughgoing skepticism. Pyrrho, according to *Brewer's Dictionary of Phrase and Fable* (1970), was a 4th-century BCE Greek philosopher: "founder of the first Greek school of sceptical philosophy. Pyrrho maintained that nothing was capable of proof and admitted the reality of nothing but sensations" (Brewer 878). [Ed.]

tions, and would fain teach us that *if we are true*, forsooth, our crimes may be lively stones out of which we shall construct the temple of the true God!

I am not careful to justify myself. I own I am gladdened by seeing the predominance of the saccharine principle throughout vegetable nature, and not less by beholding in morals that unrestrained inundation of the principle of good into every chink and hole that selfishness has left open, yea into selfishness and sin itself; so that no evil is pure, nor hell itself without its extreme satisfactions. But lest I should mislead any when I have my own head and obey my whims, let me remind the reader that I am only an experimenter. Do not set the least value on what I do, or the least discredit on what I do not, as if I pretended to settle any thing as true or false. I unsettle all things. No facts are to me sacred; none are profane; I simply experiment, an endless seeker with no Past at my back.

Yet this incessant movement and progression which all things partake could never become sensible to us but by contrast to some principle of fixture or stability in the soul. Whilst the eternal generation of circles proceeds, the eternal generator abides. That central life is somewhat superior to creation, superior to knowledge and thought, and contains all its circles. Forever it labors to create a life and thought as large and excellent as itself, but in vain, for that which is made instructs how to make a better.

Thus there is no sleep, no pause, no preservation, but all things renew, germinate and spring. Why should we import rags and relics into the new hour? Nature abhors the old, and old age seems the only disease; all others run into this one. We call it by many names, — fever, intemperance, insanity, stupidity and crime; they are all forms of old age; they are rest, conservatism, appropriation, inertia; not newness, not the way onward. We grizzle every day. I see no need of it. Whilst we converse with what is above us, we do not grow old, but grow young. Infancy, youth, receptive, aspiring, with religious eye looking upward, counts itself nothing and abandons itself to the instruction flowing from all sides. But the man and woman of seventy assume to know all, they have outlived their hope, they renounce aspiration, accept the actual for the necessary and talk down to the young. Let them then become organs of the Holy Ghost; let them be lovers; let them behold truth; and their eyes are uplifted, their wrinkles smoothed, they are perfumed again with hope and power. This old age ought not to creep on a human mind. In nature every moment is new; the past is always swallowed and forgotten; the coming only is sacred. Nothing is secure but life, transition, the energizing spirit. No love can be bound by oath or covenant to secure it against a higher love. No truth so sublime but it may be trivial tomorrow in the light of new thoughts. People wish to be settled; only as far as they are unsettled is there any hope for them.

Life is a series of surprises. We do not guess today the mood, the pleasure, the power of tomorrow, when we are building up our being. Of lower
states, of acts of routine and sense, we can tell somewhat; but the master-
pieces of God, the total growths and universal movements of the soul, he
hideth; they are incalculable. I can know that truth is divine and helpful;
but how it shall help me I can have no guess, for *so to be* is the sole inlet of
so to know. The new position of the advancing man has all the powers of
the old, yet has them all new. It carries in its bosom all the energies of the
past, yet is itself an exhalation of the morning. I cast away in this new moment all my once hoarded knowledge, as vacant and vain. Now for the first
time seem I to know any thing rightly. The simplest words, —we do not
know what they mean except when we love and aspire.

The difference between talents and character is adroitness to keep the
old and trodden round, and power and courage to make a new road to new
and better goals. Character makes an over-powering present; a cheerful,
determined hour, which fortifies all the company by making them see that
much is possible and excellent that was not thought of. Character dulls
the impression of particular events. When we see the conqueror, we do not
think much of any one battle or success. We see that we had exaggerated
the difficulty. It was easy to him. The great man is not convulsible or tor-
mentable; events pass over him without much impression. People say sometimes, "See what I have overcome; see how cheerful I am; see how completely I have triumphed over these black events." Not if they still remind
me of the black event. True conquest is the causing the calamity to fade and
disappear as an early cloud of insignificant result in a history so large and
advancing.

The one thing which we seek with insatiable desire is to forget ourselves,
to be surprised out of our propriety, to lose our sempiternal memory and
to do something without knowing how or why; in short to draw a new
circle. Nothing great was ever achieved without enthusiasm. The way of life
is wonderful; it is by abandonment. The great moments of history are the
facilities of performance through the strength of ideas, as the works of genius and religion. "A man," said Oliver Cromwell, "never rises so high as
when he knows not whither he is going." [10] Dreams and drunkenness, the
use of opium and alcohol are the semblance and counterfeit of this oracular genius, and hence their dangerous attraction for men. For the like reason they ask the aid of wild passions, as in gaming and war, to ape in some
manner these flames and generosities of the heart.

---

[10] A remark Cromwell made to "Bellievre, the French minister," according to Bishop
William Warburton (Ferguson 2:255). Cromwell was probably referring, as Emerson is,
to the unpredictability of revolutionary events and their agents. [Ed.]

Man the Reformer
A Lecture Read before the Mechanics'
Apprentices' Library Association, Boston,
at the Masonic Temple, January 25, 1841

Mr. President, and Gentlemen:

I wish to offer to your consideration some thoughts on the particular and general relations of man as a reformer. I shall assume that the aim of each young man in this association is the very highest that belongs to a rational mind. Let it be granted that our life, as we lead it, is common and mean; that some of those offices and functions for which we were mainly created are grown so rare in society that the memory of them is only kept alive in old books and in dim traditions; that prophets and poets, that beautiful and perfect men we are not now, no, nor have even seen such; that some sources of human instruction are almost unnamed and unknown among us; that the community in which we live will hardly bear to be told that every man should be open to ecstacy or a divine illumination, and his daily walk elevated by intercourse with the spiritual world. Grant all this, as we must, yet I suppose none of my auditors will deny that we ought to seek to establish ourselves in such disciplines and courses as will deserve that guidance and clearer communication with the spiritual nature. And further, I will not dissemble my hope that each person whom I address has felt his own call to cast aside all evil customs, timidities, and limitations, and to be in his place a free and helpful man, a reformer, a benefactor, not content to slip along through the world like a footman or a spy, escaping by his nimbleness and apologies as many knocks as he can, but a brave and upright man, who must find or cut a straight road to everything excellent in the earth, and not only go honorably himself, but make it easier for all who follow him to go in honor and with benefit.

In the history of the world the doctrine of Reform had never such scope as at the present hour. Lutherans, Herrnhutters, Jesuits, Monks, Quakers, Knox, Wesley, Swedenborg, Bentham,[1] in their accusations of society, all

---

The Complete Works of Ralph Waldo Emerson. Ed. Edward Waldo Emerson. Centenary Edition. Vol. 1. Boston: Houghton, 1903. (All notes are by the present editor.)

[1] Members of the Moravian Brotherhood were also called "Herrnhutters," after the town of Herrnhut in Saxony, where they settled in 1722. Moravians were active missionaries in nineteenth-century America, especially in the Northeast. The other religions or philosophical leaders are familiar examples of social reform movements or reformers in

respected something,—church or state, literature or history, domestic usages, the market town, the dinner table, coined money. But now all these and all things else hear the trumpet and must rush to judgment,—Christianity, the laws, commerce, schools, the farm, the laboratory; and not a kingdom, town, statute, rite, calling, man, or woman, but is threatened by the new spirit.

What if some of the objections whereby our institutions are assailed are extreme and speculative, and the reformers tend to idealism? That only shows the extravagance of the abuses which have driven the mind into the opposite extreme. It is when your facts and persons grow unreal and fantastic by too much falsehood, that the scholar flies for refuge to the world of ideas, and aims to recruit and replenish nature from that source. Let ideas establish their legitimate sway again in society, let life be fair and poetic, and the scholars will gladly be lovers, citizens, and philanthropists.

It will afford no security from the new ideas, that the old nations, the laws of centuries, the property and institutions of a hundred cities, are built on other foundations. The demon of reform has a secret door into the heart of every lawmaker, of every inhabitant of every city. The fact that a new thought and hope have dawned in your breast, should apprize you that in the same hour a new light broke in upon a thousand private hearts. That secret which you would fain keep,—as soon as you go abroad, lo! there is one standing on the doorstep to tell you the same. There is not the most bronzed and sharpened money-catcher who does not, to your consternation almost, quail and shake the moment he hears a question prompted by the new ideas. We thought he had some semblance of ground to stand upon, that such as he at least would die hard; but he trembles and flees. Then the scholar says, "Cities and coaches shall never impose on me again; for behold every solitary dream of mine is rushing to fulfilment. That fancy I had, and hesitated to utter because you would laugh,—the broker, the attorney, the market-man are saying the same thing. Had I waited a day longer to speak, I had been too late. Behold, State Street thinks, and Wall Street doubts, and begins to prophesy!" [2]

It cannot be wondered at that this general inquest into abuses should arise in the bosom of society, when one considers the practical impediments that stand in the way of virtuous young men. The young man on en-

---

Emerson's essays: John Knox (1505–72), founder of Presbyterianism; John Wesley, founder of the Methodists; Emanuel Swedenborg, scientist and mystic; Jeremy Bentham, English philosopher.

[2] State Street, in Boston, was the center of mercantile interests, as Wall Street, in New York, is of financial interests.

tering life finds the way to lucrative employments blocked with abuses. The ways of trade are grown selfish to the borders of theft, and supple to the borders (if not beyond the borders) of fraud. The employments of commerce are not intrinsically unfit for a man, or less genial to his faculties, but these are now in their general course so vitiated by derelictions and abuses at which all connive, that it requires more vigor and resources than can be expected of every young man, to right himself in them; he is lost in them; he cannot move hand or foot in them. Has he genius and virtue? the less does he find them fit for him to grow in, and if he would thrive in them, he must sacrifice all the brilliant dreams of boyhood and youth as dreams; he must forget the prayers of his childhood and must take on him the harness of routine and obsequiousness. If not so minded, nothing is left him but to begin the world anew, as he does who puts the spade into the ground for food. We are all implicated of course in this charge; it is only necessary to ask a few questions as to the progress of the articles of commerce from the fields where they grew, to our houses, to become aware that we eat and drink and wear perjury and fraud in a hundred commodities. How many articles of daily consumption are furnished us from the West Indies; yet it is said that in the Spanish islands the venality of the officers of the government has passed into usage, and that no article passes into our ships which has not been fraudulently cheapened.[3] In the Spanish islands, every agent or factor of the Americans, unless he be a consul, has taken oath that he is a Catholic, or has caused a priest to make that declaration for him.[4] The abolitionist has shown us our dreadful debt to the southern negro. In the island of Cuba, in addition to the ordinary abominations of slavery, it appears only men are bought for the plantations, and one dies in ten every year, of these miserable bachelors, to yield us sugar. I leave for those who have the knowledge the part of sifting the oaths of our custom-houses; I will not inquire into the oppression of the sailors; I will not pry into the usages of our retail trade. I content myself with the fact that the general system of our trade (apart from the blacker traits, which, I hope, are exceptions denounced and unshared by all reputable men) is a system of selfishness;

---

[3] Emerson begins here an extended criticism of Spanish colonialism in the Caribbean, focusing principally on slavery in Cuba and American reliance on Cuban sugar and thus slavery. Although the slave trade was banned formally in the United States in 1808, African slaves continued to be smuggled into the United States, often through Cuba, as the *Amistad* case spectacularly demonstrated.

[4] To strengthen his antislavery arguments against Spanish colonialism, especially in Cuba, Emerson plays on the strong anti-Catholic sentiments of northeastern readers. His argument that New England's economic success relied on Cuban and southern slavery was a common one among abolitionists.

is not dictated by the high sentiments of human nature; is not measured by the exact law of reciprocity, much less by the sentiments of love and hero- ism, but is a system of distrust, of concealment, of superior keenness, not of giving but of taking advantage. It is not that which a man delights to un- lock to a noble friend; which he mediates on with joy and self-approval in his hour of love and aspiration; but rather what he then puts out of sight, only showing the brilliant result, and atoning for the manner of acquiring, by the manner of expending it. I do not charge the merchant or the man- ufacturer. The sins of our trade belong to no class, to no individual. One plucks, one distributes, one eats. Every body partakes, every body con- fesses,—with cap and knee volunteers his confession, yet none feels him- self accountable. He did not create the abuse; he cannot alter it. What is he? an obscure private person who must get his bread. That is the vice,—that no one feels himself called to act for man, but only as a fraction of man. It happens therefore that all such ingenuous souls as feel within themselves the irrepressible strivings of a noble aim, who by the law of their nature must act for man, find these ways of trade unfit for them, and they come forth from it. Such cases are becoming more numerous every year.

But by coming out of trade you have not cleared yourself. The trail of the serpent reaches into all the lucrative professions and practices of man. Each has its own wrongs. Each finds a tender and very intelligent con- science a disqualification for success. Each requires of the practitioner a certain shutting of the eyes, a certain dapperness and compliance, an ac- ceptance of customs, a sequestration from the sentiments of generosity and love, a compromise of private opinion and lofty integrity. Nay, the evil cus- tom reaches into the whole institution of property, until our laws which es- tablish and protect it seem not to be the issue of love and reason, but of selfishness. Suppose a man is so unhappy as to be born a saint, with keen perceptions but with the conscience and love of an angel, and he is to get his living in the world; he finds himself excluded from all lucrative works; he has no farm, and he cannot get one; for to earn money enough to buy one requires a sort of concentration toward money, which is the selling himself for a number of years, and to him the present hour is as sacred and inviolable as any future hour. Of course, whilst another man has no land, my title to mine, your title to yours, is at once vitiated. Inextricable seem to be the twinings and tendrils of this evil, and we all involve ourselves in it the deeper by forming connections, by wives and children, by benefits and debts.

Considerations of this kind have turned the attention of many philan- thropic and intelligent persons to the claims of manual labor, as a part of the education of every young man. If the accumulated wealth of the past generations is thus tainted, —no matter how much of it is offered to us, — we must begin to consider if it were not the nobler part to renounce it, and to put ourselves into primary relations with the soil and nature, and abstaining from whatever is dishonest and unclean, to take each of us bravely his part, with his own hands, in the manual labor of the world.

But it is said, "What! will you give up the immense advantages reaped from the division of labor, and set every man to make his own shoes, bureau, knife, wagon, sails, and needle? This would be to put men back into barbarism by their own act." I see no instant prospect of a virtuous revolution; yet I confess I should not be pained at a change which threatened a loss of some of the luxuries or conveniences of society, if it proceeded from a preference of the agricultural life out of the belief that our primary duties as men could be better discharged in that calling. Who could regret to see a high conscience and a purer taste exercising a sensible effect on young men in their choice of occupation, and thinning the ranks of competition in the labors of commerce, of law, and of state?[5] It is easy to see that the inconvenience would last but a short time. This would be great action, which always opens the eyes of men. When many persons shall have done this, when the majority shall admit the necessity of reform in all these institutions, their abuses will be redressed, and the way will be open again to the advantages which arise from the division of labor, and a man may select the fittest employment for his peculiar talent again, without compromise.

But quite apart from the emphasis which the times give to the doctrine that the manual labor of society ought to be shared among all the members, there are reasons proper to every individual why he should not be deprived of it. The use of manual labor is one which never grows obsolete, and which is inapplicable to no person. A man should have a farm or a mechanical craft for his culture.[6] We must have a basis for our higher accomplishments, our delicate entertainments of poetry and philosophy, in the work of our hands. We must have an antagonism in the tough world for all the variety of our spiritual faculties, or they will not be born. Manual labor is the study of the external world. The advantage of riches remains with him who procured them, not with the heir. When I go into my garden with

---

[5] The Panic of 1837 was followed by high unemployment in America, especially in the Northeast. Emerson's call for more altruistic vocations, including a return to farming, appeals to young men's frustration with the job market.

[6] Emerson is addressing an association of mechanics, so his appeal here for every man to be trained in some manual labor makes good sense. By the same token, we can only wonder how his appeal in the rest of the essay for "higher accomplishments," such as poetry and philosophy, was received by his audience.

a spade, and dig a bed, I feel such an exhilaration and health that I discover that I have been defrauding myself all this time in letting others do for me what I should have done with my own hands. But not only health, but education is in the work. Is it possible that I, who get indefinite quantities of sugar, hominy, cotton, buckets, crockery-ware, and letter-paper, by simply signing my name once in three months to a cheque in favor of John Smith & Co. traders, get the fair share of exercise to my faculties by that act, which nature intended for me in making all these far-fetched matters important to my comfort? It is Smith himself, and his carriers, and dealers, and manufacturers; it is the sailor, the hide-drogher,[7] the butcher, the negro, the hunter, and the planter, who have intercepted the sugar of the sugar, and the cotton of the cotton. They have got the education, I only the commodity. This were all very well if I were necessarily absent, being detained by work of my own, like theirs, work of the same faculties; then should I be sure of my hands and feet; but now I feel some shame before my wood-chopper, my ploughman, and my cook, for they have some sort of self-sufficiency, they can contrive without my aid to bring the day and year round, but I depend on them, and have not earned by use a right to my arms and feet.

Consider further the difference between the first and second owner of property. Every species of property is preyed on by its own enemies, as iron by rust; timber by rot; cloth by moths; provisions by mould, putridity, or vermin; money by thieves; an orchard by insects; a planted field by weeds and the inroad of cattle; a stock of cattle by hunger; a road by rain and frost; a bridge by freshets. And whoever takes any of these things into his possession, takes the charge of defending them from this troop of enemies, or of keeping them in repair. A man who supplies his own want, who builds a raft or a boat to go a-fishing, finds it easy to caulk it, or put in a thole-pin, or mend the rudder. What he gets only as fast as he wants for his own ends, does not embarrass him, or take away his sleep with looking after. But when he comes to give all the goods he has year after year collected, in one estate to his son,—house, orchard, ploughed land, cattle, bridges, hardware, wooden-ware, carpets, cloths, provisions, books, money,—and cannot give him the skill and experience which made or collected these, and the method and place they have in his own life, the son finds his hands full,—not to use these things, but to look after them and defend them from their natural enemies. To him they are not means, but masters. Their enemies will not remit; rust, mould, vermin, rain, sun, freshet, fire, all seize

---

[7] Someone who transports hides in a drogher, a small Caribbean boat. Emerson again returns to his criticism of the commercial system's reliance on slave labor, implicating himself and other consumers for their lack of self-reliance.

their own, fill him with vexation, and he is converted from the owner into a watchman or a watch-dog to this magazine of old and new chattels. What a change! Instead of the masterly good humor and sense of power and fertility of resource in himself; instead of those strong and learned hands, those piercing and learned eyes, that supple body, and that mighty and prevailing heart, which the father had, whom nature loved and feared, whom snow and rain, water and land, beast and fish seemed all to know and to serve,—we have now a puny, protected person, guarded by walls and curtains, stoves and down beds, coaches, and men-servants and women-servants from the earth and the sky, and who, bred to depend on all these, is made anxious by all that endangers those possessions, and is forced to spend so much time in guarding them, that he has quite lost sight of their original use, namely, to help him to his ends,—to the prosecution of his love; to the helping of his friend, to the worship of his God, to the enlargement of his knowledge, to the serving of his country, to the indulgence of his sentiment, and he is now what is called a rich man,—the menial and runner of his riches.

Hence it happens that the whole interest of history lies in the fortunes of the poor. Knowledge, Virtue, Power are the victories of man over his necessities, his march to the dominion of the world. Every man ought to have this opportunity to conquer the world for himself. Only such persons interest us, Spartans, Romans, Saracens, English, Americans, who have stood in the jaws of need, and have by their own wit and might extricated themselves, and made man victorious.

I do not wish to overstate this doctrine of labor, or insist that every man should be a farmer, any more than that every man should be a lexicographer. In general one may say that the husbandman's is the oldest, and most universal profession, and that where a man does not yet discover in himself any fitness for one work more than another, this may be preferred. But the doctrine of the Farm is merely this, that every man ought to stand in primary relations with the work of the world; ought to do it himself, and not to suffer the accident of his having a purse in his pocket, or his having been bred to some dishonorable and injurious craft, to sever him from those duties; and for this reason, that labor is God's education; that he only is a sincere learner, he only can become a master, who learns the secrets of labor, and who by real cunning extorts from nature its sceptre.[8]

---

[8] Emerson's argument that only the self-reliant man who has worked can "become a master" echoes contemporary romantic ideas, such as Hegel's dialectic of the master and servant, that only through our own labor can we find identity and authority. Such ideas were crucial influences on Karl Marx and Friedrich Engels's labor theory of value in the middle of the nineteenth century.

Neither would I shut my ears to the plea of the learned professions, of the poet, the priest, the law-giver, and men of study generally; namely, that in the experience of all men of that class, the amount of manual labor which is necessary to the maintenance of a family, indisposes and disqualifies for intellectual exertion. I know it often, perhaps usually, happens that where there is a fine organization, apt for poetry and philosophy, that individual finds himself compelled to wait on his thoughts, to waste several days that he may enhance and glorify one, and is better taught by a moderate and dainty exercise, such as rambling in the fields, rowing, skating, hunting, than by the downright drudgery of the farmer and the smith. I would not quite forget the venerable counsel of the Egyptian mysteries, which declared that "there were two pairs of eyes in man, and it is requisite that the pair which are beneath should be closed, when the pair that are above them perceive, and that when the pair above are closed, those which are beneath should be opened." [9] Yet I will suggest that no separation from labor can be without some loss of power and of truth to the seer himself; that, I doubt not, the faults and vices of our literature and philosophy, their too great fineness, effeminacy, and melancholy, are attributable to the enervated and sickly habits of the literary class. Better that the book should not be quite so good, and the book-maker abler and better, and not himself often a ludicrous contrast to all that he has written.

But granting that for ends so sacred and dear some relaxation must be had, I think that if a man find in himself any strong bias to poetry, to art, to the contemplative life, drawing him to these things with a devotion incompatible with good husbandry, that man ought to reckon early with himself, and, respecting the compensations of the Universe, ought to ransom himself from the duties of economy by a certain rigor and privation in his habits. For privileges so rare and grand, let him not stint to pay a great tax. Let him be a caenobite,[10] a pauper, and if need be, celibate also. Let him learn to eat his meals standing, and to relish the taste of fair water and black bread. He may leave to others the costly conveniences of housekeeping and large hospitality and the possession of works of art. Let him feel that genius is a hospitality, and that he who can create works of art needs not collect them. He must live in a chamber, and postpone his self-indulgence, forewarned and forearmed against that frequent misfortune of men of genius, — the taste for luxury. This is the tragedy of genius; — attempting to drive

---

[9] Probably quoted from Giovanni Belzoni, *Narrative of the Operations and Recent Discoveries within the Pyramids, Temples, Tombs, and Excavations, in Egypt and Nubia,* 2 vols. (London, 1822) (Ferguson 1:261).

[10] Member of a convent. Emerson identifies the poet and philosopher with the religious monk or anchorite.

along the ecliptic with one horse of the heavens and one horse of the earth, there is only discord and ruin and downfall to chariot and charioteer.[11]

The duty that every man should assume his own vows, should call the institutions of society to account, and examine their fitness to him, gains in emphasis if we look at our modes of living. Is our housekeeping sacred and honorable? Does it raise and inspire us, or does it cripple us instead? I ought to be armed by every part and function of my household, by all my social function, by my economy, by my feasting, by my voting, by my traffic. Yet now I am almost no party to any of these things. Custom does it for me, gives me no power therefrom, and runs me in debt to boot. We spend our incomes for paint and paper, for a hundred trifles, I know not what, and not for the things of a man. Our expense is almost all for conformity. It is for cake that we run in debt; it is not the intellect, not the heart, not beauty, not worship, that costs so much. Why needs any man be rich? Why must he have horses, fine garments, handsome apartments, access to public houses, and places of amusement? Only for want of thought. Once waken in him a divine thought, and he flees into a solitary garden or garret to enjoy it, and is richer with that dream than the fee of a county could make him. But we are first thoughtless, and then find that we are moneyless. We are first sensual, and then must be rich. We dare not trust our wit for making our house pleasant to our friend, and so we buy icecreams. He is accustomed to carpets, and we have not sufficient character to put floor cloths out of his mind whilst he stays in the house, and so we pile the floor with carpets. Let the house rather be a temple of the Furies of Lacedaemon,[12] formidable and holy to all, which none but a Spartan may enter or so much as behold. As soon as there is faith, as soon as there is society, comfits and cushions will be left to slaves. Expense will be inventive and heroic. We shall eat hard and lie hard, we shall dwell like the ancient Romans in narrow tenements, whilst our public edifices, like theirs, will be worthy for their proportion of the landscape in which we set them, for conversation, for art, for music, for worship. We shall be rich to great purposes; poor only for selfish ones.

---

[11] Emerson is alluding to the Greek myth of Bellerophon, who tried to drive Pegasus's chariot (of the sun) through the heavens but could not control the horses and crashed to his death. The myth is a parable about the dangers of overreaching your abilities.

[12] Emerson is alluding to the Greek story of Orestes (subject of tragedies by Aeschylus, Sophocles, and Euripides), who was pursued by the Furies for divine punishment of his crime of killing his mother, Clytemnestra, and Aegisthus. Only when he was acquitted of his crime by a court in Athens was Orestes freed of their pursuit, and the Furies became known as the "Eumenides" or "well-meaning." Lacedaemon is another name for Sparta (Ferguson 1:261).

Now what help for these evils? How can the man who has learned but one art, procure all the conveniences of life honestly? Shall we say all we think?—Perhaps with his own hands. Suppose he collects or makes them ill;—yet he has learned their lesson. If he cannot do that?—Then perhaps he can go without. Immense wisdom and riches are in that. It is better to go without, than to have them at too great a cost. Let us learn the meaning of economy. Economy is a high, humane office, a sacrament, when its aim is grand; when it is the prudence of simple tastes, when it is practised for freedom, or love, or devotion. Much of the economy which we see in houses is of a base origin, and is best kept out of sight. Parched corn eaten to-day, that I may have roast fowl to my dinner on Sunday, is a baseness; but parched corn and a house with one apartment, that I may be free of all perturbations, that I may be serene and docile to what the mind shall speak, and girt and road-ready for the lowest mission of knowledge or goodwill, is frugality for gods and heroes.

Can we not learn the lesson of self-help? Society is full of infirm people, who incessantly summon others to serve them. They contrive everywhere to exhaust for their single comfort the entire means and appliances of that luxury to which our invention has yet attained. Sofas, ottomans, stoves, wine, game-fowl, spices, perfumes, rides, the theatre, entertainments,—all these they want, they need, and whatever can be suggested more than these they crave also, as if it was the bread which should keep them from starving; and if they miss any one, they represent themselves as the most wronged and most wretched persons on earth. One must have been born and bred with them to know how to prepare a meal for their learned stomach. Meantime they never bestir themselves to serve another person; not they! they have a great deal more to do for themselves than they can possibly perform, nor do they once perceive the cruel joke of their lives, but the more odious they grow, the sharper is the tone of their complaining and craving. Can anything be so elegant as to have few wants and to serve them one's self, so as to have somewhat left to give, instead of being always prompt to grab? It is more elegant to answer one's own needs than to be richly served; inelegant perhaps it may look to-day, and to a few, but it is an elegance forever and to all.

I do not wish to be absurd and pedantic in reform. I do not wish to push my criticism on the state of things around me to that extravagant mark that shall compel me to suicide, or to an absolute isolation from the advantages of civil society. If we suddenly plant our foot and say,—I will neither eat nor drink nor wear nor touch any food or fabric which I do not know to be innocent, or deal with any person whose whole manner of life is not clear and rational, we shall stand still. Whose is so? Not mine; not thine; not his. But

I think we must clear ourselves each one by the interrogation, whether we have earned our bread to-day by the hearty contribution of our energies to the common benefit; and we must not cease to *tend* to the correction of flagrant wrongs, by laying one stone aright every day.

But the idea which now begins to agitate society has a wider scope than our daily employments, our households, and the institutions of property. We are to revise the whole of our social structure, the State, the school, religion, marriage, trade, science, and explore their foundations in our own nature; we are to see that the world not only fitted the former men, but fits us, and to clear ourselves of every usage which has not its roots in our own mind. What is a man born for but to be a Reformer, a Remaker of what man has made; a renouncer of lies; a restorer of truth and good, imitating that great Nature which embosoms us all, and which sleeps no moment on an old past, but every hour repairs herself, yielding us every morning a new day, and with every pulsation a new life? Let him renounce everything which is not true to him, and put all his practices back on their first thoughts, and do nothing for which he has not the whole world for his reason. If there are inconveniences and what is called ruin in the way, because we have so enervated and maimed ourselves, yet it would be like dying of perfumes to sink in the effort to reattach the deeds of every day to the holy and mysterious recesses of life.

The power which is at once spring and regulator in all efforts of reform is the conviction that there is an infinite worthiness in man, which will appear at the call of worth, and that all particular reforms are the removing of some impediment. Is it not the highest duty that man should be honored in us? I ought not to allow any man, because he has broad lands, to feel that he is rich in my presence. I ought to make him feel that I can do without his riches, that I cannot be bought,—neither by comfort, neither by pride,—and though I be utterly penniless, and receiving bread from him, that he is the poor man beside me. And if, at the same time, a woman or a child discovers a sentiment of piety, or a juster way of thinking than mine, I ought to confess it by my respect and obedience, though it go to alter my whole way of life.

The Americans have many virtues, but they have not Faith and Hope. I know no two words whose meaning is more lost sight of. We use these words as if they were as obsolete as Selah and Amen.[13] And yet they have the broadest meaning, and the most cogent application to Boston in this year. The Americans have no faith. They rely on the power of a dollar; they are

---

[13]Hebrew terms for "pause and assent," archaic in Emerson's time (Ferguson 1:261).

deaf to a sentiment. They think you may talk the north wind down as easily as raise society; and no class more faithless than the scholars or intellectual men. Now if I talk with a sincere wise man, and my friend, with a poet, with a conscientious youth who is still under the dominion of his own wild thoughts, and not yet harnessed in the team of society to drag with us all in the ruts of custom, I see at once how paltry is all this generation of unbelievers, and what a house of cards their institutions are, and I see what one brave man, what one great thought executed might effect. I see that the reason of the distrust of the practical man in all theory, is his inability to perceive the means whereby we work. Look, he says, at the tools with which this world of yours is to be built. As we cannot make a planet, with atmosphere, rivers, and forests, by means of the best carpenters' or engineers' tools, with chemist's laboratory and smith's forge to boot,—so neither can we ever construct that heavenly society you prate of out of foolish, sick, selfish men and women, such as we know them to be. But the believer not only beholds his heaven to be possible, but already to begin to exist,—not by the men or materials the statesman uses, but by men transfigured and raised above themselves by the power of principles. To principles something else is possible that transcends all the power of expedients.

Every great and commanding moment in the annals of the world is the triumph of some enthusiasm. The victories of the Arabs after Mahomet, who, in a few years, from a small and mean beginning, established a larger empire than that of Rome, is an example. They did they knew not what. The naked Derar, horsed on an idea, was found an overmatch for a troop of Roman cavalry.[14] The women fought like men, and conquered the Roman men. They were miserably equipped, miserably fed. They were Temperance troops. There was neither brandy nor flesh needed to feed them. They conquered Asia, and Africa, and Spain, on barley. The Caliph Omar's walking-stick struck more terror into those who saw it than another man's sword. His diet was barley bread; his sauce was salt; and oftentimes by way of abstinence he ate his bread without salt. His drink was water. His palace was built of mud; and when he left Medina to go to the conquest of Jerusalem, he rode on a red camel, with a wooden platter hanging at his saddle, with a bottle of water and two sacks, one holding barley and the other dried fruits.[15]

---

[14]Emerson read the story of Derar Ebn Alazwar, a Moslem woman who led a troop of women that defeated the Romans, in Simon Ockley, *The History of the Saracens* (London, 1757) (Ferguson 1:261).

[15]Another story that Emerson takes from Ockley, *The History of the Saracens*, 2 vols. (London, 1718), is of the Caliph Omar, whose modesty was legendary and who conquered Jerusalem (Ferguson 1:262).

But there will dawn ere long on our politics, on our modes of living, a nobler morning than that Arabian faith, in the sentiment of love.[16] This is the one remedy for all ills, the panacea of nature. We must be lovers, and at once the impossible becomes possible. Our age and history, for these thousand years, has not been the history of kindness, but of selfishness. Our distrust is very expensive. The money we spend for courts and prisons is very ill laid out. We make, by distrust, the thief, and burglar, and incendiary, and by our court and jail we keep him so. An acceptance of the sentiment of love throughout Christendom for a season would bring the felon and the outcast to our side in tears, with the devotion of his faculties to our service. See this wide society of laboring men and women. We allow ourselves to be served by them, we live apart from them, and meet them without a salute in the streets.[17] We do not greet their talents, nor rejoice in their good fortune, nor foster their hopes, nor in the assembly of the people vote for what is dear to them. Thus we enact the part of the selfish noble and king from the foundation of the world. See, this tree always bears one fruit. In every household, the peace of a pair is poisoned by the malice, slyness, indolence, and alienation of domestics. Let any two matrons meet, and observe how soon their conversation turns on the troubles from their "*help,*" as our phrase is. In every knot of laborers, the rich man does not feel himself among his friends, — and at the polls he finds them arrayed in a mass in distinct opposition to him. We complain that the politics of masses of the people are controlled by designing men, and led in opposition to manifest justice and the common weal, and to their own interest. But the people do not wish to be represented or ruled by the ignorant and base. They only vote for these, because they were asked with the voice and semblance of kindness. They will not vote for them long. They inevitably prefer wit and probity. To use an Egyptian metaphor, it is not their will for any long time "to raise the nails of wild beasts, and to depress the heads of the sacred birds."[18] Let our affection flow out to our fellows; it would operate in a day the greatest of all revolutions. It is better to work on institutions by the sun than by the wind. The State must consider the poor man, and all voices must speak for him. Every child that is born must have a just chance for his

---

[16] Emerson's apparent admiration for Moslem religion and culture is qualified here by the conventional romantic assumption that Christianity and then Enlightenment Reason are "advances" on non-European "faiths."

[17] Emerson famously led an "experiment" in his household to invite his servants to join the family at the table.

[18] An ancient saying that Emerson found in *Treatise of Synesius on Providence,* trans. Thomas Taylor, and included with his *Select Works of Plotinus* (London, 1817).

bread. Let the amelioration in our laws of property proceed from the concession of the rich, not from the grasping of the poor. Let us begin by habitual imparting. Let us understand that the equitable rule is, that no one
should take more than his share, let him be ever so rich. Let me feel that I
am to be a lover. I am to see to it that the world is the better for me, and to
find my reward in the act. Love would put a new face on this weary old
world in which we dwell as pagans and enemies too long, and it would warm
the heart to see how fast the vain diplomacy of statesmen, the impotence
of armies, and navies, and lines of defence, would be superseded by this un-
armed child. Love will creep where it cannot go, will accomplish that by
imperceptible methods, —being its own lever, fulcrum, and power, —which
force could never achieve. Have you not seen in the woods, in a late autumn
morning, a poor fungus or mushroom, —a plant without any solidity, nay,
that seemed nothing but a soft mush or jelly, —by its constant, total, and
inconceivably gentle pushing, manage to break its way up through the
frosty ground, and actually to lift a hard crust on its head? It is the symbol
of the power of kindness. The virtue of this principle in human society in
application to great interests is obsolete and forgotten. Once or twice in
history it has been tried in illustrious instances, with signal success. This
great, overgrown, dead Christendom of ours still keeps alive at least the
name of a lover of mankind. But one day all men will be lovers; and every
calamity will be dissolved in the universal sunshine.[19]

Will you suffer me to add one trait more to this portrait of man the reformer? The finished man should have a great prospective prudence that he
may perform the high office of the mediator between the spiritual and the
actual world. An Arabian poet describes his hero by saying,

Sunshine was he
In the winter day;
And in the midsummer
Coolness and shade.[20]

He who would help himself and others should not be a subject of irregular
and interrupted impulses of virtue, but a continent, persisting, immovable
person, —such as we have seen a few scattered up and down in time for the
blessing of the world; men who have in the gravity of their nature a quality

---

[19]The idea of Christian "love" that Emerson developed in the preceding paragraph
should be understood in relation to the Christian idea of *caritas,* or "charity," in which
our love for each other represents a more profound love of God and his creation.

[20]Emerson's English translation from Goethe's German translation of the Arabic in the
latter's *Die Werke,* 40 vols. (Stuttgart and Tübingen, 1828–30), 6.13 (Ferguson 1:262).

which answers to the fly-wheel in a mill, which distributes the motion equably over all the wheels and hinders it from falling unequally and suddenly in destructive shocks. It is better that joy should be spread over all the day in the form of strength, than that it should be concentrated into ecstasies, full of danger and followed by reactions. There is a sublime prudence, which is the very highest that we know of man, which, believing in a vast future, — sure of more to come than is yet seen, — postpones always the present hour to the whole life; postpones talent to genius, and special results to character. As the merchant gladly takes money from his income to add to his capital, so is the great man very willing to lose particular powers and talents, so that he gain in the elevation of his life. The opening of the spiritual senses disposes men ever to greater sacrifices, to leave their signal talents, their best means and skill of procuring a present success, their power and their fame, — to cast all things behind, in the insatiable thirst for divine communications. A purer fame, a greater power rewards the sacrifice. It is the conversion of our harvest into seed. Is there not somewhat sublime in the act of the farmer, who casts into the ground the finest ears of his grain? The time will come when we too shall hold nothing back, but shall eagerly convert more than we now possess into means and powers, when we shall be willing to sow the sun and the moon for seeds.

The Transcendentalist
A Lecture Read at the Masonic Temple, Boston January, 1842[1]

The first thing we have to say respecting what are called *new views* here in New England, at the present time, is, that they are not new, but the very oldest of thoughts cast into the mold of these new times. The light is always identical in its composition, but it falls on a great variety of objects, and by so falling is first revealed to us, not in its own form, for it is formless, but in theirs; in like manner, thought only appears in the objects it classifies. What is popularly called Transcendentalism[2] among us, is Idealism; Idealism as it appears in 1842. As thinkers, mankind have ever divided experience, the second on consciousness; the first class beginning to think from

---

Selections from Ralph Waldo Emerson: An Organic Anthology. Ed. Stephen E. Whicher. Riverside Edition. Boston: Houghton, 1957.

[1] Emerson first delivered the lecture on 23 December 1841. [Ed.]

[2] Emerson's use of "Transcendentalism" in this paragraph is in keeping with Immanuel Kant's (1724–1804) definition of "transcendental deduction" as the process of eliminating

the data of the senses, the second class perceive that the senses are not final, and say, The senses give us representations of things, but what are the things themselves, they cannot tell. The materialist insists on facts, on history, on the force of circumstances and the animal wants of man; the idealist on the power of Thought and of Will, on inspiration, on miracle, on individual culture. These two modes of thinking are both natural, but the idealist contends that his way of thinking is in higher nature. He concedes all that the other affirms, admits the impressions of sense, admits their coherency, their use and beauty, and then asks the materialist for his grounds of assurance that things are as his senses represent them. But I, he says, affirm facts not affected by the illusions of sense, facts which are of the same nature as the faculty which reports them, and not liable to doubt; facts which in their first appearance to us assume a native superiority to material facts, degrading these into a language by which the first are to be spoken; facts which it only needs a retirement from the senses to discern. Every materialist will be an idealist; but an idealist can never go backward to be a materialist.

The idealist, in speaking of events, sees them as spirits. He does not deny the sensuous fact: by no means; but he will not see that alone. He does not deny the presence of this table, this chair, and the walls of this room, but he looks at these things as the reverse side of the tapestry, as the *other end,* each being a sequel or completion of a spiritual fact which nearly concerns him.[3] This manner of looking at things transfers every object in nature from an independent and anomalous position without there, into the consciousness. Even the materialist Condillac,[4] perhaps the most logical expounder of materialism, was constrained to say, "Though we should soar into the heavens, though we should sink into the abyss, we never go out of ourselves; it is always our own thought that we perceive." What more could an idealist say?

---

from cognition everything that is not essential to the formation of thought. According to Kant, this process results in the discovery of those mental faculties or "categories" that are independent of the external, material world. In this sense, "transcendental" does not refer to something mysteriously beyond us but refers to those faculties basic to the human mind. Emerson's "idealist" is distinguished from "materialists," who trust empirical evidence and neglect the shaping forces of the human mind. [Ed.]

[3]Kant and subsequent romantic idealists do not deny the existence of objects in the outer world, so they are not solipsists ("If a tree falls in the forest, how do you know it makes a sound?"). But the idealist "brackets" or "suspends" the sensuous data in the course of a "transcendental deduction," arguing that the only "facts" we can know with any certainty are those directly pertaining to the mind itself. [Ed.]

[4]Étienne Bonnot de Condillac (1715–1780), French Enlightenment philosopher who advocated sensationalism and associationism. [Ed.]

The materialist, secure in the certainty of sensation, mocks at fine-spun theories, at star-gazers, and dreamers, and believes that his life is solid, that he at least takes nothing for granted, but knows where he stands, and what he does. Yet how easy it is to show him that he also is a phantom walking and working amid phantoms, and that he need only ask a question or two beyond his daily questions to find his solid universe growing dim and impalpable before his sense. The sturdy capitalist, no matter how deep and square on blocks of Quincy granite he lays the foundations of his banking-house or Exchange, must set it, at last, not on a cube corresponding to the angles of his structure, but on a mass of unknown materials and solidity, red-hot or white-hot perhaps at the core, which rounds off to an almost perfect sphericity, and lies floating in soft air, and goes spinning away, dragging bank and banker with it at a rate of thousands of miles the hour, he knows not whither,—a bit of bullet, now glimmering, now darkling through a small cubic space on the edge of an unimaginable pit of emptiness. And this wild balloon, in which his whole venture is embarked, is a just symbol of his whole state and faculty. One thing at least, he says, is certain, and does not give me the headache, that figures do not lie; the multiplication table has been hitherto found unimpeachable truth; and, moreover, if I put a gold eagle[5] in my safe, I find it again tomorrow;—but for these thoughts, I know not whence they are. They change and pass away. But ask him why he believes that an uniform experience will continue uniform, or on what grounds he founds his faith in his figures, and he will perceive that his mental fabric is built up on just as strange and quaking foundations as his proud edifice of stone.

In the order of thought, the materialist takes his departure from the external world, and esteems a man as one product of that. The idealist takes his departure from his consciousness, and reckons the world an appearance. The materialist respects sensible masses, Society, Government, social art and luxury, every establishment, every mass, whether majority of numbers, or extent of space, or amount of objects, every social action. The idealist has another measure, which is metaphysical, namely the *rank* which things themselves take in his consciousness; not at all the size or appearance. Mind is the only reality, of which men and all other natures are better or worse reflectors. Nature, literature, history, are only subjective phenomena. Although in his action overpowered by the laws of action, and so, warmly coöperating with men, even preferring them to himself, yet when he speaks scientifically, or after the order of thought, he is constrained to degrade persons into representatives of truths. He does not respect labor,

---

[5] A ten-dollar gold piece. [Ed.]

or the products of labor, namely property, otherwise than as a manifold symbol, illustrating with wonderful fidelity of details the laws of being; he does not respect government, except as far as it reiterates the law of his mind; nor the church, nor charities, nor arts, for themselves; but hears, as at a vast distance, what they say, as if his consciousness would speak to him through a pantomimic scene. His thought, — that is the Universe. His experience inclines him to behold the procession of facts you call the world, as flowing perpetually outward from an invisible, unsounded center in himself, center alike of him and of them, and necessitating him to regard all things as having a subjective or relative existence, relative to that aforesaid Unknown Center of him.

From this transfer of the world into the consciousness, this beholding of all things in the mind, follow easily his whole ethics. It is simpler to be self-dependent. The height, the deity of man is to be self-sustained, to need no gift, no foreign force. Society is good when it does not violate me, but best when it is likest to solitude. Everything real is self-existent. Everything divine shares the self-existence of Deity. All that you call the world is the shadow of that substance which you are, the perpetual creation of the powers of thought, of those that are dependent and of those that are independent of your will. Do not cumber yourself with fruitless pains to mend and remedy remote effects; let the soul be erect, and all things will go well. You think me the child of my circumstances: I make my circumstance. Let any thought or motive of mine be different from that they are, the difference will transform my condition and economy. I — this thought which is called I — is the mold into which the world is poured like melted wax. The mold is invisible, but the world betrays the shape of the mold. You call it the power of circumstance, but it is the power of me. Am I in harmony with myself? my position will seem to you just and commanding. Am I vicious and insane? my fortunes will seem to you obscure and descending. As I am, so shall I associate, and so shall I act; Caesar's history will paint out Caesar. Jesus acted so, because he thought so. I do not wish to overlook or to gainsay any reality; I say I make my circumstance; but if you ask me, Whence am I? I feel like other men my relation to that Fact which cannot be spoken, or defined, nor even thought, but which exists, and will exist.

The Transcendentalist adopts the whole connection of spiritual doctrine. He believes in miracle, in the perpetual openness of the human mind to new influx of light and power; he believes in inspiration, and in ecstasy. He wishes that the spiritual principle should be suffered to demonstrate itself to the end, in all possible applications to the state of man, without the admission of anything unspiritual; that is, any thing positive, dogmatic, personal. Thus the spiritual measure of inspiration is the depth of the thought, and never, who said it? And so he resists all attempts to palm other rules and measures on the spirit than its own.

In action he easily incurs the charge of antinomianism[6] by his avowal that he, who has the Law-giver, may with safety not only neglect, but even contravene every written commandment. In the play of Othello, the expiring Desdemona absolves her husband of the murder, to her attendant Emilia. Afterwards, when Emilia charges him with the crime, Othello exclaims,

"You heard her say herself it was not I."

Emilia replies,

"The more angel she, and thou the blacker devil."[7]

Of this fine incident, Jacobi, the Transcendental moralist, makes use, with other parallel instances, in his reply to Fichte.[8] Jacobi, refusing all measure of right and wrong except the determinations of the private spirit, remarks that there is no crime but has sometimes been a virtue. "I," he says, "am that atheist, that godless person who, in opposition to an imaginary doctrine of calculation, would lie as the dying Desdemona lied; would lie and deceive, as Pylades when he personated Orestes; would assassinate like Timoleon; would perjure myself like Epaminondas and John de Witt; I would resolve on suicide like Cato; I would commit sacrilege with David; yea, and pluck ears of corn on the Sabbath, for no other reason than that I was fainting for lack of food. For I have assurance in myself that in pardoning these faults according to the letter, man exerts the sovereign right which the majesty of his being confers on him; he sets the seal of his divine nature to the grace he accords."

In like manner, if there is anything grand and daring in human thought or virtue, any reliance on the vast, the unknown; any presentiment, any extravagance of faith, the spiritualist adopts it as most in nature. The oriental mind has always tended to this largeness. Buddhism is an expression of

---

[6] Antinomianism, such as that associated with Anne Hutchinson (see in this volume "Self-Reliance," n. 16), was a heresy from orthodox Puritanism that argued God's will could be directly perceived by individuals. In Puritan debates, it was opposed to "Legalism," which may clarify Emerson's reference to "the Law-giver" here. Emerson is sensitive to the charge that his version of transcendentalism is a kind of antinomianism. [Ed.]

[7] Shakespeare, *Othello* 5.2.129–33. [Ed.]

[8] Friedrich Heinrich Jacobi (1743–1819), "Letter to Fichte" (March 1799), was partly quoted by Samuel Taylor Coleridge in *The Friend* (1818). [Orig. ed.]

it. The Buddhist, who thanks no man, who says, "Do not flatter your bene-factors,"[9] but who, in his conviction that every good deed can by no pos-sibility escape its reward, will not deceive the benefactor by pretending that he has done more than he should, is a Transcendentalist.

You will see by this sketch that there is no such thing as a Transcenden-tal *party;* that there is no pure Transcendentalist; that we know of none but prophets and heralds of such a philosophy; that all who by strong bias of nature have leaned to the spiritual side in doctrine, have stopped short of their goal. We have had many harbingers and forerunners; but of a purely spiritual life, history has afforded no example. I mean we have yet no man who has leaned entirely on his character, and eaten angels' food; who, trusting to his sentiments, found life made of miracles; who, working for universal aims, found himself fed, he knew not how clothed, sheltered, and weaponed, he knew not how, and yet it was done by his own hands. Only in the instinct of the lower animals we find the suggestion of the methods of it, and something higher than our understanding. The squirrel hoards nuts and the bee gathers honey, without knowing what they do, and they are thus provided for without selfishness or disgrace.

Shall we say then that Transcendentalism is the Saturnalia[10] or excess of Faith; the presentiment of a faith proper to man in his integrity, exces-sive only when his imperfect obedience hinders the satisfaction of his wish? Nature is transcendental, exists primarily, necessarily, ever works and ad-vances, yet takes no thought for the morrow.[11] Man owns the dignity of the life which throbs around him, in chemistry, and tree, and animal, and in the involuntary functions of his own body; yet he is balked when he tries to fling himself into this enchanted circle, where all is done without degra-dation. Yet genius and virtue predict in man the same absence of private ends and of condescension to circumstances, united with every trait and talent of beauty and power.

This way of thinking, falling on Roman times, made Stoic philosophers; falling on despotic times, made patriot Catos and Brutuses; falling on superstitious times, made prophets and apostles; on popish times, made protestants and ascetic monks, preachers of Faith against the preachers of Works; on prelatical times, made Puritans and Quakers; and falling on Unitarian and commercial times, makes the peculiar shades of Idealism which we know.

---

[9]Emerson uses this quotation frequently. He referred to Eastern religions to demon-strate the universality of transcendentalist ideas. [Ed.]

[10]Roman festival of Saturn, held in December; a time of unrestrained celebration and considered a predecessor of Christmas festivities. [Ed.]

[11]Cf. Matt. 6.34 (Ferguson 1:265). [Ed.]

It is well known to most of my audience that the Idealism of the present day acquired the name of Transcendental from the use of that term by Immanuel Kant, of Königsberg, who replied to the skeptical philosophy of Locke, which insisted that there was nothing in the intellect which was not previously in the experience of the senses, by showing that there was a very important class of ideas or imperative forms, which did not come by experience, but through which experience was acquired; that these were intuitions of the mind itself; and he denominated them *Transcendental* forms.[12] The extraordinary profoundness and precision of that man's thinking have given vogue to his nomenclature, in Europe and America, to that extent that whatever belongs to the class of intuitive thought is popularly called at the present day *Transcendental.*

Although, as we have said, there is no pure Transcendentalist, yet the tendency to respect the intuitions and to give them, at least in our creed, all authority over our experience, has deeply colored the conversation and poetry of the present day; and the history of genius and of religion in these times, though impure, and as yet not incarnated in any powerful individual, will be the history of this tendency.

It is a sign of our times, conspicuous to the coarsest observer, that many intelligent and religious persons withdraw themselves from the common labors and competitions of the market and the caucus, and betake themselves to a certain solitary and critical way of living, from which no solid fruit has yet appeared to justify their separation. They hold themselves aloof: they feel the disproportion between their faculties and the work offered them, and they prefer to ramble in the country and perish of ennui, to the degradation of such charities and such ambitions as the city can propose to them. They are striking work, and crying out for somewhat worthy to do! What they do is done only because they are over-powered by the humanities that speak on all sides; and they consent to such labor as is open to them, though to their lofty dream the writing of Iliads or Hamlets, or the building of cities or empires seems drudgery.

Now every one must do after his kind, be he asp or angel, and these must. The question which a wise man and a student of modern history will ask, is, what that kind is? And truly, as in ecclesiastical history we take so much

---

[12] Kant lived and taught most of his life in Königsberg, then part of Prussia. His "critical philosophy" responded to John Locke's (1632–1704) theory of knowledge as the "association of ideas" and of the mind as essentially a *tabula rasa* ("blank slate") to be filled with such associations. Kant's "transcendental forms" are also known as the a priori categories of the mind. For Kant, "intuition" refers to the process whereby a priori categories and external sense data are knitted together into "ideas," not to a mystical process of understanding. [Ed.]

pains to know what the Gnostics, what the Essenes, what the Manichees, and what the Reformers[13] believed, it would not misbecome us to inquire nearer home, what these companions and contemporaries of ours think and do, at least so far as these thoughts and actions appear to be not accidental and personal, but common to many, and the inevitable flower of the Tree of Time. Our American literature and spiritual history are, we confess, in the optative mood,[14] but whoso knows these seething brains, these admirable radicals, these unsocial worshippers, these talkers who talk the sun and moon away, will believe that this heresy cannot pass away without leaving its mark.[15]

They are lonely; the spirit of their writing and conversation is lonely; they repel influences; they shun general society; they incline to shut themselves in their chamber in the house, to live in the country rather than in the town, and to find their tasks and amusements in solitude. Society, to be sure, does not like this very well, it saith, Whoso goes to walk alone, accuses the whole world; he declares all to be unfit to be his companions; it is very uncivil, nay, insulting; Society will retaliate. Meantime, this retirement does not proceed from any whim on the part of these separators; but if any one will take pains to talk with them, he will find that this part is chosen both from temperament and from principle; with some unwillingness too, and as a choice of the less of two evils; for these persons are not by nature melancholy, sour, and unsocial, — they are not stockish or brute, — but joyous, susceptible, affectionate; they have even more than others a great wish to be loved. Like the young Mozart, they are rather ready to cry ten times a day, "But are you sure you love me?" Nay, if they tell you their whole thought, they will own that love seems to them the last and highest gift of nature; that there are persons whom in their hearts they daily thank for existing, — persons whose faces are perhaps unknown to them, but whose fame and spirit have penetrated their solitude, — and for whose sake they wish to exist. To behold the beauty of another character, which inspires a new inter-

---

[13] Emerson provides a list of reformist Christian sects, ranging from the Gnostics (1–3 CE) to the Protestant Reformation. [Ed.]

[14] Grammatical term for verb forms in Greek and Sanskrit that express volition, like the subjunctive in English. Emerson uses the phrase to suggest the hopeful and utopian aims of American literature and culture. [Ed.]

[15] Among the transcendentalist friends to whom he refers here, Emerson had Amos Bronson Alcott in mind, as well as the group of English reformers who established an Alcott House School at Ham, Surrey. Alcott (traveling on funds provided by Emerson) visited Surrey and returned with his plans for the American utopian community Fruitlands. Alcott founded Fruitlands in the summer of 1843. It failed the following winter. [Ed.]

est in our own; to behold the beauty lodged in a human being, with such vivacity of apprehension that I am instantly forced home to inquire if I am not deformity itself; to behold in another the expression of a love so high that it assures itself, — assures itself also to me against every possible casualty except my unworthiness; — these are degrees on the scale of human happiness to which they have ascended; and it is a fidelity to this sentiment which has made common association distasteful to them. They wish a just and even fellowship, or none. They cannot gossip with you, and they do not wish, as they are sincere and religious, to gratify any mere curiosity which you may entertain. Like fairies, they do not wish to be spoken of. Love me, they say, but do not ask who is my cousin and my uncle. If you do not need to hear my thought, because you can read it in my face and behavior, then I will tell it you from sunrise to sunset. If you cannot divine it, you would not understand what I say. I will not molest myself for you. I do not wish to be profaned.

And yet, it seems as if this loneliness, and not this love, would prevail in their circumstances, because of the extravagant demand they make on human nature. That, indeed, constitutes a new feature in their portrait, that they are the most exacting and extortionate critics. Their quarrel with every man they meet is not with his kind, but with his degree. There is not enough of him, — that is the only fault. They prolong their privilege of childhood in this wise; of doing nothing, but making immense demands on all the gladiators in the lists of action and fame. They make us feel the strange disappointment which overcasts every human youth. So many promising youths, and never a finished man! The profound nature will have a savage rudeness; the delicate one will be shallow, or the victim of sensibility; the richly accomplished will have some capital absurdity; and so every piece has a crack. 'Tis strange, but this masterpiece is the result of such an extreme delicacy that the most unobserved flaw in the boy will neutralize the most aspiring genius, and spoil the work. Talk with a seaman of the hazards to life in his profession and he will ask you, "Where are the old sailors? Do you not see that all are young men?" And we, on this sea of human thought, in like manner inquire, Where are the old idealists? where are they who represented to the last generation that extravagant hope which a few happy aspirants suggest to ours? In looking at the class of counsel, and power, and wealth, and at the matronage of the land, amidst all the prudence and all the triviality, one asks, Where are they who represented genius, virtue, the invisible and heavenly world, to these? Are they dead, — taken in early ripeness to the gods, — as ancient wisdom foretold their fate? Or did the high idea die out of them, and leave their unperfumed body as its tomb and tablet, announcing to all that the celestial inhabitant, who once gave them beauty, had departed? Will it be better with the new generation?

We easily predict a fair future to each new candidate who enters the lists, but we are frivolous and volatile, and by low aims and ill example do what we can to defeat this hope. Then these youths bring us a rough but effectual aid. By their unconcealed dissatisfaction they expose our poverty and the insignificance of man to man. A man is a poor limitary benefactor. He ought to be a shower of benefits—a great influence, which should never let his brother go, but should refresh old merits continually with new ones; so that though absent he should never be out of my mind, his name never far from my lips; but if the earth should open at my side, or my last hour were come, his name should be the prayer I should utter to the Universe. But in our experience, man is cheap and friendship wants its deep sense. We affect to dwell with our friends in their absence, but we do not; when deed, word, or letter comes not, they let us go. These exacting children advertise us of our wants. There is no compliment, no smooth speech with them; they pay you only this one compliment, of insatiable expectation; they aspire, they severely exact, and if they only stand fast in this watch-tower, and persist in demanding unto the end, and without end, then are they terrible friends, whereof poet and priest cannot choose but stand in awe; and what if they eat clouds, and drink wind, they have not been without service to the race of man.

With this passion for what is great and extraordinary, it cannot be wondered at that they are repelled by vulgarity and frivolity in people. They say to themselves, It is better to be alone than in bad company. And it is really a wish to be met,—the wish to find society for their hope and religion,—which prompts them to shun what is called society. They feel that they are never so fit for friendship as when they have quitted mankind and taken themselves to friend. A picture, a book, a favorite spot in the hills or the woods which they can people with the fair and worthy creation of the fancy, can give them often forms so vivid that these for the time shall seem real, and society the illusion.

But their solitary and fastidious manners not only withdraw them from the conversation, but from the labors of the world; they are not good citizens, not good members of society; unwillingly they bear their part of the public and private burdens; they do not willingly share in the public charities, in the public religious rites, in the enterprises of education, of missions foreign and domestic, in the abolition of the slave-trade, or in the temperance society. They do not even like to vote. The philanthropists inquire whether Transcendentalism does not mean sloth: they had as lief hear that their friend is dead, as that he is a Transcendentalist; for then is he paralyzed, and can never do anything for humanity. What right, cries the good world, has the man of genius to retreat from work, and indulge himself? The popular literary creed seems to be, "I am a sublime genius; I ought not therefore to labor." But genius is the power to labor better and more availably. Deserve thy genius: exalt it. The good, the illuminated, sit apart from the rest, censuring their dulness and vices, as if they thought that by sitting very grand in their chairs, the very brokers, attorneys, and congressmen would see the error of their ways, and flock to them. But the good and wise must learn to act, and carry salvation to the combatants and demagogues in the dusty arena below.

On the part of these children it is replied that life and their faculty seem to them gifts too rich to be squandered on such trifles as you propose to them. What you call your fundamental institutions, your great and holy causes, seem to them great abuses, and, when nearly seen, paltry matters. Each "cause" as it is called, — say Abolition, Temperance, say Calvinism, or Unitarianism, — becomes speedily a little shop, where the article, let it have been at first never so subtle and ethereal, is now made up into portable and convenient cakes, and retailed in small quantities to suit purchasers. You make very free use of these words "great" and "holy," but few things appear to them such. Few persons have any magnificence of nature to inspire enthusiasm, and the philanthropies and charities have a certain air of quackery. As to the general course of living, and the daily employments of men, they cannot see much virtue in these, since they are parts of this vicious circle; and as no great ends are answered by the men, there is nothing noble in the arts by which they are maintained. Nay, they have made the experiment and found that from the liberal professions to the coarsest manual labor, and from the courtesies of the academy and the college to the conventions of the cotillon-room and the morning call, there is a spirit of cowardly compromise and seeming which intimates a frightful skepticism, a life without love, and an activity without an aim.

Unless the action is necessary, unless it is adequate, I do not wish to perform it. I do not wish to do one thing but once. I do not love routine. Once possessed of the principle, it is equally easy to make four or forty thousand applications of it. A great man will be content to have indicated in any the slightest manner his perception of the reigning Idea of his time, and will leave to those who like it the multiplication of examples. When he has hit the white, the rest may shatter the target. Every thing admonishes us how needlessly long life is. Every moment of a hero so raises and cheers us that a twelvemonth is an age. All that the brave Xanthus brings home from his wars is the recollection that at the storming of Samos, "in the heat of the battle. Pericles smiled on me, and passed on to another detachment." [16] It

---

[16] A Greek heroic legend of the Athenian victory at Samos, recounted in Walter Savage Landor, *Pericles and Aspasia*, 2 vols. (London, 1836) (Ferguson 1:265). [Ed.]

is the quality of the moment, not the number of days, of events, or of actors, that imports.

New, we confess, and by no means happy, is our condition: if you want the aid of our labor, we ourselves stand in greater want of the labor. We are miserable with inaction. We perish of rest and rust: but we do not like your work.

"Then," says the world, "show me your own."

"We have none."

"What will you do, then?" cries the world.

"We will wait."

"How long?"

"Until the Universe beckons and calls us to work."

"But whilst you wait, you grow old and useless."

"Be it so: I can sit in a corner and *perish* (as you call it), but I will not move until I have the highest command. If no call should come for years, for centuries, then I know that the want of the Universe is the attestation of faith by my abstinence. Your virtuous projects, so called, do not cheer me. I know that which shall come will cheer me. If I cannot work, at least I need not lie. All that is clearly due today is not to lie. In other places other men have encountered sharp trials, and have behaved themselves well. The martyrs were sawn asunder, or hung alive on meat-hooks. Cannot we screw our courage to patience and truth, and without complaint, or even with good-humor, await our turn of action in the Infinite Counsels?"

But to come a little closer to the secret of these persons, we must say that to them it seems a very easy matter to answer the objections of the man of the world, but not so easy to dispose of the doubts and objections that occur to themselves. They are exercised in their own spirit with queries which acquaint them with all adversity, and with the trials of the bravest heroes. When I asked them concerning their private experience, they answered somewhat in this wise: It is not to be denied that there must be some wide difference between my faith and other faith; and mine is a certain brief experience, which surprised me in the highway or in the market, in some place, at some time, — whether in the body or out of the body, God knoweth,[17] — and made me aware that I had played the fool with fools all this time, but that law existed for me and for all; that to me belonged trust, a child's trust and obedience, and the worship of ideas, and I should never be fool more. Well, in the space of an hour probably, I was let down from this height; I was at my old tricks, the selfish member of a selfish society. My life is superficial, takes no root in the deep world; I ask, When shall I die and be re-

---

[17] Cf. 2 Cor. 12.2. [Ed.]

lieved of the responsibility of seeing a Universe I do not use? I wish to exchange this flash-of-lightning faith for continuous daylight, this fever-glow
for a benign climate.

These two states of thought diverge every moment, and stand in wild
contrast. To him who looks at his life from these moments of illumination,
it will seem that he skulks and plays a mean, shiftless and subaltern part in
the world. That is to be done which he has not skill to do, or to be said
which others can say better, and he lies by, or occupies his hands with some
plaything, until his hour comes again.[18] Much of our reading, much of our
labor, seems mere waiting: it was not that we were born for.[19] Any other
could do it as well or better. So little skill enters into these works, so little
do they mix with the divine life, that it really signifies little what we do,
whether we turn a grindstone, or ride, or run, or make fortunes, or govern
the state. The worst feature of this double consciousness[20] is, that the two
lives, of the understanding and of the soul, which we lead, really show very
little relation to each other; never meet and measure each other: one prevails now, all buzz and din; and the other prevails then, all infinitude and
paradise; and, with the progress of life, the two discover no greater disposition to reconcile themselves. Yet, what is my faith? What am I? What but
a thought of serenity and independence, an abode in the deep blue sky?
Presently the clouds shut down again; yet we retain the belief that this
pretty web we weave will at last be overshot and reticulated with veins of
the blue, and that the moments will characterize the days. Patience, then, is
for us, is it not? Patience, and still patience. When we pass, as presently we
shall, into some new infinitude, out of this Iceland of negations, it will
please us to reflect that though we had few virtues or consolations, we bore
with our indigence, nor once strove to repair it with hypocrisy or false heat
of any kind.

But this class are not sufficiently characterized if we omit to add that
they are lovers and worshippers of Beauty. In the eternal trinity of Truth,
Goodness, and Beauty, each in its perfection including the three, they prefer to make Beauty the sign and head. Something of the same taste is observ-
able in all the moral movements of the time, in the religious and benevolent

---

[18]"'His hour comes again.' A phrase used frequently with slight variation by St. John"
(Ferguson 1:265). [Ed.]

[19]"It was not that we were born for": Cf. John 18.37 (Ferguson 1:265). [Ed.]

[20]Emerson's use of "double consciousness" is typical of romantic idealist efforts to reconcile subject and object, a priori categories of the mind and the a posteriori experiences
of life. The idea influences W. E. B. Du Bois's famous use of "double consciousness" in
The Souls of Black Folk (1903) to characterize the African American experience under
conditions of racial oppression. [Ed.]

enterprises. They have a liberal, even an aesthetic spirit. A reference to Beauty in action sounds, to be sure, a little hollow and ridiculous in the ears of the old church. In politics, it has often sufficed, when they treated of justice, if they kept the bounds of selfish calculation. If they granted restitution, it was prudence which granted it. But the justice which is now claimed for the black, and the pauper, and the drunkard, is for Beauty, — is for a necessity to the soul of the agent, not of the beneficiary.[21] I say this is the tendency, not yet the realization. Our virtue totters and trips, does not yet walk firmly. Its representatives are austere; they preach and denounce; their rectitude is not yet a grace. They are still liable to that slight taint of burlesque which in our strange world attaches to the zealot. A saint should be as dear as the apple of the eye. Yet we are tempted to smile, and we flee from the working to the speculative reformer, to escape that same slight ridicule. Alas for these days of derision and criticism! We call the Beautiful the highest, because it appears to us the golden mean, escaping the dowdiness of the good and the heartlessness of the true. They are lovers of nature also, and find an indemnity in the inviolable order of the world for the violated order and grace of man.

There is, no doubt, a great deal of well founded objection to be spoken or felt against the sayings and doings of this class, some of whose traits we have selected; no doubt they will lay themselves open to criticism and to lampoons, and as ridiculous stories will be to be told of them as of any. There will be cant and pretension; there will be subtilty and moonshine. These persons are of unequal strength, and do not all prosper. They complain that everything around them must be denied; and if feeble, it takes all their strength to deny, before they can begin to lead their own life. Grave seniors insist on their respect to this institution and that usage; to an obsolete history; to some vocation, or college, or etiquette, or beneficiary, or charity, or morning or evening call, which they resist as what does not concern them. But it costs such sleepless nights, alienations and misgivings, — they have so many moods about it; these old guardians never change *their* minds; they have but one mood on the subject, namely, that Antony is very perverse, — that it is quite as much as Antony can do to assert his rights, ab-

---

[21] Emerson extends the transcendentalist idea of "Beauty" — the principle that demonstrates the harmony of the human mind with the world of nature — to political movements committed to greater social justice, including the abolition, temperance, and antipoverty movements of the 1840s. Justice in such causes is not utilitarian, Emerson argues, but in the service of the larger harmony of humanity and nature. Emerson here leaps the gap separating Kant's critiques of "practical judgment" and of "aesthetic judgment." [Ed.]

stain from what he thinks foolish, and keep his temper. He cannot help the reaction of this injustice in his own mind. He is braced-up and stilted; all freedom and flowing genius, all sallies of wit and frolic nature are quite out of the question; it is well if he can keep from lying, injustice, and suicide. This is no time for gaiety and grace. His strength and spirits are wasted in rejection. But the strong spirits overpower those around them without effort. Their thought and emotion comes in like a flood, quite withdraws them from all notice of these carping critics; they surrender themselves with glad heart to the heavenly guide, and only by implication reject the clamorous nonsense of the hour. Grave seniors talk to the deaf, — church and old book mumble and ritualize to an unheeding, preoccupied and advancing mind, and thus they by happiness of greater momentum lose no time, but take the right road at first.

But all these of whom I speak are not proficients; they are novices; they only show the road in which man should travel, when the soul has greater health and prowess. Yet let them feel the dignity of their charge, and deserve a larger power. Their heart is the ark in which the fire is concealed which shall burn in a broader and universal flame. Let them obey the Genius then most when his impulse is wildest; then most when he seems to lead to uninhabitable deserts of thought and life; for the path which the hero travels alone is the highway of health and benefit to mankind. What is the privilege and nobility of our nature but its persistency, through its power to attach itself to what is permanent?

Society also has its duties in reference to this class, and must behold them with what charity it can. Possibly some benefit may yet accrue from them to the state. In our Mechanics' Fair, there must be not only bridges, ploughs, carpenters' planes, and baking troughs, but also some few finer instruments, — rain-gauges, thermometers, and telescopes; and in society, besides farmers, sailors, and weavers, there must be a few persons of purer fire kept specially as gauges and meters of character; persons of a fine, detecting instinct, who note the smallest accumulations of wit and feeling in the bystander. Perhaps too there might be room for the exciters and monitors,[22] collectors of the heavenly spark, with power to convey the electricity to others. Or, as the storm-tossed vessel at sea speaks the frigate or "line packet"[23] to learn its longitude, so it may not be without its advantage that

---

[22] "Exciters and monitors": technical terms from the science of static electricity. Emerson uses them as metaphors for transcendentalists, who can provoke certain elective affinities, as they were called at the time, among people and between the human and natural worlds. [Ed.]

[23] Ship used by the government for dispatches or mail (Ferguson 1:265). [Ed.]

we should now and then encounter rare and gifted men, to compare the points of our spiritual compass, and verify our bearings from superior chronometers.

Amidst the downward tendency and proneness of things, when every voice is raised for a new road or another statute or a subscription of stock; for an improvement in dress, or in dentistry; for a new house or a larger business; for a political party, or the division of an estate;—will you not tolerate one or two solitary voices in the land, speaking for thoughts and principles not marketable or perishable? Soon these improvements and mechanical inventions will be superseded; these modes of living lost out of memory; these cities rotted, ruined by war, by new inventions, by new seats of trade, or the geologic changes:—all gone, like the shells which sprinkle the sea-beach with a white colony today, forever renewed to be forever destroyed. But the thoughts which these few hermits strove to proclaim by silence as well as by speech, not only by what they did, but by what they forbore to do, shall abide in beauty and strength, to reorganize themselves in nature, to invest themselves anew in other, perhaps higher endowed and happier mixed clay than ours, in fuller union with the surrounding system.

Politics
1844

Gold and iron are good
To buy iron and gold;
All earth's fleece and food
For their like are sold.
Hinted Merlin wise,
Proved Napoleon great,
Nor kind nor coinage buys
Aught above its rate.
Fear, Craft and Avarice
Cannot rear a State.
Out of dust to build
What is more than dust,—

Selections from Ralph Waldo Emerson: An Organic Anthology. Ed. Stephen E. Whicher. Riverside Edition. Boston: Houghton, 1957.

Walls Amphion piled
Phoebus stablish must.
When the Muses nine
With the Virtues meet,
Find to their design
An Atlantic seat,
By green orchard boughs
Fended from the heat,
Where the statesman ploughs
Furrow for the wheat, —
When the Church is social worth,
When the state-house is the hearth,
Then the perfect State is come,
The republican at home.

In dealing with the State we ought to remember that its institutions are not aboriginal, though they existed before we were born; that they are not superior to the citizen; that every one of them was once the act of a single man; every law and usage was a man's expedient to meet a particular case; that they all are imitable, all alterable; we may make as good, we may make better. Society is an illusion to the young citizen. It lies before him in rigid repose, with certain names, men and institutions rooted like oak-trees to the center, round which all arrange themselves the best they can. But the old statesman knows that society is fluid; there are no such roots and centers, but any particle may suddenly become the center of the movement and compel the system to gyrate round it, as every man of strong will, like Pisistratus or Cromwell, does for a time, and every man of truth, like Plato or Paul, does forever.[1] But politics rest on necessary foundations, and cannot be treated with levity. Republics abound in young civilians who believe that the laws make the city, that grave modifications of the policy and modes of living and employments of the population, that commerce, education and religion may be voted in or out; and that any measure, though it were absurd, may be imposed on a people if only you can get sufficient

---

[1] Neither the Athenian tyrant Pisistratus (d. 527 BCE) nor Oliver Cromwell was able to create a political dynasty, but Plato's and Saint Paul's teachings (and writings) have created an intellectual and spiritual heritage. [Ed.]

voices to make it a law. But the wise know that foolish legislation is a rope of sand which perishes in the twisting;[2] that the State must follow and not lead the character and progress of the citizen; the strongest usurper is quickly got rid of; and they only who build on Ideas, build for eternity; and that the form of government which prevails is the expression of what cultivation exists in the population which permits it. The law is only a memorandum. We are superstitious, and esteem the statute somewhat: so much life as it has in the character of living men is its force. The statute stands there to say, Yesterday we agreed so and so, but how feel ye this article today? Our statute is a currency which we stamp with our own portrait: it soon becomes unrecognizable, and in process of time will return to the mint. Nature is not democratic, nor limited-monarchical, but despotic, and will not be fooled or abated of any jot of her authority by the pertest of her sons; and as fast as the public mind is opened to more intelligence, the code is seen to be brute and stammering. It speaks not articulately, and must be made to. Meantime the education of the general mind never stops. The reveries of the true and simple are prophetic. What the tender poetic youth dreams, and prays, and paints today, but shuns the ridicule of saying aloud, shall presently be the resolutions of public bodies; then shall be carried as grievance and bill of rights through conflict and war, and then shall be triumphant law and establishment for a hundred years, until it gives place in turn to new prayers and pictures. The history of the State sketches in coarse outline the progress of thought, and follows at a distance the delicacy of culture and of aspiration.

The theory of politics which has possessed the mind of men, and which they have expressed the best they could in their laws and in their revolutions, considers persons and property as the two objects for whose protection government exists. Of persons, all have equal rights, in virtue of being identical in nature. This interest of course with its whole power demands a democracy. Whilst the rights of all as persons are equal, in virtue of their access to reason, their rights in property are very unequal. One man owns his clothes, and another owns a county. This accident, depending primarily on the skill and virtue of the parties, of which there is every degree, and secondarily on patrimony, falls unequally, and its rights of course are unequal. Personal rights, universally the same, demand a government framed on the ratio of the census; property demands a government framed on the ratio of owners and of owning. Laban, who has flocks and herds, wishes them looked after by an officer on the frontiers, lest the Midianites shall

---

[2] Students of the so-called Black Arts held that demons could be kept out of mischief by setting them at hopeless tasks, such as making ropes out of sand. [Orig. ed.]

drive them off, and pays a tax to that end. Jacob has no flocks or herds and no fear of the Midianites, and pays no tax to the officer. It seemed fit that Laban and Jacob should have equal rights to elect the officer who is to defend their persons, but that Laban and not Jacob should elect the officer who is to guard the sheep and cattle. And if question arise whether additional officers or watchtowers should be provided, must not Laban and Isaac, and those who must sell part of their herds to buy protection for the rest, judge better of this, and with more right, than Jacob, who, because he is a youth and a traveler, eats their bread and not his own? [3]

In the earliest society the proprietors made their own wealth, and so long as it comes to the owners in the direct way, no other opinion would arise in any equitable community than that property should make the law for property, and persons the law for persons.

But property passes through donation or inheritance to those who do not create it. Gift, in one case, makes it as really the new owner's, as labor made it the first owner's: in the other case, of patrimony, the law makes an ownership which will be valid in each man's view according to the estimate which he sets on the public tranquillity.

It was not, however, found easy to embody the readily admitted principle that property should make law for property, and persons for persons; since persons and property mixed themselves in every transaction. At last it seemed settled that the rightful distinction was that the proprietors should have more elective franchise than non-proprietors, on the Spartan principle of "calling that which is just, equal; not that which is equal, just."

That principle no longer looks so self-evident as it appeared in former times, partly because doubts have arisen whether too much weight had not been allowed in the laws to property, and such a structure given to our usages as allowed the rich to encroach on the poor, and to keep them poor; but mainly because there is an instinctive sense, however obscure and yet inarticulate, that the whole constitution of property, on its present tenures, is injurious, and its influence on persons deteriorating and degrading; that truly the only interest for the consideration of the State is persons; that property will always follow persons; that the highest end of government is the culture of men; and that if men can be educated, the institutions

---

[3] Laban, Jacob, Isaac, and the Midianites are borrowed by Emerson from Genesis 28 – 31. As a youth arriving in the land of Laban, Jacob had no property. Twenty years later, Jacob left with considerable property. Emerson's point that personal and property rights require different laws and officers responds to contemporary nineteenth-century legal debates. The division between criminal and civil law in America reflects Emerson's view here, but many have complained that property law (technically treated in civil courts) defines both criminal and civil law, as well as social attitudes. [Ed.]

will share their improvement and the moral sentiment will write the law of the land.

If it be not easy to settle the equity of this question, the peril is less when we take note of our natural defenses. We are kept by better guards than the vigilance of such magistrates as we commonly elect. Society always consists in greatest part of young and foolish persons. The old, who have seen through the hypocrisy of courts and statesmen, die and leave no wisdom to their sons. They believe their own newspaper, as their fathers did at their age. With such an ignorant and deceivable majority, States would soon run to ruin, but that there are limitations beyond which the folly and ambition of governors cannot go. Things have their laws, as well as men; and things refuse to be trifled with. Property will be protected. Corn will not grow unless it is planted and manured; but the farmer will not plant or hoe it unless the chances are a hundred to one that he will cut and harvest it. Under any forms, persons and property must and will have their just sway. They exert their power, as steadily as matter its attraction. Cover up a pound of earth never so cunningly, divide and subdivide it; melt it to liquid, convert it to gas; it will always weigh a pound; it will always attract and resist other matter by the full virtue of one pound weight: — and the attributes of a person, his wit and his moral energy, will exercise, under any law or extinguishing tyranny, their proper force, — if not overtly, then covertly; if not for the law, then against it; if not wholesomely, then poisonously; with right, or by might.

The boundaries of personal influence it is impossible to fix, as persons are organs of moral or supernatural force. Under the dominion of an idea which possesses the minds of multitudes, as civil freedom, or the religious sentiment, the powers of persons are no longer subjects of calculation. A nation of men unanimously bent on freedom or conquest can easily confound the arithmetic of statists, and achieve extravagant actions, out of all proportion to their means; as the Greeks, the Saracens, the Swiss, the Americans, and the French have done.

In like manner, to every particle of property belongs its own attraction. A cent is the representative of a certain quantity of corn or other commodity. Its value is in the necessities of the animal man. It is so much warmth, so much bread, so much water, so much land. The law may do what it will with the owner of property; its just power will still attach to the cent. The law may in a mad freak say that all shall have power except the owners of property; they shall have no vote. Nevertheless, by a higher law, the property will, year after year, write every statute that respects property. The non-proprietor will be the scribe of the proprietor. What the owners wish to do, the whole power of property will do, either through the law or else in defiance of it. Of course I speak of all the property, not merely of the great estates. When the rich are outvoted, as frequently happens, it is the joint treasury of the poor which exceeds their accumulations. Every man owns something, if it is only a cow, or a wheelbarrow, or his arms, and so has that property to dispose of.[4]

The same necessity which secures the rights of person and property against the malignity or folly of the magistrate, determines the form and methods of governing, which are proper to each nation and to its habit of thought, and nowise transferable to other states of society.[5] In this country, we are very vain of our political institutions, which are singular in this, that they sprung, within the memory of living men, from the character and condition of the people, which they still express with sufficient fidelity, — and we ostentatiously prefer them to any other in history. They are not better, but only fitter for us. We may be wise in asserting the advantage in modern times of the democratic form, but to other states of society, in which religion consecrated the monarchical, that and not this was expedient. Democracy is better for us, because the religious sentiment of the present time accords better with it. Born democrats, we are nowise qualified to judge of monarchy, which, to our fathers living in the monarchical idea, was also relatively right. But our institutions, though in coincidence with the spirit of the age, have not any exemption from the practical defects which have discredited other forms. Every actual State is corrupt. Good men must not obey the laws too well. What satire on government can equal the severity of censure conveyed in the word *politic,* which now for ages has signified *cunning,* intimating that the State is a trick?

The same benign necessity and the same practical abuse appear in the parties, into which each State divides itself, of opponents and defenders of the administration of the government. Parties are also founded on instincts, and have better guides to their own humble aims than the sagacity of their leaders. They have nothing perverse in their origin, but rudely mark some real and lasting relation. We might as wisely reprove the east wind, or the frost, as a political party, whose members, for the most part, could give no account of their position, but stand for the defense of those

---

[4] In this extended meditation on property versus personal rights, Emerson ends up universalizing both, even to the extent of justifying revolution or other military action as the political recourse for overcoming social conditions where property dominates human rights. But the position is clearly meliorist and avoids such important issues as whether citizens without land should be permitted to vote. [Ed.]

[5] Emerson seems to endorse a very modern idea of political systems as historically specific and "socially constructed," but he is making this point in order to defend dynastic monarchies, especially in Europe, as having been appropriate to their times, ignoring thereby the suffering they caused. [Ed.]

interests in which they find themselves. Our quarrel with them begins when they quit this deep natural ground at the bidding of some leader, and obeying personal considerations, throw themselves into the maintenance and defense of points nowise belonging to their system. A party is perpetually corrupted by personality. Whilst we absolve the association from dishonesty, we cannot extend the same charity to their leaders. They reap the rewards of the docility and zeal of the masses which they direct. Ordinarily our parties are parties of circumstance, and not of principle; as the planting interest in conflict with the commercial; the party of capitalists and that of operatives:[6] parties which are identical in their moral character, and which can easily change ground with each other in the support of many of their measures. Parties of principle, as, religious sects, or the party of free-trade, of universal suffrage, of abolition of slavery, of abolition of capital punishment, — degenerate into personalities, or would inspire enthusiasm. The vice of our leading parties in this country (which may be cited as a fair specimen of these societies of opinion) is that they do not plant themselves on the deep and necessary grounds to which they are respectively entitled, but lash themselves to fury in the carrying of some local and momentary measure, nowise useful to the commonwealth. Of the two great parties, which at this hour almost share the nation between them, I should say that one has the best cause, and the other contains the best men.[7] The philosopher, the poet, or the religious man, will of course wish to cast his vote with the democrat, for free-trade, for wide suffrage, for the abolition of legal cruelties in the penal code, and for facilitating in every manner the access of the young and the poor to the sources of wealth and power. But he can rarely accept the persons whom the so-called popular party propose to him as representatives of these liberalities. They have not at heart the ends which give to the name of democracy what hope and virtue are in it. The spirit of our American radicalism is destructive and aimless; it is not loving; it has no ulterior and divine ends, but is destructive only out of hatred and selfishness. On the other side, the conservative party, composed of the most moderate, able, and cultivated part of the

---

[6] Workers. [Ed.]

[7] Democrats and Whigs. At this time, Emerson favored the Democrats, who were represented by such leaders as Thomas Jefferson, Andrew Jackson, and Martin Van Buren. The Whigs were represented by John Quincy Adams, Henry Clay, and William Henry Harrison. There is no exact parallelism between today's political parties and those in Emerson's time, but it is fair to say that the Democrats were more conservative and more committed to property rights than were the Whigs, to whom Emerson is referring later in this paragraph in his remark about "American radicalism" that is "destructive and aimless." [Ed.]

population, is timid, and merely defensive of property. It vindicates no right, it aspires to no real good, it brands no crime, it proposes no generous policy; it does not build, nor write, nor cherish the arts, nor foster religion, nor establish schools, nor encourage science, nor emancipate the slave, nor befriend the poor, or the Indian, or the immigrant. From neither party, when in power, has the world any benefit to expect in science, art, or humanity, at all commensurate with the resources of the nation.

I do not for these defects despair of our republic. We are not at the mercy of any waves of chance. In the strife of ferocious parties, human nature always finds itself cherished; as the children of the convicts at Botany Bay are found to have as healthy a moral sentiment as other children.[8] Citizens of feudal states are alarmed at our democratic institutions lapsing into anarchy, and the older and more cautious among ourselves are learning from Europeans to look with some terror at our turbulent freedom. It is said that in our license of construing the Constitution, and in the despotism of public opinion, we have no anchor; and one foreign observer thinks he has found the safeguard in the sanctity of Marriage among us; and another thinks he has found it in our Calvinism.[9] Fisher Ames expressed the popular security more wisely, when he compared a monarchy and a republic, saying that a monarchy is a merchantman, which sails well, but will sometimes strike on a rock and go to the bottom; whilst a republic is a raft, which would never sink, but then your feet are always in water.[10] No forms can have any dangerous importance whilst we are befriended by the laws of things. It makes no difference how many tons' weight of atmosphere presses on our heads, so long as the same pressure resists it within the lungs. Augment the mass a thousand-fold, it cannot begin to crush us, as long as reaction is equal to action. The fact of two poles, of two forces, centripetal and centrifugal, is universal, and each force by its own activity develops the other. Wild liberty develops iron conscience. Want of liberty, by strengthening

---

[8] In his journals, Emerson commented on reports of the good health and general well-being of the children of British criminals in Botany Bay, Australia. Arguing here against hereditary criminality—an important point in an era that sought physiognomic signs of "criminal nature"—Emerson nonetheless overlooks the fact that most of the British citizens transported to Australia were simply debtors or impoverished, having thus committed "crimes" against British "property" laws. [Ed.]

[9] Emerson is probably referring to Alexis de Tocqueville, *Democracy in America* (1836–40). The Frenchman argued that democratic risks of anarchy and mob rule were mitigated by religion and marriage, reinforcing thereby a patriarchal domestic ideology that was central to gender (and racial) hierarchies of the period (Ferguson 3:219). [Ed.]

[10] Fisher Ames (1758–1808), Federalist lawyer and member of Congress (Ferguson 3:219). [Ed.]

law and decorum, stupefies conscience. "Lynch-law" prevails only where there is greater hardihood and self-subsistency in the leaders. A mob cannot be a permanency; everybody's interest requires that it should not exist, and only justice satisfies all.

We must trust infinitely to the beneficent necessity which shines through all laws. Human nature expresses itself in them as characteristically as in statues, or songs, or railroads, and an abstract of the codes of nations would be a transcript of the common conscience. Governments have their origin in the moral identity of men. Reason for one is seen to be reason for another, and for every other. There is a middle measure which satisfies all parties, be they never so many or so resolute for their own. Every man finds a sanction for his simplest claims and deeds, in decisions of his own mind, which he calls Truth and Holiness. In these decisions all the citizens find a perfect agreement, and only in these; not in what is good to eat, good to wear, good use of time, or what amount of land or of public aid each is entitled to claim. This truth and justice men presently endeavor to make application of to the measuring of land, the apportionment of service, the protection of life and property. Their first endeavors, no doubt, are very awkward. Yet absolute right is the first governor; or, every government is an impure theocracy. The idea after which each community is aiming to make and mend its law, is the will of the wise man. The wise man it cannot find in nature, and it makes awkward but earnest efforts to secure his government by contrivance; as by causing the entire people to give their voices on every measure; or by a double choice to get the representation of the whole; or by a selection of the best citizens; or to secure the advantages of efficiency and internal peace by confiding the government to one, who may himself select his agents. All forms of government symbolize an immortal government, common to all dynasties and independent of numbers, perfect where two men exist, perfect where there is only one man.[11]

Every man's nature is a sufficient advertisement to him of the character of his fellows. My right and my wrong is their right and their wrong. Whilst I do what is fit for me, and abstain from what is unfit, my neighbor and I shall often agree in our means, and work together for a time to one end. But whenever I find my dominion over myself not sufficient for me, and undertake the direction of him also, I overstep the truth, and come into false relations to him. I may have so much more skill or strength than he that he

---

[11] Emerson judged the best social and political models to be derived from the individual and his or her interpersonal relations with another individual. "Friendship," a topic on which Emerson and Thoreau wrote essays and which Margaret Fuller would incorporate into *Woman in the Nineteenth Century,* is thus an elementary social category for these transcendentalists. [Ed.]

cannot express adequately his sense of wrong, but it is a lie, and hurts like a lie both him and me. Love and nature cannot maintain the assumption; it must be executed by a practical lie, namely by force. This undertaking for another is the blunder which stands in colossal ugliness in the governments of the world. It is the same thing in numbers, as in a pair, only not quite so intelligible. I can see well enough a great difference between my setting myself down to a self-control, and my going to make somebody else act after my views; but when a quarter of the human race assume to tell me what I must do, I may be too much disturbed by the circumstances to see so clearly the absurdity of their command. Therefore all public ends look vague and quixotic beside private ones. For any laws but those which men make for themselves are laughable. If I put myself in the place of my child, and we stand in one thought and see that things are thus or thus, that perception is law for him and me. We are both there, both act. But if, without carrying him into the thought, I look over into his plot, and, guessing how it is with him, ordain this or that, he will never obey me. This is the history of governments,—one man does something which is to bind another. A man who cannot be acquainted with me, taxes me; looking from afar at me, ordains that a part of my labor shall go to this or that whimsical end,— not as I, but as he happens to fancy. Behold the consequence. Of all, debts men are least willing to pay the taxes. What a satire is this on government! Everywhere they think they get their money's worth, except for these.

Hence the less government we have the better,—the fewer laws, and the less confided power.[12] The antidote to this abuse of formal government is the influence of private character, the growth of the Individual; the appearance of the principal to supersede the proxy; the appearance of the wise man, of whom the existing government is, it must be owned, but a shabby imitation. That which all things tend to educe; which freedom, cultivation, intercourse, revolutions, go to form and deliver, is character; that is the end of Nature, to reach unto this coronation of her king. To educate the wise man the State exists, and with the appearance of the wise man, the State expires. The appearance of character makes the State unnecessary. The wise man is the State. He needs no army, fort, or navy,—he loves men too well; no bribe, or feast, or palace, to draw friends to him; no vantage ground, no favorable circumstance. He needs no library, for he has not done thinking; no church, for he is a prophet; no statute-book, for he has the lawgiver; no money, for he is value; no road, for he is at home where he is; no experience, for the life of the creator shoots through him, and looks

---

[12]Emerson articulates what would become in the twentieth century the classic "libertarian" political position. [Ed.]

from his eyes. He has no personal friends, for he who has the spell to draw the prayer and piety of all men unto him needs not husband and educate a few to share with him a select and poetic life. His relation to men is angelic; his memory is myrrh to them; his presence, frankincense and flowers.

We think our civilization near its meridian, but we are yet only at the cock-crowing and the morning star. In our barbarous society the influence of character is in its infancy. As a political power, as the rightful lord who is to tumble all rulers from their chairs, its presence is hardly yet suspected. Malthus and Ricardo quite omit it; the Annual Register is silent; in the Conversations' Lexicon, it is not set down; the President's Message, the Queen's Speech, have not mentioned it; and yet it is never nothing.[13] Every thought which genius and piety throw into the world, alters the world. The gladiators in the lists of power feel, through all their frocks of force and simulation, the presence of worth. I think the very strife of trade and ambition is confession of this divinity; and successes in those fields are the poor amends, the fig-leaf with which the shamed soul attempts to hide its nakedness. I find the like unwilling homage in all quarters. It is because we know how much is due from us that we are impatient to show some petty talent as a substitute for worth. We are haunted by a conscience of this right to grandeur of character, and are false to it. But each of us has some talent, can do somewhat useful, or graceful, or formidable, or amusing, or lucrative. That we do, as an apology to others and to ourselves, for not reaching the mark of a good and equal life. But it does not satisfy *us*, whilst we thrust it on the notice of our companions. It may throw dust in their eyes, but does not smooth our own brow, or give us the tranquillity of the strong when we walk abroad. We do penance as we go. Our talent is a sort of expiation, and we are constrained to reflect on our splendid moment with a certain humiliation, as somewhat too fine, and not as one act of many acts, a fair expression of our permanent energy. Most persons of ability meet in society with a kind of tacit appeal. Each seems to say, "I am not all here." Senators and presidents have climbed so high with pain enough, not because they think the place specially agreeable, but as an apology for real worth, and to vindicate their manhood in our eyes. This conspicuous chair is their compensation to themselves for being of a poor, cold, hard nature. They must do what they can. Like one class of forest animals, they have

---

[13] Thomas Robert Malthus (d.1834) and David Ricardo (d. 1823) were the leading English economists of the previous generation. The *Annual Register* was, like an almanach, an English account of annual events, and the *Conversations Lexicon* was a German encyclopedia (Ferguson 3:220). In Emerson's judgment, none of these sources of empirical evidence and information about societies takes into account the spiritual individualism of the self-reliant man as the basis for a well-ordered society. [Ed.]

nothing but a prehensile tail; climb they must, or crawl. If a man found himself so rich-natured that he could enter into strict relations with the best persons and make life serene around him by the dignity and sweetness of his behavior, could he afford to circumvent the favor of the caucus and the press, and covet relations so hollow and pompous as those of a politician? Surely nobody would be a charlatan, who could afford to be sincere.

The tendencies of the times favor the idea of self-government, and leave the individual, for all code, to the rewards and penalties of his own constitution, which work with more energy than we believe whilst we depend on artificial restraints. The movement in this direction has been very marked in modern history. Much has been blind and discreditable, but the nature of the revolution is not affected by the vices of the revolters; for this is a purely moral force. It was never adopted by any party in history, neither can be. It separates the individual from all party, and unites him at the same time to the race. It promises a recognition of higher rights than those of personal freedom, or the security of property. A man has a right to be employed, to be trusted, to be loved, to be revered. The power of love, as the basis of a State, has never been tried. We must not imagine that all things are lapsing into confusion if every tender protestant be not compelled to bear his part in certain social conventions; nor doubt that roads can be built, letters carried, and the fruit of labor secured, when the government of force is at an end. Are our methods now so excellent that all competition is hopeless? Could not a nation of friends even devise better ways? On the other hand, let not the most conservative and timid fear anything from a premature surrender of the bayonet and the system of force. For, according to the order of nature, which is quite superior to our will, it stands thus; there will always be a government of force where men are selfish; and when they are pure enough to abjure the code of force, they will be wise enough to see how these public ends of the post-office, of the highway, of commerce and the exchange of property, of museums and libraries, of institutions of art and science, can be answered.

We live in a very low state of the world, and pay unwilling tribute to governments founded on force. There is not, among the most religious and instructed men of the most religious and civil nations, a reliance on the moral sentiment and a sufficient belief in the unity of things, to persuade them that society can be maintained without artificial restraints, as well as the solar system; or that the private citizen might be reasonable and a good neighbor, without the hint of a jail or a confiscation. What is strange too, there never was in any man sufficient faith in the power of rectitude to inspire him with the broad design of renovating the State on the principle of right and love. All those who have pretended this design have been partial reformers, and have admitted in some manner the supremacy of the bad

State. I do not call to mind a single human being who has steadily denied the authority of the laws, on the simple ground of his own moral nature. Such designs, full of genius and full of fate as they are, are not entertained except avowedly as air-pictures. If the individual who exhibits them dare to think them practicable, he disgusts scholars and churchmen; and men of talent and women of superior sentiments cannot hide their contempt. Not the less does nature continue to fill the heart of youth with suggestions of this enthusiasm, and there are now men,—if indeed I can speak in the plural number,—more exactly, I will say, I have just been conversing with one man, to whom no weight of adverse experience will make it for a moment appear impossible that thousands of human beings might exercise towards each other the grandest and truest sentiments, as well as a knot of friends, or a pair of lovers.[14]

Experience
1844

The lords of life, the lords of life, —
I saw them pass
In their own guise,
Like and unlike,
Portly and grim, —
Use and Surprise,
Surface and Dream,
Succession swift and spectral Wrong,
Temperament without a tongue,
And the inventor of the game
Omnipresent without name; —
Some to see, some to be guessed,
They marched from east to west:

Selections from Ralph Waldo Emerson: An Organic Anthology. Ed. Stephen E. Whicher. Riverside Edition. Boston: Houghton, 1957.

[14]Emerson probably refers to the "adverse experience" of Amos Bronson Alcott, who despite the failure of his utopian community, Fruitlands, in the winter of 1843 remained committed to his progressive ideals. [Ed.]

Little man, least of all,
Among the legs of his guardians tall,
Walked about with puzzled look.

Him by the hand dear Nature took;
Dearest Nature, strong and kind,
Whispered, "Darling, never mind!
Tomorrow they will wear another face,
The founder thou; these are thy race!"

Where do we find ourselves? In a series of which we do not know the extremes, and believe that it has none. We wake and find ourselves on a stair; there are stairs below us, which seem to have ascended; there are stairs above us, many a one, which go upward and out of sight. But the Genius which according to the old belief stands at the door by which we enter, and gives us the lethe to drink, that we may tell no tales, mixed the cup too strongly, and we cannot shake off the lethargy now at noonday.[1] Sleep lingers all our lifetime about our eyes, as night hovers all day in the boughs of the fir-tree. All things swim and glimmer. Our life is not so much threatened as our perception. Ghostlike we glide through nature, and should not know our place again. Did our birth fall in some fit of indigence and frugality in nature, that she was so sparing of her fire and so liberal of her earth that it appears to us that we lack the affirmative principle, and though we have health and reason, yet we have no superfluity of spirit for new creation? We have enough to live and bring the year about, but not an ounce to impart or to invest. Ah that our Genius were a little more of a genius! We are like millers on the lower levels of a stream, when the factories above them have exhausted the water. We too fancy that the upper people must have raised their dams.

If any of us knew what we were doing, or where we are going, then when we think we best know! We do not know today whether we are busy or idle. In times when we thought ourselves indolent, we have afterwards discovered that much was accomplished and much was begun in us. All our days are so unprofitable while they pass, that 'tis wonderful where or when we ever got anything of this which we call wisdom, poetry, virtue. We never

---

[1] Plato, *Republic* 10.16, which is the concluding section. Dead souls are invited to choose the human or animal forms they wish to have in their next incarnation, then are led by the Genius (or daemon) to the River Lethe to drink forgetfulness of their past lives (Ferguson 3:181). [Ed.]

got it on any dated calendar day. Some heavenly days must have been intercalated somewhere, like those that Hermes won with dice of the Moon, that Osiris might be born.[2] It is said all martyrdoms looked mean when they were suffered. Every ship is a romantic object, except that we sail in. Embark, and the romance quits our vessel and hangs on every other sail in the horizon. Our life looks trivial, and we shun to record it. Men seem to have learned of the horizon the art of perpetual retreating and reference. "Yonder uplands are rich pasturage, and my neighbor has fertile meadow, but my field," says the querulous farmer, "only holds the world together." I quote another man's saying; unluckily that other withdraws himself in the same way, and quotes me. 'Tis the trick of nature thus to degrade today; a good deal of buzz, and somewhere a result slipped magically in. Every roof is agreeable to the eye until it is lifted; then we find tragedy and moaning women and hard-eyed husbands and deluges of lethe, and the men ask, "What's the news?" as if the old were so bad. How many individuals can we count in society? how many actions? how many opinions? So much of our time is preparation, so much is routine, and so much retrospect, that the pith of each man's genius contracts itself to a very few hours. The history of literature — take the net result of Tiraboschi, Warton, or Schlegel — is a sum of very few ideas and of very few original tales; all the rest being variation of these.[3] So in this great society wide lying around us, a critical analysis would find very few spontaneous actions. It is almost all custom and gross sense. There are even few opinions, and these seem organic in the speakers, and do not disturb the universal necessity.

What opium is instilled into all disaster! It shows formidable as we approach it, but there is at last no rough rasping friction, but the most slippery sliding surfaces; we fall soft on a thought; *Ate Dea* is gentle, —

"Over men's heads walking aloft,
With tender feet treading so soft."[4]

---

[2]Plutarch, "Of Isis and Osiris," *Morals*, tells the myth of how Hermes gambled with the Moon and won "five new days," which were the birthdays of the Egyptian gods, on the first of which Osiris was born. The only "intercalary day" that remains in the modern calendar is 29 February on leap years (Ferguson 3:181). [Ed.]

[3]Emerson is referring to three voluminous literary histories by Girolamo Tiraboschi (on Italian literature), Thomas Warton (on English poetry), and Friedrich von Schlegel (on ancient and recent literature). [Ed.]

[4]Ate Dea is the goddess Ate in Homer, who torments humankind with suffering. The quote is from Robert Burton, *Anatomy of Melancholy* (1621), in which he translates these lines from Lucian's classical Roman comedy *Podagra* (*Gout*) (Ferguson 3:182). [Ed.]

People grieve and bemoan themselves, but it is not half so bad with them as they say. There are moods in which we court suffering, in the hope that here at least we shall find reality, sharp peaks and edges of truth. But it turns out to be scene-painting and counterfeit. The only thing grief has taught me is to know how shallow it is. That, like all the rest, plays about the surface, and never introduces me into the reality, for contact with which we would even pay the costly price of sons and lovers. Was it Boscovich[5] who found out that bodies never come in contact? Well, souls never touch their objects. An innavigable sea washes with silent waves between us and the things we aim at and converse with. Grief too will make us idealists. In the death of my son, now more than two years ago, I seem to have lost a beautiful estate,—no more.[6] I cannot get it nearer to me. If tomorrow I should be informed of the bankruptcy of my principal debtors, the loss of my property would be a great inconvenience to me, perhaps, for many years; but it would leave me as it found me,—neither better nor worse. So is it with this calamity; it does not touch me; something which I fancied was a part of me, which could not be torn away without tearing me nor enlarged without enriching me, falls off from me and leaves no scar. It was caducous.[7] I grieve that grief can teach me nothing, nor carry me one step into real nature. The Indian who was laid under a curse that the wind should not blow on him, nor water flow to him, nor fire burn him, is a type of us all.[8] The dearest events are summer-rain, and we the Para coats[9] that shed every drop. Nothing is left us now but death. We look to that with a grim satisfaction, saying, There at least is reality that will not dodge us.

I take this evanescence and lubricity of all objects, which lets them slip through our fingers then when we clutch hardest, to be the most unhandsome part of our condition. Nature does not like to be observed, and likes that we should be her fools and playmates. We may have the sphere for our cricket-ball, but not a berry for our philosophy. Direct strokes she never

---

[5] R. J. Boscovich, a Jesuit mathematician and physicist who in 1758 defined matter "as composed of indivisible and mutually repulsive atoms" (Ferguson 3:182). [Ed.]

[6] Emerson's son Waldo died on 27 January 1842. [Ed.]

[7] Zoological and botanical term for organs and parts that fall off early; from the Latin *caducus* ("falling"). Emerson attempts to naturalize the death of Waldo, suggesting that it must have been part of Emerson's very being. [Ed.]

[8] In Robert Southey's poem *The Curse of Kehama* (1810), the Hindu ruler and priest Kehama curses Ladurlad with an apparent blessing—that he shall be protected from the wind, fire, and flood but thereby kept from the joys of earthly existence and thus yearn for death. [Ed.]

[9] Rubber raincoats, so named for Pará (now Belém), Brazil. [Ed.]

gave us power to make; all our blows glance, all our hits are accidents. Our relations to each other are oblique and casual.

Dream delivers us to dream, and there is no end to illusion. Life is a train of moods like a string of beads, and as we pass through them they prove to be many-colored lenses which paint the world their own hue, and each shows only what lies in its focus. From the mountain you see the mountain. We animate what we can, and we see only what we animate. Nature and books belong to the eyes that see them. It depends on the mood of the man whether he shall see the sunset or the fine poem. There are always sunsets, and there is always genius; but only a few hours so serene that we can relish nature or criticism. The more or less depends on structure or temperament. Temperament is the iron wire on which the beads are strung. Of what use is fortune or talent to a cold and defective nature? Who cares what sensibility or discrimination a man has at some time shown, if he falls asleep in his chair? or if he laugh and giggle? or if he apologize? or is infected with egotism? or thinks of his dollar? or cannot go by food? or has gotten a child in his boyhood? Of what use is genius, if the organ is too convex or too concave and cannot find a focal distance within the actual horizon of human life? Of what use, if the brain is too cold or too hot, and the man does not care enough for results, to stimulate him to experiment, and hold him up in it? or if the web is too finely woven, too irritable by pleasure and pain, so that life stagnates from too much reception without due outlet? Of what use to make heroic vows of amendment, if the same old law-breaker is to keep them? What cheer can the religious sentiment yield, when that is suspected to be secretly dependent on the seasons of the year and the state of the blood? I knew a witty physician who found the creed in the biliary duct, and used to affirm that if there was disease in the liver, the man became a Calvinist, and if that organ was sound, he became a Unitarian. Very mortifying is the reluctant experience that some unfriendly excess or imbecility neutralizes the promise of genius. We see young men who owe us a new world, so readily and lavishly they promise, but they never acquit the debt; they die young and dodge the account; or if they live, they lose themselves in the crowd.

Temperament also enters fully into the system of illusions and shuts us in a prison of glass which we cannot see. There is an optical illusion about every person we meet. In truth, they are all creatures of given temperament, which will appear in a given character, whose boundaries they will never pass; but we look at them, they seem alive, and we presume there is impulse in them. In the moment, it seems impulse; in the year, in the lifetime, it turns out to be a certain uniform tune which the revolving barrel of the music-box must play. Men resist the conclusion in the morning, but adopt it as the evening wears on, that temper prevails over everything of time, place, and condition, and is inconsumable in the flames of religion. Some modifications the moral sentiment avails to impose, but the individual texture holds its dominion, if not to bias the moral judgments, yet to fix the measure of activity and of enjoyment.

I thus express the law as it is read from the platform of ordinary life, but must not leave it without noticing the capital exception. For temperament is a power which no man willingly hears any one praise but himself. On the platform of physics we cannot resist the contracting influences of so-called science. Temperament puts all divinity to rout. I know the mental proclivity of physicians. I hear the chuckle of the phrenologists.[10] Theoretic kidnappers and slave-drivers, they esteem each man the victim of another, who winds him round his finger by knowing the law of his being; and, by such cheap signboards as the color of his beard or the slope of his occiput, reads the inventory of his fortunes and character. The grossest ignorance does not disgust like this impudent knowingness. The physicians say they are not materialists; but they are:—Spirit is matter reduced to an extreme thinness: O *so* thin!—But the definition of *spiritual* should be, *that which is its own evidence*. What notions do they attach to love! what to religion! One would not willingly pronounce these words in their hearing, and give them the occasion to profane them. I saw a gracious gentleman who adapts his conversation to the form of the head of the man he talks with! I had fancied that the value of life lay in its inscrutable possibilities; in the fact that I never know, in addressing myself to a new individual, what may befall me. I carry the keys of my castle in my hand, ready to throw them at the feet of my lord, whenever and in what disguise soever he shall appear. I know he is in the neighborhood, hidden among vagabonds. Shall I preclude my future by taking a high seat and kindly adapting my conversation to the shape of heads? When I come to that, the doctors shall buy me for a cent. — "But, sir, medical history; the report to the Institute; the proven facts!" —I distrust the facts and the inferences. Temperament is the veto or limitation-power in the constitution, very justly applied to restrain an opposite excess in the constitution, but absurdly offered as a bar to original equity. When virtue is in presence, all subordinate powers sleep. On its own level, or in view of nature, temperament is final. I see not, if one be once caught in this trap of so-called sciences, any escape for the man from the links of the

---

[10] Phrenologists claimed to read personality traits and mental faculties in the shape and bumps of the head. [Ed.]

chain of physical necessity. Given such an embryo, such a history must follow. On this platform one lives in a sty of sensualism, and would soon come to suicide. But it is impossible that the creative power should exclude itself. Into every intelligence there is a door which is never closed, through which the creator passes. The intellect, seeker of absolute truth, or the heart, lover of absolute good, intervenes for our succor, and at one whisper of these high powers, we awake from ineffectual struggles with this nightmare. We hurl it into its own hell, and cannot again contract ourselves to so base a state.

The secret of the illusoriness is in the necessity of a succession of moods or objects. Gladly we would anchor, but the anchorage is quicksand. This onward trick of nature is too strong for us: *Pero si muove*.[11] When at night I look at the moon and stars, I seem stationary, and they to hurry. Our love of the real draws us to permanence, but health of body consists in circulation, and sanity of mind in variety or facility of association. We need change of objects. Dedication to one thought is quickly odious. We house with the insane, and must humor them; then conversation dies out. Once I took such delight in Montaigne that I thought I should not need any other book; before that, in Shakespeare; then in Plutarch; then in Plotinus; at one time in Bacon; afterwards in Goethe; even in Bettine;[12] but now I turn the pages of either of them languidly, whilst I still cherish their genius. So with pictures; each will bear an emphasis of attention once, which it cannot retain, though we fain would continue to be pleased in that manner. How strongly I have felt of pictures that when you have seen one well, you must take your leave of it; you shall never see it again. I have had good lessons from pictures, which I have since seen without emotion or remark. A deduction must be made from the opinion, which even the wise express of a new book or occurrence. Their opinion gives me tidings of their mood, and some vague guess at the new fact, but is nowise to be trusted as the lasting relation between that intellect and that thing. The child asks, "Mamma, why don't I like the story as well as when you told it me yesterday?" Alas, child, it is even so with the oldest cherubim of knowledge. But will it answer thy question to say, Because thou wert born to a whole, and this story is a particular? The reason of the pain this discovery causes us (and we

---

[11] "Nevertheless it moves." Galileo was reputed to have said this just after recanting what the Inquisition termed his "heretical" theory that the earth revolves around the sun. [Ed.]

[12] Elizabeth (Bettina) Brentano von Arnim's (1785–1859) fictionalized account of her fascination with Goethe, *Goethe's Correspondence with a Child,* was popular among the transcendentalists. [Ed.]

make it late in respect to works of art and intellect) is the plaint of tragedy which murmurs from it in regard to persons, to friendship and love.

That immobility and absence of elasticity which we find in the arts, we find with more pain in the artist. There is no power of expansion in men. Our friends early appear to us as representatives of certain ideas, which they never pass or exceed. They stand on the brink of the ocean of thought and power, but they never take the single step that would bring them there. A man is like a bit of Labrador spar,[13] which has no lustre as you turn it in your hand until you come to a particular angle; then it shows deep and beautiful colors. There is no adaptation or universal applicability in men, but each has his special talent, and the mastery of successful men consists in adroitly keeping themselves where and when that turn shall be oftenest to be practised. We do what we must, and call it by the best names we can, and would fain have the praise of having intended the result which ensues. I cannot recall any form of man who is not superfluous sometimes. But is not this pitiful? Life is not worth the taking, to do tricks in.

Of course, it needs the whole society to give the symmetry we seek. The parti-colored wheel must revolve very fast to appear white. Something is learned too by conversing with so much folly and defect. In fine, whoever loses, we are always of the gaining party. Divinity is behind our failures and follies also. The plays of children are nonsense, but very educative nonsense. So it is with the largest and solemnest things, with commerce, government, church, marriage, and so with the history of every man's bread, and the ways by which he is to come by it. Like a bird which alights nowhere, but hops perpetually from bough to bough, is the Power which abides in no man and in no woman, but for a moment speaks from this one, and for another moment from that one.

But what help from these fineries or pedantries? What help from thought? Life is not dialectics. We, I think, in these times, have had lessons enough of the futility of criticism. Our young people have thought and written much on labor and reform, and for all that they have written, neither the world nor themselves have got on a step. Intellectual tasting of life will not supersede muscular activity. If a man should consider the nicety of the passage of a piece of bread down his throat, he would starve. At Education-Farm,[14] the noblest theory of life sat on the noblest figures of young men and maidens, quite powerless and melancholy. It would not rake or pitch a

---

[13] A crystalline and nonlustrous mineral, like calcite. [Ed.]

[14] The complete name of the utopian community commonly called Brook Farm (1841–47) was Brook Farm Institute of Agriculture and Education. Brook Farm was built on the principles of the French socialist, Charles Fourier (1772–1837). Nathaniel Hawthorne

ton of hay; it would not rub down a horse; and the men and maidens it left pale and hungry. A political orator wittily compared our party promises to western roads, which opened stately enough, with planted trees on either side, to tempt the traveler, but soon became narrow and narrower and ended in a squirrel-track and ran up a tree. So does culture with us; it ends in headache. Unspeakably sad and barren does life look to those, who a few months ago were dazzled with the splendor of the promise of the times. "There is now no longer any right course of action nor any self-devotion left among the Iranis."[15] Objections and criticism we have had our fill of. There are objections to every course of life and action, and the practical wisdom infers an indifferency, from the omnipresence of objection. The whole frame of things preaches indifferency. Do not craze yourself with thinking, but go about your business anywhere. Life is not intellectual or critical, but sturdy. Its chief good is for well-mixed people who can enjoy what they find, without question. Nature hates peeping, and our mothers speak her very sense when they say, "Children, eat your victuals, and say no more of it." To fill the hour,—that is happiness; to fill the hour and leave no crevice for a repentance or an approval. We live amid surfaces, and the true art of life is to skate well on them. Under the oldest mouldiest conventions, a man of native force prospers just as well as in the newest world, and that by skill of handling and treatment. He can take hold anywhere. Life itself is a mixture of power and form, and will not bear the least excess of either. To finish the moment, to find the journey's end in every step of the road, to live the greatest number of good hours, is wisdom. It is not the part of men, but of fanatics, or of mathematicians, if you will, to say that, the shortness of life considered, it is not worth caring whether for so short a duration we were sprawling in want or sitting high. Since our office is with moments, let us husband them. Five minutes of today are worth as much to me as five minutes in the next millennium. Let us be poised, and wise, and our own, today. Let us treat the men and women well; treat them as if they were real; perhaps they are. Men live in their fancy, like drunkards whose hands are too soft and tremulous for successful labor. It is a tempest of fancies, and the only ballast I know is a respect to the present hour. Without any shadow of doubt, amidst this vertigo of shows and politics, I settle myself ever the firmer in the creed that we should not postpone

---

was briefly a member, and in his novel *The Blithedale Romance* (1852) he parodied its utopian aims as well as Margaret Fuller, in the character of Zenobia. [Ed.]

[15] Quoted from *The Desatir, or Sacred Writings of the Ancient Persian Prophets*, trans. Jonathan Duncan and Mulla Firuz Bin Kaus, 2 vols. (Bombay, 1818), a compendium of Parsi (Indian Zoroastrian) sacred lore. [Ed.]

and refer and wish, but do broad justice where we are, by whomsoever we deal with, accepting our actual companions and circumstances, however humble or odious, as the mystic officials to whom the universe has delegated its whole pleasure for us. If these are mean and malignant, their contentment, which is the last victory of justice, is a more satisfying echo to the heart than the voice of poets and the casual sympathy of admirable persons. I think that however a thoughtful man may suffer from the defects and absurdities of his company, he cannot without affectation deny to any set of men and women a sensibility to extraordinary merit. The coarse and frivolous have an instinct of superiority, if they have not a sympathy, and honor it in their blind capricious way with sincere homage.

The fine young people despise life, but in me, and in such as with me are free from dyspepsia, and to whom a day is a sound and solid good, it is a great excess of politeness to look scornful and to cry for company. I am grown by sympathy a little eager and sentimental, but leave me alone and I should relish every hour and what it brought me, the potluck of the day, as heartily as the oldest gossip in the bar-room. I am thankful for small mercies. I compared notes with one of my friends who expects everything of the universe and is disappointed when anything is less than the best, and I found that I begin at the other extreme, expecting nothing, and am always full of thanks for moderate goods. I accept the clangor and jangle of contrary tendencies. I find my account in sots and bores also. They give a reality to the circumjacent picture, which such a vanishing meteorous appearance can ill spare. In the morning I awake and find the old world, wife, babes and mother, Concord and Boston, the dear old spiritual world, and even the dear old devil not far off. If we will take the good we find, asking no questions, we shall have heaping measures. The great gifts are not got by analysis. Everything good is on the highway. The middle region of our being is the temperate zone. We may climb into the thin and cold realm of pure geometry and lifeless science, or sink into that of sensation. Between these extremes is the equator of life, of thought, of spirit, of poetry, — a narrow belt. Moreover, in popular experience everything good is on the highway. A collector peeps into all the picture-shops of Europe for a landscape of Poussin, a crayon-sketch of Salvator; but the Transfiguration, the Last Judgment, the Communion of Saint Jerome,[16] and what are as transcendent as these, are on the walls of the Vatican, the Uffizi, or the Louvre, where every footman

---

[16] Salvator Rosa (1615–73); Raphael's painting *The Transfiguration of Christ* in the Vatican; Michelangelo's *The Last Judgment* in the Sistine Chapel of the Vatican; and Domenichino's *Communion of Saint Jerome* also in the Vatican (Ferguson 3:187–188). [Ed.]

may see them; to say nothing of Nature's pictures in every street, of sunsets and sunrises every day, and the sculpture of the human body never absent. A collector recently bought at public auction, in London, for one hundred and fifty-seven guineas,[17] an autograph of Shakespeare; but for nothing a school-boy can read Hamlet and can detect secrets of highest concernment yet unpublished therein. I think I will never read any but the commonest books, — the Bible, Homer, Dante, Shakespeare, and Milton. Then we are impatient of so public a life and planet, and run hither and thither for nooks and secrets. The imagination delights in the woodcraft of Indians, trappers, and bee-hunters. We fancy that we are strangers, and not so intimately domesticated in the planet as the wild man and the wild beast and bird. But the exclusion reaches them also; reaches the climbing, flying, gliding, feathered and four-footed man. Fox and woodchuck, hawk and snipe and bittern, when nearly seen, have no more root in the deep world than man, and are just such superficial tenants of the globe. Then the new molecular philosophy shows astronomical interspaces betwixt atom and atom, shows that the world is all outside; it has no inside.[18]

The mid-world is best. Nature, as we know her, is no saint. The lights of the church, the ascetics, Gentoos and corn-eaters,[19] she does not distinguish by any favor. She comes eating and drinking and sinning. Her darlings, the great, the strong, the beautiful, are not children of our law; do not come out of the Sunday School, nor weigh their food, nor punctually keep the commandments. If we will be strong with her strength, we must not harbor such disconsolate consciences, borrowed too from the consciences of other nations. We must set up the strong present tense against all the rumors of wrath, past or to come. So many things are unsettled which it is of the first importance to settle; — and, pending their settlement, we will do as we do. Whilst the debate goes forward on the equity of commerce, and will not be closed for a century or two, New and Old England may keep shop. Law of copyright and international copyright is to be discussed, and in the interim we will sell our books for the most we can.[20] Expediency of literature, reason of literature, lawfulness of writing down a thought, is questioned; much is to say on both sides, and, while the fight waxes hot, thou, dearest scholar, stick to thy foolish task, add a line every hour, and between

---

[17] British gold coins minted for trade with Africa and worth £1.05 a piece. Emerson obviously thought this was a princely sum for Shakespeare's mere autograph. [Ed.]

[18] John Dalton's (1766–1844) atomic theory. [Ed.]

[19] "Gentoos": an archaic term for Hindus, who abstain from meat. "Corn-eaters": a contemporary term for vegetarians (Ferguson 3:188). [Ed.]

[20] At that time there was no international copyright law to protect authors' rights to their publications, and cheap, pirated editions were common. [Ed.]

whiles add a line. Right to hold land, right of property, is disputed, and the conventions convene, and before the vote is taken, dig away in your garden, and spend your earnings as a waif or godsend to all serene and beautiful purposes. Life itself is a bubble and a skepticism, and a sleep within a sleep. Grant it, and as much more as they will,—but thou, God's darling! heed thy private dream; thou wilt not be missed in the scorning and skepticism; there are enough of them; stay there in thy closet and toil until the rest are agreed what to do about it. Thy sickness, they say, and thy puny habit require that thou do this or avoid that, but know that thy life is a flitting state, a tent for a night, and do thou, sick or well, finish that stint. Thou art sick, but shalt not be worse, and the universe, which holds thee dear, shall be the better.

Human life is made up of the two elements, power and form, and the proportion must be invariably kept, if we would have it sweet and sound. Each of these elements in excess makes a mischief as hurtful as its defect. Everything runs to excess; every good quality is noxious if unmixed, and, to carry the danger to the edge of ruin, nature causes each man's peculiarity to superabound. Here, among the farms, we adduce the scholars as examples of this treachery. They are nature's victims of expression. You who see the artist, the orator, the poet, too near, and find their life no more excellent than that of mechanics or farmers, and themselves victims of partiality, very hollow and haggard, and pronounce them failures, not heroes, but quacks,—conclude very reasonably that these arts are not for man, but are disease. Yet nature will not bear you out. Irresistible nature made men such, and makes legions more of such, every day. You love the boy reading in a book, gazing at a drawing or a cast; yet what are these millions who read and behold, but incipient writers and sculptors? Add a little more of that quality which now reads and sees, and they will seize the pen and chisel. And if one remembers how innocently he began to be an artist, he perceives that nature joined with his enemy. A man is a golden impossibility. The line he must walk is a hair's breadth. The wise through excess of wisdom is made a fool.

How easily, if fate would suffer it, we might keep forever these beautiful limits, and adjust ourselves, once for all, to the perfect calculation of the kingdom of known cause and effect. In the street and in the newspapers, life appears so plain a business that manly resolution and adherence to the multiplication-table through all weathers will insure success. But ah! presently comes a day, or is it only a half-hour, with its angel-whispering,— which discomfits the conclusions of nations and of years! Tomorrow again every thing looks real and angular, the habitual standards are reinstated, common-sense is as rare as genius,—is the basis of genius, and experience is hands and feet to every enterprise;—and yet, he who should do his business on this understanding would be quickly bankrupt. Power keeps quite another road than the turnpikes of choice and will, namely, the subterranean and invisible tunnels and channels of life. It is ridiculous that we are diplomatists, and doctors, and considerate people; there are no dupes like these. Life is a series of surprises, and would not be worth taking or keeping if it were not. God delights to isolate us every day, and hide from us the past and the future. We would look about us, but with grand politeness he draws down before us an impenetrable screen of purest sky, and another behind us of purest sky. "You will not remember," he seems to say, "and you will not expect." All good conversation, manners and action come from a spontaneity which forgets usages and makes the moment great. Nature hates calculators; her methods are saltatory and impulsive. Man lives by pulses; our organic movements are such; and the chemical and ethereal agents are undulatory and alternate; and the mind goes antagonizing on, and never prospers but by fits. We thrive by casualties.[21] Our chief experiences have been casual . The most attractive class of people are those who are powerful obliquely and not by the direct stroke; men of genius, but not yet accredited; one gets the cheer of their light without paying too great a tax. Theirs is the beauty of the bird or the morning light, and not of art. In the thought of genius there is always a surprise; and the moral sentiment is well called "the newness," for it is never other; as new to the oldest intelligence as to the young child; — "the kingdom that cometh without observation."[22] In like manner, for practical success, there must not be too much design. A man will not be observed in doing that which he can do best. There is a certain magic about his properest action which stupefies your powers of observation, so that though it is done before you, you wist not of it. The art of life has a pudency, and will not be exposed. Every man is an impossibility until he is born; every thing impossible until we see a success. The ardors of piety agree at last with the coldest skepticism, — that nothing is of us or our works, — that all is of God. Nature will not spare us the smallest leaf of laurel. All writing comes by the grace of God, and all doing and having. I would gladly be moral and keep due metes and bounds, which I dearly love, and allow the most to the will of man; but I have set my heart on honesty in this chapter, and I can see nothing at last, in success or failure, than more or less of vital force supplied from the Eternal. The results of life are uncalculated and uncalculable. The years teach much which the days never know. The persons who compose our company converse, and

---

[21] "Casualties" are chance occurrences or contingencies. [Orig. ed.]

[22] Cf. Luke 17.20–21. [Ed.]

come and go, and design and execute many things, and somewhat comes of it all, but an unlooked-for result. The individual is always mistaken. He designed many things, and drew in other persons as coadjutors, quarreled with some or all, blundered much, and something is done; all are a little advanced, but the individual is always mistaken. It turns out somewhat new and very unlike what he promised himself.

The ancients, struck with this irreducibleness of the elements of human life to calculation, exalted Chance into a divinity; but that is to stay too long at the spark, which glitters truly at one point, but the universe is warm with the latency of the same fire. The miracle of life which will not be expounded but will remain a miracle, introduces a new element. In the growth of the embryo, Sir Everard Home,[23] I think, noticed that the evolution was not from one central point, but coactive from three or more points. Life has no memory. That which proceeds in succession might be remembered, but that which is coexistent, or ejaculated from a deeper cause, as yet far from being conscious, knows not its own tendency. So is it with us, now skeptical or without unity, because immersed in forms and effects all seeming to be of equal yet hostile value, and now religious, whilst in the reception of spiritual law. Bear with these distractions, with this coetaneous growth of the parts; they will one day be *members,* and obey one will. On that one will, on that secret cause, they nail our attention and hope. Life is hereby melted into an expectation or a religion. Underneath the inharmonious and trivial particulars, is a musical perfection; the Ideal journeying always with us, the heaven without rent or seam. Do but observe the mode of our illumination. When I converse with a profound mind, or if at any time being alone I have good thoughts, I do not at once arrive at satisfactions, as when, being thirsty, I drink water, or go to the fire, being cold; no! but I am at first apprised of my vicinity to a new and excellent region of life. By persisting to read or to think, this region gives further sign of itself, as it were in flashes of light, in sudden discoveries of its profound beauty and repose, as if the clouds that covered it parted at intervals and showed the approaching traveler the inland mountains, with the tranquil eternal meadows spread at their base, whereon flocks graze and shepherds pipe and dance. But every insight from this realm of thought is felt as initial, and promises a sequel. I do not make it; I arrive there, and behold what was there already. I make! O no! I clap my hands in infantine joy and amazement before the first

---

[23] Sir Everard Home (1756–1832) notes in his *Lectures on Comparative Anatomy* (London, 1814–28) that the impregnated ovum is multiple (Ferguson 3:189). [Ed.]

opening to me of this august magnificence, old with the love and homage of innumerable ages, young with the life of life, the sunbright Mecca of the desert. And what a future it opens! I feel a new heart beating with the love of the new beauty. I am ready to die out of nature, and be born again into this new yet unapproachable America I have found in the West: —

"Since neither now nor yesterday began
These thoughts, which have been ever, nor yet can
A man be found who their first entrance knew." [24]

If I have described life as a flux of moods, I must now add that there is that in us which changes not and which ranks all sensations and states of mind. The consciousness in each man is a sliding scale, which identifies him now with the First Cause, and now with the flesh of his body; life above life, in infinite degrees. The sentiment from which it sprung determines the dignity of any deed, and the question ever is, not what you have done or forborne, but at whose command you have done or forborne it.

Fortune, Minerva, Muse, Holy Ghost, — these are quaint names, too narrow to cover this unbounded substance. The baffled intellect must still kneel before this cause, which refuses to be named, — ineffable cause, which every fine genius has essayed to represent by some emphatic symbol, as, Thales by water, Anaximenes by air, Anaxagoras by (Νοῦς) thought, Zoroaster by fire, Jesus and the moderns by love; and the metaphor of each has become a national religion. [25] The Chinese Mencius [26] has not been the least successful in his generalization. "I fully understand language," he said, "and nourish well my vast-flowing vigor." — "I beg to ask what you call vast-flowing vigor?" said his companion. "The explanation," replied Mencius, "is difficult. This vigor is supremely great, and in the highest degree unbending. Nourish it correctly and do it no injury, and it will fill up the vacancy between heaven and earth. This vigor accords with and assists justice and reason, and leaves no hunger." — In our more correct writing, we give to this generalization the name of Being, and thereby confess that we have arrived as far as we can go. Suffice it for the joy of the universe that we have not arrived at a wall, but at interminable oceans. Our life seems not present so much as prospective; not for the affairs on which it is wasted, but as a hint of this vast-flowing vigor. Most of life seems to be mere advertisement of faculty; information is given us not to sell ourselves cheap; that we are

---

[24] From Sophocles, *Antigone*. [Ed.]

[25] Emerson gives in this paragraph a long list of names of deities, essential elements, and philosophical essences to suggest how human consciousness has been historically represented. [Ed.]

[26] Chinese philosopher (c. 371–c. 289 BCE), grandson of Confucius. [Ed.]

very great. So, in particular, our greatness is always in a tendency or direction, not in an action. It is for us to believe in the rule, not in the exception. The noble are thus known from the ignoble. So in accepting the leading of the sentiments, it is not what we believe concerning the immortality of the soul or the like, but *the universal impulse to believe*, that is the material circumstance and is the principal fact in the history of the globe. Shall we describe this cause as that which works directly? The spirit is not helpless or needful of mediate organs. It has plentiful powers and direct effects. I am explained without explaining, I am felt without acting, and where I am not. Therefore all just persons are satisfied with their own praise. They refuse to explain themselves, and are content that new actions should do them that office. They believe that we communicate without speech and above speech, and that no right action of ours is quite unaffecting to our friends, at whatever distance; for the influence of action is not to be measured by miles. Why should I fret myself because a circumstance has occurred, which hinders my presence where I was expected? If I am not at the meeting, my presence where I am should be as useful to the commonwealth of friendship and wisdom, as would be my presence in that place. I exert the same quality of power in all places. Thus journeys the mighty Ideal before us; it never was known to fall into the rear. No man ever came to an experience which was satiating, but his good is tidings of a better. Onward and onward! In liberated moments, we know that a new picture of life and duty is already possible; the elements already exist in many minds around you of a doctrine of life which shall transcend any written record we have. The new statement will comprise the skepticisms as well as the faiths of society, and out of unbeliefs a creed shall be formed. For skepticisms are not gratuitous or lawless, but are limitations of the affirmative statement, and the new philosophy must take them in and make affirmations outside of them, just as much as it must include the oldest beliefs.

It is very unhappy, but too late to be helped, the discovery we have made that we exist. That discovery is called the Fall of Man. Ever afterwards we suspect our instruments. We have learned that we do not see directly, but mediately, and that we have no means of correcting these colored and distorting lenses which we are, or of computing the amount of their errors. Perhaps these subject-lenses have a creative power; perhaps there are no objects. Once we lived in what we saw; now, the rapaciousness of this new power, which threatens to absorb all things, engages us. Nature, art, persons, letters, religions, objects, successively tumble in, and God is but one of its ideas. Nature and literature are subjective phenomena; every evil and every good thing is a shadow which we cast. The street is full of humiliations to the proud. As the fop contrived to dress his bailiffs in his livery and make them wait on his guests at table, so the chagrins which the bad heart gives off as bubbles, at once take form as ladies and gentlemen in the street, shopmen or bar-keepers in hotels, and threaten or insult whatever is threatenable and insultable in us. 'Tis the same with our idolatries. People forget that it is the eye which makes the horizon, and the rounding mind's eye which makes this or that man a type or representative of humanity, with the name of hero or saint. Jesus, the "providential man," is a good man on whom many people are agreed that these optical laws shall take effect. By love on one part and by forbearance to press objection on the other part, it is for a time settled that we will look at him in the center of the horizon, and ascribe to him the properties that will attach to any man so seen. But the longest love or aversion has a speedy term. The great and crescive self, rooted in absolute nature, supplants all relative existence and ruins the kingdom of mortal friendship and love. Marriage (in what is called the spiritual world) is impossible, because of the inequality between every subject and every object. The subject is the receiver of Godhead, and at every comparison must feel his being enhanced by that cryptic might. Though not in energy, yet by presence, this magazine of substance cannot be otherwise than felt; nor can any force of intellect attribute to the object the proper deity which sleeps or wakes forever in every subject. Never can love make consciousness and ascription equal in force. There will be the same gulf between every me and thee as between the original and the picture. The universe is the bride of the soul. All private sympathy is partial. Two human beings are like globes, which can touch only in a point, and whilst they remain in contact all other points of each of the spheres are inert: their turn must also come, and the longer a particular union lasts, the more energy of appetency the parts not in union acquire.

Life will be imaged, but cannot be divided nor doubled. Any invasion of its unity would be chaos. The soul is not twin-born but the only begotten, and though revealing itself as child in time, child in appearance, is of a fatal and universal power, admitting no co-life. Every day, every act betrays the ill-concealed deity. We believe in ourselves as we do not believe in others. We permit all things to ourselves, and that which we call sin in others is experiment for us. It is an instance of our faith in ourselves that men never speak of crime as lightly as they think; or every man thinks a latitude safe for himself, which is nowise to be indulged to another. The act looks very differently on the inside and on the outside; in its quality and in its consequences. Murder in the murderer is no such ruinous thought as poets and romancers will have it; it does not unsettle him or fright him from his ordinary notice of trifles; it is an act quite easy to be contemplated, but in its sequel it turns out to be a horrible jangle and confounding of all relations. Especially the crimes that spring from love seem right and fair from the actor's point of view, but when acted are found destructive of society. No man at last believes that he can be lost, or that the crime in him is as black as in the felon. Because the intellect qualifies in our own case the moral judgments. For there is no crime to the intellect. That is antinomian or hypernomian, and judges law as well as fact. "It is worse than a crime, it is a blunder," said Napoleon, speaking the language of the intellect.[27] To it, the world is a problem in mathematics or the science of quantity, and it leaves out praise and blame and all weak emotions. All stealing is comparative. If you come to absolutes, pray who does not steal? Saints are sad, because they behold sin (even when they speculate) from the point of view of the conscience, and not of the intellect; a confusion of thought. Sin, seen from the thought, is a diminution, or *less;* seen from the conscience or will, it is pravity or *bad.* The intellect names it shade, absence of light, and no essence. The conscience must feel it as essence, essential evil. This it is not; it has an objective existence, but no subjective.

Thus inevitably does the universe wear our color, and every object fall successively into the subject itself. The subject exists, the subject enlarges; all things sooner or later fall into place. As I am, so I see; use what language we will, we can never say anything but what we are; Hermes, Cadmus, Columbus, Newton, Bonaparte are the mind's ministers.[28] Instead of feeling a poverty when we encounter a great man, let us treat the newcomer like a traveling geologist who passes through our estate and shows us good slate, or limestone, or anthracite, in our brush pasture. The partial action of each strong mind in one direction is a telescope for the objects on which it is pointed. But every other part of knowledge is to be pushed to the same extravagance, ere the soul attains her due sphericity. Do you see that kitten chasing so prettily her own tail? If you could look with her eyes, you might see her surrounded with hundreds of figures performing complex dramas, with tragic and comic issues, long conversations, many characters, many ups and downs of fate, —and meantime it is only puss and her tail. How long before our masquerade will end its noise of tambourines, laughter, and shouting, and we shall find it was a solitary performance? A subject and an object, —it takes so much to make the galvanic circuit complete,

---

[27] Emerson is referring to Napoleon Bonaparte's execution of the Duke D'Enghien in 1804, which incited wide opposition against Napoleon. Napoleon never admitted that the execution had been either a crime or a blunder, but many Bonapartists said so (Ferguson 3:190–191). [Ed.]

[28] Messengers of the gods, discoverers of new worlds, and political leaders are mere servants of our minds and thus kin to us. [Ed.]

but magnitude adds nothing. What imports it whether it is Kepler and the sphere, Columbus and America, a reader and his book, or puss with her tail?[29]

It is true that all the muses and love and religion hate these developments, and will find a way to punish the chemist who publishes in the parlor the secrets of the laboratory. And we cannot say too little of our constitutional necessity of seeing things under private aspects, or saturated with our humors. And yet is the God the native of these bleak rocks. That need makes in morals the capital virtue of self-trust. We must hold hard to this poverty, however scandalous, and by more vigorous self-recoveries, after the sallies of action, possess our axis more firmly. The life of truth is cold and so far mournful; but it is not the slave of tears, contritions, and perturbations. It does not attempt another's work, nor adopt another's facts. It is a main lesson of wisdom to know your own from another's. I have learned that I cannot dispose of other people's facts; but I possess such a key to my own as persuades me, against all their denials, that they also have a key to theirs. A sympathetic person is placed in the dilemma of a swimmer among drowning men, who all catch at him, and if he give so much as a leg or a finger, they will drown him. They wish to be saved from the mischiefs of their vices, but not from their vices. Charity would be wasted on this poor waiting on the symptoms. A wise and hardy physician will say, *Come out of that*, as the first condition of advice.

In this our talking America, we are ruined by our good nature and listening on all sides. This compliance takes away the power of being greatly useful. A man should not be able to look other than directly and forthright. A preoccupied attention is the only answer to the importunate frivolity of other people; an attention, and to an aim which makes their wants frivolous. This is a divine answer, and leaves no appeal, and no hard thoughts. In Flaxman's drawing of the Eumenides of Aeschylus, Orestes supplicates Apollo, whilst the Furies sleep on the threshold.[30] The face of the god expresses a shade of regret and compassion, but calm with the conviction of the irreconcilableness of the two spheres. He is born into other politics,

---

[29]Emerson's point is that every effort to link subject and object, mind and external world, is equally important, thus elevating our everyday mental acts to the discoveries of Kepler in astronomy and Columbus in the western hemisphere or lowering them to the significance of a cat chasing its tail. [Ed.]

[30]Emerson is interpreting one of John Flaxman's illustrations in *Compositions from the Tragedies of Aeschylus* (London, 1795) 24. Flaxman shows Orestes praying to the god Apollo after he has been acquitted by the court in Athens and the Furies have been turned into benign "Eumenides" (Ferguson 3:191). [Ed.]

into the eternal and beautiful. The man at his feet asks for his interest in turmoils of the earth, into which his nature cannot enter. And the Eumenides there lying express pictorially this disparity. The god is surcharged with his divine destiny.

Illusion, Temperament, Succession, Surface, Surprise, Reality, Subjectiveness, — these are threads on the loom of time, these are the lords of life. I dare not assume to give their order, but I name them as I find them in my way. I know better than to claim any completeness for my picture. I am a fragment, and this is a fragment of me. I can very confidently announce one or another law, which throws itself into relief and form, but I am too young yet by some ages to compile a code. I gossip for my hour concerning the eternal politics. I have seen many fair pictures not in vain. A wonderful time I have lived in. I am not the novice I was fourteen, nor yet seven years ago. Let who will ask, Where is the fruit? I find a private fruit sufficient. This is a fruit, — that I should not ask for a rash effect from meditations, counsels and the hiving of truths. I should feel it pitiful to demand a result on this town and county, an overt effect on the instant month and year. The effect is deep and secular as the cause. It works on periods in which mortal lifetime is lost. All I know is reception; I am and I have: but I do not get, and when I have fancied I had gotten anything, I found I did not. I worship with wonder the great Fortune. My reception has been so large, that I am not annoyed by receiving this or that superabundantly. I say to the Genius, if he will pardon the proverb, *In for a mill, in for a million.* When I receive a new gift, I do not macerate my body to make the account square, for if I should die I could not make the account square. The benefit overran the merit the first day, and has overrun the merit ever since. The merit itself, so-called, I reckon part of the receiving.

Also that hankering after an overt or practical effect seems to me an apostasy. In good earnest, I am willing to spare this most unnecessary deal of doing. Life wears to me a visionary face. Hardest roughest action is visionary also. It is but a choice between soft and turbulent dreams. People disparage knowing and the intellectual life, and urge doing. I am very content with knowing, if only I could know. That is an august entertainment, and would suffice me a great while. To know a little would be worth the expense of this world. I hear always the law of Adrastia, "that every soul which had acquired any truth, should be safe from harm until another period." [31]

---

[31] Adrastia: Greek goddess of justice and retribution. The quote is from Plato, *Phaedrus*. [Ed.]

I know that the world I converse with in the city and in the farms, is not the world I *think*. I observe that difference, and shall observe it. One day I shall know the value and law of this discrepance. But I have not found that much was gained by manipular attempts to realize the world of thought. Many eager persons successively make an experiment in this way, and make themselves ridiculous. They acquire democratic manners, they foam at the mouth, they hate and deny. Worse, I observe that in the history of mankind there is never a solitary example of success,—taking their own tests of success. I say this polemically, or in reply to the inquiry, Why not realize your world? But far be from me the despair which prejudges the law by a paltry empiricism;—since there never was a right endeavor but it succeeded. Patience and patience, we shall win at the last. We must be very suspicious of the deceptions of the element of time. It takes a good deal of time to eat or to sleep, or to earn a hundred dollars, and a very little time to entertain a hope and an insight which becomes the light of our life. We dress our garden, eat our dinners, discuss the household with our wives, and these things make no impression, are forgotten next week; but, in the solitude to which every man is always returning, he has a sanity and revelations, which in his passage into new worlds he will carry with him. Never mind the ridicule, never mind the defeat; up again, old heart!—it seems to say,—there is victory yet for all justice; and the true romance which the world exists to realize will be the transformation of genius into practical power.

The Poet
1844

A moody child and wildly wise
Pursued the game with joyful eyes,
Which chose, like meteors, their way,
And rived the dark with private ray:
They overleapt the horizon's edge,
Searched with Apollo's privilege;
Through man, and woman, and sea, and star
Saw the dance of nature forward far;

Selections from Ralph Waldo Emerson: An Organic Anthology. Ed. Stephen E. Whicher. Riverside Edition. Boston: Houghton, 1957.

Through worlds, and races, and terms, and times
Saw musical order, and pairing rhymes.[1]

Olympian bards who sung
Divine ideas below,
Which always find us young,
And always keep us so.[2]

Those who are esteemed umpires of taste are often persons who have acquired some knowledge of admired pictures or sculptures, and have an inclination for whatever is elegant; but if you inquire whether they are beautiful souls, and whether their own acts are like fair pictures, you learn that they are selfish and sensual. Their cultivation is local, as if you should rub a log of dry wood in one spot to produce fire, all the rest remaining cold. Their knowledge of the fine arts is some study of rules and particulars, or some limited judgment of color or form, which is exercised for amusement or for show. It is a proof of the shallowness of the doctrine of beauty, as it lies in the minds of our amateurs, that men seem to have lost the perception of the instant dependence of form upon soul. There is no doctrine of forms in our philosophy. We were put into our bodies, as fire is put into a pan to be carried about; but there is no accurate adjustment between the spirit and the organ, much less is the latter the germination of the former. So in regard to other forms, the intellectual men do not believe in any essential dependence of the material world on thought and volition. Theologians think it a pretty air-castle to talk of the spiritual meaning of a ship or a cloud, of a city or a contract, but they prefer to come again to the solid ground of historical evidence; and even the poets are contented with a civil and conformed manner of living, and to write poems from the fancy, at a safe distance from their own experience. But the highest minds of the world have never ceased to explore the double meaning, or shall I say the quadruple or the centuple or much more manifold meaning, of every sensuous fact; Orpheus, Empedocles, Heraclitus, Plato, Plutarch, Dante, Swedenborg, and the masters of sculpture, picture, and poetry.[3] For we are not

---

[1] From Emerson's unfinished poem "The Poet." [Ed.]

[2] This stanza comes from "Ode to Beauty," published in *The Dial*. [Orig. ed.]

[3] The mythical Orpheus stands at the head of another one of Emerson's illustrative catalogues of "representative men," because Emerson, along with many of his contemporaries, accepted the claim by Thomas Taylor, in *The Mystical Hymns of Orpheus* (1824),

pans and barrows, nor even porters of the fire and torch-bearers, but children of the fire, made of it, and only the same divinity transmuted and at two or three removes, when we know least about it. And this hidden truth, that the fountains whence all this river of Time and its creatures floweth are intrinsically ideal and beautiful, draws us to the consideration of the nature and functions of the Poet, or the man of Beauty; to the means and materials he uses, and to the general aspect of the art in the present time.

The breadth of the problem is great, for the poet is representative.[4] He stands among partial men for the complete man, and apprises us not of his wealth, but of the commonwealth. The young man reveres men of genius, because, to speak truly, they are more himself than he is. They receive of the soul as he also receives, but they more. Nature enhances her beauty, to the eye of loving men, from their belief that the poet is beholding her shows at the same time. He is isolated among his contemporaries by truth and by his art, but with this consolation in his pursuits, that they will draw all men sooner or later. For all men live by truth and stand in need of expression. In love, in art, in avarice, in politics, in labor, in games, we study to utter our painful secret. The man is only half himself, the other half is his expression.

Notwithstanding this necessity to be published, adequate expression is rare. I know not how it is that we need an interpreter, but the great majority of men seem to be minors, who have not yet come into possession of their own, or mutes, who cannot report the conversation they have had with nature. There is no man who does not anticipate a supersensual utility in the sun and stars, earth and water. These stand and wait to render him a peculiar service. But there is some obstruction or some excess of phlegm in our constitution, which does not suffer them to yield the due effect. Too feeble fall the impressions of nature on us to make us artists. Every touch should thrill. Every man should be so much an artist that he could report in conversation what had befallen him. Yet, in our experience, the rays or appulses have sufficient force to arrive at the senses, but not enough to reach the quick and compel the reproduction of themselves in speech. The poet is the person in whom these powers are in balance, the man without

---

that the "Eleusinian Mysteries" had been written by Orpheus, who was for them a historical figure (Ferguson 3:171–172). [Ed.]

[4]Emerson took the idea of the "representative man" from eighteenth-century Enlightenment philosophy, which had a profound influence on founding American political documents. In the eighteenth century, the "representative man" embodied the qualities of reason that entitled him to positions of leadership (usually in government). By claiming that the poet was also a "representative man," romantics like Emerson and Shelley tried to connect poetry, politics, and science. [Ed.]

impediment, who sees and handles that which others dream of, traverses the whole scale of experience, and is representative of man, in virtue of being the largest power to receive and to impart.

For the Universe has three children, born at one time, which reappear under different names in every system of thought, whether they be called cause, operation, and effect; or, more poetically, Jove, Pluto, Neptune; or, theologically, the Father, the Spirit, and the Son; but which we will call here the Knower, the Doer and the Sayer. These stand respectively for the love of truth, for the love of good, and for the love of beauty. These three are equal. Each is that which he is, essentially, so that he cannot be surmounted or analyzed, and each of these three has the power of the others latent in him and his own, patent.

The poet is the sayer, the namer, and represents beauty. He is a sovereign, and stands on the center. For the world is not painted or adorned, but is from the beginning beautiful; and God has not made some beautiful things, but Beauty is the creator of the universe. Therefore the poet is not any permissive potentate, but is emperor in his own right. Criticism is infested with a cant of materialism, which assumes that manual skill and activity is the first merit of all men, and disparages such as say and do not, overlooking the fact that some men, namely poets, are natural sayers, sent into the world to the end of expression, and confounds them with those whose province is action but who quit it to imitate the sayers. But Homer's words are as costly and admirable to Homer as Agamemnon's victories are to Agamemnon.[5] The poet does not wait for the hero or the sage, but, as they act and think primarily, so he writes primarily what will and must be spoken, reckoning the others, though primaries also, yet, in respect to him, secondaries and servants; as sitters or models in the studio of a painter, or as assistants who bring building-materials to an architect.

For poetry was all written before time was, and whenever we are so finely organized that we can penetrate into that region where the air is music, we hear those primal warblings and attempt to write them down, but we lose ever and anon a word or a verse and substitute something of our own, and thus miswrite the poem.[6] The men of more delicate ear write

---

[5] Emerson is tacitly responding to Plato's criticism in *Ion* and the *Republic* that poetry is a mere "imitation of an imitation," which misleads us from enduring truth and should be banished from the well-ordered state. One of Plato's targets in *Ion* was Homer, and here Emerson claims that Homer's poetic achievements are as valuable and real as Agamemnon's military victory in the Trojan War. [Ed.]

[6] It was a common belief among the romantics that language had origins in poetic utterances by primitive peoples about their circumstances, such as in the myths of the ancient Greeks. [Ed.]

down these cadences more faithfully, and these transcripts, though imperfect, become the songs of the nations. For nature is as truly beautiful as it is good, or as it is reasonable, and must as much appear as it must be done, or be known. Words and deeds are quite indifferent modes of the divine energy. Words are also actions, and actions are a kind of words.[7]

The sign and credentials of the poet are that he announces that which no man foretold. He is the true and only doctor,[8] he knows and tells; he is the only teller of news, for he was present and privy to the appearance which he describes. He is a beholder of ideas and an utterer of the necessary and causal. For we do not speak now of men of poetical talents, or of industry and skill in meter, but of the true poet. I took part in a conversation the other day concerning a recent writer of lyrics, a man of subtle mind, whose head appeared to be a music-box of delicate tunes and rhythms, and whose skill and command of language we could not sufficiently praise. But when the question arose whether he was not only a lyrist but a poet, we were obliged to confess that he is plainly a contemporary, not an eternal man.[9] He does not stand out of our low limitations, like a Chimborazo[10] under the line, running up from a torrid base through all the climates of the globe, with belts of the herbage of every latitude on its high and mottled sides; but this genius is the landscape-garden of a modern house, adorned with fountains and statues, with well-bred men and women standing and sitting in the walks and terraces. We hear, through all the varied music, the ground-tone of conventional life. Our poets are men of talents who sing, and not the children of music. The argument is secondary, the finish of the verses is primary.

For it is not meters, but a meter-making argument that makes a poem, — a thought so passionate and alive that like the spirit of a plant or an animal it has an architecture of its own, and adorns nature with a new thing. The thought and the form are equal in the order of time, but in the order of genesis the thought is prior to the form. The poet has a new thought; he has a whole new experience to unfold; he will tell us how it was with him, and

---

[7] Continuing his defense of the poet against Plato's criticism, Emerson anticipates modern theories of the performative aspects of language as constitutive of real circumstances. [Ed.]

[8] "Doctor" here means "teacher." Cf. Luke 2.46. [Ed.]

[9] The poet Emerson discusses here is Tennyson. Emerson seems again to be answering Plato's charges by distinguishing between a true poet, whose work is eternal, and a mere "rhapsode," like Ion, who merely recites poetry, or a mere "lyrist," like Emerson's Tennyson, whose work will not survive its time. [Ed.]

[10] Mount Chimborazo in Ecuador and near the equator ("under the line") was thought at the time to be the tallest of the Andes. [Ed.]

all men will be the richer in his fortune. For the experience of each new age requires a new confession, and the world seems always waiting for its poet. I remember when I was young how much I was moved one morning by tidings that genius had appeared in a youth who sat near me at table. He had left his work and gone rambling none knew whither, and had written hundreds of lines, but could not tell whether that which was in him was therein told; he could tell nothing but that all was changed, —man, beast, heaven, earth, and sea. How gladly we listened! how credulous! Society seemed to be compromised. We sat in the aurora of a sunrise which was to put out all the stars. Boston seemed to be at twice the distance it had the night before, or was much farther than that. Rome, —what was Rome? Plutarch and Shakespeare were in the yellow leaf, and Homer no more should be heard of. It is much to know that poetry has been written this very day, under this very roof, by your side. What! that wonderful spirit has not expired! These stony moments are still sparkling and animated! I had fancied that the oracles were all silent, and nature had spent her fires; and behold! all night, from every pore, these fine auroras have been streaming. Every one has some interest in the advent of the poet, and no one knows how much it may concern him. We know that the secret of the world is profound, but who or what shall be our interpreter, we know not. A mountain ramble, a new style of face, a new person, may put the key into our hands. Of course, the value of genius to us is in the veracity of its report. Talent may frolic and juggle; genius realizes and adds. Mankind in good earnest have arrived so far in understanding themselves and their work, that the foremost watchman on the peak announces his news. It is the truest word ever spoken, and the phrase will be the fittest, most musical, and the unerring voice of the world for that time.

All that we call sacred history attests that the birth of a poet is the principal event in chronology. Man, never so often deceived, still watches for the arrival of a brother who can hold him steady to a truth until he has made it his own. With what joy I begin to read a poem, which I confide in as an inspiration! And now my chains are to be broken; I shall mount above these clouds and opaque airs in which I live, —opaque, though they seem transparent, —and from the heaven of truth I shall see and comprehend my relations. That will reconcile me to life and renovate nature, to see trifles animated by a tendency, and to know what I am doing. Life will no more be a noise; now I shall see men and women, and know the signs by which they may be discerned from fools and satans. This day shall be better than my birthday: then I became an animal; now I am invited into the science of the real. Such is the hope, but the fruition is postponed. Oftener it falls that this winged man, who will carry me into the heaven, whirls me into mists, then leaps and frisks about with me as it were from cloud to cloud, still affirming that he is bound heavenward; and I, being myself a novice, am slow in perceiving that he does not know the way into the heavens, and is merely bent that I should admire his skill to rise, like a fowl or a flying fish, a little way from the ground or the water; but the all-piercing, all-feeding and ocular air[11] of heaven that man shall never inhabit. I tumble down again soon into my old nooks, and lead the life of exaggerations as before, and have lost my faith in the possibility of any guide who can lead me thither where I would be.

But, leaving these victims of vanity, let us, with new hope, observe how nature, by worthier impulses, has insured the poet's fidelity to his office of announcement and affirming, namely by the beauty of things, which becomes a new and higher beauty when expressed. Nature offers all her creatures to him as a picture-language. Being used as a type, a second wonderful value appears in the object, far better than its old value, as the carpenter's stretched cord, if you hold your ear close enough, is musical in the breeze. "Things more excellent than every image," says Jamblichus, "are expressed through images."[12] Things admit of being used as symbols, because nature is a symbol, in the whole, and in every part. Every line we can draw in the sand has expression; and there is no body without its spirit or genius. All form is an effect of character; all condition, of the quality of the life; all harmony, of health; and for this reason a perception of beauty should be sympathetic, or proper only to the good. The beautiful rests on the foundations of the necessary. The soul makes the body, as the wise Spenser teaches: —

"So every spirit, as it is more pure,
And hath in it the more of heavenly light,
So it the fairer body doth procure
To habit in, and it more fairly dight,
With cheerful grace and amiable sight.
For, of the soul, the body form doth take,
For soul is form, and doth the body make."[13]

Here we find ourselves suddenly not in a critical speculation but in a holy place, and should go very warily and reverently. We stand before the secret of the world, there where Being passes into Appearance and Unity into Variety.

---

[11] Emerson's wonderful metaphor recalls his moment of transcendentalist vision, the so-called transparent eyeball passage in *Nature* (see page 26 in this volume). [Ed.]

[12] Iamblichus (d. c. 330 CE), a Neoplatonist philosopher. [Ed.]

[13] From Edmund Spenser (1553–99), "An Hymn in Honour of Beautie." [Ed.]

The Universe is the externization of the soul. Wherever the life is, that bursts into appearance around it. Our science is sensual, and therefore superficial. The earth and the heavenly bodies, physics and chemistry, we sensually treat, as if they were self-existent; but these are the retinue of that Being we have. "The mighty heaven," said Proclus, "exhibits, in its transfigurations, clear images of the splendor of intellectual perceptions; being moved in conjunction with the unapparent periods of intellectual natures."[14] Therefore science always goes abreast with the just elevation of the man, keeping step with religion and metaphysics; or the state of science is an index of our self-knowledge. Since everything in nature answers to a moral power, if any phenomenon remains brute and dark, it is because the corresponding faculty in the observer is not yet active.

No wonder, then, if these waters be so deep, that we hover over them with a religious regard. The beauty of the fable proves the importance of the sense; to the poet, and to all others; or, if you please, every man is so far a poet as to be susceptible of these enchantments of nature; for all men have the thoughts whereof the universe is the celebration. I find that the fascination resides in the symbol. Who loves nature? Who does not? Is it only poets, and men of leisure and cultivation, who live with her? No; but also hunters, farmers, grooms, and butchers, though they express their affection in their choice of life and not in their choice of words. The writer wonders what the coachman or the hunter values in riding, in horses, and dogs. It is not superficial qualities. When you talk with him he holds these at as slight a rate as you. His worship is sympathetic; he has no definitions, but he is commanded in nature, by the living power which he feels to be there present. No imitation or playing of these things would content him; he loves the earnest of the north wind, of rain, of stone and wood and iron. A beauty not explicable is dearer than a beauty which we can see to the end of. It is nature the symbol, nature certifying the supernatural, body overflowed by life, which he worships with coarse but sincere rites.

The inwardness and mystery of this attachment drive men of every class to the use of emblems. The schools of poets and philosophers are not more intoxicated with their symbols than the populace with theirs. In our political parties, compute the power of badges and emblems. See the huge wooden ball rolled by successive ardent crowds from Baltimore to Bunker Hill! In the political processions, Lowell goes in a loom, and Lynn in a shoe, and Salem in a ship. Witness the cider-barrel, the log-cabin, the

---

[14] Proclus, a Neoplatonist philosopher, appears in this passage to be departing from a strict Platonic dualism between phenomenon and noumenon and anticipating the transcendentalist idea of the imbrication of mind and nature, spirit and matter. [Ed.]

hickory-stick, the palmetto, and all the cognizances of party.[15] See the power of national emblems. Some stars, lilies, leopards, a crescent, a lion, an eagle, or other figure, which came into credit God knows how, on an old rag of bunting, blowing in the wind on a fort at the ends of the earth, shall make the blood tingle under the rudest or the most conventional exterior. The people fancy they hate poetry, and they are all poets and mystics![16]

Beyond this universality of the symbolic language, we are apprised of the divineness of this superior use of things, whereby the world is a temple whose walls are covered with emblems, pictures, and commandments of the Deity, — in this, that there is no fact in nature which does not carry the whole sense of nature; and the distinctions which we make in events and in affairs, of low and high, honest and base, disappear when nature is used as a symbol. Thought makes everything fit for use. The vocabulary of an omniscient man would embrace words and images excluded from polite conversation. What would be base, or even obscene, to the obscene, becomes illustrious, spoken in a new connection of thought. The piety of the Hebrew prophets purges their grossness. The circumcision is an example of the power of poetry to raise the low and offensive. Small and mean things serve as well as great symbols. The meaner the type by which a law is expressed, the more pungent it is, and the more lasting in the memories of men; just as we choose the smallest box or case, in which any needful utensil can be carried. Bare lists of words are found suggestive to an imaginative and excited mind, as it is related of Lord Chatham that he was accustomed to read in Bailey's Dictionary when he was preparing to speak in Parliament.[17] The poorest experience is rich enough for all the purposes of expressing thought. Why covet a knowledge of new facts? Day and night, house and garden, a few books, a few actions, serve us as well as would all trades and all spectacles. We are far from having exhausted the significance of the few symbols we use. We can come to use them yet with a terrible simplicity. It does not need that a poem should be long. Every word was once

---

[15]Emerson is referring to emblems used in recent political campaigns, including the palmetto representing John C. Calhoun's home state of South Carolina, Andrew Jackson's hickory stick, the humble log cabin (later made famous by Lincoln) and hard-cider barrel used in William Henry Harrison's campaign against Martin Van Buren in 1840, and the great wooden balls (some twelve to thirteen feet across) that Harrison's Whigs rolled from town to town to declare their campaign a relentless juggernaut (Ferguson 3:174). [Ed.]

[16]Emerson's discussion of the poeticality of political and national symbols resembles his friend Thomas Carlyle's in *Sartor Resartus* (1836), bk 3, ch. 3 ("Symbols"). [Ed.]

[17]Statesman and prime minister William Pitt, the Earl of Chatham (1708–78). Nathan Bailey's *An Universal Etymological English Dictionary* was a widely used eighteenth-century dictionary. [Ed.]

a poem. Every new relation is a new word. Also we use defects and deformities to a sacred purpose, so expressing our sense that the evils of the world are such only to the evil eye. In the old mythology, mythologists observe, defects are ascribed to divine natures, as lameness to Vulcan, blindness to Cupid, and the like, — to signify exuberances.

For as it is dislocation and detachment from the life of God that makes things ugly, the poet, who re-attaches things to nature and the Whole, — re-attaching even artificial things, and violation of nature, to nature, by a deeper insight, — disposes very easily of the most disagreeable facts. Readers of poetry see the factory-village and the railway, and fancy that the poetry of the landscape is broken up by these; for these works of art are not yet consecrated in their reading; but the poet sees them fall within the great Order not less than the beehive or the spider's geometrical web. Nature adopts them very fast into her vital circles, and the gliding train of cars she loves like her own. Besides, in a centered mind, it signifies nothing how many mechanical inventions you exhibit. Though you add millions, and never so surprising, the fact of mechanics has not gained a grain's weight. The spiritual fact remains unalterable, by many or by few particulars; as no mountain is of any appreciable height to break the curve of the sphere. A shrewd country-boy goes to the city for the first time, and the complacent citizen is not satisfied with his little wonder. It is not that he does not see all the fine houses and know that he never saw such before, but he disposes of them as easily as the poet finds place for the railway. The chief value of the new fact is to enhance the great and constant fact of Life, which can dwarf any and every circumstance, and to which the belt of wampum and the commerce of America are alike.[18]

The world being thus put under the mind for verb and noun, the poet is he who can articulate it. For though life is great, and fascinates, and absorbs; and though all men are intelligent of the symbols through which it is named; yet they cannot originally use them. We are symbols and inhabit symbols, workmen, work, and tools, words and things, birth and death, all are emblems; but we sympathize with the symbols, and being infatuated with the economical uses of things, we do not know that they are thoughts. The poet, by an ulterior intellectual perception, gives them a power which makes their old use forgotten, and puts eyes and a tongue into every dumb and inanimate object. He perceives thought's independence of the symbol, the stability of the thought, the accidency and fugacity of the symbol. As

---

[18] References and even the rhetoric of this paragraph seem to be drawn from Henry David Thoreau's experiences on the journey he and his brother took in 1839 and later published as *A Week on the Concord and Merrimack Rivers* (1849). [Ed.]

the eyes of Lyncaeus[19] were said to see through the earth, so the poet turns the world to glass, and shows us all things in their right series and procession. For through that better perception, he stands one step nearer to things, and sees the flowing or metamorphosis; perceives that thought is multiform; that within the form of every creature is a force impelling it to ascend into a higher form; and following with his eyes the life, uses the forms which express that life, and so his speech flows with the flowing of nature. All the facts of the animal economy—sex, nutriment, gestation, birth, growth—are symbols of the passage of the world into the soul of man, to suffer there a change and reappear a new and higher fact. He uses forms according to the life, and not according to the form. This is true science. The poet alone knows astronomy, chemistry, vegetation, and animation, for he does not stop at these facts, but employs them as signs. He knows why the plain or meadow of space was strown with these flowers we call suns and moons and stars; why the great deep is adorned with animals, with men, and gods; for in every word he speaks he rides on them the horses of thought.

By virtue of this science of poet is the Namer or Language-maker, naming things sometimes after their appearance, sometimes after their essence, and giving to every one its own name and not another's, thereby rejoicing the intellect, which delights in detachment or boundary. The poets made all the words, and therefore language is the archives of history, and, if we must say it, a sort of tomb of the muses. For though the origin of most of our words is forgotten, each word was at first a stroke of genius, and obtained currency, because for the moment it symbolized the world to the first speaker and to the hearer. The etymologist finds the deadest word to have been once a brilliant picture. Language is fossil poetry. As the limestone of the continent consists of infinite masses of the shells of animalcules, so language is made up of images or tropes, which now, in their secondary use, have long ceased to remind us of their poetic origin. But the poet names the thing because he sees it, or comes one step nearer to it than any other. This expression or naming is not art, but a second nature, grown out of the first, as a leaf out of a tree.[20] What we call nature is a certain self-

---

[19] Lyncaeus was an especially sharp-eyed crewman on Jason's ship, the *Argo,* in the quest for the Golden Fleece. [Ed.]

[20] In this paragraph Emerson defends the poet as a "scientist" in his own right, anticipating modern theories that link poetic practice with linguistic study and recalling Sir Philip Sidney's conception of poetry in his *Defense of Poesie* (1595) as capable of creating a "second nature" or "golden world," which represents a more ideal (and enduring) realm of ideas. [Ed.]

regulated motion or change; and nature does all things by her own hands, and does not leave another to baptize her, but baptizes herself; and this through the metamorphosis again. I remember that a certain poet[21] described it to me thus:

> Genius is the activity which repairs the decays of things, whether wholly or partly of a material and finite kind. Nature, through all her kingdoms, insures herself. Nobody cares for planting the poor fungus; so she shakes down from the gills of one agaric countless spores, any one of which, being preserved, transmits new billions of spores tomorrow or next day. The new agaric of this hour has a chance which the old one had not. This atom of seed is thrown into a new place, not subject to the accidents which destroyed its parent two rods off. She makes a man; and having brought him to ripe age, she will no longer run the risk of losing this wonder at a blow, but she detaches from him a new self, that the kind may be safe from accidents to which the individual is exposed. So when the soul of the poet has come to ripeness of thought, she detaches and sends away from it its poems or songs, — a fearless, sleepless, deathless progeny, which is not exposed to the accidents of the weary kingdom of time; a fearless, vivacious offspring, clad with wings (such was the virtue of the soul out of which they came), which carry them fast and far, and infix them irrecoverably into the hearts of men. These wings are the beauty of the poet's soul. The songs, thus flying immortal from their mortal parent, are pursued by clamorous flights of censures, which swarm in far greater numbers and threaten to devour them; but these last are not winged. At the end of a very short leap they fall plump down and rot, having received from the souls out of which they came no beautiful wings. But the melodies of the poet ascend and leap and pierce into the deeps of infinite time.

So far the bard taught me, using his freer speech. But nature has a higher end, in the production of new individuals, than security, namely *ascension*, or the passage of the soul into higher forms. I knew in my younger days the sculptor who made the statue of the youth which stands in the public garden. He was, as I remember, unable to tell directly what made him happy or unhappy, but by wonderful indirections he could tell. He rose one day, according to his habit, before the dawn, and saw the morning break, grand as the eternity out of which it came, and for many days after, he strove to express this tranquility, and lo! his chisel has fashioned out of marble the

---

[21] The "certain poet" is probably Emerson himself. [Ed.]

form of a beautiful youth, Phosphor,[22] whose aspect is such that it is said all persons who look on it become silent. The poet also resigns himself to his mood, and that thought which agitated him is expressed, but *alter idem*,[23] in a manner totally new. The expression is organic, or the new type which things themselves take when liberated. As, in the sun, objects paint their images on the retina of the eye, so they, sharing the aspiration of the whole universe, tend to paint a far more delicate copy of their essence in his mind. Like the metamorphosis of things into higher organic forms is their change into melodies. Over everything stands its daemon or soul, and, as the form of the thing is reflected by the eye, so the soul of the thing is reflected by a melody. The sea, the mountain-ridge, Niagara, and every flower-bed, pre-exist, or super-exist, in pre-cantations, which sail like odors in the air, and when any man goes by with an ear sufficiently fine, he overhears them and endeavors to write down the notes without diluting or depraving them. And herein is the legitimation of criticism, in the mind's faith that the poems are a corrupt version of some text in nature with which they ought to be made to tally. A rhyme in one of our sonnets should not be less pleasing than the iterated nodes of a seashell, or the resembling difference of a group of flowers. The pairing of the birds is an idyl, not tedious as our idyls are; a tempest is a rough ode, without falsehood or rant; a summer, with its harvest sown, reaped, and stored, is an epic song, subordinating how many admirably executed parts. Why should not the symmetry and truth that modulate these, glide into our spirits, and we participate the invention of nature?[24]

This insight, which expresses itself by what is called Imagination, is a very high sort of seeing, which does not come by study, but by the intellect being where and what it sees, by sharing the path or circuit of things through forms, and so making them translucid to others. The path of things is silent. Will they suffer a speaker to go with them? A spy they will not suffer; a lover, a poet, is the transcendency of their own nature,—him they will suffer. The condition of true naming, on the poet's part, is his

---

[22] Greek god (also called Phosphorus) associated with the morning star. The sculptor to whom Emerson refers may be Horatio Greenough, who sculpted the monumental *Washington*, who is represented as a Greek god (but probably Zeus, not Phosphor), on display in the Capitol rotunda. [Ed.]

[23] Sameness in difference. [Ed.]

[24] Emerson's claim that poetry enables us to "participate the invention of nature" suggests that nature requires human beings for its completion and that human invention, including culture, is mandated in divine creation. This radical proposition, certainly contrary to either Puritan ideas of election or more secular Unitarian ideas of divine purpose, is part of the radical romanticism that more modern intellectuals, such as William James and Friedrich Nietzsche, found appealing in Emerson. [Ed.]

resigning himself to the divine *aura* which breathes through forms, and accompanying that.

It is a secret which every intellectual man quickly learns, that beyond the energy of his possessed and conscious intellect, he is capable of a new energy (as of an intellect doubled on itself), by abandonment to the nature of things; that beside his privacy of power as an individual man, there is a great public power on which he can draw, by unlocking, at all risks, his human doors, and suffering the ethereal tides to roll and circulate through him; then he is caught up into the life of the Universe, his speech is thunder, his thought is law, and his words are universally intelligible as the plants and animals. The poet knows that he speaks adequately, then only when he speaks somewhat wildly, or "with the flower of the mind"; not with the intellect used as an organ, but with the intellect released from all service and suffered to take its direction from its celestial life; or as the ancients were wont to express themselves, not with intellect alone, but with the intellect inebriated by nectar. As the traveler who has lost his way throws his reins on the horse's neck and trusts to the instinct of the animal to find his road, so must we do with the divine animal who carries us through this world.[25] For if in any manner we can stimulate this instinct, new passages are opened for us into nature, the mind flows into and through things hardest and highest, and the metamorphosis is possible.

This is the reason why bards love wine, mead, narcotics, coffee, tea, opium, the fumes of sandalwood and tobacco, or whatever other procurers of animal exhilaration. All men avail themselves of such means as they can, to add this extraordinary power to their normal powers; and to this end they prize conversation, music, pictures, sculpture, dancing, theaters, traveling, war, mobs, fires, gaming, politics, or love, or science, or animal intoxication,—which are several coarser or finer *quasi*-mechanical substitutes for the true nectar, which is the ravishment of the intellect by coming nearer to the fact. These are auxiliaries to the centrifugal tendency of a man, to his passage out into free space, and they help him to escape the custody of that body in which he is pent up, and of that jail-yard of individual relations in which he is enclosed. Hence a great number of such as were professionally expressers of Beauty, as painters, poets, musicians, and actors, have been more than other wont to lead a life of pleasure and indulgence; all but the few who received the true nectar; and, as it was a spurious mode of attaining freedom, as it was an emancipation not into the

---

[25] Emerson's example of the traveler who loosens his reins and lets his horse find the way recalls Samuel Taylor Coleridge's comparison, in his *Biographia Literaria* (1817), of the "organic" poet as one who can control his poetic materials with "loosened reins," "*laxis effertur habenis.*" [Ed.]

heavens but into the freedom of baser places, they were punished for that advantage they won, by a dissipation and deterioration. But never can any advantage be taken of nature by a trick. The spirit of the world, the great calm presence of the Creator, comes not forth to the sorceries of opium or of wine. The sublime vision comes to the pure and simple soul in a clean and chaste body. That is not an inspiration, which we owe to narcotics, but some counterfeit excitement and fury. Milton says that the lyric poet may drink wine and live generously, but the epic poet, he who shall sing of the gods and their descent unto men, must drink water out of a wooden bowl.[26] For poetry is not "Devil's wine," but God's wine. It is with this as it is with toys. We fill the hands and nurseries of our children with all manner of dolls, drums and horses; withdrawing their eyes from the plain face and sufficing objects of nature, the sun and moon, the animals, the water and stones, which should be their toys. So the poet's habit of living should be set on a key so low that the common influences should delight him. His cheerfulness should be the gift of the sunlight; the air should suffice for his inspiration, and he should be tipsy with water. That spirit which suffices quiet hearts, which seems to come forth to such from every dry knoll of sere grass, from every pine stump and half-imbedded stone on which the dull March sun shines, comes forth to the poor and hungry, and such as are of simple taste. If thou fill thy brain with Boston and New York, with fashion and covetousness, and wilt stimulate thy jaded senses with wine and French coffee, thou shalt find no radiance of wisdom in the lonely waste of the pine woods.

If the imagination intoxicates the poet, it is not inactive in other men. The metamorphosis excites in the beholder an emotion of joy. The use of symbols has a certain power of emancipation and exhilaration for all men. We seem to be touched by a wand, which makes us dance and run about happily, like children. We are like persons who come out of a cave or cellar into the open air. This is the effect on us of tropes, fables, oracles and all poetic forms. Poets are thus liberating gods. Men have really got a new sense, and found within their world another world, or nest of worlds; for, the metamorphosis once seen, we divine that it does not stop. I will not now consider how much this makes the charm of algebra and the mathematics, which also have their tropes, but it is felt in every definition; as when Aristotle defines *space* to be an immovable vessel in which things are contained;—or when Plato defines a *line* to be a flowing point; or *figure* to be a bound of solid; and many the like, What a joyful sense of freedom we have when Vitruvius announces the old opinion of artists that no architect

---

[26] John Milton's (1608–74) sixth *Latin Elegy*. [Ed.]

can build any house well who does not know something of anatomy. When Socrates, in Charmides, tells us that the soul is cured of its maladies by certain incantations, and that these incantations are beautiful reasons, from which temperance is generated in souls; when Plato calls the world an animal, and Timaeus affirms that the plants also are animals; or affirms a man to be a heavenly tree, growing with his root, which is his head, upward; and, as George Chapman, following him, writes,

"So in our tree of man, whose nervie root
Springs in his top;"—[27]

when Orpheus speaks of hoariness as "that white flower which marks extreme old age"; when Proclus calls the universe the statue of the intellect; when Chaucer, in his praise of "Gentilesse," compares good blood in mean condition to fire, which, though carried to the darkest house betwixt this and the mount of Caucasus, will yet hold its natural office and burn as bright as if twenty thousand men did it behold; when John saw, in the Apocalypse, the ruin of the world through evil, and the stars fall from heaven as the fig tree casteth her untimely fruit; when Aesop reports the whole catalogue of common daily relations through the masquerade of birds and beasts;—we take the cheerful hint of the immortality of our essence and its versatile habit and escapes, as when the gypsies say of themselves "it is in vain to hang them, they cannot die."[28]

The poets are thus liberating gods. The ancient British bards had for the title of their order, "Those who are free throughout the world." They are free, and they make free. An imaginative book renders us much more service at first, by stimulating us through its tropes, than afterward when we arrive at the precise sense of the author. I think nothing is of any value in books, excepting the transcendental and extraordinary. If a man is inflamed and carried away by his thought, to that degree that he forgets the authors and the public and heeds only this one dream, which holds him, like an insanity, let me read his paper, and you may have all the arguments and histories and criticism. All the value which attaches to Pythagoras, Paracelsus, Cornelius Agrippa, Cardan, Kepler, Swedenborg, Schelling, Oken, or any

---

[27] George Chapman (1559–1634), "Epistle Dedicatory," in his English translation of Homer's *Iliad*. [Ed.]

[28] In the long catalogue of examples in this paragraph, Emerson shows how poetic or figurative language is used by philosophers, architects, translators, and saints, as well as poets. The several examples from Plato (twice) and Socrates suggest an otherwise very modern claim that Plato's objections to poetic rhetoric as "imitations of imitations" are contradicted by Plato's own use of elaborate figurative language and fictional devices in his dialogues. [Ed.]

other who introduces questionable facts into his cosmogony, as angels, devils, magic, astrology, palmistry, mesmerism, and so on, is the certificate we have of departure from routine, and that here is a new witness.[29] That also is the best success in conversation, the magic of liberty, which puts the world like a ball in our hands. How cheap even the liberty then seems; how mean to study, when an emotion communicates to the intellect the power to sap and upheave nature; how great the perspective! nations, times, systems, enter and disappear like threads in tapestry of large figure and many colors; dream delivers us to dream, and while the drunkenness lasts we will sell our bed, our philosophy, our religion, in our opulence.

There is good reason why we should prize this liberation. The fate of the poor shepherd, who, blinded and lost in the snowstorm, perishes in a drift within a few feet of his cottage door, is an emblem of the state of man. On the brink of the waters of life and truth, we are miserably dying. The inaccessibleness of every thought but that we are in, is wonderful. What if you come near to it; you are as remote when you are nearest as when you are farthest. Every thought is also a prison; every heaven is also a prison. Therefore we love the poet, the inventor, who in any form, whether in an ode or in an action or in looks and behavior, has yielded us a new thought. He unlocks our chains and admits us to a new scene.

This emancipation is dear to all men, and the power to impart it, as it must come from greater depth and scope of thought, is a measure of intellect. Therefore all books of the imagination endure, all which ascend to that truth that the writer sees nature beneath him, and uses it as his exponent. Every verse or sentence possessing this virtue will take care of its own immortality. The religions of the world are the ejaculations of a few imaginative men.

But the quality of the imagination is to flow, and not to freeze. The poet did not stop at the color or the form, but read their meaning; neither may he rest in this meaning, but he makes the same objects exponents of his new thought. Here is the difference betwixt the poet and the mystic, that the last nails a symbol to one sense, which was a true sense for a moment, but soon becomes old and false. For all symbols are fluxional; all language is vehicular and transitive, and is good, as ferries and horses are, for conveyance, not as farms and houses are, for homestead.[30] Mysticism consists

---

[29] In a catalogue of ancient and Renaissance intellectuals, Emerson refers to their various superstitions to suggest that creative minds in all disciplines view the world poetically and figuratively. Emerson is also suggesting that science and imagination should not be strictly distinguished. [Ed.]

[30] Emerson's conception of thought as liberating and fluid anticipates William James's pluralism, especially in James's *A Pluralistic Universe* (1909). [Ed.]

in the mistake of an accidental and individual symbol for an universal one. The morning-redness happens to be the favorite meteor to the eyes of Jacob Behmen,[31] and comes to stand to him for truth and faith; and, he believes, should stand for the same realities to every reader. But the first reader prefers as naturally the symbol of a mother and child, or a gardener and his bulb, or a jeweler polishing a gem. Either of these, or of a myriad more, are equally good to the person to whom they are significant. Only they must be held lightly, and be very willingly translated into the equivalent terms which others use. And the mystic must be steadily told, — All that you say is just as true without the tedious use of that symbol as with it. Let us have a little algebra, instead of this trite rhetoric, — universal signs, instead of these village symbols, — and we shall both be gainers. The history of hierarchies seems to show that all religious error consisted in making the symbol too stark and solid, and was at last nothing but an excess of the organ of language.

Swedenborg, of all men in the recent ages, stands eminently for the translator of nature into thought. I do not know the man in history to whom things stood so uniformly for words. Before him the metamorphosis continually plays. Everything on which his eye rests, obeys the impulses of moral nature. The figs become grapes whilst he eats them. When some of his angels affirmed a truth, the laurel twig which they held blossomed in their hands. The noise which at a distance appeared like gnashing and thumping, on coming nearer was found to be the voice of disputants. The men in one of his visions, seen in heavenly light, appeared like dragons, and seemed in darkness; but to each other they appeared as men, and when the light from heaven shone into their cabin, they complained of the darkness, and were compelled to shut the window that they might see.

There was this perception in him, which makes the poet or seer an object of awe and terror, namely that the same man or society of men may wear one aspect to themselves and their companions, and a different aspect to higher intelligences. Certain priests, whom he describes as conversing very learnedly together, appeared to the children, who were at some distance, like dead horses; and many the like misappearances. And instantly the mind inquires whether these fishes under the bridge, yonder oxen in the pasture, those dogs in the yard, are immutably fishes, oxen, and dogs, or only so appear to me, and perchance to themselves appear upright men; and whether I appear as a man to all eyes. The Brahmins and Pythagoras propounded the same question, and if any poet has witnessed

---

[31] Jacob Boehme, seventeenth-century German mystic whose writings, along with Emanuel Swedenborg's, strongly influenced Emerson's own mysticism. [Ed.]

the transformation he doubtless found it in harmony with various experiences.[32] We have all seen changes as considerable in wheat and caterpillars. He is the poet and shall draw us with love and terror, who sees through the flowing vest the firm nature, and can declare it.

I look in vain for the poet whom I describe. We do not with sufficient plainness or sufficient profoundness address ourselves to life, nor dare we chant our own times and social circumstance. If we filled the day with bravery, we should not shrink from celebrating it. Time and nature yield us many gifts, but not yet the timely man, the new religion, the reconciler, whom all things await. Dante's praise is that he dared to write his autobiography in colossal cipher, or into universality. We have yet had no genius in America, with tyrannous eye, which knew the value of our incomparable materials, and saw, in the barbarism and materialism of the times, another carnival of the same gods whose picture he so much admires in Homer; then in the Middle Age; then in Calvinism. Banks and tariffs, the newspaper and caucus, Methodism and Unitarianism, are flat and dull to dull people, but rest on the same foundations of wonder as the town of Troy and the temple of Delphi, and are as swiftly passing away. Our log-rolling, our stumps and their politics, our fisheries, our Negroes and Indians, our boasts and our repudiations, the wrath of rogues and the pusillanimity of honest men, the northern trade, the southern planting, the western clearing, Oregon and Texas, are yet unsung.[33] Yet America is a poem in our eyes; its ample geography dazzles the imagination, and it will not wait long for meters. If I have not found that excellent combination of gifts in my countrymen which I seek, neither could I aid myself to fix the idea of the poet by reading now and then in Chalmers' collection of five centuries of English poets.[34] These are wits more than poets, though there

---

[32] The Hindus ("Brahmins") and the Greek philosopher Pythagoras speculated on metempsychosis or "the transmigration of souls," meaning that after death we might take on different human, animal, or vegetable forms and return to life. Emerson suggests that whoever hints of such natural "metamorphosis" is a poet, recalling once again Sir Philip Sidney's idea of poetry as that which represents a "golden world" that is both ideal and redemptive. [Ed.]

[33] Emerson makes an appeal for an "American literature" that would celebrate the unique qualities of American life and culture. His references to "our Negroes and Indians," as well as to "Oregon and Texas" (territories contested in the 1840s with Great Britain and Mexico, respectively), suggest that America's social and political problems, such as slavery and genocide of native peoples, should be treated in this literature, not just national glories. [Ed.]

[34] Alexander Chalmers' anthology, *The Works of the English Poets, from Chaucer to Cowper* (1810), 21 vols. [Ed.]

have been poets among them. But when we adhere to the ideal of the poet, we have our difficulties even with Milton and Homer. Milton is too literary, and Homer too literal and historical.

But I am not wise enough for a national criticism, and must use the old largeness a little longer, to discharge my errand from the muse to the poet concerning his art.

Art is the path of the creator to his work. The paths or methods are ideal and eternal, though few men ever see them; not the artist himself for years, or for a lifetime, unless he come into the conditions. The painter, the sculptor, the composer, the epic rhapsodist, the orator, all partake one desire, namely to express themselves symmetrically and abundantly, not dwarfishly and fragmentarily. They found or put themselves in certain conditions, as, the painter and sculptor before some impressive human figures; the orator into the assembly of the people; and the others in such scenes as each has found exciting to his intellect; and each presently feels the new desire. He hears a voice, he sees a beckoning. Then he is apprised, with wonder, what herds of daemons hem him in. He can no more rest; he says, with the old painter, "By God, it is in me and must go forth of me." He pursues a beauty, half seen, which flies before him. The poet pours out verses in every solitude. Most of the things he says are conventional, no doubt; but by and by he says something which is original and beautiful. That charms him. He would say nothing else but such things. In our way of talking, we say "That is yours, this is mine"; but the poet knows well that it is not his; that it is as strange and beautiful to him as to you; he would fain hear the like eloquence at length. Once having tasted this immortal ichor, [35] he cannot have enough of it, and as an admirable creative power exists in these intellections, it is of the last importance that these things get spoken. What a little of all we know is said! What drops of all the sea of our science are baled up! and by what accident it is that these are exposed, when so many secrets sleep in nature! Hence the necessity of speech and song; hence these throbs and heart-beatings in the orator, at the door of the assembly, to the end namely that thought may be ejaculated as Logos,[36] or Word.

Doubt not, O poet, but persist. Say "It is in me, and shall out." Stand there, balked and dumb, stuttering and stammering, hissed and hooted, stand and strive, until at last rage draw out of thee that *dream*-power which every night shows thee is thine own; a power transcending all limit and

---

[35] "Ichor" is Greek for the "blood of the gods," which dead souls in Hades had to drink before they could speak. [Orig. ed.]

[36] Greek for "word," associated in Genesis with the divine and creative word: "In the beginning there was the Word and the Word was [with] God." [Ed.]

privacy, and by virtue of which a man is the conductor of the whole river of electricity. Nothing walks, or creeps, or grows, or exists, which must not in turn arise and walk before him as exponent of his meaning. Comes he to that power, his genius is no longer exhaustible. All the creatures by pairs and by tribes pour into his mind as into a Noah's ark, to come forth again to people a new world. This is like the stock of air for our respiration or for the combustion of our fireplace; not a measure of gallons, but the entire atmosphere if wanted. And therefore the rich poets, as Homer, Chaucer, Shakespeare, and Raphael, have obviously no limits to their works, except the limits of their lifetime, and resemble a mirror carried through the street, ready to render an image of every created thing.

O poet! a new nobility is conferred in groves and pastures, and not in castles or by the sword-blade any longer. The conditions are hard, but equal. Thou shalt leave the world, and know the muse only. Thou shalt not know any longer the times, customs, graces, politics, or opinions of men, but shalt take all from the muse. For the time of towns is tolled from the world by funereal chimes, but in nature the universal hours are counted by succeeding tribes of animals and plants, and by growth of joy on joy. God wills also that thou abdicate a manifold and duplex life, and that thou be content that others speak for thee. Others shall be thy gentlemen and shall represent all courtesy and worldly life for thee; others shall do the great and resounding actions also. Thou shalt lie close hid with nature, and canst not be afforded to the Capitol or the Exchange. The world is full of renunciations and apprenticeships, and this is thine; thou must pass for a fool and a churl for a long season. This is the screen and sheath in which Pan has protected his well-beloved flower, and thou shalt be known only to thine own, and they shall console thee with tenderest love. And thou shalt not be able to rehearse the names of thy friends in thy verse, for an old shame before the holy ideal. And this is the reward; that the ideal shall be real to thee, and the impressions of the actual world shall fall like summer rain, copious, but not troublesome to thy invulnerable essence. Thou shalt have the whole land for thy park and manor, the sea for thy bath and navigation, without tax and without envy; the woods and the rivers thou shalt own, and thou shalt possess that wherein others are only tenants and boarders. Thou true land-lord! Sea-lord! air-lord! Wherever snow falls or water flows or birds fly, wherever day and night meet in twilight, wherever the blue heaven is hung by clouds or sown with stars, wherever are forms with transparent boundaries, wherever are outlets into celestial space, wherever is danger, and awe, and love,—there is Beauty, plenteous as rain, shed for thee, and though thou shouldst walk the world over, thou shalt not be able to find a condition inopportune or ignoble.

An Address . . . on . . . the Emancipation of the Negroes in the British West Indies
Concord, August 1, 1844[1]

Friends and Fellow Citizens,

We are met to exchange congratulations on the anniversary of an event singular in the history of civilization; a day of reason; of the clear light; of that which makes us better than a flock of birds and beasts: a day, which gave the immense fortification of a fact, — of gross history, — to ethical abstractions. It was the settlement, as far as a great Empire was concerned, of a question on which almost every leading citizen in it had taken care to record his vote; one which for many years absorbed the attention of the best and most eminent of mankind. I might well hesitate, coming from other studies, and without the smallest claim to be a special laborer in this work of humanity, to undertake to set this matter before you; which ought rather to be done by a strict cooperation of many well-advised persons; but I shall not apologize for my weakness. In this cause, no man's weakness is any prejudice; it has a thousand sons; if one man cannot speak, ten others can; and whether by the wisdom of its friends, or by the folly of the adversaries; by speech and by silence; by doing and by omitting to do, it goes forward. Therefore I will speak, — or, not I, but the might of liberty in my weakness. The subject is said to have the property of making dull men eloquent.

It has been in all men's experience a marked effect of the enterprise in behalf of the African, to generate an overbearing and defying spirit. The institution of slavery seems to its opponent to have but one side, and he feels that none but a stupid or a malignant person can hesitate on a view of the facts. Under such an impulse, I was about to say, If any cannot speak, or cannot hear the words of freedom, let him go hence, — I had almost said, Creep into your grave, the universe has no need of you! But I have thought better: let him not go. When we consider what remains to be done for this interest, in this country, the dictates of humanity make us tender of such as are not yet persuaded. The hardest selfishness is to be borne with. Let us withhold every reproachful, and, if we can, every indignant remark. In this cause, we must renounce our temper, and the risings of pride. If there be

Emerson's Anti-Slavery Writings. Ed. Len Gougeon and Joel Myerson. New Haven: Yale UP, 1995. (All notes are by the original editors.)

[1] Emerson was invited to give this address in Concord by the Women's Anti-Slavery Society. In addition to Emerson, who was "the orator of the day," Samuel Joseph May and Frederick Douglass, among others, delivered lectures.

any man who thinks the ruin of a race of men a small matter, compared with the last decoration and completions of his own comfort, —who would not so much as part with his ice-cream, to save them from rapine and manacles, I think, I must not hesitate to satisfy that man, that also his cream and vanilla are safer and cheaper, by placing the negro nation on a fair footing, than by robbing them. If the Virginian piques himself on the picturesque luxury of his vassalage, on the heavy Ethiopian manners of his house-servants, their silent obedience, their hue of bronze, their turbaned heads, and would not exchange them for the more intelligent but precarious hired-service of whites, I shall not refuse to show him, that when their free-papers are made out, it will still be their interest to remain on his estate, and that the oldest planters of Jamaica are convinced, that it is cheaper to pay wages, than to own the slave.

The history of mankind interests us only as it exhibits a steady gain of truth and right, in the incessant conflict which it records, between the material and the moral nature. From the earliest monuments, it appears, that one race was victim, and served the other races. In the oldest temples of Egypt, negro captives are painted on the tombs of kings, in such attitudes as to show that they are on the point of being executed; and Herodotus, our oldest historian, relates that the Troglodytes hunted the Ethiopians in four-horse-chariots.[2] From the earliest time, the negro has been an article of luxury to the commercial nations. So has it been, down to the day that has just dawned on the world. Language must be raked, the secrets of slaughter-houses and infamous holes that cannot front the day, must be ransacked, to tell what negro-slavery has been. These men, our benefactors, as they are producers of corn and wine, of coffee, of tobacco, of cotton, of sugar, of rum, and brandy, gentle and joyous themselves, and producers of comfort and luxury for the civilized world, —there seated in the finest climates of the globe, children of the sun, —I am heart-sick when I read how they came there, and how they are kept there. Their case was left out of the mind and out of the heart of their brothers. The prizes of society, the trumpet of fame, the privileges of learning, of culture, of religion, the decencies and joys of

---

[2]This view was common at the time. Josiah C. Nott, in *Types of Mankind, or Ethnological Researches* (Philadelphia, 1854), states that "the monuments of Egypt prove, the *Negro* races have not, during 4000 years at least, been able to make one solitary step, in Negroland, from their savage state" (p. 95). Louis Agassiz, Harvard professor of natural history and Emerson's friend, also published an essay, "Sketch of the Natural Provinces of the Animal World and Their Relation to the Different types of Man," in this volume.

Herodotus (d. ca. 424), Greek historian sometimes referred to as the father of history. Troglodytes, the name given by Greeks to various primitive tribes known for crude and uncivilized behavior.

marriage, honor, obedience, personal authority, and a perpetual melioration into a finer civility, these were for all, but not for them. For the negro,
was the slave-ship to begin with, in whose filthy hold he sat in irons, unable
to lie down; bad food, and insufficiency of that; disfranchisement; no property in the rags that covered him; no marriage, no right in the poor black
woman that cherished him in her bosom,—no right to the children of his
body; no security from the humors, none from the crimes, none from the
appetites of his master: toil, famine, insult, and flogging; and, when he
sunk in the furrow, no wind of good fame blew over him, no priest of salvation visited him with glad tidings: but he went down to death, with dusky
dreams of African shadow-catchers and Obeahs[3] hunting him. Very sad
was the negro tradition, that the Great Spirit, in the beginning, offered the
black man, whom he loved better than the buckra[4] or white, his choice of
two boxes, a big and a little one. The black man was greedy, and chose the
largest. "The buckra box was full up with pen, paper, and whip, and the negro box with hoe and bill; and hoe and bill for negro to this day."

But the crude element of good in human affairs must work and ripen,
spite of whips, and plantation-laws, and West Indian interest. Conscience
rolled on its pillow, and could not sleep. We sympathize very tenderly here
with the poor aggrieved planter, of whom so many unpleasant things are
said; but if we saw the whip applied to old men, to tender women; and, un-
deniably, though I shrink to say so,—pregnant women set in the treadmill
for refusing to work, when, not they, but the eternal law of animal nature
refused to work;—if we saw men's backs flayed with cowhides, and "hot
rum poured on, superinduced with brine or pickle, rubbed in with a corn-
husk, in the scorching heat of the sun;"—if we saw the runaways hunted
with blood-hounds into swamps and hills; and, in cases of passion, a
planter throwing his negro into a copper of boiling cane-juice,—if we saw
these things with eyes, we too should wince. They are not pleasant sights.
The blood is moral: the blood is in anti-slavery: it runs cold in the veins:
the stomach rises with disgust, and curses slavery. Well, so it happened; a
good man or woman, a country-boy or girl, it would so fall out, once in a
while saw these injuries, and had the indiscretion to tell of them. The horrid story ran and flew; the winds blew it all over the world. They who heard
it, asked their rich and great friends, if it was true, or only missionary lies.
The richest and greatest, the prime minister of England, the king's privy
council were obliged to say, that it was too true. It became plain to all men,
the more this business was looked into, that the crimes and cruelties of the

[3]Charms or fetishes, here used to mean "Obeah men" or witch doctors.
[4]Disparaging term used by blacks for those of predominantly white blood.

slave-traders and slave-owners could not be overstated. The more it was searched, the more shocking anecdotes came up, —things not to be spoken. Humane persons who were informed of the reports, insisted on proving them. Granville Sharp was accidentally made acquainted with the sufferings of a slave, whom a West Indian planter had brought with him to London, and had beaten with a pistol on his head so badly, that his whole body became diseased, and the man useless to his master, who left him to go whither he pleased.[5] The man applied to Mr. William Sharp,[6] a charitable surgeon, who attended the diseases of the poor. In process of time, he was healed. Granville Sharp found him at his brother's, and procured a place for him in an apothecary's shop. The master accidentally met his recovered slave, and instantly endeavored to get possession of him again. Sharp protected the slave. In consulting with the lawyers, they told Sharp the laws were against him. Sharp would not believe it; no prescription on earth could ever render such iniquities legal. "But the decisions are against you, and Lord Mansfield, now chief justice of England, leans to the decisions."[7] Sharp instantly sat down and gave himself to the study of English law for more than two years, until he had proved that the opinions relied on of Talbot and Yorke, were incompatible with the former English decisions, and with the whole spirit of English law.[8] He published his book in 1769, and he so filled the heads and hearts of his advocates, that when he brought the case of George Somerset,[9] another slave, before Lord Mansfield, the slavish decisions were set aside, and equity affirmed. There is a sparkle of God's righteousness in Lord Mansfield's judgment, which does the heart good. Very unwilling had that great lawyer been to reverse the late decisions; he suggested twice from the bench, in the course of the trial, how the question might be got rid of: but the hint was not taken; the case was adjourned again and again, and judgment delayed. At last judgment was demanded, and on the 22nd June, 1772, Lord Mansfield is reported to have decided in these words; "Immemorial usage preserves the memory of *positive law*, long after all traces of the occasion, reason, authority, and time of its introduction, are lost; and in a case so odious as the condition of slaves,

---

[5] Granville Sharp (1735–1813), philanthropist, pamphleteer, and scholar.

[6] William Sharp (1805–1896), physician.

[7] William Murray (1705–1793), chief justice of the King's Bench of Great Britain (1756–1788).

[8] Charles Talbot (1685–1737) and Philip Yorke (1690–1764), jurists who ruled in a slave case in 1729 that a slave did not become free by coming to England or by baptism, and that any master might compel his slave to return with him to the West Indies.

[9] Identified variously as James Somerset, Sommerset, Somersett, or Summerset.

must be taken strictly; (tracing the subject to natural principles, the claim of slavery never can be supported.) The power claimed by this return never was in use here. We cannot say the cause set forth by this return is allowed or approved of by the laws of this kingdom; and therefore the man must be discharged." [10]

This decision established the principle that the "air of England is too pure for any slave to breathe," but the wrongs in the islands were not thereby touched. Public attention, however, was drawn that way, and the methods of the stealing and the transportation from Africa, became noised abroad. The Quakers got the story. In their plain meeting-houses, and prim dwellings, this dismal agitation got entrance. They were rich: they owned for debt, or by inheritance, island property; they were religious, tender-hearted men and women; and they had to hear the news, and digest it as they could. Six Quakers met in London on the 6th July, 1783; William Dillwyn, Samuel Hoar, George Harrison, Thomas Knowles, John Lloyd, Joseph Woods, "to consider what step they should take for the relief and liberation of the negro slaves in the West Indies, and for the discouragement of the slave-trade on the coast of Africa." [11] They made friends and raised money for the slave; they interested their Yearly Meeting; and all English and all American Quakers. John Woolman of New Jersey, whilst yet an apprentice, was uneasy in his mind when he was set to write a bill of sale of a negro, for his master. [12] He gave his testimony against the traffic, in Maryland and Virginia. Thomas Clarkson was a youth at Cambridge, England, when the subject given out for a Latin prize dissertation, was, "Is it right to make slaves of others against their will?" [13] He wrote an essay, and won the prize; but he wrote too well for his own peace; he began to ask himself, if these things could be true; and if they were, he could no longer rest. He left Cambridge; he fell in with the six Quakers. They engaged him to act for them. He himself interested Mr. Wilberforce in the matter. [14] The

---

[10] Emerson apparently felt a continuing interest in Mansfield. He refers to his decision in the Somerset case again in a journal entry from 1850 (*JMN* [*Journals and Miscellaneous Notebooks*], 11:281), in a passage that he would use a year later in the Fugitive Slave Law address at concord.

[11] These six Quakers are usually credited with launching the British abolition movement in 1783. They were later joined by Granville Sharp and Thomas Clarkson (see n. 13 below).

[12] John Woolman (1720–1772), American Quaker and early advocate of the abolition of slavery, wrote *Some Considerations on the Keeping of Negroes* (1754).

[13] Thomas Clarkson (1760–1846), British philanthropist, wrote his prize essay against slavery in 1786.

[14] William Wilberforce (1759–1833), philanthropist and member of Parliament.

shipmasters in that trade were the greatest miscreants, and guilty of every barbarity to their own crews. Clarkson went to Bristol, made himself acquainted with the interior of the slaveships, and the details of the trade. The facts confirmed his sentiment, "that Providence had never made that to be wise, which was immoral, and that the slave-trade was as impolitic as it was unjust;" that it was found peculiarly fatal to those employed in it. More seamen died in that trade, in one year, than in the whole remaining trade of the country in two. Mr. Pitt and Mr. Fox were drawn into the generous enterprise.[15] In 1788, the House of Commons voted Parliamentary inquiry. In 1791, a bill to abolish the trade was brought in by Wilberforce, and supported by him, and by Fox, and Burke, and Pitt, with the utmost ability and faithfulness; resisted by the planters, and the whole West Indian interest, and lost. During the next sixteen years, ten times, year after year, the attempt was renewed by Mr. Wilberforce, and ten times defeated by the planters. The king, and all the royal family but one, were against it. These debates are instructive, as they show on what grounds the trade was assailed and defended. Every thing generous, wise, and sprightly is sure to come to the attack. On the other part, are found cold prudence, barefaced selfishness, and silent votes. But the nation was aroused to enthusiasm. Every horrid fact became known. In 1791, three hundred thousand persons in Britain pledged themselves to abstain from all articles of island produce. The planters were obliged to give way; and in 1807, on the 25th March, the bill passed, and the slave-trade was abolished.

The assailants of slavery had early agreed to limit their political action on this subject to the abolition of the trade, but Granville Sharp, as a matter of conscience, whilst he acted as chairman of the London Committee, felt constrained to record his protest against the limitation, declaring that slavery was as much a crime against the Divine law, as the slave-trade. The trade, under false flags, went on as before. In 1821, according to official documents presented to the American government by the Colonization Society, 200,000 slaves were deported from Africa.[16] Nearly 30,000 were landed in the port of Havana alone. In consequence of the dangers of the trade growing out of the act of abolition, ships were built sharp for swiftness, and with a frightful disregard of the comfort of the victims they were destined to transport. They carried five, six, even seven hundred stowed in a ship built so narrow as to be unsafe, being made just broad enough on the beam

---

[15] William Pitt (the Younger)(1759–1806), prime minister of England (1784–1801); Charles James Fox (1749–1806), member of Parliament who supported the abolition of the slave trade.
[16] The American Colonization Society was founded in 1817.

to keep the sea. In attempting to make its escape from the pursuit of a man-of-war, one ship flung five hundred slaves alive into the sea. These facts went into Parliament. In the islands, was an ominous state of cruel and licentious society; every house had a dungeon attached to it; every slave was worked by the whip. There is no end to the tragic anecdotes in the municipal records of the colonies. The boy was set to strip and to flog his own mother to blood, for a small offence. Looking in the face of his master by the negro was held to be violence by the island courts. He was worked sixteen hours, and his ration by law, in some islands, was a pint of flour and one salt herring a day. He suffered insult, stripes, mutilation, at the humor of the master: iron collars were riveted on their necks with iron prongs ten inches long; capsicum pepper was rubbed in the eyes of the females; and they were done to death with the most shocking levity between the master and manager, without fine or inquiry. And when, at last, some Quakers, Moravians, and Wesleyan and Baptist missionaries, following in the steps of Carey and Ward in the East Indies,[17] had been moved to come and cheer the poor victim with the hope of some reparation, in a future world, of the wrongs he suffered in this, these missionaries were persecuted by the planters, their lives threatened, their chapels burned, and the negroes furiously forbidden to go near them. These outrages rekindled the flame of British indignation. Petitions poured into Parliament: a million persons signed their names to these; and in 1833, on the 14th May, Lord Stanley, minister of the colonies, introduced into the House of Commons his bill for the Emancipation.[18]

The scheme of the minister, with such modification as it received in the legislature, proposed gradual emancipation; that on 1st August, 1834, all persons now slaves should be entitled to be registered as apprenticed laborers, and to acquire thereby all the rights and privileges of freemen, subject to the restriction of laboring under certain conditions. These conditions were, that the praedials should owe three fourths of the profits of their labor to their masters for six years, and the nonpraedials for four years.[19] The other fourth of the apprentice's time was to be his own, which he might sell to his master, or to other persons; and at the end of the term of years fixed, he should be free.

With these provisions and conditions, the bill proceeds, in the twelfth section, in the following terms. "Be it enacted, that all and every person

---

[17] William Carey (1761–1834) and William Ward (1769–1823), Baptist missionaries noted especially for their work in the East Indies.
[18] Edward George Stanley (1799–1869), fourteenth earl of Derby.
[19] A praedial is a slave attached to an estate.

who, on the 1st August, 1834, shall be holden in slavery within any such British colony as aforesaid, shall upon and from and after the said 1st August, become and be to all intents and purposes free, and discharged of and from all manner of slavery, and shall be absolutely and forever manumitted; and that the children thereafter born to any such person, and the offspring of such children, shall, in like manner, be free from their birth; and that from and after the 1st August, 1834, slavery shall be and is hereby utterly and forever abolished and declared unlawful throughout the British colonies, plantations, and possessions abroad."

The ministers, having estimated the slave products of the colonies in annual exports of sugar, rum, and coffee, at £1,500,000 *per annum,* estimated the total value of the slave-property at 30,000,000 pounds sterling, and proposed to give the planters, as a compensation for so much of the slaves' time as the act took from them, 20,000,000 pounds sterling, to be divided into nineteen shares for the nineteen colonies, and to be distributed to the owners of slaves by commissioners, whose appointment and duties were regulated by the Act. After much debate, the bill passed by large majorities. The apprenticeship system is understood to have proceeded from Lord Brougham, and was by him urged on his colleagues, who, it is said, were inclined to the policy of immediate emancipation.[20]

The colonial legislatures received the act of Parliament with various degrees of displeasure, and, of course, every provision of the bill was criticised with severity. The new relation between the master and the apprentice, it was feared, would be mischievous; for the bill required the appointment of magistrates, who should hear every complaint of the apprentice, and see that justice was done him. It was feared that the interest of the master and servant would now produce perpetual discord between them. In the island of Antigua, containing 37,000 people, 30,000 being negroes, these objections had such weight, that the legislature rejected the apprenticeship system, and adopted absolute emancipation. In the other islands the system of the ministry was accepted.

The reception of it by the negro population was equal in nobleness to the deed. The negroes were called together by the missionaries and by the planters, and the news explained to them. On the night of the 31st July, they met everywhere at their churches and chapels, and at midnight, when the clock struck twelve, on their knees, the silent, weeping assembly became men; they rose and embraced each other; they cried, they sung, they prayed,

---

[20]Henry Peter, Lord Brougham (1778–1868), member of Parliament, a founder of the *Edinburgh Review.*

they were wild with joy, but there was no riot, no feasting. I have never read anything in history more touching than the moderation of the negroes. Some American captains left the shore and put to sea, anticipating insurrection and general murder. With far different thoughts, the negroes spent the hour in their huts and chapels. I will not repeat to you the well-known paragraph, in which Messrs. Thome and Kimball, the commissioners sent out in the year 1837 by the American Anti-slavery Society, describe the occurrences of that night in the island of Antigua. It has been quoted in every newspaper, and Dr. Channing has given it additional fame.[21] But I must be indulged in quoting a few sentences from the pages that follow it, narrating the behavior of the emancipated people on the next day.

"The first of August came on Friday, and a release was proclaimed from all work until the next Monday. The day was chiefly spent by the great mass of the negroes in the churches and chapels. The clergy and missionaries throughout the island were actively engaged, seizing the opportunity to enlighten the people on all the duties and responsibilities of their new relation, and urging them to the attainment of that higher liberty with which Christ maketh his children free. In every quarter, we were assured, the day was like a sabbath. Work had ceased. The hum of business was still: tranquillity pervaded the towns and country. The planters informed us, that they went to the chapels where their own people were assembled, greeted them, shook hands with them and exchanged the most hearty good wishes. At Grace Hill, there were at least a thousand persons around the Moravian Chapel who could not get in. For once the house of God suffered violence, and the violent took it by force. At Grace Bay, the people, all dressed in white, formed a procession, and walked arm in arm into the chapel. We were told that the dress of the negroes on that occasion was uncommonly simple and modest. There was not the least disposition to gaiety. Throughout the island, there was not a single dance known of, either day or night, nor so much as a fiddle played."[22]

On the next Monday morning, with very few exceptions, every negro on every plantation was in the field at his work. In some places, they waited to see their master, to know what bargain he would make; but, for the most part, throughout the islands, nothing painful occurred. In June, 1835, the

[21] William Ellery Channing (1780–1842), influential Boston Unitarian minister and early antislavery advocate much admired by Emerson, published his controversial work *Slavery* in 1835.

[22] "'Emancipation in the West Indies: a Six Months Tour in Antigua, Barbadoes, and Jamaica, in the year 1837. By J. A. Thome and J. H. Kimball, New York, 1838.'—pp. 146, 147." [Emerson's note.]

ministers, Lord Aberdeen and Sir George Grey,[23] declared to the Parliament, that the system worked well; that now for ten months, from 1st August, 1834, no injury or violence had been offered to any white, and only one black had been hurt in 800,000 negroes: and, contrary to many sinister predictions, that the new crop of island produce would not fall short of that of the last year.

But the habit of oppression was not destroyed by a law and a day of jubilee. It soon appeared in all the islands, that the planters were disposed to use their old privileges, and overwork the apprentices; to take from them, under various pretences, their fourth part of their time; and to exert the same licentious despotism as before. The negroes complained to the magistrates, and to the governor. In the island of Jamaica, this ill blood continually grew worse. The governors, Lord Belmore, the Earl of Sligo, and afterwards Sir Lionel Smith, (a governor of their own class, who had been sent out to gratify the planters,) threw themselves on the side of the oppressed, and are at constant quarrel with the angry and bilious island legislature.[24] Nothing can exceed the ill humor and sulkiness of the address of this assembly.

I may here express a general remark, which the history of slavery seems to justify, that it is not founded solely on the avarice of the planter. We sometimes say, the planter does not want slaves, he only wants the immunities and the luxuries which the slaves yield him; give him money, give him a machine that will yield him as much money as the slaves, and he will thankfully let them go. He has no love of slavery, he wants luxury, and he will pay even this price of crime and danger for it. But I think experience does not warrant this favorable distinction, but shows the existence, beside the covetousness, of a bitterer element, the love of power, the voluptuousness of holding a human being in his absolute control. We sometimes observe, that spoiled children contract a habit of annoying quite wantonly those who have charge of them, and seem to measure their own sense of well-being, not by what they do, but by the degree of reaction they can cause. It is vain to get rid of them by not minding them: if purring and humming is not noticed, they squeal and screech; then if you chide and console them, they find the experiment succeeds, and they begin again. The child will sit

---

[23] George Hamilton Gordon, fourth earl of Aberdeen (1784–1860); Sir George Grey (1799–1882), under secretary for the Colonies (1834, 1835–1839).

[24] Lord Belmore, lieutenant governor of Jamaica from 1829 to 1832, arrived at a time when the slavery question was being hotly debated, and he was recalled after a rebellion broke out; Lionel Smith (1778–1842) was the first British governor-general of the Windward Islands and, nominally, of British Guiana, Trinidad, and Saint Lucia.

in your arms contented, provided you do nothing. If you take a book and read, he commences hostile operations. The planter is the spoiled child of his unnatural habits, and has contracted in his indolent and luxurious climate the need of excitement by irritating and tormenting his slave.

Sir Lionel Smith defended the poor negro girls, prey to the licentiousness of the planters; they shall not be whipped with tamarind rods, if they do not comply with their master's will; he defended the negro women; they should not be made to dig the cane-holes, (which is the very hardest of the field-work;) he defended the Baptist preachers and the stipendiary magistrates, who are the negroes' friends, from the power of the planter. The power of the planters, however, to oppress, was greater than the power of the apprentice and of his guardians to withstand. Lord Brougham and Mr. Buxton declared that the planter had not fulfilled his part in the contract, whilst the apprentices had fulfilled theirs;[25] and demanded that the emancipation should be hastened, and the apprenticeship abolished. Parliament was compelled to pass additional laws for the defence and security of the negro, and in ill humor at these acts, the great island of Jamaica, with a population of half a million, and 300,000 negroes, early in 1838, resolved to throw up the two remaining years of apprenticeship, and to emancipate absolutely on the 1st August, 1838. In British Guiana, in Dominica, the same resolution had been earlier taken with more good will; and the other islands fell into the measure; so that on the 1st August, 1838, the shackles dropped from every British slave. The accounts which we have from all parties, both from the planters, and those too who were originally most opposed to the measure, and from the new freemen, are of the most satisfactory kind. The manner in which the new festival was celebrated, brings tears to the eyes. The First of August, 1838, was observed in Jamaica as a day of thanksgiving and prayer. Sir Lionel Smith, the governor, writes to the British Ministry, "It is impossible for me to do justice to the good order, decorum, and gratitude, which the whole laboring population manifested on that happy occasion. Though joy beamed on every countenance, it was throughout tempered with solemn thankfulness to God, and the churches and chapels were everywhere filled with these happy people in humble offering of praise."

The Queen, in her speech to the Lords and Commons, praised the conduct of the emancipated population: and, in 1840, Sir Charles Metcalfe, the new governor of Jamaica, in his address to the Assembly, expressed himself

---

[25] Thomas Fowell Buxton (1786–1845), member of Parliament and philanthropist, advocated prison reforms, repression of the slave trade, and the abolition of slavery in British dominions.

to that late exasperated body in these terms.[26] "All those who are acquainted with the state of the island, know that our emancipated population are as free, as independent in their conduct, as well-conditioned, as much in the enjoyment of abundance, and as strongly sensible of the blessings of liberty, as any that we know of in any country. All disqualifications and distinctions of color have ceased; men of all colors have equal rights in law, and an equal footing in society, and every man's position is settled by the same circumstances which regulate that point in other free countries, where no difference of color exists. It may be asserted, without fear of denial, that the former slaves of Jamaica are now as secure in all social rights, as free-born Britons." He further describes the erection of numerous churches, chapels, and schools, which the new population required, and adds that more are still demanded. The legislature, in their reply, echo the governor's statement, and say, "The peaceful demeanor of the emancipated population redounds to their own credit, and affords a proof of their continued comfort and prosperity."

I said, this event is signal in the history of civilization. There are many styles of civilization, and not one only. Ours is full of barbarities. There are many faculties in man, each of which takes its turn of activity, and that faculty which is paramount in any period, and exerts itself through the strongest nation, determines the civility of that age; and each age thinks its own the perfection of reason. Our culture is very cheap and intelligible. Unroof any house, and you shall find it. The well-being consists in having a sufficiency of coffee and toast, with a daily newspaper; a well-glazed parlor, with marbles, mirrors and centre-table; and the excitement of a few parties and a few rides in a year. Such as one house, such are all. The owner of a New York manor imitates the mansion and equipage of the London nobleman; the Boston merchant rivals his brother of New York; and the villages copy Boston. There have been nations elevated by great sentiments. Such was the civility of Sparta and the Dorian race, whilst it was defective in some of the chief elements of ours.[27] That of Athens, again lay in an intellect dedicated to beauty. That of Asia Minor in poetry, music, and arts; that of Palestine in piety; that of Rome in military arts and virtues, exalted by a prodigious magnanimity; that of China and Japan in the last exaggeration of decorum and etiquette. Our civility, England determines the style of, inasmuch as England is the strongest of the family of existing nations, and as we are the expansion of that people. It is that of a trading nation; it

---

[26] Charles Metcalfe (1785–1846), governor of Jamaica (1839–1842).

[27] Sparta, also called Lacedaemon, was an ancient Greek city whose citizens were noted for their severe militaristic discipline. The Dorians were one of the three principal peoples of ancient Greece from whom the Spartans were presumed to have descended.

is a shopkeeping civility. The English lord is a retired shopkeeper, and has the prejudices and timidities of that profession. And we are shopkeepers, and have acquired the vices and virtues that belong to trade. We peddle, we truck, we sail, we row, we ride in cars, we creep in teams, we go in canals — to market, and for the sale of goods. The national aim and employment streams into our ways of thinking, our laws, our habits, and our manners. The customer is the immediate jewel of our souls. Him we flatter, him we feast, compliment, vote for, and will not contradict. It was or it seemed the dictate of trade, to keep the negro down. We had found a race who were less warlike, and less energetic shopkeepers than we; who had very little skill in trade. We found it very convenient to keep them at work, since, by the aid of a little whipping, we could get their work for nothing but their board and the cost of whips. What if it cost a few unpleasant scenes on the coast of Africa? That was a great way off; and the scenes could be endured by some sturdy, unscrupulous fellows, who could go for high wages and bring us the men, and need not trouble our ears with the disagreeable particulars. If any mention was made of homicide, madness, adultery, and intolerable tortures, we would let the church-bells ring louder, the church organ swell its peal, and drown the hideous sound. The sugar they raised was excellent: nobody tasted blood in it. The coffee was fragrant; the tobacco was incense; the brandy made nations happy; the cotton clothed the world. What! all raised by these men, and no wages? Excellent! What a convenience! They seemed created by providence to bear the heat and the whipping, and make these fine articles.

But unhappily, most unhappily, gentlemen, man is born with intellect, as well as with a love of sugar, and with a sense of justice, as well as a taste for strong drink. These ripened, as well as those. You could not educate him, you could not get any poetry, any wisdom, any beauty in woman, any strong and commanding character in man, but these absurdities would still come flashing out, — these absurdities of a demand for justice, a generosity for the weak and oppressed. Unhappily too, for the planter, the laws of nature are in harmony with each other: that which the head and the heart demand, is found to be, in the long run, for what the grossest calculator calls his advantage. The moral sense is always supported by the permanent interest of the parties. Else, I know not how, in our world, any good would ever get done. It was shown to the planters that they, as well as the negroes, were slaves; that though they paid no wages, they got very poor work; that their estates were ruining them, under the finest climate; and that they needed the severest monopoly laws at home to keep them from bankruptcy. The oppression of the slave recoiled on them. They were full of vices; their children were lumps of pride, sloth, sensuality and rottenness. The position of woman was nearly as bad as it could be, and, like other robbers, they could not sleep in security. Many planters have said, since the emancipation, that, before that day, they were the greatest slaves on the estates. Slavery is no scholar, no improver; it does not love the whistle of the railroad; it does not love the newspaper, the mailbag, a college, a book, or a preacher who has the absurd whim of saying what he thinks; it does not increase the white population; it does not improve the soil; everything goes to decay. For these reasons, the islands proved bad customers to England. It was very easy for manufacturers less shrewd than those of Birmingham and Manchester to see,[28] that if the state of things in the islands was altered, if the slaves had wages, the slaves would be clothed, would build houses, would fill them with tools, with pottery, with crockery, with hardware; and negro women love fine clothes as well as white women. In every naked negro of those thousands, they saw a future customer. Meantime, they saw further, that the slave-trade, by keeping in barbarism the whole coast of eastern Africa, deprives them of countries and nations of customers, if once freedom and civility, and European manners could get a foothold there. But the trade could not be abolished, whilst this hungry West Indian market, with an appetite like the grave, cried, "More, more, bring me a hundred a day;" they could not expect any mitigation in the madness of the poor African war-chiefs. These considerations opened the eyes of the dullest in Britain. More than this, the West Indian estate was owned or mortgaged in England, and the owner and the mortgagee had very plain intimations that the feeling of English liberty was gaining every hour new mass and velocity, and the hostility to such as resisted it, would be fatal. The House of Commons would destroy the protection of island produce, and interfere on English politics in the island legislation: so they hastened to make the best of their position, and accepted the bill.

These considerations, I doubt not, had their weight, the interest of trade, the interest of the revenue, and, moreover, the good fame of the action. It was inevitable that men should feel these motives. But they do not appear to have had an excessive or unreasonable weight. On reviewing this history, I think the whole transaction reflects infinite honor on the people and parliament of England. It was a stately spectacle, to see the cause of human rights argued with so much patience and generosity, and with such a mass of evidence before that powerful people. It is a creditable incident in the history, that when, in 1789, the first privy-council report of evidence on the trade, a bulky folio, (embodying all the facts which the London Committee had been engaged for years in collecting, and all the examinations before the council,) was presented to the House of Commons, a late day be-

---

[28] English cities known as manufacturing centers.

ing named for the discussion, in order to give members time, —Mr. Wilberforce, Mr. Pitt, the prime minister, and other gentlemen, took advantage of the postponement, to retire into the country, to read the report. For months and years the bill was debated, with some consciousness of the extent of its relations by the first citizens of England, the foremost men of the earth; every argument was weighed, every particle of evidence was sifted, and laid in the scale; and, at last, the right triumphed, the poor man was vindicated, and the oppressor was flung out. I know that England has the advantage of trying the question at a wide distance from the spot where the nuisance exists: the planters are not, excepting in rare examples, members of the legislature. The extent of the empire, and the magnitude and number of other questions crowding into court, keep this one in balance, and prevent it from obtaining that ascendancy, and being urged with that intemperance, which a question of property tends to acquire. There are causes in the composition of the British legislature, and the relation of its leaders to the country and to Europe, which exclude much that is pitiful and injurious in other legislative assemblies. From these reasons, the question was discussed with a rare independence and magnanimity. It was not narrowed down to a paltry electioneering trap, and, I must say, a delight in justice, an honest tenderness for the poor negro, for man suffering these wrongs, combined with the national pride, which refused to give the support of English soil, or the protection of the English flag, to these disgusting violations of nature.

Forgive me, fellow citizens, if I own to you, that in the last few days that my attention has been occupied with this history, I have not been able to read a page of it, without the most painful comparisons. Whilst I have read of England, I have thought of New England. Whilst I have meditated in my solitary walks on the magnanimity of the English Bench and Senate, reaching out the benefit of the law to the most helpless citizen in her world-wide realm, I have found myself oppressed by other thoughts. As I have walked in the pastures and along the edge of woods, I could not keep my imagination on those agreeable figures, for other images that intruded on me. I could not see the great vision of the patriots and senators who have adopted the slave's cause: —they turned their backs on me. No: I see other pictures— of mean men: I see very poor, very ill-clothed, very ignorant men, not surrounded by happy friends, —to be plain, —poor black men of obscure employment as mariners, cooks, or stewards, in ships, yet citizens of this our Commonwealth of Massachusetts, —freeborn as we, —whom the slave-laws of the States of South Carolina, Georgia, and Louisiana, have arrested in the vessels in which they visited those ports, and shut up in jails so long as the vessel remained in port, with the stringent addition, that if the shipmaster fails to pay the costs of this official arrest, and the board in jail, these citizens are to be sold for slaves, to pay that expense. This man, these men, I see, and no law to save them. Fellow citizens, this crime will not be hushed up any longer. I have learned that a citizen of Nantucket, walking in New Orleans, found a freeborn citizen of Nantucket, a man, too, of great personal worth, and, as it happened, very dear to him, as having saved his own life, working chained in the streets of that city, kidnapped by such a process as this. In the sleep of the laws, the private interference of two excellent citizens of Boston has, I have ascertained, rescued several natives of this State from these southern prisons. Gentlemen, I thought the deck of a Massachusetts ship was as much the territory of Massachusetts, as the floor on which we stand. It should be as sacred as the temple of God. The poorest fishing-smack, that floats under the shadow of an iceberg in the northern seas, or hunts the whale in the southern ocean, should be encompassed by her laws with comfort and protection, as much as within the arms of Cape Ann and Cape Cod. And this kidnapping is suffered within our own land and federation, whilst the fourth article of the Constitution of the United States ordains in terms, that, "The citizens of each State shall be entitled to all privileges and immunities of citizens in the several States." If such a damnable outrage can be committed on the person of a citizen with impunity, let the Governor break the broad seal of the State; he bears the sword in vain. The Governor of Massachusetts is a trifler: [29] the State-house in Boston is a play-house: the General Court is a dishonored body: if they make laws which they cannot execute. The great-hearted Puritans have left no posterity. The rich men may walk in State-street, but they walk without honor; and the farmers may brag their democracy in the country, but they are disgraced men. If the State has no power to defend its own people in its own shipping, because it has delegated that power to the Federal Government, has it no representation in the Federal Government? Are those men dumb? I am no lawyer, and cannot indicate the forms applicable to the case, but here is something which transcends all forms. Let the senators and representatives of the State, containing a population of a million freemen, go in a body before the Congress, and say, that they have a demand to make on them so imperative, that all functions of government must stop, until it is satisfied. If ordinary legislation cannot reach it, then extraordinary must be applied. The Congress should instruct the President to send to those ports of Charleston, Savannah, and New Orleans, such orders and such force, as should release, forthwith, all such citizens of Massachusetts as were holden in prison without the allegation of any crime, and should set on foot the strictest inquisition to discover where such persons, brought

---

[29] George N. Briggs (1796–1861), governor of Massachusetts (1844–1851).

into slavery by these local laws, at any time heretofore, may now be. That first;—and then, let order be taken to indemnify all such as have been incarcerated. As for dangers to the Union, from such demands!—the Union is already at an end, when the first citizen of Massachusetts is thus outraged. Is it an union and covenant in which the State of Massachusetts agrees to be imprisoned, and the State of Carolina to imprison? Gentlemen, I am loath to say harsh things, and perhaps I know too little of politics for the smallest weight to attach to any censure of mine,—but I am at a loss how to characterize the tameness and silence of the two senators and the ten representatives of the State at Washington. To what purpose, have we clothed each of those representatives with the power of seventy thousand persons, and each senator with near half a million, if they are to sit dumb at their desks, and see their constituents captured and sold;—perhaps to gentlemen sitting by them in the hall? There is a scandalous rumor that has been swelling louder of late years,—perhaps it is wholly false,—that members are bullied into silence by southern gentlemen. It is so easy to omit to speak, or even to be absent when delicate things are to be handled. I may as well say what all men feel, that whilst our very amiable and very innocent representatives and senators at Washington, are accomplished lawyers and merchants, and very eloquent at dinners and at caucuses, there is a disastrous want of *men* from New England. I would gladly make exceptions, and you will not suffer me to forget one eloquent old man, in whose veins the blood of Massachusetts rolls, and who singly has defended the freedom of speech, and the rights of the free, against the usurpation of the slave-holder. But the reader of Congressional debates, in New England, is perplexed to see with what admirable sweetness and patience the majority of the free States, are schooled and ridden by the minority of slave-holders. What if we should send thither representatives who were a particle less amiable and less innocent? I entreat you, sirs, let not this stain attach, let not this misery accumulate any longer. If the managers of our political parties are too prudent and too cold;—if, most unhappily, the ambitious class of young men and political men have found out, that these neglected victims are poor and without weight; that they have no graceful hospitalities to offer; no valuable business to throw into any man's hands, no strong vote to cast at the elections; and therefore may with impunity be left in their chains or to the chance of chains, then let the citizens in their primary capacity take up their cause on this very ground, and say to the government of the State, and of the Union, that government exists to defend the weak and the poor and the injured party; the rich and the strong can better take care of themselves. And as an omen and assurance of success, I point you to the bright example which England set you, on this day, ten years ago.

There are other comparisons and other imperative duties which come sadly to mind,—but I do not wish to darken the hours of this day by crimination; I turn gladly to the rightful theme, to the bright aspects of the occasion.

This event was a moral revolution. The history of it is before you. Here was no prodigy, no fabulous hero, no Trojan horse, no bloody war, but all was achieved by plain means of plain men, working not under a leader, but under a sentiment. Other revolutions have been the insurrection of the oppressed; this was the repentence of the tyrant. It was the masters revolting from their mastery. The slave-holder said, I will not hold slaves. The end was noble, and the means were pure. Hence, the elevation and pathos of this chapter of history. The lives of the advocates are pages of greatness, and the connexion of the eminent senators with this question, constitutes the immortalizing moments of those men's lives. The bare enunciation of the theses, at which the lawyers and legislators arrived, gives a glow to the heart of the reader. Lord Chancellor Northington is the author of the famous sentence, "As soon as any man puts his foot on English ground, he becomes free." [30] "I was a slave," said the counsel of Somerset, speaking for his client, "for I was in America: I am now in a country, where the common rights of mankind are known and regarded." Granville Sharp filled the ear of the judges with the sound principles, that had from time to time been affirmed by the legal authorities. "Derived power cannot be superior to the power from which it is derived." "The reasonableness of the law is the soul of the law." "It is better to suffer every evil, than to consent to any." Out it would come, the God's truth, out it came, like a bolt from a cloud, for all the mumbling of the lawyers. One feels very sensibly in all this history that a great heart and soul are behind there, superior to any man, and making use of each, in turn, and infinitely attractive to every person according to the degree of reason in his own mind, so that this cause has had the power to draw to it every particle of talent and of worth in England, from the beginning. All the great geniuses of the British senate, Fox, Pitt, Burke, Grenville, Sheridan, Grey, Canning, ranged themselves on its side;[31] the poet Cowper wrote for it:[32] Franklin, Jefferson, Washington, in this country, all recorded their votes. All men remember the subtlety and the fire of indignation,

---

[30] Robert Henley, first earl of Northington (1708–1772), made the remark in a British slave case, *Shanley v. Harvey*, in 1762.

[31] Edmund Burke (1729–1797), Richard Grenville (1776–1839), Charles Grey (1764–1845), and George Canning (1770–1827) were all members of Parliament who sought to abolish the slave trade and slavery.

[32] William Cowper (1731–1800).

which the Edinburgh Review contributed to the cause;[33] and every liberal mind, poet, preacher, moralist, statesman, has had the fortune to appear somewhere for this cause. On the other part, appeared the reign of pounds and shillings, and all manner of rage and stupidity; a resistance which drew from Mr. Huddlestone in Parliament the observation,[34] "That a curse attended this trade even in the mode of defending it. By a certain fatality, none but the vilest arguments were brought forward, which corrupted the very persons who used them. Every one of these was built on the narrow ground of interest, of pecuniary profit, of sordid gain, in opposition to every motive that had reference to humanity, justice, and religion, or to that great principle which comprehended them all."—This moral force perpetually reinforces and dignifies the friends of this cause. It gave that tenacity to their point which has insured ultimate triumph; and it gave that superiority in reason, in imagery, in eloquence, which makes in all countries anti-slavery meetings so attractive to the people, and has made it a proverb in Massachusetts, that, "eloquence is dog-cheap at the anti-slavery chapel?"

I will say further, that we are indebted mainly to this movement, and to the continuers of it, for the popular discussion of every point of practical ethics, and a reference of every question to the absolute standard. It is notorious, that the political, religious, and social schemes, with which the minds of men are now most occupied, have been matured, or at least broached, in the free and daring discussions of these assemblies. Men have become aware through the emancipation, and kindred events, of the presence of powers, which, in their days of darkness, they had overlooked. Virtuous men will not again rely on political agents. They have found out the deleterious effect of political association. Up to this day, we have allowed to statesmen a paramount social standing, and we bow low to them as to the great. We cannot extend this deference to them any longer. The secret cannot be kept, that the seats of power are filled by underlings, ignorant, timid, and selfish, to a degree to destroy all claim, excepting that on compassion, to the society of the just and generous. What happened notoriously to an American ambassador in England, that he found himself compelled to palter, and to disguise the fact that he was a slave-breeder, happens to men of state. Their vocation is a presumption against them, among well-meaning people. The superstition respecting power and office, is going to the ground. The stream of human affairs flows its own way, and is very little affected by the activity of legislators. What great masses of men wish done, will be done;

---

[33] *Edinburgh Review*, British quarterly periodical published from 1802 to 1929.
[34] Mr. Huddleston is unidentified.

and they do not wish it for a freak, but because it is their state and natural end. There are now other energies than force, other than political, which no man in future can allow himself to disregard. There is direct conversation and influence. A man is to make himself felt, by his proper force. The tendency of things runs steadily to this point, namely, to put every man on his merits, and to give him so much power as he naturally exerts—no more, no less. Of course, the timid and base persons, all who are conscious of no worth in themselves, and who owe all their place to the opportunities which the old order of things allowed them to deceive and defraud men, shudder at the change, and would fain silence every honest voice, and lock up every house where liberty and innovation can be pleaded for. They would raise mobs, for fear is very cruel. But the strong and healthy yeomen and husbands of the land, the self-sustaining class of inventive and industrious men, fear no competition or superiority. Come what will, their faculty cannot be spared.

The First of August marks the entrance of a new element into modern politics, namely, the civilization of the negro. A man is added to the human family. Not the least affecting part of this history of abolition, is, the annihilation of the old indecent nonsense about the nature of the negro. In the case of the ship Zong, in 1781, whose master had thrown one hundred and thirty-two slaves alive into the sea, to cheat the underwriters, the first jury gave a verdict in favor of the master and owners: they had a right to do what they had done.[35] Lord Mansfield is reported to have said on the bench, "The matter left to the jury is,—Was it from necessity? For they had no doubt,—though it shocks one very much,—that the case of slaves was the same as if horses had been thrown overboard. It is a very shocking case." But a more enlightened and humane opinion began to prevail. Mr. Clarkson, early in his career, made a collection of African productions and manufactures, as specimens of the arts and culture of the negro; comprising cloths and loom, weapons, polished stones and woods, leather, glass, dyes, ornaments, soap, pipe-bowls, and trinkets. These he showed to Mr. Pitt, who saw and handled them with extreme interest. "On sight of these," says Clarkson, "many sublime thoughts seemed to rush at once into his mind, some of which he expressed;" and hence appeared to arise a project which was always dear to him, of the civilization of Africa,—a dream which for-

---

[35] In this famous case 133 slaves who had grown ill were cast into the sea by Capt. Luke Collingwood. Only one survived. The insurance arrangement provided that if the slaves died a natural death the loss would fall on the owners of the ship and the captain, but if they were thrown alive into the sea, on any pretext of necessity for the safety of the ship, it would be the underwriters' loss. See F. O. Shyllon, *Black Slaves in Britain* (London: Oxford University Press, 1974), pp. 184–209.

ever elevates his fame. In 1791, Mr. Wilberforce announced to the House of Commons, "We have already gained one victory: we have obtained for these poor creatures the recognition of their human nature, which, for a time, was most shamefully denied them." It was the sarcasm of Montesquieu, "it would not do to suppose that negroes were men, lest it should turn out that whites were not;" for, the white has, for ages, done what he could to keep the negro in that hoggish state. His laws have been furies. It now appears, that the negro race is, more than any other, susceptible of rapid civilization. The emancipation is observed, in the islands, to have wrought for the negro a benefit as sudden as when a thermometer is brought out of the shade into the sun. It has given him eyes and ears. If, before, he was taxed with such stupidity, or such defective vision, that he could not set a table square to the walls of an apartment, he is now the principal, if not the only mechanic, in the West Indies; and is, besides, an architect, a physician, a lawyer, a magistrate, an editor, and a valued and increasing political power. The recent testimonies of Sturge, of Thome and Kimball, of Gurney, of Phillippo, are very explicit on this point, the capacity and the success of the colored and the black population in employments of skill, of profit, and of trust;[36] and, best of all, is the testimony to their moderation. They receive hints and advances from the whites, that they will be gladly received as subscribers to the Exchange, as members of this or that committee of trust. They hold back, and say to each other, that "social position is not to be gained by pushing."

I have said that this event interests us because it came mainly from the concession of the whites; I add, that in part it is the earning of the blacks. They won the pity and respect which they have received, by their powers and native endowments. I think this a circumstance of the highest import. Their whole future is in it. Our planet, before the age of written history, had its races of savages, like the generations of sour paste, or the animalcules that wriggle and bite in a drop of putrid water. Who cares for these or for their wars? We do not wish a world of bugs or of birds; neither afterward of Scythians, Caraibs, or Feejees.[37] The grand style of nature, her great periods, is all we observe in them. Who cares for oppressing whites, or oppressed blacks, twenty centuries ago, more than for bad dreams? Eaters and

---

[36] Joseph Sturge (1793–1859) published *The West Indies* (1837) to document the abuses of slaves and apprentices in the West Indies. Joseph John Gurney (1788–1847), Quaker philanthropist, wrote *Winter in the West Indies* (1840). The Reverend Phillippo (1798–1879), British Baptist missionary to the West Indies, published *Jamaica: Its Past and Present State*, which was issued in a second edition in 1843.

[37] Scythians is the name applied by the Greeks to barbarous nomadic tribes of southeastern Europe. Caraibs are black beetles. Feejees are inhabitants of the Fiji Islands.

food are in the harmony of nature; and there too is the germ forever protected, unfolding gigantic leaf after leaf, a newer flower, a richer fruit, in
every period, yet its next product is never to be guessed. It will only save
what is worth saving; and it saves not by compassion, but by power. It appoints no police to guard the lion, but his teeth and claws; no fort or city
for the bird, but his wings; no rescue for flies and mites, but their spawning numbers, which no ravages can overcome. It deals with men after the
same manner. If they are rude and foolish, down they must go. When at last
in a race, a new principle appears, an idea;—*that* conserves it; ideas only save
races. If the black man is feeble, and not important to the existing races not
on a parity with the best race, the black man must serve, and be extermi-
nated. But if the black man carries in his bosom an indispensable element
of a new and coming civilization, for the sake of that element, no wrong,
nor strength, nor circumstance, can hurt him: he will survive and play his
part. So now, the arrival in the world of such men as Toussaint,[38] and the
Haytian heroes, or of the leaders of their race in Barbadoes and Jamaica,
outweighs in good omen all the English and American humanity. The anti-
slavery of the whole world, is dust in the balance before this,—is a poor
squeamishness and nervousness: the might and the right are here: here is the
anti-slave: here is man: and if you have man, black or white is an insignificance. The intellect,—that is miraculous! Who has it, has the talisman: his
skin and bones, though they were of the color of night, are transparent, and
the everlasting stars shine through, with attractive beams. But a compassion for that which is not and cannot be useful or lovely, is degrading and
futile. All the songs, and newspapers, and money-subscriptions, and vitu-
peration of such as do not think with us, will avail nothing against a fact. I
say to you, you must save yourself, black or white, man or woman; other
help is none. I esteem the occasion of this jubilee to be the proud discovery, that the black race can contend with the white; that, in the great an-
them which we call history, a piece of many parts and vast compass, after
playing a long time a very low and subdued accompaniment, they perceive
the time arrived when they can strike in with effect, and take a master's part
in the music. The civility of the world has reached that pitch, that their more
moral genius is becoming indispensable, and the quality of this race is to
be honored for itself. For this, they have been preserved in sandy deserts,
in rice-swamps, in kitchens and shoe-shops, so long: now let them emerge,
clothed and in their own form.

---

[38] Pierre Dominique Toussaint L'Ouverture (1743–1803), soldier, statesman, and liberator of Haiti.

There remains the very elevated consideration which the subject opens, but which belongs to more abstract views than we are now taking, this namely, that the civility of no race can be perfect whilst another race is degraded. It is a doctrine alike of the oldest, and of the newest philosophy, that, man is one, and that you cannot injure any member, without a sympathetic injury to all the members. America is not civil, whilst Africa is barbarous.

These considerations seem to leave no choice for the action of the intellect and the conscience of the country. There have been moments in this, as well as in every piece of moral history, when there seemed room for the infusions of a skeptical philosophy; when it seemed doubtful, whether brute force would not triumph in the eternal struggle. I doubt not, that sometimes a despairing negro, when jumping over the ship's sides to escape from the white devils who surrounded him, has believed there was no vindication of right; it is horrible to think of, but it seemed so. I doubt not, that sometimes the negro's friend, in the face of scornful and brutal hundreds of traders and drivers, has felt his heart sink. Especially, it seems to me, some degree of despondency is pardonable, when he observes the men of conscience and of intellect, his own natural allies and champions,—those whose attention should be nailed to the grand objects of this cause, so hotly offended by whatever incidental petulances or infirmities of indiscreet defenders of the negro, as to permit themselves to be ranged with the enemies of the human race; and names which should be the alarums of liberty and the watchwords of truth, are mixed up with all the rotten rabble of selfishness and tyranny. I assure myself that this coldness and blindness will pass away. A single noble wind of sentiment will scatter them forever. I am sure that the good and wise elders, the ardent and generous youth will not permit what is incidental and exceptional to withdraw their devotion from the essential and permanent characters of the question. There have been moments, I said, when men might be forgiven, who doubted. Those moments are past. Seen in masses, it cannot be disputed, there is progress in human society. There is a blessed necessity by which the interest of men is always driving them to the right; and, again, making all crime mean and ugly. The genius of the Saxon race, friendly to liberty; the enterprise, the very muscular vigor of this nation, are inconsistent with slavery. The Intellect, with blazing eye, looking through history from the beginning onward, gazes on this blot, and it disappears. The sentiment of Right, once very low and indistinct, but ever more articulate, because it is the voice of the universe, pronounces Freedom. The Power that built this fabric of things affirms it in the heart; and in the history of the First of August, has made a sign to the ages, of his will.

The Fugitive Slave Law[1]
The Tabernacle, New York City, March 7, 1854

I do not often speak to public questions. They are odious and hurtful and it seems like meddling or leaving your work. I have my own spirits in prison,—spirits in deeper prisons, whom no man visits, if I do not. And then I see what havoc it makes with any good mind this dissipated philanthropy. The one thing not to be forgiven to intellectual persons is not to know their own task, or to take their ideas from others and believe in the ideas of others. From this want of manly rest in their own, and foolish acceptance of other people's watchwords, comes the imbecility and fatigue of their conversation. For they cannot affirm these from any original experience, and, of course, not with the natural movement and whole power of their nature and talent, but only from their memory, only from the cramp position of standing for their teacher.—They say, what they would have you believe, but which they do not quite know.

My own habitual view is to the well-being of students or scholars, and it is only when the public event affects them, that it very seriously affects me. And what I have to say is to them. For every man speaks mainly to a class whom he works with, and more or less fitly represents. It is to them I am beforehand related and engaged,—in this audience or out of this audience,—to them and not to others. And yet when I say the class of scholars and students,—that is a class which comprises in some sort all mankind,—comprises every man in the best hours of his life:—and in these days not only virtually, but actually. For who are the readers and thinkers of 1854?

Emerson's Anti-Slavery Writings. Ed. Len Gougeon and Joel Myerson. New Haven: Yale UP, 1995. (All notes are by the original editors.)

[1] Emerson delivered this, his second speech on the Fugitive Slave Law, as part of a series of antislavery lectures at the Tabernacle in New York City. At least partially in response to the recent passage of the Kansas-Nebraska Act, the presentation elicited various critiques. The *National Anti-Slavery Standard* (18 March 1854) reprinted a commentary from *Mitchel's Citizen,* which described the speech as "a tame repetition of Parker and Phillips, nay, a dilution of [Henry Ward] Beecher and a *rechauffée* of Miss Lucy." A reporter for the *Boston Transcript,* however, in an article reprinted in the *Liberator* (17 March 1854), indicated that, while some had entered the hall "thinking that the speaker would find no new form in which to exhibit his hackneyed subject . . . they found that, in the hands of the master, the old theme wears a new beauty when clothed with the graces of his thought."

Emerson himself felt that the speech was somewhat unfinished and noted in a letter to William Henry Furness that he "had to carry to New York a makeshift instead of an oracle" (*L* [*Letters*], 8:397).

Owing to the silent revolution which the newspaper has wrought, this class has come in this country to take in all classes. Look into the morning trains, which, from every suburb carry the businessmen into the city, to their shops, counting-rooms, work-yards, and warehouses. With them, enters the car the humble priest of politics, philosophy, and religion in the shape of the newsboy. He unfolds his magical sheets, two pence a head his bread of knowledge costs, and instantly the entire rectangular assembly fresh from their breakfast, are bending as one man to their second breakfast. There is, no doubt, chaff enough, in what he brings, but there is fact and thought and wisdom in the crudeness from all regions of the world.

Now I have lived all my life without suffering any known inconvenience from American slavery. I never saw it; never heard the whip; I never felt the check on my free speech and action; until the other day when Mr. Webster by his personal influence brought the Fugitive Slave law on the country. I say Mr. Webster, for though the bill was not his, yet it is notorious that he was the life and soul of it, that he gave all he had, it cost him his life. And under the shadow of his great name, inferior men sheltered themselves, and threw their ballots for it, and made the law. I say inferior men; there were all sorts of what are called brilliant men, accomplished men, men of high office, a President of the United States, senators, and of eloquent speech, but men without self-respect, without character, and it was droll to see that office, age, fame, talent, even a repute for honesty, all count for nothing. They had no opinions, they had no memory for what they had been saying like the Lord's prayer, all their lifetime; they were only looking to what their great captain did, and if he jumped, they jumped, — if he stood on his head, they did. In ordinary, the supposed sense of their district and state is their guide, and this keeps them to liberty and justice. But it is always a little difficult to decipher what this public sense is: and when a great man comes, who knots up into himself the opinions and wishes of his people, it is so much easier to follow him as an exponent of this. He, too, is responsible, they will not be. It will always suffice to say, — I followed him. I saw plainly that the great show their legitimate power in nothing more than in their power to misguide us. I saw that a great man, deservedly esteemed and admired for his powers and their general right direction, was able, fault of the total want of stamina in public men, when he failed, to break them all with him, to carry parties with him.

It showed much. It ended a great deal of nonsense we had been accustomed to hear and to repeat, on the 22nd December,[2] 19th April, 17th June,

---

[2] The Pilgrims' landing at Plymouth in December 1620 was usually commemorated on the twenty-second, which is also the anniversary day of the New-England Society.

and 4th July. It showed what reputations are made of; what straw we dignify by office and title, and how competent they are to give counsel and help in a day of trial: the shallowness of leaders; showed the divergence of parties from their alleged grounds, and that men would not stick to what they had said: that the resolutions of public bodies, and the pledges never so often given and put on record, of public men,—will not bind them. The fact comes out more plainly, that you cannot rely on any man for the defence of truth who is not constitutionally, or by blood and temperament, on that side.

In what I have to say of Mr. Webster I do not confound him with vulgar politicians of his own time or since. There is always base ambition enough, men who calculate on the immense ignorance of masses of men;—that is their quarry and farm,—they use the constituencies at home only for their shoes. And of course they can drive out from the contest any honorable man. The low can best win the low, and all men like to be made much of. There are those too who have power and inspiration only to do ill. Their talent or their faculty deserts them when they undertake anything right.

Mr. Webster had a natural ascendancy of aspect and carriage, which distinguished him over all his contemporaries. His countenance, his figure, and his manners, were all in so grand a style, that he was, without effort, as superior to his most eminent rivals, as they were to the humblest, so that his arrival in any place was an event which drew crowds of people, who went to satisfy their eyes, and could not see him enough. I think they looked at him as the representative of the American continent. He was there in his Adamitic capacity, as if he alone of all men did not disappoint the eye and ear, but was a fit figure in the landscape. I remember his appearance at Bunker Hill.[3] There was the monument, and here was Webster. He knew well that a little more or less of rhetoric signified nothing; he was only to say plain and equal things;—grand things, if he had them,—and, if he had them not, only to abstain from saying unfit things;—and the whole occasion was answered by his presence. It was a place for behavior, much more than for speech; and Webster walked through his part with entire success.

His wonderful organization, the perfection of his elocution,—and all that thereto belongs,—voice, accent, intonation, attitude, manner, we shall not soon find again. Then he was so thoroughly simple and wise in his rhetoric,—he saw through his matter,—hugged his fact so close,—went to the principal or essential, and never indulged in a weak flourish, though he

---

[3] On Webster's appearance at Bunker Hill at the dedication of the monument on 17 June 1843, see *JMN* [*Journals and Miscellaneous Notebooks*], 8:425, and *L*, 3:180–181, both of which use some of the language employed in this passage.

knew perfectly well how to make such exordiums, episodes, and perorations, as might give perspective to his harangue, without in the least embarrassing his march, or confounding his transitions. In his statement, things lay in daylight;—we saw them in order as they were. Though he knew very well how to present his own personal claims, yet in his argument he was intellectual, and stated his fact pure of all personality, so that his splendid wrath, when his eyes became lamps, was the wrath of the fact and cause he stood for. His power, like that of all great masters, was not in excellent parts, but was total. He had a great and everywhere equal propriety. He worked with that closeness of adhesion to the matter in hand, which a joiner or a chemist uses. And the same quiet and sure feeling of right to his place that an oak or a mountain have to theirs.

After all his talents have been described, there remains that perfect propriety which animated all the details of the action or speech with the character of the whole, so that his beauties of detail are endless. He seemed born for the bar, born for the senate, and took very naturally a leading part in large private and in public affairs; for his head distributed things in their right places, and what he saw so well, he compelled other people to see also. Ah! great is the privilege of eloquence. What gratitude does every human being feel to him who speaks well for the right,—who translates truth into language entirely plain and clear!

The history of this country has given a disastrous importance to the defects of this great man's mind. Whether evil influences and the corruption of politics, or whether original infirmity, it was the misfortune of this country that with this large understanding, he had not what is better than intellect, and the essential source of its health. It is the office of the moral nature to give sanity and right direction to the mind, to give centrality and unity.

Now it is a law of our nature that great thoughts come from the heart. It was for this reason I may here say as I have said elsewhere that the moral is the occult fountain of genius,—the sterility of thought, the want of generalization in his speeches, and the curious fact, that, with a general ability that impresses all the world, there is not a single general remark, not an observation on life and manners, not a single valuable aphorism that can pass into literature from his writings.

Four years ago tonight, on one of those critical moments in history when great issues are determined,—when the powers of right and wrong are mustered for conflict, and it lies with one man to give a casting vote,— Mr. Webster most unexpectedly threw his whole weight on the side of slavery, and caused by his personal and official authority the passage of the Fugitive Slave Bill.

It is remarked of the Americans, that they value dexterity too much and honor too little. That the Americans praise a man by saying that he is smart than by saying that he is right.

Now whether this defect be national or not, it is the defect and calamity of Mr. Webster and it is so far true of his countrymen that namely, they appeal to physical and mental ability, when his character is assailed. And his speeches on the 7th March, and at Albany, Buffalo, Syracuse, and Boston, are cited in justification.[4] And Mr. Webster's literary editor believes that it was his own wish to rest his fame on the Speech of 7 March. Now, though I have my own opinions on this 7th March discourse, and those others, and think them very transparent, and very open to criticisms, yet the *secondary* merits of a speech (i.e. its logic, its illustration, its points,) are not here in question. The primary quality of a speech is its *subject*. Nobody doubts that Daniel Webster could make a good speech. Nobody doubts that there were good and plausible things to be said on the part of the south. But this is not a question of ingenuity, not a question of syllogisms, but of sides. How came he there? There are always texts and thoughts and arguments; but it is the genius and temper of the man which decides whether he will stand for Right or for Might.

Who doubts the power of any clever and fluent man to defend either of our parties, or any cause in our courts? There was the same law in England for Jeffreys and Talbot and Yorke to read slavery out of, and for Lord Mansfield to read freedom.[5] And in this country one sees that there is always margin enough in the statute for a liberal judge to read one way, and a servile judge another. But the question which History will ask is broader.

In the final hour, when he was forced by the peremptory necessity of the closing armies to take a side, did he take the side of great principles, the side of humanity and justice, or the side of abuse and oppression and chaos? Mr. Webster decided for slavery; and *that*, when the aspect of the institution was no longer doubtful, no longer feeble and apologetic, and proposing soon to end itself, but when it was strong and aggressive and threatening an illimitable increase, then he listened to state reasons and hopes and

---

[4] The speeches supporting his position on the Fugitive Slave Law are: 7 March 1850, *Speech of the Hon. Daniel Webster on the Subject of Slavery* (1850; also published in 1850 as *Speech of Hon. Daniel Webster on Mr. Clay's Resolutions*); the speeches in New York State in May 1851, *Mr. Webster's Speeches at Buffalo, Syracuse, and Albany* (1851; delivered 22, 26, and 28 May, respectively; the last one was published separately as *Speech of Hon. Daniel Webster, to the Young Men of Albany* [1851]); and 20 April 1850 in Boston.

[5] The English jurist Baron George Jeffreys (1648–1689). On Talbot and Yorke, see n. 8 to the emancipation address of 1844. On Lord Mansfield (William Murray), see n. 7 to the same speech. [These notes appear on page 210 of this volume. —ED.]

left with much complacency, we are told, the testament of his speech to the astonished State of Massachusetts. *Vera pro gratis.*[6] A ghastly result of all those years of experience in affairs, this, that there was nothing better for the foremost man, the most American man in America, to tell his countrymen, than, that slavery was now at that strength, that they must beat down their conscience and become kidnappers for it. This was like the doleful speech falsely ascribed to the patriot Brutus, "Virtue, I have followed thee through life, and I find thee but a shadow."[7]

Here was a question of an immoral law, a question agitated for ages, and settled always in the same way by every great jurist, that an immoral law cannot be valid. Cicero, Grotius, Coke, Blackstone, Burlamaqui, Vattel, Burke, Jefferson do all affirm this, and I cite them not that they can give plainness to what is so clear, but because though lawyers and practical statesmen, they could not hide from themselves this truth. Here was the question: Are you for man, and for the good of man; or are you for the hurt and harm of man? It was a question, whether man shall be treated as leather? Whether the negroes shall be, as the Indians were in Spanish America, a species of money? Whether this institution, which is a kind of mill or factory for converting men into monkeys, shall be upheld and enlarged? And Mr. Webster and the country went for quadruped law. Immense mischief was done. People were all expecting a totally different course from Mr. Webster. If any man had in that hour possessed the weight with the country which he had acquired, he would have brought the whole country to its senses. But not a moment's pause was allowed. Angry parties went from bad to worse, and the decision of Webster was accompanied with every thing offensive to freedom and good morals.

There was something like an attempt to debauch the moral sentiment of the clergy and of the youth. The immense power of rectitude is apt to be forgotten in politics. But they who brought this great wrong on the country, did not forget it. They wished to avail themselves of the names of men of known probity and honor to endorse the statute. The ancient maxim is still true, that never was any injustice effected except by the help of justice.

---

[6] *Vera pro gratis* ("truth rather than pleasantness") appeared as part of a Latin passage included in the preface to Webster's publication of his speech in pamphlet form. Claude Morre Fuess reports that Webster insisted these words be printed in capitals, "a fact which proves that he was conscious of the storm which he was about to raise" (*Daniel Webster*, 2 vols. [Boston: Little, Brown, 1930], 2:222–223).

[7] Edward Waldo Emerson writes that the passage is from the Greek historian Dio Cassius (ca. 163–164 to ca. 235), gives the Greek original, and provides a translation and commentary. To Edward, it "seems very doubtful whence the Greek verses came" (*Miscellanies* [1904], p. 590).

Burke said, "he would pardon something to the spirit of liberty"—but the opposition was sharply called *treason*, by Webster and prosecuted so. He told the people at Boston, "they must conquer their prejudices," that "agitation of the subject of Slavery must be suppressed." He did, as immoral men usually do, make very low bows to the Christian Church, and went through all the Sunday decorums; but when allusion was made to the sanctions of morality, he very frankly said, at Albany, "Some higher law, something existing somewhere between here and the third heaven,—I do not know where,"—and, if the reporters say true, this wretched atheism found some laughter in the company.

I said I had never in my life suffered before from the slave institution. It was like slavery in Africa or in Japan for me. There was a fugitive law, but it had become, or was fast becoming, a dead letter; and, by the genius and laws of Massachusetts inoperative. The new Bill made it operative; required me to hunt slaves; and it found citizens in Massachusetts willing to act as judges and captors. Moreover, it disclosed the secret of the new times; that slavery was no longer mendicant, but was become aggressive and dangerous.

The way in which the country was dragged to consent to this, and the disastrous defection on the miserable cry of *Union*, of the men of letters, of the colleges, of educated men, nay of some preachers of religion shows that our prosperity had hurt us; and we can not be shocked by crime. It showed that the old religion and the sense of right had faded and gone out; that, whilst we reckoned ourselves a highly cultivated nation, our bellies had run away with our brains, and the principles of culture and progress did not exist. For I suppose that liberty is a very accurate index in men and nations of general progress.

The theory of personal liberty must always appeal to the most refined communities and to the men of the rarest perception and of delicate moral sense. For these are rights which rest on the finest sense of justice, and with every degree of civility,—it will be more truly felt and defined. A barbarous tribe of good stock will by means of their best heads secure substantial liberty. But when there is any weakness in race, as is in the black race, and it becomes in any degree matter of concession and protection from their stronger neighbors, the incompatibility and offensiveness of the wrong will, of course, be most evident to the most cultivated.

For it is, is it not? the very nature of courtesy, of politeness, of religion, of love, to prefer another, to postpone oneself, to protect another from oneself? That is the distinction of the gentleman, to defend the weak, and redress the injured, as it is of the savage and the brute to usurp and use others.

In Massachusetts, as we all know, there has always existed a predominant conservative spirit. We have more money and value of every kind than other people, and wish to keep them. The plea on which freedom was resisted was Union. I went to certain serious men who had a little more reason than the rest, and inquired why they took this part. They told me candidly that they had no confidence in their strength to resist the democratic party in this country; that they saw plainly that all was going to the utmost verge of licence; each was vying with his neighbor to lead the party by proposing the worst measure, and they threw themselves on the extreme right as a drag on the wheel; that they knew Cuba would be had, and Mexico would be had, and they stood stiffly on conservatism, and as near to monarchy as they could, only to moderate the velocity with which the car was running down the precipice: in short, their theory was despair; the whig wisdom was only reprieve, awaiting to be the last devoured. They sided with Carolina or with Arkansas, only to make a show of whig strength, wherewith to resist a little longer this general ruin.

Gentlemen, I have a respect for conservatism. I know how deeply it is founded in our nature, and how idle are all attempts to shake ourselves free of it. We are all conservatives; all half whig, half democrat, in our essences; and might as well try to jump off our planet or jump out of our skins, as to escape from our whiggery. There are two forces in nature by whose antagonism we exist: the power of Fate, of Fortune, the laws of the world, the order of things, or, however else we choose to phrase it, —the material necessities, on the one hand; and Will, or Duty, or Freedom, on the other. *May* and *must:* the sense of right and duty, on one hand; and the material necessities, on the other. *May* and *must.* In vulgar politics, the Whig goes for what has been, for the old necessities, the *musts;* the reformer goes for the better, for the ideal good, for the *mays.*

But each of these parties must of necessity take in, in some manner, the principle of the other. Each wishes to cover the whole ground, to hold fast, and to advance: only, one lays the emphasis on keeping; and the other, on advancing. I, too, think the *musts* are a safe company to follow, and even agreeable. But if we are whigs, let us be whigs of nature and science, and go for *all* the necessities. Let us know that over and above all the *musts* of poverty and appetite, is the instinct of man to rise, and the instinct to love and help his brother.

Now, Gentlemen, I think we have in this hour instruction again in the simplest lesson. Events roll, millions of men are engaged, and the result is some of those first commandments which we heard in the nursery. We never get beyond our first lesson; for really the world exists, as I understand it, to teach the science of liberty which begins with liberty from fear. The events of this month are teaching one thing plain and clear, the worthlessness of good tools to bad workmen, that papers are of no use, resolutions of public meetings, platforms of conventions, no nor laws nor Constitutions any more. These are all declaratory of the will of the moment and are passed with more levity and on grounds much less honorable than ordinary business transactions in the street. You relied on the Constitution. It has not the word slave in it and very good argument has shown that it would not warrant the crimes that are done under it. That with provisions so vague, for an object *not named,* and which would not be suffered to claim a barrel of sugar or a bushel of corn, the robbing of a man and all his posterity, — is effected. You relied on the Supreme Court. The law was right; excellent law for the lambs. But what if, unhappily, the judges were chosen from the wolves? and give to all the law a wolfish interpretation?

What is the use of admirable law forms and political forms if a hurricane of party feeling and a combination of monied interests can beat them to the ground? What is the use of courts, if judges only quote authorities, and no judge exerts original jurisdiction, or recurs to first principles? What is the use of guaranties provided by the jealousy of ages for the protection of liberty, — if these are made of no effect, when a bad act of Congress finds a willing commissioner? You relied on the Missouri Compromise: that is ridden over. You relied on state sovereignty in the free states to protect their citizens. They are driven with contempt out of the courts, and out of the territory of the slave states, if they are so happy as to get out with their lives.[8] And now, you relied on these dismal guaranties infamously made in 1850, and before the body of Webster is yet crumbled,[9] it is found that they have crumbled: this eternal monument at once of his fame and of the common Union, is rotten in four years. They are no guaranty to the free states. They are a guaranty to the slave states; that as they have hitherto met with no repulse, they shall meet with none. I fear there is no reliance to be had on any kind of form or covenant, no, not on sacred forms, — none on churches, none on bibles. For one would have said that a Christian would not keep slaves, but the Christians keep slaves. Of course, they will not dare read the bible. Won't they? They quote the bible and Christ and Paul to maintain slavery.[10] If slavery is a good, then is lying, theft, arson, incest,

---

[8] "Just ten years earlier, Hon. Samuel Hoar, the Commissioner of Massachusetts, sent to Charleston, South Carolina, in the interests of our colored citizens there constantly imprisoned and ill used, had been expelled from that state with a show of force" (Edward Waldo Emerson's note, *Miscellanies* [1904], p. 590). Ralph Waldo Emerson comments on this event at length in his sketch "Samuel Hoar," in *Lectures and Biographical Sketches* (1884).

[9] Webster had died on 24 October 1852.

[10] "The sending back of Onesimus by Paul was a precedent precious in the eyes of the proslavery preachers, North and South, in those days, ignoring, however, Paul's message, 'Not now as a servant, but above a servant, a brother beloved, specially to me, but how much more unto thee, both in the flesh and in the Lord. If thou count me therefore a

homicide, each and all goods and to be maintained by union societies. These things show that no forms, neither Constitutions nor laws nor covenants nor churches nor bibles, are of any use in themselves; the devil nestles comfortably into them all. There is no help but in the head and heart and hamstrings of a man. Covenants are of no use without honest men to keep them. Laws are of no use, but with loyal citizens to obey them. To interpret Christ, it needs Christ in the heart. The teachings of the spirit can be apprehended only by the same spirit that gave them forth. To make good the cause of Freedom you must draw off from all these foolish trusts on others. You must be citadels and warriors, yourselves Declarations of Independence, the charter, the battle, and the victory. Cromwell said, "We can only resist the superior training of the king's soldiers, by having godly men." [11] And no man has a right to hope that the laws of New York will defend him from the contamination of slaves another day, until he has made up his mind that he will not owe his protection to the laws of New York, but to his own sense and spirit. Then he protects New York. He only who is able to stand alone, is qualified for society. And that I understand to be the end for which a soul exists in this world, to be himself the counterbalance of all falsehood and all wrong. "The army of unright is encamped from pole to pole, but the road of victory is known to the just." Everything may be taken away, he may be poor, he may be homeless, yet he will know out of his arms to make a pillow and out of his breast a bolster. Why have the minority no influence? because they have not a real minority of one.

I conceive that thus to detach a man, and make him feel that he is to owe all to himself, is the way to make him strong and rich. And here the optimist must find if anywhere the benefit of slavery. We have many teachers. We are in this world for nothing else than Culture: to be instructed in nature, in realities; in the laws of moral and intelligent nature; and surely our education is not conducted by toys and luxuries, —but by austere and rugged masters, —by poverty, solitude, passions, war, slavery, —to know that paradise is under the shadow of swords; [12] that divine sentiments, which are always soliciting us, are breathed into us from on high and are a counterbalance to an universe of suffering and crime, —that self-reliance, the height and perfection of man, is reliance on God. The insight of the religious sentiment will disclose to him unexpected aids in the nature of

---

partner, receive him as myself' (*Epistle of Paul to Philemon*, i, 16, 17)"—Edward Waldo Emerson's note, *Miscellanies* (1904), p. 590.

[11] Oliver Cromwell (1599–1658), lord protector of England.

[12] Emerson was fond of this phrase from Mahomet (ca. 570–632), prophet of Islam, writing it in his journal (see *JMN*, 6:388, 7:401) and using it as the epigraph to "Heroism," in *Essays: Second Series* (1844).

things. The Persian Saadi said "Beware of hurting the orphan. When the orphan sets a crying the throne of the Almighty is rocked from side to side."[13]

Whenever a man has come to this mind, that there is no church for him but his humble morning prayer; no constitution, but his talent of dealing well and justly with his neighbor; no liberty, but his invincible will to do right, then certain aids and allies will promptly appear. For the Eternal constitution of the universe is on his side. It is of no use to vote down gravitation or morals. What is useful will last; whilst that which is hurtful to the world will sink beneath all the opposing forces which it must exasperate. The terror which the Marseillaise thunders against oppression, thunders today, —

Tout est soldat pour vous combattre.

"*Everything that can walk turns soldier to fight you down.*" The end for which man was made, is not stealing, nor crime in any form. And a man cannot steal, without incurring all the penalties of the thief; no, though all the legislatures vote that it is virtuous, and though there be a general conspiracy among scholars and official persons to hold him up, and to say, *Nothing is good but stealing.* A man who commits a crime defeats the end of his existence. He was created for benefit, and he exists for harm. And as well-doing makes power and wisdom, ill-doing takes them away. A man who steals another man's labor, (as a planter does,) steals away his own faculties; his integrity, his humanity is flowing away from him.

The habit of oppression cuts out the moral eyes, and though the intellect goes on simulating the moral as before, its sanity is invaded, and gradually destroyed. It takes away the presentiments.

I suppose, in general, this is allowed; that, if you have a nice question of right and wrong, you would not go with it to Louis Napoleon;[14] or to a political hack; or to a slave-driver. The habit of mind of traders in power would not be esteemed favorable to delicate moral perception. It is not true that there is any exception to that in American slavery, or that the system here has called out a spirit of generosity and self-sacrifice. No excess of good nature and of tenderness of moral constitution in individuals has been able to give a new character to the system, to tear down the whipping house. The plea that the negro is an inferior race sounds very oddly in my ear from a slaveholder. "The masters of slaves seem generally anxious to prove that they are not of a race superior in any noble quality to the meanest of their bond-

---

[13]The Persian poet Muslih-uh-Din Saadi (ca. 1200–ca. 1292), a longtime favorite of Emerson, who wrote a preface to an 1865 edition of *The Gulistan, or Rose Garden*. Emerson copied this sentiment into his journal (*JMN*, 9:39) and also used it in "Ethnical Scriptures," *Dial* 4 (January 1844): 404.

[14]Louis Napoleon (1808–1873) ruled France as Napoleon III from 1852 to 1871.

men." And indeed when I hear the southerner point to the anatomy of the negro, and talk of chimpanzee, — I recall Montesquieu's remark, "It will not do to say, that negroes are men, lest it should turn out that whites were not."

I know that when seen near, and in detail, slavery is disheartening. But nature is not so helpless but it can rid itself at last of every wrong. An Eastern poet, in describing the world God made pure in the beginning, said, "that God had made justice so dear to the heart of nature, that, if any injustice lurked anywhere under the sky, the blue vault would shrivel to a snakeskin and cast it out by spasms." [15] But the spasms of nature are centuries and ages and will tax the faith of short-lived men. Slowly, slowly the avenger comes, but comes surely. The proverbs of the nations affirm these delays, but affirm the arrival. They say, "God may consent, but not forever." The delay of the Divine Justice, — this was the meaning and soul of the Greek Tragedy, — this was the soul of their religion. "There has come, too, one to whom lurking warfare is dear, — Retribution, — with a soul full of wiles, a violator of hospitality, guileful without the guilt of guile, limping, late in her arrival." [16] "This happiness at its close begets itself an offspring, and does not die childless, and instead of good fortune, there sprouts forth for posterity ever-ravening calamity." [17]

For evil word, shall evil word be said,
For murderstroke, a murderstroke be paid,
Who smites must smart. [18]

These delays, — you see them now in the temper of the times. The national spirit in this country is so drowsy, preoccupied with interest, deaf to principle. The Anglo-Saxon race is proud and strong but selfish. They believe only in Anglo-Saxons. Greece found it deaf, Poland found it so, Italy found it so, Hungary found it so. England goes for trade, not for liberty; goes against Greece, against Hungary; against Schleswig-Holstein: [19] against the French Republic whilst it was yet a republic. To faint hearts the times offer no invitation. And the like torpor exists here throughout the active classes on the subject of domestic slavery and its appalling aggressions.

Yes, that is the stern edict of Providence, that liberty shall be no hasty fruit, but that event on event, population on population, age on age, shall

---

[15] Emerson also used this passage in "The Sovereignty of Ethics," in *Lectures and Biographical Sketches* (1884), pp. 184–185, and in his lectures on slavery in May 1854.

[16] Unidentified.

[17] Unidentified.

[18] Unidentified.

[19] Schleswig-Holstein, a province of Prussia, had recently engaged in a war with Denmark (1848–1850).

cast itself into the opposite scale, and not until liberty has slowly accumulated weight enough to countervail and preponderate against all this, can the sufficient recoil come. All the great cities, all the refined circles, all the statesmen, —Guizot, Palmerston, Webster, Calhoun, are sure to be found banded against liberty; they are all sure to be found befriending liberty with their words; and crushing it with their votes.

Liberty is never cheap. It is made difficult because freedom is the accomplishment and perfectness of a man. He is a finished man, earning and bestowing good, equal to the world, at home in nature and dignifying that; the sun does not see anything nobler and has nothing to teach him. Therefore mountains of difficulty must be surmounted, stern trials met, wiles of seduction, dangers, healed by a quarantine of calamities to measure his strength by before he dare say, I am free.

Whilst the inconsistency of slavery with the principles on which the world is built guarantees its downfall, I own that the patience it requires is almost too sublime for mortals and seems to demand of us more than mere hoping. And when one sees how fast the rot spreads, —it is growing serious, —I think we demand of superior men that they shall be superior in this, that the mind and the virtue give their verdict in their day and accelerate so far the progress of civilization. Possession is sure to throw its stupid strength for existing power; and appetite and ambition will go for *that*. Let the aid of virtue and intelligence and education be cast where they rightfully belong. They are organically ours. Let them be loyal to their own. English Earl Grey said, on a memorable occasion, "he should stand by his order." [20] And I wish to see the instructed or illuminated class know their own flag, and not stand for the kingdom of darkness. We should not forgive the clergy of a country, for taking on every issue the immoral side. Nor the Bench, if it throw itself on the side of the culprit. Nor the Government, if it sustain the mob against the laws. It is an immense support and ally to a brave man standing single or with few for the right, to know, when, outvoted and discountenanced and ostracised in that hour and place, yet better men in other parts of the country appreciate the service, and will rightly report him to his own age and to posterity. And without this assurance he will sooner sink; "if they do not care to be defended," he may well say, "I too will decline the controversy, from which I only reap invectives and hatred."

Yet the lovers of liberty may tax with reason the coldness and indifferentism of the scholars and literary men. They are lovers of liberty in

---

[20] This could be either Earl Charles Grey (1764–1845), English statesman, or Earl Henry George Grey (1802–1894), English politician.

Greece, and in Rome, and in the English Commonwealth, but they are very lukewarm lovers of the specific liberty of America in 1854. The universities are not now as in Hobbes's time, the core of rebellion; no, but the seat of whiggery. They have forgotten their allegiance to the muse and grown worldly and political. I remember I listened, on one of those occasions when the university chooses one of her distinguished sons returning from the political arena believing that senators and statesmen are glad to throw off the harness and to dip again in the Castalian pools.[21] But if audiences forget themselves statesmen do not. The low bows to all the crockery gods of the day were duly made. Only in one part of the discourse the orator allowed to transpire rather against his will a little sober sense.[22] It was this. I am as you see a man virtuously inclined and only corrupted by my profession of politics. I should prefer the right side. You gentlemen of these literary and scientific schools have the power to make your verdict clear and prevailing. Had you done so, you would have found me its glad organ and champion. Abstractly, I should have preferred that side. But you have not done it. You have not spoken out. You have failed to arm me. I can only deal with masses as I find them. Abstractions are not for me. I go then for such parties and opinions as have provided me with a working apparatus. I give you my word, not without regret, that I was first for you, and though I am now to deny and condemn you, you see it is not my will, but the party necessity. Having made this manifesto, and professed his adoration for liberty in the time of grandfathers, he proceeded with his work of denouncing freedom and freemen at the present day, much in the tone and spirit with which Lord Bacon prosecuted his benefactor Essex.[23] He denounced every name and aspect under which liberty and progress dared show itself in this age and country, but with a lingering conscience which qualified each sentence with a recommendation to mercy, death with a recommendation to mercy.

But I put to every noble and generous spirit in the land; to every poetic; to every heroic; to every religious heart; that not so is our learning, our

---

[21] Castalia, a fountain on Mount Parnasuss in ancient Greece sacred to the Muses and Apollo.

[22] Edward Emerson notes that the "occasion alluded to was Hon. Robert C. Winthrop's speech to the alumni of Harvard College on Commencement Day in 1852. What follows is not an abstract, but Mr. Emerson's rendering of the spirit of his address" (*Miscellanies* [1904], p. 592). Actually, much of this passage is based on Emerson's contemporaneous account in *JMN*, 13:1–73, regarding Robert Charles Winthrop (1809–1894), congressman and senator from Massachusetts.

[23] Francis Bacon (1561–1626) was befriended early in his career by the courtier Robert Devereux, second earl of Essex (1567–1601), but later served as a witness for the prosecution in Essex's trial for treason.

education, our poetry, our worship to be declared, not by heads reverted to the dying Demosthenes, Luther, or Wallace, or to George Fox,[24] or to George Washington, but to the dangers and dragons that beset the United States at this time. It is not possible to extricate oneself from the questions in which your age is involved. I hate that we should be content with standing on the defensive. Liberty is aggressive. Liberty is the Crusade of all brave and conscientious men. It is the epic poetry, the new religion, the chivalry of all gentlemen. This is the oppressed Lady whom true knights on their oath and honor must rescue and save.

Now at last we are disenchanted and shall have no more false hopes. I respect the Anti-Slavery Society. It is the Cassandra that has foretold all that has befallen,[25] fact for fact, years ago,—foretold it all, and no man laid it to heart. It seemed, as the Turks say, "Fate makes that a man should not believe his own eyes." But the Fugitive Law did much to unglue the eyes of men, and now the Nebraska Bill leaves us staring. The Anti-Slavery Society will add many members this year. The Whig party will join it. The Democrats will join it. The population of the Free States will join it. I doubt not, at last, the Slave States will join it. But be that sooner or later,—and whoever comes or stays away,—I hope we have come to an end of our unbelief, have come to a belief that there is a Divine Providence in the world which will not save us but through our own co-operation.

Woman

A Lecture Read before the Woman's Rights Convention, Boston, September 20, 1855

> The politics are base,
> The letters do not cheer,
> And 't is far in the deeps of history,
> The voice that speaketh clear.

The Complete Works of Ralph Waldo Emerson. Ed. Edward Waldo Emerson. Centenary Edition. Vol. 11. Boston: Houghton, 1904.

[24]Demosthenes (ca. 384–322 B.C.), Athenian statesman; Martin Luther (1483–1546), theologian; William Wallace (ca. 1270–1305), Scottish national hero; George Fox (1624–1691), founder of the Society of Friends, or Quakers.

[25]In the Greek legend, Cassandra was given the gift of prophecy by Apollo, but when she refused his advances, he cursed her by having no one believe her predictions.

Yet there in the parlor sits
Some figure in noble guise, —
Our Angel in a stranger's form;
Or Woman's pleading eyes.

[— Emerson]

"Lo, when the Lord made North and South,
And sun and moon ordained he,
Forth bringing each by word of mouth
In order of its dignity,
Did man from the crude clay express
By sequence, and, all else decreed,
He formed the woman; nor might less
Than Sabbath such a work succeed."[1]

Coventry Patmore

Among those movements which seem to be, now and then, endemic in the public mind, — perhaps we should say, sporadic, — rather than the single inspiration of one mind, is that which has urged on society the benefits of action having for its object a benefit to the position of Woman. And none is more seriously interesting to every healthful and thoughtful mind.

In that race which is now predominant over all the other races of men, it was a cherished belief that women had an oracular nature.[2] They are more delicate than men, — delicate as iodine to light, — and thus more impressionable. They are the best index of the coming hour. I share this belief. I think their words are to be weighed; but it is their inconsiderate word, — according to the rule, "take their first advice, not the second:" as Coleridge was wont to apply to a lady for her judgment in questions of taste, and accept it; but when she added — "I think so, because — " "Pardon me, madam," he said, "leave me to find out the reasons for myself." In this sense, as more delicate mercuries of the imponderable and immaterial influences, what

[1] From *The Angel in the House*, Bk. I, Canto iv, "The Rose of the World." A popular English Victorian poet, Patmore (1823–96) helped legitimate the ideology of feminine domesticity, sexual purity, and religious devotion. [Ed.]

[2] Emerson appeals once again to the nineteenth-century ideology of Anglo-Saxon superiority and its "destiny" to spread its "civilization" westward. See Reginald Horsman, *Race and Manifest Destiny*. [Ed.]

they say and think is the shadow of coming events. Their very dolls are indicative. Among our Norse ancestors, Frigga was worshipped as the goddess of women. "Weirdes all," said the Edda, "Frigga knoweth, though she telleth them never."[3] That is to say, all wisdoms Woman knows; though she takes them for granted, and does not explain them as discoveries, like the understanding of man. Men remark figure: women always catch the expression. They inspire by a look, and pass with us not so much by what they say or do, as by their presence. They learn so fast and convey the result so fast as to outrun the logic of their slow brother and make his acquisitions poor. 'T is their mood and tone that is important. Does their mind misgive them, or are they firm and cheerful? 'T is a true report that things are going ill or well. And any remarkable opinion or movement shared by woman will be the first sign of revolution.

Plato said, Women are the same as men in faculty, only less in degree.[4] But the general voice of mankind has agreed that they have their own strength; that women are strong by sentiment; that the same mental height which their husbands attain by toil, they attain by sympathy with their husbands. Man is the will, and Woman the sentiment. In this ship of humanity, Will is the rudder, and Sentiment the sail: when Woman affects to steer, the rudder is only a masked sail. When women engage in any art or trade, it is usually as a resource, not as a primary object. The life of the affections is primary to them, so that there is usually no employment or career which they will not with their own applause and that of society quit for a suitable marriage. And they give entirely to their affections, set their whole fortune on the die, lose themselves eagerly in the glory of their husbands and children. Man stands astonished at a magnanimity he cannot pretend to. Mrs. Lucy Hutchinson, one of the heroines of the English Commonwealth, who wrote the life of her husband, the Governor of Nottingham, says, "If he esteemed her at a higher rate than she in herself could have deserved, he was the author of that virtue he doted on, while she only reflected his own glories upon him. All that she was, was *him*, while he was hers, and all that she is now, at best, but his pale shade."[5] As for Plato's opinion, it is true that, up to recent times, in no art or science, nor in painting, poetry or

---

[3] *The Edda* is a collection of Old Norse and Icelandic mythic stories. Frigga is goddess of earth, wife of the central god, Odin, and mother of Balder, god of light. From her name comes the name of the day of the week Friday. [Ed.]

[4] Plato, *Republic,* bk. 5. [Ed.]

[5] Lucy Hutchinson in her *Memoirs of the Life of Colonel Hutchinson* (1806) records this episode in the execution of her husband, John Hutchinson (1615–64), who was condemned for signing King Charles I's death warrant and for supporting the Puritan Commonwealth. Margaret Fuller also makes several references to Hutchinson's memoir in

music, have they produced a masterpiece.[6] Till the new education and larger opportunities of very modern times, this position, with the fewest possible exceptions, has always been true. Sappho, to be sure, in the Olympic Games, gained the crown over Pindar.[7] But, in general, no mastery in either of the fine arts—which should, one would say, be the arts of women—has yet been obtained by them, equal to the mastery of men in the same. The part they play in education, in the care of the young and the tuition of older children, is their organic office in the world. So much sympathy as they have makes them inestimable as the mediators between those who have knowledge and those who want it: besides, their fine organization, their taste and love of details, makes the knowledge they give better in their hands.

But there is an art which is better than painting, poetry, music, or architecture,—better than botany, geology, or any science; namely, Conversation.[8] Wise, cultivated, genial conversation is the last flower of civilization and the best result which life has to offer us,—a cup for gods, which has no repentance. Conversation is our account of ourselves. All we have, all we can, all we know, is brought into play, and as the reproduction, in finer form, of all our havings.

Women are, by this and their social influence, the civilizers of mankind. What is civilization? I answer, the power of good women. It was Burns's remark when he first came to Edinburgh that between the men of rustic life and the polite world he observed little difference; that in the former, though unpolished by fashion and unenlightened by science, he had found much observation and much intelligence; but a refined and accomplished woman was a being almost new to him, and of which he had formed a very inadequate idea.[9] "I like women," said a clear-headed man of the world; "they are so finished." They finish society, manners, language. Form and ceremony are their realm. They embellish trifles. All these ceremonies that

Woman in the Nineteenth Century (reprinted in this volume), and it is quite possible that Emerson is relying on her example. [Ed.]

[6] Given Emerson's familiarity with Fuller's *Woman in the Nineteenth Century*, which demonstrates the diverse achievements of women in the arts throughout history, it is odd that Emerson repeats this commonplace of nineteenth-century patriarchy. [Ed.]

[7] Sappho, the classical poet from the island of Lesbos, was reputed to have defeated Pindar in one of the poetic competitions of the ancient Olympic Games. [Ed.]

[8] Emerson was aware of the seminars ("Conversations") for women that Fuller held in Boston from 1839 to 1844, but he refers here to the conversation of women in intellectual and social salons. This claim that women excelled at such conversation is another convention of the nineteenth-century ideology of feminine domesticity. [Ed.]

[9] Robert Burns (1759–96), Scottish poet known for his poems about rustic life and rural folklore. [Ed.]

hedge our life around are not to be despised, and when we have become habituated to them, cannot be dispensed with. No woman can despise them with impunity. Their genius delights in ceremonies, in forms, in decorating life with manners, with properties, order and grace. They are, in their nature, more relative; the circumstance must always be fit; out of place they lose half their weight, out of place they are disfranchised. Position, Wren [10] said, is essential to the perfecting of beauty;—a fine building is lost in a dark lane; a statue should stand in the air; much more true is it of woman.

We commonly say that easy circumstances seem somehow necessary to the finish of the female character: but then it is to be remembered that they create these with all their might. They are always making that civilization which they require; that state of art, of decoration, that ornamental life in which they best appear.

The spiritual force of man is as much shown in taste, in his fancy and imagination,—attaching deep meanings to things and to arbitrary inventions of no real value,—as in his perception of truth. He is as much raised above the beast by this creative faculty as by any other. The horse and ox use no delays; they run to the river when thirsty, to the corn when hungry, and say no thanks, but fight down whatever opposes their appetite. But man invents and adorns all he does with delays and degrees, paints it all over with forms, to please himself better; he invented majesty and the etiquette of courts and drawing-rooms; architecture, curtains, dress, all luxuries and adornments, and the elegance of privacy, to increase the joys of society. He invented marriage; and surrounded by religion, by comeliness, by all manner of dignities and renunciations, the union of the sexes.

And how should we better measure the gulf between the best intercourse of men in old Athens, in London, or in our American capitals,—between this and the hedgehog existence of diggers [11] of worms, and the eaters of clay and offal,—than by signalizing just this department of taste or comeliness? Herein woman is the prime genius and ordainer. There is no grace that is taught by the dancing-master, no style adopted into the etiquette of courts, but was first the whim and the mere action of some brilliant woman, who charmed beholders by this new expression, and made it remembered and copied. And I think they should magnify their ritual of manners. Society, conversation, decorum, flowers, dances, colors, forms, are their homes

---

[10] Sir Christopher Wren (1632–1723), English architect who designed St. Paul's Cathedral. [Ed.]

[11] Derogatory term for hunting-and-gathering peoples, especially Native Americans in California (such as the Tejon tribe), used to distinguish them from "civilized" people. [Ed.]

and attendants. They should be found in fit surroundings—with fair approaches, with agreeable architecture, and with all advantages which the means of man collect:

"The far-fetched diamond finds its home
Flashing and smouldering in her hair.
For her the seas their pearls reveal,
    Art and strange lands her pomp supply
With purple, chrome and cochineal,
    Ochre and lapis lazuli.
The worm its golden woof presents.
    Whatever runs, flies, dives or delves
All doff for her their ornaments,
    Which suit her better than themselves." [12]

There is no gift of Nature without some drawback. So, to women, this exquisite structure could not exist without its own penalty. More vulnerable, more infirm, more mortal than men, they could not be such excellent artists in this element of fancy if they did not lend and give themselves to it. They are poets who believe their own poetry. They emit from their pores a colored atmosphere, one would say, wave upon wave of rosy light, in which they walk evermore, and see all objects through this warm-tinted mist that envelops them.

But the starry crown of woman is in the power of her affection and sentiment, and the infinite enlargements to which they lead. Beautiful is the passion of love, painter and adorner of youth and early life: but who suspects, in its blushes and tremors, what tragedies, heroisms and immortalities are beyond it? The passion, with all its grace and poetry, is profane to that which follows it. All these affections are only introductory to that which is beyond, and to that which is sublime.

We men have no right to say it, but the omnipotence of Eve is in humility. The instincts of mankind have drawn the Virgin Mother—

"Created beings all in lowliness
Surpassing, as in height above them all." [13]

This is the Divine Person whom Dante and Milton saw in vision. This is the victory of Griselda, her supreme humility. And it is when love has reached this height that all our pretty rhetoric begins to have meaning. When we see that, it adds to the soul a new soul, it is honey in the mouth, music in the ear and balsam in the heart.

---

[12] Patmore, *The Angel in the House*, Bk. I, Canto iv, "The Tribute." [Ed.]

[13] John Milton (1608–74), *Paradise Lost*. [Orig. ed.]

"Far have I clambered in my mind,
But nought so great as Love I find.
What is thy tent, where dost thou dwell?
'My mansion is humility,
Heaven's vastest capability.'
The further it doth downward tend,
The higher up it doth ascend." [14]

The first thing men think of, when they love, is to exhibit their useful-
ness and advantages to the object of their affection. Women make light of
these, asking only love. They wish it to be an exchange of nobleness.

There is much in their nature, much in their social position which gives
them a certain power of divination. And women know, at first sight, the
characters of those with whom they converse. There is much that tends to
give them a religious height which men do not attain. Their sequestration
from affairs and from the injury to the moral sense which affairs often inflict,
aids this. And in every remarkable religious development in the world,
women have taken a leading part. It is very curious that in the East, where
Woman occupies, nationally, a lower sphere, where the laws resist the education and emancipation of women, —in the Mohammedan faith, Woman
yet occupies the same leading position, as a prophetess, that she has among
the ancient Greeks, or among the Hebrews, or among the Saxons. This
power, this religious character, is everywhere to be remarked in them.

The action of society is progressive. In barbarous society the position of
women is always low—in the Eastern nations lower than in the West. [15]
"When a daughter is born," says the Shiking, [16] the old Sacred Book of
China, "she sleeps on the ground, she is clothed with a wrapper, she plays
with a tile; she is incapable of evil or of good." And something like that
position, in all low society, is the position of woman; because, as before remarked, she is herself its civilizer. With the advancements of society, the
position and influence of woman bring her strength or her faults into
light. In modern times, three or four conspicuous instrumentalities may be
marked. After the deification of Woman in the Catholic Church, in the
sixteenth or seventeenth century, —when her religious nature gave her, of
course, new importance, —the Quakers have the honor of having first es-

---

[14] From Henry More (1614–1687), "Love and Humility." [Orig. ed.]

[15] Emerson once again follows the Orientalism of such romantic contemporaries as
G. W. F. Hegel, who in *The Phenomenology of Mind* (1807) and *The Philosophy of History* (1822) argues that "civilization" progresses from Asia to Europe, moving relentlessly
westward. [Ed.]

[16] *I Ching*, the ancient Chinese book of religious magic and prognostication. [Ed.]

tablished, in their discipline, the equality in the sexes. It is even more perfect in the later sect of the Shakers, where no business is broached or counselled without the intervention of one elder and one elderess.

A second epoch for Woman was in France,—entirely civil; the change of sentiment from a rude to a polite character, in the age of Louis XIV,—commonly dated from the building of the Hôtel de Rambouillet. I think another important step was made by the doctrine of Swedenborg,[17] a sublime genius who gave a scientific exposition of the part played severally by man and woman in the world, and showed the difference of sex to run through nature and through thought. Of all Christian sects this is at this moment the most vital and aggressive.

Another step was the effect of the action of the age in the antagonism to Slavery. It was easy to enlist Woman in this; it was impossible not to enlist her. But that Cause turned out to be a great scholar. He was a terrible metaphysician. He was a jurist, a poet, a divine. Was never a University of Oxford or Göttingen that made such students. It took a man from the plough and made him acute, eloquent, and wise, to the silencing of the doctors. There was nothing it did not pry into, no right it did not explore, no wrong it did not expose. And it has, among its other effects, given Woman a feeling of public duty and an added self-respect.[18]

One truth leads in another by the hand; one right is an accession of strength to take more. And the times are marked by the new attitude of Woman; urging, by argument and by association, her rights of all kinds,—in short, to one half of the world;—as the right to education, to avenues of employment, to equal rights of property, to equal rights in marriage, to the exercise of the professions and of suffrage.[19]

Of course, this conspicuousness had its inconveniences. But it is cheap wit that has been spent on this subject; from Aristophanes, in whose comedies I confess my dulness to find good joke, to Rabelais, in whom it is monstrous exaggeration of temperament, and not borne out by anything in nature,—down to English Comedy, and, in our day, to Tennyson, and the

---

[17] Emanuel Swedenborg's mystical philosophy was the basis for the early-nineteenth-century Church of Swedenborgism, still open on Tremont Street in Boston, just off Boston Common. Swedenborg's belief in the mystical correspondence between divine and earthly phenomena had a profound influence on the transcendentalists. [Ed.]

[18] Both Emerson and Fuller suggest that women's rights evolved out of women's involvement in the antislavery movement, but women's rights groups antedate abolitionist movements in the United States and should properly be said to have helped organize (rather than been organized by) the abolitionist movement. [Ed.]

[19] These are the rights listed by women's rights activists at their first national convention, held at Seneca Falls, New York, in 1848. [Ed.]

American newspapers.[20] In all, the body of the joke is one, namely, to charge women with temperament; to describe them as victims of temperament; and is identical with Mahomet's opinion that women have not a sufficient moral or intellectual force to control the perturbations of their physical structure. These were all drawings of morbid anatomy, and such satire as might be written on the tenants of a hospital or on an asylum for idiots. Of course it would be easy for women to retaliate in kind, by painting men from the dogs and gorillas that have worn our shape. That they have not, is an eulogy on their taste and self-respect. The good easy world took the joke which it liked. There is always the want of thought; there is always credulity. There are plenty of people who believe women to be incapable of anything but to cook, incapable of interest in affairs. There are plenty of people who believe that the world is governed by men of dark complexions,[21] that affairs are only directed by such, and do not see the use of contemplative men, or how ignoble would be the world that wanted them. And so without the affection of women.

But for the general charge: no doubt it is well founded. They are victims of the finer temperament. They have tears, and gayeties, and faintings, and glooms and devotion to trifles. Nature's end, of maternity for twenty years, was of so supreme importance that it was to be secured at all events, even to the sacrifice of the highest beauty. They are more personal. Men taunt them that, whatever they do, say, read or write, they are thinking of themselves and their set. Men are not to the same degree temperamented, for there are multitudes of men who live to objects quite out of them, as to politics, to trade, to letters or an art, unhindered by any influence of constitution.

The answer that lies, silent or spoken, in the minds of well-meaning persons, to the new claims, is this: that though their mathematical justice is not

---

[20] Emerson provides an odd list. Aristophanes is known for his ancient Greek comedies of manners, in which conflicts between men and women are central subjects. Rabelais is the sixteenth-century French writer known for his sexual and scatological wit, especially in *Gargantua and Pantagruel*. But Lord Alfred Tennyson (1809–92) was a British poet known for contributing to the domestic ideology endorsed elsewhere by Emerson, albeit ambivalently in this essay. Emerson simply disliked Tennyson, perhaps considering him a rival. Emerson appears to be referring here to Tennyson's poem "The Princess" (E. Emerson 417). [Ed.]

[21] Emerson probably uses the phrase "men of dark complexions" to suggest the working classes or persons involved in manual labor, but it was a nineteenth-century convention to "racialize" class distinctions, especially reserving "fair" and "white" (even "alabaster" and "ivory") as terms for upper-middle-class and aristocratic women. [Ed.]

to be denied, yet the best women do not wish these things; they are asked for by people who intellectually seek them, but who have not the support or sympathy of the truest women; and that, if the laws and customs were modified in the manner proposed, it would embarrass and pain gentle and lovely persons with duties which they would find irksome and distasteful. Very likely. Providence is always surprising us with new and unlikely instruments. But perhaps it is because these people have been deprived of education, fine companions, opportunities, such as they wished,—because they feel the same rudeness and disadvantage which offends you,—that they have been stung to say, "It is too late for us to be polished and fashioned into beauty, but, at least, we will see that the whole race of women shall not suffer as we have suffered."

They have an unquestionable right to their own property. And if a woman demand votes, offices and political equality with men, as among the Shakers an Elder and Elderess are of equal power,—and among the Quakers,—it must not be refused. It is very cheap wit that finds it so droll that a woman should vote. Educate and refine society to the highest point,—bring together a cultivated society of both sexes, in a drawing-room, and consult and decide by voices on a question of taste or on a question of right, and is there any absurdity or any practical difficulty in obtaining their authentic opinions? If not, then there need be none in a hundred companies, if you educate them and accustom them to judge. And, for the effect of it, I can say, for one, that all my points would sooner be carried in the State if women voted. On the questions that are important,—whether the government shall be in one person, or whether representative, or whether democratic; whether men shall be holden in bondage, or shall be roasted alive and eaten, as in Typee, or shall be hunted with bloodhounds, as in this country; whether men shall be hanged for stealing, or hanged at all; whether the unlimited sale of cheap liquors shall be allowed,[22]—they would give, I suppose, as intelligent a vote as the voters of Boston or New York.

We may ask, to be sure,—Why need you vote? If new power is here, of a character which solves old tough questions, which puts me and all the rest in the wrong, tries and condemns our religion, customs, laws, and opens new careers to our young receptive men and women, you can well leave voting to the old dead people. Those whom you teach, and those

---

[22]Herman Melville's *Typee, or a Peep at Polynesian Life* (1846) was a popular work that played on Euroamerican fantasies of cannibalism among the Taipi people on the Marquesas Islands in the South Pacific. Emerson interestingly indicts southern slavery on the grounds that its treatment of African Americans is as inhuman and uncivilized as such cannibalism. [Ed.]

whom you half teach, will fast enough make themselves considered and strong with their new insight, and votes will follow from all the dull.

The objection to their voting is the same as is urged, in the lobbies of legislatures, against clergymen who take an active part in politics; — that if they are good clergymen they are unacquainted with the expediencies of politics, and if they become good politicians they are worse clergymen. So of women, that they cannot enter this arena without being contaminated and unsexed.

Here are two or three objections: first, a want of practical wisdom; second, a too purely ideal view; and, third, danger of contamination. For their want of intimate knowledge of affairs, I do not think this ought to disqualify them from voting at any town-meeting which I ever attended. I could heartily wish the objection were sound. But if any man will take the trouble to see how our people vote, — how many gentlemen are willing to take on themselves the trouble of thinking and determining for you, and, standing at the door of the polls, give every innocent citizen his ticket as he comes in, informing him that this is the vote of his party; and how the innocent citizen, without further demur, goes and drops it in the ballot-box, — I cannot but think he will agree that most women might vote as wisely.

For the other point, of their not knowing the world, and aiming at abstract right without allowance for circumstances, — that is not a disqualification, but a qualification. Human society is made up of partialities. Each citizen has an interest and a view of his own, which, if followed out to the extreme, would leave no room for any other citizen. One man is timid and another rash; one would change nothing, and the other is pleased with nothing; one wishes schools, another armies, one gunboats, another public gardens. Bring all these biases together and something is done in favor of them all.

Every one is a half vote, but the next elector behind him brings the other or corresponding half in his hand: a reasonable result is had. Now there is no lack, I am sure, of the expediency, or of the interests of trade or of imperative class interests being neglected. There is no lack of votes representing the physical wants; and if in your city the uneducated emigrant vote numbers thousands, representing a brutal ignorance and mere animal wants, it is to be corrected by an educated and religious vote, representing the wants and desires of honest and refined persons. If the wants, the passions, the vices, are allowed a full vote through the hands of a half-brutal intemperate population, I think it but fair that the virtues, the aspirations should be allowed a full vote, as an offset, through the purest part of the people.

As for the unsexing and contamination, —that only accuses our existing politics, shows how barbarous we are, —that our policies are so crooked, made up of things not to be spoken, to be understood only by wink and nudge; this man to be coaxed, that man to be bought, and that other to be duped. It is easy to see that there is contamination enough, but it rots the men now, and fills the air with stench. Come out of that: it is like a dance-cellar. The fairest names in this country in literature, in law, have gone into Congress and come out dishonored. And when I read the list of men of intellect, of refined pursuits, giants in law, or eminent scholars, or of social distinction, leading men of wealth and enterprise in the commercial community, and see what they have voted for and suffered to be voted for, I think no community was ever so politely and elegantly betrayed.[23]

I do not think it yet appears that women wish this equal share in public affairs.[24] But it is they and not we that are to determine it. Let the laws be purged of every barbarous remainder, every barbarous impediment to women. Let the public donations for education be equally shared by them, let them enter a school as freely as a church, let them have and hold and give their property as men do theirs; —and in a few years it will easily appear whether they wish a voice in making the laws that are to govern them. If you do refuse them a vote, you will also refuse to tax them, —according to our Teutonic principle, No representation, no tax.

All events of history are to be regarded as growths and offshoots of the expanding mind of the race, and this appearance of new opinions, their currency and force in many minds, is itself the wonderful fact. For whatever is popular is important, shows the spontaneous sense of the hour. The aspiration of this century will be the code of the next. It holds of high and distant causes, of the same influences that make the sun and moon. When new opinions appear, they will be entertained and respected, by every fair mind, according to their reasonableness, and not according to their convenience,

---

[23] Daniel Webster's role in the Compromise of 1850 was greeted by most liberals in New England, including Emerson, as "treason" and the "great betrayal," but a group of Boston merchants signed a petition supporting Webster and published it in the local newspapers. [Ed.]

[24] Despite his earlier endorsement of women's rights, including those specified at the Seneca Falls convention, Emerson reverses his position and claims women do not really desire equal rights. His claim that women themselves will decide about complete equal rights in public affairs may refer to contemporary debates among women's rights activists concerning women's suffrage. The resolutions adopted at the women's rights convention at Seneca Falls did not include a call for women's suffrage, despite a strong minority advocating it. [Ed.]

or their fitness to shock our customs. But let us deal with them greatly; let them make their way by the upper road, and not by the way of manufacturing public opinion, which lapses continually into expediency, and makes charlatans. All that is spontaneous is irresistible, and forever it is individual force that interests. I need not repeat to you—your own solitude will suggest it—that a masculine woman is not strong, but a lady is. The loneliest thought, the purest prayer, is rushing to be the history of a thousand years.

Let us have the true woman, the adorner, the hospitable, the religious heart, and no lawyer need be called in to write stipulations, the cunning clauses of provision, the strong investitures;—for woman moulds the lawgiver and writes the law. But I ought to say, I think it impossible to separate the interests and education of the sexes. Improve and refine the men, and you do the same by the women, whether you will or no. Every woman being the wife or the daughter of a man,—wife, daughter, sister, mother, of a man, she can never be very far from his ear, never not of his counsel, if she has really something to urge that is good in itself and agreeable to nature.[25] Slavery it is that makes slavery; freedom, freedom. The slavery of women happened when the men were slaves of kings. The melioration of manners brought their melioration of course. It could not be otherwise, and hence the new desire of better laws. For there are always a certain number of passionately loving fathers, brothers, husbands and sons who put their might into the endeavor to make a daughter, a wife, or a mother happy in the way that suits best. Woman should find in man her guardian. Silently she looks for that, and when she finds that he is not, as she instantly does, she betakes her to her own defenses, and does the best she can. But when he is her guardian, fulfilled with all nobleness, knows and accepts his duties as her brother, all goes well for both.[26]

The new movement is only a tide shared by the spirits of man and woman; and you may proceed in the faith that whatever the woman's heart is prompted to desire, the man's mind is simultaneously prompted to accomplish.

---

[25] Emerson relies here on another romantic convention, especially noticeable in Hegel's writings, that women's dependency on men is evident in their various relationships to men, such as wife, daughter, sister, and mother. [Ed.]

[26] One consequence of this equation of these different subject positions was to desexualize the relationship of husband and wife and to idealize the relationship of "brother and sister." See in particular Hegel, *The Philosophy of History*. It is a convention upon which Fuller also relies in the "spiritual" relations of men and women that she advocates in *Woman in the Nineteenth Century*. [Ed.]

American Civilization
January 1, 1862

To the mizzen, the main, and the fore
Up with it once more!—
The old tri-color,
The ribbon of power,
The white, blue and red which the nations adore!
It was down at half-mast
For a grief—that is past!
To the emblem of glory no sorrow can last!

Use, labor of each for all, is the health and virtue of all beings. *Ich dien,* I serve, is a truly royal motto. And it is the mark of nobleness to volunteer the lowest service, the greatest spirit only attaining to humility. Nay, God is God because he is the servant of all. Well, now here comes this conspiracy of slavery,—they call it an institution, I call it a destitution,—this stealing of men and setting them to work, stealing their labor, and the thief sitting idle himself; and for two or three ages it has lasted, and has yielded a certain quantity of rice, cotton and sugar. And, standing on this doleful experience, these people have endeavored to reverse the natural sentiments of mankind, and to pronounce labor disgraceful, and the well-being of a man to consist in eating the fruit of other men's labor. Labor: a man coins himself into his labor; turns his day, his strength, his thought, his affection into some product which remains as the visible sign of his power; and to protect that, to secure that to him, to secure his past self to his future self, is the object of all government. There is no interest in any country so imperative as that of labor; it covers all, and constitutions and governments exist for that,—to protect and insure it to the laborer. All honest men are daily striving to earn their bread by their industry. And who is this who tosses his empty head at this blessing in disguise, the constitution of human nature, and calls labor vile, and insults the faithful workman at his daily toil? I see

---

The Complete Works of Ralph Waldo Emerson. Ed. Edward Waldo Emerson. Centenary Edition. Vol. 11. Boston: Houghton, 1904. (All notes are by the present editor.)

for such madness no hellebore,[1]—for such calamity no solution but servile war and the Africanization of the country that permits it.

At this moment in America the aspects of political society absorb attention. In every house, from Canada to the Gulf, the children ask the serious father, —"What is the news of the war to-day, and when will there be better times?" The boys have no new clothes, no gifts, no journeys; the girls must go without new bonnets; boys and girls find their education, this year, less liberal and complete.[2] All the little hopes that heretofore made the year pleasant are deferred. The state of the country fills us with anxiety and stern duties. We have attempted to hold together two states of civilization: a higher state, where labor and the tenure of land and the right of suffrage are democratical; and a lower state, in which the old military tenure of prisoners or slaves, and of power and land in a few hands, makes an oligarchy: we have attempted to hold these two states of society under one law. But the rude and early state of society does not work well with the later, nay, works badly, and has poisoned politics, public morals and social intercourse in the Republic, now for many years.

The times put this question, Why cannot the best civilization be extended over the whole country, since the disorder of the less-civilized portion menaces the existence of the country? Is this secular progress we have described, this evolution of man to the highest powers, only to give him sensibility, and not to bring duties with it? Is he not to make his knowledge practical? to stand and to withstand? Is not civilization heroic also? Is it not for action? has it not a will? "There are periods," said Niebuhr, "when something much better than happiness and security of life is attainable."[3] We live in a new and exceptionable age. America is another word for Opportunity. Our whole history appears like a last effort of the Divine Providence in behalf of the human race; and a literal, slavish following of precedents, as by a justice of the peace, is not for those who at this hour lead the destinies of this people. The evil you contend with has taken alarming proportions, and you still content yourself with parrying the blows it aims, but, as if enchanted, abstain from striking at the cause.

If the American people hesitate, it is not for want of warning or advices. The telegraph has been swift enough to announce our disasters.[4] The jour-

---

[1] Ancient name (Greek: *helleboros*) for various plants imagined to cure madness.

[2] Union blockades of Charleston and other Confederate ports made cotton and thus textiles and clothing scarce commodities during the Civil War.

[3] Barthold Georg Niebuhr (1776–1831), German historian.

[4] The new technology of the telegraph proved its military and social value during the Civil War.

nals have not suppressed the extent of the calamity. Neither was there any want of argument or of experience. If the war brought any surprise to the North, it was not the fault of sentinels on the watch-tower, who had furnished full details of the designs, the muster and the means of the enemy. Neither was anything concealed of the theory or practice of slavery. To what purpose make more big books of these statistics? There are already mountains of facts, if any one wants them. But people do not want them. They bring their opinion into the world. If they have a comatose tendency in the brain, they are pro-slavery while they live; if of a nervous sanguineous temperament, they are abolitionists. Then interests were never persuaded. Can you convince the shoe interest, or the iron interest, or the cotton interest, by reading passages from Milton or Montesquieu? You wish to satisfy people that slavery is bad economy. Why, the "Edinburgh Review" pounded on that string, and made out its case, forty years ago.[5] A democratic statesman said to me, long since, that, if he owned the State of Kentucky, he would manumit all the slaves, and be a gainer by the transaction. Is this new? No, everybody knows it. As a general economy it is admitted. But there is no one owner of the state, but a good many small owners. One man owns land and slaves; another owns slaves only. Here is a woman who has no other property,—like a lady in Charleston I knew of, who owned fifteen sweeps and rode in her carriage. It is clearly a vast inconvenience to each of these to make any change, and they are fretful and talkative, and all their friends are; and those less interested are inert, and, from want of thought, averse to innovation. It is like free trade, certainly the interest of nations, but by no means the interest of certain towns and districts, which tariff feeds fat; and the eager interest of the few overpowers the apathetic general conviction of the many. Banknotes rob the public, but are such a daily convenience that we silence our scruples and make believe they are gold. So imposts are the cheap and right taxation; but, by the dislike of people to pay out a direct tax, governments are forced to render life costly by making them pay twice as much, hidden in the price of tea and sugar.

In this national crisis, it is not argument that we want, but that rare courage which dares commit itself to a principle, believing that Nature is its ally, and will create the instruments it requires, and more than make good any petty and injurious profit which it may disturb. There never was such a combination as this of ours, and the rules to meet it are not set down

---

[5] Until 1850, Emerson was a relative meliorist on the best ways to end slavery. After Daniel Webster's "great betrayal" for his part in the passage of the Compromise of 1850, Emerson joined more radical abolitionist voices. Once war was declared, he accepted the necessity of a violent and, in his view, sacrificial end to slavery.

in any history. We want men of original perception and original action, who can open their eyes wider than to a nationality, namely, to considerations of benefit to the human race, can act in the interest of civilization. Government must not be a parish clerk, a justice of the peace. It has, of necessity, in any crisis of the state, the absolute powers of a Dictator. The existing Administration is entitled to the utmost candor. It is to be thanked for its angelic virtue, compared with any executive experiences with which we have been familiar. But the times will not allow us to indulge in compliment. I wish I saw in the people that inspiration which, if Government would not obey the same, would leave the government behind and create on the moment the means and executors it wanted. Better the war should more dangerously threaten us, — should threaten fracture in what is still whole, and punish us with burned capitals and slaughtered regiments, and so exasperate the people to energy, exasperate our nationality. There are Scriptures written invisibly on men's hearts, whose letters do not come out until they are enraged. They can be read by war-fires, and by eyes in the last peril.[6]

We cannot but remember that there have been days in American history, when, if the free states had done their duty, slavery had been blocked by an immovable barrier, and our recent calamities forever precluded. The free states yielded, and every compromise was surrender and invited new demands.[7] Here again is a new occasion which heaven offers to sense and virtue. It looks as if we held the fate of the fairest possession of mankind in our hands, to be saved by our firmness or to be lost by hesitation.

The one power that has legs long enough and strong enough to wade across the Potomac offers itself at this hour; the one strong enough to bring all the civility up to the height of that which is best, prays now at the door of Congress for leave to move.[8] Emancipation is the demand of civilization.[9] That is a principle; everything else is an intrigue. This is a progressive policy, puts the whole people in healthy, productive, amiable position, puts every man in the South in just and natural relations with every man in the North, laborer with laborer.

---

[6] The radicalism of Emerson's position in this paragraph is a major departure from his earlier considerations of how to end slavery. See "An Address . . . on . . . the Emancipation of the Negroes in the British West Indies" and "The Fugitive Slave Law," also reprinted in this volume.

[7] The Compromise of 1850 is the main "compromise" Emerson has in mind here.

[8] Although Emerson refers generally here to the collective powers of the Union to defeat the Confederacy, he is also referring to General George S. McClellan, commander of the Army of the North, who was preparing the Union Army in Washington, D.C., for an invasion of the South and demanding more assistance from Congress.

[9] Emerson is also appealing, along with many abolitionists, for immediate emancipation — a plan some thought would spark organized slave insurrections and resistance in

I shall not attempt to unfold the details of the project of emancipation. It has been stated with great ability by several of its leading advocates. I will only advert to some leading points of the argument, at the risk of repeating the reasons of others. The war is welcome to the Southerner; a chivalrous sport to him, like hunting, and suits his semi-civilized condition. On the climbing scale of progress, he is just up to war, and has never appeared to such advantage as in the last twelvemonth. It does not suit us. We are advanced some ages on the war-state, —to trade, art and general cultivation. — His laborer works for him at home, so that he loses no labor by the war. All our soldiers are laborers; so that the South, with its inferior numbers, is almost on a footing in effective war-population with the North. Again, as long as we fight without any affirmative step taken by the government, any word intimating forfeiture in the rebel states of their old privileges under the law, they and we fight on the same side, for slavery. Again, if we conquer the enemy, —what then? We shall still have to keep him under, and it will cost as much to hold him down as it did to get him down. Then comes the summer, and the fever will drive the soldiers home; next winter we must begin at the beginning, and conquer him over again. What use then to take a fort, or a privateer, or get possession of an inlet, or to capture a regiment of rebels?

But one weapon we hold which is sure. Congress can, by edict, as a part of the military defence which it is the duty of Congress to provide, abolish slavery, and pay for such slaves as we ought to pay for.[10] Then the slaves near our armies will come to us; those in the interior will know in a week what their rights are, and will, where opportunity offers, prepare to take them. Instantly, the armies that now confront you must run home to protect their estates, and must stay there, and your enemies will disappear.

There can be no safety until this step is taken. We fancy that the endless debate, emphasized by the crime and by the cannons of this war, has brought the free states to some conviction that it can never go well with us whilst this mischief of slavery remains in our politics, and that by concert or by might we must put an end to it. But we have too much experience of the futility of an easy reliance on the momentary good dispositions of the public. There does exist, perhaps, a popular will that the Union shall not be broken, —that our trade, and therefore our laws, must have the whole

---

the South to help the Union war effort. President Lincoln would not issue the Emancipation Proclamation for another year, in January 1863.

[10] Despite his radicalism in this speech, Emerson still clings to the older idea of compensating southern planters for the slaves "lost" to emancipation, which Emerson and Lincoln advocated and for which they found precedent in the British compensation of planters in the British West Indies at the end of slavery there in 1834.

breadth of the continent, and from Canada to the Gulf. But since this is the rooted belief and will of the people, so much the more are they in danger, when impatient of defeats, or impatient of taxes, to go with a rush for some peace; and what kind of peace shall at that moment be easiest attained, they will make concessions for it,—will give up the slaves, and the whole torment of the past half-century will come back to be endured anew.

Neither do I doubt, if such a composition should take place, that the Southerners will come back quietly and politely, leaving their haughty dictation. It will be an era of good feelings. There will be a lull after so loud a storm; and, no doubt, there will be discreet men from that section who will earnestly strive to inaugurate more moderate and fair administration of the government, and the North will for a time have its full share and more, in place and counsel. But this will not last;—not for want of sincere good will in sensible Southerners, but because Slavery will again speak through them its harsh necessity. It cannot live but by injustice, and it will be unjust and violent to the end of the world.

The power of Emancipation is this, that it alters the atomic social constitution of the Southern people. Now, their interest is in keeping out white labor; then, when they must pay wages, their interest will be to let it in, to get the best labor, and, if they fear their blacks, to invite Irish, German and American laborers. Thus, whilst Slavery makes and keeps disunion, Emancipation removes the whole objection to union. Emancipation at one stroke elevates the poor-white of the South, and identifies his interest with that of the Northern laborer.[11]

Now, in the name of all that is simple and generous, why should not this great right be done? Why should not America be capable of a second stroke for the well-being of the human race, as eighty or ninety years ago she was for the first,[12]—of an affirmative step in the interests of human civility, urged on her, too, not by any romance of sentiment, but by her own extreme perils? It is very certain that the statesman who shall break through the cobwebs of doubt, fear and petty cavil that lie in the way, will be greeted by the unanimous thanks of mankind. Men reconcile themselves very fast

---

[11] Emerson's argument in favor of immediate emancipation is based on a theory of labor that unites people socially by virtue of their shared labor. His appeal here to the common cause northern and southern white workers ought to share was echoed by many abolitionists, but Emerson does not mention what Frederick Douglass repeatedly advocated—the common cause of American laborers, African American and white.

[12] A common appeal by abolitionists, notably William Lloyd Garrison, was that the cause required a "second" American Revolution, which would complete the unfinished liberation of the first (specifically noting the omission of the question of slavery from the founding documents of the new nation).

to a bold and good measure when once it is taken, though they condemned it in advance. A week before the two captive commissioners were surrendered to England, every one thought it could not be done: it would divide the North.[13] It was done, and in two days all agreed it was the right action. And this action, which costs so little (the parties injured by it being such a handful that they can very easily be indemnified), rids the world, at one stroke, of this degrading nuisance, the cause of war and ruin to nations. This measure at once puts all parties right. This is borrowing, as I said, the omnipotence of a principle. What is so foolish as the terror lest the blacks should be made furious by freedom and wages?[14] It is denying these that is the outrage, and makes the danger from the blacks. But justice satisfies everybody,—white man, red man, yellow man and black man. All like wages, and the appetite grows by feeding.

But this measure, to be effectual, must come speedily. The weapon is slipping out of our hands. "Time," say the Indian Scriptures, "drinketh up the essence of every great and noble action which ought to be performed, and which is delayed in the execution."

I hope it is not a fatal objection to this policy that it is simple and beneficent thoroughly, which is the tribute of a moral action. An unprecedented material prosperity has not tended to make us Stoics or Christians. But the laws by which the universe is organized reappear at every point, and will rule it. The end of all political struggle is to establish morality as the basis of all legislation.[15] It is not free institutions, it is not a republic, it is not a democracy, that is the end,—no, but only the means. Morality is the object of government. We want a state of things in which crime shall not pay. This is the consolation on which we rest in the darkness of the

[13] On November 8, 1861, Captain Charles Wilkes of the U.S.S. *San Jacinto* boarded the British mail ship *Trent* and removed two Confederate commissioners, James Murray Mason and James Slidell. The British government and public protested the boarding of a neutral ship, and there were fears Great Britain might enter the Civil War on the side of the South, but political tension was relieved when the U.S. released the commissioners to the British on December 26, 1861.

[14] An argument against emancipation (one traceable to antebellum proslavery interests) was that liberated slaves would run wild with "freedom and wages." Some advocates of this position pointed to Afro-Caribbean riots at the conclusion of slavery in the British West Indies, but those riots were generally directed at the ten-year "apprenticeship" the British government required former slaves to serve under their former masters.

[15] Following his arguments for the economic, political, and military practicality of immediate emancipation, Emerson's appeal to an older transcendentalist morality at the conclusion of his speech sounds a strange note. To be sure, the cause of abolition is moral for all the practical reasons Emerson cites. What sounds discordant is Emerson's apparent abandonment of these self-evidently moral claims for the sake of an irrelevant transcendentalist ethics.

264 // RALPH WALDO EMERSON

future and the afflictions of to-day, that the government of the world is moral, and does forever destroy what is not. It is the maxim of natural philosophers that the natural forces wear out in time all obstacles, and take place: and it is the maxim of history that victory always falls at last where it ought to fall; or, there is perpetual march and progress to ideas. But in either case, no link of the chain can drop out. Nature works through her appointed elements; and ideas must work through the brains and the arms of good and brave men, or they are no better than dreams.

Since the above pages were written, President Lincoln has proposed to Congress that the government shall co-operate with any state that shall enact a gradual abolishment of slavery. In the recent series of national successes, this message is the best. It marks the happiest day in the political year. The American Executive ranges itself for the first time on the side of freedom. If Congress has been backward, the President has advanced. This state-paper is the more interesting that it appears to be the President's individual act, done under a strong sense of duty. He speaks his own thought in his own style. All thanks and honor to the Head of the State! The message has been received throughout the country with praise, and, we doubt not, with more pleasure than has been spoken. If Congress accords with the President, it is not yet too late to begin the emancipation; but we think it will always be too late to make it gradual. All experience agrees that it should be immediate. More and better than the President has spoken shall, perhaps, the effect of this message be, — but, we are sure, not more or better than he hoped in his heart, when, thoughtful of all the complexities of his position, he penned these cautious words.

Thoreau

1862[1]

Henry David Thoreau was the last male descendant of a French ancestor who came to this country from the Isle of Guernsey. His character exhibited occasional traits drawn from this blood, in singular combination with a very strong Saxon genius.

Selections from Ralph Waldo Emerson: An Organic Anthology. Ed. Stephen E. Whicher. Riverside Edition. Boston: Houghton, 1957.

[1] Thoreau died on May 6, 1862, and on May 9 Emerson read a eulogy, a revised version of which was published in August in *The Atlantic Monthly*. [Orig. ed.]

He was born in Concord, Massachusetts, on the 12th of July, 1817. He was graduated at Harvard College in 1837, but without any literary distinction. An iconoclast in literature, he seldom thanked colleges for their service to him, holding them in small esteem, whilst yet his debt to them was important. After leaving the University, he joined his brother in teaching a private school, which he soon renounced. His father was a manufacturer of leadpencils, and Henry applied himself for a time to this craft, believing he could make a better pencil than was then in use. After completing his experiments, he exhibited his work to chemists and artists in Boston, and having obtained their certificates to its excellence and to its equality with the best London manufacture, he returned home contented. His friends congratulated him that he had now opened his way to fortune. But he replied that he should never make another pencil. "Why should I? I would not do again what I have done once." He resumed his endless walks and miscellaneous studies, making every day some new acquaintance with Nature, though as yet never speaking of zoölogy or botany, since, though very studious of natural facts, he was incurious of technical and textual science.

At this time, a strong, healthy youth, fresh from college, whilst all his companions were choosing their profession, or eager to begin some lucrative employment, it was inevitable that his thoughts should be exercised on the same question, and it required rare decision to refuse all the accustomed paths and keep his solitary freedom at the cost of disappointing the natural expectations of his family and friends: all the more difficult that he had a perfect probity, was exact in securing his own independence, and in holding every man to the like duty. But Thoreau never faltered. He was a born protestant. He declined to give up his large ambition of knowledge and action for any narrow craft or profession, aiming at a much more comprehensive calling, the art of living well. If he slighted and defied the opinions of others, it was only that he was more intent to reconcile his practice with his own belief. Never idle or self-indulgent, he preferred, when he wanted money, earning it by some piece of manual labor agreeable to him, as building a boat or a fence, planting, grafting, surveying or other short work, to any long engagements. With his hardy habits and few wants, his skill in wood-craft, and his powerful arithmetic, he was very competent to live in any part of the world. It would cost him less time to supply his wants than another. He was therefore secure of his leisure.

A natural skill for mensuration, growing out of his mathematical knowledge and his habit of ascertaining the measures and distances of objects which interested him, the size of trees, the depth and extent of ponds and rivers, the height of mountains and the airline distance of his favorite summits,—this, and his intimate knowledge of the territory about Concord, made him drift into the profession of land-surveyor. It had the advantage for him that it led him continually into new and secluded grounds, and helped his studies of Nature. His accuracy and skill in this work were readily appreciated, and he found all the employment he wanted.

He could easily solve the problems of the surveyor, but he was daily beset with graver questions, which he manfully confronted. He interrogated every custom, and wished to settle all his practice on an ideal foundation. He was a protestant à *outrance*,[2] and few lives contain so many renunciations. He was bred to no profession; he never married; he lived alone; he never went to church; he never voted; he refused to pay a tax to the State; he ate no flesh, he drank no wine, he never knew the use of tobacco; and, though a naturalist, he used neither trap nor gun. He chose, wisely no doubt for himself, to be the bachelor of thought and Nature. He had no talent for wealth, and knew how to be poor without the least hint of squalor or inelegance. Perhaps he fell into his way of living without forecasting it much, but approved it with later wisdom. "I am often reminded," he wrote in his journal, "that if I had bestowed on me the wealth of Croesus, my aims must be still the same, and my means essentially the same." He had no temptations to fight against, — no appetites, no passions, no taste for elegant trifles. A fine house, dress, the manners and talk of highly cultivated people were all thrown away on him. He much preferred a good Indian, and considered these refinements as impediments to conversation, wishing to meet his companion on the simplest terms. He declined invitations to dinner-parties, because there each was in every one's way, and he could not meet the individuals to any purpose. "They make their pride," he said, "in making their dinner cost much; I make my pride in making my dinner cost little." When asked at table what dish he preferred, he answered, "The nearest." He did not like the taste of wine, and never had a vice in his life. He said, — "I have a faint recollection of pleasure derived from smoking dried lily-stems, before I was a man. I had commonly a supply of these. I have never smoked anything more noxious."

He chose to be rich by making his wants few, and supplying them himself. In his travels, he used the railroad only to get over so much country as was unimportant to the present purpose, walking hundreds of miles, avoiding taverns, buying a lodging in farmers' and fishermen's houses, as cheaper, and more agreeable to him, and because there he could better find the men and the information he wanted.

There was somewhat military in his nature, not to be subdued, always manly and able, but rarely tender, as if he did not feel himself except in

---

[2] "To the very limit" (E. Emerson 380). [Ed.]

opposition. He wanted a fallacy to expose, a blunder to pillory, I may say required a little sense of victory, a roll of the drum, to call his powers into full exercise. It cost him nothing to say No; indeed he found it much easier than to say Yes. It seemed as if his first instinct on hearing a proposition was to controvert it, so impatient was he of the limitations of our daily thought. This habit, of course, is a little chilling to the social affections; and though the companion would in the end acquit him of any malice or untruth, yet it mars conversation. Hence, no equal companion stood in affectionate relations with one so pure and guileless. "I love Henry," said one of his friends, "but I cannot like him; and as for taking his arm, I should as soon think of taking the arm of an elm-tree."[3]

Yet, hermit and stoic as he was, he was really fond of sympathy, and threw himself heartily and childlike into the company of young people whom he loved, and whom he delighted to entertain, as he only could, with the varied and endless anecdotes of his experiences by field and river: and he was always ready to lead a huckleberry-party or a search for chestnuts or grapes. Talking, one day, of a public discourse, Henry remarked that whatever succeeded with the audience was bad. I said, "Who would not like to write something which all can read, like Robinson Crusoe? and who does not see with regret that his page is not solid with a right materialistic treatment, which delights everybody?" Henry objected, of course, and vaunted the better lectures which reached only a few persons. But, at supper, a young girl, understanding that he was to lecture at the Lyceum,[4] sharply asked him, "Whether his lecture would be a nice, interesting story, such as she wished to hear, or whether it was one of those old philosophical things that she did not care about." Henry turned to her, and bethought himself, and, I saw, was trying to believe that he had matter that might fit her and her brother, who were to sit up and go to the lecture, if it was a good one for them.

He was a speaker and actor of the truth, born such, and was ever running into dramatic situations from this cause. In any circumstance it interested all bystanders to know what part Henry would take, and what he would say; and he did not disappoint expectation, but used an original judgment on each emergency. In 1845 he built himself a small framed house on the shores of Walden Pond, and lived there two years alone, a life of labor and study. This action was quite native and fit for him. No one who knew him would tax him with affectation. He was more unlike his neighbors in his thought than in his action. As soon as he had exhausted the

---

[3] The friend was Emerson himself. [Ed.]

[4] The Lyceum was an organization that sponsored public lectures in towns and villages in the Northeast. Emerson lectured regularly in the Lyceum series. [Ed.]

advantages of that solitude, he abandoned it. In 1847, not approving some uses to which the public expenditure was applied, he refused to pay his town tax, and was put in jail.[5] A friend paid the tax for him, and he was released. The like annoyance was threatened the next year. But as his friends paid the tax, notwithstanding his protest, I believe he ceased to resist. No opposition or ridicule had any weight with him. He coldly and fully stated his opinion without affecting to believe that it was the opinion of the company. It was of no consequence if every one present held the opposite opinion. On one occasion he went to the University Library to procure some books. The librarian refused to lend them. Mr. Thoreau repaired to the President, who stated to him the rules and usages, which permitted the loan of books to resident graduates, to clergymen who were alumni, and to some others resident within a circle of ten miles' radius from the College. Mr. Thoreau explained to the President that the railroad had destroyed the old scale of distances, — that the library was useless, yes, and President and College useless, on the terms of his rules, — that the one benefit he owed to the College was its library, — that, at this moment, not only his want of books was imperative, but he wanted a large number of books, and assured him that he, Thoreau, and not the librarian, was the proper custodian of these. In short, the President found the petitioner so formidable, and the rules getting to look so ridiculous, that he ended by giving him a privilege which in his hands proved unlimited thereafter.

No truer American existed than Thoreau. His preference of his country and condition was genuine, and his aversation from English and European manners and tastes almost reached contempt. He listened impatiently to news or *bonmots* gleaned from London circles; and though he tried to be civil, these anecdotes fatigued him. The men were all imitating each other, and on a small mold. Why can they not live as far apart as possible, and each be a man by himself? What he sought was the most energetic nature; and he wished to go to Oregon, not to London. "In every part of Great Britain," he wrote in his diary, "are discovered traces of the Romans, their funereal urns, their camps, their roads, their dwellings. But New England, at least, is not based on any Roman ruins. We have not to lay the foundations of our houses on the ashes of a former civilization."

But idealist as he was, standing for abolition of slavery, abolition of tariffs, almost for abolition of government, it is needless to say he found

---

[5] Thoreau refused to pay a poll tax because the funds would contribute to the U.S. war with Mexico over Texas. His "Civil Disobedience" was first published, under the title "Resistance to Civil Government," in 1849 and since that time has had a wide influence on such thinkers and activists as Mahatma Gandhi and Martin Luther King, Jr. [Ed.]

himself not only unrepresented in actual politics, but almost equally opposed to every class of reformers. Yet he paid the tribute of his uniform respect to the Anti-Slavery party. One man, whose personal acquaintance he had formed, he honored with exceptional regard. Before the first friendly word had been spoken for Captain John Brown, he sent notices to most houses in Concord that he would speak in a public hall on the condition and character of John Brown, on Sunday evening, and invited all people to come.[6] The Republican Committee, the Abolitionist Committee, sent him word that it was premature and not advisable. He replied,—"I did not send to you for advice, but to announce that I am to speak." The hall was filled at an early hour by people of all parties, and his earnest eulogy of the hero was heard by all respectfully, by many with a sympathy that surprised themselves.[7]

It was said of Plotinus that he was ashamed of his body, and 'tis very likely he had good reason for it,—that his body was a bad servant, and he had not skill in dealing with the material world, as happens often to men of abstract intellect.[8] But Mr. Thoreau was equipped with a most adapted and serviceable body. He was of short stature, firmly built, of light complexion, with strong, serious blue eyes, and a grave aspect,—his face covered in the late years with a becoming beard. His senses were acute, his frame well-knit and hardy, his hands strong and skilful in the use of tools. And there was a wonderful fitness of body and mind. He could pace sixteen rods more accurately than another man could measure them with rod and chain.[9] He could find his path in the woods at night, he said, better by his feet than his eyes. He could estimate the measure of a tree very well by his eye; he could estimate the weight of a calf or a pig, like a dealer. From a box containing a bushel or more of loose pencils, he could take up with his hands fast enough just a dozen pencils at every grasp.[10] He was a good swimmer, runner, skater, boatman, and would probably outwalk most countrymen in a

---

[6]Captain John Brown (1800–59), the abolitionist, on 18 October 1859 led a group of armed men and seized the U.S. arsenal at Harpers Ferry, Virginia. He was tried in Virginia, convicted of treason and murder, and executed. [Ed.]

[7]Thoreau was invited to attend a memorial service for John Brown on 4 July 1860. He declined the invitation but sent a section of his journal in which he had written his views of John Brown. Those words were read at the memorial service and then published in July 1860 in William Lloyd Garrison's abolitionist newspaper, *The Liberator*. [Ed.]

[8]Plotinus, the Neoplatonist philosopher, would have criticized the body for its materiality, regardless of its fitness. [Ed.]

[9]A rod is a measure of 5.5 yards or 5.03 meters. Thoreau was trained and worked briefly as a surveyor. [Ed.]

[10]Thoreau's family manufactured and sold pencils. [Ed.]

day's journey. And the relation of body to mind was still finer than we have indicated. He said he wanted every stride his legs made. The length of his walk uniformly made the length of his writing. If shut up in the house he did not write at all.

He had a strong common sense, like that which Rose Flammock, the weaver's daughter in Scott's romance,[11] commends in her father, as resembling a yardstick, which, whilst it measures dowlas[12] and diaper, can equally well measure tapestry and cloth of gold. He had always a new resource. When I was planting forest trees, and had procured half a peck of acorns, he said that only a small portion of them would be sound, and proceeded to examine them and select the sound ones. But finding this took time, he said, "I think if you put them all into water the good ones will sink"; which experiment we tried with success. He could plan a garden or a house or a barn; would have been competent to lead a "Pacific Exploring Expedition"; could give judicious counsel in the gravest private or public affairs.

He lived for the day, not cumbered and mortified by his memory. If he brought you yesterday a new proposition, he would bring you today another not less revolutionary. A very industrious man, and setting, like all highly organized men, a high value on his time, he seemed the only man of leisure in town, always ready for any excursion that promised well, or for conversation prolonged into late hours. His trenchant sense was never stopped by his rules of daily prudence, but was always up to the new occasion. He liked and used the simplest food, yet, when some one urged a vegetable diet, Thoreau thought all diets a very small matter, saying that "the man who shoots the buffalo lives better than the man who boards at the Graham House." He said, — "You can sleep near the railroad, and never be disturbed: Nature knows very well what sounds are worth attending to, and has made up her mind not to hear the railroad-whistle. But things respect the devout mind, and a mental ecstasy was never interrupted." He noted what repeatedly befell him, that, after receiving from a distance a rare plant, he would presently find the same in his own haunts. And those pieces of luck which happen only to good players happened to him. One day, walking with a stranger, who inquired where Indian arrow-heads could be found, he replied, "Everywhere," and, stooping forward, picked one on the instant from the ground. At Mount Washington, in Tuckerman's Ravine, Thoreau had a bad fall, and sprained his foot. As he was in the act of getting up from his fall, he saw for the first time the leaves of the *Arnica mollis.*[13]

---

[11] Sir Walter Scott, *The Betrothed* (1825). [Ed.]

[12] "Dowlas" is linen or calico, which together with "diaper" means ordinary fabric. [Ed.]

[13] Medicinal plant used for sprains and bruises. [Ed.]

His robust common sense, armed with stout hands, keen perceptions and strong will, cannot yet account for the superiority which shone in his simple and hidden life. I must add the cardinal fact, that there was an excellent wisdom in him, proper to a rare class of men, which showed him the material world as a means and symbol. This discovery, which sometimes yields to poets a certain casual and interrupted light, serving for the ornament of their writing, was in him an unsleeping insight; and whatever faults or obstructions of temperament might cloud it, he was not disobedient to the heavenly vision. In his youth, he said, one day, "The other world is all my art; my pencils will draw no other; my jack-knife will cut nothing else; I do not use it as a means." This was the muse and genius that ruled his opinions, conversation, studies, work and course of life. This made him a searching judge of men. At first glance he measured his companion, and, though insensible to some fine traits of culture, could very well report his weight and calibre. And this made the impression of genius which his conversation sometimes gave.

He understood the matter in hand at a glance, and saw the limitations and poverty of those he talked with, so that nothing seemed concealed from such terrible eyes. I have repeatedly known young men of sensibility converted in a moment to the belief that this was the man they were in search of, the man of men, who could tell them all they should do. His own dealing with them was never affectionate, but superior, didactic, scorning their petty ways, —very slowly conceding, or not conceding at all, the promise of his society at their houses, or even at his own. "Would he not walk with them?" "He did not know. There was nothing so important to him as his walk; he had no walks to throw away on company." Visits were offered him from respectful parties, but he declined them. Admiring friends offered to carry him at their own cost to the Yellowstone River, —to the West Indies, —to South America. But though nothing could be more grave or considered than his refusals, they remind one, in quite new relations, of that fop Brummel's reply to the gentleman who offered him his carriage in a shower, "But where will *you* ride, then?" [14]—and what accusing silences, and what searching and irresistible speeches, battering down all defenses, his companions can remember!

Mr. Thoreau dedicated his genius with such entire love to the fields, hills and waters of his native town, that he made them known and interesting to all reading Americans, and to people over the sea. The river on whose banks he was born and died he knew from its springs to its confluence with

----

[14]George (Beau) Brummel (1778–1840), a British gentleman who was dandyish in dress and manners. [Ed.]

the Merrimack. He had made summer and winter observations on it for many years, and at every hour of the day and night. The result of the recent survey of the Water Commissioners appointed by the State of Massachusetts he had reached by his private experiments, several years earlier. Every fact which occurs in the bed, on the banks or in the air over it; the fishes, and their spawning and nests, their manners, their food; the shad-flies which fill the air on a certain evening once a year, and which are snapped at by the fishes so ravenously that many of these die of repletion; the conical heaps of small stones on the river-shallows, the huge nests of small fishes, one of which will sometimes overfill a cart; the birds which frequent the stream, heron, duck, sheldrake, loon, osprey; the snake, muskrat, otter, woodchuck and fox, on the banks; the turtle, frog, hyla and cricket, which make the banks vocal, — were all known to him, and, as it were, townsmen and fellow creatures; so that he felt an absurdity or violence in any narrative of one of these by itself apart, and still more of its dimensions on an inch-rule, or in the exhibition of its skeleton, or the specimen of a squirrel or a bird in brandy. He liked to speak of the manners of the river, as itself a lawful creature, yet with exactness, and always to an observed fact. As he knew the river, so the ponds in this region.

One of the weapons he used, more important to him than microscope or alcohol-receiver to other investigators, was a whim which grew on him by indulgence, yet appeared in gravest statement, namely, of extolling his own town and neighborhood as the most favored center for natural observation. He remarked that the Flora of Massachusetts embraced almost all the important plants of America, — most of the oaks, most of the willows, the best pines, the ash, the maple, the beech, the nuts. He returned Kane's Arctic Voyage[15] to a friend of whom he had borrowed it, with the remark, that "Most of the phenomena noted might be observed in Concord." He seemed a little envious of the Pole, for the coincident sunrise and sunset, or five minutes' day after six months: a splendid fact, which Annursnuc[16] had never afforded him. He found red snow in one of his walks, and told me that he expected to find yet the *Victoria regia*[17] in Concord. He was the attorney of the indigenous plants, and owned to a preference of the weeds to the imported plants, as of the Indian to the civilized man, and noticed, with pleasure, that the willow bean-poles of his neighbor had grown more than his beans. "See these weeds," he said, "which have been hoed at by a million farmers all spring and summer, and yet have prevailed, and just

---

[15] Elisha Kent Kane (1820–57), *Arctic Explorations* (1856). [Ed.]

[16] A hill in Concord. [Ed.]

[17] A water-lily, native to South America. [Ed.]

now come out triumphant over all lanes, pastures, fields and gardens, such is their vigor. We have insulted them with low names, too,—as Pigweed, Wormwood, Chickweed, Shad-blossom." He says, "They have brave names, too,—Ambrosia, Stellaria, Amelanchier, Amaranth, etc."

I think his fancy for referring everything to the meridian of Concord did not grow out of any ignorance or depreciation of other longitudes or latitudes, but was rather a playful expression of his conviction of the indifferency of all places, and that the best place for each is where he stands. He expressed it once in this wise: "I think nothing is to be hoped from you, if this bit of mold under your feet is not sweeter to you to eat than any other in this world, or in any world."

The other weapon with which he conquered all obstacles in science was patience. He knew how to sit immovable, a part of the rock he rested on, until the bird, the reptile, the fish, which had retired from him, should come back and resume its habits, nay, moved by curiosity, should come to him and watch him.

It was a pleasure and a privilege to walk with him. He knew the country like a fox or a bird, and passed through it as freely by paths of his own. He knew every track in the snow or on the ground, and what creature had taken this path before him. One must submit abjectly to such a guide, and the reward was great. Under his arm he carried an old music-book to press plants; in his pocket, his diary and pencil, a spy-glass for birds, microscope, jack-knife and twine. He wore a straw hat, stout shoes, strong gray trousers, to brave scrub-oaks and smilax, and to climb a tree for a hawk's or a squirrel's nest. He waded into the pool for the water-plants, and his strong legs were no insignificant part of his armor. On the day I speak of he looked for the Menyanthes,[18] detected it across the wide pool, and, on examination of the florets, decided that it had been in flower five days. He drew out of his breast-pocket his diary, and read the names of all the plants that should bloom on this day, whereof he kept account as a banker when his notes fall due. The Cypripedium[19] not due till tomorrow. He thought that, if waked up from a trance, in this swamp, he could tell by the plants what time of the year it was within two days. The redstart was flying about, and presently the fine grosbeaks,[20] whose brilliant scarlet "makes the rash gazer wipe his eye," and whose fine clear note Thoreau compared to that of a tanager which has got rid of its hoarseness. Presently he heard a note which he called that of the night-warbler, a bird he had never identified, had been in search of twelve

---

[18] Scientific name for the buckbean, a plant that grows in bogs. [Ed.]

[19] Scientific name for the "lady's slipper" orchid. [Ed.]

[20] Finches. The quotation is from George Herbert's (1593–1633) poem "Vertue." [Ed.]

years, which always, when he saw it, was in the act of diving down into a tree or bush, and which it was vain to seek; the only bird which sings indifferently by night and by day. I told him he must beware of finding and booking it, lest life should have nothing more to show him. He said, "What you seek in vain for, half your life, one day you come full upon, all the family at dinner. You seek it like a dream, and as soon as you find it you become its prey."

His interest in the flower or the bird lay very deep in his mind, was connected with Nature, —and the meaning of Nature was never attempted to be defined by him. He would not offer a memoir of his observations to the Natural History Society. "Why should I? To detach the description from its connections in my mind would make it no longer true or valuable to me: and they do not wish what belongs to it." His power of observation seemed to indicate additional senses. He saw as with microscope, heard as with eartrumpet, and his memory was a photographic register of all he saw and heard. And yet none knew better than he that it is not the fact that imports, but the impression or effect of the fact on your mind. Every fact lay in glory in his mind, a type of the order and beauty of the whole.

His determination on Natural History was organic. He confessed that he sometimes felt like a hound or a panther, and, if born among Indians, would have been a fell hunter. But, restrained by his Massachusetts culture, he played out the game in this mild form of botany and ichthyology. His intimacy with animals suggested what Thomas Fuller records of Butler the apiologist, that "either he had told the bees things or the bees had told him." Snakes coiled round his legs; the fishes swam into his hand, and he took them out of the water; he pulled the woodchuck out of its hole by the tail, and took the foxes under his protection from the hunters. Our naturalist had perfect magnanimity; he had no secrets: he would carry you to the heron's haunt, or even to his most prized botanical swamp, —possibly knowing that you could never find it again, yet willing to take his risks.

No college ever offered him a diploma, or a professor's chair; no academy made him its corresponding secretary, its discoverer or even its member. Perhaps these learned bodies feared the satire of his presence. Yet so much knowledge of Nature's secret and genius few others possessed; none in a more large and religious synthesis. For not a particle of respect had he to the opinions of any man or body of men, but homage solely to the truth itself; and as he discovered everywhere among doctors some leaning of courtesy, it discredited them. He grew to be revered and admired by his townsmen, who had at first known him only as an oddity. The farmers who employed him as a surveyor soon discovered his rare accuracy and skill, his knowledge of their lands, of trees, of birds, of Indian remains and the like, which enabled him to tell every farmer more than he knew before of his own farm; so that he began to feel a little as if Mr. Thoreau had better rights in his land than he. They felt, too, the superiority of character which addressed all men with a native authority.

Indian relics abound in Concord, — arrow-heads, stone chisels, pestles and fragments of pottery; and on the river-bank, large heaps of clam-shells and ashes mark spots which the savages frequented. These, and every circumstance touching the Indian, were important in his eyes. His visits to Maine were chiefly for love of the Indian. He had the satisfaction of seeing the manufacture of the bark canoe, as well as of trying his hand in its management on the rapids. He was inquisitive about the making of the stone arrow-head, and in his last days charged a youth setting out for the Rocky Mountains to find an Indian who could tell him that: "It was well worth a visit to California to learn it." Occasionally, a small party of Penobscot Indians would visit Concord, and pitch their tents for a few weeks in summer on the river-bank. He failed not to make acquaintance with the best of them; though he well knew that asking questions of Indians is like catechizing beavers and rabbits. In his last visit to Maine he had great satisfaction from Joseph Polis, an intelligent Indian of Oldtown, who was his guide for some weeks.

He was equally interested in every natural fact. The depth of his perception found likeness of law throughout Nature, and I know not any genius who so swiftly inferred universal law from the single fact. He was no pedant of a department. His eye was open to beauty, and his ear to music. He found these, not in rare conditions, but wheresoever he went. He thought the best of music was in single strains; and he found poetic suggestion in the humming of the telegraph-wire.

His poetry might be bad or good; he no doubt wanted a lyric facility and technical skill, but he had the source of poetry in his spiritual perception. He was a good reader and critic, and his judgment on poetry was to the ground of it. He could not be deceived as to the presence or absence of the poetic element in any composition, and his thirst for this made him negligent and perhaps scornful of superficial graces. He would pass by many delicate rhythms, but he would have detected every live stanza or line in a volume and knew very well where to find an equal poetic charm in prose. He was so enamoured of the spiritual beauty that he held all actual written poems in very light esteem in the comparison. He admired Aeschylus and Pindar; but when some one was commending them, he said that Aeschylus and the Greeks, in describing Apollo and Orpheus, had given no song, or no good one. "They ought not to have moved trees, but to have chanted to the gods such a hymn as would have sung all their old ideas out of their heads, and new ones in." His own verses are often rude and defective. The gold does not yet run pure, is drossy and crude. The thyme and marjoram are not yet honey. But if he want lyric fineness and technical merits, if he have not the poetic temperament, he never lacks the causal thought, showing that his genius was better than his talent. He knew the worth of the Imagination for the uplifting and consolation of human life, and liked to throw every thought into a symbol. The fact you tell is of no value, but only the impression. For this reason his presence was poetic, always piqued the curiosity to know more deeply the secrets of his mind. He had many reserves, an unwillingness to exhibit to profane eyes what was still sacred in his own, and knew well how to throw a poetic veil over his experience. All readers of Walden will remember his mythical record of his disappointments:—

"I long ago lost a hound, a bay horse and a turtle-dove, and am still on their trail. Many are the travelers I have spoken concerning them, describing their tracks, and what calls they answered to. I have met one or two who have heard the hound, and the tramp of the horse, and even seen the dove disappear behind a cloud; and they seemed as anxious to recover them as if they had lost them themselves."

His riddles were worth the reading, and I confide that if at any time I do not understand the expression, it is yet just. Such was the wealth of his truth that it was not worth his while to use words in vain. His poem entitled "Sympathy" reveals the tenderness under that triple steel of stoicism, and the intellectual subtility it could animate. His classic poem on "Smoke" suggests Simonides, but is better than any poem of Simonides.[21] His biography is in his verses. His habitual thought makes all his poetry a hymn to the Cause of causes, the Spirit which vivifies and controls his own:—

"I hearing get, who had but ears,
And sight, who had but eyes before;
I moments live, who lived but years,
And truth discern, who knew but learning's lore."

And still more in these religious lines:—

"Now chiefly is my natal hour,
And only now my prime of life;
I will not doubt the love untold,
Which not my worth nor want have bought,
Which wooed me young, and wooes me old,
And to this evening hath me brought."[22]

---

[21] Greek poet of the sixth century BCE. [Ed.]
[22] Both quotations are from Thoreau's poem "Inspiration." [Ed.]

Whilst he used in his writings a certain petulance of remark in reference to churches or churchmen, he was a person of a rare, tender and absolute religion, a person incapable of any profanation, by act or by thought. Of course, the same isolation which belonged to his original thinking and living detached him from the social religious forms. This is neither to be censured nor regretted. Aristotle long ago explained it, when he said, "One who surpasses his fellow citizens in virtue is no longer a part of the city. Their law is not for him, since he is a law to himself."

Thoreau was sincerity itself, and might fortify the convictions of prophets in the ethical laws by his holy living. It was an affirmative experience which refused to be set aside. A truth-speaker he, capable of the most deep and strict conversation; a physician to the wounds of any soul; a friend, knowing not only the secret of friendship, but almost worshipped by those few persons who resorted to him as their confessor and prophet, and knew the deep value of his mind and great heart. He thought that without religion or devotion of some kind nothing great was ever accomplished: and he thought that the bigoted sectarian had better bear this in mind.

His virtues, of course, sometimes ran into extremes. It was easy to trace to the inexorable demand on all for exact truth that austerity which made this willing hermit more solitary even than he wished. Himself of a perfect probity, he required not less of others. He had a disgust at crime, and no worldly success would cover it. He detected paltering as readily in dignified and prosperous persons as in beggars, and with equal scorn. Such dangerous frankness was in his dealing that his admirers called him "that terrible Thoreau," as if he spoke when silent, and was still present when he had departed. I think the severity of his ideal interfered to deprive him of a healthy sufficiency of human society.

The habit of a realist to find things the reverse of their appearance inclined him to put every statement in a paradox. A certain habit of antagonism defaced his earlier writings,—a trick of rhetoric not quite outgrown in his later, of substituting for the obvious word and thought its diametrical opposite. He praised wild mountains and winter forests for their domestic air, in snow and ice he would find sultriness, and commended the wilderness for resembling Rome and Paris. "It was so dry, that you might call it wet."

The tendency to magnify the moment, to read all the laws of Nature in the one object or one combination under your eye, is of course comic to those who do not share the philosopher's perception of identity. To him there was no such thing as size. The pond was a small ocean; the Atlantic, a large Walden Pond. He referred every minute fact to cosmical laws. Though he meant to be just, he seemed haunted by a certain chronic assumption that the science of the day pretended completeness, and he had just found out that the *savans*[23] had neglected to discriminate a particular botanical variety, had failed to describe the seeds or count the sepals.[24] "That is to say," we replied, "the blockheads were not born in Concord; but who said they were? It was their unspeakable misfortune to be born in London, or Paris, or Rome; but, poor fellows, they did what they could, considering that they never saw Bateman's Pond, or Nine-Acre Corner, or Becky Stow's Swamp; besides, what were you sent into the world for, but to add this observation?

Had his genius been only contemplative, he had been fitted to his life, but with his energy and practical ability he seemed born for great enterprise and for command; and I so much regret the loss of his rare powers of action, that I cannot help counting it a fault in him that he had no ambition. Wanting this, instead of engineering for all America, he was the captain of a huckleberry-party. Pounding beans is good to the end of pounding empires one of these days; but if, at the end of years, it is still only beans!

But these foibles, real or apparent, were fast vanishing in the incessant growth of a spirit so robust and wise, and which effaced its defeats with new triumphs. His study of Nature was a perpetual ornament to him, and inspired his friends with curiosity to see the world through his eyes, and to hear his adventures. They possessed every kind of interest.

He had many elegancies of his own, whilst he scoffed at conventional elegance. Thus, he could not bear to hear the sound of his own steps, the grit of gravel; and therefore never willingly walked in the road, but in the grass, on mountains and in woods. His senses were acute, and he remarked that by night every dwelling-house gives out bad air like a slaughter-house. He liked the pure fragrance of melilot.[25] He honored certain plants with special regard, and, over all, the pond-lily,—then, the gentian, and the *Mikania scandens*,[26] and "life-everlasting," and a bass-tree which he visited every year when it bloomed, in the middle of July. He thought the scent a more oracular inquisition than the sight,—more oracular and trustworthy. The scent, of course, reveals what is concealed from the other senses. By it he detected earthiness. He delighted in echoes, and said they were almost the only kind of kindred voices that he heard. He loved Nature so well, was so happy in her solitude, that he became very jealous of cities and the sad work which their refinements and artifices made with man and his dwelling. The axe was always destroying his forest. "Thank God," he said, "they can-

---

[23] French: scholars. [Ed.]
[24] Leaves constituting the calyx of a flower. [Ed.]
[25] Sweet clover. [Ed.]
[26] Climbing hempweed, a vine. [Ed.]

not cut down the clouds!" "All kinds of figures are drawn on the blue ground with this fibrous white paint."

I subjoin a few sentences taken from his unpublished manuscripts, not only as records of his thought and feeling, but for their power of description and literary excellence: —

"Some circumstantial evidence is very strong, as when you find a trout in the milk."

"The chub is a soft fish, and tastes like boiled brown paper salted."

"The youth gets together his materials to build a bridge to the moon, or, perchance, a palace or temple on the earth, and, at length the middle-aged man concludes to build a wood-shed with them."

"The locust z-ing."

"Devil's-needles zigzagging along the Nut-Meadow brook."

"Sugar is not so sweet to the palate as sound to the healthy ear."

"I put on some hemlock-boughs, and the rich salt crackling of their leaves was like mustard to the ear, the crackling of uncountable regiments. Dead trees love the fire."

"The bluebird carries the sky on his back."

"The tanager flies through the green foliage as if it would ignite the leaves."

"If I wish for a horse-hair for my compass-sight I must go to the stable; but the hair-bird, with her sharp eyes, goes to the road."

"Immortal water, alive even to the superficies."

"Fire is the most tolerable third party."

"Nature made ferns for pure leaves, to show what she could do in that line."

"No tree has so fair a bole and so handsome an instep as the beech."

"How did these beautiful rainbow-tints get into the shell of the fresh-water clam, buried in the mud at the bottom of our dark river?"

"Hard are the times when the infant's shoes are second-foot."

"We are strictly confined to our men to whom we give liberty."

"Nothing is so much to be feared as fear. Atheism may comparatively be popular with God himself."

"Of what significance the things you can forget? A little thought is sexton to all the world."

"How can we expect a harvest of thought who have not had a seed-time of character?"

"Only he can be trusted with gifts who can present a face of bronze to expectations."

"I ask to be melted. You can only ask of the metals that they be tender to the fire that melts them. To nought else can they be tender."

There is a flower known to botanists, one of the same genus with our summer plant called "Life-Everlasting," a *Gnaphalium* like that, which grows on the most inaccessible cliffs of the Tyrolese mountains, where the chamois dare hardly venture, and which the hunter, tempted by its beauty, and by his love (for it is immensely valued by the Swiss maidens), climbs the cliffs to gather, and is sometimes found dead at the foot, with the flower in his hand. It is called by botanists the *Gnaphalium leontopodium,* but by the Swiss *Edelweisse,* which signifies *Noble Purity.* Thoreau seemed to me living in the hope to gather this plant, which belonged to him of right. The scale on which his studies proceeded was so large as to require longevity, and we were the less prepared for his sudden disappearance. The country knows not yet, or in the least part, how great a son it has lost. It seems an injury that he should leave in the midst his broken task which none else can finish, a kind of indignity to so noble a soul that he should depart out of Nature before yet he has been really shown to his peers for what he is. But he, at least, is content. His soul was made for the noblest society; he had in a short life exhausted the capabilities of this world; wherever there is knowledge, wherever there is virtue, wherever there is beauty, he will find a home.

Part Two

———◆———

SELECTED POEMS

Selected Poems

Ralph Waldo Emerson

Each and All
1834/1839[1]

Little thinks, in the field, yon red-cloaked clown[2]
Of thee from the hill-top looking down;
The heifer that lows in the upland farm,
Far-heard, lows not thine ear to charm;
5 The sexton, tolling his bell at noon,
Deems not that great Napoleon
Stops his horse, and lists with delight,
Whilst his files sweep round yon Alpine height;
Nor knowest thou what argument
10 Thy life to thy neighbor's creed has lent.
All are needed by each one;
Nothing is fair or good alone.
I thought the sparrow's note from heaven,
Singing at dawn on the alder bough;
15 I brought him home, in his nest, at even;
He sings the song, but it cheers not now,
For I did not bring home the river and sky; —
He sang to my ear — they sang to my eye.
The delicate shells lay on the shore;
20 The bubbles of the latest wave
Fresh pearls to their enamel gave,
And the bellowing of the savage sea
Greeted their safe escape to me.
I wiped away the weeds and foam,
25 I fetched my sea-born treasures home;
But the poor, unsightly, noisome things
Had left their beauty on the shore
With the sun and the sand and the wild uproar.
The lover watched his graceful maid,

The Complete Works of Ralph Waldo Emerson. Ed. Edward Waldo Emerson. Centenary Edition. Vol. 9. Boston: Houghton, 1903. (*The Complete Works* serves as the source for all poems reprinted here. All notes are by the present editor.)

[1] When two dates are given for a poem, the left-hand date indicates when the poem was composed, the right-hand date indicates when it was first published.

[2] An Italian peasant whom Emerson described in his journal during his travels in Italy and who gives charm to the landscape.

30 As 'mid the virgin train she strayed,
Nor knew her beauty's best attire
Was woven still by the snow-white choir.
At last she came to his hermitage,
Like the bird from the woodlands to the cage; —
35 The gay enchantment was undone,
A gentle wife, but fairy none.
Then I said, "I covet truth;
Beauty is unripe childhood's cheat;
I leave it behind with the games of youth:" —
40 As I spoke, beneath my feet
The ground-pine curled its pretty wreath,
Running over the club-moss burrs;
I inhaled the violet's breath;
Around me stood the oaks and firs;
45 Pine-cones and acorns lay on the ground;
Over me soared the eternal sky,
Full of light and of deity;
Again I saw, again I heard,
The rolling river, the morning bird; —
50 Beauty through my senses stole;
I yielded myself to the perfect whole.

Concord Hymn
Sung at the Completion
of the Battle Monument, July 4, 1837 [1]

By the rude bridge that arched the flood,
    Their flag to April's breeze unfurled,
Here once the embattled farmers stood
    And fired the shot heard round the world.

5 The foe long since in silence slept;
    Alike the conqueror silent sleeps;
And Time the ruined bridge has swept
    Down the dark stream which seaward creeps.

---

[1] Written for the dedication of the monument commemorating the Battle of Concord. The poem was sung by the townspeople of Concord at the dedication ceremony on 4 July 1837.

On this green bank, by this soft stream,
10   We set to-day a votive stone;
That memory may their deed redeem,
    When, like our sires, our sons are gone.

Spirit, that made those heroes dare
    To die, and leave their children free,
15   Bid Time and Nature gently spare
    The shaft we raise to them and thee.

Ode, Inscribed to W. H. Channing[1]
1846/1847

Though loath to grieve
The evil time's sole patriot,
I cannot leave
My honied thought
5   For the priest's cant,
Or statesman's rant.

If I refuse
My study for their politique,
Which at the best is trick,
10   The angry Muse
Puts confusion in my brain.

But who is he that prates
Of the culture of mankind,
Of better arts and life?
15   Go, blindworm, go,
Behold the famous States
Harrying Mexico
With rifle and with knife![2]

---

[1] William Henry Channing (1810–84), nephew of the Unitarian minister William Ellery Channing, was himself a Unitarian minister, Christian socialist, and abolitionist. He had urged Emerson to become an activist in the cause of abolition, and Emerson's poem is a response to this call.

[2] The Mexican-American War (1846–48) had just begun, and Emerson uses it to remind the reader (and subject of the ode) that antislavery states have little cause for moral self-righteousness, given their involvement in this unjust war.

Or who, with accent bolder,
20 Dare praise the freedom-loving mountaineer?
I found by thee, O rushing Contoocook!
And in thy valleys, Agiochook!
The jackals of the negro-holder.[3]

The God who made New Hampshire
25 Taunted the lofty land
With little men; —
Small bat and wren
House in the oak: —
If earth-fire cleave
30 The upheaved land, and bury the folk,
The southern crocodile would grieve.[4]
Virtue palters; Right is hence;
Freedom praised, but hid;
Funeral eloquence
35 Rattles the coffin-lid.

What boots thy zeal,
O glowing friend,
That would indignant rend
The northland from the south?
40 Wherefore? to what good end?
Boston Bay and Bunker Hill
Would serve things still; —
Things are of the snake.[5]

The horseman serves the horse,
45 The neatherd serves the neat,[6]
The merchant serves the purse,
The eater serves his meat;

---

[3] Opening this stanza with an allusion to the New Hampshire state motto "Live free or die!" and mentioning two New Hampshire rivers, Emerson implicates New Englanders in the sins of slavery, especially Daniel Webster, a native of New Hampshire, whose accommodation of slavery interests increasingly disillusioned Emerson. When Webster supported the Compromise of 1850 three years later, Emerson branded him the "Great Betrayer."

[4] The "southern crocodile" would grieve "crocodile tears."

[5] Emerson explains more clearly why New England is implicated in the sin of slavery: the ruling commercial interests of Boston are inseparable from the slave labor of the South and its cotton and from the slave labor of the Caribbean and its sugar.

[6] "Neatherd": cowherd. "Neat": cow.

'T is the day of the chattel,[7]
Web to weave, and corn to grind;
50 Things are in the saddle,
And ride mankind.

There are two laws discrete,
Not reconciled, —
Law for man, and law for thing;
55 The last builds town and fleet,
But it runs wild,
And doth the man unking.

'T is fit the forest fall,
The steep be graded,
60 The mountain tunnelled,
The sand shaded,
The orchard planted,
The glebe tilled,
The prairie granted,
65 The steamer built.

Let man serve law for man;
Live for friendship, live for love,
For truth's and harmony's behoof;
The state may follow how it can,
70 As Olympus follows Jove.

    Yet do not I implore
The wrinkled shopman to my sounding woods,
Nor bid the unwilling senator
Ask votes of thrushes in the solitudes.
75 Every one to his chosen work; —
Foolish hands may mix and mar;[8]
Wise and sure the issues are.
Round they roll till dark is light,
Sex to sex, and even to odd; —
80 The over-god
Who marries Right to Might,

---

[7] Emerson seems to be arguing that every person is a slave, a sentiment he invokes in several early essays, including *Nature* (reprinted in this volume).

[8] Emerson rationalizes his refusal to become an activist for abolition on the grounds that poets and philosophers should not do the work of others, such as statesmen and lawyers.

Who peoples, unpeoples, —
He who exterminates
Races by stronger races,
85 Black by white faces,—
Knows to bring honey
Out of the lion;
Grafts gentlest scion
On pirate and Turk.[9]

90 The Cossack eats Poland[10]
Like stolen fruit;
Her last noble is ruined,
Her last poet mute:
Straight, into double band
95 The victors divide;
Half for freedom strike and stand; —
The astonished Muse finds thousands at her side.

Waldeinsamkeit[1]
1857/1858

I do not count the hours I spend
In wandering by the sea;
The forest is my loyal friend,
Like God it useth me.

5 In plains that room for shadows make
Of skirting hills to lie,
Bound in by streams which give and take
Their colors from the sky;

Or on the mountain-crest sublime,
10 Or down the oaken glade,

---

[9] Emerson further rationalizes slavery by arguing that progress eventually will replace the rule of "Right to Might" with the nobler heirs of such pirates as steal human labor and lives.

[10] Russia took over most of Poland in 1796. The Polish insurrection of 1830 –31 was hailed as an emancipatory revolution by many around the world, but it was brutally suppressed by Russia.

[1] German: forest solitude.

O what have I to do with time?
For this the day was made.

Cities of mortals woe-begone
Fantastic care derides,
15 But in the serious landscape lone
Stern benefit abides.

Sheen will tarnish, honey cloy,
And merry is only a mask of sad,
But, sober on a fund of joy,
20 The woods at heart are glad.

There the great Planter plants
Of fruitful worlds the grain,
And with a million spells enchants
The souls that walk in pain.

25 Still on the seeds of all he made
The rose of beauty burns;
Through times that wear and forms that fade,
Immortal youth returns.

The black ducks mounting from the lake,
30 The pigeon in the pines,
The bittern's boom, a desert make[2]
Which no false art refines.

Down in yon watery nook,
Where bearded mists divide,
35 The gray old gods whom Chaos knew,
The sires of Nature, hide.

Aloft, in secret veins of air,
Blows the sweet breath of song,
O, few to scale those uplands dare,
40 Though they to all belong!

See thou bring not to field or stone
The fancies found in books;
Leave authors' eyes, and fetch your own,
To brave the landscape's looks.

---

[2] A bittern is a small heron.

45 Oblivion here thy wisdom is,
Thy thrift, the sleep of cares;
For a proud idleness like this
Crowns all thy mean affairs.

Boston Hymn
Read in Music Hall, January 1, 1863[1]

The word of the Lord by night
To the watching Pilgrims came,
As they sat by the seaside,
And filled their hearts with flame.

5 God said, I am tired of kings,
I suffer them no more;
Up to my ear the morning brings
The outrage of the poor.

Think ye I made this ball
10 A field of havoc and war,
Where tyrants great and tyrants small
Might harry the weak and poor?

My angel, — his name is Freedom, —
Choose him to be your king;
15 He shall cut pathways east and west
And fend you with his wing.

Lo! I uncover the land
Which I hid of old time in the West
As the sculptor uncovers the statue
20 When he has wrought his best;

I show Columbia, of the rocks
Which dip their foot in the seas
And soar to the air-borne flocks
Of clouds and the boreal fleece.

---

[1] Emerson read the poem at the Jubilee Concert in The Boston Music Hall to celebrate the Emancipation Proclamation. By all accounts, the celebration that evening was stirring, and Emerson was loudly cheered as he recited the poem.

25 I will divide my goods;
Call in the wretch and slave:
None shall rule but the humble,
And none but Toil shall have.

I will have never a noble,
30 No lineage counted great;
Fishers and choppers and ploughmen
Shall constitute a state.

Go, cut down trees in the forest
And trim the straightest boughs;
35 Cut down trees in the forest
And build me a wooden house.

Call the people together,
The young men and the sires,
The digger in the harvest-field,
40 Hireling and him that hires;

And here in a pine state-house
They shall choose men to rule
In every needful faculty,
In church and state and school.

45 Lo, now! if these poor men
Can govern the land and sea
And make just laws below the sun,
As planets faithful be.

And ye shall succor men;
50 'Tis nobleness to serve;
Help them who cannot help again;
Beware from right to swerve.

I break your bonds and masterships,
And I unchain the slave:
55 Free be his heart and hand henceforth
As wind and wandering wave.

I cause from every creature
His proper good to flow:
As much as he is and doeth,
60 So much he shall bestow.

292 // RALPH WALDO EMERSON

But, laying hands on another
To coin his labor and sweat,
He goes in pawn to his victim
For eternal years in debt.

65 To-day unbind the captive,
So only are ye unbound;
Lift up a people from the dust,
Trump of their rescue, sound!

Pay ransom to the owner
70 And fill the bag to the brim.
Who is the owner? The slave is owner,
And ever was. Pay him.[2]

O North! give him beauty for rags,
And honor, O South! for his shame;
75 Nevada! coin thy golden crags
With Freedom's image and name.

Up! and the dusky race
That sat in darkness long, —
Be swift their feet as antelopes,
80 And as behemoth strong.

Come, East and West and North,
By races, as snow-flakes,
And carry my purpose forth,
Which neither halts nor shakes.

85 My will fulfilled shall be,
For, in daylight or in dark,
My thunderbolt has eyes to see
His way home to the mark.

---

[2] Responding to arguments that slave-owners should be compensated for the "loss" of their slaves—a position Emerson himself had advocated in earlier writings—Emerson resoundingly makes the point that slaves deserve compensation for the labor and life stolen from them. The crowd rose to its feet as Emerson read this stanza.

Voluntaries[1]
1863

I

Low and mournful be the strain,
Haughty thought be far from me;
Tones of penitence and pain,
Moanings of the tropic sea;
5 Low and tender in the cell
Where a captive sits in chains,
Crooning ditties treasured well
From his Afric's torrid plains.
Sole estate his sire bequeathed, —
10 Hapless sire to hapless son, —
Was the wailing song he breathed,
And his chain when life was done.

    What his fault, or what his crime?
Or what ill planet crossed his prime?
15 Heart too soft and will too weak
To front the fate that crouches near, —
Dove beneath the vulture's beak; —
Will song dissuade the thirsty spear?
Dragged from his mother's arms and breast,
20 Displaced, disfurnished here,
His wistful toil to do his best
Chilled by a ribald jeer.
Great men in the Senate sate,
Sage and hero, side by side,
25 Building for their sons the State,
Which they shall rule with pride.
They forbore to break the chain
Which bound the dusky tribe,
Checked by the owners' fierce disdain,
30 Lured by "Union" as the bribe.

---

[1] Written in honor of Colonel Robert Gould Shaw and the Massachusetts 54th Regiment, the first Union regiment to enlist African Americans, many of them ex-slaves. Shaw and many of his men were killed in an assault on Fort Wagner, South Carolina on 18 July 1863.

Destiny sat by, and said,
"Pang for pang your seed shall pay,
Hide in false peace your coward head,
I bring round the harvest day."

II

35 Freedom all winged expands,
Nor perches in a narrow place;
Her broad van seeks unplanted lands;
She loves a poor and virtuous race.
Clinging to a colder zone
40 Whose dark sky sheds the snowflake down,
The snowflake is her banner's star,
Her stripes the boreal streamers are.
Long she loved the Northman well;[2]
Now the iron age is done,
45 She will not refuse to dwell
With the offspring of the Sun;
Foundling of the desert far,
Where palms plume, siroccos blaze,
He roves unhurt the burning ways
50 In climates of the summer star.
He has avenues to God
Hid from men of Northern brain,
Far beholding, without cloud,
What these with slowest steps attain.
55 If once the generous chief arrive
To lead him willing to be led,
For freedom he will strike and strive,
And drain his heart till he be dead.

III

In an age of fops and toys,
60 Wanting wisdom, void of right,
Who shall nerve heroic boys
To hazard all in Freedom's fight, —
Break sharply off their jolly games,
Forsake their comrades gay

---

[2]Emerson seems to repudiate his earlier Anglo-Saxonism.

65 And quit proud homes and youthful dames
For famine, toil and fray?
Yet on the nimble air benign
Speed nimbler messages,
That waft the breath of grace divine
70 To hearts in sloth and ease.
So nigh is grandeur to our dust,
So near is God to man,
When Duty whispers low, *Thou must*,
The youth replies, *I can.*

IV

75 O, well for the fortunate soul
Which Music's wings infold,
Stealing away the memory
Of sorrows new and old!
Yet happier he whose inward sight,
80 Stayed on his subtile thought,
Shuts his sense on toys of time,
To vacant bosoms brought.
But best befriended of the God
He who, in evil times,
85 Warned by an inward voice,
Heeds not the darkness and the dread,
Biding by his rule and choice,
Feeling only the fiery thread
Leading over heroic ground,
90 Walled with mortal terror round,
To the aim which him allures,
And the sweet heaven his deed secures.
Peril around, all else appalling,
Cannon in front and leaden rain
95 Him duty through the clarion calling
To the van called not in vain.

Stainless soldier on the walls,
Knowing this,—and knows no more,—
Whoever fights, whoever falls,
100 Justice conquers evermore,
Justice after as before,—
And he who battles on her side,
God, though he were ten times slain,

Crowns him victor glorified,
105 Victor over death and pain.

V

Blooms the laurel which belongs
To the valiant chief who fights;
I see the wreath, I hear the songs
Lauding the Eternal Rights,
110 Victors over daily wrongs:
Awful victors, they misguide
Whom they will destroy,
And their coming triumph hide
In our downfall, or our joy:
115 They reach no term, they never sleep,
In equal strength through space abide;
Though, feigning dwarfs, they crouch and creep,
The strong they slay, the swift outstride:
Fate's grass grows rank in valley clods,
120 And rankly on the castled steep, —
Speak it firmly, these are gods,
All are ghosts beside.

Part Three

—⟨●⟩—

WOMAN IN THE NINETEENTH CENTURY AND SELECTED *DISPATCHES FROM EUROPE, 1846–1850*

Woman in the Nineteenth Century (1845)

Margaret Fuller

Woman in the Nineteenth Century [1]

"Frei durch Vernunft, stark durch Gesetze,
Durch Sanftmuth gross, und reich durch Schätze,
Die lange Zeit dein Busen dir verschwieg." [2]

"I meant the day-star should not brighter rise,
Nor lend like influence from its lucent seat;
I meant she should be courteous, facile, sweet,
Free from that solemn vice of greatness, pride;
I meant each softest virtue there should meet,
Fit in that softer bosom to reside;
Only a (heavenward and instructed) soul
I purposed her, that should, with even powers,
The rock, the spindle, and the shears control
Of destiny, and spin her own free hours." [3]

Preface

The following essay is a reproduction, modified and expanded, of an article published in "The Dial, Boston, July, 1843," under the title of "The Great Lawsuit. Man versus Men: Woman versus Women."

This article excited a good deal of sympathy, and still more interest. It is in compliance with wishes expressed from many quarters, that it is prepared for publication in its present form.

Objections having been made to the former title, as not sufficiently easy to be understood, the present has been substituted as expressive of the main purpose of the essay; though, by myself, the other is preferred, partly for the reason others do not like it, *i.e.*, that it requires some thought to see what it means, and might thus prepare the reader to meet me on my own

---

Woman in the Nineteenth Century. New York: Greeley & McElrath, 1845.

[1] The following text is based on the first edition with obvious printer's errors corrected. [Ed.]

[2] German from an unknown source: "Free through Reason, strong through Law, / Through gentleness great, and rich through wealth, / For a long time your heart kept you secret." [Ed.]

[3] Ben Jonson (1572–1637), "On Lucy, Countess of Bedford." [Ed.]

ground. Beside, it offers a larger scope, and is, in that way, more just to my desire. I meant, by that title, to intimate the fact that, while it is the destiny of Man, in the course of the Ages, to ascertain and fulfil the law of his being, so that his life shall be seen, as a whole, to be that of an angel or messenger, the action of prejudices and passions, which attend, in the day, the growth of the individual, is continually obstructing the holy work that is to make the earth a part of heaven. By Man I mean both man and woman: these are the two halves of one thought. I lay no especial stress on the welfare of either. I believe that the development of the one cannot be effected without that of the other. My highest wish is that this truth should be distinctly and rationally apprehended, and the conditions of life and freedom recognized as the same for the daughters and the sons of time; twin exponents of a divine thought.

I solicit a sincere and patient attention from those who open the following pages at all. I solicit of women that they will lay it to heart to ascertain what is for them the liberty of law. It is for this, and not for any, the largest, extension of partial privileges that I seek. I ask them, if interested by these suggestions, to search their own experience and intuitions for better, and fill up with fit materials the trenches that hedge them in. From men I ask a noble and earnest attention to any thing that can be offered on this great and still obscure subject, such as I have met from many with whom I stand in private relations.

And may truth, unpolluted by prejudice, vanity, or selfishness, be granted daily more and more, as the due inheritance, and only valuable conquest for us all!

November, 1844

WOMAN IN THE NINETEENTH CENTURY

"Frailty, thy name is WOMAN."[4]
"The Earth waits for her Queen."

The connection between these quotations may not be obvious, but it is strict. Yet would any contradict us, if we made them applicable to the other side, and began also

Frailty, thy name is MAN.
The Earth waits for its King.

---

[4] Shakespeare, *Hamlet* 1.2.146. [Ed.]

Yet man, if not yet fully installed in his powers, has given much earnest of his claims. Frail he is indeed, how frail! how impure! Yet often has the vein of gold displayed itself amid the baser ores, and Man has appeared before us in princely promise worthy of his future.

If, oftentimes, we see the prodigal son feeding on the husks in the fair field no more his own, anon, we raise the eyelids, heavy from bitter tears, to behold in him the radiant apparition of genius and love, demanding not less than the all of goodness, power and beauty.[5] We see that in him the largest claim finds a due foundation. That claim is for no partial sway, no exclusive possession. He cannot be satisfied with any one gift of life, any one department of knowledge or telescopic peep at the heavens. He feels himself called to understand and aid nature, that she may, through his intelligence, be raised and interpreted; to be a student of, and servant to, the universe-spirit; and king of his planet, that as an angelic minister, he may bring it into conscious harmony with the law of that spirit.

In clear triumphant moments, many times, has rung through the spheres the prophecy of his jubilee, and those moments, though past in time, have been translated into eternity by thought; the bright signs they left hang in the heavens, as single stars or constellations, and, already, a thickly sown radiance consoles the wanderer in the darkest night. Other heroes since Hercules have fulfilled the zodiac of beneficent labors, and then given up their mortal part to the fire without a murmur; while no God dared deny that they should have their reward.

> Siquis tamen, Hercule, siquis
> Forte Deo doliturus erit, data præmia nollet,
> Sed meruise dari sciet, invitus que probabit,
> Assensere Dei.[6]

Sages and lawgivers have bent their whole nature to the search for truth, and thought themselves happy if they could buy, with the sacrifice of all temporal ease and pleasure, one seed for the future Eden. Poets and priests have strung the lyre with the heart-strings, poured out their best blood upon the altar, which, reared anew from age to age shall at last sustain the flame pure enough to rise to highest heaven. Shall we not name with as

---

[5] Cf. Luke 15.11–32. [Ed.]

[6] Ovid, *Metamorphoses,* bk. 9, in which Jove makes the following statement after Hercules has been killed: "If any God dissent, and judge too great / The sacred honors of the heavenly seat, / Even he shall own his deeds deserve the sky, / Even he, reluctant, shall at length comply." Fuller provided this translation from John Gay (1685–1732) in "The Great Lawsuit" (Reynolds, *Woman* 8). [Ed.]

deep a benediction those who, if not so immediately, or so consciously, in connection with the eternal truth, yet, led and fashioned by a divine instinct, serve no less to develope and interpret the open secret of love passing into life, energy creating for the purpose of happiness; the artist whose hand, drawn by a pre-existent harmony to a certain medium, moulds it to forms of life more highly and completely organized than are seen elsewhere, and, by carrying out the intention of nature, reveals her meaning to those who are not yet wise enough to divine it; the philosopher who listens steadily for laws and causes, and from those obvious, infers those yet unknown; the historian who, in faith that all events must have their reason and their aim, records them, and thus fills archives from which the youth of prophets may be fed. The man of science dissects the statements, tests the facts, and demonstrates order, even where he cannot its purpose.

Lives, too, which bear none of these names, have yielded tones of no less significance. The candle-stick set in a low place has given light as faithfully, where it was needed, as that upon the hill.[7] In close alleys, in dismal nooks, the Word has been read as distinctly, as when shown by angels to holy men in the dark prison. Those who till a spot of earth scarcely larger than is wanted for a grave, have deserved that the sun should shine upon its sod till violets answer.

So great has been, from time to time, the promise, that, in all ages, men have said the gods themselves came down to dwell with them; that the All-Creating wandered on the earth to taste, in a limited nature, the sweetness of virtue; that the All-Sustaining incarnated himself to guard, in space and time, the destinies of this world; that heavenly genius dwelt among the shepherds, to sing to them and teach them how to sing. Indeed

"Der stets den Hirten gnadig sich bewies."

"He has constantly shown himself favorable to shepherds."

And the dwellers in green pastures and natural students of the stars were selected to hail, first among men, the holy child, whose life and death were to present the type of excellence, which has sustained the heart of so large a portion of mankind in these later generations.

Such marks have been made by the footsteps of *man,* (still alas! to be spoken of as the *ideal* man,) wherever he has passed through the wilderness of *men,* and whenever the pigmies stepped in one of those they felt dilate within the breast somewhat that promised nobler stature and purer blood.

---

[7] Cf. Matt. 5.14–15, the source of the old saying "Don't hide your light under a bushel." The "city on a hill" is a metaphor for heaven, the earthly Jerusalem, and—for the Puritans—the founding of the Massachusetts Bay Colony. [Ed.]

They were impelled to forsake their evil ways of decrepit scepticism, and covetousness of corruptible possessions. Conviction flowed in upon them. They, too, raised the cry; God is living, now, to-day; and all beings are brothers, for they are his children. Simple words enough, yet which only angelic nature, can use or hear in their full free sense.

These were the triumphant moments, but soon the lower nature took its turn, and the era of a truly human life was postponed.

Thus is man still a stranger to his inheritance, still a pleader, still a pilgrim. Yet his happiness is secure in the end. And now, no more a glimmering consciousness, but assurance begins to be felt and spoken, that the highest ideal man can form of his own powers, is that which he is destined to attain. Whatever the soul knows how to seek, it cannot fail to obtain. This is the law and the prophets.[8] Knock and it shall be opened, seek and ye shall find.[9] It is demonstrated; it is a maxim. Man no longer paints his proper nature in some form and says, "Prometheus had it; it is God-like;" but "Man must have it; it is human." However disputed by many, however ignorantly used, or falsified by those who do receive it, the fact of an universal, unceasing revelation has been too clearly stated in words to be lost sight of in thought, and sermons preached from the text, "Be ye perfect," are the only sermons of a pervasive and deep-searching influence.[10]

But, among those who meditate upon this text, there is a great difference of view, as to the way in which perfection shall be sought.

Through the intellect, say some. Gather from every growth of life its seed of thought; look behind every symbol for its law; if thou canst *see* clearly, the rest will follow.

Through the life, say others. Do the best thou knowest to-day. Shrink not from frequent error in this gradual fragmentary state. Follow thy light for as much as it will show thee, be faithful as far as thou canst, in hope that faith presently will lead to sight. Help others, without blaming their need of thy help. Love much and be forgiven.

It needs not intellect, needs not experience, says a third. If you took the true way, your destiny would be accomplished in a purer and more natural order. You would not learn through facts of thought or action, but express through them the certainties of wisdom. In quietness yield thy soul to the causal soul. Do not disturb thy apprenticeship by premature effort; neither check the tide of instruction by methods of thy own. Be still, seek not, but wait in obedience. Thy commission will be given.

---

[8] Cf. Matt. 7.12. [Ed.]

[9] Cf. Matt. 7.8. [Ed.]

[10] Cf. Matt. 5.48. [Ed.]

Could we indeed say what we want, could we give a description of the child that is lost, he would be found. As soon as the soul can affirm clearly that a certain demonstration is wanted, it is at hand. When the Jewish prophet described the Lamb,[11] as the expression of what was required by the coming era, the time drew nigh. But we say not, see not as yet, clearly, what we would. Those who call for a more triumphant expression of love, a love that cannot be crucified, show not a perfect sense of what has already been given. Love has already been expressed, that made all things new, that gave the worm its place and ministry as well as the eagle; a love to which it was alike to descend into the depths of hell, or to sit at the right hand of the Father.

Yet, no doubt, a new manifestation is at hand, a new hour in the day of man. We cannot expect to see any one sample of completed being, when the mass of men still lie engaged in the sod, or use the freedom of their limbs only with wolfish energy. The tree cannot come to flower till its root be free from the cankering worm, and its whole growth open to air and light. While any one is base, none can be entirely free and noble. Yet something new shall presently be shown of the life of man, for hearts crave, if minds do not know how to ask it.

Among the strains of prophecy, the following, by an earnest mind of a foreign land, written some thirty years ago, is not yet outgrown; and it has the merit of being a positive appeal from the heart, instead of a critical declaration what man should *not* do.

"The ministry of man implies, that he must be filled from the divine fountains which are being engendered through all eternity, so that, at the mere name of his master, he may be able to cast all his enemies into the abyss; that he may deliver all parts of nature from the barriers that imprison them; that he may purge the terrestrial atmosphere from the poisons that infect it; that he may preserve the bodies of men from the corrupt influences that surround, and the maladies that afflict them; still more, that he may keep their souls pure from the malignant insinuations which pollute, and the gloomy images that obscure them; that he may restore its serenity to the Word, which false words of men fill with mourning and sadness; that he may satisfy the desires of the angels, who await from him the development of the marvels of nature; that, in fine, his world may be filled with God, as eternity is."[12]

---

[11] An incarnation of Jesus. Cf. Isa. 7.14 (Reynolds, *Woman* 10). [Ed.]

[12] Louis Claude de Saint-Martin (1743–1803), *The Ministry of Man and Spirit* (1802) (Reynolds, *Woman* 11). [Ed.]

Another attempt we will give, by an obscure observer of our own day and country, to draw some lines of the desired image. It was suggested by seeing the design of Crawford's Orpheus,[13] and connecting with the circumstance of the American, in his garret at Rome, making choice of this subject, that of Americans here at home, showing such ambition to represent the character, by calling their prose and verse "Orphic sayings" — "Orphics."[14] We wish we could add that they have shown that musical apprehension of the progress of nature through her ascending gradations which entitled them so to do, but their attempts are frigid, though sometimes grand; in their strain we are not warmed by the fire which fertilized the soil of Greece.

Orpheus was a law-giver by theocratic commission. He understood nature, and made her forms move to his music. He told her secrets in the form of hymns, nature as seen in the mind of God. His soul went forth toward all beings, yet could remain sternly faithful to a chosen type of excellence. Seeking what he loved, he feared not death nor hell, neither could any shape of dread daunt his faith in the power of the celestial harmony that filled his soul.

It seemed significant of the state of things in this country, that the sculptor should have represented the seer at the moment when he was obliged with his hand to shade his eyes.

> Each Orpheus must to the depths descend,
> For only thus the Poet can be wise,
>   Must make the sad Persephone his friend,
> And buried love to second life arise;
>   Again his love must lose through too much love,
> Must lose his life by living life too true,
>   For what he sought below is passed above,
> Already done is all that he would do;
>   Must tune all being with his single lyre,
> Must melt all rocks free from their primal pain,
>   Must search all nature with his one soul's fire,
> Must bind anew all forms in heavenly chain.

---

[13] Thomas Crawford's (1814–57) neoclassical sculpture *Orpheus and Cerebus* shows the mythic Orpheus hunting with Cerebus, dog of the Underworld, for the lost Eurydice. Crawford was one of the American expatriate sculptors and artists in Rome. Several important American women artists, such as Harriet Hosmer (1830–1908) and Maria Louisa Lander (1826–1923), worked in Crawford's studio. [Ed.]

[14] Amos Bronson Alcott's (1799–1888) "Orphic Sayings" were published in *The Dial* while Fuller was editor. (Reynolds, *Woman* 11). [Ed.]

If he already sees what he must do,
Well may he shade his eyes from the far-shining view.[15]

A better comment could not be made on what is required to perfect man, and place him in that superior position for which he was designed, than by the interpretation of Bacon upon the legends of the Syren coast. When the wise Ulysses passed, says he, he caused his mariners to stop their ears with wax, knowing there was in them no power to resist the lure of that voluptuous song. But he, the much experienced man, who wished to be experienced in all, and use all to the service of wisdom, desired to hear the song that he might understand its meaning. Yet, distrusting his own power to be firm in his better purpose, he caused himself to be bound to the mast, that he might be kept secure against his own weakness.[16] But Orpheus passed unfettered, so absorbed in singing hymns to the gods that he could not even hear those sounds of degrading enchantment.

Meanwhile not a few believe, and men themselves have expressed the opinion, that the time is come when Eurydice is to call for an Orpheus, rather than Orpheus for Eurydice: that the idea of Man, however imperfectly brought out, has been far more so than that of Woman, that she, the other half of the same thought, the other chamber of the heart of life, needs now to take her turn in the full pulsation, and that improvement in the daughters will best aid in the reformation of the sons of this age.

It should be remarked that, as the principle of liberty is better understood, and more nobly interpreted, a broader protest is made in behalf of Woman. As men become aware that few men have had a fair chance, they are inclined to say that no women have had a fair chance. The French Revolution, that strangely disguised angel, bore witness in favor of woman, but interpreted her claims no less ignorantly than those of man. Its idea of happiness did not rise beyond outward enjoyment, unobstructed by the tyranny of others. The title it gave was citoyen, citoyenne, and it is not unimportant to woman that even this species of equality was awarded her. Before, she could be condemned to perish on the scaffold for treason, not as a citizen, but as a subject. The right with which this title then invested a human being, was that of bloodshed and license. The Goddess of Liberty was impure. As we read the poem addressed to her not long since, by Beranger, we can scarcely refrain from tears as painful as the tears of blood

---

[15] Indented quotations not enclosed in quotation marks are Fuller's own works. [Ed.]

[16] Fuller cites Francis Bacon (1561–1626) to support a conventional interpretation of Ulysses' episode with the Sirens in Homer's *Odyssey*. She uses citation as Emerson does, to bolster the authority of her text by displaying her learning. [Ed.]

that flowed when "such crimes were committed in her name." [17] Yes! man, born to purify and animate the unintelligent and the cold, can, in his madness, degrade and pollute no less the fair and the chaste. Yet truth was prophesied in the ravings of that hideous fever, caused by long ignorance and abuse. Europe is conning a valued lesson from the blood-stained page. The same tendencies, farther unfolded, will bear good fruit in this country.

Yet, by men in this country, as by the Jews, when Moses was leading them to the promised land, every thing has been done that inherited depravity could do, to hinder the promise of heaven from its fulfilment. The cross here as elsewhere, has been planted only to be blasphemed by cruelty and fraud. The name of the Prince of Peace has been profaned by all kinds of injustice toward the Gentile whom he said he came to save. But I need not speak of what has been done towards the red man, the black man. Those deeds are the scoff of the world; and they have been accompanied by such pious words that the gentlest would not dare to intercede with "Father, forgive them, for they know not what they do." [18]

Here, as elsewhere, the gain of creation consists always in the growth of individual minds, which live and aspire, as flowers bloom and birds sing, in the midst of morasses; and in the continual development of that thought, the thought of human destiny, which is given to eternity adequately to express, and which ages of failure only seemingly impede. Only seemingly, and whatever seems to the contrary, this country is as surely destined to elucidate a great moral law, as Europe was to promote the mental culture of man.

Though the national independence be blurred by the servility of individuals, though freedom and equality have been proclaimed only to leave room for a monstrous display of slave-dealing and slave-keeping; though the free American so often feels himself free, like the Roman, only to pamper his appetites and his indolence through the misery of his fellow beings,

---

[17] For Fuller, like most romantics, the American and French Revolutions ushered in a new, modern age. The French Revolution included the elevation of women from "subjects" (of the monarch but also of men) to "citizens" (*citoyennes*, a title conferred on women during the Revolution). But the French Revolution also resulted in the Reign of Terror, which remained for many romantics a warning of the excesses of revolutionary zeal and threats of mob rule (in fact, the Terror had less to do with rule by the masses than by a powerful oligarchy). Fuller here alludes to the last words of the French revolutionary leader Madame Roland (1754–93) on the guillotine and to Pierre-Jean de Béranger's (1780–1857) poem about Madame Roland. [Ed.]

[18] Cf. Luke 23.34. Fuller identifies Native American and African American victims of missionaries and Euroamerican expansion with Moses and the Jews, cast out of the Promised Land, and suggests that the American Revolution also had its "Reign of Terror" and failed in its promise of liberty and justice for all. [Ed.]

still it is not in vain, that the verbal statement has been made, "All men are born free and equal." There it stands, a golden certainty wherewith to encourage the good, to shame the bad. The new world may be called clearly to perceive that it incurs the utmost penalty, if it reject or oppress the sorrowful brother. And, if men are deaf, the angels hear. But men cannot be deaf. It is inevitable that an external freedom, an independence of the encroachments of other men, such as has been achieved for the nation, should be so also for every member of it. That which has once been clearly conceived in the intelligence cannot fail sooner or later to be acted out. It has become a law as irrevocable as that of the Medes in their ancient dominion; men will privately sin against it, but the law, as expressed by a leading mind of the age,

> "Tutti fatti a sembianza d'un Solo,
> Figli tutti d'un solo riscatto,
> In qual'ora, in qual parte del suolo
> Trascorriamo quest' aura vital,
> Siam fratelli, siam stretti ad un patto:
> Maladetto colui che lo infrange,
> Che s'innalza sul fiacco che piange
> Che contrista uno spirto immortal."

> "All made in the likeness of the One,
> All children of one ransom,
> In whatever hour, in whatever part of the soil,
> We draw this vital air,
> We are brothers; we must be bound by one compact,
> Accursed he who infringes it,
> Who raises himself upon the weak who weep,
> Who saddens an immortal spirit." [19]

This law cannot fail of universal recognition. Accursed be he who willingly saddens an immortal spirit, doomed to infamy in later, wiser ages, doomed in future stages of his own being to deadly penance, only short of death. Accursed be he who sins in ignorance, if that ignorance be caused by sloth.

We sicken no less at the pomp than the strife of words. We feel that never were lungs so puffed with the wind of declamation, on moral and religious subjects, as now. We are tempted to implore these "word-heroes," these

---

[19] Fuller's translation of the preceding lines by the Italian poet Alessandro Manzoni (1785–1873). [Ed.]

word-Catos, word-Christs, to beware of cant [20] above all things; to remember that hypocrisy is the most hopeless as well as the meanest of crimes, and that those must surely be polluted by it, who do not reserve a part of their morality and religion for private use. Landor [21] says that he cannot have a great deal of mind who cannot afford to let the larger part of it lie fallow and what is true of genius is not less so of virtue. The tongue is a valuable member, but should appropriate but a small part of the vital juices that are needful all over the body. We feel that the mind may "grow black and rancid in the smoke" even "of altars." We start up from the harangue to go into our closet and shut the door. There inquires the spirit, "Is this rhetoric the bloom of healthy blood or a false pigment artfully laid on?" And yet again we know where is so much smoke, must be some fire; with so much talk about virtue and freedom, must be mingled some desire for them; that it cannot be in vain that such have become the common topics of conversation among men, rather than schemes for tyranny and plunder, that the very newspapers see it best to proclaim themselves Pilgrims, Puritans, Heralds of Holiness. The king that maintains so costly a retinue cannot be a mere boast, or Carabbas fiction. [22] We have waited here long in the dust; we are tired and hungry, but the triumphal procession must appear at last.

Of all its banners, none has been more steadily upheld, and under none have more valor and willingness for real sacrifices been shown, than that of the champions of the enslaved African. And this band it is, which, partly from a natural following out of principles, partly because many women have been prominent in that cause, makes, just now, the warmest appeal in behalf of woman.

Though there has been a growing liberality on this subject, yet society at large is not so prepared for the demands of this party, but that they are and will be for some time, coldly regarded as the Jacobins of their day. [23]

"Is it not enough," cries the irritated trader, "that you have done all you could to break up the national union, and thus destroy the prosperity of our country, but now you must be trying to break up family union, to take

---

[20] Dr. Johnson's one piece of advice should be written on every door; "Clear your mind of cant." But Byron, to whom it was so acceptable, in clearing away the noxious vine, shook down the building. Sterling's emendation is worthy of honor: "Realize your cant, not cast it off." [Fuller's note.]

[21] Walter Savage Landor (1775–1864), English poet (Reynolds, *Woman* 15). [Ed.]

[22] Marquess of Carabas is the title the cat invents for his master in Charles Perrault's (1628–1703) fairy tale "Puss in Boots" (Reynolds, *Woman* 15). [Ed.]

[23] Women's rights activists and abolitionists generally shared common goals in antebellum America and often were viewed as "Jacobins" or political radicals. [Ed.]

my wife away from the cradle and the kitchen hearth to vote at polls, and preach from a pulpit? Of course, if she does such things, she cannot attend to those of her own sphere. She is happy enough as she is. She has more leisure than I have, every means of improvement, every indulgence."

"Have you asked her whether she was satisfied with these *indulgences?*"

"No, but I know she is. She is too amiable to wish what would make me unhappy, and too judicious to wish to step beyond the sphere of her sex. I will never consent to have our peace disturbed by any such discussions."

"'Consent—you?' it is not consent from you that is in question, it is assent from your wife."

"Am not I the head of my house?"

"You are not the head of your wife. God has given her a mind of her own."

"I am the head and she the heart."

"God grant you play true to one another then. I suppose I am to be grateful that you did not say she was only the hand. If the head represses no natural pulse of the heart, there can be no question as to your giving your consent. Both will be of one accord, and there needs but to present any question to get a full and true answer. There is no need of precaution, of indulgence, or consent. But our doubt is whether the heart does consent with the head, or only obeys its decrees with a passiveness that precludes the exercise of its natural powers, or a repugnance that turns sweet qualities to bitter, or a doubt that lays waste the fair occasions of life. It is to ascertain the truth, that we propose some liberating measures."

Thus vaguely are these questions proposed and discussed at present. But their being proposed at all implies much thought and suggests more. Many women are considering within themselves, what they need that they have not, and what they can have, if they find they need it. Many men are considering whether women are capable of being and having more than they are and have, *and*, whether, if so, it will be best to consent to improvement in their condition.

This morning, I open the Boston "Daily Mail," and find in its "poet's corner," a translation of Schiller's "Dignity of Woman." [24] In the advertisement of a book on America, I see in the table of contents this sequence, "Republican Institutions. American Slavery. American Ladies."

I open the "*Deutsche Schnellpost,*" published in New-York, and find at the head of a column, *Juden-und Frauen-emancipation in Ungarn,* Emancipation of Jews and Women in Hungary. [25]

---

[24] Friedrich Schiller's (1759–1805) poem. [Ed.]

[25] Emancipatory movements throughout Europe, leading up to the revolutionary events

The past year has seen action in the Rhode-Island legislature, to secure married women rights over their own property, where men showed that a very little examination of the subject could teach them much; an article in the Democratic Review[26] on the same subject more largely considered, written by a woman impelled, it is said, by glaring wrong to a distinguished friend having shown the defects in the existing laws, and the state of opinion from which they spring; and an answer from the revered old man, J. Q. Adams, in some respects the Phocion of his time, to an address made him by some ladies.[27] To this last I shall again advert in another place.

These symptoms of the times have come under my view quite accidentally: one who seeks, may, each month or week, collect more.

The numerous party, whose opinions are already labelled and adjusted too much to their mind to admit of any new light, strive, by lectures on some model-woman of bride-like beauty and gentleness, by writing and lending little treatises, intended to mark out with precision the limits of woman's sphere, and woman's mission, to prevent other than the rightful shepherd from climbing the wall, or the flock from using any chance to go astray.

Without enrolling ourselves at once on either side, let us look upon the subject from the best point of view which to-day offers. No better, it is to be feared, than a high house-top. A high hill-top, or at least a cathedral spire, would be desirable.

It may well be an Anti-Slavery party that pleads for woman, if we consider merely that she does not hold property on equal terms with men; so that, if a husband dies without making a will, the wife, instead of taking at once his place as head of the family, inherits only a part of his fortune, often brought him by herself, as if she were a child, or ward only, not an equal partner.

We will not speak of the innumerable instances in which profligate and idle men live upon the earnings of industrious wives; or if the wives leave them, and take with them the children, to perform the double duty of mother and father, follow from place to place, and threaten to rob them of the children, if deprived of the rights of a husband, as they call them, planting themselves in their poor lodgings, frightening them into paying tribute

---

of 1848, were often cited by American political rights' activists as precedents for abolition and women's rights in the United States. [Ed.]

[26] "The Legal Wrongs of Women," *United States Magazine and Democratic Review* 14 (May 1844): 477–83 (Reynolds, *Woman* 16). [Ed.]

[27] Phocion (c. 402–318 BCE) was an honorable Athenian statesman. John Quincy Adams (1767–1848) was sixth president of the United States. Fuller quotes and discusses his address on pp. 386–389. [Ed.]

by taking from them the children, running into debt at the expense of these otherwise so overtasked helots.[28] Such instances count up by scores within my own memory. I have seen the husband who had stained himself by a long course of low vice, till his wife was wearied from her heroic forgiveness, by finding that his treachery made it useless, and that if she would provide bread for herself and her children, she must be separate from his ill fame. I have known this man come to instal himself in the chamber of a woman who loathed him and say she should never take food without his company. I have known these men steal their children whom they knew they had no means to maintain, take them into dissolute company, expose them to bodily danger, to frighten the poor woman, to whom, it seems, the fact that she alone had borne the pangs of their birth, and nourished their infancy, does not give an equal right to them. I do believe that this mode of kidnapping, and it is frequent enough in all classes of society, will be by the next age viewed as it is by Heaven now, and that the man who avails himself of the shelter of men's laws to steal from a mother her own children, or arrogate any superior right in them, save that of superior virtue, will bear the stigma he deserves, in common with him who steals grown men from their mother land, their hopes, and their homes.

I said, we will not speak of this now, yet I have spoken, for the subject makes me feel too much. I could give instances that would startle the most vulgar and callous, but I will not, for the public opinion of their own sex is already against such men, and where cases of extreme tyranny are made known, there is private action in the wife's favor. But she ought not to need this, nor, I think, can she long. Men must soon see that, on their own ground, that woman is the weaker party, she ought to have legal protection, which would make such oppression impossible. But I would not deal with "atrocious instances" except in the way of illustration, neither demand from men a partial redress in some one matter, but go to the root of the whole. If principles could be established, particulars would adjust themselves aright. Ascertain the true destiny of woman, give her legitimate hopes, and a standard within herself; marriage and all other relations would by degrees be harmonized with these.

But to return to the historical progress of this matter. Knowing that there exists in the minds of men a tone of feeling towards women as towards slaves, such as is expressed in the common phrase, "Tell that to women and

---

[28] Many nineteenth-century American women left their abusive or alcoholic husbands, and many of these husbands pursued their wives and tried to steal back their children. Nineteenth-century temperance advocates were motivated in part by the widespread damage to the family caused by the abuse of alcohol. [Ed.]

children," that the infinite soul can only work through them in already ascertained limits,[29] that the gift of reason, man's highest prerogative, is allotted to them in much lower degree; that they must be kept from mischief and melancholy by being constantly engaged in active labor, which is to be furnished and directed by those better able to think, &c. &c.; we need not multiply instances, for who can review the experience of last week without recalling words which imply, whether in jest or earnest, these views or views like these; knowing this, can we wonder that many reformers think that measures are not likely to be taken in behalf of women, unless their wishes could be publicly represented by women?

That can never be necessary, cry the other side. All men are privately influenced by women; each has his wife, sister, or female friends, and is too much biased by these relations to fail of representing their interests, and, if this is not enough, let them propose and enforce their wishes with the pen. The beauty of home would be destroyed, the delicacy of the sex be violated, the dignity of halls of legislation degraded by an attempt to introduce them there. Such duties are inconsistent with those of a mother; and then we have ludicrous pictures of ladies in hysterics at the polls, and senate chambers filled with cradles.

But if, in reply, we admit as truth that woman seems destined by nature rather for the inner circle, we must add that the arrangements of civilized life have not been, as yet, such as to secure it to her. Her circle, if the duller, is not the quieter. If kept from "excitement," she is not from drudgery. Not only the Indian squaw carries the burdens of the camp, but the favorites of Louis the Fourteenth accompany him in his journeys, and the washerwoman stands at her tub and carries home her work at all seasons, and in all states of health. Those who think the physical circumstances of woman would make a part in the affairs of national government unsuitable, are by no means those who think it impossible for the negresses to endure field work, even during pregnancy, or the sempstresses to go through their killing labors.

As to the use of the pen, there was quite as much opposition to woman's possessing herself of that help to free agency, as there is now to her seizing on the rostrum or the desk; and she is likely to draw, from a permission to plead her cause that way, opposite inferences to what might be wished by those who now grant it.

---

[29] Fuller here follows Mary Wollstonecraft (1759–97), who argued in *Vindication of the Rights of Woman* (1792) that woman's reason could be as well developed by education as man's, and extends the argument to include the rights of children to education. [Ed.]

As to the possibility of her filling with grace and dignity, any such position, we should think those who had seen the great actresses, and heard the Quaker preachers of modern times, would not doubt, that woman can express publicly the fulness of thought and creation, without losing any of the peculiar beauty of her sex. What can pollute and tarnish is to act thus from any motive except that something needs to be said or done. Women could take part in the processions, the songs, the dances of old religion; no one fancied their delicacy was impaired by appearing in public for such a cause.

As to her home, she is not likely to leave it more than she now does for balls, theatres, meetings for promoting missions, revival meetings, and others to which she flies, in hope of an animation for her existence, commensurate with what she sees enjoyed by men. Governors of ladies' fairs are no less engrossed by such a change, than the Governor of the state by his; presidents of Washingtonian societies no less away from home than presidents of conventions. If men look straitly to it, they will find that, unless their lives are domestic, those of the women will not be. A house is no home unless it contain food and fire for the mind as well as for the body. The female Greek, of our day, is as much in the street as the male to cry, What news? We doubt not it was the same in Athens of old. The women, shut out from the market place, made up for it at the religious festivals. For human beings are not so constituted that they can live without expansion. If they do not get it one way, they must another, or perish.

As to men's representing women fairly at present, while we hear from men who owe to their wives not only all that is comfortable or graceful, but all that is wise in the arrangement of their lives, the frequent remark, "You cannot reason with a woman," when from those of delicacy, nobleness, and poetic culture, the contemptuous phrase "women and children," and that in no light sally of the hour, but in works intended to give a permanent statement of the best experiences, when not one man, in the million, shall I say? no, not in the hundred million, can rise above the belief that woman was made *for man*, when such traits as these are daily forced upon the attention, can we feel that man will always do justice to the interests of woman? Can we think that he takes a sufficiently discerning and religious view of her office and destiny, *ever* to do her justice, except when prompted by sentiment, accidentally or transiently, that is, for the sentiment will vary according to the relations in which he is placed. The lover, the poet, the artist, are likely to view her nobly. The father and the philosopher have some chance of liberality; the man of the world, the legislator for expediency, none.

Under these circumstances, without attaching importance, in themselves, to the changes demanded by the champions of woman, we hail them as signs of the times. We would have every arbitrary barrier thrown down. We would have every path laid open to woman as freely as to man. Were this done and a slight temporary fermentation allowed to subside, we should see crystallizations more pure and of more various beauty. We believe the divine energy would pervade nature to a degree unknown in the history of former ages, and that no discordant collision, but a ravishing harmony of the spheres would ensue.

Yet, then and only then, will mankind be ripe for this, when inward and outward freedom for woman as much as for man shall be acknowledged as a right, not yielded as a concession. As the friend of the negro assumes that one man cannot by right, hold another in bondage, so should the friend of woman assume that man cannot, by right, lay even well-meant restrictions on woman. If the negro be a soul, if the woman be a soul, appareled in flesh, to one Master only are they accountable. There is but one law for souls, and if there is to be an interpreter of it, he must come not as man, or son of man, but as son of God.

Were thought and feeling once so far elevated that man should esteem himself the brother and friend, but nowise the lord and tutor of woman, were he really bound with her in equal worship, arrangements as to function and employment would be of no consequence. What woman needs is not as a woman to act or rule, but as a nature to grow, as an intellect to discern, as a soul to live freely and unimpeded, to unfold such powers as were given her when we left our common home. If fewer talents were given her, yet if allowed the free and full employment of these, so that she may render back to the giver his own with usury,[30] she will not complain; nay I dare to say she will bless and rejoice in her earthly birth-place, her earthly lot. Let us consider what obstructions impede this good era, and what signs give reason to hope that it draws near.

I was talking on this subject with Miranda,[31] a woman, who, if any in the world could, might speak without heat and bitterness of the position of her sex. Her father was a man who cherished no sentimental reverence for woman, but a firm belief in the equality of the sexes. She was his eldest child, and came to him at an age when he needed a companion. From the time she could speak and go alone, he addressed her not as a plaything, but as a living mind. Among the few verses he ever wrote was a copy addressed

---

[30] Cf. Matt. 25.14–30, the parable of the talents, in which gifts or abilities are equated with the ancient monetary measure, a talent. "Usury" means here "interest," not excessive or unfair interest. [Ed.]

[31] The learned daughter of Prospero in Shakespeare's *The Tempest* and Fuller's alter-ego throughout *Woman in the Nineteenth Century*. [Ed.]

to this child, when the first locks were cut from her head, and the reverence expressed on this occasion for that cherished head, he never belied. It was to him the temple of immortal intellect. He respected his child, however, too much to be an indulgent parent. He called on her for clear judgment, for courage, for honor and fidelity; in short, for such virtues as he knew. In so far as he possessed the keys to the wonders of this universe, he allowed free use of them to her, and by the incentive of a high expectation, he forbade, as far as possible, that she should let the privilege lie idle.

Thus this child was early led to feel herself a child of the spirit. She took her place easily, not only in the world of organized being, but in the world of mind. A dignified sense of self-dependence was given as all her portion, and she found it a sure anchor. Herself securely anchored, her relations with others were established with equal security. She was fortunate in a total absence of those charms which might have drawn to her bewildering flatteries, and in a strong electric nature, which repelled those who did not belong to her, and attracted those who did. With men and women her relations were noble, affectionate without passion, intellectual without coldness. The world was free to her, and she lived freely in it. Outward adversity came, and inward conflict, but that faith and self-respect had early been awakened which must always lead at last, to an outward serenity and an inward peace.

Of Miranda I had always thought as an example, that the restraints upon the sex were insuperable only to those who think them so, or who noisily strive to break them. She had taken a course of her own, and no man stood in her way. Many of her acts had been unusual, but excited no uproar. Few helped, but none checked her, and the many men, who knew her mind and her life, showed to her confidence, as to a brother, gentleness as to a sister. And not only refined, but very coarse men approved and aided one in whom they saw resolution and clearness of design. Her mind was often the leading one, always effective.

When I talked with her upon these matters, and had said very much what I have written, she smilingly replied: "and yet we must admit that I have been fortunate, and this should not be. My good father's early trust gave the first bias, and the rest followed of course. It is true that I have had less outward aid, in after years, than most women, but that is of little consequence. Religion was early awakened in my soul, a sense that what the soul is capable to ask it must attain, and that, though I might be aided and instructed by others, I must depend on myself as the only constant friend. This self dependence, which was honored in me, is deprecated as a fault in most women. They are taught to learn their rule from without, not to unfold it from within.

"This is the fault of man, who is still vain, and wishes to be more important to woman than, by right, he should be."

"Men have not shown this disposition toward you," I said.

"No! because the position I early was enabled to take was one of self-reliance. And were all women as sure of their wants as I was, the result would be the same. But they are so overloaded with precepts by guardians, who think that nothing is so much to be dreaded for a woman as originality of thought or character, that their minds are impeded by doubts till they lose their chance of fair free proportions. The difficulty is to get them to the point from which they shall naturally develop self-respect, and learn self-help.

"Once I thought that men would help to forward this state of things more than I do now. I saw so many of them wretched in the connections they had formed in weakness and vanity. They seemed so glad to esteem women whenever they could.

"The soft arms of affection," said one of the most discerning spirits, "will not suffice for me, unless on them I see the steel bracelets of strength."

But early I perceived that men never, in any extreme of despair, wished to be women. On the contrary they were ever ready to taunt one another at any sign of weakness, with,

"Art thou not like the women, who" — [32]

The passage ends various ways, according to the occasion and rhetoric of the speaker. When they admired any woman they were inclined to speak of her as "above her sex." Silently I observed this, and feared it argued a rooted scepticism, which for ages had been fastening on the heart, and which only an age of miracles could eradicate. Ever I have been treated with great sincerity; and I look upon it as a signal instance of this, that an intimate friend of the other sex said, in a fervent moment, that I "deserved in some star to be a man." He was much surprised when I disclosed my view of my position and hopes, when I declared my faith that the feminine side, the side of love, of beauty, of holiness, was now to have its full chance, and that, if either were better, it was better now to be a woman, for even the slightest achievement of good was furthering an especial work of our time. He smiled incredulous. "She makes the best she can of it,"

---

[32] Conventional thinking about gender divisions in antebellum America did not acknowledge either homosexual desire or homosocial bonding among men, despite considerable social evidence to the contrary. [Ed.]

thought he. "Let Jews believe the pride of Jewry, but I am of the better sort, and know better."

Another used as highest praise, in speaking of a character in literature, the words "a manly woman."

So in the noble passage of Ben Jonson:

"I meant the day-star should not brighter ride,
  Nor shed like influence from its lucent seat;
I meant she should be courteous, facile, sweet,
  Free from that solemn vice of greatness, pride;
I meant each softest virtue there should meet,
  Fit in that softer bosom to abide,
Only a learned and a *manly* soul,
  I purposed her, that should with even powers,
The rock, the spindle, and the shears control
Of destiny, and spin her own free hours."[33]

"Methinks," said I, "you are too fastidious in objecting to this. Jonson in using the word 'manly' only meant to heighten the picture of this, the true, the intelligent fate, with one of the deeper colors." "And yet," said she, "so invariable is the use of this word where a heroic quality is to be described, and I feel so sure that persistence and courage are the most womanly no less than the most manly qualities, that I would exchange these words for others of a larger sense at the risk of marring the fine tissue of the verse. Read, 'a heavenward and instructed soul,' and I should be satisfied. Let it not be said, wherever there is energy or creative genius, 'She has a masculine mind.'"[34]

This by no means argues a willing want of generosity toward woman. Man is as generous toward her, as he knows how to be.

Wherever she has herself arisen in national or private history, and nobly shone forth in any form of excellence, men have received her, not only willingly, but with triumph. Their encomiums indeed, are always, in some sense, mortifying; they show too much surprise. Can this be you? he cries to the transfigured Cinderella; well I should never have thought it, but I am very glad. We will tell every one that you have "*surpassed your sex.*"

---

[33] Jonson, "On Lucy, Countess of Bedford" (Reynolds, *Woman* 23). [Ed.]

[34] In her imaginary dialogue with Miranda, Fuller anticipates the relationship between literary interpretation (and the politics of language) and feminism so crucial to the work of such second-wave twentieth-century feminists as Simone de Beauvoir, Kate Millett, Germaine Greer, Sandra Gilbert, and Susan Gubar. Reinterpretation of the masculine literary canon in terms of hidden gender politics and divisions is one of Fuller's tasks in this work. [Ed.]

In every-day life the feelings of the many are stained with vanity. Each wishes to be lord in a little world, to be superior at least over one; and he does not feel strong enough to retain a life-long ascendancy over a strong nature. Only a Theseus could conquer before he wed the Amazonian Queen. Hercules wished rather to rest with Dejanira, and received the poisoned robe, as a fit guerdon.[35] The tale should be interpreted to all those who seek repose with the weak.

But not only is man vain and fond of power, but the same want of development, which thus affects him morally, prevents his intellectually discerning the destiny of woman. The boy wants no woman, but only a girl to play ball with him, and mark his pocket handkerchief.

Thus, in Schiller's Dignity of Woman, beautiful as the poem is, there is no "grave and perfect man," but only a great boy to be softened and restrained by the influence of girls. Poets, the elder brothers of their race, have usually seen farther; but what can you expect of every-day men, if Schiller was not more prophetic as to what women must be? Even with Richter,[36] one foremost thought about a wife was that she would "cook him something good." But as this is a delicate subject, and we are in constant danger of being accused of slighting what are called "the functions," let me say in behalf of Miranda and myself, that we have high respect for those who cook something good, who create and preserve fair order in houses, and prepare therein the shining raiment for worthy inmates, worthy guests. Only these "functions" must not be a drudgery, or enforced necessity, but a part of life. Let Ulysses drive the beeves home while Penelope there piles up the fragrant loaves; they are both well employed if these be done in thought and love, willingly. But Penelope is no more meant for a baker or weaver solely, than Ulysses for a cattle-herd.[37]

The sexes should not only correspond to and appreciate, but prophesy to one another. In individual instances this happens. Two persons love in one another the future good which they aid one another to unfold. This is imperfectly or rarely done in the general life. Man has gone but little way;

---

[35] A reward. In Greek myth, Theseus defeated the Amazons and abducted their queen, Antiope; and Hercules' jealous wife, Dejanira, sent Hercules a robe she thought dipped in love potion but which actually poisoned him. [Ed.]

[36] Jean Paul Friedrich Richter (1763–1825), German writer. Like Emerson, Fuller identifies with German romantics, even though she criticizes two of her favorites here. [Ed.]

[37] In the predominantly agrarian economy of antebellum America, the division of labor into farming and domestic tasks did not suggest a hierarchy, as Fuller suggests here with her example from Homer's *Odyssey*. By the same token, Fuller argues against any essentializing masculine and feminine roles, questioning thereby a prevailing belief in woman's "nature" as nurturer and thus "angel in the house." [Ed.]

now he is waiting to see whether woman can keep step with him, but instead of calling out, like a good brother, "you can do it, if you only think so," or impersonally; "any one can do what he tries to do;" he often discourages with school-boy brag: "Girls can't do that; girls can't play ball." But let any one defy their taunts, break through and be brave and secure, they rend the air with shouts.

This fluctuation was obvious in a narrative I have lately seen, the story of the life of Countess Emily Plater, the heroine of the last revolution in Poland.[38] The dignity, the purity, the concentrated resolve, the calm, deep enthusiasm, which yet could, when occasion called, sparkle up a holy, an indignant fire, make of this young maiden the figure I want for my frontispiece. Her portrait is to be seen in the book, a gentle shadow of her soul. Short was the career—like the maid of Orleans,[39] she only did enough to verify her credentials, and then passed from a scene on which she was, probably, a premature apparition.

When the young girl joined the army where the report of her exploits had preceded her, she was received in a manner that marks the usual state of feeling. Some of the officers were disappointed at her quiet manners; that she had not the air and tone of a stage-heroine. They thought she could not have acted heroically unless in buskins; had no idea that such deeds only showed the habit of her mind. Others talked of the delicacy of her sex, advised her to withdraw from perils and dangers, and had no comprehension of the feelings within her breast that made this impossible. The gentle irony of her reply to these self-constituted tutors, (not one of whom showed himself her equal in conduct or reason,) is as good as her indignant reproof at a later period to the general, whose perfidy ruined all.

But though, to the mass of these men, she was an embarrassment and a puzzle, the nobler sort viewed her with a tender enthusiasm worthy of her. "Her name," said her biographer, "is known throughout Europe. I paint her character that she may be as widely loved."

With pride, he shows her freedom from all personal affections; that,

---

[38] Fuller refers to "Emily Plater, the Polish Heroine," *United States Magazine and Democratic Review* 11 (July 1842): 23–28. Plater (1806–31) was a Polish nationalist who resisted the Russian invasion (see Emerson's "Ode, Inscribed to W. H. Channing," n. 10, on p. 288) and died two months after the Russians crushed the rebellion (Reynolds, *Woman* 24). While identifying the limitations of patriarchal views of women's inferiority in life and literature, Fuller will offer her own examples of historical and literary women of heroic stature. [Ed.]

[39] Joan of Arc (c. 1412–31), who resisted the English (and French aristocracy in league with them). [Ed.]

though tender and gentle in an uncommon degree, there was no room for a private love in her consecrated life. She inspired those who knew her with a simple energy of feeling like her own. We have seen, they felt, a woman worthy the name, capable of all sweet affections, capable of stern virtue.

It is a fact worthy of remark, that all these revolutions in favor of liberty have produced female champions that share the same traits, but Emily alone has found a biographer. Only a near friend could have performed for her this task, for the flower was reared in feminine seclusion, and the few and simple traits of her history before her appearance in the field could only have been known to the domestic circle. Her biographer has gathered them up with a brotherly devotion.

No! man is not willingly ungenerous. He wants faith and love, because he is not yet himself an elevated being. He cries, with sneering skepticism, Give us a sign. But if the sign appears, his eyes glisten, and he offers not merely approval, but homage.

The severe nation [40] which taught that the happiness of the race was forfeited through the fault of a woman, and showed its thought of what sort of regard man owed her, by making him accuse her on the first question to his God; who gave her to the patriarch as a handmaid, and by the Mosaical law, bound her to allegiance like a serf; even they greeted, with solemn rapture, all great and holy women as heroines, prophetesses, judges in Israel; and if they made Eve listen to the serpent, gave Mary as a bride to the Holy Spirit. In other nations it has been the same down to our day. To the woman who could conquer, a triumph was awarded. And not only those whose strength was recommended to the heart by association with goodness and beauty, but those who were bad, if they were steadfast and strong, had their claims allowed. In any age a Semiramis, an Elizabeth of England, a Catharine of Russia, makes her place good, whether in a large or small circle.[41] How has a little wit, a little genius, been celebrated in a woman! What an intellectual triumph was that of the lonely Aspasia, and how heartily acknowledged! She, indeed, met a Pericles.[42] But what annalist, the rudest of men, the most plebeian of husbands, will spare from his page one

---

[40] Biblical Israel. It was a nineteenth-century convention to refer to all other societies as "nations," despite the relatively recent development of the nation-state. Fuller here questions the myth of the Fall (and Original Sin), told principally in Genesis. [Ed.]

[41] Queen Semiramis (ninth century BCE) ruled Assyria and was the founder of Babylon. Elizabeth I (1533–1603) ruled England from 1558 to 1603. Catherine the Great (1729–96) ruled Russia from 1762 to 1796. [Ed.]

[42] Aspasia (c. 470–410 BCE) ruled over a circle of intellectuals and politicians, including Pericles, the Athenian leader, who was also her lover (Reynolds, *Woman* 26). [Ed.]

of the few anecdotes of Roman women — Sappho! Eloisa![43] The names are of threadbare celebrity. Indeed they were not more suitably met in their own time than the Countess Colonel Plater on her first joining the army. They had much to mourn, and their great impulses did not find due scope. But with time enough, space enough, their kindred appear on the scene. Across the ages, forms lean, trying to touch the hem of their retreating robes. The youth here by my side cannot be weary of the fragments from the life of Sappho. He will not believe they are not addressed to himself, or that he to whom they were addressed could be ungrateful. A recluse of high powers devotes himself to understand and explain the thought of Eloisa; he asserts her vast superiority in soul and genius to her master; he curses the fate that cast his lot in another age than hers. He could have understood her: he would have been to her a friend, such as Abelard never could. And this one woman he could have loved and reverenced, and she, alas! lay cold in her grave hundreds of years ago. His sorrow is truly pathetic. These responses that come too late to give joy are as tragic as any thing we know, and yet the tears of later ages glitter as they fall on Tasso's prison bars.[44] And we know how elevating to the captive is the security that somewhere an intelligence must answer to his.

The man habitually most narrow towards women will be flushed, as by the worst assault on Christianity, if you say it has made no improvement in her condition. Indeed, those most opposed to new acts in her favor, are jealous of the reputation of those which have been done.

We will not speak of the enthusiasm excited by actresses, improvisatrici, female singers, for here mingles the charm of beauty and grace; but female authors, even learned women, if not insufferably ugly and slovenly, from the Italian professor's daughter, who taught behind the curtain, down to Mrs. Carter and Madame Dacier,[45] are sure of an admiring audience, and what is far better, chance to use what they have learned, and to learn more, if they can once get a platform on which to stand.

But how to get this platform, or how to make it of reasonably easy access is the difficulty. Plants of great vigor will almost always struggle into

---

[43] Sappho (c. 600 BCE) was a Greek poet from the island of Lesbos. Eloisa (c. 1098–1164) was a French abbess who corresponded with her teacher and love, Peter Abélard (1079–1142). [Ed.]

[44] Torquato Tasso (1544–95), Italian poet, was imprisoned for insulting his patron Duke Alfonso II of Ferrara (Reynolds, *Woman* 26). [Ed.]

[45] Elizabeth Carter (1717–1806), English poet and translator; Anne Lefevre Dacier (1647–1720), French classical scholar and translator (Reynolds, *Woman* 27). [Ed.]

blossom, despite impediments. But there should be encouragement, and a free genial atmosphere for those of more timid sort, fair play for each in its own kind. Some are like the little, delicate flowers which love to hide in the dripping mosses, by the sides of mountain torrents, or in the shade of tall trees. But others require an open field, a rich and loosened soil, or they never show their proper hues.

It may be said that man does not have his fair play either; his energies are repressed and distorted by the interposition of artificial obstacles. Ay, but he himself has put them there; they have grown out of his own imperfections. If there *is* a misfortune in woman's lot, it is in obstacles being interposed by men, which do *not* mark her state; and, if they express her past ignorance, do not her present needs. As every man is of woman born, she has slow but sure means of redress, yet the sooner a general justness of thought makes smooth the path, the better.

Man is of woman born, and her face bends over him in infancy with an expression he can never quite forget. Eminent men have delighted to pay tribute to this image, and it is an hacknied observation, that most men of genius boast some remarkable development in the mother. The rudest tar brushes off a tear with his coat-sleeve at the hallowed name. The other day, I met a decrepit old man of seventy, on a journey, who challenged the stage-company to guess where he was going. They guessed aright, "To see your mother." "Yes," said he, "she is ninety-two, but has good eye-sight still, they say. I have not seen her these forty years, and I thought I could not die in peace without." I should have liked his picture painted as a companion piece to that of a boisterous little boy, whom I saw attempt to declaim at a school exhibition —

"O that those lips had language. Life has passed
With me but roughly since I heard thee last."[46]

He got but very little way before sudden tears shamed him from the stage.

Some gleams of the same expression which shone down upon his infancy, angelically pure and benign, visit man again with hopes of pure love, of a holy marriage. Or, if not before, in the eyes of the mother of his child they again are seen, and dim fancies pass before his mind, that woman may not have been born for him alone, but have come from heaven, a commissioned

---

[46] William Cowper (1731–1800), "On the Receipt of My Mother's Picture out of Norfolk" (Reynolds, *Woman* 28). [Ed.]

soul, a messenger of truth and love; that she can only make for him a home in which he may lawfully repose, in so far as she is

"True to the kindred points of Heaven and home."[47]

In gleams, in dim fancies, this thought visits the mind of common men. It is soon obscured by the mists of sensuality, the dust of routine, and he thinks it was only some meteor, or ignis fatuus that shone.[48] But, as a Rosicrucian lamp,[49] it burns unwearied, though condemned to the solitude of tombs; and to its permanent life, as to every truth, each age has in some form borne witness. For the truths, which visit the minds of careless men only in fitful gleams, shine with radiant clearness into those of the poet, the priest, and the artist.

Whatever may have been the domestic manners of the ancients, the idea of woman was nobly manifested in their mythologies and poems, where she appears as Sita in the Ramayana, a form of tender purity, as the Egyptian Isis,[50] of divine wisdom never yet surpassed. In Egypt, too, the Sphynx, walking the earth with lion tread, looked out upon its marvels in the calm, inscrutable beauty of a virgin's face, and the Greek could only add wings to the great emblem. In Greece, Ceres and Proserpine, significantly termed "the great goddesses," were seen seated, side by side. They needed not to rise for any worshipper or any change; they were prepared for all things, as those initiated to their mysteries knew. More obvious is the meaning of these three forms, the Diana, Minerva, and Vesta.[51] Unlike in the expres-

---

[47] William Wordsworth (1770–1850), "To a Skylark" (Reynolds, *Woman* 28). [Ed.]

[48] Halley's comet was visible in 1835, and several meteors were interpreted in the antebellum period as signs of significant social changes (especially abolition). "Ignis fatuus": marsh-fire, or phosphorescent light seen around swamps and bogs. [Ed.]

[49] The Rosicrucian Order was a mystical religious sect of the seventeenth and eighteenth centuries, originally founded in 1484 by Christian Rosenkreutz. The Rosicrucians were reputed to have a lamp that could burn indefinitely. The idea of the soul as an "eternal" light is an old Christian belief, but the idea of "inner illumination" as the source of truth is typical of Fuller and other romantics. [Ed.]

[50] For an adequate description of the Isis, see Appendix A. [Fuller's note. Like Emerson, Fuller provides long catalogues of examples to illustrate her arguments. In the Hindu epic poem *Ramayana* (c. 300 BCE), Sita is goddess of the earth and companion of Rama, the incarnation of the god Vishnu (Reynolds, *Woman* 28). Isis is the Egyptian goddess of fertility, and she gives birth to the mythic twins, Set(h) and Osiris, after being impregnated by Osiris, whom she is already carrying in her womb. Set(h) seasonally dismembers Osiris, and Isis wanders the Nile gathering his limbs, reassembling him as spring renewal. — Ed.]

[51] Fuller's long catalogue of goddesses — from the hybrid Egyptian Sphinx to the winged Greek (Theban) Sphinx through the numerous Roman goddesses of agriculture, the moon, the hunt, war, wisdom, the arts, and fire (or the household hearth) — have in

sion of their beauty, but alike in this,—that each was self-sufficing. Other forms were only accessories and illustrations, none the complement to one like these. Another might, indeed, be the companion, and the Apollo and Diana set off one another's beauty. Of the Vesta, it is to be observed, that not only deep-eyed, deep-discerning Greece, but ruder Rome, who represents the only form of good man, (the always busy warrior,) that could be indifferent to woman, confided the permanence of its glory to a tutelary goddess, and her wisest legislator spoke of meditation as a nymph.

Perhaps in Rome the neglect of woman was a reaction on the manners of Etruria,[52] where the priestess Queen, warrior Queen, would seem to have been so usual a character.

An instance of the noble Roman marriage, where the stern and calm nobleness of the nation was common to both, we see in the historic page through the little that is told us of Brutus and Portia.[53] Shakespeare has seized on the relation in its native lineaments, harmonizing the particular with the universal; and, while it is conjugal love, and no other, making it unlike the same relation, as seen in Cymbeline, or Othello, even as one star differeth from another in glory.

> "By that great vow
> Which did incorporate and make us one,
> Unfold to me, yourself, your half,
> Why you are heavy   *   *   *
> Dwell I but in the suburbs
> Of your good pleasure? If it be no more,
> Portia is Brutus' harlot, not his wife."

Mark the sad majesty of his tone in answer. Who would not have lent a life-long credence to that voice of honor?

> "You are my true and honorable wife,
> As dear to me as are the ruddy drops
> That visit this sad heart."

---

common virginity and thus self-reliance, in particular independence from gods/men. In passages such as this, Fuller anticipates late-twentieth-century feminists interested in goddesses as alternatives to patriarchal mythologies as "founding," usually violent, cultural rituals and narratives. [Ed.]

[52] Etruria of the Etruscans, who preceded the Romans. Fuller suggests that the Romans' generally negative attitudes toward women in politics, society, and religion may have been a defensive effort to distinguish their culture from the Etruscans'. [Ed.]

[53] The historical Marcus Junius Brutus (c. 84–42 BCE) was supported by his wife, Portia, in his assassination of Julius Caesar. [Ed.]

It is the same voice that tells the moral of his life in the last words—

"Countrymen,
My heart doth joy, that yet in all my life,
I found no man but he was true to me."

It was not wonderful that it should be so.

Shakespeare, however, was not content to let Portia rest her plea for confidence on the essential nature of the marriage bond;

"I grant I am a woman; but withal,
A woman that lord Brutus took to wife.
I grant I am a woman; but withal,
A woman well reputed—Cato's daughter.
Think you I am *no stronger than my sex*,
Being so fathered and so husbanded?"

And afterwards in the very scene where Brutus is suffering under that "insupportable and touching loss," the death of his wife, Cassius pleads—

"Have you not love enough to bear with me,
When that rash humor which my mother gave me
Makes me forgetful?
Brutus.—Yes, Cassius; and henceforth,
When you are over-earnest with your Brutus,
He'll think your mother chides and leave you so." [54]

As indeed it was a frequent belief among the ancients, as with our Indians, that the *body* was inherited from the mother, the *soul* from the father. As in that noble passage of Ovid, already quoted, where Jupiter, as his divine synod are looking down on the funeral pyre of Hercules, thus triumphs—

Nic nisi *maternâ* Vulcanum parte potentem.
Sentiet. Aeternum est, à me quod traxit, et expers
At que immune necis, nullaque domabile flamma
Idque ego defunctum terrâ cœlestibus oris
Accipiam, cunctisque meum lætabile factum
Dis fore confido.
"The part alone of gross *maternal* frame
Fire shall devour, while that from me he drew
Shall live immortal and its force renew;

---

[54] The five preceding quotations are from Shakespeare, *Julius Caesar*: 2.1.272–75, 285–87; 2.1.288–90; 5.4.33–35; 2.1.292–97; 4.2.119–24 (Reynolds 29). Fuller's method of literary "close reading" is remarkably similar to modern approaches to literary analysis. [Ed.]

That, when he's dead, I'll raise to realms above;
Let all the powers the righteous act approve." [55]

It is indeed a god speaking of his union with an earthly woman, but it expresses the common Roman thought as to marriage, the same which permitted a man to lend his wife to a friend, as if she were a chattel.

"She dwelt but in the suburbs of his good pleasure." [56]

Yet the same city as I have said leaned on the worship of Vesta, the Preserver, and in later times was devoted to that of Isis. In Sparta, thought, in this respect as in all others, was expressed in the characters of real life, and the women of Sparta were as much Spartans as the men. The citoyen, citoyenne of France was here actualized. Was not the calm equality they enjoyed as honorable as the devotion of chivalry? They intelligently shared the ideal life of their nation.

Like the men they felt

"Honor gone, all's gone,
Better never have been born."

They were the true friends of men. The Spartan, surely, would not think that he received only his body from his mother. The sage, had he lived in that community, could not have thought the souls of "vain and foppish men will be degraded after death, to the forms of women, and, if they do not there make great efforts to retrieve themselves, will become birds."

(By the way it is very expressive of the hard intellectuality of the merely *mannish* mind, to speak thus of birds, chosen always by the *feminine* poet as the symbols of his fairest thoughts.)

We are told of the Greek nations in general, that woman occupied there an infinitely lower place than man. It is difficult to believe this when we see such range and dignity of thought on the subject in the mythologies, and find the poets producing such ideals as Cassandra, Iphiginia, Antigone, Macaria, where Sibylline priestesses told the oracle of the highest god, and he could not be content to reign with a court of fewer than nine muses. Even victory wore a female form. [57]

---

[55] Ovid, *Metamorphoses* bk. 9 (Reynolds, *Woman* 30). [Ed.]

[56] Cf. Shakespeare, *Julius Caesar* 2.1.285–86. [Ed.]

[57] Fuller offers a long catalogue of ancient Greek heroines, most of whom are subjects of Greek tragedy and epic. Cassandra, daughter of King Priam, was given the gift of prophecy by Apollo but was doomed never to be believed after she resisted him (see Homer, *Iliad*). Iphigenia, daughter of King Priam, was to be sacrificed by her father to obtain the gods' blessing on his campaign against Troy, but she was saved by Artemis (see Euripides,

But whatever were the facts of daily life, I cannot complain of the age and nation, which represents its thought by such a symbol as I see before me at this moment. It is a zodiac of the busts of gods and goddesses, arranged in pairs. The circle breathes the music of a heavenly order. Male and female heads are distinct in expression, but equal in beauty, strength and calmness. Each male head is that of a brother and a king—each female of a sister and a queen. Could the thought, thus expressed, be lived out, there would be nothing more to be desired. There would be unison in variety, congeniality in difference.

Coming nearer our own time, we find religion and poetry no less true in their revelations. The rude man, just disengaged from the sod, the Adam, accuses woman to his God, and records her disgrace to their posterity. He is not ashamed to write that he could be drawn from heaven by one beneath him, one made, he says, from but a small part of himself. But in the same nation, educated by time, instructed by a succession of prophets, we find woman in as high a position as she has ever occupied. No figure that has ever arisen to greet our eyes has been received with more fervent reverence than that of the Madonna. Heine calls her the *Dame du Comptoir* of the Catholic church, and this jeer well expresses a serious truth.[58]

And not only this holy and significant image was worshipped by the pilgrim, and the favorite subject of the artist, but it exercised an immediate influence on the destiny of the sex. The empresses who embraced the cross, converted sons and husbands. Whole calendars of female saints, heroic dames of chivalry, binding the emblem of faith on the heart of the best-beloved, and wasting the bloom of youth in separation and loneliness, for the sake of duties they thought it religion to assume, with innumerable forms of poesy, trace their lineage to this one. Nor, however imperfect may be the action, in our day, of the faith thus expressed, and though we can scarcely think it nearer this ideal, than that of India or Greece was near their ideal, is it in vain that the truth has been recognized, that woman is not only a part of man, bone of his bone, and flesh of his flesh, born that men might not be lonely, but that women are in themselves possessors of and possessed by immortal souls. This truth undoubtedly received a greater outward stability from the belief of the church that the earthly parent of the Saviour of souls was a woman.

Iphigenia at Aulis). Antigone, daughter of Oedipus, disobeyed King Creon and buried her brother, Polyneices (see Sophocles, *Antigone*). Macaria, daughter of Hercules, sacrificed herself to save Athens (see Euripides, *Children of Hercules*). Ancient Greek monuments to Victory, such as the *Winged Victory of Nike,* were feminine in form. [Ed.]

[58] Heinrich Heine (1797–1856), German poet. "Dame du comptoir": French for "saleswoman," meaning that the Virgin Mary promotes Catholicism. [Ed.]

The assumption of the Virgin, as painted by sublime artists, Petrarch's Hymn to the Madonna,[59] cannot have spoken to the world wholly without result, yet, oftentimes those who had ears heard not.

See upon the nations the influence of this powerful example. In Spain look only at the ballads. Woman in these is "very woman;" she is the betrothed, the bride, the spouse of man, there is on her no hue of the philosopher, the heroine, the savante, but she looks great and noble; why? because she is also, through her deep devotion, the betrothed of heaven. Her up-turned eyes have drawn down the light that casts a radiance round her. See only such a ballad as that of "Lady Teresa's Bridal."[60]

Where the Infanta, given to the Moorish bride-groom, calls down the vengeance of Heaven on his unhallowed passion, and thinks it not too much to expiate by a life in the cloister, the involuntary stain upon her princely youth.[61] It was this constant sense of claims above those of earthly love or happiness that made the Spanish lady who shared this spirit, a guerdon to be won by toils and blood and constant purity, rather than a chattel to be bought for pleasure and service.

Germany did not need to *learn* a high view of woman; it was inborn in that race. Woman was to the Teuton warrior his priestess, his friend, his sister, in truth, a wife. And the Christian statues of noble pairs, as they lie above their graves in stone, expressing the meaning of all the by-gone pilgrimage by hands folded in mutual prayer, yield not a nobler sense of the place and powers of woman, than belonged to the altvater day. The holy love of Christ which summoned them, also, to choose "the better part, that which could not be taken from them," refined and hallowed in this nation a native faith, thus showing that it was not the warlike spirit alone that left the Latins so barbarous in this respect.

But the Germans, taking so kindly to this thought, did it the more justice. The idea of woman in their literature is expressed both to a greater height and depth than elsewhere.

I will give as instances the themes of three ballads.

One is upon a knight who had always the name of the Virgin on his lips. This protected him all his life through, in various and beautiful modes, both from sin and other dangers, and, when he died, a plant sprang from

---

[59] Appendix, B. [Fuller's note.]

[60] A ballad published in John Gibson Lockhart's (1794–1854) *Ancient Spanish Ballads: Historical and Romantic* (1823) about Princess Theresa, sister of King Alfonso V (994–1028) and not to be confused with the Spanish mystic, Saint Theresa of Avila (1515–82) (Dickenson 230). [Ed.]

[61] Appendix, C. [Fuller's note.]

his grave, which so gently whispered the Ave Maria that none could pass it by with an unpurified heart.

Another is one of the legends of the famous Drachenfels.[62] A maiden, one of the earliest converts to Christianity, was carried by the enraged populace to this dread haunt of "the dragon's fabled brood," to be their prey. She was left alone, but unafraid, for she knew in whom she trusted. So, when the dragons came rushing towards her, she showed them a crucifix and they crouched reverently at her feet. Next day the people came, and seeing these wonders, are all turned to the faith which exalts the lowly.

The third I have in mind is another of the Rhine legends. A youth is sitting with the maid he loves on the shore of an isle, her fairy kingdom, then perfumed by the blossoming grape vines, which draped its bowers. They are happy; all blossoms with them, and life promises its richest wine. A boat approaches on the tide; it pauses at their feet. It brings, perhaps, some joyous message, fresh dew for their flowers, fresh light on the wave. No! it is the usual check on such great happiness. The father of the Count departs for the crusade; will his son join him, or remain to rule their domain, and wed her he loves? Neither of the affianced pair hesitate a moment. "I must go with my father." "Thou must go with thy father." It was one thought, one word. "I will be here again," he said, "when these blossoms have turned to purple grapes." "I hope so," she sighed, while the prophetic sense said "no."

And there she waited, and the grapes ripened, and were gathered into the vintage, and he came not. Year after year passed thus, and no tidings; yet still she waited.

He, meanwhile, was in a Moslem prison. Long he languished there without hope, till, at last, his patron saint appeared in vision and announced his release, but only on condition of his joining the monastic order for the service of the saint.

And so his release was effected, and a safe voyage home given. And once more he sets sail upon the Rhine. The maiden, still watching beneath the vines, sees at last the object of all this patient love approach. Approach, but not to touch the strand to which she, with outstretched arms, has rushed. He dares not trust himself to land, but in low, heart-broken tones, tells her of heaven's will; and that he, in obedience to his vow, is now on his way to a convent on the river bank, there to pass the rest of his earthly life in the service of the shrine. And then he turns his boat, and floats away from her

---

[62]Dragon Rock, a legendary peak on the Rhine. Fuller's treatment of Greek, Roman, Spanish, and German myths and legends is her way of showing by comparative cultural analyses how pervasively women have figured in the defining stories of the world's societies. Modern comparative literary study certainly draws much of its strength from romantic interpreters of myth like Fuller. [Ed.]

and hope of any happiness in this world, but urged, as he believes, by the breath of heaven.

The maiden stands appalled, but she dares not murmur, and cannot hesitate long. She also bids them prepare her boat. She follows her lost love to the convent gate, requests an interview with the abbot, and devotes her Elysian isle, where vines had ripened their ruby fruit in vain for her, to the service of the monastery where her love was to serve. Then, passing over to the nunnery opposite, she takes the veil, and meets her betrothed at the altar; and for a life long union, if not the one they had hoped in earlier years.

Is not this sorrowful story of a lofty beauty? Does it not show a sufficiently high view of woman, of marriage? This is commonly the chivalric, still more the German view.

Yet, wherever there was a balance in the mind of man of sentiment, with intellect, such a result was sure. The Greek Xenophon has not only painted as a sweet picture of the domestic woman, in his Economics, but in the Cyropedia has given, in the picture of Panthea, a view of woman which no German picture can surpass, whether lonely and quiet with veiled lids, the temple of a vestal loveliness, or with eyes flashing, and hair flowing to the free wind, cheering on the hero to fight for his God, his country, or whatever name his duty might bear at the time. This picture I shall copy by and by.[63] Yet Xenophon grew up in the same age with him who makes Iphigenia say to Achilles —

"Better a thousand women should perish than one man cease to see the light."[64]

This was the vulgar Greek sentiment. Xenophon, aiming at the ideal man, caught glimpses of the ideal woman also. From the figure of a Cyrus, the Pantheas stand not afar. They do not in thought; they would not in life.

I could swell the catalogue of instances far beyond the reader's patience. But enough have been brought forward to show that, though there has been great disparity betwixt the nations as between individuals in their culture on this point, yet the idea of woman has always cast some rays and often been forcibly represented.

Far less has woman to complain that she has not had her share of power. This, in all ranks of society, except the lowest, has been hers to the extent that vanity would crave, far beyond what wisdom would accept. In the very

---

[63] Fuller develops the story of Panthea below (see pp. 349–353), basing her account on Xenophon's (c. 431–354 BCE) *Cyropedia,* which deals with the education of Cyrus the Great and responds to Plato's ideas of education in the *Republic.* Xenophon also wrote *Economics,* which deals with estate and domestic management. [Ed.]

[64] Euripides, *Iphigenia at Aulis;* see Appendix G. [Ed.]

lowest, where man, pressed by poverty, sees in woman only the partner of toils and cares, and cannot hope, scarcely has an idea of, a comfortable home, he often maltreats her, and is less influenced by her. In all ranks, those who are gentle and uncomplaining, too candid to intrigue, too delicate to encroach, suffer much. They suffer long, and are kind; verily, they have their reward. But wherever man is sufficiently raised above extreme poverty or brutal stupidity, to care for the comforts of the fireside, or the bloom and ornament of life, woman has always power enough, if she choose to exert it, and is usually disposed to do so, in proportion to her ignorance and childish vanity. Unacquainted with the importance of life and its purposes, trained to a selfish coquetry and love of petty power, she does not look beyond the pleasure of making herself felt at the moment, and governments are shaken and commerce broken up to gratify the pique of a female favorite. The English shopkeeper's wife does not vote, but it is for her interest that the politician canvasses by the coarsest flattery. France suffers no woman on her throne, but her proud nobles kiss the dust at the feet of Pompadour and Dubarry; for such flare in the lighted foreground where a Roland would modestly aid in the closet.[65] Spain, (that same Spain which sang of Ximena and the Lady Teresa,) shuts up her women in the care of duennas, and allows them no book but the Breviary, but the ruin follows only the more surely from the worthless favorite of a worthless queen.[66] Relying on mean precautions, men indeed cry peace, peace, where there is no peace.

It is not the transient breath of poetic incense that women want; each can receive that from a lover. It is not life-long sway; it needs but to become a coquette, a shrew, or a good cook, to be sure of that. It is not money, nor notoriety, nor the badges of authority that men have appropriated to themselves. If demands, made in their behalf, lay stress on any of these particulars, those who make them have not searched deeply into the need. It is for that which at once includes these and precludes them; which would not be forbidden power, lest there be temptation to steal and misuse it; which

---

[65] France may not have had a ruling queen, but Louis XV's mistresses, Madame de Pompadour (1721–64) and the Countess du Barry (1743–93), wielded enormous state power. Madame Roland, the French revolutionary, helped bring down the monarchy. [Ed.]

[66] Catholic Spain may treat women as inferior to men, but the Princess Theresa (see n. 60) and Ximena, wife of the epic soldier El Cid, give contrary evidence. On the other hand, if the Spanish treat women as weak and inferior, then they will get what they deserve, such as Manuel de Godoy (1767–1851), lover of Queen Maria Louisa and chief minister of Charles IV of Spain. Allying Spain with Napoleon Bonaparte against England, de Godoy helped bring about the Spanish naval defeat at Trafalgar (1805) and the subsequent invasion of Spain by Napoleon's army (Reynolds, *Woman* 36). [Ed.]

would not have the mind perverted by flattery from a worthiness of esteem. It is for that which is the birthright of every being capable to receive it, — the freedom, the religious, the intelligent freedom of the universe, to use its means; to learn its secret as far as nature has enabled them, with God alone for their guide and their judge.

Ye cannot believe it, men; but the only reason why women ever assume what is more appropriate to you, is because you prevent them from finding out what is fit for themselves. Were they free, were they wise fully to develop the strength and beauty of woman; they would never wish to be men, or man-like. The well-instructed moon flies not from her orbit to seize on the glories of her partner. No; for she knows that one law rules, one heaven contains, one universe replies to them alike. It is with women as with the slave.

"Vor dem Sklaven, wenn er die Kette bricht
Vor dem freien Menschen erzittert nicht."

Tremble not before the free man, but before the slave who has chains to break.[67]

In slavery, acknowledged slavery, women are on a par with men. Each is a work-tool, an article of property, no more! In perfect freedom, such as is painted in Olympus, in Swedenborg's angelic state, in the heaven where there is no marrying nor giving in marriage, each is a purified intelligence, an enfranchised soul, — no less![68]

Jene himmlische Gestalten
Sie fragen nicht nach Mann und Weib,
Und keine kleider, keine Falten
Umgeben den verklarten Leib.[69]

The child who sang this was a prophetic form, expressive of the longing for a state of perfect freedom, pure love. She could not remain here, but was transplanted to another air. And it may be that the air of this earth will

---

[67] English translation of the German poetic lines from Friedrich Schiller, "Words of Faith" (1798). [Ed.]

[68] Returning to the theme of women's rights and abolition, Fuller notes ironically that enslaved women are equal with men, both turned into commodities or tools, and she makes thereby an important point about the relationship beween women's rights, abolition, and international rights to one's own labor—common themes among contemporary abolitionists. [Ed.]

[69] From Johann Wolfgang von Goethe (1749–1832), *Wilhelm Meister's Apprenticeship:* "Those heavenly forms/ Do not wonder about man and woman/And no clothing, no ruffles/Surround the transfigured body" (Reynolds, *Woman* 37). [Ed.]

never be so tempered that such can bear it long. But, while they stay, they must bear testimony to the truth they are constituted to demand.

That an era approaches which shall approximate nearer to such a temper than any has yet done, there are many tokens, indeed so many, that only a few of the most prominent can here be enumerated.

The reigns of Elizabeth of England and Isabella of Castile foreboded this era.[70] They expressed the beginning of the new state, while they forwarded its progress. These were strong characters and in harmony with the wants of their time. One showed that this strength did not unfit a woman for the duties of a wife and a mother, the other that it could enable her to live and die alone, a wide energetic life, a courageous death. Elizabeth is certainly no pleasing example. In rising above the weakness, she did not lay aside the weaknesses ascribed to her sex; but her strength must be respected now, as it was in her own time.[71]

Elizabeth and Mary Stuart[72] seem types, moulded by the spirit of the time, and placed upon an elevated platform to show to the coming ages, woman such as the conduct and wishes of man in general is likely to make her, lovely even to allurement, quick in apprehension and weak in judgment, with grace and dignity of sentiment, but no principle; credulous and indiscreet, yet artful; capable of sudden greatness or of crime, but not of a steadfast wisdom, or self-restraining virtue; and woman half-emancipated and jealous of her freedom, such as she has figured before and since in many a combative attitude, mannish, not equally manly, strong and prudent more than great or wise; able to control vanity, and the wish to rule through coquetry and passion, but not to resign these dear deceits, from the very foundation, as unworthy a being capable of truth and nobleness. Elizabeth, taught by adversity, put on her virtues as armor, more than produced them in a natural order from her soul. The time and her position called on her to act the wise sovereign, and she was proud that she could do so, but her tastes and inclinations would have led her to act the weak woman. She was without magnanimity of any kind.

---

[70]Queen Isabella I (1451–1504) of Castille and León established the unified Spanish kingdom by marrying Ferdinand V of Aragon (Reynolds, *Woman* 37). [Ed.]

[71]Although Queen Elizabeth I was known as the "Virgin Queen," she also was known for her love-affairs with such noblemen as Robert Dudley, the Earl of Leicester (1531–58). Fuller's prudish condemnation of sexually liberated women reflects her commitment as a transcendentalist to "purified" or "spiritual" love and nineteenth-century middle-class social mores. [Ed.]

[72]Mary Stuart, "Mary Queen of Scots" (1542–87), was a central figure in the Catholic plots against Elizabeth, several aided by the Spanish. She was arrested and executed by Elizabeth. [Ed.]

We may accept as an omen for ourselves, that it was Isabella who furnished Columbus with the means of coming hither. This land must pay back its debt to woman, without whose aid it would not have been brought into alliance with the civilized world.

A graceful and meaning figure is that introduced to us by Mr. Prescott, in the Conquest of Mexico, in the Indian girl Marina, who accompanied Cortes, and was his interpreter in all the various difficulties of his career.[73] She stood at his side, on the walls of the besieged palace, to plead with her enraged countrymen. By her name he was known in New Spain, and, after the conquest, her gentle intercession was often of avail to the conquered. The poem of the Future may be read in some features of the story of "Malinche."

The influence of Elizabeth on literature was real, though, by sympathy with its finer productions, she was no more entitled to give name to an era than Queen Anne.[74] It was simply that the fact of having a female sovereign on the throne affected the course of a writer's thoughts. In this sense, the presence of a woman on the throne always makes its mark. Life is lived before the eyes of men, by which their imaginations are stimulated as to the possibilities of woman. "We will die for our King, Maria Theresa,"[75] cry the wild warriors, clashing their swords, and the sounds vibrate through the poems of that generation. The range of female character in Spenser alone might content us for one period. Britomart and Belphoebe have as much room on the canvass as Florimel; and where this is the case, the haughtiest amazon will not murmur that Una should be felt to be the fairest type.[76]

---

[73] William H. Prescott (1796–1859) in *History of the Conquest of Mexico* (1843) grandly romanticizes the story of the relationship between Cortés and his Aztec guide, translator, and mistress, Malinche, whom Cortés baptized as "Marina" (Dickenson 231). Today, Malinche is viewed as the prototypical victim of imperial domination, the subaltern "betrayer"(often with witchlike powers) of her own people, or both. [Ed.]

[74] Although Queen Anne (r. 1702–14) is associated with specific styles in crafts and architecture and ruled when the Act of Union (1707) united England, Wales, and Scotland, her era is hardly comparable in cultural achievement to the Elizabethan era in Fuller's judgment. [Ed.]

[75] Maria Theresa (1717–80) was ruler of the Austro-Hungarian Empire and initiated the Seven Years War — probably where the cheering soldiers are headed — to regain territory lost to Prussia and Russia. [Ed.]

[76] Allegorical feminine characters in Edmund Spenser's *The Faerie Queene* (1590–96): Britomart, an allegory for Britain, is the chaste (and feminine) knight. Belphoebe, representing the young Queen Elizabeth, is the chaste huntress. Florimel typifies perfect femininity as chaste and virtuous. Una represents the ideal of spiritual and transcendent truth. [Ed.]

Unlike as was the English Queen to a fairy queen, we may yet conceive that it was the image of *a* queen before the poet's mind, that called up this splendid court of women. Shakespeare's range is also great; but he has left out the heroic characters, such as the Macaria of Greece, the Britomart of Spenser. Ford and Massinger have, in this respect, soared to a higher flight of feeling than he.[77] It was the holy and heroic woman they most loved, and if they could not paint an Imogen, a Desdemona, a Rosalind, yet, in those of a stronger mould, they showed a higher ideal, though with so much less poetic power to embody it, than we see in Portia or Isabella. The simple truth of Cordelia, indeed, is of this sort. The beauty of Cordelia is neither male nor female; it is the beauty of virtue.[78]

The ideal of love and marriage rose high in the mind of all the Christian nations who were capable of grave and deep feeling. We may take as examples of its English aspect, the lines,

"I could not love thee, dear, so much,
Loved I not honor more."[79]

Or the address of the Commonwealth's man to his wife, as she looked out from the Tower window to see him for the last time, on his way to the scaffold. He stood up in the cart, waved his hat, and cried, "To Heaven, my love, to Heaven, and leave you in the storm?"[80]

Such was the love of faith and honor, a love which stopped, like Colonel Hutchinson's, "on this side idolatry," because it was religious. The meeting of two such souls Donne describes as giving birth to an "abler soul."[81]

Lord Herbert wrote to his love,

"Were not our souls immortal made,
Our equal loves can make them such."[82]

---

[77] John Ford (1586-c.1640) and Philip Massinger (1583–1640) are English Renaissance dramatists who focused on victimized women characters. [Ed.]

[78] Imogen, Desdemona, Rosalind, Portia, Isabella, and Cordelia are female characters in Shakespeare's *Cymbeline, Othello, As You Like It, The Merchant of Venice, Measure for Measure,* and *King Lear,* respectively. (Dickenson 232). [Ed.]

[79] Richard Lovelace (1618–58), "To Locasta, Going to the Wars." [Ed.]

[80] Lucy Hutchinson, in her *Memoirs of the Life of Colonel Hutchinson* (1806), records this episode in the execution of her husband, John Hutchinson (1615–64), who was condemned for signing King Charles I's death warrant and for supporting the Puritan Commonwealth (Dickenson 232). [Ed.]

[81] John Donne (1572–1631), "The Exstacie." [Ed.]

[82] Lord Edward Herbert (1583–1648), "An Ode upon a Question Moved, Whether Love Should Continue Forever?" In general, Fuller is providing a revisionary interpretation of Elizabethan, Jacobean, and Restoration literature by recalling the role women played as historical agents, inspirations, and characters in this cultural tradition. [Ed.]

In the "Broken Heart" of Ford, Penthea, a character which engages my admiration even more deeply than the famous one of Calanthe, is made to present to the mind the most beautiful picture of what these relations should be in their purity.[83] Her life cannot sustain the violation of what she so clearly felt.

Shakespeare, too, saw that, in true love as in fire, the utmost ardor is coincident with the utmost purity. It is a true lover that exclaims in the agony of Othello,

"If thou art false, O then Heaven mocks itself."[84]

The son, framed like Hamlet, to appreciate truth in all the beauty of relations, sinks into deep melancholy, when he finds his natural expectations disappointed. He has no mother. She to whom he gave the name, disgraces from his heart's shrine all the sex.

"Frailty, thy name is woman."

It is because a Hamlet could find cause to say so, that I have put the line, whose stigma has never been removed, at the head of my work. But, as a lover, surely a Hamlet would not have so far mistook, as to have finished with such a conviction. He would have felt the faith of Othello, and that faith could not, in his more dispassionate mind, have been disturbed by calumny.

In Spain, this thought is arrayed in a sublimity, which belongs to the sombre and passionate genius of the nation. Calderón's Justina[85] resists all the temptation of the Demon, and raises her lover, with her, above the sweet lures of mere temporal happiness. Their marriage is vowed at the stake; their souls are liberated together by the martyr flame into "a purer state of sensation and existence."

In Italy, the great poets wove into their lives an ideal love which answered to the highest wants. It included those of the intellect and the affections, for it was a love of spirit for spirit. It was not ascetic, or superhuman, but, interpreting all things, gave their proper beauty to details of the common life, the common day; the poet spoke of his love, not as a flower to place in his bosom, or hold carelessly in his hand, but as a light towards which he must find wings to fly, or "a stair to heaven." He delighted to speak of her, not

---

[83] Penthea and Calanthe are female characters in John Ford's play *The Broken Heart* (1633). [Ed.]

[84] Shakespeare, *Othello* 3.3.278. [Ed.]

[85] Justina is the heroine in Pedro Calderón de la Barca's (1600–81) play *El Magico Prodigioso* (1637). She "sacrifices" herself and her lover, Cyprian, to death at the stake in order to resist temptation—another story of sacrificial and transcendent love. [Ed.]

only as the bride of his heart, but the mother of his soul; for he saw that, in cases where the right direction had been taken, the greater delicacy of her frame, and stillness of her life, left her more open to spiritual influx than man is. So he did not look upon her as betwixt him and earth, to serve his temporal needs, but rather, betwixt him and heaven, to purify his affections and lead him to wisdom through love. He sought, in her, not so much the Eve, as the Madonna.

In these minds the thought, which gleams through all the legends of chivalry, shines in broad intellectual effulgence, not to be misinterpreted, and their thought is reverenced by the world, though it lies so far from the practice of the world as yet, so far, that it seems as though a gulf of death yawned between.

Even with such men, the practice was, often, widely different from the mental faith. I say mental, for if the heart were thoroughly alive with it, the practice could not be dissonant. Lord Herbert's was a marriage of convention, made for him at fifteen; he was not discontented with it, but looked only to the advantages it brought of perpetuating his family on the basis of a great fortune. He paid, in act, what he considered a dutiful attention to the bond; his thoughts travelled elsewhere; and while forming a high ideal of the companionship of minds in marriage, he seems never to have doubted that its realization must be postponed to some other state of being. Dante, almost immediately after the death of Beatrice, married a lady chosen for him by his friends, and Boccaccio, in describing the miseries that attended, in this case,

"The form of an union where union is none,"

speaks as if these were inevitable to the connection, and the scholar and poet, especially, could expect nothing but misery and obstruction in a domestic partnership with woman.[86]

Centuries have passed since, but civilized Europe is still in a transition state about marriage; not only in practice, but in thought. It is idle to speak with contempt of the nations where polygamy is an institution, or seraglios a custom, when practices far more debasing haunt, well nigh fill, every city and every town. And so far as union of one with one is believed to be the

---

[86] Having discussed the use of women to represent spiritual purity in Italian Renaissance poetry—Fuller undoubtedly has Petrarch and Dante in mind—she cites the harsh reality of arranged marriages and marriages of convenience for some of the greatest of these poets, including Lord Herbert and Dante Alighieri (1265–1321), who married Gemma Donati after the death of his poetic inspiration, Beatrice. Fuller is anticipating her own argument later in the text for more spiritual relations between husband and wife, such as the relationship of William Godwin and Mary Wollstonecraft. [Ed.]

only pure form of marriage, a great majority of societies and individuals are still doubtful whether the earthly bond must be a meeting of souls, or only supposes a contract of convenience and utility. Were woman established in the rights of an immortal being, this could not be. She would not, in some countries, be given away by her father, with scarcely more respect for her feelings than is shown by the Indian chief, who sells his daughter for a horse, and beats her if she runs away from her new home.[87] Nor, in societies where her choice is left free, would she be perverted, by the current of opinion that seizes her, into the belief that she must marry, if it be only to find a protector, and a home of her own.

Neither would man, if he thought the connection of permanent importance, form it so lightly. He would not deem it a trifle, that he was to enter into the closest relations with another soul, which, if not eternal in themselves, must eternally affect his growth.

Neither, did he believe woman capable of friendship,[88] would he, by rash haste, lose the chance of finding a friend in the person who might, probably, live half a century by his side. Did love, to his mind, stretch forth into infinity, he would not miss his chance of its revelations, that he might, the sooner, rest from his weariness by a bright fireside, and secure a sweet and graceful attendant "devoted to him alone." Were he a step higher, he would not carelessly enter into a relation where he might not be able to do the duty of a friend, as well as a protector from external ill, to the other party, and have a being in his power pining for sympathy, intelligence and aid, that he could not give.

What deep communion, what real intercourse is implied by the sharing the joys and cares of parentage, when any degree of equality is admitted between the parties! It is true that, in a majority of instances, the man looks upon his wife as an adopted child, and places her to the other children in the relation of nurse or governess, rather than of parent. Her influence with them is sure, but she misses the education which should enlighten that influence, by being thus treated. It is the order of nature that children should complete the education, moral and mental, of parents, by making them think what is needed for the best culture of human beings, and conquer all faults and impulses that interfere with their giving this to these dear objects,

---

[87] Although Fuller considered herself an advocate of Native American rights, she also subscribed to antebellum conventions about "Indian savagery," none more telling than the accounts of Native American fathers "trading" their daughters for a "horse." Yet most nineteenth-century English marriages involved financial "settlements" and "dowries," which are principally what Lakota demands for "horses" (or other wealth) as part of an engagement signify. [Ed.]

[88] See Appendix D, Spinoza's view. [Fuller's note.]

who represent the world to them. Father and mother should assist one another to learn what is required for this sublime priesthood of nature. But, for this, a religious recognition of equality is required.

Where this thought of equality begins to diffuse itself, it is shown in four ways.

The household partnership. In our country, the woman looks for a "smart but kind" husband; the man for a "capable, sweet-tempered" wife.

The man furnishes the house; the woman regulates it. Their relation is one of mutual esteem, mutual dependence. Their talk is of business, their affection shows itself by practical kindness. They know that life goes more smoothly and cheerfully to each for the other's aid; they are grateful and content. The wife praises her husband as a "good provider;" the husband, in return, compliments her as a "capital housekeeper." This relation is good, as far as it goes.

Next comes a closer tie, which takes the two forms, either of mutual idolatry, or of intellectual companionship. The first, we suppose, is to no one a pleasing subject of contemplation. The parties weaken and narrow one another; they lock the gate against all the glories of the universe, that they may live in a cell together. To themselves they seem the only wise, to all others steeped in infatuation; the gods smile as they look forward to the crisis of cure; to men, the woman seems an unlovely syren; to women, the man an effeminate boy.

The other form, of intellectual companionship, has become more and more frequent. Men engaged in public life, literary men, and artists, have often found in their wives companions and confidants in thought no less than in feeling. And as the intellectual development of woman has spread wider and risen higher, they have, not unfrequently, shared the same employment. As in the case of Roland and his wife,[89] who were friends in the household and in the nation's councils, read, regulated home affairs, or prepared public documents together, indifferently.

It is very pleasant, in letters begun by Roland, and finished by his wife, to see the harmony of mind, and the difference of nature; one thought, but various ways of treating it.

This is one of the best instances of a marriage of friendship. It was only friendship, whose basis was esteem; probably neither party knew love, except by name.

Roland was a good man, worthy to esteem, and be esteemed; his wife as

---

[89] Jean-Marie Roland de la Platière (1734–93) married Jeanne-Marie Roland in 1780. He was minister of the interior in 1792, and both sided with the Girondists against Danton and Robespierre, Jacobin leaders. When his wife was executed during the Reign of Terror, Roland committed suicide. [Ed.]

deserving of admiration, as able to do without it. Madame Roland is the fairest specimen we have yet of her class, as clear to discern her aim, as valiant to pursue it, as Spenser's Britomart; austerely set apart from all that did not belong to her, whether as woman or as mind. She is an antetype of a class to which the coming time will afford a field, the Spartan matron, brought by the culture of the age of Books to intellectual consciousness and expansion.

Self-sufficingness, strength, and clear-sightedness were, in her, combined with a power of deep and calm affection. She, too, would have given a son or husband the device for his shield, "Return with it or upon it;" and this, not because she loved little, but much. The page of her life is one of unsullied dignity.

Her appeal to posterity is one against the injustice of those who committed such crimes in the name of Liberty. She makes it in behalf of herself and her husband. I would put beside it, on the shelf, a little volume, containing a similar appeal from the verdict of contemporaries to that of mankind, made by Godwin in behalf of his wife, the celebrated, the, by most men, detested, Mary Wolstonecraft. In his view, it was an appeal from the injustice of those who did such wrong in the name of virtue.[90]

Were this little book interesting for no other cause, it would be so for the generous affection evinced under the peculiar circumstances. This man had courage to love and honor this woman in the face of the world's sentence, and of all that was repulsive in her own past history. He believed he saw of what soul she was, and that the impulses she had struggled to act out were noble, though the opinions to which they had led might not be thoroughly weighed. He loved her, and he defended her for the meaning and tendency of the inner life. It was a good fact.

Mary Wolstonecraft, like Madame Dudevant, (commonly known as George Sand,)[91] in our day, was a woman whose existence better proved the need of some new interpretation of woman's rights, than any thing she wrote. Such beings as these, rich in genius, of most tender sympathies, capable of high virtue and a chastened harmony, ought not to find themselves,

---

[90]Fuller is referring to William Godwin's (1756–1836) memoir of his wife, Mary Wollstonecraft (1759–97), author of *A Vindication of the Rights of Woman* (1792), who died of pueral fever after giving birth to their daughter, Mary (who as Mary Shelley later wrote *Frankenstein*). In his memoir, Godwin reveals Wollstonecraft's earlier affair with Gilbert Imlay in 1793–95 and their illegitimate daughter—facts that damaged Wollstonecraft's nineteenth-century reputation among both men and women. [Ed.]

[91]Amandine Lucile Aurore Dupin, Baroness Dudevant (1804–76), wrote under the pen name "George Sand" and scandalized many with her male attire and love affairs. Sand mocked contemporary women's rights activists, but Fuller embraces her as an early feminist (Dickenson 233). [Ed.]

by birth, in a place so narrow, that, in breaking bonds, they become out-laws. Were there as much room in the world for such, as in Spenser's poem for Britomart, they would not run their heads so wildly against the walls, but prize their shelter rather. They find their way, at last, to light and air, but the world will not take off the brand it has set upon them. The champion of the Rights of Woman found, in Godwin, one who would plead that cause like a brother. He who delineated with such purity of traits the form of woman in the Marguerite, of whom the weak St. Leon could never learn to be worthy, a pearl indeed whose price was above rubies, was not false in life to the faith by which he had hallowed his romance.[92] He acted as he wrote, like a brother. This form of appeal rarely fails to touch the basest man. "Are you acting towards other women in the way you would have men act to-wards you sister?" George Sand smokes, wears male attire, wishes to be ad-dressed as "Mon frère;"—perhaps, if she found those who were as broth-ers, indeed, she would not care whether she were brother or sister.[93]

---

[92] Characters in William Godwin's novel *St. Leon* (1799) (Dickenson 234). Fuller's em-phasis on Godwin's and Wollstonecraft's relationship as that of "brother and sister" fol-lows romantic conventions regarding the ideal of desexualized, spiritual relationships between men and women, such as one finds in G. W. F. Hegel's *Phenomenology of Mind* (1807) and *The Philosophy of History* (1822). [Ed.]

[93] Since writing the above, I have read with great satisfaction, the following sonnets ad-dressed to George Sand by a woman who has precisely the qualities that the author of Si-mon and Indiana lacks. It is such a woman, so unblemished in character, so high in aim, and pure in soul, that should address this other, as noble in nature, but clouded by er-ror, and struggling with circumstances. It is such women that will do such justice. They are not afraid to look for virtue and reply to aspiration, among those who have *not* "dwelt in decencies forever." It is a source of pride and happiness to read this address from the heart of Elizabeth Barrett.

TO GEORGE SAND

A Desire

Thou large-brained woman and large-hearted man,
    Self-called George Sand! whose soul, amid the lions
    Of thy tumultous senses moans defiance,
And answers roar for roar, as spirits can:
I would some mild miraculous thunder ran
    Above the applauded circus, in appliance
    Of thine own nobler nature's strength and science,
        Drawing two pinions, white as wings of swan,
From the strong shoulders, to amaze the place
    With holier light! that thou to woman's claim,
And man's might join, beside, the angel's grace
    Of a pure genius sancitified from blame;
Till child and maiden pressed to thine embrace,
    To kiss upon thy lips a stainless fame.

We rejoice to see that she, who expresses such a painful contempt for men in most of her works, as shows she must have known great wrong from them, depicting in "La Roche Mauprat," a man raised by the workings of love, from the depths of savage sensualism, to a moral and intellectual life.[94] It was love for a pure object, for a steadfast woman, one of those who, the Italian said, could make the stair to heaven.

This author, beginning like the many in assault upon bad institutions, and external ills, yet deepening the experience through comparative freedom, sees at last, that the only efficient remedy must come from individual character. These bad institutions, indeed, it may always be replied, prevent individuals from forming good character, therefore we must remove them. Agreed, yet keep steadily the higher aim in view. Could you clear away all the bad forms of society, it is vain, unless the individual begin to be ready for better. There must be a parallel movement in these two branches of life. And all the rules left by Moses availed less to further the best life than the living example of one Messiah.

Still, still the mind of the age struggles confusedly with these problems, better discerning as yet the ill it can no longer bear, than the good by which it may supersede it. But women, like Sand, will speak now and cannot be silenced; their characters and their eloquence alike foretell an era when such as they shall easier learn to lead true lives. But though such forebode,

---

TO THE SAME

A Recognition

True genius, but true woman! dost deny
    Thy woman's nature with a manly scorn,
And break away the gauds and armlets worn
    By weaker women in capitivity?
Ah, vain denial! that revolted cry
    Is sobbed in by a woman's voice forlorn:—
Thy woman's hair, my sister, all unshorn,
    Floats back dishevelled strength in agony,
Disproving thy man's name, and while before
    The world thou burnest in a poet-fire,
We see thy woman-heart beat evermore
    Through the large flame. Beat purer, heart, and higher,
Till God unsex thee on the spirit-shore;
    To which alone unsexing, purely aspire.

This last sonnet seems to have been written after seeing the picture of Sand, which represents her in a man's dress, but with long loose hair, and an eye whose mournful fire is impressive even in the caricatures. [Fuller's note.]

[94] George Sand, *La Roche Mauprat* (1837). [Ed.]

not such shall be the parents of it.[95] Those who would reform the world must show that they do not speak in the heat of wild impulse; their lives must be unstained by passionate error; they must be severe lawgivers to themselves. They must be religious students of the divine purpose with regard to man, if they would not confound the fancies of a day with the requisitions of eternal good. Their liberty must be the liberty of law and knowledge. But, as to the transgressions against custom which have caused such outcry against those of noble intention, it may be observed, that the resolve of Eloisa to be only the mistress of Abelard, was that of one who saw in practice around her, the contract of marriage made the seal of degradation. Shelley feared not to be fettered, unless so to be was to be false.[96] Wherever abuses are seen, the timid will suffer; the bold will protest. But society has a right to outlaw them till she has revised her law; and this she must be taught to do, by one who speaks with authority, not in anger or haste.

If Godwin's choice of the calumniated authoress of the "Rights of Woman," for his honored wife, be a sign of a new era, no less so is an article to which I have alluded some pages back, published five or six years ago in one of the English Reviews, where the writer, in doing full justice to Eloisa, shows his bitter regret that she lives not now to love him, who might have known better how to prize her love than did the egotistical Abelard.

These marriages, these characters, with all their imperfections, express an onward tendency. They speak of aspiration of soul, of energy of mind, seeking clearness and freedom. Of a like promise are the tracts lately published by Goodwyn Barmby, (the European Pariah, as he calls himself,) and his wife Catharine.[97] Whatever we may think of their measures, we see in them wedlock; the two minds are wed by the only contract that can permanently avail, of a common faith and a common purpose.

We might mention instances, nearer home, of minds, partners in work and in life, sharing together, on equal terms, public and private interests, and which were not, on any side, the aspect of offence shown by those last-named: persons who steer straight onward, yet, in our comparatively free life, have not been obliged to run their heads against any wall. But the prin-

---

[95] Appendix, E. [Fuller's note.]

[96] Percy Bysshe Shelley (1792–1822) married Harriet Westbrook in 1811 even though he was an atheist and opposed to the institution of marriage. In 1814, he left Harriet for Mary Godwin, whom he married after Harriet committed suicide (Dickenson 234). [Ed.]

[97] John Goodwyn Barmby (1820–81), Christian socialist and Unitarian minister, and his wife Catharine. [Ed.]

ciples which guide them might, under petrified and oppressive institutions, have made them warlike, paradoxical, and in some sense, Pariahs. The phenomena are different, the law is the same, in all these cases. Men and women have been obliged to build up their house anew from the very foundation. If they found stone ready in the quarry, they took it peaceably, otherwise they alarmed the country by pulling down old towers to get materials.

These are all instances of marriage as intellectual companionship. The parties meet mind to mind, and a mutual trust is produced, which can buckler them against a million. They work together for a common purpose, and, in all these instances, with the same implement, the pen. The pen and the writing-desk furnish forth as naturally the retirement of woman as of man.

A pleasing expression, in this kind, is afforded by the union in the names of the Howitts. William and Mary Howitt we heard named together for years, supposing them to be brother and sister; the equality of labors and reputation, even so, was auspicious; more so, now we find them man and wife. In his late work on Germany, Howitt mentions his wife,[98] with pride, as one among the constellation of distinguished English-women, and in a graceful simple manner.

Our pleasure, indeed, in this picture, is marred by the vulgar apparition which has of late displaced the image, which we had from her writings cherished of a pure and gentle Quaker poetess. The surprise was painful as that of the little sentimentalist in the tale of "L'Amie Inconnue" when she found her correspondent, the poetess, the "adored Araminta," scolding her servants in Welsh, and eating toasted cheese and garlic. Still, we cannot forget what we have thought of the partnership in literature and affection between the Howitts, the congenial pursuits and productions, the pedestrian tours where the married pair showed that marriage, on a wide enough basis, does not destroy the "inexhaustible" entertainment which lovers found in one another's company.

In naming these instances, I do not mean to imply that community of employment is essential to union of husband and wife, more than to the union of friends. Harmony exists in difference, no less than in likeness, if only the same key-note govern both parts. Woman the poem, man the

---

[98] William Howitt (1792–1879), Quaker poet and author of *The Rural and Domestic Life of Germany* (1842), and his wife Mary Botham Howitt (1799–1888), Quaker poet and political activist, author of "The Spider and the Fly," and a member of the English women's rights group that advocated married women's rights to their earnings and property (Dickenson 235). [Ed.]

poet! Woman the heart, man the head! Such divisions are only important when they are never to be transcended. If nature is never bound down, nor the voice of inspiration stifled, that is enough. We are pleased that women should write and speak, if they feel the need of it, from having something to tell; but silence for ages would be no misfortune, if that silence be from divine command, and not from man's tradition.

While Goetz Von Berlichigen rides to battle, his wife is busy in the kitchen; but difference of occupation does not prevent that community of inward life, that perfect esteem, with which he says—

"Whom God loves, to him gives he such a wife." [99]

Manzoni thus dedicates his "Adelchi." [100]

"To his beloved and venerated wife, Enrichetta Luigia Blondel, who, with conjugal affection and maternal wisdom, has preserved a virgin mind, the author dedicates this "Adelchi," grieving that he could not, by a more splendid and more durable monument, honor the dear name, and the memory of so many virtues."

The relation could not be fairer, or more equal, if she, too, had written poems. Yet the position of the parties might have been the reverse as well; the woman might have sung the deeds, given voice to the life of the man, and beauty would have been the result, as we see, in pictures of Arcadia, the nymph singing to the shepherds, or the shepherd, with his pipe, alluring the nymphs; either makes a good picture. The sounding lyre requires, not muscular strength, but energy of soul to animate the hand which would control it. Nature seems to delight in varying the arrangements, as if to show that she will be fettered by no rule, and we must admit the same varieties that she admits.

The fourth and highest grade of marriage union, is the religious, which may be expressed as pilgrimage towards a common shrine. This includes the others; home sympathies and household wisdom, for these pilgrims must know how to assist each other along the dusty way; intellectual communion, for how sad it would be on such a journey to have a companion to whom you could not communicate thoughts and aspirations as they sprang to life; who would have no feeling for the prospects that open, more and more glorious as we advance; who would never see the flowers that may be gathered by the most industrious traveller. It must include all these.

---

[99] Goethe's play *Goetz von Berlichingen* (1773), about a German knight (Dickenson 253). [Ed.]

[100] Manzoni's tragedy *Adelchi* (1822). [Ed.]

Such a fellow-pilgrim Count Zinzendorf seems to have found in his Countess, of whom he thus writes: [101]

"Twenty-five years' experience has shown me that just the help-mate whom I have, is the only one that could suit my vocation. Who else could have so carried through my family affairs? Who lived so spotlessly before the world? Who so wisely aided me in my rejection of a dry morality? Who so clearly set aside the Pharisaism which, as years passed, threatened to creep in among us? Who so deeply discerned as to the spirits of delusion, which sought to bewilder us? Who would have governed my whole economy so wisely, richly, and hospitably, when circumstances commanded? Who have taken indifferently the part of servant or mistress, without, on the one side, affecting an especial spirituality; on the other, being sullied by any worldly pride? Who, in a community where all ranks are eager to be on a level, would, from wise and real causes, have known how to maintain inward and outward distinctions? Who, without a murmur, have seen her husband encounter such dangers by land and sea? Who undertaken with him, and *sustained* such astonishing pilgrimages? Who, amid such difficulties, always held up her head and supported me? Who found such vast sums of money, and acquitted them on her own credit? And, finally, who, of all human beings, could so well understand and interpret to others my inner and outer being as this one, of such nobleness in her way of thinking, such great intellectual capacity, and free from the theological perplexities that enveloped me!"

Let any one peruse, with all their power, the lineaments of this portrait, and see if the husband had not reason, with this air of solemn rapture and conviction, to challenge comparison? We are reminded of the majestic cadence of the line whose feet step in the just proportions of Humanity,

"Daughter of God and Man, accomplished Eve!" [102]

An observer [103] adds this testimony:

"We may, in many marriages, regard it as the best arrangement, if the man has so much advantage over his wife, that she can, without much thought of her own, be, by him, led and directed as by a father. But it was

---

[101] Nicolaus Ludwig, Graf von Zinzendorf (1700–60), and his wife Erdmute, who collaborated in his work as a German religious and social reformer. He founded the Moravian Brotherhood, which had wide influence as missionaries in Europe and America (especially in the Northeast). [Ed.]

[102] John Milton, *Paradise Lost* 4.660. [Ed.]

[103] Spangenberg [Fuller's note]. August Gottlieb Spangenberg (1704–92) succeeded Zinzendorf as head of the German Moravians. [Ed.]

not so with the Count and his consort. She was not made to be a copy; she was an original; and, while she loved and honored him, she thought for herself, on all subjects, with so much intelligence, that he could and did look on her as sister and friend also."

Compare with this refined specimen of a religiously civilized life, the following imperfect sketch of a North American Indian, and we shall see that the same causes will always produce the same results. The Flying Pigeon (Ratchewaine) was the wife of a barbarous chief, who had six others, but she was his only true wife, because the only one of a strong and pure character, and, having this, inspired a veneration, as like as the mind of the man permitted, to that inspired by the Countess Zinzendorf. She died when her son was only four years old, yet left on his mind a feeling of reverent love worthy the thought of Christian chivalry. Grown to manhood, he shed tears on seeing her portrait.

THE FLYING PIGEON[104]

"Ratchewaine was chaste, mild, gentle in her disposition, kind, generous, and devoted to her husband. A harsh word was never known to proceed from her mouth; nor was she ever known to be in a passion. Mahaskah used to say of her, after her death, that her hand was shut, when those, who did not want, came into her presence; but when the really poor came in, it was like a strainer full of holes, letting all she held in it pass through. In the exercise of generous feeling she was uniform. It was not indebted for its exercise to whim, to caprice, or partiality. No matter of what nation the applicant for her bounty was, or whether at war or peace with her nation; if he were hungry, she fed him; if naked, she clothed him; and if houseless, she gave him shelter. The continued exercise of this generous feeling kept her poor. And she has known to give away her last blanket—all the honey that was in the lodge, the last bladder of bear's oil, and the last piece of dried meat.

"She was scrupulously exact in the observance of all the religious rites which her faith imposed upon her. Her conscience is represented to have been extremely tender. She often feared that her acts were displeasing to the Great Spirit, when she would blacken her face, and retire to some lone place, and fast and pray."

To these traits should be added, but for want of room, anecdotes which show the quick decision and vivacity of her mind. Her face was in harmony

---

[104] The next two paragraphs are from Thomas McKenney and James Hall, *History of the Indian Tribes of North America* (1836–44). Hall compiled his own collections of Native American legends and stories, such as *The Wilderness and the War-Path* (1846), and he is infamously represented as "Judge James Hall," the "Indian-Hater," in Herman Melville's *The Confidence-Man: His Masquerade* (1857). [Ed.]

with this combination. Her brow is as ideal and the eyes and lids as devout and modest as the Italian pictures of the Madonna, while the lower part of the face has the simplicity and childish strength of the Indian race. Her picture presents the finest specimen of Indian beauty we have ever seen.

Such a woman is the sister and friend of all beings, as the worthy man is their brother and helper.

With like pleasure we survey the pairs wedded on the eve of missionary effort. They, indeed, are fellow pilgrims on a well-made road, and whether or not they accomplish all they hope for the sad Hindoo, or the nearer savage, we feel that, in the burning waste, their love is like to be a healing dew, in the forlorn jungle, a tent of solace to one another. They meet, as children of one Father, to read together one book of instruction.[105]

We must insert in this connection the most beautiful picture presented by ancient literature of wedded love under this noble form.

It is from the romance in which Xenophon, the chivalrous Greek, presents his ideal of what human nature should be.[106]

The generals of Cyrus had taken captive a princess, a woman of unequalled beauty, and hastened to present her to the prince as the part of the spoil he would think most worthy of his acceptance.

Cyrus visits the lady, and is filled with immediate admiration by the modesty and majesty with which she receives him. He finds her name is Panthea, and that she is the wife of Abradatus, a young king whom she entirely loves. He protects her as a sister, in his camp, till he can restore her to her husband.

After the first transports of joy at this re-union, the heart of Panthea is bent on showing her love and gratitude to her magnanimous and delicate protector. And as she has nothing so precious to give as the aid of Abradatus, that is what she most wishes to offer. Her husband is of one soul with her in this, as in all things.

The description of her grief and self-destruction, after the death which ensued upon this devotion, I have seen quoted, but never that of their parting when she sends him forth to battle. I shall copy both. If they have been read by any of my readers, they may be so again with profit in this connexion, for never were the heroism of a true woman, and the purity of love, in a true marriage, painted in colors more delicate or more lively.

---

[105] Fuller fails to recognize that the spiritual love of such married missionaries disguises their colonial purposes in their efforts to convert "the sad Hindoo[s]" or "the nearer savage." [Ed.]

[106] In the next few pages, Fuller combines quotations from and paraphrase of Xenophon's *Cyropaedia* to tell the story of King Cyrus and Panthea. [Ed.]

"The chariot of Abradatus, that had four perches and eight horses, was completely adorned for him; and when he was going to put on his linen corslet, which was a sort of armor used by those of his country, Panthea brought him a golden helmet, and arm-pieces, broad bracelets for his wrists, a purple habit that reached down to his feet, and hung in folds at the bottom, and a crest dyed of a violet color. These things she had made unknown to her husband, and by taking the measure of his armor. He wondered when he saw them, and inquired thus of Panthea: 'And have you made me these arms, woman, by destroying your own ornaments?' 'No, by Jove,' said Panthea, 'not what is the most valuable of them; for it is you, if you appear to others to be what I think you, that will be my greatest ornament.' And, saying that, she put on him the armor, and, though she endeavored to conceal it, the tears poured down her cheeks. When Abradatus, who was before a man of fine appearance, was set out in those arms, he appeared the most beautiful and noble of all, especially, being likewise so by nature. Then, taking the reins from the driver, he was just preparing to mount the chariot, when Panthea, after she had desired all that were there to retire, thus said:

"'O Abradatus! if ever there was a woman who had a greater regard to her husband than to her own soul, I believe you know that I am such an one; what need I therefore speak of things in particular? for I reckon that my actions have convinced you more than any words I can now use. And yet, though I stand thus affected towards you, as you know I do, I swear by this friendship of mine and yours, that I certainly would rather choose to be put under ground jointly with you, approving yourself a brave man, than live with you in disgrace and shame; so much do I think you and myself worthy of noblest things. Then I think that we both lie under great obligations to Cyrus, that, when I was a captive, and chosen out for himself, he thought fit to treat me neither as a slave, nor, indeed, as a woman of mean account, but he took and kept me for you, as if I were his brother's wife. Besides, when Araspes, who was my guard, went away from him, I promised him, that, if he would allow me to send for you, you would come to him, and approve yourself a much better and more faithful friend than Araspes.'

"Thus she spoke; and Abradatus being struck with admiration at her discourse, laying his hand gently on her head, and lifting up his eyes to heaven, made this prayer: 'Do thou, O greatest Jove! grant me to appear a husband worthy of Panthea, and a friend worthy of Cyrus, who has done us so much honor!'

"Having said this, he mounted the chariot by the door of the driver's seat; and, after he had got up, when the driver shut the door, Panthea, who had now no other way to salute him, kissed the seat of the chariot. The chariot then moved, and she, unknown to him, followed, till Abradatus turning about, and seeing her, said: 'Take courage, Panthea! Fare you happily and well, and now go your ways.' On this her women and servants carried her to her conveyance, and, laying her down, concealed her by throwing the covering of a tent over her. The people, though Abradatus and his chariot made a noble spectacle, were not able to look at him till Panthea was gone."

After the battle—

"Cyrus calling to some of his servants, 'Tell me,' said he, 'has any one seen Abradatus? for I admire that he now does not appear.' One replied, 'My sovereign, it is because he is not living, but died in the battle as he broke in with his chariot on the Egyptians. All the rest, except his particular companions, they say, turned off when they saw the Egyptians' compact body. His wife is now said to have taken up his dead body, to have placed it in the carriage that she herself was conveyed in, and to have brought it hither to some place on the river Pactolus, and her servants are digging a grave on a certain elevation. They say that his wife, after setting him out with all the ornaments she has, is sitting on the ground with his head on her knees.' Cyrus, hearing this, gave himself a blow on the thigh, mounted his horse at a leap, and taking with him a thousand horse, rode away to this scene of affliction; but gave orders to Gadatas and Gobryas to take with them all the rich ornaments proper for a friend and an excellent man, deceased, and to follow after him; and whoever had herds of cattle with him, he ordered them to take both oxen, and horses, and sheep in good number, and to bring them away to the place where, by inquiry, they should find him to be, that he might sacrifice these to Abradatus.

"As soon as he saw the woman sitting on the ground, and the dead body there lying, he shed tears at the afflicting sight, and said: 'Alas! thou brave and faithful soul, hast thou left us, and art thou gone?' At the same time he took him by the right hand, and the hand of the deceased came away, for it had been cut off, with a sword, by the Egyptians. He, at the sight of this, became yet much more concerned than before. The woman shrieked out in a lamentable manner, and, taking the hand from Cyrus, kissed it, fitted it to its proper place again, as well as she could, and said, 'The rest, Cyrus, is in the same condition, but what need you see it? And I know that I was not one of the least concerned in these his sufferings, and, perhaps, you were not less so, for I, fool that I was! frequently exhorted him to behave in such a manner as to appear a friend to you, worthy of notice; and I know he never thought of what he himself should suffer, but of what he should do to please you. He is dead, therefore,' said she, 'without reproach, and I, who urged him on, sit here alive.' Cyrus shedding tears for some time in silence, then spoke—'He has died, woman, the noblest death; for he has died victorious! do you adorn him with these things that I furnish you with.'

(Gobryas and Gadatas were then come up and had brought rich ornaments in great abundance with them.) 'Then,' said he, 'be assured that he shall not want respect and honor in all other things: but, over the above, multitudes shall concur in raising him a monument that shall be worthy of us, and all the sacrifices shall be made him that are proper to be made in honor of a brave man. You shall not be left destitute, but, for the sake of your modesty and every other virtue, I will pay you all other honors, as well as place those about you who will conduct you wherever you please. Do you but make it known to me where it is that you desire to be conveyed to.' And Panthea replied, 'Be confident, Cyrus,' said she, 'I will not conceal from you to whom it is that I desire to go.'

"He, having said this, went away with great pity for her that she should have lost such a husband, and for the man that he should have left such a wife behind him, never to see her more. Panthea then gave orders for her servants to retire, 'Till such time,' said she, 'as I shall have lamented my husband, as I please.' Her nurse she bid to stay, and gave orders that, when she was dead, she would wrap her and her husband up in one mantle together. The nurse, after having repeatedly begged her not to do this, and meeting with no success, but observing her to grow angry, sat herself down, breaking out into tears. She, being before-hand provided with a sword, killed herself, and, laying her head down on her husband's breast, she died. The nurse set up a lamentable cry, and covered them both as Panthea had directed.[107]

"Cyrus, as soon as he was informed of what the woman had done, being struck with it, went to help her if he could. The servants, three in number, seeing what had been done, drew their swords and killed themselves, as they stood at the place where she had ordered them. And the monument is now said to have been raised by continuing the mount on to the servants; and on a pillar above, they say, the names of the man and woman were written in Syriac letters.

"Below were three pillars, and they were inscribed thus, 'Of the servants.' Cyrus, when he came to this melancholy scene, was struck with admiration of the woman, and, having lamented over her, went away. He took care, as was proper, that all the funeral rites should be paid them in the noblest manner, and the monument, they say, was raised up to a very great size."

These be the ancients, who, so many assert had no idea of the dignity of woman, or of marriage. Such love Xenophon could paint as subsisting be-

---

[107] Fuller's celebration of Panthea falling on her dead husband's sword contributes to the romantic ideology of feminine sacrifice that was part of the gender hierarchies of the nineteenth century. [Ed.]

tween those who after death "would see one another never more." Thousands of years have passed since, and with the reception of the cross, the nations assume the belief that those who part thus, may meet again and forever, if spiritually fitted to one another, as Abradatus and Panthea were, and yet do we see such marriages among them? If at all, how often?

I must quote two more short passages from Xenophon, for he is a writer who pleases me well.

Cyrus receiving the Armenians whom he had conquered.

"Tigranes," said he, "at what rate would you purchase the regaining of your wife?" Now Tigranes happened to be *but lately married*, and had a very great love for his wife," (that clause perhaps sounds *modern*.)

"Cyrus," said he, "I would ransom her at the expense of my life."

"Take then your own to yourself," said he. * * *

When they came home, one talked of Cyrus' wisdom, another of his patience and resolution, another of his mildness. One spoke of his beauty and the smallness of his person, and, on that, Tigranes asked his wife, "And do you, Armenian dame, think Cyrus handsome?" "Truly," said she, "I did not look at him." "At whom, then, did you look?" said Tigranes. "At him who said that, to save me from servitude, he would ransom me at the expense of his own life."

From the Banquet. — [108]

Socrates, who observed her with pleasure, said, "This young girl has confirmed me in the opinion I have had, for a long time, that the female sex are nothing inferior to ours, excepting only in strength of body, or, perhaps, in steadiness of judgment."

In the Economics, the manner in which the husband gives counsel to his young wife, presents the model of politeness and refinement.[109] Xenophon is thoroughly the gentleman, gentle in breeding and in soul. All the men he describes are so, while the shades of manner are distinctly marked. There is the serene dignity of Socrates, with gleams of playfulness thrown across its cool religious shades, the princely mildness of Cyrus, and the more domestic elegance of the husband in the Economics.

There is no way that men sin more against refinement, as well as discretion, than in their conduct towards their wives. Let them look at the men of Xenophon. Such would know how to give counsel, for they would know how to receive it. They would feel that the most intimate relations claimed most, not least, of refined courtesy. They would not suppose that confidence

---

[108] Plato, *Symposium*. [Ed.]

[109] Xenophon, *Economics*. [Ed.]

justified carelessness, nor the reality of affection want of delicacy in the expression of it.

Such men would be too wise to hide their affairs from the wife and then expect her to act as if she knew them. They would know that if she is expected to face calamity with courage, she must be instructed and trusted in prosperity, or, if they had failed in wise confidence such as the husband shows in the Economics, they would be ashamed of anger or querulous surprise at the results that naturally follow.

Such men would not be exposed to the bad influence of bad wives, for all wives, bad or good, loved or unloved, inevitably influence their husbands, from the power their position not merely gives, but necessitates, of coloring evidence and infusing feelings in hours when the patient, shall I call him? is off his guard. Those who understand the wife's mind, and think it worth while to respect her springs of action, know better where they are. But to the bad or thoughtless man who lives carelessly and irreverently so near another mind, the wrong he does daily back upon himself recoils. A Cyrus, an Abradatus knows where he stands.

But to return to the thread of my subject.

Another sign of the times is furnished by the triumphs of female authorship. These have been great and constantly increasing. Women have taken possession of so many provinces for which men had pronounced them unfit, that though these still declare there are some inaccessible to them, it is difficult to say just *where* they must stop.

The shining names of famous women have cast light upon the path of the sex, and many obstructions have been removed. When a Montague[110] could learn better than her brother, and use her lore afterward to such purpose, as an observer, it seemed amiss to hinder woman from preparing themselves to see, or from seeing all they could, when prepared. Since Somerville[111] has achieved so much, will any young girl be prevented from seeking a knowledge of the physical sciences, if she wishes it? De Stael's[112]

---

[110] "Lady Mary Wortley Montague (1689–1762), English travel writer, feminist, and sister of novelist Henry Fielding. She eloped with Edward Wortley Montague, ambassador to Turkey (1716–18)," and wrote about Turkish life and culture, including knowledge about inoculation against smallpox, which she introduced to England (Dickenson 236). [Ed.]

[111] Mary Fairfax Somerville (1780–1872), Scottish mathematician. Her second husband, surgeon William Somerville, introduced her to London's intellectual circles. She presented work to the Royal Society and was elected an honorary member (Dickenson 236). [Ed.]

[112] Anne Louise Germaine Necker (1766–1817), Baroness de Staël, known as "Madame de Staël." A French novelist, political reformer, and literary critic, she was best known for her novel and its heroine, *Corinne* (1807). Fuller was known as the "New England Corinne." In this paragraph, Fuller criticizes Madame de Staël for her affairs, notably with the French novelist Benjamin Constant (Dickenson 236). [Ed.]

name was not so clear of offence; she could not forget the woman in the thought; while she was instructing you as a mind, she wished to be admired as a woman; sentimental tears often dimmed the eagle glance. Her intellect too, with all its splendor, trained in a drawing-room, fed on flattery, was tainted and flawed; yet its beams make the obscurest school-house in New-England warmer and lighter to the little rugged girls, who are gathered together on its wooden bench. They may never through life hear her name, but she is not the less their benefactress.

The influence has been such, that the aim certainly is, now, in arranging school instruction for girls, to give them as fair a field as boys. As yet, indeed, these arrangements are made with little judgment or reflection; just as the tutors of Lady Jane Grey,[113] and other distinguished women of her time, taught them Latin and Greek, because they knew nothing else themselves, so now the improvement in the education of girls is to be made by giving them young men as teachers, who only teach what has been taught themselves at college, while methods and topics need revision for these new subjects, which could better be made by those who had experienced the same wants. Women are, often, at the head of these institutions, but they have, as yet, seldom been thinking women, capable to organize a new whole for the wants of the time, and choose persons to officiate in the departments. And when some portion of instruction is got of a good sort from the school, the far greater proportion which is infused from the general atmosphere of society contradicts its purport. Yet books and a little elementary instruction are not furnished, in vain. Women are better aware how great and rich the universe is, not so easily blinded by narrowness or partial views of a home circle.[114] "Her mother did so before her," is no longer a sufficient excuse. Indeed, it was never received as an excuse to mitigate the severity of censure, but was adduced as a reason, rather, why there should be no effort made for reformation.

Whether much or little has been done or will be done, whether women will add to the talent of narration, the power of systematizing, whether they will carve marble, as well as draw and paint, is not important. But that it should be acknowledged that they have intellect which needs developing, that they should not be considered complete, if beings of affection and habit alone, is important.

---

[113] Lady Jane Grey (1537–54), great granddaughter of Henry VII of England. A claimant to the Crown, she ruled for nine days in 1553. Educated by tutors hired by Henry VIII's wife Catherine Parr, Jane Grey was noted for her learning (Dickenson 236). [Ed.]

[114] Fuller argues that women's formal education remains governed by patriarchal values even when the teachers are women. She argues that the curriculum for women must take into account a different social order without conventional gender divisions. [Ed.]

Yet even this acknowledgement, rather conquered by woman than proffered by man, has been sullied by the usual selfishness. So much is said of women being better educated, that they may become better companions and mothers *for men*. They should be fit for such companionship, and we have mentioned, with satisfaction, instances where it has been established. Earth knows no fairer, holier relation than that of a mother. It is one which, rightly understood, must both promote and require the highest attainments. But a being of infinite scope must not be treated with an exclusive view to any one relation. Give the soul free course, let the organization, both of body and mind, be freely developed, and the being will be fit for any and every relation to which it may be called. The intellect, no more than the sense of hearing, is to be cultivated merely that she may be a more valuable companion to man, but because the Power who gave a power, by its mere existence, signifies that it must be brought out towards perfection.

In this regard of self-dependence, and a greater simplicity and fulness of being, we must hail as a preliminary the increase of the class contemptuously designated as old maids.

We cannot wonder at the aversion with which old bachelors and old maids have been regarded. Marriage is the natural means of forming a sphere, of taking root on the earth; it requires more strength to do this without such an opening; very many have failed, and their imperfections have been in every one's way. They have been more partial, more harsh, more officious and impertinent than those compelled by severer friction to render themselves endurable. Those, who have a more full experience of the instincts, have a distrust, as to whether they can be thoroughly human and humane, such as is hinted in the saying, "Old maids' and bachelors' children are well cared for," which derides at once their ignorance and their presumption.

Yet the business of society has become so complex, that it could now scarcely be carried on without the presence of these despised auxiliaries; and detachments from the army of aunts and uncles are wanted to stop gaps in every hedge. They rove about, mental and moral Ishmaelites, pitching their tents amid the fixed and ornamented homes of men.[115]

In a striking variety of forms, genius of late, both at home and abroad, has paid its tribute to the character of the Aunt, and the Uncle, recognizing in these personages the spiritual parents, who had supplied defects in the treatment of the busy or careless actual parents.

---

[115] Ishmael and Hagar, his mother, Abraham's mistress, were cast out of the family after the birth of Abraham's legitimate son, Isaac, and were forced to wander. Cf. Gen. 21.14 – 21 and the narrator of Herman Melville's *Moby-Dick* (1851), Ishmael. [Ed.]

They also gain a wider, if not so deep experience. Those who are not intimately and permanently linked with others, are thrown upon themselves, and, if they do not there find peace and incessant life, there is none to flatter them that they are not very poor and very mean.

A position which so constantly admonishes, may be of inestimable benefit. The person may gain, undistracted by other relationships, a closer communion with the one. Such a use is made of it by saints and sybils. Or she may be one of the lay sisters of charity, a Caness, bound by an inward vow! Or the useful drudge of all men, the Martha,[116] much sought, little prized. Or the intellectual interpreter of the varied life she sees; the Urania[117] of a half-formed world's twilight.

Or she may combine all these. Not "needing to care that she may please a husband," a frail and limited being, her thoughts may turn to the centre, and she may, by steadfast contemplation entering into the secret of truth and love, use it for the use of all men, instead of a chosen few, and interpret through it all the forms of life. It is possible, perhaps, to be at once a priestly servant, and a loving muse.

Saints and geniuses have often chosen a lonely position in the faith that if, undisturbed by the pressure of near ties, they would give themselves up to the inspiring spirit, it would enable them to understand and reproduce life better than actual experience could.

How many old maids take this high stand, we cannot say: it is an unhappy fact, that too many who have come before the eye are gossips rather, and not always good-natured gossips. But if these abuse, and none make the best of their vocation, yet it has not failed to produce some good results. It has been seen by others, if not by themselves, that beings, likely to be left alone, need to be fortified and furnished within themselves, and education and thought have tended more and more to regard these beings as related to absolute Being, as well as to other men. It has been seen that, as the breaking of no bond ought to destroy a man, so ought the missing of none to hinder him from growing. And thus a circumstance of the time, which springs rather from its luxury than its purity, has helped to place women on the true platform.

Perhaps the next generation, looking deeper into this matter, will find that contempt is put upon old maids, or old women at all, merely because they do not use the elixir which would keep them always young. Under its influence a gem brightens yearly which is only seen to more advantage

---

[116] The common name in nineteenth-century America given to a reliable, subservient wife, probably in reference to Luke 10.40. [Ed.]

[117] The Greek muse of astronomy (Dickenson 237). [Ed.]

through the fissures Time makes in the casket.[118] No one thinks of Michael Angelo's Persican Sibyl, or St. Theresa, or Tasso's Leonora, or the Greek Electra, as an old maid, more than of Michael Angelo or Canova as old bachelors, though all had reached the period in life's course appointed to take that degree.[119]

See a common woman at forty; scarcely has she the remains of beauty, of any soft poetic grace which gave her attraction as woman, which kindled the hearts of those who looked on her to sparkling thoughts, or diffused round her a roseate air of gentle love. See her, who was, indeed, a lovely girl, in the coarse full-blown dahlia flower of what is commonly called matron-beauty, fat, fair, and forty, showily dressed, and with manners as broad and full as her frill or satin cloak. People observe, "how well she is preserved;" "she is a fine woman still," they say. This woman, whether as a duchess in diamonds, or one of our city dames in mosaics, charms the poet's heart no more, and would look much out of place kneeling before the Madonna. She "does well the honors of her house," "leads society," is, in short, always spoken and thought of upholstery-wise.

Or see that care-worn face, from which every soft line is blotted, those faded eyes from which lonely tears have driven the flashes of fancy, the mild white beam of a tender enthusiasm. This woman is not so ornamental to a tea party; yet she would please better, in picture. Yet surely she, no more than the other, looks as a human being should at the end of forty years. Forty years! have they bound those brows with no garland? shed in the lamp no drop of ambrosial oil?

Not so looked the Iphigenia in Aulis.[120] Her forty years had seen her in anguish, in sacrifice, in utter loneliness. But those pains were borne for her father and her country; the sacrifice she had made pure for herself and those around her. Wandering alone at night in the vestal solitude of her im-

---

[118] Appendix, F. [Fuller's note.]

[119] Michelangelo's fresco of the Persican Sibyl, oldest of the ancient oracles, is on the ceiling of the Sistine Chapel. Saint Theresa of Avila (1515–82) was a Spanish mystic. Leonora d'Este was a patron of the Italian poet Torquato Tasso. Electra was the daughter of Agamemnon and Clytemnestra and helps her brother avenge their father's murder by Clytemnestra and her lover Aegisthus (Dickenson 237). Antonio Canova (1757–1822) was an Italian sculptor who helped promote the neoclassical revival in sculpture, in which many American women sculptors, such as Harriet Hosmer and Louisa Lander, participated. [Ed.]

[120] See Euripides, *Iphigenia in Aulis* and *Iphigenia at Tauris*. As Fuller reads the figure of Iphigenia in these Greek tragedies, then turns to an interpretation of Michelangelo's Persican Sibyl, she epitomizes the sort of cultural criticism that interprets the political and social consequences of different media. [Ed.]

prisoning grove, she has looked up through its "living summits" to the stars, which shed down into her aspect their own lofty melody. At forty she would not misbecome the marble.

Not so looks the Persica. She is withered, she is faded; the drapery that enfolds her has, in its dignity an angularity, too, that tells of age, of sorrow, of a stern composure to the *must*. But her eye, that torch of the soul, is untamed, and in the intensity of her reading, we see a soul invincibly young in faith and hope. Her age is her charm, for it is the night of the Past that gives this beacon fire leave to shine. Wither more and more, black Chrysalid![121] thou dost but give the winged beauty time to mature its splendors.

Not so looked Victoria Colonna,[122] after her life of a great hope, and of true conjugal fidelity. She had been, not merely a bride, but a wife, and each hour had helped to plume the noble bird. A coronet of pearls will not shame her brow; it is white and ample, a worthy altar for love and thought.

Even among the North American Indians, a race of men as completely engaged in mere instinctive life as almost any in the world, and where each chief, keeping many wives as useful servants, of course looks with no kind eye on celibacy in woman, it was excused in the following instance mentioned by Mrs. Jameson.[123] A woman dreamt in youth that she was betrothed to the Sun. She built her a wigwam apart, filled it with emblems of her alliance, and means of an independent life. There she passed her days, sustained by her own exertions, and true to her supposed engagement.

In any tribe, we believe, a woman, who lived as if she was betrothed to the Sun, would be tolerated, and the rays which made her youth blossom sweetly, would crown her with a halo in age.

There is, on this subject, a nobler view than heretofore, if not the noblest, and improvement here must coincide with that in the view taken of marriage.

We must have units before we can have union, says one of the ripe thinkers of the times.

If larger intellectual resources begin to be deemed needful to woman, still more is a spiritual dignity in her, or even the mere assumption of it,

---

[121] A chrysalid is the insect larva inside a cocoon, hence anticipating some natural metamorphosis. [Ed.]

[122] Vittoria Colonna (1490–1549) wrote over one hundred elegies about her husband, who died from battle wounds in 1525. In the late 1530s, she began a long friendship with Michelangelo, with whom she exchanged letters and sonnets (Dickenson 237). [Ed.]

[123] Anna Brownell Jameson (1794–1860) relates this story of a Chippewa woman in *Winter Studies and Summer Rambles in Canada* (1838). [Ed.]

360 // MARGARET FULLER

looked upon with respect. Joanna Southcote and Mother Anne Lee are sure of a band of disciples; Ecstatica, Dolorosa, of enraptured believers who will visit them in their lowly huts, and wait for days to revere them in their trances. The foreign noble traverses land and sea to hear a few words from the lips of the lowly peasant girl, whom he believes especially visited by the Most High.[124] Very beautiful, in this way, was the influence of the invalid of St. Petersburg, as described by De Maistre.

Mysticism, which may be defined as the brooding soul of the world, cannot fail of its oracular promise as to woman. "The mothers" — "The mother of all things," are expressions of thought which lead the mind towards this side of universal growth. Whenever a mystical whisper was heard, from Behmen down to St. Simon,[125] sprang up the thought, that, if it be true, as the legend says, that humanity withers through a fault committed by and a curse laid upon woman, through her pure child, or influence, shall the new Adam, the redemption, arise. Innocence is to be replaced by virtue, dependence by a willing submission, in the heart of the Virgin Mother of the new race.

The spiritual tendency is towards the elevation of woman, but the intellectual by itself is not so. Plato sometimes seems penetrated by that high idea of love, which considers man and woman as the two-fold expression of one thought. This the angel of Swedenborg, the angel of the coming age, cannot surpass, but only explain more fully. But then again Plato, the man of intellect, treats woman in the Republic as property, and, in the Timæus, says that man, if he misuse the privileges of one life, shall be degraded into the form of woman, and then, if he do not redeem himself, into that of a bird. This, as I said above, expresses most happily how anti-poetical is this state of mind. For the poet, contemplating the world of things, selects various birds as the symbols of his most gracious and ethereal thoughts, just as he calls upon his genius, as muse, rather than as God. But the intellect, cold, is ever more masculine than feminine; warmed by emotion, it rushes towards mother earth, and puts on the forms of beauty.

The electrical, the magnetic element in woman has not been fairly

---

[124] A catalogue of holy, saintly, mystical women in history, each of whom has had some sort of antinomian experience of the divine: Joanna Southcote (1750–1814), English prophet and religious leader, claimed she would give birth to Christ's Second Coming. Mother Anne Lee (1736–84), English founder of the Shakers, claimed she was the Second Coming. Ecstatica and Dolorosa are mythic types of Christian transcendence and mourning, respectively, crucial for our apprehension of Christ's Passion. [Ed.]

[125] Jakob Boehme (1575–1624), German mystic. Claude-Henri de Rouvroy, Comte de Saint-Simon (1760–1825), French socialist and religious figure. [Ed.]

brought out at any period. Every thing might be expected from it; she has far more of it than man. This is commonly expressed by saying that her intuitions are more rapid and more correct. You will often see men of high intellect absolutely stupid in regard to the atmospheric changes, the fine invisible links which connect the forms of life around them, while common women, if pure and modest, so that a vulgar self do not overshadow the mental eye, will seize and delineate these with unerring discrimination. Women who combine this organization with creative genius, are very commonly unhappy at present. They see too much to act in conformity with those around them, and their quick impulses seem folly to those who do not discern the motives. This is an usual effect of the apparition of genius, whether in man or woman, but is more frequent with regard to the latter, because a harmony, an obvious order and self-restraining decorum, is most expected from her.

Then women of genius, even more than men, are likely to be enslaved by an impassioned sensibility. The world repels them more rudely, and they are of weaker bodily frame.

Those, who seem overladen with electricity, frighten those around them. "When she merely enters the room, I am what the French call *herissé*," [126] said a man of petty feelings and worldly character of such a woman, whose depth of eye and powerful motion announced the conductor of the mysterious fluid.

Wo to such a woman who finds herself linked to such a man in bonds too close. It is the cruellest of errors. He will detest her with all the bitterness of wounded self-love. He will take the whole prejudice of manhood upon himself, and to the utmost of his power imprison and torture her by its imperious rigors.

Yet, allow room enough, and the electric fluid will be found to invigorate and embellish, not destroy life. Such women are the great actresses, the songsters. Such traits we read in a late searching, though too French analysis of the character of Mademoiselle Rachel, by a modern La Rochefoucoult. [127] The Greeks thus represent the muses; they have not the golden serenity of

---

[126] Unnerved. [Ed.]

[127] The popular nineteenth-century actress, Rachel Félix (1821–58), born Élissa Félix to poor Jewish parents, rose from humble origins to great celebrity, playing leading roles in plays by Racine, Corneille, and Shakespeare. Miriam Rooth, the protagonist of Henry James's *The Tragic Muse* (1890), is modeled on Rachel Félix. The "modern La Rochefoucoult" must refer to the author of the essay on Rachel Félix to which Fuller is referring. Rochefoucault (1613–80) was a famous French writer of moral exempla and maxims. [Ed.]

Apollo; they are *over*-flowed with thought; there is something tragic in their air. Such are the Sibyls of Guercino,[128] the eye is over-full of expression, dilated and lustrous; it seems to have drawn the whole being into it.

Sickness is the frequent result of this over-charged existence. To this region, however misunderstood, or interpreted with presumptuous carelessness, belong the phenomena of magnetism, or mesmerism, as it is now often called, where the trance of the Ecstatica purports to be produced by the agency of one human being on another, instead of, as in her case, direct from the spirit.

The worldling has his sneer at this as at the services of religion. "The churches can always be filled with women." "Show me a man in one of your magnetic states, and I will believe."

Women are, indeed, the easy victims both of priest-craft and self-delusion, but this would not be, if the intellect was developed in proportion to the other powers. They would, then, have a regulator, and be more in equipoise, yet must retain the same nervous susceptibility, while their physical structure is such as it is.

It is with just that hope, that we welcome every thing that tends to strengthen the fibre and develope the nature on more sides. When the intellect and affections are in harmony; when intellectual consciousness is calm and deep; inspiration will not be confounded with fancy.

Then, "she who advances
   With rapturous, lyrical glances,
Singing the song of the earth, singing
   Its hymn to the Gods,"

will not be pitied, as a madwoman, nor shrunk from as unnatural.

The Greeks, who saw every thing in forms, which we are trying to ascertain as law, and classify as cause, embodied all this in the form of Cassandra. Cassandra was only unfortunate in receiving her gift too soon. The remarks, however, that the world still makes in such cases, are well expressed by the Greek dramatist.

In the Trojan Dames, there are fine touches of nature with regard to Cassandra. Hecuba[129] shows that mixture of shame and reverence that prosaic kindred always do towards the inspired child, the poet, the elected sufferer for the race.

---

[128]Giovanni Francesco Barbieri (1591–1666), Italian painter also known as "Guercino." [Ed.]

[129]Cassandra and Hecuba are characters in Euripides' *The Trojan Women* (415 BCE). Fuller interprets the play in the next paragraphs and quotations. [Ed.]

When the herald announces that Cassandra is chosen to be the mistress of Agamemnon, Hecuba answers, with indignation, betraying the pride and faith she involuntarily felt in this daughter.

Hec. "The maiden of Phoebus, to whom the golden haired
    Gave as a privilege a virgin life!
Tal. Love of the inspired maiden hath pierced him.
Hec. Then cast away, my child, the sacred keys, and from thy person
    The consecrated garlands which thou wearest."

Yet, when a moment after, Cassandra appears, singing, wildly, her inspired song, Hecuba calls her, "My *frantic* child."
Yet how graceful she is in her tragic *raptus*,[130] the chorus shows.

Chor. "How sweetly at thy house's ills thou smil'st,
    Chanting what, haply, thou wilt not show true."

If Hecuba dares not trust her highest instinct about her daughter, still less can the vulgar mind of the herald Talthybius, a man not without feeling, but with no princely, no poetic blood, abide the wild prophetic mood which insults all his prejudices.

Tal. "The venerable, and that accounted wise,
    Is nothing better than that of no repute,
    For the greatest king of all the Greeks,
    The dear son of Atreus, is possessed with the love
    Of this madwoman. I, indeed, am poor,
    Yet, I would not receive her to my bed."

The royal Agamemnon could see the beauty of Cassandra, HE was not afraid of her prophetic gifts.

The best topic for a chapter on this subject in the present day, would be the history of the Seeress of Prevorst,[131] the best observed subject of magnetism in our present times, and who, like her ancestresses of Delphos, was roused to ecstacy or phrenzy by the touch of the laurel.

---

[130] Possessed, in a trance. [Ed.]

[131] Friederike Hauffe (1801–27), a young woman from the German village of Prevorst, experienced mesmeric trances and was the subject of several treatises, including her physician's, the German Justinus Kerner's *The Seeress of Prevorst* (1829), and Fuller's *Summer on the Lakes in 1843* (1844), ch. 5. Mesmerism, including hypnotic and mystical trances and various "elective affinities," was a popular topic among American transcendentalists and European romantics. The Delphic oracle was one of the famous oracular sources of the classical Greek world. [Ed.]

I observe in her case, and in one known to me here, that, what might have been a gradual and gentle disclosure of remarkable powers, was broken and jarred into disease by an unsuitable marriage. Both these persons were unfortunate in not understanding what was involved in this relation, but acted ignorantly as their friends desired. They thought that this was the inevitable destiny of woman. But when engaged in the false position, it was impossible for them to endure its dissonances, as those of less delicate perceptions can, and the fine flow of life was checked and sullied. They grew sick, but, even so, learnt and disclosed more than those in health are wont to do.

In such cases, worldlings sneer, but reverent men learn wondrous news, either from the person observed, or by thoughts caused in themselves by the observation. Fenelon learns from Guyon,[132] Kerner, from his Seeress, what we fain would know. But to appreciate such disclosures one must be a child, and here the phrase, "women and children" may, perhaps, be interpreted aright, that only little children shall enter into the kingdom of heaven.

All these motions of the time, tides that betoken a waxing moon, overflow upon our land. The world, at large, is readier to let woman learn and manifest the capacities of her nature than it ever was before, and here is a less encumbered field and freer air than any where else. And it ought to be so; we ought to pay for Isabella's jewels.[133]

The names of nations are feminine—religion, virtue, and victory are feminine. To those who have a superstition, as to outward reigns, it is not without significance that the name of the queen of our mother-land should at this crisis be Victoria—Victoria the First. Perhaps to us it may be given to disclose the era thus outwardly presaged.

Another Isabella[134] too at this time ascends the throne. Might she open a new world to her sex! But, probably, these poor little women are, least of any, educated to serve as examples or inspirers for the rest. The Spanish queen is younger; we know of her that she sprained her foot the other day, dancing in her private apartments; of Victoria, that she reads aloud, in a distinct voice and agreeable manner, her addresses to parliament on certain solemn days, and, yearly, that she presents to the nation some new prop of royalty. These ladies have, very likely, been trained more completely to

---

[132] François Fénélon (1651–1715), French writer, defended Jeanne Marie Guyon (1648–1717), founder of Quietism, which taught an utter disregard for salvation (Dickenson 239). [Ed.]

[133] Queen Isabella I of Spain (1451–1504), who reportedly sold her jewels to help finance Columbus's voyages. [Ed.]

[134] Isabella II (1830–1904), queen of Spain (r. 1833–70). [Ed.]

the puppet life than any other. The queens, who have been queens indeed, were trained by adverse circumstances to know the world around them and their own powers.

It is moving, while amusing, to read of the Scottish peasant measuring the print left by the queen's foot as she walks, and priding himself on its beauty. It is so natural to wish to find what is fair and precious in high places, so astonishing to find the Bourbon a glutton, or the Guelph a dullard or gossip.[135]

In our own country, women are, in many respects, better situated than men. Good books are allowed, with more time to read them. They are not so early forced into the bustle of life, nor so weighed down by demands for outward success. The perpetual changes, incident to our society, make the blood circulate freely through the body politic, and, if not favorable at present to the grace and bloom of life, they are so to activity, resource, and would be to reflection, but for a low materialist tendency, from which the women are generally exempt in themselves, though its existence, among the men, has a tendency to repress their impulses and make them doubt their instincts, thus, often, paralyzing their action during the best years.

But they have time to think, and no traditions chain them, and few conventionalities compared with what must be met in other nations. There is no reason why they should not discover that the secrets of nature are open, the revelations of the spirit waiting for whoever will seek them. When the mind is once awakened to this consciousness, it will not be restrained by the habits of the past, but fly to seek the seeds of a heavenly future.

Their employments are more favorable to meditation than those of men.

Woman is not addressed religiously here, more than elsewhere. She is told she should be worthy to be the mother of a Washington, or the companion of some good man. But in many, many instances, she has already learnt that all bribes have the same flaw; that truth and good are to be sought solely for their own sakes. And, already, an ideal sweetness floats over many forms, shines in many eyes.

Already deep questions are put by young girls on the great theme: What shall I do to enter upon the eternal life?[136]

Men are very courteous to them. They praise them often, check them seldom. There is chivalry in the feeling towards "the ladies," which gives them the best seats in the stage-coach, frequent admission, not only to lectures

---

[135] The Bourbons were a French royal family, struggling to reestablish that French monarchy in the nineteenth century. Guelphs originated as dukes of Saxony and Bavaria in the twelfth century and were best known as one of the ruling factions in Dante's Italy. [Ed.]

[136] Cf.: Matt. 19.16. [Ed.]

of all sorts, but to courts of justice, halls of legislature, reform conventions. The newspaper editor "would be better pleased that the Lady's Book[137] should be filled up exclusively by ladies. It would then, indeed, be a true gem, worthy to be presented by young men to the mistresses of their affections." Can gallantry go further?

In this country is venerated, wherever seen, the character which Goethe spoke of an Ideal, which he saw actualized in his friend and patroness, the Grand Duchess Amelia. "The excellent woman is she, who, if the husband dies, can be a father to the children." And this, if read aright, tells a great deal.

Women who speak in public, if they have a moral power, such as has been felt from Angelina Grimke and Abby Kelly;[138] that is, if they speak for conscience' sake, to serve a cause which they hold sacred, invariably subdue the prejudices of their hearers, and excite an interest proportionate to the aversion with which it had been the purpose to regard them.

A passage in a private letter so happily illustrates this, that it must be inserted here.

Abby Kelly in the Town-House of ———.

"The scene was not unheroic — to see that woman, true to humanity and her own nature, a centre of rude eyes and tongues, even gentlemen feeling licensed to make part of a species of mob around a female out of her sphere. As she took her seat in the desk amid the great noise, and in the throng, full, like a wave, of something to ensue, I saw her humanity in a gentleness and unpretension, tenderly open to the sphere around her, and, had she not been supported by the power of the will of genuineness and principle, she would have failed. It led her to prayer, which, in woman especially, is childlike; sensibility and will going to the side of God and looking up to him; and humanity was poured out in aspiration.

"She acted like a gentle hero, with her mild decision and womanly calmness. All heroism is mild and quiet and gentle, for it is life and possession, and combativeness and firmness show a want of actualness. She is as earnest, fresh, and simple as when she first entered the crusade. I think she did much good, more than the men in her place could do, for woman feels more as being and reproducing, this brings the subject more into home relations. Men speak through, and mostly from intellect, and this addresses itself in others, which creates and is combative."

---

[137] *Godey's Lady's Book,* a popular women's magazine. [Ed.]

[138] Angelina Grimké (1805–79), one of the two abolitionist, feminist Grimké sisters. Her *An Appeal to the Women of the Nominally Free States* (1837) links women's rights and abolition. Abby Kelly (1811–67), women's rights activist and abolitionist best known for violating the rule of "woman's silence" at the Connecticut Anti-Slavery Society in 1840. [Ed.]

Not easily shall we find elsewhere, or before this time, any written observations on the same subject, so delicate and profound.

The late Dr. Channing,[139] whose enlarged and tender and religious nature, shared every onward impulse of his time, though his thoughts followed his wishes with a deliberative caution, which belonged to his habits and temperament, was greatly interested in these expectations for women. His own treatment of them was absolutely and thoroughly religious. He regarded them as souls, each of which had a destiny of its own, incalculable to other minds, and whose leading it must follow, guided by the light of a private conscience. He had sentiment, delicacy, kindness, taste; but they were all pervaded and ruled by this one thought, that all beings had souls, and must vindicate their own inheritance. Thus all beings were treated by him with an equal, and sweet, though solemn, courtesy. The young and unknown, the woman and the child, all felt themselves regarded with an infinite expectation, from which there was no reaction to vulgar prejudice. He demanded of all he met, to use his favorite phrase, "great truths."

His memory, every way dear and reverend, is, by many, especially cherished for this intercourse of unbroken respect.

At one time, when the progress of Harriet Martineau[140] through this country, Angelina Grimké's appearance in public, and the visit of Mrs. Jameson had turned his thoughts to this subject, he expressed high hopes as to what the coming era would bring to woman. He had been much pleased with the dignified courage of Mrs. Jameson in taking up the defence of her sex, in a way from which women usually shrink, because, if they express themselves on such subjects with sufficient force and clearness to do any good, they are exposed to assaults whose vulgarity makes them painful. In intercourse with such a woman, he had shared her indignation at the base injustice, in many respects, and in many regions, done to the sex; and been led to think of it far more than ever before. He seemed to think that he might some time write upon the subject. That his aid is withdrawn from the cause is a subject of great regret, for, on this question as on others, he would have known how to sum up the evidence and take, in the noblest spirit, middle ground. He always furnished a platform on which

---

[139] William Ellery Channing (1780–1842), Unitarian minister and transcendentalist, uncle of William Henry Channing. The poet [William] Ellery Channing (1818–1901) was Fuller's brother-in-law. [Ed.]

[140] Harriet Martineau's (1802–76) *Society in America* (1837) was criticized by Fuller, although Martineau was a leading English abolitionist and women's rights activist. Martineau, in turn, criticized Fuller and her students in the Boston "conversations" as "gorgeous pedants" and Fuller herself as excessively abstract (Dickenson 241). [Ed.]

opposing parties could stand, and look at one another under the influence of his mildness and enlightened candor.

Two younger thinkers, men both, have uttered noble prophecies, auspicious for woman. Kinmont,[141] all whose thoughts tended towards the establishment of the reign of love and peace, thought that the inevitable means of this would be an increased predominance given to the idea of woman. Had he lived longer, to see the growth of the peace party, the reforms in life and medical practice which seek to substitute water for wine and drugs, pulse for animal food, he would have been confirmed in his view of the way in which the desired changes are to be effected.

In this connection, I must mention Shelley,[142] who, like all men of genius, shared the feminine development, and, unlike many, knew it. His life was one of the first pulse-beats in the present reform-growth. He, too, abhorred blood and heat, and, by his system and his song, tended to reinstate a plant-like gentleness in the development of energy. In harmony with this, his ideas of marriage were lofty, and, of course, no less so of woman, her nature, and destiny.

For woman, if, by a sympathy as to outward condition she is led to aid the enfranchisement of the slave, must be no less so, by inward tendency, to favor measures which promise to bring the world more thoroughly and deeply into harmony with her nature. When the lamb takes place of the lion as the emblem of nations, both women and men will be as children of one spirit, perpetual learners of the word and doers thereof, not hearers only.

A writer in the New-York Pathfinder, in two articles headed "Femality,"[143] has uttered a still more pregnant word than any we have named. He views woman truly from the soul, and not from society, and the depth and leading of his thoughts are proportionably remarkable. He views the feminine nature as a harmonizer of the vehement elements, and this has often

---

[141] Alexander Kinmont (1799–1838), Scottish abolitionist, feminist, and educator, came to America in 1823 and established a school in Cincinnati. In her review of Frederick Douglass's *Narrative of the Life of Frederick Douglass, An American Slave* (1845), Fuller notes that Kinmont and William Ellery Channing advocated the assimilation of African Americans into American society and the involvement of women in the public ("male") sphere as ways of improving American civilization "beyond what has been seen heretofore in the history of the world." Kinmont also advocated temperance, regular exercise, and a vegetarian diet (Dickenson 241). [Ed.]

[142] Percy Bysshe Shelley (1792–1822), English romantic poet. It is some measure of Fuller's double standards in evaluating predecessors that she continues to praise male reformers, like Shelley, whose relations with women are hardly exemplary, and condemns George Sand and Mary Wollstonecraft, among other women, for their love affairs. [Ed.]

[143] By "V.," "Femality," *Pathfinder* 18 Mar. 1843: 35–36, 51–52 (Reynolds, *Woman* 68). [Ed.]

been hinted elsewhere; but what he expresses most forcibly is the lyrical, the inspiring, and inspired apprehensiveness of her being.

This view being identical with what I have before attempted to indicate, as to her superior susceptibility to magnetic or electric influence, I will now try to express myself more fully.

There are two aspects of woman's nature, represented by the ancients as Muse and Minerva. It is the former to which the writer in the Pathfinder looks. It is the latter which Wordsworth has in mind, when he says —

> "With a placid brow,
> Which woman ne'er should forfeit, keep thy vow." [144]

The especial genius of woman I believe to be electrical in movement, intuitive in function, spiritual in tendency. She excels not so easily in classification, or re-creation, as in an instinctive seizure of causes, and a simple breathing out of what she receives that has the singleness of life, rather than the selecting and energizing of art.

More native is it to her to be the living model of the artist than to set apart from herself any one form in objective reality; more native to inspire and receive the poem, than to create it. In so far as soul is in her completely developed, all soul is the same; but as far as it is modified in her as woman, it flows, it breathes, it sings, rather than deposits soil, or finishes work, and that which is especially feminine flushes, in blossom, the face of earth, and pervades, like air and water, all this seeming solid globe, daily renewing and purifying its life. Such may be the especially feminine element, spoken of as Femality. But it is no more the order of nature that it should be incarnated pure in any form, than that the masculine energy should exist unmingled with it in any form.

Male and female represent the two sides of the great radical dualism. But, in fact, they are perpetually passing into one another. Fluid hardens to solid, solid rushes to fluid. There is no wholly masculine man, no purely feminine woman. [145]

History jeers at the attempts of physiologists to bind great original laws by the forms which flow from them. They make a rule; they say from observation, what can and cannot be. In vain! Nature provides exceptions to

---

[144] Cf. William Wordsworth, "Liberty" (1835). [Ed.]

[145] This often quoted line from Fuller anticipates Sigmund Freud's claims, apparently supported by modern biology, that every human being has male and female qualities and that there is no strict sexual boundary. The entire paragraph anticipates modern feminists' interpretations of gender roles as social constructions, rather than human essences or universals. [Ed.]

every rule. She sends women to battle, and sets Hercules spinning;[146] she enables women to bear immense burdens, cold, and frost; she enables the man, who feels maternal love, to nourish his infant like a mother. Of late she plays still gayer pranks. Not only she deprives organizations, but organs, of a necessary end. She enables people to read with the top of the head, and see with the pit of the stomach. Presently she will make a female Newton, and a male Syren.

Man partakes of the feminine in the Apollo, woman of the masculine as Minerva.

What I mean by the Muse is the unimpeded clearness of the intuitive powers which a perfectly truthful adherence to every admonition of the higher instincts would bring to a finely organized human being. It may appear as prophecy or as poesy. It enabled Cassandra to foresee the results of actions passing round her; the Seeress to behold the true character of the person through the mask of his customary life. (Sometimes she saw a feminine form behind the man, sometimes the reverse.) It enabled the daughter of Linnaeus to see the soul of the flower exhaling from the flower.[147] It gave a man, but a poet man, the power of which he thus speaks: "Often in my contemplation of nature, radiant intimations, and as it were sheaves of light appear before me as to the facts of cosmogony in which my mind has, perhaps, taken especial part." He wisely adds, "but it is necessary with earnestness to verify the knowledge we gain by these flashes of light." And none should forget this. Sight must be verified by life before it can deserve the honors of piety and genius. Yet sight comes first, and of this sight of the world of causes, this approximation to the region of primitive motions, women I hold to be especially capable. Even without equal freedom with the other sex, they have already shown themselves so, and should these faculties have free play, I believe they will open new, deeper and purer sources of joyous inspiration than have as yet refreshed the earth.

Let us be wise and not impede the soul. Let her work as she will. Let us have one creative energy, one incessant revelation. Let it take what form it

---

[146] In Greek myth, Hercules was condemned to a year's slavery by the Delphic oracle and was purchased by Omphale, queen of Lydia, who set him to spinning wool and in turn wore his lion's skin (Reynolds, *Woman* 69). [Ed.]

[147] The daughter of Linnaeus states, that, while looking steadfastly at the red lily, she saw its spirit hovering above it, as a red flame. It is true, this, like many fair spirit-stories, may be explained away as an optical illusion, but its poetic beauty and meaning would, even then, make it valuable, as an illustration of the spiritual fact [Fuller's note]. Carolus Linnaeus (1707–78), Swedish botanist who developed the classificatory system for plants and animals (Reynolds, *Woman* 69). [Ed.]

will, and let us not bind it by the past to man or woman, black or white. Jove sprang from Rhea, Pallas from Jove.[148] So let it be.

If it has been the tendency of these remarks to call woman rather to the Minerva side, — if I, unlike the more generous writer, have spoken from society no less than the soul, — let it be pardoned! It is love that has caused this, love for many incarcerated souls, that might be freed, could the idea of religious self-dependence be established in them, could the weakening habit of dependence on others be broken up.

Proclus[149] teaches that every life has, in its sphere, a totality or wholeness of the animating powers of the other spheres; having only, as its own characteristic, a predominance of some one power. Thus Jupiter comprises, within himself, the other twelve powers, which stand thus: The first triad is *demiurgic or fabricative*, i.e., Jupiter, Neptune, Vulcan; the second, *defensive*, Vesta, Minerva, Mars; the third, *vivific*, Ceres, Juno, Diana; and the fourth, Mercury, Venus, Apollo, *elevating and harmonic*. In the sphere of Jupiter, energy is predominant — with Venus, beauty; but each comprehends and apprehends all the others.

When the same community of life and consciousness of mind begins among men, humanity will have, positively and finally, subjugated its brute elements and Titanic childhood; criticism will have perished; arbitrary limits and ignorant censure be impossible; all will have entered upon the liberty of law, and the harmony of common growth.

Then Apollo will sing to his lyre what Vulcan forges on the anvil, and the Muse weave anew the tapestries of Minerva.

It is, therefore, only in the present crisis that the preference is given to Minerva. The power of continence must establish the legitimacy of freedom, the power of self-poise the perfection of motion.

Every relation, every gradation of nature is incalculably precious, but only to the soul which is poised upon itself, and to whom no loss, no change, can bring dull discord, for it is in harmony with the central soul.

If any individual live too much in relations, so that he becomes a stranger to the resources of his own nature, he falls, after a while, into a distraction, or imbecility, from which he can only be cured by a time of isolation, which gives the renovating fountains time to rise up. With a society it is the same.

---

[148] Fuller again anticipates modern feminists who study goddesses by noting that the Greek male gods, such as Jove, are born of goddesses (Jove was born of Rhea, daughter of the Earth and Sky), but Pallas Athena, virgin goddess of wisdom and courage, had no mother and sprang directly from the head of her father, Jove, not unlike the miracle of "virgin birth" in Christianity (but with a different gendering). [Ed.]

[149] Proclus (410–85 CE), Neoplatonist philosopher. [Ed.]

Many minds, deprived of the traditionary or instinctive means of passing a cheerful existence, must find help in self-impulse, or perish. It is therefore that, while any elevation, in the view of union, is to be hailed with joy, we shall not decline celibacy as the great fact of the time. It is one from which no vow, no arrangement, can at present save a thinking mind. For now the rowers are pausing on their oars; they wait a change before they can pull together. All tends to illustrate the thought of a wise cotemporary. Union is only possible to those who are units. To be fit for relations in time, souls, whether of man or woman, must be able to do without them in the spirit.[150]

It is therefore that I would have woman lay aside all thought, such as she habitually cherishes, of being taught and led by men. I would have her, like the Indian girl, dedicate herself to the Sun, the Sun of Truth, and go no where if his beams did not make clear the path. I would have her free from compromise, from complaisance, from helplessness, because I would have her good enough and strong enough to love one and all beings, from the fulness, not the poverty of being.

Men, as at present instructed, will not help this work, because they also are under the slavery of habit. I have seen with delight their poetic impulses. A sister is the fairest ideal, and how nobly Wordsworth, and even Byron, have written of a sister.[151]

There is no sweeter sight than to see a father with his little daughter. Very vulgar men become refined to the eye when leading a little girl by the hand. At that moment the right relation between the sexes seems established, and you feel as if the man would aid in the noblest purpose, if you ask him in behalf of his little daughter. Once two fine figures stood before me, thus. The father of very intellectual aspect, his falcon eye softened by affection as he looked down on his fair child, she the image of himself, only more graceful and brilliant in expression. I was reminded of Southey's Kehama;[152] when lo, the dream was rudely broken. They were talking of education, and he said,

---

[150] Fuller refers to the transcendentalist idea of basic human and social relations as based on monadic, self-reliant individuals. For many transcendentalists, "friendship" would be the model for interpersonal and for wider social interactions. Both Emerson and Thoreau wrote essays on friendship. [Ed.]

[151] Byron's "Epistle to Augusta" was for his half-sister, Augusta Leigh (1783–1851). Wordsworth's close relationship with his sister, Dorothy (1771–1855), is represented well in poems such as "To My Sister" and "Tintern Abbey" (Reynolds, *Woman* 71). Once again Fuller subscribes to the spiritualized "brother and sister" relations between men and women advocated by the romantics. Fuller herself was the eldest sister of seven children surviving their father's death in 1835, and she did much to help bring up the other six children. [Ed.]

[152] Robert Southey (1774–1843), *The Curse of Kehama* (1810) (see n. 8, on p. 169). [Ed.]

"I shall not have Maria brought too forward. If she knows too much, she will never find a husband; superior women hardly ever can."

"Surely," said his wife, with a blush, "you wish Maria to be as good and wise as she can, whether it will help her to marriage or not."

"No," he persisted, "I want her to have a sphere and a home, and some one to protect her when I am gone."

It was a trifling incident, but made a deep impression. I felt that the holiest relations fail to instruct the unprepared and perverted mind. If this man, indeed, could have looked at it on the other side, he was the last that would have been willing to have been taken himself for the home and protection he could give, but would have been much more likely to repeat the tale of Alcibiades with his phials.[153]

But men do *not* look at both sides, and women must leave off asking them and being influenced by them, but retire within themselves, and explore the ground-work of life till they find their peculiar secret. Then, when they come forth again, renovated and baptized, they will know how to turn all dross to gold, and will be rich and free though they live in a hut, tranquil, if in a crowd. Then their sweet singing shall not be from passionate impulse, but the lyrical overflow of a divine rapture, and a new music shall be evolved from this many-chorded world.

Grant her, then, for a while, the armor and the javelin. Let her put from her the press of other minds and meditate in virgin loneliness. The same idea shall re-appear in due time as Muse, or Ceres, the all-kindly patient Earth-Spirit.

Among the throng of symptoms which denote the present tendency to a crisis in the life of woman, which resembles the change from girlhood with its beautiful instincts, but unharmonized thoughts, its blind pupilage and restless seeking, to self-possessed, wise, and graceful womanhood, I have attempted to select a few.

One of prominent interest is the unison of three male minds, upon the subject, which, for width of culture, power of self-concentration and dignity of aim, take rank as the prophets of the coming age, while their histories and labors are rooted in the past.

---

[153] Alcibiades (c. 450–04 BCE), Athenian statesman, was invited by an admirer, Anytus, to a dinner party but refused, got drunk at home with friends, then marched to Anytus' house and ordered his slaves to take half of Anytus' gold and silver cups (*phials*). The meaning of Fuller's allusion seems to be that if the father had looked correctly at the education of his daughter, he would have understood that for him to "protect" her by marrying her to another man was a violation of her own self-reliant spirit, of her own "home" (and thus his desire like Alcibiades' violation of Anytus' home). [Ed.]

Swedenborg came, he tells us, to interpret the past revelation and unfold a new. He announces the new church that is to prepare the way for the New Jerusalem, a city built of precious stones, hardened and purified by secret processes in the veins of earth through the ages.

Swedenborg approximated to that harmony between the scientific and poetic lives of mind, which we hope from the perfected man. The links that bind together the realms of nature, the mysteries that accompany her births and growths, were unusually plain to him. He seems a man to whom insight was given at a period when the mental frame was sufficiently matured to retain and express its gifts.

His views of woman are, in the main, satisfactory. In some details, we may object to them as, in all his system, there are still remains of what is arbitrary and seemingly groundless; fancies that show the marks of old habits, and a nature as yet not thoroughly leavened with the spiritual leaven. At least so it seems to me now. I speak reverently, for I find such reason to venerate Swedenborg, from an imperfect knowledge of his mind, that I feel one more perfect might explain to me much that does not now secure my sympathy.

His idea of woman is sufficiently large and noble to interpose no obstacle to her progress. His idea of marriage is consequently sufficient. Man and woman share an angelic ministry, the union is from one to one, permanent and pure.

As the New Church extends its ranks, the needs of woman must be more considered.

Quakerism also establishes woman on a sufficient equality with man. But though the original thought of Quakerism is pure, its scope is too narrow, and its influence, having established a certain amount of good and made clear some truth, must, by degrees, be merged in one of wider range.[154] The mind of Swedenborg appeals to the various nature of man and allows room for æsthetic culture and the free expression of energy.

As apostle of the new order, of the social fabric that is to rise from love,

---

[154]In worship at stated periods, in daily expression, whether by word or deed, the Quakers have placed woman on the same platform as men. Can any one assert that they have reason to repent this? [Fuller's note]. George Fox (1624–91) founded the Religious Society of Friends, the Quakers, and advocated the spiritual equality of women, and his wife Margaret Fell advocated the ordination of women ministers in *Women's Speaking* (1666). By the nineteenth century, Quakers had a long tradition of female ministry (Dickenson 243). They were active in abolition and women's rights, although they were commonly viewed in the antebellum period as provinicial and antimodern, which may explain Fuller's criticism of Quaker's "narrow" scope. [Ed.]

and supersede the old that was based on strife, Charles Fourier[155] comes next, expressing, in an outward order, many facts of which Swedenborg saw the secret springs. The mind of Fourier, though grand and clear, was, in some respects, superficial. He was a stranger to the highest experiences. His eye was fixed on the outward more than the inward needs of man. Yet he, too, was a seer of the divine order, in its musical expression, if not in its poetic soul. He has filled one department of instruction for the new era, and the harmony in action, and freedom for individual growth he hopes shall exist; and if the methods he proposes should not prove the true ones, yet his fair propositions shall give many hints, and make room for the inspiration needed for such.

He, too, places woman on an entire equality with man, and wishes to give to one as to the other that independence which must result from intellectual and practical development.

Those who will consult him for no other reason, might do so to see how the energies of woman may be made available in the pecuniary way. The object of Fourier was to give her the needed means of self help, that she might dignify and unfold her life for her own happiness, and that of society. The many, now, who see their daughters liable to destitution, or vice to escape from it, may be interested to examine the means, if they have not yet soul enough to appreciate the ends he proposes.

On the opposite side of the advancing army, leads the great apostle of individual culture, Goethe.[156] Swedenborg makes organization and union the necessary results of solitary thought. Fourier, whose nature was, above all, constructive, looked to them too exclusively. Better institutions, he thought, will make better men. Goethe expressed, in every way, the other side. If one man could present better forms, the rest could not use them till ripe for them.

Fourier says, As the institutions, so the men! All follies are excusable and natural under bad institutions.

Goethe thinks, As the man, so the institutions! There is no excuse for ignorance and folly. A man can grow in any place, if he will.

---

[155] Charles Fourier (1772–1837), French utopian socialist. His theories were applied at Brook Farm (1841–47), where Fuller visited (but did not live and work) and where she tried to get her youngest brother Lloyd (who had learning disabilities) a place. Fourier was a committed women's rights activist (Dickenson 243). [Ed.]

[156] Fuller contrasts the romantic individualist, Goethe, with the romantic socialist, Fourier, criticizing both in the following paragraphs. Her criticism of Goethe's self-reliance is interesting, insofar as she departs from transcendentalist colleagues, such as Emerson and Thoreau in this respect. [Ed.]

Ay! but Goethe, bad institutions are prison walls and impure air that make him stupid, so that he does not will.

And thou, Fourier, do not expect to change mankind at once, or even "in three generations" by arrangement of groups and series, or flourish of trumpets for attractive industry. If these attempts are made by unready men, they will fail.

Yet we prize the theory of Fourier no less than the profound suggestion of Goethe. Both are educating the age to a clearer consciousness of what man needs, what man can be, and better life must ensue.

Goethe, proceeding on his own track, elevating the human being in the most imperfect states of society, by continual efforts at self-culture, takes as good care of women as of men. His mother, the bold, gay Frau Aja, with such playful freedom of nature; the wise and gentle maiden, known in his youth, over whose sickly solitude "the Holy Ghost brooded as a dove;" his sister, the intellectual woman *par excellence:* the Duchess Amelia; Lili, who combined the character of the woman of the world with the lyrical sweetness of the shepherdess, on whose chaste and noble breast flowers and gems were equally at home; all these had supplied abundant suggestions to his mind, as to the wants and the possible excellencies of woman.[157] And, from his poetic soul, grew up forms new and more admirable than life has yet produced, for whom his clear eye marked out paths in the future.

In Faust, we see the redeeming power, which, at present, upholds woman, while waiting for a better day, in Margaret. The lovely little girl, pure in instinct, ignorant in mind, is misled and profaned by man abusing her confidence.[158] To the Mater *Dolorosa* she appeals for aid. It is given to the soul, if not against outward sorrow; and the maiden, enlightened by her sufferings, refusing to receive temporal salvation by the aid of an evil power, obtains the eternal in its stead.

In the second part, the intellectual man, after all his manifold strivings, owes to the interposition of her whom he had betrayed *his* salvation. She intercedes, this time herself a glorified spirit, with the Mater *Gloriosa*.

Leonora, too, is woman, as we see her now, pure, thoughtful, refined by much acquaintance with grief.

---

[157] This long catalogue of the women in Goethe's life is cited in anticipation of Fuller's interpretation of the genesis of the characters of Margaret, Faust's lover and the model of woman's love in Goethe's *Faust* (1808), Leonora in his *Torquato Tasso* (1790), and Iphigenia in his *Iphigenie auf Tauris* (1787). Fuller here anticipates genetic criticism, which explains how literary characters and devices have evolved in an author's work and life, and the specific use of such criticism by modern psychoanalytic critics of literature and culture. [Ed.]

[158] As Faust says, her only fault was a "Kindly delusion," — "ein guter wahn." [Fuller's note.]

Iphigenia he speaks of in his journals as his "daughter," and she is the daughter[159] whom a man will wish, even if he has chosen his wife from very mean motives. She is the virgin, steadfast soul, to whom falsehood is more dreadful than any other death.

But it is to Wilhelm Meister's Apprenticeship and Wandering Years[160] that I would especially refer, as these volumes contain the sum of the Sage's observations during a long life, as to what man should do, under present circumstances, to obtain mastery over outward, through an initiation into inward life, and severe discipline of faculty.

As Wilhelm advances in the upward path he becomes acquainted with better forms of woman by knowing how to seek, and how to prize them when found. For the weak and immature man will, often, admire a superior woman, but he will not be able to abide by a feeling, which is too severe a tax on his habitual existence. But, with Wilhelm, the gradation is natural and expresses ascent in the scale of being. At first he finds charm in Mariana and Philina, very common forms of feminine character, not without redeeming traits, no less than charms, but without wisdom or purity. Soon he is attended by Mignon, the finest expression ever yet given to what I have called the lyrical element in woman. She is a child, but too full-grown for this man; he loves, but cannot follow her; yet is the association not without an enduring influence. Poesy has been domesticated in his life, and, though he strives to bind down her heavenward impulse, as art or apothegm, these are only the tents, beneath which he may sojourn for a while, but which may be easily struck, and carried on limitless wanderings.

Advancing into the region of thought, he encounters a wise philanthropy in Natalia, (instructed, let us observe, by an *uncle*,) practical judgment and the outward economy of life in Theresa, pure devotion in the Fair Saint.

---

[159] Goethe was as false to his ideas in practice, as Lord Herbert. And his punishment was the just and usual one of connections formed beneath the standard of right, from the impulses of the baser self. Iphigenia was the worthy daughter of his mind, but the son, child of his degrading connection in actual life, corresponded with that connection. This son, on whom Goethe vainly lavished so much thought and care, was like his mother, and like Goethe's attachment for his mother, "This young man," says a late well informed writer, (M. Henri Blaze,) "Wieland, with good reason, called the son of the servant, *der Sohn der Magd*. He inherited from his father only his name and his *physique*." [Fuller's note. Fuller refers here to Goethe's relationship with Christiane Vulpius, who was his common-law wife from 1788 to 1806, when he formally married her, and their illegitimate son, Wieland (b. 1789), adding to her erratic criticism of "scandalous" relationships out of formal marriage (Dickenson 244). —Ed.]

[160] Fuller now turns to Goethe's famous novels of education, *Wilhelm Meister's Apprenticeship* (1795–96) and *Wilhelm Meister's Wandering Years* (1829). [Ed.]

Farther and last he comes to the house of Macaria, the soul of a star, *i.e.* a pure and perfected intelligence embodied in feminine form, and the centre of a world whose members revolve harmoniously round her. She instructs him in the archives of a rich human history, and introduces him to the contemplation of the heavens.

From the hours passed by the side of Mariana to these with Macaria, is a wide distance for human feet to traverse. Nor has Wilhelm travelled so far, seen and suffered so much in vain. He now begins to study how he may aid the next generation; he sees objects in harmonious arrangement, and from his observations deduces precepts by which to guide his course as a teacher and a master, "help-full, comfort-full."

In all these expressions of woman, the aim of Goethe is satisfactory to me. He aims at a pure self-subsistence, and free development of any powers with which they may be gifted by nature as much for them as for men. They are units, addressed as souls. Accordingly the meeting between man and woman, as represented by him, is equal and noble, and, if he does not depict marriage, he makes it possible.

In the Macaria, bound with the heavenly bodies in fixed revolutions, the centre of all relations, herself unrelated, he expresses the Minerva side of feminine nature. It was not by chance that Goethe gave her this name. Macaria, the daughter of Hercules, who offered herself as a victim for the good of her country, was canonized by the Greeks, and worshipped as the Goddess of true Felicity. Goethe has embodied this Felicity as the Serenity that arises from Wisdom, a Wisdom, such as the Jewish wise man venerated, alike instructed in the designs of heaven, and the methods necessary to carry them into effect upon earth.

Mignon is the electrical, inspired, lyrical nature. And wherever it appears we echo in our aspirations that of the child,

> "So let me seem until I be:—
> Take not the *white robe* away."
> *　　*　　*　　*　　*
> "Though I lived without care and toil,
> Yet felt I sharp pain enough,
> Make me again forever young."[161]

All these women, though we see them in relations, we can think of as unrelated. They all are very individual, yet seem, nowhere, restrained. They satisfy for the present, yet arouse an infinite expectation.

---

[161] *Wilhelm Meister's Apprenticeship*, bk. 8, ch. 2. [Ed.]

The economist Theresa, the benevolent Natalia, the fair Saint, have chosen a path, but their thoughts are not narrowed to it. The functions of life to them are not ends, but suggestions.

Thus, to them, all things are important, because none is necessary. Their different characters have fair play, and each is beautiful in its minute indications, for nothing is enforced or conventional, but every thing, however slight, grows from the essential life of the being.

Mignon and Theresa wear male attire when they like, and it is graceful for them to do so, while Macaria is confined to her arm-chair behind the green curtain, and the Fair Saint could not bear a speck of dust on her robe.

All things are in their places in this little world, because all is natural and free, just as "there is room for everything out of doors." Yet all is rounded in by natural harmony, which will always arise where Truth and Love are sought in the light of Freedom.

Goethe's book bodes an era of freedom like its own of "extraordinary generous seeking," and new revelations. New individualities shall be developed in the actual world, which shall advance upon it as gently as the figures come out upon his canvass.

I have indicated on this point the coincidence between his hopes and those of Fourier, though his are directed by an infinitely higher and deeper knowledge of human nature. But, for our present purpose, it is sufficient to show how surely these different paths have conducted to the same end two earnest thinkers. In some other place I wish to point out similar coincidences between Goethe's model school and the plans of Fourier, which may cast light upon the page of prophecy.

Many women have observed that the time drew nigh for a better care of the sex, and have thrown out hints that may be useful. Among these may be mentioned—

Miss Edgeworth,[162] who, although restrained by the habits of her age and country, and belonging more to the eighteenth than the nineteenth century, has done excellently as far as she goes. She had a horror of sentimentalism, and the love of notoriety, and saw how likely women, in the early stages of culture, were to aim at these. Therefore she bent her efforts to recommending domestic life. But the methods she recommends are such as will fit a character for any position to which it may be called. She taught a contempt of falsehood, no less in its most graceful, than in its meanest apparitions; the cultivation of a clear, independent judgment, and

---

[162] Maria Edgeworth (1767–1849), Anglo-Irish novelist and women's rights advocate and education reformer, best known for her gothic novel *Castle Rackrent* (1800). [Ed.]

adherence to its dictates; habits of various and liberal study and employment, and a capacity for friendship. Her standard of character is the same for both sexes. Truth, honor, enlightened benevolence, and aspiration after knowledge. Of poetry, she knows nothing, and her religion consists in honor and loyalty to obligations once assumed, in short, in "the great idea of duty which holds us upright." Her whole tendency is practical.

Mrs. Jameson is a sentimentalist, and, therefore, suits us ill in some respects, but she is full of talent, has a just and refined perception of the beautiful, and a genuine courage when she finds it necessary. She does not appear to have thought out, thoroughly, the subject on which we are engaged, and her opinions, expressed as opinions, are sometimes inconsistent with one another. But from the refined perception of character, admirable suggestions are given in her "Women of Shakespeare," and "Loves of the Poets." [163]

But that for which I most respect her is the decision with which she speaks on a subject which refined women are usually afraid to approach, for fear of the insult and scurril jest they may encounter; but on which she neither can nor will restrain the indignation of a full heart. I refer to the degradation of a large portion of women into the sold and polluted slaves of men, and the daring with which the legislator and man of the world lifts his head beneath the heavens, and says "this must be; it cannot be helped; it is a necessary accompaniment of *civilization.*"

So speaks the *citizen.* Man born of woman, the father of daughters, declares that he will and must buy the comforts and commercial advantages of his London, Vienna, Paris, New-York, by conniving at the moral death, the damnation , so far as the action of society can insure it, of thousands of women for each splendid metropolis. [164]

O men! I speak not to you. It is true that your wickedness (for you must not deny that, at least, nine thousand out of the ten fall through the vanity you have systematically flattered, or the promises you have treacherously broken;) yes, it is true that your wickedness is its own punishment. Your forms degraded and your eyes clouded by secret sin; natural harmony broken and fineness of perception destroyed in your mental and bodily organization; God and love shut out from your hearts by the foul visitants you have permitted there; incapable of pure marriage; incapable of pure parentage; incapable of worship; oh wretched men, your sin is its own punishment! You have lost the world in losing yourselves. Who ruins another has admitted the worm to the root of his own tree, and the fuller ye fill the cup of evil, the deeper must be your own bitter draught. But I speak not to

---

[163] See n. 123. [Ed.]

[164] Fuller directly addresses nineteenth-century prostitution and links it with slavery. [Ed.]

you—you need to teach and warn one another. And more than one voice rises in earnestness. And all that *women* say to the heart that has once chosen the evil path, is considered prudery, or ignorance, or perhaps, a feebleness of nature which exempts from similar temptations.

But to you, women, American women, a few words may not be addressed in vain. One here and there may listen.

You know how it was in the Oriental clime. One man, if wealth permitted, had several wives and many hand-maidens. The chastity and equality of genuine marriage, with "the thousand decencies that flow," from its communion, the precious virtues that gradually may be matured, within its enclosure, were unknown.

But this man did not wrong according to his light. What he did, he might publish to God and Man; it was not a wicked secret that hid in vile lurking-places and dens, like the banquets of beasts of prey. Those women were not lost, not polluted in their own eyes, nor those of others. If they were not in a state of knowledge and virtue, they were at least in one of comparative innocence.

You know how it was with the natives of this continent. A chief had many wives whom he maintained and who did his household work; those women were but servants, still they enjoyed the respect of others and their own. They lived together in peace. They knew that a sin against what was in their nation esteemed virtue, would be as strictly punished in man as in woman.

Now pass to the countries where marriage is between one and one. I will not speak of the Pagan nations, but come to those which own the Christian rule. We all know what that enjoins; there is a standard to appeal to.[165]

See now, not the mass of the people, for we all know that it is a proverb and a bitter jest to speak of the "down-trodden million." We know that, down to our own time, a principle never had so fair a chance to pervade the mass of the people, but that we must solicit its illustration from select examples.

Take the Paladin,[166] take the Poet. Did *they* believe purity more impossible to man than to woman? Did they wish woman to believe that man was less amenable to higher motives, that pure aspirations would not guard him against bad passions, that honorable employments and temperate habits would not keep him free from slavery to the body. O no! Love was to them a part of heaven, and they could not even wish to receive its happiness,

---

[165] Although Fuller excuses Moslem men and Native American men for polygamy, she displays here an Orientalism that reflects on her conviction of the civilized superiority of "Christian rule" and betrays her ignorance of marriage customs in Islam and the many different Native American tribes. [Ed.]

[166] Chivalric knight. [Ed.]

unless assured of being worthy of it. Its highest happiness to them was, that it made them wish to be worthy. They courted probation. They wished not the title of knight, till the banner had been upheld in the heats of battle, amid the rout of cowards.

I ask of you, young girls—I do not mean *you*, whose heart is that of an old coxcomb, though your locks have not yet lost their sunny tinge. Not of you whose whole character is tainted with vanity, inherited or taught, who have early learnt the love of coquettish excitement, and whose eyes rove restlessly in search of a "conquest" or a "beau." You who are ashamed *not* to be seen by others the mark of the most contemptuous flattery or injurious desire. To such I do not speak. But to thee, maiden, who, if not so fair, art yet of that unpolluted nature which Milton saw when he dreamed of Comus and the Paradise.[167] Thou, child of an unprofaned wedlock, brought up amid the teachings of the woods and fields, kept fancy-free by useful employment and a free flight into the heaven of thought, loving to please only those whom thou wouldst not be ashamed to love; I ask of thee, whose cheek has not forgotten its blush nor thy heart its lark-like hopes, if he whom thou mayst hope the Father will send thee, as the companion of life's toils and joys, is not to thy thought pure? Is not manliness to thy thought purity, *not* lawlessness? Can his lips speak falsely? Can he do, in secret, what he could not avow to the mother that bore him? O say, dost thou not look for a heart free, open as thine own, all whose thoughts may be avowed, incapable of wronging the innocent, or still farther degrading the fallen. A man, in short, in whom brute nature is entirely subject to the impulses of his better self.

Yes! it was thus that thou didst hope, for I have many, many times seen the image of a future life, of a destined spouse, painted on the tablets of a virgin heart.

It might be that she was not true to these hopes. She was taken into what is called "the world," froth and scum as it mostly is on the social caldron. There, she saw fair woman carried in the waltz close to the heart of a being who appeared to her a Satyr. Being warned by a male friend that he was in fact of that class, and not fit for such familiar nearness to a chaste being, the advised replied that "women should know nothing about such things." She saw one fairer given in wedlock to a man of the same class. "Papa and mamma said that 'all men were faulty, at some time in their lives; they had a great many temptations. Frederick would be so happy at home; he would not want to do wrong.'" She turned to the married women; they, oh tenfold horror! laughed at her supposing "men were like women." Sometimes,

---

[167] The heroine of John Milton's *Comus* (1684) resists the attempted seduction by the pagan god, Comus, and preserves her chastity. [Ed.]

I say, she was not true and either sadly accommodated herself to "woman's lot," or acquired a taste for satyr-society, like some of the Nymphs, and all the Bacchanals of old. But to these who could not and would not accept a mess of pottage, or a Circe cup, in lieu of their birthright, and to these others who have yet their choice to make, I say, Courage! I have some words of cheer for you. A man, himself of unbroken purity, reported to me the words of a foreign artist, that "the world would never be better till men subjected themselves to the same laws they had imposed on women;" that artist, he added, was true to the thought. The same was true of Canova, the same of Beethoven. "Like each other demi-god, they kept themselves free from stain," and Michael Angelo, looking over here from the loneliness of his century, might meet some eyes that need not shun his glance.[168]

In private life, I am assured by men who are not so sustained and occupied by the worship of pure beauty, that a similar consecration is possible, is practiced. That many men feel that no temptation can be too strong for the will of man, if he invokes the aid of the Spirit instead of seeking extenuation from the brute alliances of his nature. In short, what the child fancies is really true, though almost the whole world declares it a lie. Man is a child of God; and if he seek His guidance to keep the heart with diligence, it will be so given that all the issues of life may be pure. Life will then be a temple.

> The temple round
> Spread green the pleasant ground;
> The fair colonnade
> Be of pure marble pillars made;
> 5   Strong to sustain the roof,
> Time and tempest proof,
> Yet, amidst which, the lightest breeze
> Can play as it please;
> The audience hall
> 10   Be free to all
> Who revere
> The Power worshipped here,
> Sole guide of youth
> Unswerving Truth:
> 15   In the inmost shrine

---

[168] Fuller seems to be citing great artists, such as Canova, Beethoven, and Michelangelo, whose personal lives mirrored their aesthetic idealization of women in their art. This is another instance of Fuller's "spiritualization" (here "aestheticization") of relations between men and women. The nineteenth-century and early-modern "cult of beauty" was certainly one of the most pernicious factors working to hold women in cultural, political, and personal bondage. [Ed.]

Stands the image divine,
Only seen
By those whose deeds have worthy been —
Priestlike clean.
20 Those, who initiated are,
Declare,
As the hours
Usher in varying hopes and powers;
It changes its face,
25 It changes its age,
Now a young beaming Grace,
Now Nestorian Sage: [169]
But, to the pure in heart,
This shape of primal art
30 In age is fair,
In youth seems wise,
Beyond compare,
Above surprise;
What it teaches native seems
35 Its new lore our ancient dreams;
Incense rises from the ground,
Music flows around;
Firm rest the feet below, clear gaze the eyes above,
When Truth to point the way through Life assumes the wand of Love;
40 But, if she cast aside the robe of green,
Winter's silver sheen,
White, pure as light,
Makes gentle shroud as worthy weed as bridal robe had been. [170]

We are now in a transition state, and but few steps have yet been taken. From polygamy, Europe passed to the marriage *de convenance*. [171] This was scarcely an improvement. An attempt was then made to substitute genuine

---

[169] Nestor is the wise counselor in Homer's *Iliad* and *Odyssey*. [Ed.]

[170] (*As described by the historian.*)

The temple of Juno is like what the character of woman should be.
Columns! graceful decorums, attractive yet sheltering.
Porch! noble inviting aspect of the life.
Kaos! receives the worshippers. See here the statue of the Divinity.
Ophistodomos! Sanctuary where the most precious possessions were kept safe from the hand of the spoiler and the eye of the world. [Fuller's note. The poem is Fuller's.]

[171] French: arranged marriage. Fuller is again subscribing to the progressive rhetoric of the romantics and transcendentalists. [Ed.]

marriage, (the mutual choice of souls inducing a permanent union,) as yet baffled on every side by the haste, the ignorance, or the impurity of man. Where man assumes a high principle to which he is not yet ripened; it will happen, for a long time, that the few will be nobler than before; the many worse. Thus now. In the country of Sidney and Milton, the metropolis is a den of wickedness, and a stye of sensuality; in the country of Lady Russell, the custom of English Peeresses, of selling their daughters to the highest bidder, is made the theme and jest of fashionable novels by unthinking children who would stare at the idea of sending them to a Turkish slave dealer, though the circumstances of the bargain are there less degrading, as the will and thoughts of the person sold are not so degraded by it, and it is not done in defiance of an acknowledged law of right in the land and the age.[172]

I must here add that I do not believe there ever was put upon record more depravation of man, and more despicable frivolity of thought and aim in woman, than in the novels which purport to give the picture of English fashionable life, which are read with such favor in our drawing rooms, and give the tone to the manners of some circles. Compared with the hardhearted cold folly there described, crime is hopeful, for it, at least, shows some power remaining in the mental constitution.

To return: Attention has been awakened among men to the stains of celibacy, and the profanations of marriage. They begin to write about it and lecture about it. It is the tendency now to endeavor to help the erring by showing them the physical law. This is wise and excellent; but forget not the better half. Cold bathing and exercise will not suffice to keep a life pure, without an inward baptism and noble and exhilarating employment for the thoughts and the passions. Early marriages are desirable, but if, (and the world is now so out of joint that there are a hundred thousand chances to one against it,) a man does not early, or at all, find the person to whom he can be united in the marriage of souls, will you give him in the marriage *de convenance,* or if not married, can you find no way for him to lead a virtuous and happy life? Think of it well, ye who think yourselves better than pagans, for many of *them* knew this sure way.[173]

To you, women of America, it is more especially my business to address myself on this subject, and my advice may be classed under three heads:

---

[172] Lady Rachel Russell (1636–1723) was the wife of Lord William Russell and an aristocratic woman of letters. Lady Russell is also the name of the marriage-arranger in Jane Austen's *Persuasion* (1818) (Dickenson 245–246). [Ed.]

[173] The Persian sacred books, the Desatir, describe the great and holy prince Ky Khosrou, as being "an angel, and the son of an angel," one to whom the Supreme says, "Thou art not absent from before me for one twinkling of an eye. I am never out of thy heart. And I am contained in nothing but in thy heart, and in a heart like thy heart. And I am nearer

Clear your souls from the taint of vanity.

Do not rejoice in conquests, either that your power to allure may be seen by other women, or for the pleasure of rousing passionate feelings that gratify your love of excitement.

It must happen, no doubt, that frank and generous women will excite love they do not reciprocate, but, in nine cases out of ten, the woman has, half consciously, done much to excite. In this case she shall not be held guiltless, either as to the unhappiness or injury to the lover. Pure love, inspired by a worthy object, must ennoble and bless, whether mutual or not; but that which is excited by coquettish attraction of any grade of refinement, must cause bitterness and doubt, as to the reality of human goodness, so soon as the flush of passion is over. And that you may avoid all taste for these false pleasures

"Steep the soul
In one pure love, and it will last thee long."

The love of truth, the love of excellence, which, whether you clothe them in the person of a special object or not, will have power to save you from following Duessa, and lead you in the green glades where Una's feet have trod.[174]

It was on this one subject that a venerable champion of good, the last representative of the spirit which sanctified the revolution and gave our country such a sunlight of hope in the eyes of the nations, the same who lately in Boston offered anew to the young men the pledge taken by the young men of his day, offered, also, his counsel, on being addressed by the principal of a girl's school, thus:

REPLY OF MR. ADAMS [175]

Mr. Adams was so deeply affected by the address of Miss Foster,[176] as to be for some time inaudible. When heard, he spoke as follows:

---

unto thee than thou art to thyself." This Prince had in his Golden Seraglio three ladies of surpassing beauty, and all four, in this royal monastery, passed their lives, and left the world, as virgins.

The Persian people had no scepticism when the history of such a mind was narrated. They were Catholics. [Fuller's note. See Emerson's essay "Experience," n. 15, on p. 174.—Ed.]

[174] Una allegorizes Truth and Duessa Evil in Edmund Spenser's *The Faerie Queene*. [Ed.]

[175] John Quincy Adams (1767–1848), sixth president of the United States, loyally supported by Fuller's father Timothy, who was a U.S. congressman until 1825. When Andrew Jackson was elected president in 1828, Timothy Fuller's political hopes were dashed. [Ed.]

[176] Hannah Foster (1759–1840), novelist and educator, author of *The Coquette* (1797) and *The Boarding School; or, Lessons of a Preceptress to Her Pupils* (1798) (Reynolds, *Woman* 84). [Ed.]

"This is the first instance in which a lady has thus addressed me personally; and I trust that all the ladies present will be able sufficiently to enter into my feelings to know, that I am more affected by this honor, than by any other I could have received.

"You have been pleased, Madam, to allude to the character of my father,[177] and the history of my family, and their services to the country. It is indeed true, that from the existence of the Republic as an independent nation, my father and myself have been in the public service of the country, almost without interruption. I came into the world, as a person having personal responsibilities, with the Declaration of Independence, which constituted us a nation. I was a child at that time, and had then perhaps the greatest of blessings that can be bestowed on man — a mother who was anxious and capable to form her children to what they ought to be.[178] From that mother I derived whatever instruction — religious especially, and moral — has pervaded a long life; I will not say perfectly, and as it ought to be; but I will say, because it is justice only to the memory of her whom I revere, that if, in the course of my life, there has been any imperfection, or deviation from what she taught me, the fault is mine, and not hers.

"With such a mother, and such other relations with the sex, of sister, wife, and daughter, it has been the perpetual instruction of my life to love and revere the female sex. And in order to carry that sentiment of love and reverence to its highest degree of perfection, I know of nothing that exists in human society better adapted to produce that result, than institutions of the character that I have now the honor to address.

"I have been taught, as I have said, through the course of my life, to love and to revere the female sex; but I have been taught, also — and that lesson has perhaps impressed itself on my mind even more strongly, it may be, than the other — I have been taught not to flatter them. It is not unusual in the intercourse of man with the other sex — and especially for young men — to think, that the way to win the hearts of ladies is by flattery. — To love and to revere the sex, is what I think the duty of man; but *not to flatter them;* and this I would say to the young ladies here; and if they, and others present, will allow me, with all the authority which nearly four score years may have with those who have not yet attained one score — I would say to them what I have no doubt they say to themselves, and are taught here, not to take the flattery of men as proof of perfection.

"I am now, however, I fear, assuming too much of a character that does

---

[177] John Adams (1735–1826), second president of the United States. [Ed.]

[178] Abigail Smith Adams (1744–1818), known from her published letters as prose stylist and historian of the American Revolution. [Ed.]

not exactly belong to me. I therefore conclude, by assuring you, Madam, that your reception of me has affected me, as you perceive, more than I can express in words; and that I shall offer my best prayers, till my latest hour, to the Creator of us all, that this institution especially, and all others of a similar kind, designed to form the female mind to wisdom and virtue, may prosper to the end of time."

It will be interesting to add here the character of Mr. Adams's mother, as drawn by her husband, the first John Adams, in a family letter[179] written just before his death.

"I have reserved for the last the life of Lady Russell. This I have not yet read, because I read it more than forty years ago. On this hangs a tale which you ought to know and communicate it to your children. I bought the life and letters of Lady Russell, in the year 1775, and sent it to your grand-mother, with an express intent and desire, that she should consider it a mirror in which to contemplate herself; for, at that time, I thought it ex-tremely probable, from the daring and dangerous career I was determined to run, that she would one day find herself in the situation of Lady Russell, her husband without a head.[180] This lady was more beautiful than Lady Russell, had a brighter genius, more information, a more refined taste, and, at least, her equal in the virtues of the heart; equal fortitude and firm-ness of character, equal resignation to the will of Heaven, equal in all the virtues and graces of the christian life. Like Lady Russell, she never, by word or look, discouraged me from running all hazards for the salvation of my country's liberties; she was willing to share with me, and that her children should share with us both, in all the dangerous consequences we had to hazard."

Will a woman who loves flattery or an aimless excitement, who wastes the flower of her mind on transitory sentiments, ever be loved with a love like that, when fifty years trial have entitled to the privileges of "the golden marriage?"

Such was the love of the iron-handed warrior for her, not his hand-maid, but his help-meet:

"Whom God loves, to him gives he such a wife."

I find the whole of what I want in this relation, in the two epithets by which Milton makes Adam address *his* wife.

---

[179] Journal and Correspondence of Miss Adams, vol. i. p. 246. [Fuller's note. John Adams's letter is dated 12 July 1820 (Reynolds, *Woman* 85). —Ed.]

[180] See n. 172. Lord Russell was beheaded for treason in 1683, and Adams imagines he may suffer the same fate during the American Revolution. [Ed.]

In the intercourse of every day he begins:

"Daughter of God and man, *accomplished* Eve." [181]

In a moment of stronger feeling,

"Daughter of God and man, IMMORTAL Eve."

What majesty in the cadence of the line; what dignity, what reverence in the attitude, both of giver and receiver!

The woman who permits, in her life, the alloy of vanity; the woman who lives upon flattery, coarse or fine, shall never be thus addressed. She is *not* immortal as far as her will is concerned, and every woman who does so creates miasma, [182] whose spread is indefinite. The hand, which casts into the waters of life a stone of offence, knows not how far the circles thus caused, may spread their agitations.

A little while since, I was at one of the most fashionable places of public resort. I saw there many women, dressed without regard to the season or the demands of the place, in apery, or, as it looked, in mockery of European fashions. I saw their eyes restlessly courting attention. I saw the way in which it was paid, the style of devotion, almost an open sneer, which it pleased those ladies to receive from men whose expression marked their own low position in the moral and intellectual world. Those women went to their pillows with their heads full of folly, their hearts of jealousy, or gratified vanity: those men, with the low opinion they already entertained of woman confirmed. These were American *ladies;* i.e., they were of that class who have wealth and leisure to make full use of the day, and confer benefits on others. They were of that class whom the possession of external advantages makes of pernicious example to many, if these advantages be misused.

Soon after, I met a circle of women, stamped by society as among the most degraded of their sex. "How," it was asked of them, "did you come here?" for, by the society that I saw in the former place, they were shut up in a prison. [183] The causes were not difficult to trace: love of dress, love of flattery, love of excitement. They had not dresses like the other ladies, so they stole them; they could not pay for flattery by distinctions, and the

---

[181] See Appendix, H [Fuller's note. The quotations are from Milton's *Paradise Lost,* bk. 4, line 660, and bk. 9, line 291, respectively (Reynolds, *Woman* 86). —Ed.]

[182] An infectious or noxious emanation, such as swamp gas. [Ed.]

[183] In 1844, Fuller visited women inmates at Sing Sing Prison in New York (see her "Letter to the Women Inmates at Sing Sing" [Reynolds, *Woman* 205]), thus anticipating modern feminists involved in prison reform. [Ed.]

dower of a worldly marriage, so they paid by the profanation of their persons. In excitement, more and more madly sought from day to day, they drowned the voice of conscience.

Now I ask you, my sisters, if the women at the fashionable house be not answerable for those women being in the prison?

As to position in the world of souls, we may suppose the women of the prison stood fairest, both because they had misused less light, and because loneliness and sorrow had brought some of them to feel the need of better life, nearer truth and good. This was no merit in them, being an effect of circumstance, but it was hopeful. But you, my friends, (and some of you I have already met,) consecrate yourselves without waiting for reproof, in free love and unbroken energy, to win and to diffuse a better life. Offer beauty, talents, riches, on the altar; thus shall ye keep spotless your own hearts, and be visibly or invisibly the angels to others.

I would urge upon those women who have not yet considered this subject, to do so. Do not forget the unfortunates who dare not cross your guarded way. If it do not suit you to act with those who have organized measures of reform, then hold not yourself excused from acting in private. Seek out these degraded women, give them tender sympathy, counsel, employment. Take the place of mothers, such as might have saved them originally.

If you can do little for those already under the ban of the world, and the best considered efforts have often failed, from a want of strength in those unhappy ones to bear up against the sting of shame and the prejudices of the world, which makes them seek oblivion again in their old excitements, you will at least leave a sense of love and justice in their hearts that will prevent their becoming utterly imbittered and corrupt. And you may learn the means of prevention for those yet uninjured. There will be found in a diffusion of mental culture, simple tastes, best taught by your example, a genuine self-respect, and above all, what the influence of man tends to hide from woman, the love and fear of a divine, in preference to a human tribunal.

But suppose you save many who would have lost their bodily innocence (for as to mental, the loss of that is incalculably more general,) through mere vanity and folly; there still remain many, the prey and spoil of the brute passions of man. For the stories frequent in our newspapers outshame antiquity, and vie with the horrors of war.

As to this, it must be considered that, as the vanity and proneness to seduction of the imprisoned women represented a general degradation in their sex; so do these acts a still more general and worse in the male. Where so many are weak it is natural there should be many lost, where legislators admit that ten thousand prostitutes are a fair proportion to one city, and husbands tell their wives that it is folly to expect chastity from men, it is inevitable that there should be many monsters of vice.

I must in this place mention, with respect and gratitude, the conduct of Mrs. Child in the case of Amelia Norman.[184] The action and speech of this lady was of straight-forward nobleness, undeterred by custom or cavil from duty towards an injured sister. She showed the case and the arguments the counsel against the prisoner had the assurance to use in their true light to the public. She put the case on the only ground of religion and equity. She was successful in arresting the attention of many who had before shrugged their shoulders, and let sin pass as necessarily a part of the company of men. They begin to ask whether virtue is not possible, perhaps necessary, to man as well as to woman. They begin to fear that the perdition of a woman must involve that of a man. This is a crisis. The results of this case will be important.

In this connection I must mention Eugène Sue,[185] the French novelist, several of whose works have been lately transplanted among us, as having the true spirit of reform as to women. Like every other French writer, he is still tainted with the transmissions of the old regime. Still falsehood may be permitted for the sake of advancing truth, evil as the way to good. Even George Sand, who would trample on every graceful decorum, and every human law for the sake of a sincere life, does not see that she violates it by making her heroines able to tell falsehoods in a good cause. These French writers need ever to be confronted by the clear perception of the English and German mind, that the only good man, consequently the only good reformer, is he

"Who bases good on good alone, and owes
To virtue every triumph that he knows."

Still, Sue has the heart of a reformer, and especially towards women, he sees what they need, and what causes are injuring them. From the histories of Fleur de Marie and La Louve, from the lovely and independent character of Rigolette, from the distortion given to Matilda's mind, by the present views of marriage, and from the truly noble and immortal character of the "hump-backed Sempstress" in the "Wandering Jew," may be gathered

---

[184] Abolitionist, feminist, and advocate of Native American rights, Lydia Maria Child (1802–80), a close friend of Fuller's, championed the cause of Amelia Norman, a young woman acquitted of publicly stabbing her seducer (Reynolds, *Woman* 87). [Ed.]

[185] Eugène Sue's (1804–57) popular novels about the French underclass sensationalize and sentimentalize the victimization of poor women, such as Fleur de Marie and La Louve and Rigolette in *Mysteries of Paris* (1842–43) and the seamstress in *The Wandering Jew* (1844–45). [Ed.]

much that shall elucidate doubt and direct inquiry on this subject. In reform, as in philosophy, the French are the interpreters to the civilized
world. Their own attainments are not great, but they make clear the past,
and break down barriers to the future.

Observe that the good man of Sue is pure as Sir Charles Grandison.[186]

Apropos to Sir Charles, women are accustomed to be told by men that
the reform is to come *from them*. "You," say the men, "must frown upon
vice, you must decline the attentions of the corrupt, you must not submit to
the will of your husband when it seems to you unworthy, but give the laws
in marriage, and redeem it from its present sensual and mental pollutions."

This seems to us hard. Men have, indeed, been, for more than a hundred
years, rating women for countenancing vice. But at the same time, they
have carefully hid from them its nature, so that the preference often shown
by women for bad men, arises rather from a confused idea that they are
bold and adventurous, acquainted with regions which women are forbidden to explore, and the curiosity that ensues, than a corrupt heart in the
woman. As to marriage it has been inculcated on women for centuries, that
men have not only stronger passions than they, but of a sort that it would be
shameful for them to share or even understand. That, therefore, they must
"confide in their husbands," i.e., submit implicitly to their will. That the
least appearance of coldness or withdrawal, from whatever cause, in the wife
is wicked, because liable to turn her husband's thoughts to illicit indulgence; for a man is so constituted that he must indulge his passions or die!

Accordingly a great part of women look upon men as a kind of wild
beasts, but "suppose they are all alike;" the unmarried are assured by the
married that, "if they knew men as they do," i.e., by being married to them,
"they would not expect continence or self-government from them."

I might accumulate illustrations on this theme, drawn from acquaintance with the histories of women, which would startle and grieve all thinking men, but I forbear. Let Sir Charles Grandison preach to his own sex, or
if none there be, who feels himself able to speak with authority from a life
unspotted in will or deed, let those who are convinced of the practicability
and need of a pure life, as the foreign artist was, advise the others, and warn
them by their own example, if need be.

The following passage from a female writer on female affairs, expresses
a prevalent way of thinking on this subject.

"It may be that a young woman, exempt from all motives of vanity, determines to take for a husband a man who does not inspire her with a very

---

[186] The self-righteous protagonist of Samuel Richardson's (1689–1761) novel *The History
of Sir Charles Grandison* (1754), which Fuller proceeds in the next few paragraphs to analyze. [Ed.]

decided inclination. Imperious circumstances, the evident interest of her family, or the danger of a suffering celibacy, may explain such a resolution. If, however, she were to endeavor to surmount a personal repugnance, we should look upon this as *injudicious*. Such a rebellion of nature marks the limit that the influence of parents, or the self-sacrifice of the young girl, should never pass. *We shall be told that this repugnance is an affair of the imagination;* it may be so; but imagination is a power which it is temerity to brave; and its antipathy is more difficult to conquer than its preference." [187]

Among ourselves, the exhibition of such a repugnance from a woman who had been given in marriage "by advice of friends," was treated by an eminent physician as sufficient proof of insanity. If he had said sufficient cause for it, he would have been nearer right.

It has been suggested by men who were pained by seeing bad men admitted, freely, to the society of modest women, thereby encouraged to vice by impunity, and corrupting the atmosphere of homes; that there should be a senate of the matrons in each city and town, who should decide what candidates were fit for admission to their houses and the society of their daughters. [188]

Such a plan might have excellent results, but it argues a moral dignity and decision, which does not yet exist, and needs to be induced by knowledge and reflection. It has been the tone to keep women ignorant on these subjects, or when they were not, to command that they should seem so. "It is indelicate," says the father or husband, "to inquire into the private character of such an one. It is sufficient that I do not think him unfit to visit you." And so, this man, who would not tolerate these pages in his house, "unfit for family reading," because they speak plainly, introduces there a man whose shame is written on his brow, as well as the open secret of the whole town, and, presently, if *respectable* still, and rich enough, gives him his daughter to wife. The mother affects ignorance, "supposing he is no worse than most men." The daughter *is* ignorant; something in the mind of the new spouse seems strange to her, but she supposes it is "woman's lot" not to be perfectly happy in her affections; she has always heard, "men could not understand women," so she weeps alone, or takes to dress and the duties of the house. The husband, of course, makes no avowal, and dreams of no redemption.

"In the heart of every young woman," says the female writer, above quoted, addressing herself to the husband, "depend upon it, there is a fund

---

[187] Madame Necker de Saussure. [Fuller's note. Albertine Necker de Saussure (1766–1841), cousin, friend, and biographer of Madame de Staël (Dickenson 247).—Ed.]

[188] See Goethe's Tasso. "A synod of good women should decide,"—if the golden age is to be restored. [Fuller's note. Goethe's *Torquato Tasso* (see n. 157).—Ed.]

of exalted ideas; she conceals, represses, without succeeding in smothering them. *So long as these ideas in your wife are directed to* YOU, *they are, no doubt, innocent,* but take care that they be not accompanied with *too much* pain. In other respects, also, spare her delicacy. Let all the antecedent parts of your life, if there are such, which would give her pain, be concealed from her; *her happiness and her respect for you would suffer from this misplaced confidence.* Allow her to retain that flower of purity, *which should distinguish her in your eyes from every other woman.*" We should think so, truly, under this canon. Such a man must esteem purity an exotic that could only be preserved by the greatest care. Of the degree of mental intimacy possible, in such a marriage, let every one judge for himself!

On this subject, let every woman, who has once begun to think, examine herself, see whether she does not suppose virtue possible and necessary to man, and whether she would not desire for her son a virtue which aimed at a fitness for a divine life, and involved, if not asceticism, that degree of power over the lower self, which shall "not exterminate the passions, but keep them chained at the feet of reason." The passions, like fire, are a bad master; but confine them to the hearth and the altar, and they give life to the social economy, and make each sacrifice meet for heaven.

When many women have thought upon this subject, some will be fit for the Senate, and one such Senate in operation would affect the morals of the civilized world.

At present I look to the young. As preparatory to the Senate, I should like to see a society of novices, such as the world has never yet seen, bound by no oath, wearing no badge. In place of an oath they should have a religious faith in the capacity of man for virtue; instead of a badge, should wear in the heart a firm resolve not to stop short of the destiny promised him as a son of God. Their service should be action and conservatism, not of old habits, but of a better nature, enlightened by hopes that daily grow brighter.

If sin was to remain in the world, it should not be by their connivance at its stay, or one moment's concession to its claims.

They should succor the oppressed, and pay to the upright the reverence due in hero-worship by seeking to emulate them. They would not denounce the willingly bad, but they could not be with them, for the two classes could not breathe the same atmosphere.

They would heed no detention from the time-serving, the worldly and the timid.

They could love no pleasures that were not innocent and capable of good fruit.

I saw, in a foreign paper, the title now given to a party abroad, "Los Exaltados." Such would be the title now given these children by the world: Los

Exaltados, Las Exaltadas;[189] but the world would not sneer always, for from them would issue a virtue by which it would, at last, be exalted too.

I have in my eye a youth and a maiden whom I look to as the nucleus of such a class. They are both in early youth, both as yet uncontaminated, both aspiring, without rashness, both thoughtful, both capable of deep affection, both of strong nature and sweet feelings, both capable of large mental development. They reside in different regions of earth, but their place in the soul is the same. To them I look, as, perhaps, the harbingers and leaders of a new era, for never yet have I known minds so truly virgin, without narrowness or ignorance.

When men call upon women to redeem them, they mean such maidens. But such are not easily formed under the present influences of society. As there are more such young men to help give a different tone, there will be more such maidens.

The English novelist, D'Israeli, has, in his novel of the "Young Duke,"[190] made a man of the most depraved stock be redeemed by a woman who despises him when he has only the brilliant mask of fortune and beauty to cover the poverty of his heart and brain, but knows how to encourage him when he enters on a better course. But this woman was educated by a father who valued character in women.

Still there will come now and then, one who will, as I hope of my young Exaltada, be example and instruction to the rest. It was not the opinion of woman current among Jewish men that formed the character of the mother of Jesus.

Since the sliding and backsliding men of the world, no less than the mystics declare that, as through woman man was lost, so through woman must man be redeemed, the time must be at hand. When she knows herself indeed as "accomplished," still more as "immortal Eve," this may be.

As an immortal, she may also know and inspire immortal love, a happiness not to be dreamed of under the circumstances advised in the last quotation. Where love is based on concealment, it must, of course, disappear when the soul enters the scene of clear vision!

And, without this hope, how worthless every plan, every bond, every power!

---

[189] Spanish liberal political party of the 1820s. Fuller anticipates feminists of the National Organization for Women and others in the New Left by insisting on the feminine form of the group's name to recognize the inclusion of women and thus acknowledge the sexual politics of language (Dickenson 247). [Ed.]

[190] Benjamin Disraeli (1804–1881), author of the autobiographical novel *The Young Duke* (1831) and later Conservative prime minister of Great Britain (Dickenson 248). [Ed.]

"The giants," said the Scandinavian Saga, "had induced Loke, (the spirit that hovers between good and ill,) to steal for them Iduna, (Goddess of Immortality,) and her apples of pure gold." He lured her out, by promising to show, on a marvellous tree he had discovered, apples beautiful as her own, if she would only take them with her for a comparison. Thus, having lured her beyond the heavenly domain, she was seized and carried away captive by the powers of misrule.

As now the gods could not find their friend Iduna, they were confused with grief; indeed they began visibly to grow old and gray. Discords arose, and love grew cold. Indeed, Odur, spouse of the goddess of love and beauty, wandered away and returned no more. At last, however, the gods, discovering the treachery of Loke, obliged him to win back Iduna from the prison in which she sat mourning. He changed himself into a falcon, and brought her back as a swallow, fiercely pursued by the Giant King, in the form of an eagle. So she strives to return among us, light and small as a swallow. We must welcome her form as the speck on the sky that assures the glad blue of Summer. Yet one swallow does not make a summer. Let us solicit them in flights and flocks!

Returning from the future to the present, let us see what forms Iduna takes, as she moves along the declivity of centuries to the valley where the lily flower may concentrate all its fragrance.

It would seem as if this time were not very near to one fresh from books, such as I have of late been—no: *not* reading, but sighing over. A crowd of books having been sent me since my friends knew me to be engaged in this way, on Woman's "Sphere," Woman's "Mission," and Woman's "Destiny," I believe that almost all that is extant of formal precept has come under my eye. Among these I read with refreshment, a little one called "The Whole Duty of Woman," "indited by a noble lady at the request of a noble lord," and which has this much of nobleness, that the view it takes is a religious one.[191] It aims to fit woman for heaven, the main bent of most of the others is to fit her to please, or, at least, not to disturb a husband.

Among these I select as a favorable specimen, the book I have already quoted, "The Study[192] of the Life of Woman, by Madame Necker de Saus-

---

[191] Eighteenth- and nineteenth-century "conduct" books offered exempla for women's conduct, developed in part out of anchorites' (or nuns') medieval conduct books. They powerfully influenced the development of the modern novel and its characters and plots. [Ed.]

[192] This title seems to be incorrectly translated from the French. I have not seen the original. [Fuller's note. *L'Éducation progressive; ou, Étude du cours de la vie, par Mme Necker de Saussure* (Paris, 1828–32) (Dickenson 248).—Ed.]

sure, of Geneva, translated from the French." This book was published at Philadelphia, and has been read with much favor here. Madame Necker is the cousin of Madame de Stael, and has taken from her works the motto prefixed to this.

"Cette vie n'a quelque prix que si elle sert a' l'education morale de notre coeur." [193]

Mde. Necker is, by nature, capable of entire consistency in the application of this motto, and, therefore, the qualifications she makes, in the instructions given to her own sex, show forcibly the weight which still paralyzes and distorts the energies of that sex.

The book is rich in passages marked by feeling and good suggestions, but taken in the whole the impression it leaves is this:

Woman is, and *shall remain* inferior to man and subject to his will, and, in endeavoring to aid her, we must anxiously avoid any thing that can be misconstrued into expression of the contrary opinion, else the men will be alarmed, and combine to defeat our efforts.

The present is a good time for these efforts, for men are less occupied about women than formerly. Let us, then, seize upon the occasion, and do what we can to make our lot tolerable. But we must sedulously avoid encroaching on the territory of man. If we study natural history, our observations may be made useful, by some male naturalist; if we draw well, we may make our services acceptable to the artists. But our names must not be known, and, to bring these labors to any result, we must take some man for our head, and be his hands.

The lot of woman is sad. She is constituted to expect and need a happiness that cannot exist on earth. She must stifle such aspirations within her secret heart, and fit herself, as well as she can, for a life of resignations and consolations.

She will be very lonely while living with her husband. She must not expect to open her heart to him fully, or that, after marriage, he will be capable of the refined service of love. The man is not born for the woman, only the woman for the man. "Men cannot understand the hearts of women." The life of woman must be outwardly a well-intentioned, cheerful dissimulation of her real life.

Naturally, the feelings of the mother, at the birth of a female child, resemble those of the Paraguay woman, described by Southey as lamenting in such heart-breaking tones that her mother did not kill her the hour she was born. "Her mother, who knew what the life of a woman must be;" — or

---

[193] French: This life has value only if it serves the moral education of our heart. [Ed.]

those women seen at the north by Sir A. Mackenzie,[194] who performed this pious duty towards female infants whenever they had an opportunity.

"After the first delight, the young mother experiences feelings a little different, according as the birth of a son or a daughter has been announced.

"Is it a son? A sort of glory swells at this thought the heart of the mother; she seems to feel that she is entitled to gratitude. She has given a citizen, a defender to her country. To her husband an heir of his name, to herself a protector. And yet the contrast of all these fine titles with this being, so humble, soon strikes her. At the aspect of this frail treasure, opposite feelings agitate her heart; she seems to recognize in him *a nature superior to her own*, but subjected to a low condition, and she honors a future greatness in the object of extreme compassion. Somewhat of that respect and adoration for a feeble child, of which some fine pictures offer the expression in the features of the happy Mary, seem reproduced with the young mother who has given birth to a son.

"Is it a daughter? There is usually a slight degree of regret; so deeply rooted is the idea of the superiority of man in happiness and dignity, and yet, as she looks upon this child, she is more and more *softened* towards it—a deep sympathy—a sentiment of identity with this delicate being takes possession of her; an extreme pity for so much weakness, a more pressing need of prayer stirs her heart. Whatever sorrows she may have felt, she dreads for her daughter; but she will guide her to become much wiser, much better than herself. And then the gayety, the frivolity of the young woman have their turn. This little creature is a flower to cultivate, a doll to decorate."

Similar sadness at the birth of a daughter I have heard mothers express not unfrequently.

As to this living so entirely for men, I should think when it was proposed to women they would feel, at least, some spark of the old spirit of races allied to our own. If he is to be my bridegroom *and lord*, cries Brunhilda,[195] he must first be able to pass through fire and water. I will serve at the banquet, says the Valkyrie, but only him who, in the trial of deadly combat, has shown himself a hero.

---

[194] Sir Alexander Mackenzie (c. 1755–1820), Scottish explorer of northern and western Canada. (Dickenson 248). [Ed.]

[195] See the Nibelungen Lays. [Fuller's note. In the medieval German epic *Das Niebelungenlied*, Brünhilda is a Valkyrie, or goddess, who decides the life and death of warriors. Punished by Odin, she is rescued by the epic hero, Siegfried, who rides through the magic fire and moats surrounding her castle.—Ed.]

If women are to be bond-maids, let it be to men superior to women in fortitude, in aspiration, in moral power, in refined sense of beauty! You who give yourselves "to be supported," or because "one must love something," are they who make the lot of the sex such that mothers are sad when daughters are born.

It marks the state of feeling on this subject that it was mentioned, as a bitter censure on a woman who had influence over those younger than herself. "She makes those girls want to see heroes?"

"And will that hurt them?"

"Certainly; how *can* you ask? They will find none, and so they will never be married."

"*Get* married" is the usual phrase, and the one that correctly indicates the thought, but the speakers, on this occasion, were persons too outwardly refined to use it. They were ashamed of the word, but not of the thing. Madame Necker, however, sees good possible in celibacy.

Indeed, I know not how the subject could be better illustrated, than by separating the wheat from the chaff in Madame Necker's book; place them in two heaps and then summon the reader to choose; giving him first a near-sighted glass to examine the two; it might be a christian, an astronomical, or an artistic glass, any kind of good glass to obviate acquired defects in the eye. I would lay any wager on the result.

But time permits not here a prolonged analysis. I have given the clues for fault-finding.

As a specimen of the good take the following passage, on the phenomena of what I have spoken of, as the lyrical or electric element in woman.

"Women have been seen to show themselves poets in the most pathetic pantomimic scenes, where all the passions were depicted full of beauty; and these poets used a language unknown to themselves, and the performance once over, their inspiration was a forgotten dream. Without doubt there is an interior development to beings so gifted, but their sole mode of communication with us is their talent. They are, in all besides, the inhabitants of another planet."

Similar observations have been made by those who have seen the women at Irish wakes, or the funeral ceremonies of modern Greece or Brittany, at times when excitement gave the impulse to genius; but, apparently, without a thought that these rare powers belonged to no other planet, but were a high development of the growth of this, and might by wise and reverent treatment, be made to inform and embellish the scenes of every day. But, when woman has her fair chance, they will do so, and the poem of the hour will vie with that of the ages. I come now with satisfaction to my own country, and to a writer, a female writer, whom I have selected as the clearest, wisest, and kindliest, who has as yet, used pen here on these subjects. This is Miss Sedgwick.[196]

Miss Sedgwick, though she inclines to the private path, and wishes that, by the cultivation of character, might should vindicate right, sets limits nowhere, and her objects and inducements are pure. They are the free and careful cultivation of the powers that have been given, with an aim at moral and intellectual perfection. Her speech is moderate and sane, but never palsied by fear or sceptical caution.

Herself a fine example of the independent and beneficent existence that intellect and character can give to woman, no less than man; if she know how to seek and prize it; also that the intellect need not absorb or weaken, but rather will refine and invigorate the affections, the teachings of her practical good sense come with great force, and cannot fail to avail much. Every way her writings please me both as to the means and the ends. I am pleased at the stress she lays on observance of the physical laws, because the true reason is given. Only in a strong and clean body can the soul do its message fitly.

She shows the meaning of the respect paid to personal neatness both in the indispensable form of cleanliness, and of that love of order and arrangement, that must issue from a true harmony of feeling.

The praises of cold water seem to me an excellent sign in the age. They denote a tendency to the true life. We are now to have, as a remedy for ills, not orvietan, or opium, or any quack medicine, but plenty of air and water, with due attention to warmth and freedom in dress, and simplicity of diet.

Every day we observe signs that the natural feelings on these subjects are about to be reinstated, and the body to claim care as the abode and organ of the soul, not as the tool of servile labor, or the object of voluptuous indulgence.

A poor woman who had passed through the lowest grades of ignominy, seemed to think she had never been wholly lost, "for," said she, "I would always have good under-clothes;" and, indeed, who could doubt that this denoted the remains of private self-respect in the mind?

A woman of excellent sense said, "it might seem childish, but to her one of the most favorable signs of the times, was that the ladies had been persuaded to give up corsets."

Yes! let us give up all artificial means of distortion. Let life be healthy, pure, all of a piece. Miss Sedgwick, in teaching that domestics must have

---

[196] Catharine Maria Sedgwick (1789–1867), American novelist and essayist of such works as *Hope Leslie* (1827) and *Tales and Sketches* (1835), both of which Fuller read (Dickenson 248). [Ed.]

the means of bathing as much as their mistresses, and time, too, to bathe, has symbolized one of the most important of human rights.

Another interesting sign of the time is the influence exercised by two women, Miss Martineau and Miss Barrett, from their sick rooms.[197] The lamp of life which, if it had been fed only by the affections, depended on precarious human relations, would scarce have been able to maintain a feeble glare in the lonely prison, now shines far and wide over the nations, cheering fellow sufferers and hallowing the joy of the healthful.

These persons need not health or youth, or the charms of personal presence, to make their thoughts available. A few more such, and old woman[198] shall not be the synonyme for imbecility, nor old maid a term of contempt, nor woman be spoken of as a reed shaken in the wind.

It is time, indeed, that men and women both should cease to grow old in any other way than as the tree does, full of grace and honor. The hair of the artist turns white, but his eye shines clearer than ever, and we feel that age brings him maturity, not decay. So would it be with all were the springs of immortal refreshment but unsealed within the soul, then like these women they would see, from the lonely chamber window, the glories of the universe; or, shut in darkness, be visited by angels.

I now touch on my own place and day, and, as I write, events are occurring that threaten the fair fabric approached by so long an avenue. Week before last the Gentile was requested to aid the Jew to return to Palestine, for the Millennium, the reign of the Son of Mary, was near. Just now, at high and solemn mass, thanks were returned to the Virgin for having delivered O'Connell[199] from unjust imprisonment, in requital of his having consecrated to her the league formed in behalf of Liberty on Tara's Hill. But, last week brought news which threatens that a cause identical with the enfranchisement of Jews, Irish, women, ay, and of Americans in general, too, is in danger, for the choice of the people threatens to rivet the chains

---

[197] Elizabeth Barrett (1806–91), English poet, was an invalid before she married Robert Browning. Harriet Martineau was an invalid between 1839 and 1844, during which period she completed two novels (Reynolds, *Woman* 97). Fuller is reacting here to patriarchal clichés about women as frail and subject to their physical and emotional vagaries, as well as to pseudo-medical diagnoses of women's "neurasthenia," or "nervous disorders" incapacitating them for a wide range of tasks. [Ed.]

[198] An apposite passage is quoted in appendix F. [Fuller's note. Fuller anticipates criticism of ageism and other forms of discrimination against people, especially women, because of their advanced ages.—Ed.]

[199] Daniel O'Connell (1775–1847), Irish nationalist. He was arrested in 1844 for sedition after organizing at Tara's Hill a meeting in which he argued for the repeal of the Act of Union linking Ireland with Wales, Scotland, and England in Great Britain (Dickenson 248–249). [Ed.]

of slavery and the leprosy of sin permanently on this nation, through the annexation of Texas![200]

Ah! if this should take place, who will dare again to feel the throb of heavenly hope, as to the destiny of this country? The noble thought that gave unity to all our knowledge, harmony to all our designs; — the thought that the progress of history had brought on the era, the tissue of prophecies pointed out the spot, where humanity was, at last, to have a fair chance to know itself, and all men be born free and equal for the eagle's flight, flutters as if about to leave the breast, which, deprived of it, will have no more a nation, no more a home on earth.

Women of my country! — Exaltadas! If such there be, — Women of English, old English nobleness, who understand the courage of Boadicea, the sacrifice of Godiva, the power of Queen Emma to tread the red hot iron unharmed. Women who share the nature of Mrs. Hutchinson, Lady Russell, and the mothers of our own revolution: have you nothing to do with this?[201] You see the men, how they are willing to sell shamelessly, the happiness of countless generations of fellow-creatures, the honor of their country, and their immortal souls, for a money market and political power. Do you not feel within you that which can reprove them, which can check, which can convince them? You would not speak in vain; whether each in her own home, or banded in unison.

Tell these men that you will not accept the glittering baubles, spacious dwellings, and plentiful service, they mean to offer you through these means. Tell them that the heart of women demands nobleness and honor in man, and that, if they have not purity, have not mercy, they are no longer fathers, lovers, husbands, sons of yours.

This cause is your own, for as I have before said, there is a reason why the foes of African slavery seek more freedom for women; but put it not upon that ground, but on the ground of right.

---

[200] The U.S. annexation of Texas was considered by many, especially abolitionists, to be an effort of proslavery interests to extend their territory. Most transcendentalists vigorously opposed Texas annexation, which occurred in December 1845, shortly after Fuller completed this text (Reynolds, *Woman* 97). [Ed.]

[201] In another catalogue of famous women reformers, Fuller demonstrates once again the international scope of her cultural contribution to the women's rights movement. Boadicea (d. 62 CE) led resistance to the Roman conquest of Britain. Lady Godiva (c. 1040–1080) rode naked through the Coventry countryside to convince her husband to remit a tax levied on his tenants. Queen Emma of England (d. 1052) was reputed to have undergone torture by hot iron to prove her chastity. Anne Hutchinson (1591–1643) was exiled from the Puritan Massachusetts Bay Colony to Rhode Island because of her antinomianism. (Dickenson 249). [Ed.]

If you have a power, it is a moral power. The films of interest are not so close around you as around the men. If you will but think, you cannot fail to wish to save the country from this disgrace. Let not slip the occasion, but do something to lift off the curse incurred by Eve.

You have heard the women engaged in the abolition movement accused of boldness, because they lifted the voice in public, and lifted the latch of the stranger. But were these acts, whether performed judiciously or no, *so* bold as to dare before God and man to partake the fruits of such offence as this?

You hear much of the modesty of your sex. Preserve it by filling the mind with noble desires that shall ward off the corruptions of vanity and idleness. A profligate woman, who left her accustomed haunts and took service in a New-York boarding-house, said "she had never heard talk so vile at the Five Points,[202] as from the ladies at the boarding-house." And why? Because they were idle; because, having nothing worthy to engage them, they dwelt, with unnatural curiosity, on the ill they dared not go to see.

It will not so much injure your modesty to have your name, by the unthinking, coupled with idle blame, as to have upon your soul the weight of not trying to save a whole race of women from the scorn that is put upon *their* modesty.

Think of this well! I entreat, I conjure you, before it is too late. It is my belief that something effectual might be done by women, if they would only consider the subject, and enter upon it in the true spirit, a spirit gentle, but firm, and which feared the offence of none, save One who is of purer eyes than to behold iniquity.

And now I have designated in outline, if not in fulness, the stream which is ever flowing from the heights of my thought.

In the earlier tract,[203] I was told, I did not make my meaning sufficiently clear. In this I have consequently tried to illustrate it in various ways, and may have been guilty of much repetition. Yet, as I am anxious to leave no room for doubt, I shall venture to retrace, once more, the scope of my design in points, as was done in old-fashioned sermons.

Man is a being of two-fold relations, to nature beneath, and intelligences above him. The earth is his school, if not his birth-place: God his object: life and thought, his means of interpreting nature, and aspiring to God.

Only a fraction of this purpose is accomplished in the life of any one man. Its entire accomplishment is to be hoped only from the sum of the lives of men, or man considered as a whole.

---

[202] A poor section of New York City known for its high rate of crime (Dickenson 250). [Ed.]

[203] "The Great Lawsuit." In the new sections Fuller wrote for *Woman in the Nineteenth Century*, she places much greater emphasis on specific political reforms and action. [Ed.]

As this whole has one soul and one body, any injury or obstruction to a part, or to the meanest member, affects the whole. Man can never be perfectly happy or virtuous, till all men are so.

To address man wisely, you must not forget that his life is partly animal, subject to the same laws with nature.

But you cannot address him wisely unless you consider him still more as soul, and appreciate the conditions and destiny of soul.

The growth of man is two-fold, masculine and feminine.

As far as these two methods can be distinguished they are so as

Energy and Harmony.

Power and Beauty.

Intellect and Love.

Or by some such rude classification, for we have not language primitive and pure enough to express such ideas with precision.

These two sides are supposed to be expressed in man and woman, that is, as the more and less, for the faculties have not been given pure to either, but only in preponderance. There are also exceptions in great number, such as men of far more beauty than power, and the reverse. But as a general rule, it seems to have been the intention to give a preponderance on the one side, that is called masculine, and on the other, one that is called feminine.

There cannot be a doubt that, if these two developments were in perfect harmony, they would correspond to and fulfil one another, like hemispheres, or the tenor and bass in music.

But there is no perfect harmony in human nature; and the two parts answer one another only now and then, or, if there be a persistent consonance, it can only be traced, at long intervals, instead of discoursing an obvious melody.

What is the cause of this?

Man, in the order of time, was developed first; as energy comes before harmony; power before beauty.

Woman was therefore under his care as an elder. He might have been her guardian and teacher.

But as human nature goes not straight forward, but by excessive action and then reaction in an undulated course, he misunderstood and abused his advantages, and became her temporal master instead of her spiritual sire.

On himself came the punishment. He educated woman more as a servant than a daughter, and found himself a king without a queen.

The children of this unequal union showed unequal natures, and, more and more, men seemed sons of the hand-maid, rather than princes.

At last there were so many Ishmaelites that the rest grew frightened and indignant. They laid the blame on Hagar, and drove her forth into the wilderness.

But there were none the fewer Ishmaelites for that.

At last men became a little wiser, and saw that the infant Moses was, in every case, saved by the pure instincts of woman's breast. For, as too much adversity is better for the moral nature than too much prosperity, woman, in this respect, dwindled less than man, though in other respects, still a child in leading strings.

So man did her more and more justice, and grew more and more kind.

But yet, his habits and his will corrupted by the past, he did not clearly see that woman was half himself, that her interests were identical with his, and that, by the law of their common being, he could never reach his true proportions while she remained in any wise shorn of hers.

And so it has gone on to our day; both ideas developing, but more slowly than they would under a clearer recognition of truth and justice, which would have permitted the sexes their due influence on one another, and mutual improvement from more dignified relations.

Wherever there was pure love, the natural influences were, for the time, restored.

Wherever the poet or artist gave free course to his genius, he saw the truth, and expressed it in worthy forms, for these men especially share and need the feminine principle. The divine birds need to be brooded into life and song by mothers.

Wherever religion (I mean the thirst for truth and good, not the love of sect and dogma,) had its course, the original design was apprehended in its simplicity, and the dove presaged sweetly from Dodona's oak.[204]

I have aimed to show that no age was left entirely without a witness of the equality of the sexes in function, duty and hope.

Also that, when there was unwillingness or ignorance, which prevented this being acted upon, women had not the less power for their want of light and noble freedom. But it was power which hurt alike them and those against whom they made use of the arms of the servile; cunning, blandishment, and unreasonable emotion.

That now the time has come when a clearer vision and better action are possible. When man and woman may regard one another as brother and sister, the pillars of one porch, the priests of one worship.

I have believed and intimated that this hope would receive an ampler fruition, than ever before, in our own land.

And it will do so if this land carry out the principles from which sprang our national life.

---

[204] Dodona in ancient Greece was the site of the oldest sanctuary to Zeus, who reputedly spoke through the rustlings of an oak tree's leaves (Reynolds, *Woman* 101). [Ed.]

I believe that, at present, women are the best helpers of one another. Let them think; let them act; till they know what they need.

We only ask of men to remove arbitrary barriers. Some would like to do more. But I believe it needs for woman to show herself in her native dignity, to teach them how to aid her; their minds are so encumbered by tradition.

When Lord Edward Fitzgerald[205] travelled with the Indians, his manly heart obliged him at once, to take the packs from the squaws and carry them. But we do not read that the red men followed his example, though they are ready enough to carry the pack of the white woman, because she seems to them a superior being.

Let woman appear in the mild majesty of Ceres, and rudest churls will be willing to learn from her.

You ask, what use will she make of liberty, when she has so long been sustained and restrained?

I answer; in the first place, this will not be suddenly given. I read yesterday a debate of this year on the subject of enlarging women's rights over property. It was a leaf from the class-book that is preparing for the needed instruction. The men learned visibly as they spoke. The champions of woman saw the fallacy of arguments, on the opposite side, and were startled by their own convictions. With their wives at home, and the readers of the paper, it was the same. And so the stream flows on; thought urging action, and action leading to the evolution of still better thought.

But, were this freedom to come suddenly, I have no fear of the consequences. Individuals might commit excesses, but there is not only in the sex a reverence for decorums and limits inherited and enhanced from generation to generation, which many years of other life could not efface, but a native love, in woman as woman, of proportion, of "the simple art of not too much," a Greek moderation, which would create immediately a restraining party, the natural legislators and instructors of the rest, and would gradually establish such rules as are needed to guard, without impeding, life.

The Graces would lead the choral dance, and teach the rest to regulate their steps to the measure of beauty.

But if you ask me what offices they may fill; I reply—any. I do not care what case you put; let them be sea-captains, if you will. I do not doubt there

---

[205] Lord Edward Fitzgerald (1763–98), an Irish aristocrat who traveled throughout the Mississippi Valley, served in the British army during the American Revolution, and later planned a French invasion of Ireland (Reynolds, *Woman* 101). Fuller's comments on the behaviors of Native American men toward their women relies on her observations in *Summer on the Lakes in 1843* (1844) and extends her inaccurate generalization of Native American patriarchy as "primitive."

are women well fitted for such an office, and, if so, I should be glad to see them in it, as to welcome the maid of Saragossa, or the maid of Missolonghi, or the Suliote heroine, or Emily Plater.[206]

I think women need, especially at this juncture, a much greater range of occupation than they have, to rouse their latent powers. A party of travellers lately visited a lonely hut on a mountain. There they found an old woman that told them she and her husband had lived there forty years. "Why," they said, "did you choose so barren a spot?" She "did not know; *it was the man's notion.*"

And, during forty years, she had been content to act, without knowing why, upon "the man's notion." I would not have it so.

In families that I know, some little girls like to saw wood, others to use carpenters' tools. Where these tastes are indulged, cheerfulness and good humor are promoted. Where they are forbidden, because "such things are not proper for girls," they grow sullen and mischievous.

Fourier had observed these wants of women, as no one can fail to do who watches the desires of little girls, or knows the ennui that haunts grown women, except where they make to themselves a serene little world by art of some kind. He, therefore, in proposing a great variety of employments, in manufactures or the care of plants and animals, allows for one third of women, as likely to have a taste for masculine pursuits, one third of men for feminine.

Who does not observe the immediate glow and serenity that is diffused over the life of women, before restless or fretful, by engaging in gardening, building, or the lowest department of art. Here is something that is not routine, something that draws forth life toward the infinite.

I have no doubt, however, that a large proportion of women would give themselves to the same employments as now, because there are circumstances that must lead them. Mothers will delight to make the nest soft and warm. Nature would take care of that; no need to clip the wings of any bird that wants to soar and sing, or finds in itself the strength of pinion for a migratory flight unusual to its kind. The difference would be that *all* need not be constrained to employments, for which *some* are unfit.

---

[206] Fuller provides another list of women who fought for liberty: Maria Agustín, the maid of Saragossa (modern Zaragoza), defended the city against the French invasion of 1808–09 and is a character in Byron's *Childe Harold's Pilgrimage* (1812) (canto 1, st. 55 ff.). Missolonghi, Greece, was besieged by the Turks during the war of Greek independence and was the site of Byron's death in 1824. He had gone there to join the Greek struggle. Who the maid was remains unclear. The Suliotes were inhabitants of the Greek island of Suli, who rebelled in 1820 against the Turks and were defeated in 1822. Emily Plater rebelled against Russian rule of Poland (see n. 38) (Dickenson 251). [Ed.]

I have urged upon the sex self-subsistence in its two forms of self-reliance and self-impulse, because I believe them to be the needed means of the present juncture.

I have urged on woman independence of man, not that I do not think the sexes mutually needed by one another, but because in woman this fact has led to an excessive devotion, which has cooled love, degraded marriage, and prevented either sex from being what it should be to itself or the other.

I wish woman to live, *first* for God's sake. Then she will not make an imperfect man her god, and thus sink to idolatry. Then she will not take what is not fit for her from a sense of weakness and poverty. Then, if she finds what she needs in man embodied, she will know how to love, and be worthy of being loved.

By being more a soul, she will not be less woman, for nature is perfected through spirit.

Now there is no woman, only an overgrown child.

That her hand may be given with dignity, she must be able to stand alone. I wish to see men and women capable of such relations as are depicted by Landor in his Pericles and Aspasia, where grace is the natural garb of strength, and the affections are calm, because deep. The softness is that of a firm tissue, as when

"The gods approve
The depth, but not the tumult of the soul,
A fervent, not ungovernable love." [207]

A profound thinker has said, "no married woman can represent the female world, for she belongs to her husband. The idea of woman must be represented by a virgin."

But that is the very fault of marriage, and of the present relation between the sexes, that the woman does belong to the man, instead of forming a whole with him. Were it otherwise, there would be no such limitation to the thought.

Woman, self-centred, would never be absorbed by any relation; it would be only an experience to her as to man. It is a vulgar error that love, *a* love to woman is her whole existence; she also is born for Truth and Love in their universal energy. Would she but assume her inheritance, Mary would not be the only virgin mother. Not Manzoni alone would celebrate in his wife the virgin mind with the maternal wisdom and conjugal affections. The soul is ever young, ever virgin.

And will not she soon appear? The woman who shall vindicate their birthright for all women; who shall teach them what to claim, and how to

---

[207] William Wordsworth, "Laodamia" (1814). [Ed.]

use what they obtain? Shall not her name be for her era Victoria, for her country and life Virginia? Yet predictions are rash; she herself must teach us to give her the fitting name.

An idea not unknown to ancient times has of late been revived; that, in the metamorphoses of life, the soul assumes the form, first of man, then of woman, and takes the chances, and reaps the benefits of either lot. Why then, say some, lay such emphasis on the rights or needs of woman? What she wins not, as woman, will come to her as man.

That makes no difference. It is not woman, but the law of right, the law of growth, that speaks in us, and demands the perfection of each being in its kind, apple as apple, woman as woman. Without adopting your theory I know that I, a daughter, live through the life of man; but what concerns me now is, that my life be a beautiful, powerful, in a word, a complete life in its kind. Had I but one more moment to live, I must wish the same.

Suppose, at the end of your cycle, your great world-year, all will be completed, whether I exert myself or not (and the supposition is *false,*) but suppose it true, am I to be indifferent about it? Not so! I must beat my own pulse true in the heart of the world; for *that* is virtue, excellence, health.

Thou, Lord of Day! didst leave us to-night so calmly glorious, not dismayed that cold winter is coming, not postponing thy beneficence to the fruitful summer! Thou didst smile on thy day's work when it was done, and adorn thy down-going as thy up-rising, for thou art loyal, and it is thy nature to give life, if thou canst, and shine at all events!

I stand in the sunny noon of life. Objects no longer glitter in the dews of morning, neither are yet softened by the shadows of evening. Every spot is seen, every chasm revealed. Climbing the dusty hill, some fair effigies that once stood for symbols of human destiny have been broken; those I still have with me, show defects in this broad light. Yet enough is left, even by experience, to point distinctly to the glories of that destiny; faint, but not to be mistaken streaks of the future day. I can say with the bard,

"Though many have suffered shipwreck, still beat noble hearts."

Always the soul says to us all: Cherish your best hopes as a faith, and abide by them in action. Such shall be the effectual fervent means to their fulfilment,

> For the Power to whom we bow
> Has given its pledge that, if not now,
> They of pure and stedfast mind,
> By faith exalted, truth refined,
> 5   *Shall* hear all music loud and clear,
> Whose first notes they ventured here.

Then fear not thou to wind the horn,
Though elf and gnome thy courage scorn;
Ask for the Castle's King and Queen;
10 Though rabble rout may rush between,
Beat thee senseless to the ground,
In the dark beset thee round;
Persist to ask and it will come,
Seek not for rest in humbler home;
15 So shalt thou see what few have seen,
The palace home of King and Queen.[208]

15th November, 1844

APPENDIX[209]

A.

Apparition of the goddess Isis to her votary, from Apuleius.[210]

"Scarcely had I closed my eyes, when behold (I saw in a dream) a divine form emerging from the middle of the sea, and raising a countenance venerable, even to the gods themselves. Afterwards, the whole of the most splendid image seemed to stand before me, having gradually shaken off the sea. I will endeavor to explain to you its admirable form, if the poverty of human language will but afford me the power of an appropriate narration; or if the divinity itself, of the most luminous form, will supply me with a liberal abundance of fluent diction. In the first place, then, her most copious and long hairs, being gradually intorted, and promiscuously scattered on her divine neck, were softly defluous. A multiform crown, consisting of various flowers, bound the sublime summit of her head. And in the middle of the crown, just on her forehead, there was a smooth orb resembling a mirror, or rather a white refulgent light, which indicated that she was the moon. Vipers rising up after the manner of furrows, environed the crown on the right hand and on the left, and Cerealian ears of corn were also ex-

---

[208] Fuller's poem. [Ed.]

[209] Fuller's appendixes anticipate the work of modern revisionary literary and cultural historians, especially feminist and ethnic studies scholars, who consider the reintroduction of neglected or repressed work by women and minorities to be at least as important as their own interpretations of such work. [Ed.]

[210] Lucius Apuleius (b. c. 123 CE), the Roman author of *The Golden Ass*. This selection comes from bk. 11 (Reynolds, *Woman* 109). [Ed.]

tended from above. Her garment was of many colors, and woven from the finest flax, and was at one time lucid with a white splendor, at another yellow from the flower of crocus, and at another flaming with a rosy redness. But that which most excessively dazzled my sight, was a very black robe, fulgid with a dark splendor, and which, spreading round and passing under her right side, and ascending to her left shoulder, there rose protuberant, like the centre of a shield, the dependent part of her robe falling in many folds, and having small knots of fringe, gracefully flowing in its extremities. Glittering stars were dispersed through the embroidered border of the robe, and through the whole of its surface, and the full moon, shining in the middle of the stars, breathed forth flaming fires. A crown, wholly consisting of flowers and fruits of every kind, adhered with indivisible connexion to the border of the conspicuous robe, in all its undulating motions.

"What she carried in her hands also consisted of things of a very different nature. Her right hand bore a brazen rattle, through the narrow lamina of which, bent like a belt, certain rods passing, produced a sharp triple sound through the vibrating motion of her arm. An oblong vessel, in the shape of a boat, depended from her left hand, on the handle of which, in that part which was conspicuous, an asp raised its erect head and largely swelling neck. And shoes, woven from the leaves of the victorious palm tree, covered her immortal feet. Such, and so great a goddess, breathing the fragrant odour of the shores of Arabia the happy, deigned thus to address me."

The foreign English of the translator, Thomas Taylor,[211] gives the description the air of being, itself, a part of the Mysteries. But its majestic beauty requires no formal initiation to be enjoyed.

B.

I give this, in the original, as it does not bear translation. Those who read Italian will judge whether it is not a perfect description of a perfect woman.

LODI E PREGHIERE' A MARIA[212]

Vergine bella che di sol vestita,
Coronata di stelle, al sommo Sole

---

[211]Thomas Taylor (1758–1835), English classical scholar and Neoplatonist (Reynolds, *Woman* 110). [Ed.]

[212]Fuller gives the title in Italian, "Praise and Prayer to the Virgin Mary," to the poem that concludes Petrarch's *Canzoniere,* the collection of 366 lyrics that focus on his love

Piacesti si, che'n te sua luce ascose;
Amor mi spinge a dir di te parole:
5 Ma non so 'ncominciar senza tu' aita,
E di Colui che amando in te si pose.
Invoco lei che ben sempre rispose,
Chi la chiamò con fede.
Vergine, s'a mercede
10 Miseria extrema dell' smane cose
Giammai ti volse, al mio prego t'inchina:
Soccorri alla mia guerra;
Bench' i' sia terra, e tu del ciel Regina.

Vergine saggia, e del bel numero una
15 Delle beate vergini prudenti;
Anzi la prima, e con più chiara lampa;
O saldo scudo dell' afflitte gente
Contra colpi di Morte e di Fortuna,
Sotto' l qual si trionfa, non pur scampa:
20 O refrigerio alcieco ardor ch' avvampa
Qui fra mortali sciocchi,
Vergine, que' begli occhi
Che vider tristi la spietata stampa
Ne' dolci membri del tuo caro figlio,
25 Volgi al mio dubbio stato;
Che sconsigliato a te vien per consiglio.

Vergine pura, d'ogni parte intera,
Del tuo parto gentil figliuola e madre;
Che allumi questa vita, e l'altra adorni;
30 Per te il tuo Figlio e quel del sommo Padre,
O finestra del ciel lucente altera,
Venne a salvarne in su gli estremi giorni,
E fra tutt' i terreni altri soggiorni
Sola tu fusti eletta,

---

for Laura, who in these poems is an anticipation of the spiritual love represented by the Virgin. Fuller or the printer introduced several mistakes into the Italian text reproduced here, none of which has been corrected (Dickenson 252). The so-called cult of medievalism, with special focus on the Virgin Mary as a central figure in medieval European Catholicism, is a motif in nineteenth-century Anglo-American writing that extends from the transcendentalists through the Victorian Pre-Raphaelites and culminates in Henry Adams's (1838–1918) *Mont-Saint-Michel and Chartres* (1904). [Ed.]

35 Vergine benedetta;
Che 'l pianto d' Eva in allegrezza torni';
Fammi; che puoi; della sua grazia degno,
Senza fine o beata,
Già coronata nel superno regno.

40 Vergine santa d'ogni grazia piena;
Che per vera e altissima umiltate
Salisti al ciel, onde miei preghi ascolti;
Tu partoristi il fonte di pietate,
E di giustizia il Sol, che rasserena
45 Il secol pien d'errori oscuri e folti:
Tre dolci e eari nomi ha' in te raccolti,
Madre, Figliuola, e Sposa;
Vergine gloriosa,
Donna del Re che nostri lacci ha sciolti,
50 E fatto'l mondo libero e felice;
Nelle cui sante piaghe
Prego ch'appaghe il cor, vera beatrice.

Vergine sola al mondo senza esempio,
Che 'l ciel di tue bellezze innamorasti,
55 Cui nè prima fu simil, nè seconda;
Santi pensieri, atti pietosi e casti
Al vero Dio sacrato, e vivo tempio
Fecero in tua virginita feconda.
Per te può la mia vita esser gioconda,
60 S' a' tuoi preghi, o MARIA
Vergine dolce, e pia.
Ove 'l fallo abbondò, la grazia abbonda.
Con le ginocchia della mente inchine
Prego che sia mia scorta;
65 E la mia torta via drizzi a buon fine.

Vergine chiara, e stabile in eterno,
Di questo tempestoso mare stella;
D'ogni fedel nocchier fidata guida;
Pon mente in che terribile procella
70 I mi ritrovo sol senza governo,
Ed ho gia' da vicin l'ulti me strida:
Ma pur' in te l'anima mia si fida;
Peccatrice; i' nol nego,
Vergine: ma te prego

75 Che 'l tuo nemico del mia mal non rida:
   Ricorditi che fece il peccar nostro
   Prender Dio, per scamparne,
   Umana carne al tuo virginal christro.

   Vergine, quante lagrime ho già sparte,
80 Quante lusinghe, e quanti preghi indarno,
   Pur per mia pena, e per mio grave danno!
   Da poi ch' i' nacqui in su la riva d' Arno;
   Cercando or questa ed or quell altra parte,
   Non è stata mia vita altro ch' affanno.
85 Mortal bellezza, atti, e parole m' hanno
   Tutta ingombrata l' alma.
   Vergine sacra, ed alma,
   Non tardar; ch' i' non forse all' ultim 'ann,
   I di miei piu correnti che saetta,
90 Fra miserie e peccati
   Sonsen andati, e sol Morte n'aspetta.

   Vergine, tale è terra, e posto ha in doglia
   Lo mio cor; che vivendo in pianto il tenne;
   E di mille miei mali un non sapea;
95 E per saperlo, pur quel che n'avvenne,
   Fora avvenuto: ch' ogni altra sua voglia
   Era a me morte, ed a lei fama rea
   Or tu, donna del ciel, tu nostra Dea,
   Se dir lice, e conviensi;
100 Vergine d'alti sensi,
   Tu vedi it tutto; e quel che non potea
   Far altri, è nulla a e la tua gran virtute;
   Pon fine al mio dolore;
   Ch'a te onore ed a me fia salute.

105 Vergine, in cui ho tutta mia speranza
   Che possi e vogli al gran bisogno aitarme;
   Non mi lasciare in su l'estremo passo.
   Non guardar me, ma chi degnò crearme;
   No'l mio valor, ma l'alta sua sembianza;
110 Che in me ti mova a curar d'uorm si basso.
   Medusa, e l'error mio io han fatto un sasso
   D'umor vano stillante;
   Vergine, tu di sante

Lagrime, e pie adempi 'l mio cor lasso;
115   Ch' almen l'ultimo pianto sia divoto,
    Senza terrestro limo;
    Come fu'l primo non d'insania voto.

    Vergine umana, e nemica d'orgoglio,
    Del comune principio amor t'induca;
120   Miserere d' un cor contrito umile;
    Che se poca mortal terra caduca
    Amar con si mirabil fede soglio;
    Che devro far di te cosa gentile?
    Se dal mio stato assai misero, e vile
125 Per le me man resurgo,
    Vergine; è' sacro, e purgo
    Al tuo nome e pens ieri e'ngegno, e stile;
    La lingua, e'l cor, le lagrime, e i sospiri,
    Scorgimi al miglior guado;
130   E prendi in grado i cangiati desiri.

    Il di s'appressa, e non pote esser lunge;
    Si corre il tempo, e vola,
    Vergine unica, e sola;
    E'l cor' or conscienza, or morte punge.
135 Raccommandami al tuo Figliuol, verace
    Uomo, e verace Dio;
    Ch accolga l mio spirto ultimo in pace.

As the Scandinavian represented Frigga the Earth, or World mother, knowing all things, yet never herself revealing them, though ready to be called to counsel by the gods.[213] It represents her in action, decked with jewels and gorgeously attended. But, says the Mythos, when she ascended the throne of Odin, her consort (Haaven) she left with mortals, her friend, the Goddess of Sympathy, to protect them in her absence.

Since, Sympathy goes about to do good. Especially she devotes herself to the most valiant and the most oppressed. She consoled the Gods in some degree even for the death of their darling Baldur. Among the heavenly powers she has no consort.

---

[213] Frigga is the Old Norse goddess of the earth, wife of the central god, Odin, and mother to Balder, god of light. [Ed.]

C.

"THE WEDDING OF THE LADY THERESA"

From Lockhart's Spanish Ballads[214]

"'Twas when the fifth Alphonso in Leon held his sway,
    King Abdalla of Toledo an embassy did send;
He asked his sister for a wife, and in an evil day
    Alphonso sent her, for he feared Abdalla to offend;
5 He feared to move his anger, for many times before
    He had received in danger much succor from the Moor.

Sad heart had fair Theresa, when she their paction knew;
    With streaming tears she heard them tell she 'mong the Moors
        must go;
That she, a Christian damsel, a Christian firm and true,
10   Must wed a Moorish husband, it well might cause her wo;
But all her tears and all her prayers they are of small avail;
    At length she for her fate prepares, a victim sad and pale.

The king hath sent his sister to fair Toledo town,
    Where then the Moor Abdalla his royal state did keep;
15 When she drew near, the Moslem from his golden throne came down,
    And courteously received her, and bade her cease to weep;
With loving words he pressed her to come his bower within;
    With kisses he caressed her, but still she feared the sin.

"Sir King, Sir King, I pray thee," — 'twas thus Theresa spake,
20   "I pray thee, have compassion, and do to me no wrong;
For sleep with thee I may not, unless the vows I break,
    Whereby I to the holy church of Christ my Lord belong;
For thou hast sworn to serve Mahoun, and if this thing should be,
    The curse of God it must bring down upon thy realm and thee.

25 "The angel of Christ Jesu, to whom my heavenly Lord
    Hath given my soul in keeping, is ever by my side;
If thou dost me dishonor, he will unsheath his sword,
    And smite thy body fiercely, at the crying of thy bride;
Invisible he standeth; his sword like fiery flame,
30 Will penetrate thy bosom, the hour that sees my shame."

---

[214] John Gibson Lockhart, *Ancient Spanish Ballads: Historical and Romantic* (1823). [Ed.]

The Moslem heard her with a smile; the earnest words she said,
   He took for bashful maiden's wile, and drew her to his bower:
In vain Theresa prayed and strove,—she pressed Abdalla's bed,
   Perforce received his kiss of love, and lost her maiden flower.
35 A woful woman there she lay, a loving lord beside,
   And earnestly to God did pray, her succor to provide.

The angel of Christ Jesu her sore complaint did hear,
   And plucked his heavenly weapon from out his sheath unseen,
He waved the brand in his right hand, and to the King came near,
40   And drew the point o'er limb and joint, beside the weeping Queen:
A mortal weakness from the stroke upon the King did fall;
   He could not stand when daylight broke, but on his knees must crawl.

Abdalla shuddered inly, when he this sickness felt,
   And called upon his barons, his pillow to come high;
45 "Rise up," he said "my liegemen," as round his bed they knelt,
   "And take this Christian lady, else certainly I die;
Let gold be in your girdles, and precious stones beside,
   And swiftly ride to Leon, and render up my bride."

When they were come to Leon, Theresa would not go
50   Into her brother's dwelling, where her maiden years were spent;
But o'er her downcast visage a white veil she did throw,
   And to the ancient nunnery of Las Huelgas went.
There, long, from worldly eyes retired, a holy life she led;
   There she, an aged saint, expired; there sleeps she with the dead."

D.

The following extract from Spinoza is worthy of attention, as expressing the view which a man of the largest intellectual scope may take of
woman, if that part of his life to which her influence appeals, has been left
unawakened.[215]

He was a man of the largest intellect, of unsurpassed reasoning powers,
yet he makes a statement false to history, for we well know how often men
and women have ruled together without difficulty, and one in which very

---

[215] Benedict Spinoza (1632–77), Dutch philosopher who had a strong influence on the
transcendentalists. (Dickenson 252–253). [Ed.]

few men even at the present day, I mean men who are thinkers, like him, would acquiesce.

I have put in contrast with it three expressions of the latest literature. 1st. From the poems of W. E. Channing, a poem called "Reverence," equally remarkable for the deep wisdom of its thought and the beauty of its utterance, and containing as fine a description of one class of women as exists in literature.[216]

In contrast with this picture of woman, the happy Goddess of Beauty, the wife, the friend, "the summer queen," I add one by the author of "Festus," of a woman of the muse, the sybil kind, which seems painted from living experience.[217]

And thirdly, I subjoin Eugene Sue's description of a wicked, but able woman of the practical sort,[218] and appeal to all readers whether a species that admits of three such varieties is so easily to be classed away, or kept within prescribed limits, as Spinoza, and those who think like him, believe.

SPINOZA. TRACTATUS POLITICI, DE DEMOCRATIA, CAPUT XI

"Perhaps some one will here ask, whether the supremacy of man over woman is attributable to nature or custom? For if it be human institutions alone to which this fact is owing, there is no reason why we should exclude women from a share in government. Experience, however, most plainly teaches that it is woman's weakness which places her under the authority of man. Since it has nowhere happened that men and women ruled together; but wherever men and women are found the world over, there we see the men ruling and the women ruled, and in this order of things men and women live together in peace and harmony. The Amazons, it is true, are reputed formerly to have held the reins of government, but they drove men from their dominions; the male of their offspring they invariably destroyed, permitting their daughters alone to live. Now if women were by nature upon an equality with men, if they equalled men in fortitude, in genius (qualities which give to men might, and consequently, right) it surely would be the case, that among the numerous and diverse nations of the

---

[216] [William] Ellery Channing (1818–1901), transcendentalist poet, Fuller's brother-in-law, and author of *Poems* (1843), from which "Reverence" is taken. [Ed.]

[217] The selection is taken from Philip James Bailey's (1816–1902) *Festus* (1839), a retelling of the Faust legend (Dickenson 253). [Ed.]

[218] A selection from Eugène Sue (see n. 185). [Ed.]

earth, some would be found where both sexes ruled conjointly, and others where the men were ruled by the women, and so educated as to be mentally inferior: since this state of things no where exists, it is perfectly fair to infer that the rights of women are not equal to those of men; but that women must be subordinate, and therefore cannot have an equal, far less a superior place in the government. If, too, we consider the passions of men — how the love men feel towards women is seldom any thing but lust and impulse, and much less a reverence for qualities of soul than an admiration of physical beauty, observing, too, how men are afflicted when their sweethearts favor other wooers, and other things of the same character, — we shall see at a glance that it would be, in the highest degree, detrimental to peace and harmony, for men and women to possess an equal share in government."

"REVERENCE"

"As an ancestral heritage revere
All learning, and all thought. The painter's fame
Is thine, whate'er thy lot, who honorest grace.
And need enough in this low time, when they,
5 Who seek to captivate the fleeting notes
Of heaven's sweet beauty, must despair almost,
So heavy and obdurate show the hearts
Of their companions. Honor kindly then
Those who bear up in their so generous arms
10 The beautiful ideas of matchless forms;
For were these not portrayed, our human fate, —
Which is to be all high, majestical,
To grow to goodness with each coming age,
Till virtue leap and sing for joy to see
15 So noble, virtuous men, — would brief decay;
And the green, festering slime, oblivious, haunt
About our common fate. Oh honor them!

But what to all true eyes has chiefest charm,
And what to every breast where beats a heart
20 Framed to one beautiful emotion, — to
One sweet and natural feeling, lends a grace
To all the tedious walks of common life
This is fair woman, — woman, whose applause
Each poet sings, — woman the beautiful.

25 Not that her fairest brow, or gentlest form
   Charm us to tears; not that the smoothest check,
   Where ever rosy tints have made their home,
   So rivet us on her; but that she is
   The subtle, delicate grace, — the inward grace,
30 For words too excellent; the noble, true,
   The majesty of earth; the summer queen:
   In whose conceptions nothing but what's great
   Has any right. And, O! her love for him,
   Who does but his small part in honoring her;
35 Discharging a sweet office, sweeter none,
   Mother and child, friend, counsel and repose; —
   Nought matches with her, nought has leave with her
   To highest human praise. Farewell to him
   Who reverences not with an excess
40 Of faith the beauteous sex; all barren he
   Shall live a living death of mockery.

   Ah! had but words the power, what could we say
   Of woman! We, rude men, of violent phrase,
   Harsh action, even in repose inwardly harsh;
45 Whose lives walk blustering on high stilts, removed
   From all the purely gracious influence
   Of mother earth. To single from the host
   Of angel forms one only, and to her
   Devote our deepest heart and deepest mind
50 Seems almost contradiction. Unto her
   We owe our greatest blessings, hours of cheer,
   Gay smiles, and sudden tears, and more than these
   A sure perpetual love. Regard her as
   She walks along the vast still earth; and see!
55 Before her flies a laughing troop of joys,
   And by her side treads old experience,
   With never-failing voice admonitory;
   The gentle, though infallible, kind advice,
   The watchful care, the fine regardfulness,
60 Whatever mates with what we hope to find,
   All consummate in her — the summer queen.

   To call past ages better than what now
   Man is enacting on life's crowded stage,
   Cannot improve our worth; and for the world

65 Blue is the sky as ever, and the stars
   Kindle their crystal flames at soft-fallen eve
   With the same purest lustre that the east
   Worshipped. The river gently flows through fields
   Where the broad-leaved corn spreads out, and loads
70 Its car as when the Indian tilled the soil.
   The dark green pine, — green in the winter's cold,
   Still whispers meaning emblems, as of old;
   The cricket chirps, and the sweet, eager birds
   In the sad woods crowd their thick melodies;
75 But yet, to common eyes, life's poetry
   Something has faded, and the cause of this
   May be that man, no longer at the shrine
   Of woman, kneeling with true reverence,
   In spite of field, wood, river, stars and sea
80 Goes most disconsolate. A babble now,
   A huge and wind-swelled babble, fills the place
   Of that great adoration which of old
   Man had for woman. In these days no more
   Is love the pith and marrow of man's fate.

85 Thou who in early years feelest awake
   To finest impulses from nature's breath,
   And in thy walk hearest such sounds of truth
   As on the common ear strike without heed,
   Beware of men around thee. Men are foul,
90 With avarice, ambition and deceit;
   The worst of all, ambition. This is life
   Spent in a feverish chase for selfish cads,
   Which has no virtue to redeem its toil
   But one long, stagnant hope to raise the self.
95 The miser's life to this seems sweet and fair;
   Better to pile the glittering coin, than seek
   To overtop our brothers and our loves.
   Merit in this? Where lies it, though thy name
   Ring over distant lands, meeting the wind
100 Even on the extremest verge of the wide world.
   Merit in this? Better be hurled abroad
   On the vast whirling tide, than in thyself
   Concentrated, feed upon thy own applause.
   Thee shall the good man yield no reverence;
105 But, while the idle, dissolute crowd are loud

In voice to send thee flattery, shall rejoice
That he has scaped thy fatal doom, and known
How humble faith in the good soul of things
Provides amplest enjoyment. O my brother,
110 If the Past's counsel any honor claim
From thee, go read the history of those
Who a like path have trod, and see a fate
Wretched with fears, changing like leaves at noon,
When the new wind sings in the white birch wood.
115 Learn from the simple child the rule of life,
And from the movements of the unconscious tribes
Of animal nature, those that bend the wing
Or cleave the azure tide, content to be.
What the great frame provides, — freedom and grace.
120 Thee, simple child, do the swift winds obey,
And the white waterfalls with their bold leaps
Follow thy movements. Tenderly the light
Thee watches, girding with a zone of radiance,
And all the swinging herbs love thy soft steps."

DESCRIPTION OF ANGELA, FROM "FESTUS"

"I loved her for that she was beautiful,
And that to me she seemed to be all nature
And all varieties of things in one;
Would set at night in clouds of tears, and rise
5 All light and laughter in the morning; fear
No petty customs nor appearances,
But think what others only dreamed about;
And say what others did but think; and do
What others would but say; and glory in
10 What others dared but do; it was these which won me;
And that she never schooled within her breast
One thought or feeling, but gave holiday
To all; and that she told me all her woes
And wrongs and ills; and so she made them mine
15 In the communion of love; and we
Grew like each other, for we loved each other;
She, mild and generous as the sun in spring;
And I, like earth, all budding out with love.

*　　*　　*

The beautiful are never desolate:
20 For some one always loves them; God or man;
If man abandons, God Himself takes them:
And thus it was. She whom I once loved died,
The lightning loathes its cloud; the soul its clay.
Can I forget that hand I took in mine,
25 Pale as pale violets; that eye, where mind
And matter met alike divine?—ah, no!
May God that moment judge me when I do!
Oh! she was fair; her nature once all spring
And deadly beauty, like a maiden sword,
30 Startlingly beautiful. I see her now!
Wherever thou art thy soul is in my mind;
Thy shadow hourly lengthens o'er my brain
And peoples all its pictures with thyself;
Gone, not forgotten; passed, not lost; thou wilt shine
35 In heaven like a bright spot in the sun!
She said she wished to die, and so she died,
For, cloudlike, she poured out her love, which was
Her life, to freshen this parched heart. It was thus;
I said we were to part, but she said nothing;
40 There was no discord; it was music ceased,
Life's thrilling, bursting, bounding joy. She sate,
Like a house-god, her hands fixed on her knee,
And her dark hair lay loose and long behind her,
Through which her wild bright eye flashed like a flint;
45 She spake not, moved not, but she looked the more,
As if her eye were action, speech, and feeling.
I felt it all, and came and knelt beside her,
The electric touch solved both our souls together;
Then came the feeling which unmakes, undoes;
50 Which tears the sealike soul up by the roots,
And lashes it in scorn against the skies.

*　　*　　*

It is the saddest and the sorest sight,
One's own love weeping. But why call on God?
But that the feeling of the boundless bounds
55 All feeling; as the welkin does the world;
It is this which ones us with the whole and God.
Then first we wept; then closed and clung together;

And my heart shook this building of my breast
Like a live engine booming up and down:
60 She fell upon me like a snow-wreath thawing.
Never were bliss and beauty, love and wo,
Ravelled and twined together into madness,
As in that one wild hour to which all else
The past, is but a picture. That alone
65 Is real, and forever there in front.

         *   *   *

*   *   *   After that I left her,
And only saw her once again alive."

"Mother Saint Perpetua, the superior of the convent, was a tall woman, of about forty years, dressed in dark gray serge, with a long rosary hanging at her girdle; a white mob cap, with a long black veil, surrounded her thin wan face with its narrow hooded border. A great number of deep transverse wrinkles plowed her brow, which resembled yellowish ivory in color and substance. Her keen and prominent nose was curved like the hooked beak of a bird of prey; her black eye was piercing and sagacious; her face was at once intelligent, firm, and cold.

"For comprehending and managing the material interests of the society, Mother Saint Perpetua could have vied with the shrewdest and most wily lawyer. When women are possessed of what is called *business talent,* and when they apply thereto the sharpness of perception, the indefatigable perseverance, the prudent dissimulation, and above all, the correctness and rapidity of judgment at first sight, which are peculiar to them, they arrive at prodigious results.

"To mother Saint Perpetua, a woman of a strong and solid head, the vast monied business of the society was but child's play. None better than she understood how to buy depreciated properties, to raise them to their original value, and sell them to advantage; the average purchase of rents, the fluctuations of exchange, and the current prices of shares in all the leading speculations, were perfectly familiar to her. Never had she directed her agents to make a single false speculation, when it had been the question how to invest funds, with which good souls were constantly endowing the society of Saint Mary. She had established in the house a degree of order, of discipline, and, above all, of economy, that were indeed remarkable; the constant aim of all her exertions being, not to enrich herself, but the community over which she presided; for the spirit of association, when it is directed to an object of *collective selfishness,* gives to corporations all the faults and vices of individuals."

E.

The following is an extract from a letter addressed to me by one of the monks of the 19th century.[219] A part I have omitted, because it does not express my own view, unless with qualifications which I could not make, except by full discussion of the subject.

"Woman in the 19th century should be a pure, chaste, holy being.

This state of being in woman is no more attained by the expansion of her intellectual capacity, than by the augmentation of her physical force.

Neither is it attained by the increase or refinement of her love for man, or for any object whatever, or for all objects collectively; but

This state of being is attained by the reference of all her powers and all her actions to the source of Universal Love, whose constant requisition is a pure, chaste and holy life.

So long as woman looks to man (or to society) for that which she needs, she will remain in an indigent state, for he himself is indigent of it, and as much needs it as she does.

So long as this indigence continues, all unions or relations constructed between man and woman are constructed in indigence, and can produce only indigent results or unhappy consequences.

The unions now constructing, as well as those in which the parties constructing them were generated, being based on self-delight, or lust, can lead to no more happiness in the 20th, than is found in the 19th century.

It is not amended institutions, it is not improved education, it is not another selection of individuals for union, that can meliorate the sad result, but the *basis* of the union must be changed.

If in the natural order Woman and Man would adhere strictly to physiological or natural laws, in physical chastity, a most beautiful amendment of the human race, and human condition, would in a few generations adorn the world.

Still, it belongs to Woman in the spiritual order, to devote herself wholly to her eternal husband, and become the Free Bride of the One who alone

---

[219] Fuller probably uses the phrase "one of the monks of the 19th century" to refer to an advocate of the chastity and sexual abstinence she endorses throughout this text (Dickenson 253). Reynolds speculates that Fuller refers to Charles Lane (1800–70), English transcendentalist and social reformer, who joined the Shakers in Harvard, Massachusetts, in 1844 and who later reviewed *Woman in the Nineteenth Century* (*Woman* 122). [Ed.]

can elevate her to her true position, and reconstruct her a pure, chaste, and holy being."

F.

I have mislaid an extract from "The Memoirs of an American Lady"[220] which I wished to use on this subject, but its import is, briefly, this:

Observing of how little consequence the Indian women are in youth, and how much in age, because in that trying life, good counsel and sagacity are more prized than charms, Mrs. Grant expresses a wish that Reformers would take a hint from observation of this circumstance.

In another place she says: "The misfortune of our sex is, that young women are not regarded as the material from which old women must be made."

I quote from memory, but believe the weight of the remark is retained.

G.

EURIPIDES. SOPHOCLES.

As many allusions are made in the foregoing pages to characters of women drawn by the Greek dramatists, which may not be familiar to the majority of readers, I have borrowed from the papers of Miranda,[221] some notes upon them. I trust the girlish tone of apostrophizing rapture may be excused. Miranda was very young at the time of writing, compared with her present mental age. *Now,* she would express the same feelings, but in a worthier garb—if she expressed them at all.

Iphigenia! Antigone! you were worthy to live! *We* are fallen on evil times, my sisters! our feelings have been checked; our thoughts questioned; our forms dwarfed and defaced by a bad nurture. Yet hearts, like yours, are in our breasts, living, if unawakened; and our minds are capable of the same resolves. You, we understand at once, those who stare upon us pertly in the street, we cannot—could never understand.

You knew heroes, maidens, and your fathers were kings of men. You believed in your country, and the gods of your country. A great occasion was given to each, whereby to test her character.

---

[220] Anne Grant (1755–1838), *Memoirs of an American Lady* (1808). Fuller uses this example to extend her critique of ageism in nineteenth-century culture, especially as applied to women, subject as they are to the cult of beauty and youth. [Ed.]

[221] As noted earlier, "Miranda" is Fuller's fictional alter-ego. [Ed.]

You did not love on earth; for the poets wished to show us the force of woman's nature, virgin and unbiassed. You were women; not wives, or lovers, or mothers. Those are great names, but we are glad to see *you* in untouched flower.

Were brothers so dear, then, Antigone? We have no brothers. We see no men into whose lives we dare look steadfastly, or to whose destinies we look forward confidently. We care not for their urns; what inscription could we put upon them? They live for petty successes; or to win daily the bread of the day. No spark of kingly fire flashes from their eyes.

None! are there *none?*

It is a base speech to say it. Yes! there are some such; we have sometimes caught their glances. But rarely have they been rocked in the same cradle as we, and they do not look upon us much; for the time is not yet come.

Thou art so grand and simple! we need not follow thee; thou dost not need our love.

But, sweetest Iphigenia; who knew *thee,* as to me thou art known. I was not born in vain, if only for the heavenly tears I have shed with thee. She will be grateful for them. I have understood her wholly; as a friend should, better than she understood herself.

With what artless art the narrative rises to the crisis. The conflicts in Agamemnon's mind, and the imputations of Menelaus give us, at once, the full image of him, strong in will and pride, weak in virtue, weak in the noble powers of the mind that depend on imagination. He suffers, yet it requires the presence of his daughter to make him feel the full horror of what he is to do.

"Ah me! that breast, those cheeks, those golden tresses!" [222]

It is her beauty, not her misery, that makes the pathos. This is noble. And then, too, the injustice of the gods, that she, this creature of unblemished loveliness, must perish for the sake of a worthless woman. Even Menelaus feels it, the moment he recovers from his wrath.

> "What hath she to do,
> The virgin daughter, with my Helena!
> *   *   Its former reasonings now
> My soul foregoes.   *   *   *   *
>   For it is not just

---

[222] The following quotes are from Euripides, *Iphigenia at Aulis*. Fuller's interpretations of Iphigenia and of Sophocles' Antigone anticipate modern feminist efforts to construct an alternative "classical mythology" that draws principally on the powers of ancient Greek feminine heroic figures and goddesses. [Ed.]

That thou shouldst groan, but my affairs go pleasantly,
That those of thy house should die, and mine see the light."

Indeed the overwhelmed aspect of the king of men might well move him.

Men.   "Brother, give me to take thy right hand,
Aga.   I give it, *for* the victory is thine, and I am wretched.
      I am, indeed, ashamed to drop the tear,
      And not to drop the tear I am ashamed."

How beautifully is Iphigenia introduced; beaming more and more softly on us with every touch of description. After Clytemnestra has given Orestes (then an infant,) out of the chariot, she says:

      "Ye females, in your arms,
Receive her, for she is of tender age.
Sit here by my feet, my child,
By thy mother, Iphigenia, and show
These strangers how I am blessed in thee,
And here address thee to thy father.
Iphi.   Oh mother, should I run, wouldst thou be angry? And embrace
      my father breast to breast?"

With the same sweet timid trust she prefers the request to himself, and as he holds her in his arms, he seems as noble as Guido's Archangel; as if he never could sink below the trust of such a being!

The Achilles, in the first scene, is fine. A true Greek hero; not too good; all flushed with the pride of youth; but capable of god-like impulses. At first, he thinks only of his own wounded pride, (when he finds Iphigenia has been decoyed to Aulis under the pretext of becoming his wife;) but the grief of the queen soon makes him superior to his arrogant chafings. How well he says:—

"*Far as a young man may,* I will repress
So great a wrong."

By seeing him here, we understand why he, not Hector, was the hero of the Iliad. The beautiful moral nature of Hector was early developed by close domestic ties, and the cause of his country. Except in a purer simplicity of speech and manner, he might be a modern and a christian. But Achilles is cast in the largest and most vigorous mould of the earlier day: his nature is one of the richest capabilities, and therefore less quickly unfolds its meaning. The impression it makes at the early period is only of power and pride; running as fleetly with his armor on, as with it off; but sparks of pure lustre are struck, at moments, from the mass of ore. Of this sort is his refusal to see the beautiful virgin he has promised to protect. None of the Grecians must have the right to doubt his motives. How wise and prudent, too, the advice he gives as to the queen's conduct! He will not show himself, unless needed. His pride is the farthest possible remote from vanity. His thoughts are as free as any in our own time.

> "The prophet? what is he? a man
> Who speaks 'mong many falsehoods, but few truths,
> Whene'er chance leads him to speak true; when false,
> The prophet is no more."

Had Agamemnon possessed like clearness of sight, the virgin would not have perished, but also, Greece would have had no religion and no national existence.

When, in the interview with Agamemnon, the Queen begins her speech, in the true matrimonial style, dignified though her gesture be, and true all she says, we feel that truth, thus sauced with taunts, will not touch his heart, nor turn him from his purpose. But when Iphigenia begins her exquisite speech, as with the breathings of a lute,

> "Had I, my father, the persuasive voice
> Of Orpheus, &c.
>   Compel me not
> What is beneath to view. I was the first
> To call thee father; me thou first didst call
> Thy child: I was the first that on thy knees
> Fondly caressed thee, and from thee received
> The fond caress: this was thy speech to me: —
> 'Shall I, my child, e'er see thee in some house
> Of splendor, happy in thy husband, live
> And flourish, as becomes my dignity?'
> My speech to thee was, leaning 'gainst thy cheek,
> (Which with my hand I now caress:) 'And what
> Shall I then do for thee? shall I receive
> My father when grown old, and in my house
> Cheer him with each fond office, to repay
> The careful nurture which he gave my youth?'
> These words are in my memory deep impressed,
> Thou hast forgot them and will kill thy child."

Then she adjures him by all the sacred ties, and dwells pathetically on the circumstance which had struck even Menelaus.

> "If Paris be enamored of his bride,
> His Helen, what concerns it me? and how

Comes he to my destruction?
                    Look upon me;
Give me a smile, give me a kiss, my father;
That if my words persuade thee not, in death
I may have this memorial of thy love."

Never have the names of father and daughter been uttered with a holier tenderness than by Euripides, as in this most lovely passage, or in the "Supplicants," after the voluntary death of Evadne; Iphis says [223]

"What shall this wretch now do? Should I return
To my own house?—sad desolation there
I shall behold, to sink my soul with grief.
Or go I to the house of Capaneus?
That was delightful to me, when I found
My daughter there; but she is there no more:
Oft would she kiss my cheek, with fond caress
Oft soothe me. To a father, waxing old,
Nothing is dearer than a daughter! none
Have spirits of higher pitch, but less inclined
To sweet endearing fondness. Lead me then,
Instantly lead me to my house, consign
My wretched age to darkness, there to pine
And waste away.
                    Old age,
Struggling with many griefs, O how I hate thee!"

But to return to Iphigenia.—how infinitely melting is her appeal to Orestes, whom she holds in her robe.

"My brother, small assistance canst thou give
Thy friends; yet for thy sister with thy tears
Implore thy father that she may not die:
Even infants have a sense of ills; and see,
My father! silent though he be, he sues
To thee: be gentle to me; on my life
Have pity: thy two children by this beard
Entreat thee, thy dear children: one is yet
An infant, one to riper years arrived."

The mention of Orestes, then an infant, all through, though slight, is of a domestic charm that prepares the mind to feel the tragedy of his after lot. When the Queen says

---

[223] In Euripides' *Suppliant Women,* Evadne is the tragic character who throws herself on her husband's funeral pyre and is grieved by her father, Iphis. [Ed.]

"Dost thou sleep,
My son? The rolling chariot hath subdued thee;
Wake to thy sister's marriage happily."

We understand the horror of the doom which makes this cherished child a parricide. And so when Iphigenia takes leave of him after her fate is by herself accepted.

Iphi. "To manhood train Orestes,
Cly. Embrace him, for thou ne'er shalt see him more.
Iphi. (*To Orestes.*) For as thou couldst, thou didst assist thy friends."

We know not how to blame the guilt of the maddened wife and mother. In her last meeting with Agamemnon, as in her previous expostulations and anguish, we see that a straw may turn the balance, and make her his deadliest foe. Just then, came the suit of Aegisthus, then, when every feeling was uprooted or lacerated in her heart.

Iphigenia's moving address has no further effect than to make her father turn at bay and brave this terrible crisis. He goes out, firm in resolve; and she and her mother abandon themselves to a natural grief.

Hitherto nothing has been seen in Iphigenia, except the young girl, weak, delicate, full of feeling and beautiful as a sunbeam on the full green tree. But, in the next scene, the first impulse of that passion which makes and unmakes us, though unconfessed even to herself, though hopeless and unreturned, raises her at once into the heroic woman, worthy of the goddess who demands her.

Achilles appears to defend her, whom all others clamorously seek to deliver to the murderous knife. She sees him, and fired with thoughts, unknown before, devotes herself at once for the country which has given birth to such a man.

"To be too fond of life
Becomes not me; nor for myself alone,
But to all Greece, a blessing didst thou bear me.
Shall thousands, when their country's injured, lift
Their shields; shall thousands grasp the oar, and dare,
Advancing bravely 'gainst the foe, to die
For Greece? And shall my life, my single life,
Obstruct all this? Would this be just? What word
Can we reply? Nay more, it is not right
That he with all the Grecians should contest
In fight, should die, *and for a woman.* No:
More than a thousand women is one man
Worthy to see the light of day.
 * * * for Greece I give my life.

Slay me; demolish Troy: for these shall be
Long time my monuments, my children these,
My nuptials and my glory."

This sentiment marks woman, when she loves enough to feel what a creature of glory and beauty a true *man* would be, as much in our own time as
that of Euripides. Cooper makes the weak Hetty say to her beautiful sister:
"Of course, I don't compare you with Harry. A handsome man is always
far handsomer than any woman." [224] True, it was the sentiment of the age,
but it was the first time Iphigenia had felt it. In Agamemnon she saw *her
father*, to him she could prefer her claim. In Achilles she saw *a man*, the
crown of creation, enough to fill the world with his presence, were all other
beings blotted from its spaces. [225]

The reply of Achilles is as noble. Here is his bride, he feels it now, and
all his vain vauntings are hushed.

"Daughter of Agamemnon, highly blessed
Some god would make me, if I might attain
Thy nuptials. Greece in thee I happy deem,
And thee in Greece.   *   *
     *   *   *   in thy thought
Revolve this well; death is a dreadful thing."

How sweet is her reply, and then the tender modesty with which she addresses him here and elsewhere as "*stranger*."

                "Reflecting not on any, thus I speak:
                Enough of wars and slaughters from the charms
                Of Helen rise; but die not thou for me,
                O Stranger, nor distain thy sword with blood,
                But let me save my country if I may."
Achilles.   "O glorious spirit! nought have I 'gainst this

---

[224] In James Fenimore Cooper's (1789–1851) novel *The Deerslayer* (1841), Hetty Hutter
says this to her beautiful sister, Judith, with whom the frontiersman Hurry Harry is in
love. Of course, Cooper contributed not only to the "cult of womanhood" but also to
the mythology of the frontier, including such related myths as the "Noble Savage" and
"Vanishing American." [Ed.]

[225] Men do not often reciprocate this pure love.

"Her prentice han' she tried on man,
     and then she made the lasses o',"

Is a fancy, not a feeling, in their more frequently passionate and strong, than noble or
tender natures. [Fuller's note. Fuller quotes Robert Burns's (1759–96) "Green Grow the
Rashes."—Ed.]

To urge, since such thy will, for what thou sayst
Is generous. Why should not the truth be spoken?"

But feeling that human weakness may conquer yet, he goes to wait at the altar, resolved to keep his promise of protection thoroughly.

In the next beautiful scene she shows that a few tears might overwhelm her in his absence. She raises her mother beyond weeping them, yet her soft purity she cannot impart.

Iphi. "My father, and thy husband do not hate:
Cly. For thy dear sake fierce contests must he bear.
Iphi. For Greece reluctant me to death he yields;
Cly. Basely, with guile unworthy Atreus' son."

This is truth incapable of an answer and Iphigenia attempts none. She begins the hymn which is to sustain her,

"Lead me; mine the glorious fate,
To o'erturn the Phrygian state."

After the sublime flow of lyric heroism, she suddenly sinks back into the tenderer feeling of her dreadful fate.

"O my country, where these eyes
Opened on Pelasgic skies!
O ye virgins, once my pride,
In Mycenæ who abide!
   CHORUS
Why of Perseus name the town,
Which Cyclopean ramparts crown?
   IPHIGENIA.
Me you rear'd a beam of light,
Freely now I sink in night."

Freely; as the messenger afterwards recounts it.

    * * *

"Imperial Agamemnon, when he saw
His daughter, as a victim to the grave,
Advancing, groan'd, and bursting into tears,
Turned from the sight his head, before his eyes,
Holding his robe. The virgin near him stood,
And thus addressed him: 'Father, I to thee
Am present; for my country, and for all
The land of Greece, I freely give myself
A victim: to the altar let them lead me,
Since such the oracle. If aught on me
Depends, be happy, and obtain the prize

Of glorious conquest, and revisit safe
Your country. Of the Grecians, for this cause,
Let no one touch me; with intrepid spirit
Silent will I present my neck.' She spoke,
And all that heard revered the noble soul
And virtue of the virgin."

How quickly had the fair bud bloomed up into its perfection. Had she lived a thousand years, she could not have surpassed this. Goethe's Iphigenia, the mature woman, with its myriad delicate traits, never surpasses, scarcely equals what we know of her in Euripides.

Can I appreciate this work in a translation? I think so, impossible as it may seem to one who can enjoy the thousand melodies, and words in exactly the right place and cadence of the original. They say you can see the Apollo Belvidere[226] in a plaster cast, and I cannot doubt it, so great the benefit conferred on my mind, by a transcript thus imperfect. And so with these translations from the Greek. I can divine the original through this veil, as I can see the movements of a spirited horse by those of his coarse grasscloth muffler. Beside, every translator who feels his subject is inspired, and the divine Aura informs even his stammering lips.

Iphigenia is more like one of the women Shakespeare loved than the others; she is a tender virgin, ennobled and strengthened by sentiment more than intellect, what they call a woman *par excellence*.

Macaria is more like one of Massinger's women. She advances boldly, though with the decorum of her sex and nation:

Macaria.   "Impute not boldness to me that I come
Before you, strangers; this my first request
I urge; for silence and a chaste reserve
Is woman's genuine praise, and to remain
Quiet within the house. But I come forth,
Hearing thy lamentations, Iolaus:
Though charged with no commission, yet perhaps,
I may be useful."   *   *

Her speech when she offers herself as the victim, is reasonable, as one might speak to-day. She counts the cost all through. Iphigenia is too timid and delicate to dwell upon the loss of earthly bliss, and the due experience of life, even as much as Jeptha's daughter did,[227] but Macaria is explicit, as well befits the daughter of Hercules.

---

[226] *Apollo Belvedere* is a famous Roman sculpture copied from a Greek original. [Ed.]

[227] In Judg. 10–12, the Israelite king Jeptha promises to sacrifice the first creature he sees on returning home from battle. He sees his young daughter and sacrifices her. Fuller's

"Should *these* die, myself
Preserved, of prosperous future could I form
One cheerful hope?
A poor forsaken virgin who would deign
To take in marriage? Who would wish for sons
From one so wretched? Better then to die,
Than bear such undeserved miseries:
One less illustrious this might more beseem.

*   *   *

I have a soul that unreluctantly
Presents itself, and I proclaim aloud
That for my brothers and myself I die,
I am not fond of life, but think I gain
An honorable prize to die with glory."

Still nobler when Iolaus proposes rather that she shall draw lots with her sisters.

"*By lot* I will not die, for to such death
No thanks are due, or glory—name it not.
If you accept me, if my offered life
Be grateful to you, willingly I give it
For these, but by constraint I will not die."

Very fine are her parting advice and injunctions to them all:

"Farewell! revered old man, farewell! and teach
These youths in all things to be wise, like thee,
Naught will avail them more."

Macaria has the clear Minerva eye: Antigone's is deeper, and more capable of emotion, but calm. Iphigenia's, glistening, gleaming with angel truth, or dewy as a hidden violet.

I am sorry that Tennyson, who spoke with such fitness of all the others in his "Dream of fair women," has not of Iphigenia. Of her alone he has not made a fit picture, but only of the circumstances of the sacrifice. He can never have taken to heart this work of Euripides, yet he was so worthy to feel it. Of Jeptha's daughter, he has spoken as he would of Iphigenia, both in her beautiful song, and when

---

emphasis on feminine sacrifice is certainly in keeping with the nineteenth-century cult of the "angel in the house," who looks beyond this world for her value and significance. Admittedly, Fuller revises this rhetoric and tries to adapt it to women's rights politics, but the aura remains. [Ed.]

"I heard Him, for He spake, and grief became
  A solemn scorn of ills.

It comforts me in this one thought to dwell
  That I subdued me to my father's will;
Because the kiss he gave me, ere I fell,
  Sweetens the spirit still.

Moreover it is written, that my race
  Hewed Ammon, hip and thigh from Arroer
Or Arnon unto Minneth. Here her face
  Glow'd as I look'd on her.

She locked her lips; she left me where I stood;
  "Glory to God," she sang, and past afar,
Thridding the sombre boskage of the woods,
  Toward the morning-star." [228]

In the "Trojan dames" there are fine touches of nature with regard to Cassandra. Hecuba shows that mixture of shame and reverence, that prose kindred always do, towards the inspired child, the poet, the elected sufferer for the race.

When the herald announces that she is chosen to be the mistress of Agamemnon, Hecuba answers indignant, and betraying the involuntary pride and faith she felt in this daughter.

"The virgin of Apollo, whom the God,
  Radiant with golden locks, allowed to live
  In her pure vow of maiden chastity?
Tal. With love the raptured virgin smote his heart.
Hec. Cast from thee, O my daughter, cast away
  Thy sacred wand, rend off the honored wreaths,
  The splendid ornaments that grace thy brows."

Yet the moment Cassandra appears, singing wildly her inspired song, Hecuba calls her

"My *frantic* child."

Yet how graceful she is in her tragic phrenzy, the chorus shows—

"How sweetly at thy house's ills thou smil'st,
  Chanting what haply thou wilt not show true?"

---

[228] Alfred, Lord Tennyson (1801–92), "A Dream of Fair Women" (1832) (Reynolds, *Woman* 132). [Ed.]

But if Hecuba dares not trust her highest instinct about her daughter, still less can the vulgar mind of the herald (a man not without tenderness of heart, but with no princely, no poetic blood,) abide the wild prophetic mood which insults his prejudices both as to country and decorums of the sex. Yet Agamemnon, though not a noble man, is of large mould and could admire this strange beauty which excited distaste in common minds.

> *Tal.* "What commands respect, and is held high
> As wise, is nothing better than the mean
> Of no repute: for this most potent king
> Of all the Grecians, the much honored son
> Of Atreus, is enamored with his prize,
> This frantic raver. I am a poor man,
> Yet would I not receive her to my bed."

Cassandra answers with a careless disdain,

"This is a busy slave."

With all the lofty decorum of manners among the ancients, how free was their intercourse, man to man, how full the mutual understanding between prince and "busy slave!" Not here in adversity only, but in the pomp of power, it was so. Kings were approached with ceremonious obeisance, but not hedged round with etiquette, they could see and know their fellows.

The Andromache here is just as lovely as that of the Iliad.

To her child whom they are about to murder, the same that was frightened at the "glittering plume."

> "Dost thou weep,
> My son? Hast thou a sense of thy ill fate?
> Why dost thou clasp me with thy hands, why hold
> My robes, and shelter thee beneath my wings,
> Like a young bird? No more my Hector comes,
> Returning from the tomb; he grasps no more
> His glittering spear, bringing protection to thee."
>   *   *   *
> *   *   "O soft embrace,
> And to thy mother dear. O fragrant breath!
> In vain I swathed thy infant limbs, in vain
> I gave thee nurture at this breast, and toiled,
> Wasted with care. *If ever,* now embrace,
> Now clasp thy mother; throw thine arms around
> My neck and join thy cheek, thy lips to mine."

As I look up I meet the eyes of Beatrice Cenci.[229] Beautiful one, these woes, even, were less than thine, yet thou seemest to understand them all. Thy clear melancholy gaze says, they, at least, had known moments of bliss, and the tender relations of nature had not been broken and polluted from the very first. Yes! the gradations of wo are all but infinite: only good can be infinite.

Certainly the Greeks knew more of real home intercourse, and more of woman than the Americans. It is in vain to tell me of outward observances. The poets, the sculptors always tell the truth. In proportion as a nation is refined, women *must* have an ascendancy, it is the law of nature.

Beatrice! thou wert not "fond of life," either, more than those princesses. Thou wert able to cut it down in the full flower of beauty, as an offering to *the best* known to thee. Thou wert not so happy as to die for thy country or thy brethren, but thou wert worthy of such an occasion.

In the days of chivalry woman was habitually viewed more as an ideal, but I do not know that she inspired a deeper and more home-felt reverence than Iphigenia in the breast of Achilles, or Macaria in that of her old guardian, Iolaus.

We may, with satisfaction, add to these notes the words to which Haydn has adapted his magnificent music in "The Creation."[230]

"In native worth and honor clad, with beauty, courage, strength adorned, erect to heaven, and tall, he stands, a Man!—the lord and king of all! The large and arched front sublime of wisdom deep declares the seat, and in his eyes with brightness shines the soul, the breath and image of his God. With fondness leans upon his breast the partner for him formed, a woman fair, and graceful spouse. Her softly smiling virgin looks, of flowery spring the mirror, bespeak him love, and joy and bliss."

Whoever has heard this music must have a mental standard as to what man and woman should be. Such was marriage in Eden, when "erect to heaven *he* stood," but since, like other institutions, this must be not only reformed, but revived, may be offered as a picture of something intermediate,—the seed of the future growth,—

---

[229] Beatrice Cenci (1577–99), daughter of Francesco Cenci, who was reputed to have sexually abused Beatrice (and perhaps his other twelve children). Beatrice was reputed to have conspired to murder her father (in the various legends, she conspired with family members or with her lover), for which crime she was imprisoned in Rome's Castello Saint'Angelo, tortured, and executed. Guido Reni's famous painting *Beatrice Cenci* (Orientalized with a turban) was enormously popular in the nineteenth century, perhaps thanks also to Percy Bysshe Shelley's poetic drama *The Cenci* (1819), in which Shelley turns her into a proto-revolutionary figure. Henry James compares Margaret Fuller to Beatrice Cenci—both "doomed" women—in *William Wetmore Story and His Friends* (1903). [Ed.]

[230] Franz Joseph Haydn's (1732–1809) oratorio of 1798 (Reynolds, *Woman* 134). [Ed.]

H.

THE SACRED MARRIAGE[231]

And has another's life as large a scope?
It may give due fulfilment to thy hope,
And every portal to the unknown may ope.

If, near this other life, thy inmost feeling
5   Trembles with fateful prescience of revealing
The future Deity, time is still concealing.

If thou feel thy whole force drawn more and more
To launch that other bark on seas without a shore;
And no still secret must be kept in store;

10   If meannesses that dim each temporal deed,
The dull decay that mars the fleshly weed,
And flower of love that seems to fall and leave no seed —

Hide never the full presence from thy sight
Of mutual aims and tasks, ideals bright,
15   Which feed their roots to-day on all this seeming blight.

Twin stars that mutual circle in the heaven,
Two parts for spiritual concord given,
Twin Sabbaths that inlock the Sacred Seven;

Still looking to the centre for the cause,
20   Mutual light giving to draw out the powers,
And learning all the other groups by cognizance of one another's laws:

The parent love the wedded love includes,
The one permits the two their mutual moods,
The two each other know mid myriad multitudes;

25   With child-like intellect discerning love,
And mutual action energizing love,
In myriad forms affiliating love.

A world whose seasons bloom from pole to pole,
A force which knows both starting-point and goal,
30   A Home in Heaven, — the Union in the Soul.

---

[231] Fuller's poem. [Ed.]

Selected *Dispatches from Europe, 1846–1850*

Margaret Fuller

Dispatch 18
NEW AND OLD WORLD DEMOCRACY

[Undated][1]

This letter will reach the United States about the 1st of January; and it may not be impertinent to offer a few New-Year's reflections. Every new year, indeed, confirms the old thoughts, but also presents them under some new aspects.

The American in Europe, if a thinking mind, can only become more American. In some respects it is a great pleasure to be here. Although we have an independent political existence, our position toward Europe, as to Literature and the Arts, is still that of a colony, and one feels the same joy here that is experienced by the colonist in returning to the parent home. What was but picture to us becomes reality; remote allusions and derivations trouble no more: we see the pattern of the stuff, and understand the whole tapestry. There is a gradual clearing up on many points, and many baseless notions and crude fancies are dropped. Even the post-haste passage of the business American through the great cities, escorted by cheating couriers, and ignorant *valets de place,* unable to hold intercourse with the natives of the country, and passing all his leisure hours with his countrymen, who know no more than himself, clears his mind of some mistakes—lifts some mists from his horizon.

There are three species: first, the servile American—a being utterly shallow, thoughtless, worthless. He comes abroad to spend his money and indulge his tastes. His object in Europe is to have fashionable clothes, good foreign cookery, to know some titled persons, and furnish himself with coffee-house gossip, which he wins importance at home by retailing among those less traveled, and as uninformed as himself.

I look with unspeakable contempt on this class—a class which has all the thoughtlessness and partiality of the exclusive classes in Europe, without any of their refinement, or the chivalric feeling which still sparkles among them here and there. However, though these willing serfs in a free age do some little hurt, and cause some annoyance at present, it cannot last: our

"These Sad but Glorious Days": Dispatches from Europe, 1846–1850. Ed. Larry J. Reynolds and Susan Belasco Smith. New Haven: Yale UP, 1992). (*These Sad but Glorious Days* serves as the source for all dispatches reprinted here. All notes are by the original editors.)

[1] First published as "Things and Thoughts in Europe. No. XVIII" in *New-York Daily Tribune,* 1 January 1848, p. 1:1–3.

country is fated to a grand, independent existence, and as its laws develop, these parasites of a bygone period must wither and drop away.

Then there is the conceited American, instinctively bristling and proud of—he knows not what—He does not see, not he, that the history of Humanity for many centuries is likely to have produced results it requires some training, some devotion, to appreciate and profit by. With his great clumsy hands only fitted to work on a steam-engine, he seizes the old Cremona violin, makes it shriek with anguish in his grasp, and then declares he thought it was all humbug before he came, and now he knows it; that there is not really any music in these old things; that the frogs in one of our swamps make much finer, for *they* are young and alive. To him the etiquettes of courts and camps, the ritual of the Church, seem simply silly—and no wonder, profoundly ignorant as he is of their origin and meaning. Just so the legends which are the subjects of pictures, the profound myths which are represented in the antique marbles, amaze and revolt him; as, indeed, such things need to be judged of by another standard from that of the Connecticut Blue-Laws. He criticizes severely pictures, feeling quite sure that his natural senses are better means of judgment than the rules of connoisseurs—not feeling that to see such objects mental vision as well as fleshly eyes are needed, and that something is aimed at in Art beyond the imitation of the commonest forms of Nature.

This is Jonathan in the sprawling state, the booby truant, not yet aspiring enough to be a good school-boy. Yet in his folly there is meaning; add thought and culture to his independence, and he will be a man of might: he is not a creature without hope, like the thick-skinned dandy of the class first specified.

The Artistes form a class by themselves. Yet among them, though seeking special aims by special means may also be found the lineaments of these two classes, as well as of the third, of which I am to speak.

3d. The thinking American—a man who, recognizing the immense advantage of being born to a new world and on a virgin soil, yet does not wish one seed from the Past to be lost. He is anxious to gather and carry back with him all that will bear a new climate and new culture. Some will dwindle; others will attain a bloom and stature unknown before. He wishes to gather them clean, free from noxious insects. He wishes to give them a fair trial in his new world. And that he may know the conditions under which he may best place them in that new world, he does not neglect to study their history in this.

The history of our planet in some moments seems so painfully mean and little, such terrible bafflings and failures to compensate some brilliant successes—such a crashing of the mass of men beneath the feet of a few, and these, too, of the least worthy—such a small drop of honey to each cup of gall, and, in many cases, so mingled, that it is never one moment in life purely tasted,—above all, so little achieved for Humanity as a whole, such tides of war and pestilence intervening to blot out the traces of each triumph, that no wonder if the strongest soul sometimes pauses aghast! No wonder if the many indolently console themselves with gross joys and frivolous prizes. Yes! Those men *are* worthy of admiration who can carry this cross faithfully through fifty years; it is a great while for all the agonies that beset a lover of good, a lover of men; it makes a soul worthy of a speedier ascent, a more productive ministry in the next sphere. Blessed are they who ever keep that portion of pure, generous love with which they began life! How blessed those who have deepened the fountains, and have enough to spare for the thirst of others! Some such there are; and, feeling that, with all the excuses for failure, still only the sight of those who triumph gives a meaning to life or makes its pangs endurable, we must arise and follow.

Eighteen hundred years of this Christian culture in these European Kingdoms, a great theme never lost sight of, a mighty idea, an adorable history to which the hearts of men invariably cling, yet are genuine results rare as grains of gold in the river's sandy bed! Where is the genuine Democracy to which the rights of all men are holy? where the child-like wisdom learning all through life more and more of the will of God? where the aversion to falsehood in all its myriad disguises of cant, vanity, covetousness, so clear to be read in all the history of Jesus of Nazareth? Modern Europe is the sequel to that history, and see this hollow England, with its monstrous wealth and cruel poverty, its conventional life and low, practical aims; see this poor France, so full of talent, so adroit, yet so shallow and glossy still, which could not escape from a false position with all its baptism of blood; see that lost Poland and this Italy bound down by treacherous hands in all the force of genius; see Russia with its brutal Czar and innumerable slaves; see Austria and its royalty that represents nothing, and its people who, as people, are and have nothing! If we consider the amount of truth that has really been spoken out in the world, and the love that has beat in private hearts—how Genius has decked each spring-time with such splendid flowers, conveying each one enough of instruction in its life of harmonious energy, and how continually, unquenchably the spark of faith has striven to burst into flame and light up the Universe—the public failure seems amazing, seems monstrous.

Still Europe toils and struggles with her idea, and, at this moment, all things bode and declare a new outbreak of the fire, to destroy old palaces of crime! May it fertilize also many vineyards!—Here at this moment a successor of St. Peter, after the lapse of near two thousand years, is called "Utopian" by a part of this Europe, because he strives to get some food to the mouths of the *leaner* of his flock. A wonderful state of things, and which leaves as the best argument against despair that men do not, *cannot* despair amid such dark experiences—and thou, my country! will thou not be more true? does no greater success await thee? All things have so conspired to teach, to aid! A new world, a new chance, with oceans to wall in the new thought against interference from the old!—Treasures of all kinds, gold, silver, corn, marble, to provide for every physical need! A noble, constant, starlike soul, an Italian, led the way to its shores, and, in the first days, the strong, the pure, those too brave, too sincere for the life of the Old World hastened to people them. A generous struggle then shook off what was foreign and gave the nation a glorious start for a worthy goal. Men rocked the cradle of its hopes, great, firm, disinterested men who saw, who wrote, as the basis of all that was to be done, a statement of the rights, the inborn rights of men, which, if fully interpreted and acted upon, leaves nothing to be desired.

Yet, oh Eagle, whose early flight showed this clear sight of the Sun, how often dost thou near the ground, how show the vulture in these later days! Thou wert to be the advance-guard of Humanity, the herald of all Progress; how often hast thou betrayed this high commission! Fain would the tongue in clear triumphant accents draw example from thy story, to encourage the hearts of those who almost faint and die beneath the old oppressions. But we must stammer and blush when we speak of many things. I take pride here that I may really say the Liberty of the Press works well, and that checks and balances naturally evolve from it which suffice to its government. I may say the minds of our people are alert, and that Talent has a free chance to rise. It is much. But dare I say that political ambition is not as darkly sullied as in other countries? Dare I say that men of most influence in political life are those who represent most virtue or even intellectual power? Is it easy to find names in that career of which I can speak with enthusiasm? Must I not confess in my country to a boundless lust of gain? Must I not confess to the weakest vanity, which bristles and blusters at each foolish taunt of the foreign press; and must I not admit that the men who make these undignified rejoinders seek and find popularity so? Must I not confess that there is as yet no antidote cordially adopted that will defend even that great, rich country against the evils that have grown out of the commercial system in the old world? Can I say our social laws are generally better, or show a nobler insight into the wants of man and woman? I do, indeed, say what I believe, that voluntary association for improvement in these particulars will be the grand means for my nation to grow and give a nobler harmony to the coming age. But it is only of a small minority that I can say they as yet seriously take to heart these things; that they earnestly meditate on what is wanted for their country,—for mankind,—for our cause is, indeed, the cause of all mankind at present. Could we succeed, really succeed, combine a deep religious love with practical development, the achievements of Genius with the happiness of the multitude, we might believe Man had now reached a commanding point in his ascent, and would stumble and faint no more. Then there is this horrible cancer of Slavery, and this wicked War, that has grown out of it.[2] How dare I speak of these things here? I listen to the same arguments against the emancipation of Italy, that are used against the emancipation of our blacks; the same arguments in favor of the spoliation of Poland as for the conquest of Mexico. I find the cause of tyranny and wrong everywhere the same—and lo! my Country the darkest offender, because with the least excuse, foresworn to the high calling with which she was called,—no champion of the rights of men, but a robber and a jailer; the scourge hid behind her banner; her eyes fixed, not on the stars, but on the possessions of other men.

How it pleases me here to think of the Abolitionists! I could never endure to be with them at home, they were so tedious, often so narrow, always so rabid and exaggerated in their tone.[3]

But, after all, they had a high motive, something eternal in their desire and life; and, if it was not the only thing worth thinking of it was really something worth living and dying for to free a great nation from such a terrible blot, such a threatening plague. God strengthen them and make them wise to achieve their purpose!

I please myself, too, with remembering some ardent souls among the American youth who, I trust, will yet expand and help to give soul to the huge, over fed, too hastily grown-up body. May they be constant. "Were Man but constant he were perfect!" it has been said; and it is true that he who could be constant to those moments in which he has been truly human—not brutal, not mechanical—is on the sure path to his perfection and to effectual service of the Universe.

It is to the youth that Hope addresses itself, to those who yet burn with aspiration, who are not hardened in their sins. But I dare not expect too

---

[2] Fuller alludes to the Mexican War (1846–48), viewed by many in America as a means to extend slavery territory. It was precipitated by the annexation of Texas by the United States in December 1845. Hostilities began in April 1846 when Mexicans resisted the crossing of the disputed boundary of southern Texas by American troops. The treaty of Guadalupe-Hildalgo, signed on 2 February 1848, gave the United States two-fifths of Mexico's territory, including California (*OCAL*). [Hart, James D. *The Oxford Companion to American Literature*. 5th ed. New York: Oxford UP, 1983.]

[3] In the early 1840s Fuller expressed indifference toward the antislavery movement and refused to devote one of her "conversations" to abolition when Maria Weston Chapman asked her to do so. In 1845, however, she published seven pieces in the *Tribune* against slavery, and she twice reviewed Chapman's annual abolition anthology (Chevigny 238–39, 286, 288, 340–42).

much of them. I am not very old, yet of those who, in life's morning, I saw touched by the light of a high hope, many have seceded. Some have become voluptuaries; some mere family men, who think it is quite life enough to win bread for half a dozen people and treat them decently; others are lost through indolence and vacillation. Yet some remain constant. "I have witnessed many a shipwreck, yet still beat noble hearts."

I have found many among the youth of England, of France—of Italy also—full of high desire, but will they have courage and purity to fight the battle through in the sacred, the immortal band? Of some of them I believe it and await the proof. If a few succeed amid the trial, we have not lived and loved in vain.

To these, the heart of my country, a Happy New Year! I do not know what I have written. I have merely yielded to my feelings in thinking of America; but something of true love must be in these lines—receive them kindly, my friends; it is, by itself, some merit for printed words to be sincere.

Dispatch 23
THE SPRINGTIME REVOLUTIONS OF '48

ROME, 29th March, 1848[1]

It is long since I have written; my health entirely gave way beneath the Roman Winter. The rain was constant, commonly falling in torrents from the 16th December to the 19th March. Nothing could surpass the dirt, the gloom, the desolation of Rome. Let no one fancy he has seen her who comes here only in the Winter. It is an immense mistake to do so. I cannot sufficiently rejoice that I did not first see Italy in the Winter.

The climate of Rome at this time of extreme damp I have found equally exasperating and weakening. I have had constant nervous headache without strength to bear it, nightly fever, want of appetite. Some constitutions bear it better, but the complaint of weakness and extreme dejection of spirits is general among foreigners in the wet season. The English say they become acclimated in two or three years and cease to suffer, though never so strong as at home.

Now this long dark dream—to me the most idle and most suffering season of my life—seems past.[2] The Italian heavens wear again their deep

---

[1] First published as "Things and Thoughts in Europe. No. XXIII" in *New-York Daily Tribune*, 4 May 1848, p. 1:1–3.

[2] Fuller would not, of course, explain that the main reason for her illness was the first few months of her pregnancy, which she kept secret from family and friends.

blue; the sun shines gloriously; the melancholy lustres are stealing again over the Campagna, and hundreds of larks sing unwearied above its ruins. Nature seems in sympathy with the great events that are transpiring; with the emotions which are swelling the hearts of men. The morning sun is greeted by the trumpets of the Roman Legions marching out once more, but now not to oppress but to defend. The stars look down on their jubilees over the good news which nightly reaches them from their brothers of Lombardy.[3] This week has been one of nobler, sweeter feeling of a better hope and faith than Rome in her greatest days ever knew. How much has happened since I wrote!—First, the victorious resistance of Sicily and the revolution of Naples. This has led us yet only to half measures, but even these have been of great use to the progress of Italy. The Neapolitans will, probably, have to get rid at last of the stupid crowned head who is at present their puppet, but their bearing with him has led to the wiser sovereigns granting these Constitutions, which, if eventually inadequate to the wants of Italy, will be so useful, are so needed, to educate her to seek better, completer forms of administration.

In the midst of all this serious work came the play of Carnival, in which there was much less interest felt than usual, but enough to dazzle and captivate a stranger. One thing, however, had been omitted in the description of the Roman Carnival; *i.e.* that it rains every day. Almost every day came on violent rain just as the tide of gay masks was fairly engaged in the Corso. This would have been well worth bearing once or twice for the sake of seeing the admirable good humor of this people. Those who had laid out all their savings in the gayest, thinnest dresses, on carriages and chairs for the Corso, and found themselves suddenly drenched, their finery spoiled, and obliged to ride and sit shivering all the afternoon. But they never murmured, never scolded, never stopped throwing their flowers. Their strength of constitution is wonderful. While I, in my shawl and boa, was coughing at the open window from the moment I inhaled the wet sepulchral air, the servant girls of the house had taken off their woolen gowns, and arrayed in white muslins and roses, sat in the drenched street beneath the drenching rain, quite happy, and have suffered nothing in consequence.

---

[3] Milan had just experienced her "Five Glorious Days." The revolution began on the morning of 18 March, and after five days of furious street fighting during which the Milanese used barricades and homemade weapons to combat the 18,000 to 20,000 Austrian troops, the Austrian general Radetzky abandoned the city. On 22 March his army retreated to the Quadrilateralo, a district between the mountains and the sea. On this same day, Venice staged its successful revolution, forcing the governor and military commandant to evacuate the town and the surrounding forts (*Cambridge Modern History* 11: 81–82). [Ward, A. W., G. W. Prothero, and Stanley Leathes, eds. *Cambridge Modern History*. Vol. 2. New York: Macmillan, 1903.]

The Romans renounced the *moccaletti*,[4] ostensibly as an expression of sympathy for the sufferings of the Milanese, but really because, at that time, there was great disturbance about the Jesuits, and the Government feared that difficulties would arise in the excitement of the evening. But, since, we have had this entertainment in honor of the Revolutions of France and Austria, and nothing could be more beautiful. The fun usually consists in all the people blowing one another's lights out; we had not this; all the little tapers were left to blaze, and the long Corso swarmed with tall fire-flies. — Lights crept out over the surface of all the houses, and such merry little twinkling lights, laughing and flickering with each slightest movement of those who held them. Up and down the Corso, they twinkled, they swarmed, they streamed, while a surge of gay triumphant sound ebbed and flowed beneath that glittering surface. Here and there danced men carrying aloft *moccoli*, and clanking chains, emblem of the tyrannic power now vanquished by the people. The people, sweet and noble, who, in the intoxication of their joy, were guilty of no rude or unkindly word or act, and who, no signal being given as usual for the termination of their diversion, closed, of their own accord and with one consent, singing the hymns for Pio, by nine o'clock, and retired peacefully to their homes, to dream of hopes they yet scarce understand.

This happened last week. The news of the dethronement of Louis Philippe reached us just after the close of the Carnival. It was just a year from my leaving Paris.[5] I did not think, as I looked with such disgust on the empire of sham he had established in France, and saw the soul of the people

---

[4]Story was quite taken with the *moccoletti*, the feast of the tapers that ends the Roman Carnival. He explains what Fuller had observed: "Thousands of little waxen tapers then flutter about like living things, dancing along balconies and open windows, quivering up and down the entire length of the Corso, flickering from carriage to carriage, flying backwards and forwards at the ends of long *canne*, and pursued by flapping handkerchiefs that seek to extinguish them. A soft yellow light glows over the brown palace façades, gleaming on the window-panes, and illuminating below a sea of merry faces. Up the Corso, far as the eye can reach, the *moccoletti* sparkle like swarms of brilliant fire-flies. The street resounds with a tumultuous cry of '*Ecco il moccolo — moccolo*,' as the little tapers are brandished and shaken in the air, and the loud jeers of '*Senza moccolo — senza moccolo*,' as dexterous hands and lips suddenly extinguish them. The scene is always gay; but the wild, glad exultation of the spectacle in 1848, when the news of Italian victories came in from Lombardy, and the people, waving their *moccoletti*, poured into the Corso, cheering and singing their national songs, surpassed for enthusiasm anything I ever saw" (2:552–53). [Story, William Wetmore. *Roba di Roma*. 8th ed. Vol. 2. Boston: Houghton, 1887.]

[5]On 22–24 February the French workers, joined by students and members of the bourgeoisie, especially urban artisans, overthrew the monarchy of Louis Philippe and proclaimed France a republic. A provisional government was established with the poet-statesman Alphonse de Lamartine at its head.

imprisoned and held fast as in an iron vice, that it would burst its chains so soon. Whatever be the result, France has done gloriously; she has declared that she will not be satisfied with pretexts while there are facts in the world—that to stop her march is a vain attempt, though the onward path be dangerous and difficult. It is vain to cry Peace, peace, when there is no peace. The news from France, in these days, sounds ominous, though still vague; it would appear that the political is being merged in the social struggle: it is well; whatever blood is to be shed, whatever altars cast down. Those tremendous problems MUST be solved, whatever be the cost! That cost cannot fail to break many a bank, many a heart in Europe, before the good can bud again out of a mighty corruption. To you, people of America, it may perhaps be given to look on and learn in time for a preventive wisdom. You may learn the real meaning of the words FRATERNITY, EQUALITY: you may, despite the apes of the Past, who strive to tutor you, learn the needs of a true Democracy. You may in time learn to reverence, learn to guard, the true aristocracy of a nation, the only really noble—the LABORING CLASSES.[6]

And Metternich, too, is crushed; the seed of the Woman has had his foot on the serpent. I have seen the Austrian arms dragged through the streets of Rome and burned in the Piazza del Popolo.—The Italians embraced one another and cried *Miracolo, Providenza!* the modern Tribune Ciceruacchio fed the flame with faggots; Adam Mickiewicz, the great Poet of Poland, long exiled from his country or the hopes of a country, looked on, while Polish women, exiled too, or who, perhaps, like one nun who is here, had been daily scourged by the orders of a tyrant, brought little pieces that had been scattered in the street and threw into the flames—an offering received by the Italians with loud plaudits.[7] It was a transport of the people, who found no way to vent their joy, but the symbol, the poesy, natural to the Italian mind; the ever-too-wise "upper classes" regret it, and the Germans choose to resent as an insult to Germany; but it was nothing of the kind; the insult

---

[6] In Paris communist and socialist ideas had become familiar to the working classes and contributed to the prevailing social unrest. *The Communist Manifesto,* which appeared in February 1848, was just one of many calls for the overthrow of existing social conditions in Europe. During her stay in Paris in the winter of 1846–47, Fuller encountered socialist revolutionary thought at first hand, but several years before, she had gotten an early sense of it. In the summer of 1845 she translated a letter from the Paris correspondent of the *Deutsche Schnellpost,* A German immigrants' newspaper, which discussed Marx and ended with a long quotation from Engels's *Condition of the Working Class in England.* According to Chevigny, who sees Fuller becoming more Marxist in Europe, "this is surely among the very earliest notices of Marx and Engels in America" (294).

[7] On 14 March 1848 Fuller wrote Emerson that Mickiewicz "is with me here, and will remain some time" (Hudspeth 5: 55). [Hudspeth, Robert N., ed. *The Letters of Margaret Fuller.* Vol. 5. Ithaca: Cornell UP, 1983.]

was to the prisons of Spielberg, to those who commanded the massacres of Milan; a base tyranny little congenial to the native German heart, as the true Germans of Germany are at this moment showing by their struggles, by their resolves.

When the double-headed eagle was pulled down from above the lofty portal of the Palazzo di Venezia, the people placed there in its stead one of white and gold inscribed with the name ALTA ITALIA, and quick upon the emblem followed the news that Milan was fighting against her tyrants— that Venice had driven them out and freed from their prisons the courageous Protestants in favor of truth, Tommaseo and Manin—that Manin, descendant of the last Doge, had raised the Republican banner on the Place St. Mark—and that Modena, that Parma, were driving out the unfeeling and imbecile creatures who had mocked Heaven and Man by the pretence of Government there.

With indescribable rapture these news were received in Rome. Men were seen dancing, women weeping with joy along the street. The youth rushed to enrol themselves in regiments to go to the frontier. In the Colosseum their names were received. Father Gavazzi,[8] a truly patriotic monk, gave them the cross to carry on a new, a better, because defensive crusade. Sterbini, long exiled, addressed them; he said, "Romans, do you wish to go; do you wish to go with all your hearts? If so, you *may*, and those who do not wish to go themselves may give money. To those who will go, the government gives bread and fifteen baiocchi a day." The people cried "We too wish to go, but we do not wish so much; the Government is very poor; we can live on a paul[9] a day." The princes answered by giving, one sixty thousand, others twenty, fifteen, ten thousand dollars. The people answered by giving at the benches which are opened in the piazzas literally everything; street-peddlers gave the gains of each day; women gave every ornament— from the splendid necklace and bracelet down to the poorest bit of coral; servant girls gave five pauls, two pauls, even half a paul, if they had no more; a man all in rags gave two pauls; "it is," said he, "all I have." "Then," said Torlonia, "take from me this dollar;" the man of rags thanked him warmly and handed that also to the bench, which refused to receive it. "No! *that* must stay with you," shouted all present. These are the people whom the traveler accuses of being unable to rise above selfish considerations. Na-

---

[8] Alessandro Gavazzi (1809–89), a priest born at Bologna, became a Barnabite monk and a supporter of Pius IX. After the fall of Rome in 1849, he escaped to England and founded the (Protestant) Italian Free Church (*Chambers's Biographical Dictionary*). [Thorne, J. D., ed. *Chamber's Biographical Dictionary*. New York: St. Martin's, 1968.]

[9] The baiocchi was the smallest unit of money minted in the Papal States. The paul was a silver coin, originally minted by Pope Paul III. Both coins were worth very little.

tion, rich and glorious by nature as ever, capable, like all nations, all men, of being degraded by slavery, capable as are few nations, few men, of kindling into pure flame at the touch of a ray from the Sun of Truth, of Life.

The two or three days that followed, the troops were marching about by detachments, followed always by the people, to Ponte Malle, often farther. The women wept; for the habits of the Romans are so domestic, that it seemed a great thing to have their sons and lovers gone even for a few months. The English — or, at least those of the illiberal, bristling nature — too often met here, which casts out its porcupine quills against everything like enthusiasm (of the more generous Saxon blood I know some noble examples,) laughed at all this. They have said that this people would not fight; when the Sicilians, men and women, did so nobly they said, "Oh! the Sicilians are quite unlike the Italians; you will see when the struggle comes on in Lombardy, they cannot resist the Austrian force a moment." I said, "That force is only physical; do not you think a sentiment can sustain them?" They reply, "All stuff and poetry; it will fade the moment their blood flows." When news came that the Milanese, men and women, fight as the Sicilians did, they said, "Well, the Lombards are a better race, but these Romans are good for nothing; it is a farce for a Roman to try to walk even; they never walk a mile; they will not be able to support the first day's march of thirty miles, and not to have their usual minestra to eat either." Now the troops were not willing to wait for the Government to make the necessary arrangements for their march, so at the first night's station — Monterose — they did *not* find food or bedding, yet the second night, at Civita Castellana, they were so well alive as to remain dancing and vivaing Pio Nino in the piazza till after midnight. No, Messieurs, Soul is not quite nothing, if Matter be a clog upon its transports.

The Americans show a better, warmer feeling than they did; the meeting in New-York was of use in instructing the Americans abroad! The dinner given here on Washington's birthday, was marked by fine expressions of sentiment and a display of talent unusual on such occasions. There was a poem from Mr. Story of Boston, which gave great pleasure; a speech by Mr. Hillard, said to be very good, and one by Mr. Hedge of Bangor, exceedingly admired for the felicity of thought and image and the finished beauty of style.[10]

---

[10] Although Fuller apparently did not attend this dinner, her friends were clearly leaders. She saw the Storys virtually every day; George Stillman Hillard, who was Charles Sumner's law partner, was an old friend, and Frederic Henry Hedge (1805–90) was the Unitarian clergyman whose name was attached to Hedge's Club, known also as the Transcendental Club, the group of New England intellectuals with whom Fuller associated during her years in Boston (*DAB*) [Johnson, Allen, and Dumas Malone, ed. *The Dictionary of American Biography*. 20 vols. New York: Scribner's, 1928–36.]

Next week we shall have more news, and I shall try to write and mention also some interesting things want of time obliges me to omit in this letter.[11] I annex a poem of Cranch's, descriptive of a picture he sends to Mr. Ogden Haggerty of your City, interesting in itself and not irrelevant to this present communication:

THE CASTLE OF THE COLONNAS

BY C. P. CRANCH

High on a rugged mountain, gray and old,
Gray like the rocks themselves—where heat and cold
For centuries with the battlements have striven,
As Man did once—its walls all bare and riven,
5   The castle stands—a mass of frowning stone,
With dark-green vines and ivy over-grown,
Through the gray rifts the deep Italian day
Smiles as it ever smiles on all decay.
Here in the olden days of feudal might
10 The proud Colonna donned his armor bright
And strode upon the ramparts, to survey
The vassal plains that far beneath him lay,
And mustering his brave knights, held them intent
To guard each oft-assaulted battlement.
15 Here bristling up the steep and narrow path
Host after host came flaming in fierce wrath.
Through the bright day and through the starlit night
Thundered the tempest of the bloody fight;
And those far Volscian mounta'ns, soft and blue,
20 Smiled through their purple haze, as now they do
On the deep stillness of this peaceful day,—
When nought is heard save—faint and far away,
Down by the vineyards green—the shepherd's song
Floating the vale and mountain side along;
25 Or cawing rooks that clamor hour by hour
Sailing around the Ruin's topmost tower.

---

[11]The rest of this paragraph and the poem are omitted in *AHA*. [Margaret Fuller, *At Home and Abroad*, or *Things and Thoughts in Europe*. Ed. Arthur B. Fuller. Boston: Crosby, Nichols, 1856.]

Up the gray rocks no more the files advance;
No more the battle stern, the wild romance.
Peace hath her victories now, perchance as famed
30 As those in olden time the Warrior claimed.
All Italy hath breathed a freer air
Since good Mastai fills Saint Peter's chair:
More mildly seems to bend the Summer sky
Its infinite dome of blue; the morning's eye
35 Opens more hopefully, and evening closes
With tinted clouds like dropping leaves of roses,
Over the Roman streets and shrines and fountains,
O'er the Campagna and the purple mountains
Love, Freedom, Truth may yet extend their wing,
40 And all be realized that poets sing.

When great Colonna, driven from his home,
Landless, and stripped of all, went forth to roam,
"Where is thy fortress now?" they asked. With pride,
His hand upon his heart, the chief replied
45 "'Tis here!"—And thou around whose onward course
Threaten the legions of tyrannic force,
Sovereign whom God hath surely blest and sent
To be of future good His instrument,
Though all desert thee in thine hour of need,
50 And leave thee houseless on the rocks to bleed,
Let thy soul's watchword be a truer light
Than even his who ruled by fear and might.
Thy Heart thy Fortress! An unfading youth
Shall yearly crown its battlements of truth.
55 In the bright panoply of God encased
No years shall molder and no tyrant waste.
No Ruin of the Past that heart shall be,
But a great Beacon-tower for the good and free.

Rome, February, 1848

———*April 1.*

Yesterday I passed at Ostia and Castle Fusano. A million birds sang; the woods teemed with blossoms: the sod grew green hourly over the graves of the mighty Past; the surf rushed in on a fair shore; the Tiber majestically retreated to carry inland her share from the treasures of the deep; the sea breezes burnt my face, but revived my heart; I felt the calm of thought, the sublime hopes of the Future, Nature, Man—so great, though so little—so dear, though incomplete.[12] Returning to Rome, I find the news, pronounced official, that the viceroy Ranieri has capitulated at Verona; that Italy is free, independent, and One.[13] I trust this will prove no April foolery, no premature news; it seems too good, too speedy a realization of hope, to have come on earth, and can only be answered in the words of the proclamation made yesterday by Pius IX.:

"The events which these two months past have seen rush after one another in so rapid succession, are no human work. Woe to him who in this wind, which shakes and tears up alike the lofty cedars and humble shrubs, hears not the voice of God! Woe to human pride, if to the fault or merit of any man whatsoever it refer these wonderful changes, instead of adoring the mysterious designs of Providence."

Dispatch 26
REVOLUTION IN ROME

ROME, *December 2, 1848*[1]

Messrs. Greeley & McElrath:

Not till I saw the snow on the mountains grow rosy in the Autumn sunset did I turn my steps again toward Rome. I was very ready to return. After three or four years of constant excitement this six months of seclusion had been welcome; but now I felt the need of meeting other eyes beside those, so bright and so shallow, of the Italian peasant. Indeed, I left what was most precious that I could not take with me; still it was a compensation that I was again to see Rome.[2] Rome that almost killed me with her cold breath

---

[12] Castle Fusano, a seventeenth-century villa, is two miles south of Ostia, near Italy's west coast. Fuller's biographer Madeleine B. Stern believes that "Margaret Fuller and Giovanni Ossoli were married in a civil ceremony of April 4, 1848, in one of the towns near Rome." She bases this conjecture on the fact that "April 4 seems to have been an anniversary for the Ossolis. Their letters of April 3 and 4, 1849, express keen regret that they cannot be together on the fourth and hope that the next year will being them better luck on that day" (430). [Stern, Madeleine B. *The Life of Margaret Fuller*. New York: Dutton, 1942.]

[13] Archduke Rainier, the Hapsburg viceroy of Lombardy and Venetia, was outmaneuvered by Manin, who established a civic guard on March 22 (Fejtö ix). [Fejtö, François, ed. *The Opening of an Era: 1848*. New York: Howard Fertig, 1966.]

[1] First published as "Things and Thoughts in Europe. No. XXVI" in *New-York Daily Tribune*, 26 January 1849, p. 1:1–4.

[2] Fuller refers to her son; she had not yet written to her family and friends of his birth.

of last Winter, yet still with that cold breath whispered a tale of import so divine. Rome so beautiful, so great; her presence stupifies, and one has to withdraw to prize the treasures she has given. City of the Soul! yes, it is *that;* the very dust magnetizes you, and thousand spells have been chaining you in every careless, every murmuring moment. Yes! Rome, however seen, thou must be still adored; and every hour of absence or presence must deepen love with one who has known what it is to repose in thy arms.

Repose! for whatever be the revolutions, tumults, panics, hopes of the present day, still the temper of life here is Repose. The great Past enfolds us, and the emotions of the moment cannot here importantly disturb that impression. From the wild shout and throng of the streets the setting sun recalls us as it rests on a hundred domes and temples—rests on the Campagna, whose grass is rooted in departed human greatness. Burial-place so full of spirit that Death itself seems no longer cold; oh let me rest here, too! Rest, here, seems possible; meseems myriad lives still linger here, awaiting some one great summons.

The rivers had burst their bounds, and beneath the moon the fields round Rome lay, one sheet of silver.[3] Entering the gate while the baggage was under examination I walked to the gate of a villa. Far stretched its overarching shrubberies, its deep-green bowers; two statues with foot advanced and uplifted finger, seemed to greet me; it was near the scene of great revels, great splendors in the old time; there lay the gardens of Sallust, where were combined palace, theater, library, bath and villa. Strange things have happened now, the most attractive part of which—the secret heart—lies buried or has fled to animate other forms: for of that part historians have rarely given a hint, more than they do now of the truest life of our day, that refuses to be embodied by the pen; it craves forms more mutable, more eloquent than the pen can give.

I found Rome empty of foreigners: most of the English have fled in affright—the Germans and French are wanted at home—the Czar has recalled many of his younger subjects; he does not like the schooling they get here.[4] That large part of the population which lives by the visits of foreigners

---

[3] In a long letter to her mother, dated 16 November 1848, Fuller described her arrival in Rome, which was made difficult because of the flooding she describes here: "As we approached the Tiber, the towers and domes of Rome could be seen, like a cloud lying low on the horizon. The road and the meadows, alike under water, lay between us and it, one sheet of silver. The horses entered; they behaved nobly; we proceeded, every moment uncertain if the water would not become deep; but the scene was beautiful, and I enjoyed it highly" (Hudspeth 5: 48–49). The Tiber flooded frequently until embankments were constructed in the late nineteenth century.

[4] The depopulation of Rome made it possible for Fuller to locate inexpensive accommodations, very important to her at this time because of her very slender means. She found

was suffering very much — trade, industry, for every reason, stagnant. The people were every moment becoming more exasperated by the impudent measures of the Minister Rossi, and their mortification at seeing Rome represented and betrayed by a foreigner.[5] And what foreigner? A pupil of Guizot and Louis Philippe. The news had just reached them of the bombardment and storm of Vienna. Zucchi, the Minister-of-War, left Rome to put down over-free manifestations in the Provinces, and impede the entrance of the troops of the Patriot Chief, Garibaldi, into Bologna.[6] From the Provinces came soldiery, called by Rossi to keep order at the opening of the Chamber of Deputies. He reviewed them in the face of the Civic Guard; the Press began to be restrained; men were arbitrarily seized and sent out of the kingdom; the public indignation rose to its height; the cup overflowed.

The 15th was a beautiful day and I had gone out for a long walk. Returning at night, the old Padrona met me with her usual smile a little clouded, "Do you know," said she, "that the Minister Rossi has been killed?"[7]

"Killed!"

"Yes — with a thrust in the back. A wicked man, surely, but is that the way to punish CHRISTIANS?"[8]

"I cannot," observed a Philosopher, "sympathize under any circumstances with so immoral a deed; but surely the manner of doing it was *grandiose.*"

The people at large was not so refined in their comments as either the Padrona or the Philosopher; but soldiers and populace alike ran up and down singing "Blessed the hand that rids the earth of a tyrant."

---

a large, sunny room on the upper story of 60 Piazza Barberini, which she rented by the month. From one side, she could see the Barberini Palace and the pope's gardens, from the other the piazza and the Street of the Four Fountains (Stern 442).

[5] Pellegrino Rossi (1787–1848), a lawyer and professor, was an Italian political exile naturalized in France whom Guizot appointed the French ambassador to Rome in 1845. He had become a friend and advisor to the pope, who appointed him prime minister of the Papal States on 16 September 1848. Though a brilliant statesman, he was disliked and distrusted by many in Rome who considered him arrogant and retrogressive (Robertson 363–64; Hudspeth 5: 50). [Robertson, Priscilla. *Revolutions of 1848: A Social History.* Princeton: Princeton UP, 1952.]

[6] General Carlo Zucchi had unsuccessfully led a troup of rebels against the Austrians in March 1831 and had been imprisoned (*New Cambridge Modern History* 10: 554–55). Zucchi had been involved in the defense of Palmanova against the Austrians and accepted an invitation from Rossi to maintain order in the Papal army (Berkeley 3: 400). [Berkeley, G. F. H. and J. Berkeley. *Italy in the Making: January 1st 1848 to November 16th 1848.* 1940. London: Cambridge UP, 1968.]

[7] No Roman said *murdered.* [Fuller's note.]

[8] Arthur Fuller changed this phrase to read "to punish even the wicked?" in *AHA.*

"Certainly, the manner *was* grandiose."

The Chamber was awaiting the entrance of Rossi. Had he lived to enter, he would have found the Assembly, without a single exception, ranged upon the Opposition benches. His carriage approached, attended by a howling, hissing multitude. He smiled, affected unconcern, but must have felt relieved when his horses entered the courtyard gate of the *Cancelleria*.[9] He did not know he was entering the place of his execution. The horses stopped; he alighted in the midst of a crowd; it jostled him as if for the purpose of insult; he turned abruptly and received as he did so the fatal blow. It was dealt by a resolute, perhaps experienced, hand; he fell and spoke no word more.

The crowd, as if all previously acquainted with the plan, as no doubt most of them were, issued quietly from the gate and passed through the outside crowd—its members, among whom was he who dealt the blow, dispersing in all directions.—For two or three minutes this outside crowd did not know that anything special had happened.—When they did, the news was at the moment received in silence. The soldiers in whom Rossi had trusted, whom he had hoped to flatter and bribe, stood at their posts and said not a word.—Neither they nor any one asked "Who did this? Where is he gone?"[10] The sense of the people certainly was that it was an act of summary justice on an offender whom the laws could not reach, but they felt it to be indecent to shout or exult on the spot where he was breathing his last. Rome, so long supposed the Capital of Christendom, certainly took a very pagan view of this act, and the piece represented on the occasion at the theaters was "The Death of Nero."

The next morning I went to the church of St. Andrea della Valle, where was to be performed a funeral service, with fine music, in honor of the victims of Vienna; for this they do here for the victims all round—"victims of Milan," "victims of Paris," "victims of Naples," and now "victims of Vienna." But today I found the church closed, the service put off—Rome was thinking about her own victims.

---

[9] The Palazzo della Cancelleria was built in the fifteenth century. The gate to the courtyard was added by Domenico Fontana (Baedeker 2: 218). [Baedeker, Karl. *Italy: Handbook for Travellers*. 11th ed. Vol. 2. Leipzig: Baedeker, 1899.]

[10] Apparently the murderer was Luigi Brunetti, the oldest son of Ciceraucchio, acting at the instigation of the politician Sterbini and with the cooperation of a group of volunteers returned from the Lombard campaign, known as the Reduci. An associate of theirs named Grandoni was unjustly condemned for the murder in May 1854 and died in prison a month later (Trevelyan 80–81). [Trevelyan, George Macaulay. *Garibaldi's Defense of the Roman Republic, 1848–49*. London: Longmans, Green, 1941.]

I passed into the church of *San Luigi dei Francesi*. The Republican flag was flying at the door; the young Sacristan said the fine musical service which this church gave formerly on St. Philip's day, in honor of Louis Philippe, would now be transferred to the Republican Anniversary, the 25th of February. I looked at the monument Chateaubriand erected when here, to a poor girl, who died last of her family, having seen all the others perish round her.[11] I entered the Domenichino Chapel, and gazed anew on those magnificent representations of the Life and Death of St. Cecilia. She and St. Agnes are my favorite saints. I love to think of those angel visits which her husband knew by the fragrance of roses and lilies left behind in the apartment. I love to think of his visit to the Catacombs, and all that followed. In this picture St. Cecilia, as she stretches out her arms toward the suffering multitude, seems as if an immortal fount of purest love sprung from her heart. She gives very strongly the sense of an inexhaustible love — the only love that is much worth thinking about.

Leaving the church I passed along, toward the *Piazza del Popolo*, "Yellow Tiber rose," but not high enough to cause "distress," as he does when in a swelling mood rather than "mantle" it. I heard the drums beating, and, entering the Piazza, I found the troops of the line already assembled, and the Civic Guard marching in by platoons; each *battaglione* saluted as it entered by trumpets and a fine strain from the hand of the Carbineers.

I climbed the Pincian to see better. There is no place so fine for anything of this kind as the Piazza del Popolo, it is so full of light, so fair and grand, the obelisk and fountain make so fine a center to all kinds of groups.

The object of the present meeting was for the Civic Guard and troops of the line to give pledges of sympathy preparatory to going to the Quirinal to demand a change of Ministry and of measures. The flag of the Union was placed in front of the obelisk; all present saluted it; some officials made addresses; the trumpets sounded, and all moved toward the Quirinal.

Nothing could be gentler than the disposition of the crowd. They were resolved to be played with no longer, but no threat was heard or thought. — They believed that the Court would be convinced by the fate of Rossi that the retrograde movement it had attempted was impracticable. They knew the retrograde party were panic-struck, and hoped to use the occasion to free the Pope from their meshes. All felt that Pius IX. had fallen irrevocably from his high place of the friend of Progress and father of Italy: but still he

---

[11]Vicomte François-Auguste-René de Chateaubriand (1768–1848), an important precursor of romanticism, won fame with *Le Génie du christianisme* (1802) (*OCFL*) [Harvey, Paul, and J. E. Heseltine. *The Oxford Companion to French Literature*. New York: Oxford UP, 1959.]

was personally beloved, and still his name, so often shouted in hope and joy, had not quite lost its *prestige*.

I returned to the house, which is very near the Quirinal. On one side I could see the Palace and gardens of the Pope, on the other the Piazza Barberini and street of the Four Fountains. Presently I saw the carriage of Prince Barberini drive hurriedly into his court-yard gate, the footman signing to close it, a discharge of firearms was heard, and the drums of the Civic Guard beat to arms.[12]

The Padrona ran up and down crying with every round of shot, "Jesu Maria, they are killing the Pope! O! poor Holy Father—Tita, Tita, (out of the window to her husband,) what *is* the matter?"

The lord of creation disdained to reply.

"Oh! Signora, pray, pray, ask Tita what is the matter?" I did so. "I don't know, Signora; nobody knows."

"Why don't you go on the mount and see?"

"It would be an imprudence, Signora; nobody will go."

I was just thinking to go myself when I saw a poor man borne by, badly wounded, and heard that the Swiss were firing on the people. Their doing so was the cause of whatever violence there was, and it was not much.

The people had assembled, as usual, at the Quirinal, only with more form and solemnity than usual. They had taken with them several of the Chamber of Deputies, and they sent an embassy, headed by Galetti,[13] who had been in the late Ministry, to state their wishes. They received a peremptory negative. They then insisted on seeing the Pope, and pressed on the palace. The Swiss became alarmed, and fired from the windows, from the roof. They did this, it is said, without orders, but who could, at the time, suppose that? If it had been planned to exasperate the people to blood,

---

[12] Fuller wrote her mother a detailed account of this scene: "To-day, all the troops and the people united and went to the Quirinal to demand a change of measures. They found the Swiss Guard drawn out, and the Pope dared not show himself. They attempted to force the door of his palace, to enter his presence, and the guard fired. I saw a man borne by wounded. The drum beat to call out the National Guard. The carriage of Prince Barberini [Francesco-Maria Barberini-Colona (1772–1853)] has returned with its frightened inmates and liveried retinue, and they have suddenly barred up the court-yard gate" (Hudspeth 5: 49–50).

[13] Giuseppe Galletti (1798–1873), a Bolognese lawyer who was serving a life sentence for his revolutionary activities in 1844, was freed by Pius IX in the general amnesty of 1846. Galletti was made minister of the interior by the pope in 1848 and, after the pope's flight, worked to organize the election of a constituent assembly for the entire country (Berkeley 2: 39; Hearder 198, 109; Zorzi 207). [Hearder, Harry. *Italy in the Age of Risorgimento, 1790–1870*. New York: Longman, 1983. Zorzi, Rosella Mamoli. *Margaret Fuller: Un'americana a Roma, 1847–1849*. Pordenone: Studio Tesi, 1986.]

what more could have been done? As it was, very little was shed; but the Pope, no doubt, felt great panic. He heard the report of fire-arms—heard that they tried to burn a door of the palace. I would lay my life that he could have shown himself without the slightest danger; nay, that the habitual respect for his presence would have prevailed, and hushed all tumult. He did not think so, and to still it once more degraded himself and injured his people, by making promises he did not mean to keep.

He protests now against those promises as extorted by violence, a strange plea, indeed, for the representative of St. Peter!

Rome is all full of effigies of those over whom violence had no power. There is an early Pope about to be thrown into the Tiber; violence had no power to make him say what he did not mean. Delicate girls, men in the prime of hope and pride of power—they were all alike about that. They could be done to death in boiling oil, roasted on coals, or cut to pieces; but they could not say what they did not mean. These formed the true Church; it was these who had power to disseminate the religion of Him, the Prince of Peace, who died a bloody death of torture between sinners, because He never could say what He did not mean.

A little church outside the gate of St. Sebastian commemorates this affecting tradition of the Church; Peter, alarmed at the persecution of the Christians, had gone forth to fly, when in this spot he saw a bright figure in his path and recognized his Master traveling toward Rome.

"Lord," he said, "whither goest thou?"

"I go," replied Jesus, "to die, with my people."

Peter comprehended the reproof. He felt that he must not a fourth time deny his Master, yet hope for salvation. He returned to Rome to offer his life in attestation of his faith.

The Roman Catholic Church has risen a monument to the memory of such facts. And has the present Head of that Church quite failed to understand their monition?

Not all the Popes have so failed, though the majority have been intriguing, ambitious men of the world. But even the mob of Rome—and in Rome there *is* a true mob of unheeding cabbage-sellers, who never had a thought before beyond contriving how to satisfy their animal instincts for the day—said, on hearing the protest, "There was another Pius, not long since, who talked in a very different style. When the French threatened him, he said, 'You may do with me as you see fit, but I cannot consent to act against my convictions.'"

In fact, the only dignified course for the Pope to pursue was to resign his temporal power. He could no longer hold it on his own terms; but to that he clung; and the counselors around him were men to wish him to regard *that* as the first of duties. When the question was of waging war for the independence of Italy, they regarded him solely the head of the Church; but when the demand was to satisfy the wants of his people, and ecclesiastical goods were threatened with taxes, then he was the Prince of the State, bound to maintain all the selfish prerogative of by-gone days for the benefit of his successors. Poor Pope! how has his mind been torn to pieces in these later days. It moves compassion. There can be no doubt that all his natural impulses are generous and kind, and in a more private station he would have died beloved and honored; but to this he was unequal; he has suffered bad men to surround; and by their misrepresentations and insidious suggestions, at last entirely to cloud his mind. I believe he really thinks now the Progress movement tends to anarchy, blood, all that looked worst in the first French Revolution. However that may be I cannot forgive him some of the circumstances of this flight.[14] To fly to Naples to throw himself in the arms of the bombarding monarch, blessing him and thanking his soldiery for preserving that part of Italy from anarchy—to protest that all his promises at Rome were null and void, when he thought himself in safety to choose a commission for governing in his absence, composed of men of princely blood, but as to character so null that everybody laughed and said he chose those who could best be spared if they were killed; (but they all ran away directly;) when Rome was thus left without any Government, to refuse to see any deputation, even the Senator of Rome, whom he had so gladly sanctioned,—these are the acts either of a fool or a foe. They are not his acts, to be sure, but he is responsible, he lets them stand as such in the face of the world, and weeps and prays for their success.

No more of him! His day is over. He has been made, it seems unconsciously, an instrument of good his regrets cannot destroy. Nor can he be made so important an instrument of ill. These acts have not had the effect the foes of freedom hoped. Rome remained quite cool and composed; all felt that they had not demanded more than was their duty to demand, and were willing to accept what might follow. In a few days all began to say, "Well, who would have thought it? The Pope, the Cardinals, the Princes are gone, and Rome is perfectly tranquil, and one does not miss anything, except that there are not so many rich carriages and liveries."

The Pope may regret too late that he ever gave the people a chance to make this reflection. Yet the best fruits of the movement may not ripen for long. It is one which requires radical measures, clear-sighted, resolute men: these last, as yet, do not show themselves in Rome. The new Tuscan

---

[14] The pope fled, disguised as an ordinary priest, on 24 November 1848.

Ministry has three men of superior force in various ways: Montanelli, Guerrazzi, D'Aguila; such are not as yet to be found in Rome.[15]

But should she fall this time, (and she must either advance with decision and force, or fall—since to stand still is impossible,) the people have learned much; ignorance and servility of thought are lessened—the way is paving for final triumph.

And my country, what does she? You have chosen a new President from a Slave State, representative of the Mexican War. But he seems to be honest, a man that can be esteemed, and is one really known to the people; which is a step upward after having sunk last time to choosing a mere tool of party.[16]

Pray send here a good Ambassador—one that has experience of foreign life, that he may act with good judgement; and, if possible, a man that has knowledge and views which extend beyond the cause of party politics in the United States; a man of unity in principles, but capable of understanding variety in forms. And send a man capable to prize the luxury of living in, or knowing Rome: it is one that should not be thrown away on a person who cannot prize or use it. Another century, and I might ask to be made Ambassador myself ('tis true, like other Ambassadors, I would employ clerks to do the most of the duty,) but woman's day has not come yet. They hold their clubs in Paris, but even George Sand will not act with women as they are. They say she pleads they are too mean, too treacherous. She should not abandon them for that, which is not nature but misfortune. How much I shall have to say on that subject if I live, which I hope I shall not,[17] for I am very tired of the battle with giant wrongs, and would like to have some one younger and stronger arise to say what ought to be said, still more to do what ought to be done. Enough! if I felt these things in privileged America, the cries of mothers and wives beaten at night by sons and husbands for their diversion after drinking, as I have repeatedly heard them these past months, the excuse for falsehood, "I *dare not* tell my husband, he would be ready to kill me," have sharpened my perception as to the ills of

---

[15]Giuseppe Montanelli (1813–62) and Francesco Domenico Guerrazzi (1804–73) were actively working for a constituent assembly in Tuscany (Berkeley 3: 407). The third man Fuller refers to is probably their colleague Mariano d'Ayala (1807–77) (Zorzi 208).

[16]General Zachary Taylor, a Virginian, had just been elected president of the United States on the Whig ticket. The *Tribune* under Greeley's editorship was, of course, a Whig newspaper. The outgoing president, James K. Polk, a "dark horse" candidate at the 1844 Democratic convention, had gained the nomination due to then-President Martin Van Buren's opposition to the annexation of Texas. The militantly nationalistic Polk narrowly defeated the Whig candidate Henry Clay, who also opposed the annexation of Texas (*OCAL*).

[17]Arthur Fuller changed this phrase to "if I live which I desire not" in *AHA*.

Woman's condition and remedies that must be applied. Had I but genius, had I but energy, to tell what I know as it ought to be told! God grant them me, or some other more worthy woman, I pray.[18]

But the hour of sending to the post approaches, and I must leave these great matters for some practical details. I wish to observe to my friends and all others, whom it may concern, that a banking-house here having taken Mr. Hooker, an American, into partnership, some facilities are presented for intercourse with Rome, which they may value.[19] Mr. Hooker undertakes to have pictures copied, and to purchase those little objects of virtu peculiar to Rome, for those who cannot come themselves, as I suppose few would wish to at this time. He has the advantage of a general acquaintance with the artist to be employed, and an experience, that, no doubt, would enable him to do all this with better advantage than any stranger can for himself. It is also an excellent house to have to do with in money matters, reasonable, exact, and where none of the petty trickery or neglect so common at Torlonia's need be apprehended. They have now made arrangements with Livingston, Wells & Co. for the transmission of letters. Many addressed to me have been lost, I know not how; and I should like my friends to send to me when they can through this channel. Men who feel able can pay their letters through in this way, which has been impossible before. I have received many letters marked *paid through,* and I fear my friends in America have often paid what was quite useless, as no arrangements had been made for forwarding the letters post-paid to Rome. Those who write now can pay their letters to Florence, if they have friends there, through *Livingston, Wells & Co.* to care *Maquay, Pakenham & Co. Florence.* To us of Rome they can be sent through the same, to care of *Pakenham, Hooker & Co. Rome.*

Those of our friends, (I speak of the poor artists as well as myself,) who cannot afford to pay, should at least forbear to write on thick paper and under an envelop, the unnecessary use of which doubles the expense of the letter. I am surprised to find even those who have been abroad so negligent in these respects. I might have bought all the books of reference I needed, and have been obliged to do without money that could have been saved by attention from my friends to these particulars.

Write us two, three, four sheets if you will, on this paper, without crossing. Then if one pays a couple of dollars for a letter, at least one has

---

[18] The following three paragraphs are omitted from *AHA*.

[19] A constant source of irritation to Fuller was the difficulty of getting her mail regularly. She continually wrote sets of instructions to her correspondents about where and how to send letters. James Clinton Hooker (1818–94), of Vermont, was associated with the banking firm of Maquay, Packenham in Rome (Hudspeth 5: 76).

something for the money: and letters are too important to happiness; we cannot afford to be without knowledge of your thoughts, your lives; but it is hard, in people who can scarcely find bread, to pay for coarse paper and an envelop the price of a beautiful engraving, and know at the same time that they are doomed to leave Rome unable to carry away a single copy of what they have most loved here, for possession or for gift. So write, dear friends, much and often, but don't ruin us for nothing.

Don Tirlone, the *Punch* of Rome, has just come in. This number represents the Fortress of Gaeta; outside hangs a cage containing a parrot (Pappagallo), the plump body of the bird is surmounted by a noble large head with benign face and Papal head-dress. He sits on the perch now with folded wings, but the cage door, in likeness of a loggia, shows there is convenience to come forth for the purposes of benediction, when wanted. Outside, the King of Naples, dressed as Harlequin, plays the organ for instruction of the bird (unhappy penitent, doomed to penance,) and grinning with sharp teeth observes: "He speaks in my way now." In the background a young Republican holds ready the match for a barrel of gunpowder, but looks at his watch waiting the moment to ignite it.

A happy New-Year to my country! may she be worthy of the privileges she possesses, while others are lavishing their blood to win them—that is all that need be wished for her at present.

Dispatch 29
KINGS, REPUBLICANS, AND AMERICAN ARTISTS

ROME, *March 20, 1849* [1]

The Roman Republic moves on better than could have been expected. There are great difficulties about money, necessarily, as the Government, so beset with difficulties and dangers, cannot command confidence in that respect. The solid coin has crept out of the country or lies hid, and in the use of paper there are the corresponding difficulties. But the poor, always the chief sufferers from such a state of things, are wonderfully patient, and I doubt not that the new form, if Italy could be left to itself, would be settled for the advantage of all. Tuscany would soon be united with Rome, and to the Republic of Central Italy, no longer broken asunder by petty restrictions and sacrificed to the interests of a few persons, would come that prosperity natural to a region so favored by Nature.

---

[1] First published as "Things and Thoughts in Europe. No. XXIX" in *New-York Daily Tribune,* 16 May 1849, p. 1:1–5.

Could Italy be left alone! but treacherous, selfish men at home strive to betray, and foes threaten her from without on every side. Even France, her natural ally, promises to prove foolishly and basely faithless. The dereliction from principle of her Government seems certain, and thus far the nation, despite the remonstrance of a few worthy men, gives no sign of effective protest. There would be little hope for Italy, were not the thrones of her foes in a tottering state, their action liable at every moment to be distracted by domestic difficulties. The Austrian Government seems as destitute of support from the nation as is possible for a Government to be, and the army is no longer what it was, being made up so largely of new recruits. The Croats are uncertain in their adhesion, the war in Hungary likely to give them much to do, and if the Russian is called in, the rest of Europe becomes hostile. All these circumstances give Italy a chance she otherwise could not have; she is in great measure disfurnished of arms and money; her King in the South is a bloody, angry, well-armed foe; her King in the North, a proved traitor. Charles Albert has now declared war because he could not do otherwise; but his sympathies are in fact all against Liberty; the splendid lure that he might become King of Italy glitters no more; the Republicans are in the ascendant, and he may well doubt, should the stranger be driven out, whether Piedmont could escape the contagion. Now, his people insisting on war, he has the air of making it with a good grace, but should he be worsted, probably he will know some loop-hole by which to steal out. The rat will steal out and leave the lions in the trap.

The "illustrious Gioberti" has fallen—fallen forever from his high scaffold of words. His demerits were too unmistakable for rhetoric to hide. That he sympathized with the Pope rather than the Roman people, and could not endure to see him stripped of his temporal power, no one could blame in the author of the "*Primato.*" That he refused the Italian General Assembly, if it was to be based on the so-called Montanelli system [2] instead of his own, might be conviction or it might be littleness and vanity. But that he privily planned, without even adherence of the council of Ministers, an armed intervention of the Piedmontese troops in Tuscany, thus willing to cause civil war, and, at this great moment, to see Italian blood shed by Italian hands, was treachery. I think, indeed, he has been probably made the scape-goat in that affair; that Charles Albert planned the measure, and finding himself unable to carry it out, in consequence of the vigilance and indignant opposition of the Chamber of Deputies, was somewhat consoled

---

[2] Professor Montanelli, who had been imprisoned by the Austrians, had been allowed to return to Tuscany, where he devised a plan for a constituent assembly that would include all of Italy (Maurice 419). [Maurice, C. Edmund. *The Revolutionary Movement of 1848–49 in Italy, Austria-Hungary, and Germany.* New York: Putnam, 1887].

by making it an occasion to victimize the "Illustrious," whom four weeks before the people had forced him to accept as his Minister.

Now the name of Gioberti is erased from the corners of the streets to which it was affixed a year ago; he is stripped of all his honorary degrees, and proclaimed an unworthy son of the country. Mazzini is the idol of the people. "Soon to be hunted out," sneered the skeptical American. Possibly yes! for no man is secure of his palm till the fight is over. The civic wreath may be knocked from his head a hundred times in the ardor of the contest. No matter, if he can always keep the forehead pure and lofty, as will Mazzini.

In thinking of Mazzini, I always remember Petrarch's invocation to Rienzi.[3] Mazzini comes at a riper period in the world's history, with the same energy of soul, but of purer temper and more enlarged views to answer them.

I do not know whether I mentioned a kind of poetical correspondence about Mazzini and Rossi. Rossi was also an exile for liberal principles, but he did not value his birthright; he alienated it, and as a French citizen became Peer of France and Representative of Louis Philippe in Italy. When, with the fatuity of those whom the gods have doomed to perish, Pius IX. took the representative of the fallen Guizot policy for his Minister, he made him a Roman citizen. He was proclaimed such the 14th of November. On the 15th he perished before he could enter the parliament he had called. He fell at the door of the Cancelleria when it was sitting.

Mazzini, in his exile, remained absolutely devoted to his native country. Because, though feeling as few can, that the interests of humanity in all nations are identical, he felt also that, born of a race so suffering, so much needing devotion and energy, his first duty was to that. The only powers he acknowledged were *God and the People,* the special scope of his acts the unity and independence of Italy. Rome was the theme of his thoughts, but, very early exiled, he had never seen that home to which all the orphans of the soul so naturally turn. Now he entered it as a Roman citizen, elected representative of the people by universal suffrage. His motto, *Dio e Popolo,*

---

[3] Fuller refers to Petrarch's letter to Francesco Calvo da Napoli, apostolic prothonotary for Clement VI and Innocent VI from 1347 to 1359. In this letter, Petrarch warmly defends Cola di Rienzo, who was brought to Avignon for judgment by the Papal Court. In defending Rienzo, Petrarch celebrates the autonomy of the Roman people and, in a passage that must have reminded Fuller of Mazzini, exclaims, "A crime worthy of the cross and vultures, that a Roman citizen should grieve to see his land, the rightful mistress of all others, enslaved to the basest of men!" (*Letters on Familiar Matters,* vol. 2, book 13, letter 6, trans. Aldo S. Bernardo [Baltimore: Johns Hopkins University Press, 1982], 196; Kenelon Foster, *Petrarch: Poet and Humanist* [Edinburgh: Edinburgh University Press, 1984], 14; Morris Bishop, trans., *Letters from Petrarch* [Bloomington: Indiana University Press, 1966], 116).

is put upon the coin with the Roman eagle; unhappily this first-issued coin is of brass, or else of silver, with much alloy. *Dei, avertite omen,*[4] and may peaceful days turn it all to pure gold!

On his first entrance to the house Mazzini, received with fervent applause and summoned to take his place beside the President, spoke as follows:

> "It is from me, colleagues, that should come these tokens of applause, these tokens of affection, because the little good I have not done, but tried to do, has come to me from Rome. Rome was always a sort of talisman for me; a youth, I studied the history of Italy, and found while all the other nations were born, grew up, played their part in the world, then fell to reappear no more in the same power, a single city was privileged by God to die only to rise again greater than before, to fulfill a mission greater than the first. I saw the Rome of the Empire extend her conquests from the confines of Africa to the confines of Asia. I saw Rome perish, crushed by the barbarians, by those whom even yet the world calls barbarians. I saw her rise again after having chased away these same barbarians, reviving in its sepulchre the germ of Civilization. I saw her rise more great for conquest, not with arms, but with words — rise in the name of the Popes to repeat her grand mission. I said in my heart, the city which, alone in the world, has had two grand lives, one greater than the other, will have a third. After the Rome which wrought by conquest of arms, the Rome which wrought by conquest of words, must come a third which shall work by virtue of example. After the Rome of the Emperors — after the Rome of the Popes, will come the Rome of the People. The Rome of the People is arisen; do not salute with applauses, but let us rejoice together! I cannot promise anything for myself, except concurrence in all you shall do for the good of Rome, of Italy, of Mankind. Perhaps we shall have to pass through great crises; perhaps we shall have to fight a sacred battle against the only enemy that threatens us, Austria. We will fight it, and we will conquer. I hope, please God, that foreigners may not be able to say any more that which so many of them repeat to-day, speaking of our affairs, that the light which comes from Rome is only an *ignis fatuus* wandering among the tombs; the world shall see that it is a starry light, eternal, pure and resplendent as those we look up to in the Heavens!"

On a later day he spoke more fully of the difficulties that threaten at home the young Republic, and said:

> "Let us not hear of right, of left, of center; these terms express the three powers in a constitutional monarchy; for us they have no meaning; the only divisions for us are of Republicans or non-Republicans — or of

---

[4]The Italian motto is: "God and the People." The Latin is: "Oh gods, turn aside the omen."

sincere men and temporizing men. Let us not hear so much of the Republicans of to-day and of yesterday; I am a Republican of twenty years' standing. Entertaining such hopes for Italy, when many excellent, many sincere men held them as Utopian, shall I denounce these men because they are now convinced of their practicability?"

This last I quote from memory. In hearing the gentle tone of remonstrance with those of more petty mind, or influenced by the passions of the partisan, I was forcibly reminded of the parable by Jesus of the Vineyard and the discontent of the laborers that those who came at the eleventh hour "received also a penny."[5] Mazzini also is content that all should fare alike as brethren, if only they will come into the vineyard. He is not an orator, but the simple conversational tone of his address is in refreshing contrast with the boyish rhetoric and academic swell common to Italian speakers in the present unfledged state. As they have freer use of the power of debate they will become more simple and manly. The speech of Mazzini is laden with mind—it goes straight to the mark by the shortest path and moves without effort from the irresistible impression of deep conviction and fidelity in the speaker. Mazzini is a man of genius, an elevated thinker, but the most powerful and first impression from his presence must always be of the religion of his soul, of his *virtue*, both in the modern and antique sense of that word.[6]

If clearness of right, if energy, if indefatigable perseverance, can steer the ship through this dangerous pass, it will be done. He said "we will conquer;" whether Rome will this time is not to me certain, but such men as Mazzini conquer always—conquer in defeat. Yet Heaven grant that no more blood, no more corruption of priestly government, be for Italy. It could only be for once more, for the strength of her present impulse would not fail to triumph at last; but even one more trial seems too intolerably much when I think of the holocaust of broken hearts, baffled lives, that must attend it.

But enough of politics for the present; this letter goes by private hand, and as news, will be superseded before it can arrive.

Let me rather take the opportunity to say some things that I have let lie by, while writing of political events. Especially of our Artists I wish to say something. I know many of them, if not all, and see with pleasure our young country so fairly represented.

---

[5]Matthew 20:1–16

[6]Fuller had written to Mazzini on March 3 to offer a "tribute of affection" (Hudspeth 5: 196–97). In a long letter to Caroline Sturgis Tappan, Fuller combined additional information about her son, Nino, with some details about her great affection for Mazzini (Hudspeth 5: 207–11).

Among the painters I saw of Brown only two or three pictures at the exhibition in Florence; they were coarse, flashy things.[7] I was told he could do better, but a man who indulges himself with such coarse sale-work, cannot surely do well at any time.

The merits of Terry and Freeman are not my merits; they are beside both favorites in our country, and have a sufficient number of pictures there for every one to judge.[8] I am no connoisseur as regards the technical merits of paintings; it is only poetic invention, or a tender feeling of nature which captivates me.

Terry loves grace, and consciously works from the model. The result is a pleasing transposition of the hues of this clime. But the design of the picture is never original, nor is it laden with any message from the heart. Of Freeman I know less; as the two or three pictures of his that I have seen never interested me. I have not visited his studio.

Of Hicks I think very highly.[9] He is a man of ideas, an original observer, and with a poetic heart. His system of coloring is derived from a thoughtful study, not a mere imitation of nature, and shows the fineness of his organization. Struggling unaided to pursue the expensive studies of his art, he has had only a small studio, and received only orders for little cabinet pictures.—Could he carry out adequately his ideas, in him would be found the treasure of genius. He has made the drawings for a large picture of many figures; the design is original and noble, the grouping highly effective. Could he paint this picture I believe it would be a real boon to the lovers of Art, the lovers of Truth. I hope very much that when he returns to the United States, some competent patron of art—one of the few who has mind as well as purse, will see the drawings and order the picture. Otherwise he cannot paint it, as the expenses attendant on models for so many

---

[7] Henry Kirke Brown (1814–86), a sculptor and portrait painter, lived in Europe from 1844 to 1848 (Groce). [Groce, George C., and David H. Wallace. *The New-York Historical Society's Dictionary of Artists in America, 1564–1860.* New Haven: Yale UP, 1957.]

[8] James Edward Freeman (1808–84) was a genre and portrait painter who settled in Italy in the late 1830s. From 1840 to 1849 he was the American consul at Ancona, though he resided in Rome and performed his duties by proxy (Groce).

[9] Fuller had been very friendly with Hicks during his stay in Rome. She wrote to Samuel G. Ward to encourage him to visit Hicks in New York, where Hicks had returned in the fall of 1849: "When you are in N.Y. do me the pleasure of visiting the studio of Hicks and seeing him, if you can. I have loved him very much; we have been very intimate; I should like to have you see him; perhaps an acquaintance will spring up; in his soul is real greatness; his life has been a battle but waged on his side with great calmness" (Hudspeth 5: 279). After returning to the United States, Hicks became a prosperous portraitist (Chevigny 424).

figures, &c. are great, and the time demanded could not otherwise be taken from the claims of the day.

Among landscape painters Cropsey and Cranch have the true artist spirit. In faculties, each has what the other wants. Cropsey is a reverent and careful student of nature in detail; it is no pedantry, but a true love he has, and his pictures are full of little gentle signs of intimacy. They please and touch, but yet, in poetic feeling of the heart of nature, he is not equal to Cranch, who produces fine effects by means more superficial, and, on examination, less satisfactory. Each might take somewhat from the other to advantage, could he do it without diminishing his own original dower. Both are artists of high promise, and deserve to be loved and cherished by a country which may, without presumption, hope to carry landscape painting to a pitch of excellence unreached before. For the historical painter, the position with us is, for many reasons, not favorable, but there is no bar in the way of the landscape painter, and fate, bestowing such a prodigality of subject, seems to give us a hint not to be mistaken. I think the love of landscape painting is genuine in our nation, and as it is a branch of art where achievement has been comparatively low, we may not unreasonably suppose it has been left for us. I trust it will be undertaken in the highest spirit. —Nature, it seems to me, reveals herself more freely in our land; she is true, virgin and confiding—she smiles upon the vision of a true Endymion. I hope to see not only copies upon canvas of our magnificent scenes, but a transfusion of the spirit which is their divinity.

Then why should the American landscape-painter come to Italy?—cry many. I think, myself, he ought not to stay here very long. Yet a few years' study is precious, for here Nature herself has worked with Man, as if she wanted to help him in the composition of pictures. The ruins of Italy, in their varied relations with vegetation and the heavens, make speeches from every stone for the instruction of the artist; the greatest variety here is found with the greatest harmony; to know how this union may be accomplished is a main secret of art, and though the coloring is not the same, yet he who has the key to its mysteries of beauty is the more initiated to the same in other climates, and will easily attune afresh his more instructed eye and mind to the contemplation of that which molded his childhood.

I may observe of the two artists I have named, that Cranch has entered more into the spirit of Italian landscape, while Cropsey is still more distinguished on subjects such as he first loved. He seemed to find the Scotch lake and mountain scenery very congenial; his sketches and pictures taken from a short residence there are impressive. Perhaps a melancholy or tender subject suits him best; something rich, bold and mellow is more adapted to call out the genius of Cranch.

Among the Sculptors new names rise up to show that this is decidedly a province for hope in America. I look upon this as the natural talent of an American, and have no doubt that glories will be displayed by our sculptors unknown to classic art. The facts of our history, ideal and social, will be grand and of new import; it is perfectly natural to the American to mold in clay and carve in stone. The permanence of material and solid relief in the forms correspond to the positiveness of his nature better than the mere ephemeral and even tricky methods of the painter—to his need of motion and action, better than the chambered scribbling of the poet. He will thus record his best experiences, and these records will adorn the noble structures that must naturally arise for the public uses of our society.

It is particularly gratifying to see men that might amass far more money and attain more temporary power in other parts, despise those lower lures too powerful in our country, and aim only at excellence in the expression of thought. Among these I may mention Story and Mozier.[10] Story has made in Florence the model for a statue of his father. This I have not seen, but two statuettes that he modeled here from the "Fisher" of Goethe pleased me extremely. The languid, meditative revery of the boy, the morbid tenderness of his nature, is most happily expressed in the first, as is the fascinated surrender to the syren murmur of the flood in the second. He has taken the moment

"Half drew she him; half sank he in,"[11] &c.

I hope some one will give him an order to make them in marble. Mozier seemed to have an immediate success. The fidelity and spirit of his portrait-busts could be appreciated by every one; for an ideal head of Pocahontas

---

[10] Joseph Mozier (1812–70) was a successful merchant in New York, who abandoned his business career in 1845 and went to Italy to become a sculptor (Groce). He was exceptionally kind to Fuller during her sickness in Florence in the summer of 1847 but gossiped maliciously about her and Ossoli to Nathaniel Hawthorne some eleven years later, provoking an infamous entry in Hawthorne's Italian notebooks. According to Hawthorne, Mozier said that Ossoli was a handsome man but "destitute of manners" and "half an idiot." He also said that Fuller, before her return to America, "had quite lost all power of literary production" and that her manuscript "History of the Roman Revolution . . . never had existence." This information led Hawthorne to declare, "There appears to have been a total collapse in poor Margaret, morally and intellectually" and to comment on "her strange, heavy, unpliable, and, in many respects, defective and evil nature" (Chevigny 416–19; Nathaniel Hawthorne, *The French and Italian Notebooks,* ed. Thomas Woodson [Columbus: Ohio State University Press, 1980], 155–56).

[11] Another translation of this part of Goethe's "The Fisherman" reads: "She spoke to him, she sang to him; / The fellow, done for then, / Half yielded too as half she drew, / Was never seen again" (Goethe, *Selected Poems,* ed. Christopher Middleton [Boston: Suhrkamp / Insel, 1983], 75).

too, he had at once orders for many copies. It was not an Indian head, but in the union of sweetness and strength with a princelike, childlike dignity, very happily expressive of his idea of her character. I think he has modeled a Rebecca at the Well, but this I did not see.

These have already a firm hold on the affections of our people; every American who comes to Italy visits their studios, and speaks of them with pride, as indeed they well may, in comparing them with artists of other nations. It will not be long before you see Greenough's group; it is in spirit a pendent to Cooper's novels. I confess I wish he had availed himself of the opportunity to immortalize the real noble Indian in marble. This is only the man of the woods—no Metamora, no Uncas.[12] But the group should be very instructive to our people.

You seem as crazy about Powers's Greek Slave as the Florentines were about Cimabue's Madonnas, in which we still see the spark of genius, but not fanned to its full flame.[13] If your enthusiasm be as genuine as that of the lively Florentines, we will not quarrel with it; but I am afraid a great part is drawing-room raptures and newspaper echoes. Genuine enthusiasm, however crude the state of mind from which it springs, always elevates, always educates, but in the same proportion talking and writing for effect stultifies and debases. I shall not judge the adorers of the Greek Slave, but only observe that they have not kept in reserve any higher admiration for works even now extant, which are, in comparison with that statue, what that statue is compared with any weeping marble on a common monument.

I consider the Slave as a form of simple and sweet beauty, but that neither as an ideal expression or a specimen of plastic power is it transcendent. Powers stands far higher in his busts than in any ideal statue. His conception of what is individual in character is clear and just; his power of execution almost unrivaled; but he has had a lifetime of discipline for the bust, while his studies on the human body are comparatively limited; nor is his treatment of it free and masterly. To me, his conception of subject is not striking: I do not consider him rich in artistic thought.

He, no less than Greenough and Crawford, would feel it a rich reward for many labors, and a happy climax to their honors to make an equestrian

---

[12] Fuller refers to heroic portrayals of Native Americans. Metamora was another name for King Philip (?–1676), chief of the Wampanoag tribe of the Plymouth colony from 1662. The actor Edwin Forrest starred in the popular romantic tragedy about him by J. A. Stone, revised by R. M. Bird, entitled *Metamora* (1836) (*OCAL*). Uncas (1600–1683) was chief of the Mohigan tribe and appears as a heroic figure in Cooper's Leatherstocking tales.

[13] Powers's *The Greek Slave* was exhibited at the Great Exhibition in 1851 and became one of the most talked about statues in the nineteenth century (*OCA*). [Osborne, Harold, ed. *The Oxford Companion to Art*. Oxford: Oxford UP, 1970.]

statue of Washington for our country. I wish they might all do it, as each would show a different kind of excellence. To present the man on horseback, the wise centaur, the tamer of horses, may well be deemed a highest achievement of modern as it was of ancient art. The study of the anatomy and action of the horse, so rich in suggestions, is naturally most desirable to the artist; happy he who, obliged by the brevity of life and the limitations of fortune, to make his studies conform to his "orders," finds himself justified by a national behest in entering on this department.

At home one gets callous about the character of Washington, from a long experience of 4th of July bombast in his praise. But seeing the struggles of other nations, and the deficiencies of the leaders who try to sustain them, the heart is again stimulated and puts forth buds of praise. One appreciates the wonderful combination of events and influences that gave our independence so healthy a birth, and the almost miraculous merits of the men who tended its first motions. In the combination of excellences needed at such a period with the purity and modesty which dignify the private man in the humblest station, Washington as yet stands alone. No country has ever had such a good future; no other is so happy as to have a pattern of spotless worth which will remain in her latest day venerable as now.

Surely then that form should be immortalized in material solid as its fame; and, happily for the artist, that form was of natural beauty and dignity, and he who places him on horseback simply represents his habitual existence. Everything concurs to make an equestrian statue of Washington desirable.

The dignified way to manage that affair would be to have a Committee chosen of impartial judges, men who would look only to the merits of the work and the interests of the country, unbiased by any personal interest in favor of some one artist. It is said it is impossible to find such a one, but I cannot believe it. Let there be put aside the mean squabbles and jealousies, the vulgar pushing of unworthy friends, with which, unhappily, the artist's career seems more rife than any other, and a fair concurrence established; let each artist offer his design for an equestrian statue of Washington, and let the best have the preference.

Mr. Crawford has made a design which he takes with him to America, and which, I hope, will be generally seen. He has represented Washington in his actual dress; a figure of Fame, winged, presents the laurel and civic wreath; his gesture declines them; he seems to say, "For me the deed is enough — I need no badge, no outward token in reward."

This group has no insipid allegorical air, as might be supposed; and its composition is very graceful, simple, and harmonious. The costume is very happily managed. The angel figure is draped, and with the Liberty cap, which as a badge both of ancient and modern times, seems to connect the two figures, and in an artistic point of view balances well the cocked hat; there is a similar harmony between the angel's wings and the extremities of the horse. The action of the winged figure induces a natural and spirited action of the horse and rider. I thought of Goethe's remark, that a fine work of art will always have, at a distance, where its details cannot be discerned, a beautiful effect, as of architectural ornament, and that this excellence the groups of Rapheal share with the antique. He would have been pleased with the beautiful balance of forms in this group, with the freedom with which light and air play in and out, the management of the whole being clear and satisfactory at the first glance. But one should go into a great number of studies, as you can in Rome or Florence, and see the abundance of heavy and inharmonious designs to appreciate the merits of this; anything really good seems so simple and so a matter of course to the unpracticed observer.

Some say the Americans will not want a group, but just the fact; the portrait of Washington riding straight onward like Marcus Aurelius, or making an address, or lifting his sword. I do not know about that—it is a matter of feeling. This winged figure not only gives a poetic sense to the group, but a natural support and occasion for action to the horse and rider. Uncle Sam must send Major Downing[14] to look at it, and then, if he wants other designs, let him establish a concurrence, as I have said, and choose what is best. I am not particularly attached to Mr. Greenough, Mr. Powers or Mr. Crawford. I admire various excellencies in the works of each, and should be glad if each received an order for an equestrian statue. Nor is there any reason why they should not. There is money enough in the country, and the more good things there are for the people to see freely in open daylight the better. That makes artists germinate.

I love the artists, though I cannot speak of their works in a way to content their friends or even themselves, often. Who can, that has a standard of excellence in the mind and a delicate conscience in the use of words? My highest tribute is meager of superlatives in comparison with the hackneyed puffs with which artists submit to be besmeared. Submit, alas! often they court them, rather. I do not expect any kindness from my contemporaries. I know that what is to me justice and honor is to them only a hateful coldness. Still I love them, I wish for their good, I feel deeply for their sufferings, annoyances, privations, and would lessen them if I could. I have thought it might perhaps be of use to publish some account of the expenses of the art-

---

[14]Major Jack Downing is the pseudonym of Seba Smith (1792–1868). Fuller alludes to Major Downing's penchant for commenting on current events with a shrewdness that belies his rustic simplicity. *The Life and Writings of Major Jack Downing* appeared in 1834 (*OCAL*).

ist. There is a general impression that the artist lives very cheaply in Italy. This is a mistake. Italy, compared with America, is not so very cheap, except for those who have iron constitutions to endure bad food, eaten in bad air, damp and dirty lodgings. The expenses, even in Florence, of a simple but clean and wholesome life, are little less than in New-York. The great difference is for people that are rich. An Englishman of rank and fortune does not need the same amount of luxury as at home to be on a footing with the nobles of Italy. The Broadway merchant would find his display of mahogany and carpets thrown away in a country where a higher kind of ornament is the only one available. But poor people who can, at any rate, buy only the necessaries of life, will find them in the Italian cities, where all sellers live by cheating foreigners, very little cheaper than in America.

The patron of Art in America, ignorant of these facts, and not knowing the great expenses which attend the study of Art and the production of its wonders, are often guilty of most undesigned cruelty, and do things which it would grieve their hearts to have done, if they only knew the facts. They have read essays on the uses of adversity in developing genius, and they are not sufficiently afraid to administer a dose of adversity beyond what the forces of the patient can bear. Laudanum in drops is useful as a medicine, but a cup-full kills downright.

Beside this romantic idea about letting artists suffer to develop their genius, the American Maecenas is not sufficiently aware of the expenses attendant on producing the work he wants. He does not consider that the painter, the sculptor, must be paid for the time he spends in designing and molding, no less than in painting and carving; that he must have his bread and sleeping-house, his workhouse or studio, his marbles and colors; the sculptor his workmen; so that if the price be paid he asks, a modest and delicate man very commonly receives *no* guerdon for his thought—the real essence of the work—except the luxury of seeing it embodied which he could not otherwise have afforded. The American Maecenas often pushes the price down, not from want of generosity, but from a habit of making what are called good bargains—*i.e.* bargains for one's own advantage at the expense of a poorer brother. Those who call these good do not believe that

"Mankind is one,
And beats with one great heart."

They have not read the life of Jesus Christ.

Then the American Maecenas sometimes, after ordering a work, has been known to change his mind when the statue is already modeled. It is the American who does these things, because an American, who either from taste or vanity buys a picture, is often quite uneducated as to the arts and cannot understand why a little picture or figure costs so much money. The

Englishman or Frenchman, of a suitable position to seek these adornments for his house, usually understands better than the visitor of Powers who, on hearing the price of the Proserpine, wonderingly asked, "Isn't statuary riz lately?" Queen Victoria of England, and her Albert, it is said, use their royal privilege to get works of art at a price below their value, but their subjects would be ashamed to do so.

To supply means of judging to the American merchant, (full of kindness and honorable sympathy as beneath the crust he so often is) who wants pictures and statues not merely from ostentation, but as means of delight and improvement to himself and his friends, who has a soul to respect the genius and desire the happiness of the artist, and who, if he errs, does so from ignorance of the circumstances, I give the following memorandum, made at my desire by an artist, my neighbor:

> The rent of a suitable studio for modeling in clay and executing statues in marble may be estimated at $200 a year.
> The best journeyman carver in marble at Rome receives $60 a month. Models are paid $1 a day. The cost of marble varies according to the size of the block, being generally sold by the cubic palm, a square of 9 inches English. As a general guide regarding the prices established among the higher sculptors of Rome I may mention that for a statue of life-size the demand is from $1,000 to $5,000, varying according to the composition of the figure and the number of accessories.
> It is a common belief in the United States that a student of art can live in Italy and pursue his studies on an income of $300 or $400 a year. This is a lamentable error; the Russian Government allows its pensioners $700, which is scarcely sufficient. $1000 per annum should be placed at the disposal of every young artist leaving our country for Europe.

Let it be remembered, in addition to considerations inevitable from this memorandum, that you may, in your work of art, for years and months of uncheered and difficult waiting on the part of the artist, after he has gone through the earlier stages of an education, too largely based and of aim too high to finish in this world.

The Prussian artist here on my left hand, learned not only his art, but reading and writing, after he was thirty. A farmer's son, he was allowed no freedom to learn anything till the death of the head of the house left him a beggar, but set him free; on foot he walked hundreds of miles to Berlin, attracted by his first works some attention, and received some assistance in money, earned more by invention of a plowshare, walked to Rome, struggled through every privation, and has now a reputation which has secured him the means of putting his thoughts into marble. True, at 49 years of age he is still severely poor; he cannot marry because he cannot maintain a family; but he is cheerful, because he can work in his own way, trusts with childlike reliance in God, and is still sustained by the vigorous health he won laboring in his father's fields. Not every man could continue to work, circumstanced as he is, at the end of the half century. For him the only sad thing in my mind is that his works are not worth working, though of merit in composition and execution, yet ideally a product of the galvanized piety of the German school, more mutton-like than lamb-like to my unchurched eyes.

You are likely to have a work by the great master of that school, Overbeck, to look at in the United States, Mr. Perkins of Boston, who knows how to spend his money with equal generosity and discretion, having bought his *Wise and Foolish Virgins*. It will be precious to the country from great artistic merits. As to the spirit, "blessed are the poor in spirit." That kind of severity is, perhaps has become, the nature of Overbeck. He seems like a monk, but a really pious and pure one.—This spirit is not what I seek; I deem it too narrow for our day, but being deeply sincere in him, its expression is at times also deeply touching.—Barrabbas borne in triumph, and the child Jesus who, playing with his father's tools, has made himself a cross, are subjects best adapted for expression of this spirit. I have written too carelessly—much writing hath made me mad of late. Forgive if the "style be not neat, terse, and sparkling," if there be nought of the "thrilling," if the sentences seem not "written with a diamond pen," like all else that is published in America. Sometime I must try to do better. For this time

"Forgive my faults; forgive my virtues too."

21st.—Day before yesterday was the feast of St. Joseph.[15] He is supposed to have acquired a fondness for fried rice-cakes, during his residence in Egypt. Many are eaten in the open street, in arbors made for the occasion. One was made beneath my window, on Piazza Barberini. All day and the evening men cleanly dressed in white aprons and liberty caps, quite new, of fine, red cloth, were frying them for crowds of laughing, gesticulating customers. It rained a little, and they held an umbrella over the frying-pan, but not over themselves. The arbor is still there, and little children are playing in and out of it; one still lesser runs in its leading strings, followed by the bold, gay nurse, to the brink of the fountain after its orange which has rolled before it. Tenerani's workmen are coming out of his studio, the priests are coming home from Ponta Pio, the contadini beginning to play at *mora*, for the setting sun has just lit up the magnificent range of windows

---

[15] The Feast of St. Joseph, celebrated on 19 March, was introduced in Rome by Pope Sixtus IV in 1479 (*NCE*). [*The New Catholic Encyclopedia*. 18 vols. Washington, D.C.: Catholic University of America, 1967.]

in Palazzo Barberini, and then faded tenderly, sadly away, and the mellow bells have chimed the Ave Maria.[16]

Rome looks as Roman, that is to say, as tranquil as ever, despite the trouble that tugs at her heart-strings. There is a report that Mazzini is to be made Dictator, as Manin is in Venice, for a short time, so as to provide hastily and energetically for the war. Ave Maria Santissima! when thou didst gaze on thy babe with such infinite hope, thou didst not dream that so many ages after blood would be shed and curses uttered in his name. Madonna Addolorata! hadst thou not hoped peace and good will would spring from his bloody woes, couldst thou have borne these hours at the foot of the cross. O Stella! woman's heart of love, send yet a ray of pure light on this troubled deep!

Dispatch 30
ARRIVAL OF THE FRENCH

ROME, *6th May, 1849*[1]

I write you from barricaded Rome. The Mother of Nations is now at bay against them all.[2]

---

[16]The *contadini* were peasants, working men, or farm workers. *Morra* (or *mora*) is an old game, popular with the contadini. Fuller was not the only American visitor to Italy in the nineteenth century to be struck by its pervasiveness. According to Story, the game was so absorbing that beggars would play away their earnings; the usual stakes were, however, a bottle of wine. [William Wetmore Story] describes it thus: "Two persons place themselves opposite each other, holding their right hands closed before them. They then simultaneously and with a sudden gesture throw out their hands, some of the fingers being extended, and others shut up on the palm,—each calling out in a loud voice, at the same moment, the number he guesses the fingers extended by himself and his adversary to make. If neither cry out aright, or if both cry out aright, nothing is gained or lost; but if only one guess the true number, he wins a point. Thus, if one throw out four fingers and the other two, he who cries out six makes a point, unless the other cry out the same number. The points are generally five, though sometimes they are doubled; and as they are made, they are marked by the left hand, which during the whole game is held stiffly in the air at about the shoulders' height, one finger being extended for every point. When the *partito* is won, the winner cries out '*Fatto!*' or '*Guadagnato!*' or '*Vinto!*' or else strikes his hands across each other in sign of triumph. This last sign is also used when Double *Morra* is played, to indicate that five points are made" (1: 119–24). [Story, William Wetmore. *Roba di Roma*. 8th ed. Vol. 1. Boston: Houghton, 1887.]

[1]First published as "Undaunted Rome" in *New-York Daily Tribune*, 5 June 1849, p. 2:3. Arthur Fuller did not include this letter in *AHA*.

[2]Fuller had just returned to Rome after spending the end of March and most of April in Rieti with her son (see her letters to Ossoli in Hudspeth 5: 218–26).

Rome was suffering before. The misfortunes of other regions of Italy, the defeat at *Novara*, preconcerted in hope to strike the last blow at Italian independence, the surrender and painful condition of Genoa, the money difficulties—insuperable, unless the Government could secure confidence abroad as well as at home—prevented her people from finding that foothold for which they were ready.[3] The vacillations of France agitated them, still they could not seriously believe she would ever act the part she has.[4] We must say France, because, though many honorable men have washed their hands of all share in the perfidy, the Assembly voted funds to sustain the expedition to Città Vecchia, and the Nation, the Army have remained quiescent.

No one was, no one could be, deceived as to the scope of this expedition. It was intended to restore the Pope to the temporal sovereignty, from which the People, by the use of suffrage, had deposed him. No doubt the French, in case of success, proposed to temper the triumph of Austria and Naples, and stipulate for conditions that might soothe the Romans and make their act less odious. Also they were probably deceived by the representations of Gaeta, and believed that a large party, which had been intimidated by the republicans, would declare in favor of the Pope when they found themselves likely to be sustained. But this last pretext may in no way avail them. They landed at Città Vecchia, and no one declared for the Pope. They marched on Rome. Placards were affixed within the walls by hands unknown, calling upon the Papal party to rise within the town. Not a soul stirred. The French had no excuse left for pretending to believe that the present Government was not entirely acceptable to the people. Notwithstanding, they assail the gates, they fire upon St. Peter's, and their balls pierced the Vatican. They were repulsed as they deserved, retired in quick and shameful defeat, as surely the brave French soldiery could not, if they had not been demoralized by a sense of what an infamous course they were pursuing. France, eager to destroy the last hope of Italian emancipation, France the alguazil[5] of Austria, the soldiers of republican France, firing upon

---

[3] On 23 March Radetzky and the Austrian army defeated Charles Albert at Novara; Charles Albert was forced to abdicate (Fejtö xii).

[4] On 31 March the French Chamber of Deputies authorized an invasion of Italy. The French general Nicolas Charles Victor Oudinot arrived at Città Vecchia on 24 April, pretending to be on a mission to save Italy from the Austrians. On 30 April the French attacked the Roman defenses outside the city and were defeated by Garibaldi. A truce was declared. In the meantime, Ferdinand II had crossed the border with 9000 troops, and Garibaldi moved to attack the Neapolitans, who were forced back across their own borders and were defeated on 19 May (Fejtö xii; Hudspeth 5: 227, 230).

[5] Police officer.

republican Rome! If there be angel as well as demon powers that interfere in the affairs of men, those bullets could scarcely fail to be turned back against their own breasts. Yet Roman blood has flowed also; I saw how it stained the walls of the Vatican Gardens on the 30th April[6]—the first anniversary of the appearance of Pius IX's too famous encyclic letter. Shall he, shall any Pope ever again walk peacefully in these gardens. Impossible! The temporal sovereignty of the Popes was gone, by their shameless, merciless measures taken to restore it. The spiritual dominion falls too into irrevocable ruin.

What may be the issue, at this moment we cannot guess. The French have retired to Città Vecchia, but whether to re-embark or to await re-inforcements we know not. The Neapolitan force has halted within a few miles of the walls; it is not large, and they are undoubtedly surprised at the discomfiture of the French. Perhaps they wait for the Austrians, but we do not yet hear that these have entered Romana.[7] Meanwhile Rome is strongly barricaded, and, though she cannot stand always against a world in arms, she means at least to try. Mazzini is at her head; she has now a guide "who understands his faith," and all there is of noble spirit will show itself. We all feel very sad, because the idea of bombs barbarously thrown in, and street-fight in Rome is peculiarly dreadful. Apart from all the blood and anguish inevitable at such times, the glories of Art may perish, and mankind be forever despoiled of the most beautiful inheritance. Yet I would defend Rome to the last moment. She must not be false to the higher hope that has dawned upon her. She must not fall back again into servility and corruption. And no one is willing. The interference of the French has roused the weakest to resistance. "From the Austrians, from the Neapolitans," they cried, "we expected this; but from the French, it is too infamous, it cannot be borne," and they all ran to arms and fought nobly.

The Americans here are not in a pleasant situation. Mr. Cass, the Chargé of the United States, stays here without recognizing the Government.[8] Of course, he holds no position at the present moment that can enable him to

---

[6] Fuller wrote an essay about this, which appeared as "Recollections of the Vatican," *United States Magazine and Democratic Review*, 27 (July 1850): 64–71.

[7] The province of Romagna, also known as the Legations, historically had opposed the rule of the popes and was shortly to be occupied by the Austrians (Derek Beales, *The Risorgimento and the Unification of Italy* [New York: Barnes and Noble, 1971], 23, 45, 59, 65).

[8] Lewis Cass, Jr. (1813?–78), was the American chargé d'affaires to the Papal States. He had become a close friend of Fuller's at this time (Hudspeth 5: 13, 228). Cass was sent to Rome in January 1849 with instructions from the secretary of state not to deliver his credentials either to the minister of foreign affairs of Pope Pius IX, or to the revolutionary government, until he should receive further instructions from the State Department (Marraro 26). [Marraro, Howard R. *American Opinion on the Unification of Italy*. New York: Columbia UP, 1932.]

act for us. Beside, it gives us pain that our country, whose policy it justly is to avoid physical interference with the affairs of Europe, should not use a moral influence. Rome has, as we did, thrown off a Government no longer tolerable; she has made use of the suffrage to form another; she stands on the same basis as ourselves. Mr. Rush did us great honor by his ready recognition of a principle as represented by the French Provisional Government;[9] had Mr. Cass been empowered to do the same, our country would have acted nobly, and all that is most truly American in America would have spoken to sustain the sickened hopes of European democracy. But of this more when I write next. Who knows what I may have to tell another week?

Dispatch 31
BETWEEN THE HEAVES OF STORM

ROME, *May 27, 1849*[1]

I have suspended writing in the expectation of some decisive event, but none such comes yet. The French, entangled in a web of falsehood, abashed by a defeat that Oudinot has vainly tried to gloss over, the expedition disowned by all honorable men at home, disappointed by Gaeta, because it dares not go the length the Papal infatuation demands, knows not what to do. The Neapolitans have been decidedly driven back, the last time in a most shameful rout; the King flying in front into their own borders. We have heard for several days that the Austrians were advancing, but they come not. They also, it is probable, meet with unexpected embarrassments. They find that the sincere movement of the Italian people is very unlike that of troops commanded by princes and generals who never wished to conquer and were always waiting to betray. Then their troubles at home are constantly increasing, and, should the Russian intervention quell them to-day, it is only to raise a storm far more terrible to-morrow.[2]

---

[9] Richard Rush (1780–1859), a lawyer, diplomat, and statesman, was appointed ambassador to France on 3 March 1847 by President Polk. Rush witnessed the February revolution and, without waiting for instructions from Washington, formally recognized the new republic (*DAB*).

[1] First published as "Things and Thoughts in Europe. No. XXX" in *New-York Daily Tribune*, 23 June 1849, p. 1:2–4.

[2] A series of events had taken place since Fuller's twenty-ninth dispatch. On 30 April 1849 the first encounter between French and Italian armies took place outside Città Vecchia and the French were driven back. Garibaldi then defeated the Neapolitans at Velletri. Throughout May, the Austrian army advanced and besieged Ancona. Pius IX remained

The struggle is now fairly, thoroughly commenced between the principle of Democracy and the old powers, no longer legitimate. That struggle may last fifty years, and the earth be watered with the blood and tears of more than one generation, but the result is sure. All Europe, including Great Britain, where the most bitter resistance of all will be made, is to be under Republican Government in the next century.

'God works in a mysterious way.'[3]

Every struggle made by the old tyrannies, all their Jesuitical deceptions, their rapacity, their imprisonments and executions of the most generous men, only sow more Hydra teeth; the crop shoots up daily more and more plenteous.[4]

When I first arrived in Italy, the vast majority of this people had no wish beyond limited monarchies, constitutional governments. They still respected the famous names of the nobility; they despised the priests, but were still fondly attached to the dogmas and ritual of the Roman Catholic Church. It required King Bomba, it required the triple treachery of Charles Albert, it required Pio IX, and the 'illustrious Gioberti,' it required the naturally kind-hearted, but, from the necessity of his position, cowardly and false Leopold of Tuscany, it required the vagabond "serene" meannesses of Parma and Modena, the "fatherly" Radetzky, and finally the imbecile Louis Bonaparte, "would-be Emperor of France," to convince this people that no transition is possible between the old and the new. *The work is done;* the revolution in Italy is now radical, nor can it stop till Italy become independent and united as a republic. Protestant she already is. The memory of saints and martyrs may continue to be revered, the ideal of Woman to be adored under the name of Maria.—Christ will now begin to be a little thought of; *his* idea was always kept carefully out of sight under the old re-

---

in Gaeta, where he had taken refuge. The Russians, fearing the further spread of revolution in Europe, were prepared to bring pressure to bear on Austria to preserve the status quo (Hearder 118).

[3] William Cowper, "Light Shining Out of Darkness," line 1: "God moves in a mysterious way" (*The Poems of William Cowper*, vol. 1, ed. John D. Baird and Charles Ryskamp [Oxford: Oxford University Press, 1974], 174).

[4] Fuller may have two myths in mind. In the Greek myth about Hercules, the Hydra is a dragon (or in some versions, a water snake) that has many heads. As Hercules chops off one head, two grow in its place. Hercules defeats the monster by chopping off the center head and burying it. The more likely reference is to book 3 of Ovid's *Metamorphoses*, in which Cadmus kills a serpent and, according to the directions of Pallas, buries the teeth. As soon as the seeds are buried, warriors appear as if sprung from the ground and begin a fierce battle. The survivors found a new state (Harry Thurston Peck, ed., *Harper's Dictionary of Classical Literature and Antiquities* [New York: American Book Co., 1923]).

gime; all the worship was for Madonna and Saints, who were to be well paid for interceding for sinners. An example which might make men cease to be such was no way to be coveted. Now the New Testament has been translated into Italian; copies are already dispersed far and wide; men calling themselves Christians will no longer be left entirely ignorant of the precepts and life of Jesus.

The people of Rome have burnt the Cardinals' carriages. They took the confessionals out of the churches, and made mock confessions in the piazzas, the scope of which was, "I have sinned, father, so and so." "Well, my son, how much will you pay to the church for absolution?" Afterward the people thought of burning the confessionals or using them for barricades, but at the request of the Triumvirate they desisted, and even put them back into the churches.[5] But it was from no reaction of feeling that they stopped short, only from respect for the government. The "Tartuffe" of Molière has been translated into Italian, and was last night performed with great applause at the Valle.[6] Can all this be forgotten? Never! Should guns and bayonets replace the Pope on the throne, he will find its foundations, once deep as modern civilization, now so undermined that it falls with the least awkward movement.

But I cannot believe he will be replaced there. France alone could consummate that crime, that for her cruelest, most infamous treason. The Elections in France will decide. In three or four days we shall know whether the French nation at large be guilty or no—whether it be the will of the Nation to aid or strive to ruin a Government founded precisely on the same basis as their own.

I do not dare to trust that people. The peasant is yet very ignorant. The suffering workman is frightened as he thinks of the punishments that ensued on the insurrections of May and June. The man of property is full of horror, at the brotherly scope of Socialism. The aristocrat dreams of the guillotine always when he hears speak of the people. The influence of the Jesuits is still immense in France. Both in France and England the grossest falsehoods have been circulated with unwearied diligence about the state of things in Italy. An amusing specimen of what is still done in this line I find just now in a foreign journal, where it says there are red flags on all the houses of Rome, meaning to imply that the Romans are athirst for blood. Now, the fact is, that these flags are put up at the entrance of those streets where there is no barricade, as a signal to coachmen and horsemen that they

---

[5] Rome at this time was governed by the triumvirate of Mazzini, Aurelio Saffi, and Carlo Armellini, but Mazzini was de facto head of state.

[6] Story considered the Valle one of the better theaters in Rome, where "the drama is played by an excellent company" (1: 210).

can pass freely. There is one on the house where I am, in which is no person but myself who thirst for peace, and the *padrone* who thirsts for money. Meanwhile the French troops are encamped at a little distance from Rome. Some attempts at fair and equal treaty when their desire to occupy Rome was firmly resisted, Oudinot describes in his dispatches as a readiness for *submission*. Having tried in vain to gain this point, he has sent to France for fresh orders. These will be decided by the turn the election takes. Meanwhile the French troops are much exposed to the Roman force where they are. Should the Austrians come up, what will they do? Will they shamelessly fraternize with them, after pretending and proclaiming that they came here as a check upon their aggressions? Will they oppose them in defence of Rome with which they are at war?

Ah! the way of falsehood, the way of treachery, how dark—how full of pitfalls and traps! Heaven defend from it all who are not yet engaged therein!

War near at hand seems to me even more dreadful than I had fancied it. True! it tries men's souls, lays bare selfishness in undeniable deformity. Here, it has produced much fruit of noble sentiment, noble act; but still it breeds vice, too, drunkenness, mental dissipation, tears asunder the tenderest ties, lavishes the productions of earth for which her starving poor stretch out their hands in vain, in the most unprofitable manner. And the ruin that ensues, how terrible. Let those who have ever passed happy days in Rome grieve to hear that the beautiful plantations of *Villa Borghese*—that chief delight and refreshment of citizens, foreigners, and little children, are laid low, as far as the obelisk.[7] The fountain, singing alone amid the fallen groves, cannot be seen and heard without tears; it seems like some innocent infant calling and crowing amid dead bodies on a field which battle has strewn with the bodies of those that once cherished it. Also, the plantations of *Villa Salvage* on the Tiber, the beautiful avenue on the way from St. John Lateran to *La Maria Maggiore,* the trees of the Forum are fallen. Rome is shorn of the locks which lent grace to her venerable brow. She looks desolate, profaned. I feel what I never expected to, as if I might by and by be willing to leave Rome.

Then I have, for the first time, seen what wounded men suffer.[8] The night of the 30th April I passed in the hospital, and saw the terrible agonies

---

[7] The Villa Borghese, one of the Roman park villas, consists of formal gardens, plots of trees, and a variety of buildings, including the Borghese Gallery (Masson 217–18). [Masson, Georgina. *The Companion Guide to Rome.* 6th ed. New York: Prentice-Hall, 1986.] The park lies adjacent to the Piazza del Popolo, which has an obelisk and fountain at its center.

[8] By this time, Fuller had accepted the position of *regolatrice,* or director, of the Hospital of the Fate Bene Fratelli, offered to her by Princess Christina Trivulzio di Belgiojoso.

of those dying or who needed amputation, felt their mental pains, and longing for the loved ones who were away, — for many of these were Lombards, who had come from the field of Novara to fight upon a fairer chance — many were students of the University, who had enlisted and threw themselves into the front of the engagement. (N.B. — The impudent falsehoods of the French general's dispatches are incredible. The French were never decoyed on in any way. They were received with every possible mark of hostility. They were defeated in open field, the Garibaldi legion rushing out to them, and though they suffered much from the walls, they sustained themselves nowhere. — They never put up a white flag till they wished to surrender. The vanity that strives to cover over these facts is unworthy men. The only excuse for the impudent conduct of the expedition is that they were deceived, not by the Romans here, but by the priests of Gaeta leading them to expect action in their favor within the walls. These priests themselves were deluded by their hopes and old habits of mind. The troops did not fight well, and Gen. Oudinot abandoned his wounded without proper care. All this says nothing against French valor, proved by ages of glory, beyond the doubt of their worst foes. They were demoralized because they fought in so bad a cause, and there was no sincere ardor or clear hope in any breast.)

But to return to the hospitals: these were put in order, and have been kept so by the Princess Belgiojoso.[9] The Princess was born of one of the noblest families of the Milanese, a descendant of the great Trivulzio, and inherited a large fortune. Very early she compromised it in liberal movements, and, on their failure, was obliged to fly to Paris, where for a time she maintained herself by writing, and I think by painting also. A Princess so placed naturally excited great interest, and she drew around her a little court of celebrated men. After recovering her fortune, she still lived in Paris, distinguished for her talents and munificence, both toward literary men and her exiled countrymen. Later, on her estate, called Locate, between Pavia and Milan, she had made experiments in the Socialist direction with fine judgment and success. Association for education, for labor, for transaction of household affairs, had been carried on for several years; she had spared no devotion of time and money to this object, loved and was much beloved by those objects of her care, and said she hoped to die there. All is now despoiled and broken up, though it may be hoped that some seeds of peaceful reform have been sown which will spring to light when least expected.

---

[9] Fuller had written her brother, Richard, on 8 February 1848 that she intended to write about the princess in the *Tribune* (Hudspeth 5: 52). Deiss has called the princess "a sophisticated, aristocratic, strangely beautiful, European Margaret Fuller. . . . She was the fantasy Margaret Fuller of the real Margaret Fuller" (120).

The Princess returned to Italy in 1847–48, full of hope in Pius IX and Charles Albert. She showed her usual energy and truly princely heart, sustaining, at her own expense, a company of soldiers and a journal up to the last sad betrayal of Milan, August 6. These days undeceived all the people, but few of the noblesse; she was one of the few with mind strong enough to understand the lesson, and is now warmly interested in the Republican movement. From Milan she went to France, but, finding it impossible to effect anything serious there in behalf of Italy, returned, and has been in Rome about two months. Since leaving Milan she receives no income, her possessions being in the grasp of Radetsky, and cannot know when, if ever, she will again. But as she worked so largely and well with money, so can she without. She published an invitation to the Roman women to make lint and bandages and offer their services to the wounded; she put the hospitals in order; the central one, Trinita de Pellegrini, (once the abode where the Pilgrims were received during Holy week, and where foreigners were entertained by seeing their feet washed by the noble dames and dignitaries of Rome,) she has remained day and night since the wounded were first there, on the 30th of April. Some money she procured at first by going through Rome, accompanied by two other ladies veiled, to beg it. Afterward the voluntary contributions were generous; among the rest, I am proud to say, the Americans in Rome gave $250, of which a handsome portion came from Mr. Brown, the Consul.

I value this mark of sympathy more because of irritation and surprise occasioned here by the position of Mr. Cass, the Envoy. It is most unfortunate that we should have an envoy here for the first time, just to offend and disappoint the Romans. When all the other ambassadors are at Gaeta ours is in Rome, as if by his presence to discountenance the Republican Government which he does not recognize. Mr. Cass, it seems, is limited by his instructions not to recognize the Government till sure it can be sustained. Now, it seems to me the only dignified ground for our Government, the only legitimate ground for any Republican Government, is to recognize for any nation the Government chosen by itself. The suffrage had been correct here, and the proportion of votes to the whole population was much larger, it was said, by Americans here, than it is in our country at the time of contested elections. It had elected an Assembly, that Assembly had appointed, to meet the exigencies of this time, the Triumvirate. If any misrepresentations have induced America to believe, as France affects to have believed, that so large a vote could have been obtained by moral intimidation, the present unanimity of the population in resisting such immense odds, and the enthusiasm of their every expression in favor of the present Government, puts the matter beyond a doubt. The Roman people claims once more to have a national existence. It declines farther serfdom to an ecclesiastical court. It claims liberty of conscience, of action and of thought. Should it fall from its present position, it will not be from internal dissent, but from foreign oppression.

Since this is the case, surely our country, if no other, is bound to recognize the present Government *so long as it can sustain itself.* This position is that to which we have a right: being such, it is no matter how it is viewed by others. But I dare assert it is the only respectable one for our country, in the eyes of the Emperor of Russia himself.

The first best occasion is past, when Mr. Cass might, had he been empowered to act as Mr. Rush did in France, have morally strengthened the staggering Republic, which would have found sympathy where alone it is of permanent value on the basis of principle. Had it been in vain, what then? America would have acted honorably; as to his being compromised thereby with the Papal Government, that fear is idle. Pope and Cardinals have great hopes from America; the giant influence there is kept up with the greatest care; the number of Catholic writers in the United States, too, carefully counted. Had our Republican Government acknowledged this Republican Government, the Papal Camarilla[10] would have respected us more, but not loved us less, for have we not the loaves and fishes to give as well as the precious souls to be saved? Ah! here, indeed, America might go straight forward with much to-be-deprecated impunity. Bishop Hughes himself need not be anxious.[11] The first best occasion has passed, and the unrecognized, unrecognizing Envoy has given offense and not comfort, by a presence that seemed constantly to say, I do not think you can sustain yourselves. It has wounded both the heart and the pride of Rome. Some of the lowest people have asked me, "Is it not true that your country had a war to become free?" — "Yes." "Then why do they not feel for us?" Yet even now it is not too late. If America would only hail triumphant, if she

---

[10] In the sense Fuller uses the term here, a *camarilla* is an unflattering name for a close adviser of the pope. It implies that the adviser molds policies to benefit himself.

[11] Bishop John Joseph Hughes (1797–1864) worked throughout his life for the development of the Roman Catholic church in America. He traveled frequently in Europe to recruit priests and nuns and became well known for his fight against the Public School Society and for the establishment of Catholic schools (*DAB*). He was an avid supporter of Pius IX, and in response to the Roman revolution, he claimed that the republicans had established "a reign of terror over the Roman people." Hughes took particular offense at the *Tribune*'s coverage and declared, "And this is the phalanx recognized by Mr Greeley as the Roman republic! Yet no ambassador from foreign countries has recognised such a republic, except it be the female plenipotentiary who furnishes the Tribune with diplomatic correspondence" (*New York Herald,* 17 June 1849, p. 2).

would not sustain injured Rome, that would be something. "Can you suppose Rome will triumph," you say, "without money, and against so potent a league of foes?" I am not sure, but I hope, for I believe something in the heart of a people when fairly awakened. I have also a lurking confidence in what our fathers spoke of so constantly, a providential order of things, by which brute force and selfish enterprises are sometimes set at nought by aid which seems to descend from a higher sphere. Even old Pagans believed in that, you know, and I was born in America, Christianized by the Puritans—America, freed by eight years' patient suffering, poverty and struggle—America, so cheered in dark days by one spark of sympathy from a foreign shore—America, first "recognized" by Lafayette. I saw him in traversing our country, then great, rich, and free. Millions of men who owed in part their happiness to what, no doubt, was once sneered at as romantic sympathy, threw garlands on his path. It is natural that I should have some faith.[12]

Send, dear America, a talisman to thy ambassadors, precious beyond all that boasted gold of California. Let it loose his tongue to cry "Long live the Republic, and may God bless the cause of the People, the brotherhood of nations and of men—the equality of rights for all." *Viva America!*

Hail to my country! May she live a free, a glorious, a loving life, and not perish, like the old dominions, from the leprosy of selfishness.

EVENING.

I am alone in the ghostly silence of a great house, not long since full of gay faces and echoing with gay voices, now deserted by every one but me—for almost all foreigners are gone now, driven by force either of the Summer heats or the foe. I hear all the Spaniards are going now, that twenty-one have taken passports to-day; why that is, I do not know.

I shall not go till the last moment; my only fear is of France. I cannot think in any case there would be found men willing to damn themselves to latest posterity by bombarding Rome. Other cities they may, careless of destroying the innocent and helpless, the babe and old grandsire who cannot war against them. But Rome, precious inheritance of mankind, will they run the risk of marring their shrined treasures? Would they dare do it?

Two of the balls that struck St. Peter's have been sent to Pio IX. by his children, who find themselves so much less "beloved" than were the Austrians.

---

[12] Fuller had probably seen General Lafayette (1757–1834) in Cambridge, Massachusetts, during his celebrated tour of the United States in 1824.

These two days, days of solemn festivity in the kalends of the Church, have been duly kept, and the population looks cheerful as it swarms through the streets. The order of Rome, thronged as it is with troops, is amazing. I go from one end to the other, and where the poorest and most barbarous of the population (barbarously ignorant, I mean) alone and on foot. My friends send out their little children alone with their nurses. The amount of crime is almost nothing, what it was. The Roman, no longer pent in ignorance and crouching beneath espionage, no longer stabs in the dark. His energies have true vent; his better feelings are roused; he has thrown aside the stiletto. The power here is indeed miraculous, since no doubt still lurk within the walls many who are eager to incite brawls, if only to give an excuse for slander.

To-day I suppose twelve thousand Austrians marched into Florence. The Florentines have humbled and disgraced themselves in vain. They recalled the Grand Duke to ward off the entrance of the Austrians, but in vain went the deputation to Gaeta (in an American steamer!). Leopold was afraid to come till his dear cousins of Austria had put everything in perfect order; then the Austrians entered to take Leghorn, but the Florentines still kept on imploring they would not come there; Florence was as subdued, as good as possible already; they have had the answer they deserved. Now they crown their work by giving over Guerrazzi and Petracci to be tried by an Austrian Court Martial.[13] Truly the cup of shame brims over.

I have been out on the *loggia* to look over the city. All sleeps with that peculiar air of serene majesty known to this city only.—This city that has grown, not out of the necessities of commerce nor the luxuries of wealth, but first out of heroism, then out of faith. Swelling domes, roofs softly tinted with yellow moss—what deep meaning, what deep repose, in your faintly seen outline!

The young Moon climbs among clouds—the clouds of a departing thunderstorm. Tender, smiling Moon! can it be that thy full orb may look down on a smoking, smoldering Rome, and see her best blood run along the stones without one in the world to defend, one to aid—scarce one to cry out a tardy "Shame?" We will wait, whisper the nations, and see if they can bear it. Rack them well to see if they are brave. *If they can do without us,* we will help them. Is it thus ye would be served in your turn? Beware!

---

[13] Francesco Domenico Guerrazzi, a confirmed revolutionary, had become one of the triumvirs of the Florentine republic in October 1848 (Berkeley 390; *New Cambridge Modern History* 10: 408). [Ward, A. W., G. W. Prothero, and Stanley Leathes, eds. *Cambridge Modern History.* Vol. 10. New York: MacMillian, 1911.]

Dispatch 34
Bombardment and Defeat

[...]The following Address has been circulated from hand to hand:

TO THE PEOPLE OF ROME

Misfortune, brothers, has fallen upon us anew. But it is trial of brief duration—it is the stone of the sepulcher which we shall throw away after three days, rising victorious and renewed, an immortal Nation. For with us are God and Justice—God and Justice, who cannot die, but always triumph, while Kings and Popes, once dead, revive no more.

As you have been great in the combat, be so in the days of sorrow—great in your conduct as citizens, of generous disdain, of sublime silence. Silence is the weapon we have now to use against the Cossacks of France and the Priests, their masters.

In the streets do not look at them; do not answer if they address you.

In the cafés, in the eating-houses, if they enter, rise and go out.

Let your windows remain closed as they pass.

Never attend their feasts, their parades.

The harmony of their musical bands be for you tones of slavery, and, when you hear them, fly.

Let the liberticide soldier be condemned to isolation; let him atone in solitude and contempt for having served priests and kings.

And you, Roman women—master-piece of God's work!—deign no look, no smile to those satellites of an abhorred Pope! Cursed be she who, before the odious satellites of Austria, forgets that she is Italian! Her name shall be published for the execration of all her people! And even the courtezans! let them show love for their country, and thus regain the dignity of citizens!

And our word of order, our cry of reunion and emancipation, be now and ever, VIVA LA REPUBLICA!

This incessant cry, which not even French slaves can dispute, shall prepare us to administer the bequest of our martyrs, shall be consoling dew to the immaculate and holy bones that repose, sublime holocaust of faith and of love, near our walls, and make doubly divine the Eternal City. In this cry we shall find ourselves always brothers, and we shall conquer. Viva Rome, the Capital of Italy! Viva the Italy of the People! Viva the Roman Republic!   A ROMAN
Dated *Rome, July 4*, 1849.

For this day's anniversary, so joyously celebrated in our land, was that of the entrance of the French into Rome.

I know not whether the Romans will follow out this programme with constancy as the sterner Milanese have done. If they can, it will draw upon them endless persecutions, countless exactions, but at once educate and prove them worthy of a nobler life.

Yesterday I went over the scene of conflict. It was fearful even to *see* the casinos *Quattro Venti* and *Vascello* where the French and Romans had been several days so near one another, all shattered to pieces, with fragments of rich stucco and painting still sticking to rafters between the great holes made by the cannonade, and think that men had stayed and fought in them when only a mass of ruins. The French, indeed, were entirely sheltered the last days; to my unpracticed eyes the extent and thoroughness of their works seemed miraculous, and gave me first clear idea of the incompetency of the Italians to resist organized armies. I saw their commanders had not even known enough of the art of war to understand how the French were conducting the siege. — It is true their resources were at any rate inadequate to resistance; only continual sorties would have arrested the progress of the foe, and to make them and man the wall their forces were inadequate. I was struck more than ever by the heroic valor of *ours*, let me say, as I have said all along, for go where I may, a large part of my heart will ever remain in Italy. I hope her children will always acknowledge me as a sister, though I drew not my first breath here. A contadini showed me where thirty-seven braves are buried beneath a heap of wall that fell upon them in the shock of one cannonade. A marble nymph, with broken arm, looked sadly that way from her sun-dried fountain, some roses were blooming still, some red oleanders amid the ruin. The sun was casting its last light on the mountains on the tranquil, sad Campagna, that sees one leaf turned more in the book of Woe. This was in the Vascello. I then entered the French ground, all mapped and hollowed like a honey-comb. A pair of skeleton legs protruded from a bank of one barricade; lower a dog had scratched away its light covering of earth from the body of a man, and discovered it lying face upward all dressed; the dog stood gazing on it with an air of stupid amazement. I thought at that moment, recalling some letters received, "O men and women of America, spared these frightful sights, these sudden wrecks of every hope, what angel of Heaven do you suppose has time to listen to your tales of morbid woe? If any find leisure to work for men to-day, think you not they have enough to do to care for the victims here."

I see you have meetings, where you speak of the Italians, the Hungarians. I pray you *do something;* let it not end in a mere cry of sentiment. That is better than to sneer at all that is liberal, like the English; than to talk of the holy victims of patriotism as "anarchists" and "brigands," —but it is not enough. It ought not to content your consciences. Do you owe no tithe to Heaven for the privileges it has showered on you, for whose achievement so many here suffer and perish daily? Deserve to retain them, by helping your fellow-men to acquire them. Our Government must abstain from interference, but private action is practicable, is due. For Italy, it is in this moment too late, but all that helps Hungary helps her also, helps all who wish the freedom of men from an hereditary yoke now become intolerable. Send money, send cheer—acknowledge as the legitimate leaders and rulers those men who represent the people, who understand its wants, who are ready to die or to live for its good. Kossuth I know not, but his people recognize him;[1] Manin I know not, but with what firm nobleness, what persevering virtue, he has acted for Venice!—Mazzini I know, the man and his acts, great, pure and constant,—a man to whom only the next age can do justice, as it reaps the harvest of the seed he has sown in this.[2]—Friends, countrymen, and lovers of virtue, lovers of freedom, lovers of truth!—be on the alert; rest not supine in your easier lives, but remember

"Mankind is one,
And beats with one great heart."

Dispatch 37
THE NEXT REVOLUTION

FLORENCE, *Jan. 6, 1850*[1]

Last winter began with meteors and the rose-colored Aurora Borealis. All the winter was steady sunshine, and the Spring that followed no less glorious, as if Nature rejoiced in and daily smiled upon the noble efforts and tender, generous impulses of the Italian people. This winter, Italy is shrouded

---

[1] Kossuth delivered a fiery speech against Austrian hegemony in the Hungarian Diet on 3 March 1848, which inflamed the students' demonstrations in Vienna and led to the demand for a constitution from Emperor Ferdinand I. In October 1848 Kossuth and his peoples' army drove Austrian imperial troops out of his country. Elected governor of the newly proclaimed Hungarian Republic in April 1849, Kossuth fought with his countrymen against overwhelming military odds; in August 1849 the republican forces were defeated by the combined armies of Austria and Russia (Reynolds 154).

[2] After the French entered Rome and the fate of the republic was sealed, Mazzini escaped to England. From London he planned new attempts at uprisings at Mantua in 1852, at Milan in 1853, and at Genoa and Leghorn in 1857. With Kossuth he founded the Republican European Association and the Society of Friends of Italy. In 1861 he greeted the news of the establishment of a unified kingdom of Italy with little joy; he continued to work for a unified republic and refused a seat in the Italian parliament in protest. In 1870 he was arrested and imprisoned at Gaeta. He died at Pisa on 10 March 1872 (*Chambers's Biographical Dictionary*).

[1] First published as "Italy" in *New-York Daily Tribune,* 13 February 1850, Supplement, p. 1:2–3. This dispatch was not included in *AHA.*

with snow. Here in Florence the oil congeals in the closet beside the fire—the water in the chamber—just as in our country-houses of New-England, as yet uncomforted by furnaces. I was supposing this to be confined to colder Florence, but a letter, this day received, from Rome says the snow lies there two feet deep, and water freezes instantly if thrown upon the pavement. I hardly know how to believe it—I who never saw but one slight powdering of snow all my two Roman winters, scarce enough to cover a Canary bird's wing.

Thus Nature again sympathizes with this injured people, though, I fear me, many a houseless wanderer wishes she did not. For many want both bread, and any kind of shelter this winter, an extremity of physical deprivation that had seemed almost impossible in this richest land. It had seemed that Italians might be subjected to the extreme of mental and moral suffering, but that the common beggar's plea, "*I am hungry*," must remain a mere poetic expression. 'Tis no longer so, for it proves possible for the wickedness of man to mar to an indefinite extent the benevolent designs of God. Yet, indeed, if indefinitely not infinitely. I feel now that we are to bless the very extremity of ill with which Italy is afflicted. The cure is sure, else death would follow.

The barbarities of reaction have reached their hight in the kingdom of Naples and Sicily. Bad government grows daily worse in the Roman dominions. The French have degraded themselves there enough to punish them even for the infamous treachery of which they were guilty. Their foolish national vanity, which prefers the honor of the uniform to the honor of the man, has received its due reward, in the numberless decisions and small insults it has received from a bitterer, blacker vice, the arrogance of the priests. President, envoys, ministers, officers, have all debased themselves; have told the most shameless lies; have bartered the fair fame slowly built up by many years of seeming consistency, for a few days of brief authority, in vain. Their schemes, thus far, have ended in disunion, and should they now win any point upon the right reverend cardinal vices, it is too late. The seeds for a vast harvest of hatreds and contempts are sown over every inch of Roman ground, nor can that malignant growth be extirpated, till the wishes of Heaven shall waft a fire that will burn down all, root and branch, and prepare the earth for an entirely new culture. The next revolution, here and elsewhere, will be radical. Not only Jesuitism must go, but the Roman Catholic religion must go. The Pope cannot retain even his spiritual power. The influence of the clergy is too perverting, too foreign to every hope of advancement and health. Not only the Austrian, and every potentate of foreign blood, must be deposed, but every man who assumes an arbitrary lordship over fellow man, must be driven out. It will be an uncompromising revolution. England cannot reason nor ratify nor criticize it—France cannot betray it—Germany cannot bungle it—Italy cannot bubble it away—Russia cannot stamp it down nor hide it in Siberia. The New Era is no longer an embryo; it is born; it begins to walk—this very year sees its first giant steps, and can no longer mistake its features. Men have long been talking of a transition state—it is over—the power of positive, determinate effort is begun. A faith is offered—men are everywhere embracing it; the film is hourly falling from their eyes and they see, not only near but far, duties worthy to be done. God be praised! It was a dark period of that sceptical endeavor and work, only worthy as helping to educate the next generation, was watered with much blood and tears. God be praised! that time is ended, and the noble band of teachers who have passed this last ordeal of the furnace and den of lions, are ready now to enter their followers for the elementary class.

At this moment all the worst men are in power, and the best betrayed and exiled. All the falsities, the abuses of the old political forms, the old social compact, seem confirmed. Yet it is not so: the struggle that is now to begin will be fearful, but even from the first hours not doubtful. Bodies rotten and trembling cannot long contend with swelling life. Tongue and hand cannot be permanently employed to keep down hearts. Sons cannot be long employed in the conscious enslavement of their sires, fathers of their children. That advent called EMMANUEL begins to be understood, and shall no more so foully be blasphemed. Men shall now be represented as souls, not hands and feet, and governed accordingly. A congress of great, pure, loving minds, and not a congress of selfish ambitions, shall preside. Do you laugh, Editor of the "*Times?*" (Times of the Iron Age.) Do you laugh, Roman Cardinal, as you shut the prison-door on woman weeping for her son martyred in the cause of his country? Do you laugh, Austrian officer, as you drill the Hungarian and Lombard youth to tremble at your baton? Soon you, all of you, shall "*believe* and tremble."

I take little interest now in what is going on here in Italy.[2] It is all leavened with the same leaven, and ferments to the same end. Tuscany is stupified. They are not discontented here, if they can fold the hands yet a little while to slumber. The Austrian tutelage is mild. In Lombardy and Venice they

---

[2] Fuller was, at this time, busy with taking care of her son and planning her return to the United States. She wrote a number of letters to friends and family members in December, explaining that she and Ossoli would come to America together (see Hudspeth 5: 286–307). She was, of course, saddened at the thought of leaving Italy; she wrote her mother: "Weary in spirit with the deep disappointments of the last year, I wish to dwell little on these things for the moment, but seek some consolation in the affections of my little boy is quite well now, and I often feel happy in seeing how joyous and full of activity he seems. Ossoli, too, feels happier here. The future is full of difficulties for us; but having settled our plans for the present we shall set it aside while we may" (Hudspeth 5: 298).

would gladly make it so, but the case is too difficult. The sick man tosses and tumbles. The so-called Italian moderates are fighting at last, (not battles, they have not energy for that,) but skirmishes in Piedmont. The result cannot be doubtful; we need not waste time and paper in predicting it.

Joy to those born in this day: In America is open to them the easy chance of a noble, peaceful growth, in Europe of a combat grand in its motives, and in its extent beyond what the world ever before so much as dreamed. Joy to them; and joy to those their heralds, who, if their path was desert, their work unfinished, and their heads in the power of a prostituted civilization, to throw as toys at the feet of flushed, triumphant wickedness, yet holy-hearted in unasking love, great and entire in their devotion, fall or fade, happy in the thought that there come after them greater than themselves, who may at last string the harp of the world to full concord, in glory to God in the highest, for peace and love from man to man is become the bond of life.

WORKS CITED

Arnim, Bettina von. *Correspondence of Fräulein Günderrode and Bettina von Arnim*. Trans. Margaret Fuller and Minna Wesselhoeft. Boston: Burnham, 1842.

Auerbach, Erich. *Mimesis: The Representation of Reality in Western Literature*. 1946. Trans. Willard R. Trask. Princeton: Princeton UP, 1953.

Brewer, Ebenezer Cobham. "Pyrrhonism." *Brewer's Dictionary of Phrase and Fable*. Revised by Ivor H. Evans. Centenary Edition. New York: Harper, 1970.

Cabot, James Elliot, ed. *The Complete Works of Ralph Waldo Emerson*. Riverside Edition. 12 vols. Boston: Houghton, 1893.

Chevigny, Bell. *The Woman and the Myth: Margaret Fuller's Life and Writings*. Old Westbury, NY: Feminist Press, 1976.

Curtius, Ernst Robert. *Europäische Literatur und Lateinisches Mittelalter*. Bern: Francke Verlag, 1948.

Dickenson, Donna, ed. *"Woman in the Nineteenth Century" and Other Writings*. By Margaret Fuller. World's Classics. New York: Oxford UP, 1994.

Douglass, Frederick. *Narrative of the Life of Frederick Douglass, An American Slave, Written by Himself*. 1845. Ed. Houston Baker, Jr. Baltimore: Penguin, 1982.

Ellison, Julie. *Emerson's Romantic Style*. Princeton: Princeton UP, 1984.

Emerson, Edward Waldo, ed. *The Complete Works of Ralph Waldo Emerson*. Centenary Edition. 12 vols. Boston: Houghton, 1903–04.

Emerson, Ralph Waldo. "To Margaret Fuller." 11 July 1843. Rusk. Vol. 3, 183.

———, William Henry Channing, and James Freeman Clarke, eds. *Memoirs of Margaret Fuller Ossoli*. 2 vols. London: Richard Bentley, 1852. Rpt. New York: Burt Franklin, 1972.

Ferguson, Alfred R., ed. *The Collected Works of Ralph Waldo Emerson.* 5 vols. to date. Cambridge: Harvard UP, 1971–.

"Freedom." Def. l.e. *Webster's New World Dictionary of American English.* 3rd ed. 1988.

Fuller, Margaret. *Papers on Literature and Art.* 2 vols. New York: Wiley and Putnam, 1846.

———. *Summer on the Lakes in 1843.* Boston: C. C. Little and James Brown, 1844.

Gilman, William H., et al., eds. *The Journals and Miscellaneous Notebooks of Ralph Waldo Emerson.* 16 vols. Cambridge: Harvard UP, 1960–84.

Gougeon, Len, and Joel Myerson, eds. *Emerson's Anti-Slavery Writings.* New Haven: Yale UP, 1995.

Hall, James. *The Wilderness and the War-Path.* 1846. New York: Garrett, 1969.

Hawthorne, Nathaniel. *The Blithedale Romance.* 1852. Ed. Fredson Bowers. Centenary Edition of the Works of Nathaniel Hawthorne. Vol. 3. Columbus: Ohio State UP, 1964.

———. *The French and Italian Notebooks.* Centenary Edition of the Works of Nathaniel Hawthorne. Ed. William Charvat et al. Vol. 14. Columbus: Ohio State UP, 1980.

———. *The Scarlet Letter.* 1850. The Centenary Edition of the Works of Nathaniel Hawthorne. Ed. William Charvat et al. Columbus: Ohio State UP, 1962.

Hegel, Georg Wilhelm Friedrich. *The Phenomenology of Mind.* 1807. Trans. J. B. Baillie. New York: Harper, 1967.

———. *The Philosophy of History.* 1899. Trans. J. Sibree. New York: Dover, 1956.

Horsman, Reginald. *Race and Manifest Destiny: The Origins of American Racial Anglo-Saxonism.* Cambridge: Harvard UP, 1981.

Hudspeth, Robert N., ed. *The Letters of Margaret Fuller.* 6 vols. Ithaca: Cornell UP, 1983–95.

James, Henry. *William Wetmore Story and His Friends: From Letters, Diaries, and Recollections.* 2 vols. Boston: Houghton, 1903.

James, William. *"Essays in Radical Empiricism" and "A Pluralistic Universe."* Boston: Peter Smith, 1961.

Kant, Immanuel. *The Conflict of the Faculties.* Trans. Mary J. Gregor. Lincoln: U of Nebraska P, 1992.

——. *Education*. Trans. Annette Churton. Ann Arbor: U of Michigan P, 1960.

Marcuse, Herbert. *One Dimensional Man: Studies in the Ideology of Advanced Industrial Society*. Boston: Beacon, 1964.

"Maugre." Def. 3. *Oxford English Dictionary*. The Compact Edition. 1971.

Melville, Herman. *The Confidence-Man: His Masquerade*. 1857. *The Writings of Herman Melville*. Eds. Harrison Hayford, Hershel Parker, and G. Thomas Tanselle. Vol. 10. Evanston: Northwestern UP, 1984.

——. *Moby-Dick, or The Whale*. 1851. *The Writings of Herman Melville*. Eds. Harrison Hayford, Hershel Parker, and G. Thomas Tanselle. Vol. 6. Evanston: Northwestern UP, 1988.

——. *Typee: A Peep at Polynesian Life*. 1846. *The Writings of Herman Melville*. Ed. Harrison Hayford, Hershel Parker, and G. Thomas Tanselle. Vol. 1. Evanston: Northwestern UP, 1968.

Myerson, Joel B., ed. *Woman in the Nineteenth Century*. 1845. By Margaret Fuller. Facsim. ed. Introd. by Madeline B. Stern. Columbia: U of South Carolina P, n.d.

Packer, Barbara. "The Transcendentalists." *The Cambridge History of American Literature, Vol. 2, 1820–1865*. Ed. Sacvan Bercovitch and Cyrus N. Patell. New York: Cambridge UP, 1995. 525–47.

"Plantation." Def. 2. *Oxford English Dictionary*. The Compact Edition. 1971.

Reynolds, Larry J., ed. *Woman in the Nineteenth Century*. 1845. By Margaret Fuller. Norton Critical Edition. New York: Norton, 1998.

——, and Susan Belasco Smith, eds. *"These Sad but Glorious Days": Dispatches from Europe, 1846–1850*. By Margaret Fuller. New Haven: Yale UP, 1992.

Rowe, John Carlos. *At Emerson's Tomb: The Politics of Classic American Literature*. New York: Columbia UP, 1997.

——. *The New American Studies*, Minneapolis: U of Minnesota P, 2002.

——. *The Other Henry James*. Durham: Duke UP, 1998.

Rusk, Ralph L., ed. *The Letters of Ralph Waldo Emerson*. 10 vols. New York: Columbia UP, 1939.

Smith, Susan Belasco, ed. *Summer on the Lakes in 1843*. 1844. By Margaret Fuller. Urbana: U of Illinois P, 1991.

Stern, Madeline B. Introduction. Myerson, *Woman*.

Thoreau, Henry David. "Civil Disobedience." 1849. *The Reform Papers. The Writings of Henry David Thoreau*. Ed. Carl S. Hovde, William L.

Howarth, and Elizabeth Hall Witherall. Vol. 3. Princeton: Princeton UP, 1973.

——. *A Week on the Concord and Merrimack Rivers*. 1849. *The Writings of Henry David Thoreau*. Ed. Carl S. Hovde. Vol. 5. Princeton: Princeton UP, 1980.

——. *Walden, or Life in the Woods*. 1854. *The Writings of Henry David Thoreau*. Ed. Carl F. Hovde, William L. Howarth, Elizabeth Hall Witherell. Vol. 1. Princeton: Princeton UP, 1971.

von Frank, Albert J. *The Trials of Anthony Burns: Freedom and Slavery in Emerson's Boston*. Cambridge: Harvard UP, 1998.

Whicher, Stephen E. *Freedom and Fate: An Inner Life of Ralph Waldo Emerson*. Philadelphia: U of Pennsylvania P, 1953.

——, ed. *Selections from Ralph Waldo Emerson: An Organic Anthology*. Riverside Edition. Boston: Houghton, 1957.

Wollstonecraft, Mary. *A Vindication of the Rights of Woman*. 1792. Ed. Miriam Brody Kramnick. Harmondsworth: Penguin, 1975.

FOR FURTHER READING

Allen, Gay Wilson. *Waldo Emerson: A Biography*. New York: Viking, 1981.

Allen, Margaret Vanderhaar. *The Achievement of Margaret Fuller*. University Park: Pennsylvania State UP, 1979.

Anderson, Quentin. *The Imperial Self: An Essay in American Literary and Cultural History*. New York: Knopf, 1971.

Bercovitch, Sacvan, and Cyrus N. Patell, eds. *The Cambridge History of American Literature. Vol. 2, 1820–1865*. New York: Cambridge UP, 1995.

Bishop, Jonathan. *Emerson on the Soul*. Cambridge: Harvard UP, 1964.

Blanchard, Paula. *Margaret Fuller: From Transcendentalism to Revolution*. New York: Delacorte, 1978.

Bloom, Harold. *A Map of Misreading*. New York: Oxford UP, 1975.

Buell, Lawrence. *Literary Transcendentalism: Style and Vision in the American Renaissance*. Ithaca: Cornell UP, 1973.

———. *New England Literary Culture: From Revolution through Renaissance*. New York: Cambridge UP, 1986.

Cadava, Eduardo. *Emerson and the Climates of History*. Stanford: Stanford UP, 1997.

Cameron, Kenneth. *Emerson's Reading*. 1941. New York: Haskell House, 1973.

———. *Emerson the Essayist*. 2 vols. Raleigh: Thistle, 1945.

Capper, Charles. *Margaret Fuller: The Private Years*. New York: Oxford UP, 1992. Vol. 1 of *Margaret Fuller: An American Romantic Life*.

Chevigny, Bell. *The Woman and the Myth: Margaret Fuller's Life and Writings*. Rev. ed. Boston: Northeastern UP, 1994.

Cheyfitz, Eric. *The Trans-Parent: Sexual Politics in the Language of Emerson.* Baltimore: Johns Hopkins UP, 1981.

Cott, Nancy F. *The Bonds of Womanhood: "Woman's Sphere" in New England, 1780–1835.* New Haven: Yale UP, 1977.

Deiss, Joseph Jay. *The Roman Years of Margaret Fuller: A Biography.* New York: T. Y. Crowell, 1969.

Ellison, Julie. *Delicate Subjects: Romanticism, Gender, and the Ethics of Understanding.* Ithaca: Cornell UP, 1990.

Feidelson, Charles, Jr. *Symbolism and American Literature.* Chicago: U of Chicago P, 1953.

Flexner, Eleanor. *Century of Struggle: The Women's Rights Movement in the United States.* Cambridge: Harvard UP, 1975.

Gougeon, Len. *Virtue's Hero: Emerson, Antislavery, and Reform.* Athens: U of Georgia P, 1990.

Harding, Walter. *Emerson's Library.* Charlottesville: U of Virginia P, 1967.

Jehlen, Myra. *American Incarnation: The Individual, the Nation, and the Continent.* Cambridge: Harvard UP, 1986.

Kolodny, Annette. *The Land before Her: Fantasy and Experience on the American Frontiers, 1630–1860.* Chapel Hill: U of North Carolina P, 1984.

Matthiessen, F[rancis] O[tto]. *American Renaissance: Art and Expression in the Age of Emerson and Whitman.* New York: Oxford UP, 1941.

McAleer, John. *Ralph Waldo Emerson: Days of Encounter.* Boston: Little, Brown, 1984.

Myerson, Joel. *The New England Transcendentalists and the "Dial": A History of the Magazine and Its Contributors.* Rutherford: Fairleigh Dickinson UP, 1980.

——, ed. *Critical Essays on Margaret Fuller.* Boston: Hall, 1980.

Newfield, Christopher. *The Emerson Effect: Individualism and Submission in America.* Chicago: U of Chicago P, 1997.

Packer, Barbara. *Emerson's Fall: A New Interpretation of the Major Essays.* New York: Continuum, 1982.

Pease, Donald. *Visionary Compacts: American Renaissance Writers in Cultural Context.* Madison: U of Wisconsin P, 1987.

Poirier, Richard. *The Renewal of Literature: Emersonian Reflections.* New York: Random, 1987.

Porte, Joel. *Representative Man: Ralph Waldo Emerson in His Time.* New York: Oxford UP, 1979.

Porter, David. *Emerson and Literary Change.* Cambridge: Harvard UP, 1978.

Reynolds, Larry J. *European Revolutions and the American Literary Renaissance.* New Haven: Yale UP, 1988.

Rose, Anne. *Transcendentalism as a Social Movement: 1830–1850.* New Haven: Yale UP, 1981.

Smith-Rosenberg, Carroll. *Disorderly Conduct: Visions of Gender in Victorian America.* New York: Oxford UP, 1985.

Steele, Jeffrey. *The Representation of the Self in the American Renaissance.* Chapel Hill: U of North Carolina P, 1987.

Urbanski, Marie Mitchell Olesen. *Margaret Fuller's "Woman in the Nineteenth Century": A Literary Study of Form and Content, of Sources and Influence.* Westport: Greenwood, 1980.

Yoder, Ralph A. *Emerson and the Orphic Poet in America.* Berkeley: U of California P, 1978.

Zink, Harriet Rodgers. *Emerson's Use of the Bible.* Lincoln: U of Nebraska P, 1935.

Zwarg, Christina. *Feminist Conversations: Fuller, Emerson, and the Play of Reading.* Ithaca: Cornell UP, 1995.